Eugen Ehrlich

FUNDAMENTAL PRINCIPLES OF THE SOCIOLOGY OF LAW

〔奥〕尤根·埃利希 著

法律社会学基本原理

曹阳 导读 注释

上海译文出版社

World Academic Classics
世界学术经典·英文版

总策划／总主编
庄智象　林骧华

上海时代教育出版研究中心
Shanghai Epoch Education Publishing Research Center 研发

世界学术经典（英文版）
总　序

书之成为经典，乃人类在不同时代的思想、智慧与学术的结晶，优秀文化之积淀，具有不随时代变易的永恒价值。有道是读书须读经典，这是智者的共识。

对于中外经典著作中的思想表述，仅读外文书的中译本或文言著作的白话释文是不够的，尤其是当误译、误释发生的时候，读者容易被误导，或望文生义，或以讹传讹，使原有的文化差异变成更深的文化隔阂。因此，在“世界学术经典（英文版）”的选目中，大部分作品为英文原著；原作是其他语种的经典，则选用相对可靠的英文译本；至于中国古代经典，则采用汉英对照的方式呈现，旨在向西方阐释中国的思想和文化。其中，精选的中国经典是整个系列的重要组成部分。有了这一部分的经典，才真正体现出“世界性”。

以原典和英文方式出版，是为了使读者通过研读，准确理解以英文表达的思想、理论和方法，力求避免舛误，进而通过批判和接受，化为智慧力量。这有利于思想的传播，裨益于新思想的产生，同时亦可提高英语修养。

经典名著的重要性是不言而喻的，但是以下几点意义值得一再重申。

（一）学术经典提供思想源泉

两千六百年来的世界学术经典凝聚了人类思想的精华，世世代代的优秀思想家以他们独特的见识和智慧，留给后人取之不竭、用之不尽的思想源泉。从老子、孔子、柏拉图、亚里士多德以降，天才辈出，思想闪光，精彩纷呈。思想界的大师、名家们在人类思想史传统链条上的每一个环节，都启发后人开拓新的思想领域，探究生命的本质，直抵人性的深层。随着人类思想的不断成熟和完善，各个学科领域的理论从本体论、认识论、方法论、实践论、价值论等维度不断深化。后人继承前人的思想，借经典的滋养保持思想活力，丰富和发展前人的观点，使之形成一波又一波的思想洪流，从而改变人的思想和世界观，改变人类社会的进程。历史已经证明：人类社会的进步，思想的力量大于一切。

（二）学术经典传承精神力量

经典名著中蕴含的人类精神，传承的人类守望的共同价值原则和社会理想，在每一个具体领域里都有诸多丰富的表述，它们从整体上构成了推动人类进步的精神力量。研习和传承人类两千六百多年来的优秀思想，并将它化作求新求变的灵感，是人类文明的要义所在。仅有技术进步，还不足以表明人类的文明程度。若无优秀的思想底蕴，人类存在的意义将大打折扣。

中国思想传统中的基本理念和西方思想传统中的基本理念分别形成了东西方两大具有普遍价值的道德观念和价值系统。值得注意的是：（1）这两大道德系统应该是一个互补、互鉴的整体，两者都不可偏废，因为人类的思想是个多元整体。任何一个民族，缺少其中之一，在精神上都可能是不完整的；(2) 这些基本理念都不是抽象概念，它们都具有很强的实践意义，并且必须由实践来考察，否则就很难体现其价值。

精神传承必然是一种自觉的过程，它靠习得，不靠遗传，因此我们需要研读经典。

(三) 学术经典构成文化积淀

“文化”包含三大部分：(1) 思想与精神现象；(2) 制度与习俗；(3) 有形的事物。学术经典是对思想与精神现象的归纳和提炼，对制度与习俗的探究和设计，对有形事物的形而上思考和描述。

每一个学科领域的经典著作中都会提出一些根本性的问题，这些问题直面人的困惑，思考人类社会的疑难，在新思想和新知识中展现人类的智慧。当这些思想成果积淀下来，就构成人类文化的主要组成部分。文化不只是制度或器物的外在形式，更重要的是凝结在其背后的精神与思想。

每一个学科的学术本身都要面对一些形而上的（超越性的、纯理论性的）文化问题。在很多人看来，理性的思考和理论的表述都是很枯燥的，但是热爱真理并且对思想情有独钟的人会从学术经典的理论中发现无限生动的天地，从而产生获得真理的快乐，这才是我们追求的真正文化。

大量阅读经典名著是一种学习、积累文化的根本方法，深度阅读和深刻记忆能使文化积淀在人的身上，并且代代相传。假如这一过程中断了，人世间只剩下花天酒地、歌舞升平，文化也就湮灭了。

（四）学术经典推动社会进步

毫无疑问，凡属学术经典，都必须含有新的学术成果——新思想、新理论、新方法，或者新探索。这样的原创性学术成果越多，人类的思想就越深邃，视野越开阔，理论更全面、完美，方法更先进、有效，社会的进步才能获得新的动力和保障。

人文主义推翻神学，理性主义旨在纠正人的偏激，启蒙精神主张打破思想束缚，多元主义反抗绝对理念。各种新思想层出不穷，带来了学术的进步，启发并推动了更大的社会变革。这些原创思想在历史长河中经过漫长的时间考验，成为经典，在任何一种文明中都是社会进步和发展的动力。

当我们研读完一部学术经典，分析和归纳其原创的思想观点时，可以很清晰地理解和感悟它在同时代的环境里对于社会的变革和进步有着何种意义，以及它对当下有哪些启迪。

相比技术的发展，思想并不浮显在社会的表层，它呈现在书本的字里行间，渗透于人的心智，在人的灵魂中闪光。每当社会需要时，它能让我们看到无形的巨大力量。

温故而知新。今日世界纷乱依旧，但时代已不再朦胧。人类思想史上的各种主张，在实践中都已呈现清晰的面貌。当我们重新梳理各种思想和理论时，自然不会再返回到“全盘接受”或者“全盘否定”的幼稚阶段。二十一世纪人类正确的世界观、人生观、价值观需要优秀思想传统的支撑，并通过批判继承，不断推陈出新，滋衍出磅礴之推力。

我们所选的这些学术经典，成书于不同的时代，代表了不同的思想与理论主张。有些著作带有时代烙印，有其局限性或片面性；有些观点不一定正确，但从另一个方面显示出人类思想的丰富性和复杂性。各门学科建立、各种主张提出之后，都曾经在历代思想的实验场上经受碰撞和检验，被接受或者被批判。我们的学者需要研读这些书，而青年学生们的思想成长更需要读这些书。当然，批评与分析是最有效和最有益的阅读方法。

有鉴于此，我们希望“世界学术经典（英文版）”能够真正做到“开卷有益”，使我们自己在潜移默化中都成长为有思想、有理想、有品位的人。

上海时代教育出版研究中心

2018 年 10 月

目录

导　读

曹　阳

尤根·埃利希（1862—1922），奥地利法学家，欧洲社会法学与自由法学创始人，在全世界享有盛誉。尤根·埃利希于 1886 年在维也纳大学获得法学博士学位，1897 年担任切尔诺维茨大学罗马法教授，1906 年升任校长，直至去世。尤根·埃利希一生著作等身，出版了大量在法律社会学领域具有广泛影响的作品。其著作主要包括《法律的自由发现和自由法学》《法学逻辑》《法和生活》以及《法律社会学基本原理》等。其中《法律社会学基本原理》一书是集其法律社会学思想之大成之作，亦被称为社会法学的开山之作，对社会法学的创建有着深远影响。他与德国的马克斯·韦伯和美国的罗斯科·庞德并称为社会法学派的三大奠基人。

在《法律社会学基本原理》一书中，尤根·埃利希第一次系统地对社会法学理论作出了详细阐释，提出了社会法学的研究对象和研究方法，尤其是提出了“活法”（living law）论、法律自由发现论、法社会学研究方法等基本理论与方法。他的核心观点是：无论现在还是其他任何时候，法律发展的重心都不在立法、法学，也不在司法裁决，而在社会本身。美国著名法学家庞德在为《法律社会学基本原理》英译本所写的导论中指出，“与 19 世纪形而上学的法学和历史法学形成鲜明对照，埃利希认为在法律上，应当研究的不是抽象的个人，而是社会关系、集团和团体”。“活法”是尤根·埃利希法律社会学的基石。“活法”是指在现实生活中被各成员所认同、最终支配各成员的法律规范，包括各种规则、制度、秩序、行为过程和其他非规则性要素。“活法”不是法院裁判案件时认为具有约束力的内容，亦即“不限于对法院适用的、供判决之用的规范”。“活法”必须在婚姻契约、购销契约、遗嘱、继承、社会联合体章程、商业章程中而不是在法典条款中寻求。在所有这些契约中，除仅适用于特别交易的个别内容外，还存在典型的、反复出现的内容，而这些典型内容基本上是文件中最重要的东西。埃利希认为，“活法”知识具有独立的价值，它构成了人类社会法律秩序的基础。

《法律社会学基本原理》一书共分为二十一章。从方法论角度看，本书以历史法学为基础，以社会学研究方法为核心，建立了法律社会学体系；从具体结构看，作者以罗马法、普通法、欧陆共同法为基础，以法律结构与功能为线索，阐释了联合体内部秩序，并以此为基础提出了“活法”概念，构建了“活法”的框架体系与研究方法。

在本书中，作者首先回答了什么是法律并提出了法律的社会属性，且用较大篇幅分析、介绍了实证主义法学的一些基本理论，如法律事实、裁判规范、国家与法的命题。作者指出，依据目前流行的法律定义，法律不仅是行为规则，法院据以裁判的规则就是人们应当用以规范行为的规则，而且也是强制性规则。承认可执行请求权与强加可执行义务是法律的基本元素。作者同时也指出，法律更是一种规整（ordering），是一种构造方式，是一种为联合体每个成员分配在团体中地位和职责的规则。埃利希认为，法官和法学家应当意识到法律规则和法律文件背后的社会事实，因为社会内在秩序的强大力量是法律效力的真正来源。人类社会是彼此具有相互关系的人类联合体的总和，构成人类社会的社会联合体性质迥异。不同的地域存在不同的社会联合体，且规模大小不同。不同的社会联合体从侧面反映了人类社会的演变形式，即家庭到家族再到民族的进程。家庭与家族是社会联合体的原初形态。基于互助精神与血缘关系形成的纽带促进了家族的形成与发展。随着社会发展，人们以更多元的方式发生联系与互动，从而促进民族国家等新的联合体的涌现。

为了进一步论证法律的社会性，埃里希探讨了法律三要素：法律事实（legal facts）、法律规范（legal norms）和法律命题（legal propositions）。在埃利希看来，人类群体通过组织构造而变成了联合体，组织构造是为每个个体分配位置和职能的规则。而联结这些规则的就是法律事实。埃利希认为，如果我们将注意力集中于社会生活原初的法律事实，我们会发现法律事实存在两种情况：作为主体存在的联合体与作为客体存在的占有。埃利希进而认为，所有的法律都产生于如下事实：联合体内的成员因占有而受到额外尊重，这是一般秩序和一般行为规则的基础。后来，对人的占有变成了对人的权利（支配关系和家庭关系），进而变成了要求他人履行的权利（个人责任）；对物的占有变成了对物的权利或获取物的各种收益的权利（所有权和物权）。再后来，基于契约的对物占有变成为基于前占有人宣告而产生的物权。概而言之，人类整个经济与社会秩序建立在习惯、支配、占有与处分等有限的法律事实之上。

法律规范是对典型法律事实的确认。埃里希认为，社会得以维持的前提就是内部秩序的平衡，而维持这种平衡的要求就是社会联合体中的每一种法律事实都能在法律秩序中得到完美解决。而在所有的法律联合体中，法律规范构成了内部秩序的支柱，是它们的构造方法的最强有力支撑。埃里希认为，没有任何一个法律上的联合体能完全依靠法律规范来维持其存在，宗教、道德、惯例等法律之外的规范也发挥着重要作用。

每一个作为司法裁判基础的法律命题，本身也是一种裁判规范。每一个法律命题都需要用语言清晰表达，通过权威方式发布，并宣布其具有普遍约束力。埃利希认为，我们必须区分法律命题的三种不同类型。第一种是与法院和其他裁决机构对社会中现存法律事实保护一致的法律命题；第二种是与这种法律命题不同的、否定现存法律事实或者自身积极创造法律事实的法律命题；第三种法律命题为法律事实规定了法律后果，完全独立于由习惯、支配和占有关系以及这些法律事实所创造之处分而产生的规范。

埃利希认为，不应该混淆法律规范和法律命题。法律命题是制定法卷册或法律书籍中法律规定精确的、具有普遍约束力的系统表达。而法律规范是一种落实到实践中的法律命令，如同在一个确定的联合体内获得普遍遵守的法律命令，即使没有任何语言对它作出清晰的阐明也必须遵守。

在介绍与分析了实证主义法学的基本理论后，埃利希提出了法学功能的新理论。埃利希认为，法学功能不同于法学的历史作用，其从来不是指导人们依照法律规制的基本原理行事的行为规制。法学并不为人们的行为提供法律指引，其主要是为解决人们日常生活的法律需求。僵化的法律命题显然无法应对纷繁复杂的社会现实，必须通过创造性的法学以发现法律。法学的功能包含律师功能、法律行为、司法功能三个要素。律师功能即说服法院，社会已经为他所代表的利益提供了救济，向法院论证为何某种利益值得法律保护。法律行为通常并不仅仅是为了在法律诉讼程序中使用而存在，其主要功能是提供法律关系的秩序。处理法律行为的法学分支的目标与涉及律师功能的法律分支的目标，二者并无本质不同，都是为了利用手边工具，为涉争利益提供最佳保护可能。司法功能赋予法官通过利益权衡，对该利益是否值得保护作出判定，从而发现规范与统一规范适用。

埃利希坚持法的二源理论：即法源于制定法或习惯法。传统观点认为法律起源于国家。法源的一源论认为，国家成为权威的、唯一的法律来源。埃里希指出，所有法律都来源于制定法或者习惯法，国家在法律创制中发挥的作用十分有限。习惯法更具有生命力、包容性和适应性，它的庞杂内容是制定法根本没有开垦过的活动领域；另一方面，即使有制定法的存在，人们更多的时候还是愿意按照自己习惯中的做法生活。习惯法、制定法、法学家法都是源自同一幼枝（即民众意识）上的芽苗。“法的自由发现运动”则从社会中寻找可以解决新问题的原则性习惯规范，来应对法律的滞后性问题。由此，埃利希完成了对完全以国家立法为基础的法源学说的批判。埃利希同时也指出，历史法学派关于法源理论的观点也存在错误。历史法学派认为，法律的生命力来自于民族情感与民族意识，立法活动无任何意义，其仅仅是发现民族的“共同信念”与“共同意识”。埃利希虽然认同历史法学派对于非国家法的关注，但其反对仅仅强调法律意识而不关注法律意识在现实法律生活中的运用。

在本书最后两章，作者试图系统阐释法律社会学研究方法。

在对传统实证主义法学相关概念作出分析后，埃里希提出了法源“二元”论理论，阐释了习惯法规则在社会规制中的重要价值，提出了法律社会学的两种方法：(1) 法律史和实用法学运用；(2)“活法”研究。至此，作者完成了法社会学的理论与方法构建，开创了法律研究的社会学视野。法律研究的社会学视野将社会学概念、理论、研究方法引入法学研究中，不仅研究制定法的价值，更重视研究在现实社会中实际起作用、发挥实效的“活法”。

埃利希认为，法律社会学是一门观察的科学。要理解具有重要意义的法律领域内的社会现象，必须关注法律本身的事实与法律命题。埃利希指出，理解和解释法律命题而引据的事实，毫无例外取自历史和文化人类学。法律史的主要功能是为法律社会学提供题材。法律命题和法律制度是从民族生活中成长起来、从作为整体的社会和经济构造中成长起来的。法律社会学正是从社会和经济的历史中提取素材。

埃利希认为，实用法学的成果对于法律社会学同样重要。实用法学家首先要处理的是裁判规范。裁判规范从社会构造中产生，要理解裁判规范就必须理解相关的社会构造。要解释物权法就必须说明生活中可以见到何种物权。另外，实用法学与其表达的规范一道，必定呈现一幅社会图景。法学实际上是社会生活的法律信息的形态学。

对于“活法”研究，埃利希认为，并非所有的法律均包含在法律命题中。现代法典的编撰者往往不关心对自身所处时代、所处社会之法律有关的事物作出表述。《德国民法典》的相关立法资料几乎都来自于潘德克顿法教科书。然而，我们的法典要处理的法律关系错综复杂、千变万化。“活法”事实上超越了法典，独立生长。“活法”与法庭和其他裁判机构所执行的法律并不一致。即使“活法”未以法律命题的形式提出，但它仍是支配生活本身的法律。埃利希认为，我们的法律知识首先来源于现代法律文件，其次来源于对生活、商业、习惯、管理、联合体的直接观察。这种直接观察不仅是对那些法律已经认可的事项，而且也是对那些法律遗漏和忽略的事项，甚至对那些实际上遭到法律反对的事项进行观察。埃利希认为，“法”的概念已经发生变化，判例不再是制定法的仆人，而是制定法的竞争者与替代者。司法裁判显然无法勾画出法律生活的完整图景，“活法”必须在婚姻关系、购销契约、附用益权契约等实际存在而不是在法典条款中去探寻。

埃利希认为，法理学的社会学学派用来检测法律命题和法律文件的标准是现实生活。“活法”内容除了睁开眼睛细心观察生活、访寻民众并记录下他们的回答外，并无他途。法律是永无止境的发展过程。对于法学家而言，有生命力的新法萌芽远比垂死的法律残余更重要。因而，法律社会学必须从探明“活法”开始，它的注意力将主要指向具体的而非抽象的东西。

通过《法律社会学基本原理》一书，埃利希希望完成对法律社会学理论体系化的阐释。事实上，他在书中花了大量篇幅完成的仅是对传统实证主义法学的相关理论与概念分析以及传统法学过于注重对“死法”研究的弊端，忽视了社会的真正运作机制，忽视了在社会运转中真正发挥作用的是“活法”而不是书面文字上的法律。埃里希反对僵化的法典化运动，指出从法典化的那一刻起，正是“活法”生长之时。从内容与逻辑结构上看，本书只是一系列与法律社会学主题相关的文章集合，而不是一个具有完整体系的法律社会学系统性的诠释。在一定程度上，这也是该书的不足之处。

《法律社会学基本原理》一书无疑为我们提供了理解法律规范的不同视角。在传统上占据主导地位的实证主义法学强调对制定法的理解与适用，较少关注社会规范的实际运作机理；而《法律社会学基本原理》一书提出要关注社会规范如何真正在社会生活中发挥作用，要研究这些真正的社会规范，而不是僵化的书面法律。埃里希强调需从社会学角度理解法律，需要通过观察去了解法律运作的方法、效果，这无疑提供了法律研究的新视野与新方法。他提出的“活法”理论无疑对现今的法典化浪潮具有特殊的启发意义。立法者希望通过法典建立社会生活中法律、法规的“百科全书”。然而，社会生活远比立法者的描述更加丰富、多元，立法者与司法者必须关注“社会学视野的法律世界”。

FUNDAMENTAL PRINCIPLES OF THE SOCIOLOGY OF LAW

I THE PRACTICAL CONCEPT OF LAW

There was a time, and indeed it does not lie very far behind us, when the university trained the physician for his future profession by requiring him to commit to memory the symptoms of the various diseases and the names of such remedies for them as were known at thc timc. This time is past. The modem physician is a natural scientist who has chosen the human body as his field of investigation. Similarly, not much more than a century ago, the mechanical engineer was little more than a mechanician to whom his master had imparted the manual skill required for the building of machines. Here too a change has taken place. The present-day mechanical engineer is a physicist who studies the nature of the materials which he is to use and the extent to which their reactions to various external influences take place in conformity with observed and observable laws. Neither the physician nor the mechanical engineer any longer, in a purely craftsmanlike manner, acquires merely the skill required for his profession, but chiefly an understanding of its scientific basis. The same development has taken place long ago in countless other fields.

In jurisprudence, however, the distinction between the theoretical science of law[1] (*Rechtswissenschaft*) and the practical science of law (*Rechtslehre*)[2], i.e. practical juristic science, is being made only just now, and, for the time being, the greater number of those that are working in this field are not aware that it is being made. This distinction,

---

1. the theoretical science of law（*Rechtswissenschaft*）：理论法学（* 括号内德语同英文意，文中相似情况不再一一注明）
2. the practical science of law (*Rechtslehre*)：实践法学

however, is the basis of an independent science of law, whose purpose is not to subserve practical ends but to serve pure knowledge, which is concerned not with words but with facts. This change, then, which has taken place long since in the natural sciences is taking place in jurisprudence also, in the science which Anton Menger[1] has called the most backward of all sciences, "to be likened to an out-of-the-way town in the provinces, where the discarded fashions of the metropolis are being worn as novelties." And it will not be barren of good results. The new science of law will bring about much enlightenment as to the nature of law and of legal institutions that has hitherto been withheld from us, and doubtless it will also yield results that are of practical usefulness.

There is little that is more instructive to the jurist than the study of those spheres of juristic knowledge in which the change hasalready taken place, e.g. that of the general theory of the state or that of history of law. Let us glance at the latter for a moment. The idea that the law is to be interpreted in its historical relations was not unknown to the Romans. Both Gaius[2] and the fragments of the Digest[3] abound with historical references. Even the glossators[4] and the postglossators[5] have made abundant use of the data of legal history. Moreover the great French scholars and the fine Dutch scholars of the sixteenth, seventeenth, and eighteenth centuries can properly be referred to as historical and philological jurists. The German publicists of the seventeenth century have also worked along historical lines. The

---

1. Anton Menger：安东·门格尔（1841—1906），奥地利法学家，长期任维也纳大学法学院院长、校长，著有《民法与无产阶级》等著作。
2. Gaius：盖尤斯，古罗马帝国前期著名法学家。
3. Digest：《学说汇编》
4. glossators：注释法学派，是指西欧中世纪中后期以研究罗马法为中心的学派。
5. postglossators：后注释法学派。是继注释法学派之后兴起的又一支研究罗马法的法学流派。

same is truc of thc English, possibly from the days of Fortescue[1]. Blackstone is a perfect master of the art of explaining historically such parts of existing law as appear to be inexplicable. But it was the Historical School of jurisprudence[2] that first made the history of law, which until then had been studied exclusively for the sake of a better understanding of the positive law, an independent science; made her the mistress of her own household. To the modern legal historian it is a matter of indifference whether the results of his investigations are of any practical usefulness or not. They are to him not a means, but an end. Nevertheless, ever since legal history ceased to be a handmaiden to dogmatic legal scicncc[3], shc has rcndcrcd the most invaluable services to the latter. Present-day dogmatics owes its greatest scientific achievements to fructification by legal history. The importance of legal history for legal science, however, rests not so much upon the fact that it is history as upon the fact that it is a pure science, perhaps the only science of law that is in existence today. And what an inexhaustible source of stimulation and instruction legal history has become for theorctical and practical economics, as well as for legislation! Would this have been possible if it had not given up its original limited aims and methods?

Human thinking is necessarily dominated by the concept of purpose, which determines its direction, the selection of its materials, and its methods. And with reference to these things the thinking of the jurist is conditioned by the practical purposes pursued by juristic science. When a structural-iron engineer is thinking of iron, he does

1. Fortescue：福蒂斯丘（1394—1479），15 世纪英国著名的政治理论家与法学家。
2. Historical School of jurisprudence：历史法学派。以萨维尼（1779—1861）为代表的历史法学派认为法的本质是世代相传的民族精神，法的最好来源是习惯。
3. dogmatic legal science：法教义学。是对法规范构成的实定法秩序做出体系化解释的法学方法。

not have the chemical element in mind, but the article of commerce with which the foundries are supplying him for his buildings. He will be interested only in those properties of iron that are of moment for iron construction, and when he studies these properties he will employ such met hods as are suitable for the workshop of the builder who erects iron structures. He will not take thought to develop methods of scientific investigation, for the structural-iron engineer is not interested in scientific results; for practical purposes scientific exactness would be not only superfluous, but too expensive, time-consuming, and difi&cult. It is sufficient if the structural-iron engineer does those things which he can do best, and leaves to others the things which they can do better. This, of course, is not, in itself, a detriment. It is true that, because of this necessary limitation, the structural-iron engineer fails to observe many a thing that might be of importance not only for science but for the technic of iron construction. But as soon as men of science and specialists in other branches of iron work find something that is of value for iron construction, he will avail himself of it. Good work done by him within his narrow sphere and with the limited means at his disposal is of scientific as well as of practical value. The observations of the practical man have at all times been providing nourishment for science; a great deal of the scientific botany of our time has been derived from the old herbalism of the apothecaries.

The situation would be quite different if there were no science dealing with iron but structural-iron engineering; if there were no botany but the herbalism of the apothecaries: not only research but practical work as well would suffer tremendously. In addition to pharmacognosy and pharmacology, which have replaced the herbalism of the apothecaries, the nature of plants is being studied by the sciences of agriculture, forestry, horticulture, and many others. Scientific botany studies it qidte independently, and the results of its investigations, of course, avail the practical sciences referred to; and at the same time the results of the labor of the practical men working in all of these fields offer to the botanist a multitude of suggestions.

It is the tragic fate of juristic science that, though at the present time it is an exclusively practical science of law, it is at the same time the only science of law in existence. The result of this situation is that its teaching on the subject of law and legal relations is, as to tendency, subject matter, and method, only that which the practical science of law can give. Indeed it is as if mineralogy and chemistry could teach us no more about iron than that which has been discovered for the purposes of structural-iron engineering; as if botany could teach us no more about plants than is contained in the text-books on pharmacognosy and pharmacology. This state of the science of law is an extremely sad one, particularly in view of the fact that the present-day practical science of law is far from covering the whole field of the practical activity of the jurist. Properly speaking there ought to be as many practical sciences of law as there are juristic activities. The Romans divided the activity of the jurist into *respondere*[1], *agere*[2], *cavere*[3]; which, being expressed in modern terminology is: the activity of the judge, of the draftsman of legal documents, and of the attorney; and it seems that in the days of the Republic at least, research, literature, and instruction were engaged in the service of each of these three activities. In England practical juristic science (*Rechtslehre*)[4] is concerned with the activity of the judge and the attorney; whereas the art of drafting legal documents (conveyancing[5]) exists as a distinct, highly developed branch of legal science. But the judge, the draftsman of legal documents, and the attorney are by no means the only representatives

---

1. *respondere*：〈拉〉解答
2. *agere*：〈拉〉协助
3. *cavere*：〈拉〉提供
4. practical juristic science (*Rechtslehre*)：实用法学。是关注法官与律师的法律实践。
5. conveyancing：产权转让

of professional juristic activity. In addition to the administration of the affairs of the state, the administration of private affairs is a fruitful sphere of juristic activity, e.g. agriculture, commerce, and industry. To these may be added participation in legislation, politics, journalism.

The practical juristic science of the Continent is considerably poorer than that of the Romans and of the English. Since the reception of Roman law, it has made its abode exclusively at the universities, which, for the most part, were founded, and are being maintained, by the state, and to which, after the rise of a learned judiciary, the task of training the future judge for his calling has chiefly been assigned. Had legal instruction been given in private schools, undoubtedly there would have been schools for attorneys and notaries in addition to schools for judges, and the various practical sciences of law would have enjoyed a corresponding development. As it was, a juristic science arose whose content can be defined exhaustively as practical instruction in the performance of the duties of a judge. Slowly and haltingly there was added the preparation for the diplomatic and administrative services. Accordingly the practical and the theoretical science of law began to comprise also international law and public law. Paulsen therefore quite properly described the present-day juristic faculties as technical training schools for judges and administrative officials. Since the majority of students, however, were bent upon a career on the bench, the law that the judge requires remained in the center of legal teaching. This may perhaps account for the fact that the study of public law and international law became a scientific study long before private law, penal law, and procedure. Public law in the narrow sense (*allgemeines Staatsrecht,* later called *allgemeine Staatslehre*[1]) was the first branch of juristic science, which, disregarding the practical utility of its results, pursued purely scientific aims. But the juristic faculties

---

1. *allgemeine Staatslehre*：〈德〉狭义上的公法，区分于国家法（Staatsrecht）与国际法，而国家法包括宪法和行政法。

could and would not become anything but training schools for judges and government ofi&cials; and this aim became the determining factor not only in legal education but also in research and literature. For this reason it is not very likely that the draftsman of legal documents or the attorney-at-law[1] will find a book from which he can learn how to perform the duties of his profession, difficult, important, and involving grave responsibilities though they be. Most of the information he needs he must obtain in a purely tradesmanlike fashion in the practice, and the most valuable knowledge gained by professional experience dies with him who has acquired it. But — and this is the important consideration here — these things are also being ignored by the science of law, which knows only the law required by the judge, although even a hasty glance at legal life shows that a great deal of the administration of justice and of the development of law takes place in the offices of attorneys and notaries, and that legal science can gather valuable material therefrom. Moreover the modern jurist can, if need be, get all the information he requires as to the importance of the legal document as a lever for the development of law from any handbook of legal history. The fact that practical juristic science limits itself in its own sphere in accordance with the same point of view is quite in keeping with this. It excludes important matters from discussion if the judge does not generally concern himself with them in his professional capacity. About a decade ago, Lotmar[2] first discovered for juristic science the existence of law concerning contracts of labor — after the great industrial development in Germany had begun to make it a matter of ever-increasing concern to the administration of justice. The most significant juristic problems of our time, the problems of trade unions, of trusts, and of cartels, do not exist for practical juristic science; doubtless for the simple reason that, although they play an

1. attorney-at-law：律师
2. Lotmar：洛特曼（1850—1922），德国著名劳动法学家。

important part in legal life, their role is not nearly so important in the administration of justice.

The most disastrous consequence of this state of affairs has been its effect on the method of juristic science. The first and foremost function of all research is to find a method adapted to its subject matter. The life of many a great scholar has been spent in the endeavor to find a method. Once the method was found, the work could be carried on by inferior minds. Ultimately, even the analysis of the spectrum is nothing more than a method. With the sole exception of the general theory of the state[1] (*Staaislehre*), which is already infused with a scientific spirit, the science of law knows no other method than that which has been developed by practical juristic science for the application of law by the judge. According to the prevailing conception of the judicial office, which arose in the sixteenth century, the judge must derive his decision of the individual case from the existing general propositions[2]. Practical juristic science, which had been designed for the use of the judge, was to supply the judge with legal propositions, formulated in the most general terms possible, in order that the greatest possible number of decisions might be derived from them. It was to teach the judge how to apply the general propositions to the specific cases. Its method therefore had to be a method of abstraction and deduction. With the exception of public law[3] in the narrow sense, however, juristic science as a whole proceeds by abstraction and deduction just as if the human mind were incapable of any higher attainment than the creation of bloodless shapes that lose contact with reality proportionately to the measure of abstractness that they attain. In this respect it is altogether different from true science, the prevailing

1. general theory of the state：国家的一般理论，是关于国家学说的广义理论。
2. general propositions：一般命题
3. public law：公法

method of which is inductive, and which seeks to increase the depth of our insight into the nature of things through observation and experience.

Accordingly juristic science has no scientific concept of law, Just as the technical expert in iron construction, when speaking of iron, is not thinking of the chemically pure substance which the chemist or the mineralogist refers to as iron, but rather of the chemically very impure compound that is used in iron construction, so the jurist does not mean by law that which lives and is operative in human society as law, but, apart from a few branches of public law, exclusively that which is of importance as law in the judicial administration of justice. An occasional flash of deeper insight ought not to mislead anyone. A technical expert in iron construction may perhaps, in making an attempt to be scientific, state the chemical formula of the compound which is being used in iron construction as iron, but in the course of his practical discussion he will deal only with this compound; for iron in the scientific sense is of no interest to him. The important thing is not the definitions that are found in the introductory chapters of handbooks or monographs, but the concept of law with which juristic science actually works; for concepts are not merely external ornamentation, but implements for the erection of a structure of scientific thought.

From the point of view of the judge, the law is a rule according to which the judge must decide the legal disputes that are brought before him. According to the definition which is current in juristic science, particularly in Germany, the law is a rule of human conduct. The rule of human conduct and the rule according to which the judges decide legal disputes may be two quite distinct things; for men do not always act according to the rules that will be applied in settling their disputes. No doubt the legal historian conceives of law as a rule of human conduct; he states the rules according to which, in antiquity or in the Middle Ages, marriages were entered into, husband and wife, parents and children lived together in the family; he tells whether property was held individually or in common, whether the soil was tilled by the owner or by a lessee paying rent or by a serf rendering services; how contracts were entered into, and how property descended. One would hear the same thing if one should ask a traveler returning from foreign lands to give an account of the law of the peoples he has become acquainted with. He will tell of marriage customs, of family life, of the manner of entering into contracts; but he will have little to say about the rules according to which law-suits are being decided.

This concept of law, which the jurist adopts quite instinctively when he is studying the law of a foreign nation or of remote times for a purely scientific purpose, he will give up at once when he turns to the positive law of his own country and of his own time. Without his becoming aware of it, secretly as it were, the rule according to which men act becomes the rule according to which their acts are being adjudged by courts and other tribunals. The latter, indeed, is also a rule of conduct, but it is such for but a small part of the people, i.e. for the authorities, entrusted with the application of the law; but not like the former, for the generality of the people. The scientific view has given way to the practical view, adapted to the requirements of the judicial official, who, to be sure, is interested in knowing the rule according to which he must proceed. It is true, jurists look upon these rules as rules of conduct as well, but they arrive at this view by a jump in their thinking. They mean to say that the rules according to which courts decide are the rules according to which men ought to regulate their conduct. To this is added a vague notion that in the course of time men will actually regulate their conduct in accordance with the rules according to which the courts render their decisions. Now it is true that a rule of conduct is not only a rule according to which men customarily regulate their conduct, but also a rule according to which they ought to do so, but it is an altogether inadmissible assumption that this "ought" is determined either exclusively or even preponderantly by the courts. Daily experience teaches the contrary. Surely no one denies that judicial decisions influence the conduct of men, but we must first of all inquire to what extent this is true and upon what circumstances it depends.

Every page of a law book, every lecture on a legal subject, bears out the statement just made. Each and every word shows that the jurist who is discussing a legal relation invariably has in mind the problem how the legal disputes arising from this relation are to be adjudged, and not the totally different question how men conduct themselves, and how they ought to conduct themselves in this relation. Even a man of the mental stature of a Maitland[1] said that to write the history of the English actions is to write the history of English law. This juristic line of thought has been given a positively naive expression in the doctrine of error in law. A juristic science which conceives of law as a rule of conduct could not consistently have laid down a principle that men are bound by the law even though they do not know it; for one cannot act according to a rule that one does not know. On the contrary, it ought to have discussed the question how much of a given legal material is known as a rule of conduct and is followed as such, and, at most, what can be done to make it known. In fact, Binding understood the whole problem in this way years ago, and posited the proposition that only the norms of penal law[2], not the penal law itself, are generally known, and in fact regulate human conduct. Only Max Ernst Mayer[3] has followed him, without however adding anything to the requisite experiential material. But if we say, as is usually done, that the law binds him who does not know the law as well as him who

1. Maitland：梅特兰（1850—1906），英国法学家，是开创英国法律史学的现代法学家。
2. penal law：刑法
3. Max Ernst Mayer：马克斯・欧内斯特・迈耶（1875—1923），德国刑法学家。

does, we are evidently giving up the concept of law as a rule of human conduct altogether; we are laying down a rule for the courts and other tribunals, which the latter are to apply whether the person concerned knew it or not. We are not improving the situation by requiring everyone to know the law or by setting up the fiction that the law, if properly published, is known to everyone.

The prevailing notion as to the origin of law is a result of this very line of thought. Whence comes the rule of law, and who breathes life and efficacy into it? It is extremely interesting to note the answers that have been made in reply to these questions; for they clearly and unambiguously reflect the fact that even perfectly correct scientific knowledge is not sufficient to guide the human mind when the necessity of serving a practical need suggests another path. Today, a century after Savigny[1] and Puchta[2], no scientifically trained jurist doubts that a considerable part of the law of the past was not created by the state, and that even today it is derived to a great extent from other sources. That is the theory. Now comes the question: Where is this non-state law[3] to be studied? Where is an exposition of it to be found? Where is it being taught? Perhaps we are not too daring if we make the assertion that today research, literature, and legal education on the Continent know of no other law than statute law[4].

To be sure one soothes one's conscience by saying that customary law[5] — a collective term, an expression which for centuries has been used to lump together the whole heterogeneous mass of non-state law — is a "negligible quantity[6]" at the present time. This statement is found in the writings of Savigny and Puchta themselves. Since that time it

1. Savigny：萨维尼（1779—1861），德国法学家，历史法学派代表人物。
2. Puchta：普赫塔（1798—1846），德国法学家，概念法学代表人物。
3. non-state law：非国家法，意指非国家创设的法律。
4. statute law：制定法。由立法机关通过的成文法，与判例法相对。
5. customary law：习惯法
6. negligible quantity：微不足道的数量

has been repeated time and again in various forms, and even writers who do not make the statement in so many words adhere to it. A jurist who holds this opinion has ceased to look upon law as a rule of general human conduct; he has clearly demonstrated that law is to him, preponderantly at least, a rule for the conduct of courts and other tribunals; for even the believers in the doctrine of the omnipotence of the state have not very often seriously thought that the state can make rules to regulate the whole field of human conduct. Perhaps the only exception within the whole range of European civilization was the Emperor Josef II[1], whose program split on the rock of this idea. For this reason the relation of juristic science to non-state law, quite independently of scientific conviction, has been undergoing changes in accordance with the changing attitude of the state toward the courts. And if juristic science today is devoted exclusively to state law, the reason for this must be sought in the fact that the state, in the course of historical development, has come to believe that it is able to add to the monopoly of the administration of law, which it acquired long ago, a monopoly of the creation of law. And I do not doubt, therefore, that the modern free-finding-of-law movement[2] marks not only an advance in scientific insight, but also an actual shift in the relation of the state and society — a shift which has taken place long ago in other spheres.

Where the judge renders his decisions chiefly according to custom, as was done almost everywhere down to a very late stage of development, e.g. in Rome in the days of the Republic, or in Germany in the Middle Ages, the idea, self-evidently[3], does not enter the head of anyone to derive the law as such from the state. As late as the end

---

1. Emperor Josef II：约瑟夫二世皇帝（1741—1790），1765—1790 任神圣罗马帝国皇帝。
2. free-finding-of-law movement：法律自由发现运动。批判概念法学，强调法的妥当性价值。
3. self-evidently：不证自明

of the Republic, the Romans considered their national customary law, the *ius civile*[1], at least as valuable as a source of law as the *leges*[2]. And the law-books of the Middle Ages mention provisions of statutes or regulations only in exceptional instances. In the Middle Ages, the *corpus iuris civilis*[3], the *corpus iuris canonici*[4], even the Golden Bull[5], are merely very high authorities to which one turns for aid in the solution of difficult and important problems as one might turn to any other authorities, e.g. the Bible or the ancient writers — for in the Middle Ages scientific work was done chiefly on the basis of authority, in law no less than in theology, philosophy, or medicine. It is only after the state has grown extremely powerful, and has begun to tend toward an absolute form of government, that the thought begins to germinate, and the impulse awakens, to make the state the authoritative, and in the course of time the sole, source of law. This was done in Rome in the days of the Empire and in western Europe in the sixteenth century. Attempts were made to tie non-state creation of law to authorization by the state, particularly in the very earliest days of the Empire, by means of the *ius respondendi*[6], which was conferred by the Emperor upon jurists empowered to create law. The power to create law was limited to questions not yet regulated by law. Very strict precepts as to the validity of customary law were embodied in the statutes. Attempts were made to render it superfluous by means of codifications, which purported to comprise the whole law; occasionally, even to exclude it in express terms. Even the scientific legal work of the jurists was looked upon askance, and occasionally was expressly forbidden because the powers that were realized that it gave rise to a new sort

---

1. *ius civile*：〈拉〉市民法
2. *leges*：〈拉〉法律
3. *corpus iuris civilis*：〈拉〉《民法大全》
4. *corpus iuris canonici*：〈拉〉《教会法大全》
5. the Golden Bull：《金玺诏书》，盖有金印的特许状。
6. *ius respondendi*：〈拉〉法律解答权，法学家对法律提出解答的权利。

of non-state law, i.e. to juristic law. The final word of this trend was spoken, perhaps, by Justinian[1]: *Tam conditor quam interpret legum solus imperator iuste existimabitur, nihil hac lege derogante veteris iuris condiloribus, quia et eis hoc maiestas imperialis permisit.*[2]

Juristic science steadfastly follows in the path of this development of state law, paying very little attention to the progress of scientific knowledge. Having made a curt obeisance to the teachings of science, she returns at once to the task which she considers her true function, i.e. to furnish that which the administration of law requires. The decisive step had already been taken when the judge was no longer required to know both non-state and state law; when only a knowledge of state law was presupposed, while non-state law had to be proved by the parties. Henceforth only state law is "law" in the full sense of the term; every other kind of law is merely "fact." Juristic science arrived at this stage when the judge became a learned official of the state, i.e., in Germany, as early as the sixteenth century. The doctrine, which was becoming more and more firmly established, was that customary law, which today comprises all non-state law with the exception of juristic law, is law of an inferior kind, which, as to its origin and as to its validity, is conditioned upon authorization, recognition, or confirmation by the legislator, who could, if he chose, forbid its use altogether. It was held in low esteem, even ridiculed occasionally, proof of it was made more difficult, and the conditions upon which it was recognized were insisted upon with increasing strictness. Studies investigating and presenting non-state law became fewer and fewer in number, until, finally, in the eighteenth century they ceased to

---

1. Justinian：优士丁尼，527—565年担任东罗马帝国皇帝，编纂《优士丁尼法典》。
2. *Tam conditor quam ... imperialis permisit.*：〈拉〉皇帝应被正当地看做是唯一的立法者和法律的解释者。这一规定不损害古法的建构者，因为他们的特权本来就是由皇帝授予的。

appear altogether. In the teaching of law, customary law became a mere name. This was the state of affairs at the beginning of the nineteenth century. Juristic science thought that it was its function not to determine what is law, but to point out to the judge, who was appointed and commissioned by the state, what he should apply as law according to the will of his employer. There never was a time when the law promulgated by the state in statutory form was the only law, even for the courts and other tribunals, and there has always been an undercurrent, therefore, which strove to secure proper recognition for law that was not promulgated by the state. This undercurrent forced its way to the surface at two different periods: in the writings of the teachers of the law of nature school[1] in the seventeenth and eighteenth centuries, and again in the writings of Savigny and Puchta, the founders of the Historical School[2]. To what extent the teachers of the law of nature were the precursors of the historical conception of law, and to what extent the pioneers of the Historical School were carrying out the ideas of the Natural Law School, has, unfortunately, been realized only very rarely, and has never been properly investigated by anyone. These two schools have this in common: neither has blindly accepted as law what the state declared to be law; both have sought to ascertain the nature of law in a scientific manner. Both have found its origin outside of the state: one, in the nature of man; the other, in the legal consciousness of the people.

Neither of these schools has fully followed out its ideas. Doubtless they were hindered by the idea which has dominated all juristic thinking down to our day, i.e. the idea that only that is law which the judge applies in the administration of justice. In spite of their radicalism[3],

1. law of nature school：自然法学派。主张自然法为正义的标准，坚持正义的绝对法。
2. Historical School：即历史法学派
3. radicalism：激进主义

the teachers of the law of nature, particularly those outside of France, where the situation was somewhat different from that in the other countries of Europe, never dared to assert, with any show of firmness at least, that a judge can ever be under a duty to apply a rule of law that has not, tacitly at least, been approved by the state. Accordingly the law of nature is, in fact, suspended in mid-air. Only that is law which is binding on the judge; but the law of nature is not binding on the judge. At this point the doctrine of the school of the law of nature completely reverses itself. The protagonists of natural law as non-state law based on the nature of man in the end demand legislation by the state in order that the law of nature may be realized.

Savigny and Puchta perhaps were the first to conceive, vaguely at least, the idea of a science of law the exclusive object of which is to promote knowledge. Their whole life-work bears witness to a disdain, unconscious perhaps, never expressly admitted certainly, clearly marked however, for a science of law which serves only practical purposes. Even in their studies in the common law[1], i.e. the positive law[2] of their day, they sought to arrive at a scientific understanding of that element of the common law which constitutes the nature of all law; they sought to comprehend not a system of law, but law itself. Far in advance of their time, they turned away from the insignificant figure of the personal legislator and directed their attention to the great elemental forces that are at work in the creation of law. These natural forces prevail in customary law, which, it is true, was to them a symbol of all that is superhuman in law rather than a clearly discerned concept. Nevertheless the task of creating a science of law proved too great even for them. They made a beginning, but were unable to carry it out.

The founders of the Historical School never attempted actually to

1. common law：共同法，与英美法的普通法不同。
2. positive law：实证法

apply in their dogmatic works[1] the methodological principles which they professed in theory. Their interest in non-state law led them to strive for a clear understanding of the concept of customary law; but they never took the trouble to investigate the customary law of Germany; they made no attempt to perfect the methods, highly imperfect then as well as now, for the ascertainment of customary law; they rejected Beseler's suggestions, which, inadequate to be sure, were nevertheless worthy of serious consideration; they did not discuss a single case taken from the living customary law that was not already known in legal literature. They do indeed insist that the law develops in the popular legal consciousness (*Rechtsbewusstsein des Volkes*)[2], but barring the much decried method of legislation, they cannot tell us how new law is received into the body of already existing positive law; they never express an opinion as to the method by which legal science recognizes and receives new law, unless, indeed, it is supplied ready-made by legislation. The legal material that they deal with is comprised in its entirety in the common law juristic science of the eighteenth century. They arrange it much more carefully, observe much more closely, occasionally merely more subtly, the states of fact previously discussed by their predecessors; they test it by the content of the sources which they have re-examined historically and, occasionally, doctrinally; they often correct the traditional definitions with remarkable acumen; but they make no attempt to enrich it or to introduce new methods.

They have had few continuators[3] and no followers. Beseler, it is true, in obedience to a splendid inspiration, made an attempt to begin afresh where the thread had been cut. But though he saw many things in their true relations, he thought few of them out to their logical

---

1. dogmatic works：教义学著作
2. legal consciousness (*Rechtsbewusstsein des Volkes*)：法律意识
3. continuators：承继者

conclusions; at any rate, he did not express his thoughts clearly, and therefore the general judgment as to the value of his work was easily misled by malevolent critics. Only a few Germanists and a few teachers of ecclesiastical law[1] are actually working in the field of legal dogmatic in the spirit of the Historical School. The former confine themselves to searching out the vestiges of ancient German legal institutions that have been received into the codifications[2] of German particular law, i.e. the so-called common German private law. The latter limit themselves to a very narrow field.

Particularly as to the all-important matter of customary law, retrogression rather than progress is observable. The epigoni[3] of the Historical School who are working in the field of historical dogmatic pass by Savigny and Puchta's doctrine of customary law, which is one of the great achievements of the human mind, with little or no appreciation of its importance. Ignoring Savigny and Puchta, they start from the common law juristic science of the eighteenth century. To them customary law no longer is a power which governs the creation of law, the laws of which must be made the subject of scientific inquiry. The only question in their minds is: What are the conditions under which, according to the intention of the legislator, which is to be ascertained by interpretation of the *corpus iuris civilis* and *canonici* or of a modern statute, customary law is binding upon the judge? That is to say, it still is nothing more than a practical juristic science which is concerned only with the duties of the judge. At the same time, it manifests no interest in non-state law. The doctrine of customary law is disposed of in a few introductory paragraphs of the institutional books and of the handbooks; a few smaller works discuss the controversial questions that are sufficiently well known. There is

1. ecclesiastical law：教会法
2. codifications：法典化
3. epigoni：追随者

no thought of systematic inquiry. They do not even know of a method for it. The small number of scholars who did examine individual cases of customary law (Bruns, Fitting) dealt only with written sources, especially with juristic literature, i.e. they proceeded very much as if they were dealing with a statute. Under the heading *The Interpretation of the Rules of Law*[1], they actually discuss only the interpretation of statutes. To introduce, as Windscheid[2] and Baehr have done, the course of judicial decisions into the presentation of the positive law is considered a pioneering innovation.

Accordingly practical juristic science has, in spite of Savigny and Puchta, remained what it has been ever since the rise of the state-controlled judiciary, i.e. the science of the application of the law created by the state. Practically all modern juristic writing and teaching, within the sphere of private law[3] at least, pretends to be nothing but a setting forth, as clear, as faithful, as complete, as is possible, of the content of statute law in its finest ramifications and its remotest applications. Such a literature and such teaching cannot, however, be termed scientific; in fact, they are merely a more emphatic form of publication of statutes. The ultimate inference which is drawn by the exponents of this school is the doctrine of the perfection and completeness of the legal system. When the Historical School makes this assertion, it reverses itself just as the Law of Nature School did when it demanded legislation by the state. This conception of law, which was first stated in express terms by Brinz[4], but which had actually been applied at an earlier date by the exponents of the Historical School, so effectively brought down the fate of the Historical School upon its head on lines parallel to the fate of the Law of Nature

1. *The Interpretation of the Rules of Law*：《法律规则的解释》
2. Windscheid：温德沙伊德（1817—1892），《德国民法典》起草者。
3. private law：私法
4. Brinz：布林兹（1820—1887），德国法学家和政治家。

School that one is tempted to see the sway of a higher justice therein. There is a veritable gulf fixed between the *Weltanschauung* (world-view, or philosophy) of the two great vanquishers[1] of the Law of Nature School, who founded the Historical School, and the proposition that there is within the positive law an answer for every question that might arise, and that one need but find it. And this theorem — for it is nothing more than a practically meaningless theorem[2] — makes it perfectly obvious that practical juristic science, in its entirety, does not purport to be anything but a system of norms according to which the judge must render his decisions; for surely no man has ever entertained the preposterous thought that the law in its entiret is a complete system of rules which regulate in advance all human conduct in all possible relations. Jellinek[3] has made the remark that the dogma of the logical perfection of the legal system does not apply to public law "but only to those parts of the legal order in which the final decision of the individual case lies in the hands of the judge." By way of proof, Jellinek adduces a great number of problems of public law for which the existing public law offers no solution whatever. But the situation would be the same if the final decision did lie in the hands of a judge — and this is possible in each and every one of the cases adduced by Jellinek. Only, if that were the case, it would be incumbent upon the judge to find a solution, but he would not find it on the basis of the logically perfect system; for it is not contained therein. What Jellinek considers a peculiarity of public law, therefore, holds true, in fact, for every department of law, and the principle of the logically perfect system of law does not state a scientifically established fact, but merely expresses the practical endeavor to supply the judge with a store of

1. vanquishers：征服者
2. theorem：定理
3. Jellinek：耶里内克（1851—1911），德国著名法学家，著有《人权与公民权利宣言——现代宪法史论》。

norms for decision sufficient for all cases that might arise and to make them binding upon him as effectively as possible.

In the light of these considerations, it is possible to understand the view; which still prevails at the present time, that the law is a compulsory order, that it is an essential element of the law to recognize enforceable claims[1] and to impose enforceable duties. First of all we must arrive at a clear understanding of what is meant by compulsion. It cannot mean psychological compulsion of any kind; for man always acts under some kind of psychological compulsion[2], even quite outside of the legal sphere. It can, therefore, mean only such compulsion as is considered characteristic of law; i.e. only such psychological compulsion as is exercised by threat of penalty or of compulsory execution. That these two kinds of compulsion have been considered essential characteristics of law can be explained only by the fact that law has always been believed to be the rule to be applied by the judge. With rare exceptions, cases are brought before the judge solely in order to have the judge impose a penalty or in order to secure compulsory enforcement of the claim after the judge has recognized its validity, and, with rare exceptions, a judgment of a court of law can actually be executed in our day. Law applied by the court and law that can be enforced by compulsion are practically synonymous to day. To a person, however, whose conception of law is that of a rule of conduct, compulsion by threat of penalty as well as of compulsory execution becomes a secondary matter. To him the scene of all human life is not the court room. It is quite obvious that a man lives in innumerable legal relations, and that, with few exceptions, he quite voluntarily performs the duties incumbent upon him because of these relations. One performs one's duties as father or son, as husband or wife; does not interfere with one's neighbor's enjoyment of his property, pays

1. enforceable claims：可执行请求权
2. compulsion：制裁，强制

one's debts, delivers that which one has sold, and renders to one's employer the performance to render which one has obligated oneself. The jurist, of course, is ready with the objection that all men perform their duties only because they know that the courts could eventually compel them to perform them. If he should take the pains, to which, indeed, he is not accustomed, to observe what men do and leave undone, he would soon be convinced of the fact that, as a rule, the thought of compulsion by the courts does not even enter the minds of men. In so far as they do not simply act instinctively, as indeed is usually the case, their conduct is determined by quite different motives: they might otherwise have quarrels with their relatives, lose their positions, lose custom, get the reputation of being quarrelsome, dishonest, irresponsible persons. The jurist ought to be the last person of all to overlook the fact that that which men do or leave undone as a legal duty in this sense often is something quite different from, occasionally is much more than, that which the authorities could ever compel them to do or leave undone. The rule of conduct, not infrequently, is quite different from the rule that is obeyed because of compulsion (*Zwangsnorm*[1]).

It was observed long ago that in a considerable part of public law in the narrow sense (*Staatsrecht*[2]) and administrative law[3] there is no compulsion in this sense whatever. If, in reply to this argument, one would urge the compulsion that lies in the responsibility of cabinet ministers or in the parliamentary or the disciplinary responsibility of officials, one should show whether or not this compulsion can, at this stage, be said to be identical with the compulsion that lies in compulsory execution. These two things seem to lie pretty far apart from each other. At this point we may disregard altogether

1. *Zwangsnorm*：〈德〉强制性规则
2. *Staatsrecht*：〈德〉狭义上的公法
3. administrative law：行政法

the psychological question whether or not a weapon so dull as the impeachment of a minister practically always turns out to be, or as the parliamentary and the disciplinary responsibility of an official turns out to be in many cases can be said to amount to a means of compulsion. But even this resource will fail in the case of international law, ecclesiastical law, and public law in the narrow sense (*Staatsrecht*), as well as in a considerable part of the administrative law of an absolute or of a non-parliamentary constitutional state, and particularly in the case of almost all precepts regulating the competence and the order of business of parliamentary representative bodies. It has often been said that almost any breach of the constitution may be perpetrated without the perpetrators being held to account, provided the majority of the parliament or of any other representative body and the presiding officer are in agreement. It is true, in such case there remains the "restraint exercised by public opinion" popular indignation or resentment," and, lastly, the possibility of revolution. But can a sanction of this kind, which is not prescribed by law and is not regulated by law, be considered an essential characteristic of law? There are no social norms[1], whether they be norms of morality, of ethical custom, of honor, of tact, of etiquette, or of fashion, but have recourse to a sanction of this kind whenever they are being transgressed[2]. And in the case of a few of these non-legal norms, this sanction is often more effective than in the case of a legal norm; occasionally it is so powerful as to overcome even the compulsion exercised by legal execution. Many a man pays his gambling debts although he fails to pay his tailor, fights a duel with the person who challenges him, contemptuous[3] of the criminal law, but blindly obedient to the social sanction.

---

1. social norms：社会规范
2. transgressed：违反的
3. contemptuous：蔑视的

All of this has been stated often enough, and it is perhaps superfluous to revert to it here. Therefore I will emphasize but one point — a point which has been neglected hitherto, i.e. the great number of situations in private law for which no effective legal sanction has been provided. This is true particularly in the case of all purely personal claims strictly limited to a certain time which arise from permanent legal relations. Many precepts that determine the mutual rights and duties of the members of a family or of a partnership, the duties of the organs of a corporation, of the board of directors[1], of the members, or of the meeting of the members, fail to create an enforceable legal situation because, as the jurists say, they create no subjective law: there is no legal remedy to enforce them. And in many cases of this kind there is no possibility of availing oneself of an existing legal remedy. Would a member of an association sue the board of directors because the reading room has not been placed at his disposal? Would an employer sue a servant girl for not tidying the house? What would a suit of this kind avail him? The claim for damages would not afford relief, for no matter how much importance he may have attached to his right at the moment, in the end he will not be able to prove damage that is worth mentioning. It is only where the obligor[2] has, by his conduct, made the relation unendurable, that the obligee[3] is given an effectual legal remedy, i.e. the right to demand the dissolution of the relation and damages. But this does not involve a legal sanction which effectively compels the other party to perform his duties; for the latter very often embarks upon his illegal course of conduct in order to bring about the dissolution of the relation in exchange for the payment of damages. The order of human society is based upon the fact that, in general, legal duties are being performed,

---

1. board of directors：董事会
2. obligor：债务人
3. obligee：债权人

not upon the fact that failure to perform gives rise to a cause of action.

Three elements therefore must, under all circumstances, be excluded from the concept of law as a compulsory order maintained by the state — a concept to which the traditional juristic science has clung tenaciously in substance, though not always in form. It is not an essential element of the concept of law that it be created by the state, nor that it constitute the basis for the decisions of the courts or other tribunals, nor that it be the basis of a legal compulsion consequent upon such a decision. A fourth element remains, and that will have to be the point of departure, i.e. the law is an ordering. It is the deathless merit of Gierke[1] that he discovered this characteristic of law in the bodies which he called associations (*Genossenschaften*), and among which he numbered the state, and that he gave an account of it in a det ailed study. As a result of his labors, we may consider it established that, within the scope of the concept of the association, the law is an organization, that is to say, a rule which assigns to each and every member of the association his position in the community, whether it be of domination or of subjection (*Uberordnung*[2], *Unterordnung*[3]), and his duties; and that it is now quite impossible to assume that law exists within these associations chiefly for the purpose of deciding controversies that arise out of the communal relation. The legal norm according to which legal disputes are being decided, the norm for decision, is merely a species of legal norm with limited functions and purposes.

Gierke's doctrine is open to the objection that it is taking a partial view of things, but only inasmuch as it presents as applying only to the

---

1. Gierke：基尔克（1841—1921），德国法学家、政治家。其为德国历史法学派中日耳曼学派最后一位代表性人物。其主要著作有《德国合作社法》(4卷本)、《德国私法》(3卷本)、《自然法和德国法》、《约翰斯・阿尔图修斯与国家理论在自然法上的发展》等。
2. *Überordnung*：〈德〉支配者
3. *Unterordnung*：〈德〉被支配者

law of associations that which holds true for the whole legal sphere. His own book shows plainly that the law of associations does not organize human beings only, but things as well. It is a question not only of what the members of the association do or leave undone, but of the extent to which they should be permitted to avail themselves of the property of the association. It was observed long ago that Gierke has formula ted his concept so broadly as to include practically the entire German law within its scope. And herein lies the germ of a true and great conception of the nature of law. Just as we find the ordered community wherever we follow its traces, far beyond the limits set by Gierke, so we also find law everywhere, ordering and upholding every human association.

The term social sciences, at the present time, comprises every manner of science of human society, theoretical as well as practical; and therefore it includes not only the theoretical science of economics but the practical science (*Nationalökonomie*[1], as it is called), statistics, and politics as well. At the beginning of the last century, the French philosopher Auguste Comte[2] created the term sociology to designate the totality of the theoretical social sciences. Attempts are making to give to sociology a specific content, to make it an independent science, the function of which is to present a synthesis of the content of all theoretical social sciences, which might constitute a unitary "general part" of the social sciences. The existence of such a science may be justified, but it would not be advisable to call it sociology, for in that case it would be necessary to find a new term for the social sciences as a whole. The term *Jurisprudenz*[3] hitherto has comprised both the theoretical and the practical science of law; and it is likely that this

---

1. *Nationalökonomie*：〈德〉国民经济学
2. Auguste Comte：奥古斯特·孔德（1798—1857），法国著名哲学家、社会学和实证主义创始人。
3. *Jurisprudenz*：〈德〉法学

customary terminology will be retained, but it will be necessary to distinguish between the theory of law in the proper sense of the term, the science of law, on the one hand, and the practical juristic science (*Jurisprudenz*) and, where there is no danger of misunderstanding, juristic science (*Jurisprudenz*) simply, on the other. Since the law is a social phenomenon, every kind of legal science (*Jurisprudenz*) is a social science; but legal science in the proper sense of the term is a part of the theoretical science of society, of sociology. The sociology of law is the theoretical science of law (*die wissenschaftliche Lehre vom Recht*[1]).

1. *die wissenschaftliche Lehre vom Recht*：〈德〉理论性法学

II THE INNER ORDER OF THE SOCIAL ASSOCIATIONS

It is axiomatic that all study in the field of social science is based on the concept of human society. Society is the sum total of the human associations that have mutual relations with one another. And these associations that constitute human society are very heterogeneous[1]. The state, the nation, the commurdty of states which are bound together by the ties of international law, i.e. the political, economic, intellectual, and social association of the civilized nations of the earth extending far beyond the bounds of the individual state and nation, the religious communions and the individual churches, the various sects and religious groups, the corporations, the classes, the professions, the political parties within the state, the families in the narrowest and in the widest sense, the social groups and cliques — this universe of interlacing rings and intersecting circles — constitute a society to the extent that acting and reacting upon one another is at all perceptible among them. There is then, first of all, a society consisting of the civilized nations of the earth; within this society are various narrower societies, e.g. a society of the Christian and of the Mohammedan nations[2], and lastly societies that comprise only the individual civilized nations. Nations that are altogether outside of this sphere of mutual action and reaction are beyond the pale of human society, e.g. the savage and the barbarous nations of the earth, and,

1. heterogeneous：多样化
2. Mohammedan nations：伊斯兰民族

until recent times, the Japanese and the Chinese, who, however, in their seclusion, constituted a society of their own.

From these various kinds of groups of human beings, we must select, first of all, a certain kind of organized association, which we shall hereafter designate as the primitive (genetic) association. We meet with it in primitive times in various forms as clan (*Geschlecht, Gens, Sippe*[1]), family, house community. The clan and the family are its original forms. It cannot as yet be determined which of these two must be considered the true original form (*Urform*[2]); whether the clan is nothing more than a full-grown, enlarged family, or whether the family developed at a much later time than, and within, the clan. It is self-evident that, from the moment in which men begin to form associations, increased capacity for association with others becomes a weapon in the struggle for existence. It effects the gradual exclusion and extinction of those in whom self-seeking and predatory instincts predominate, and the survival of those that have capacity for socialization, who henceforth are the stronger because they can avail themselves of the strength of the whole association. Accordingly natural selection and heredity produce a race of human beings which is increasingly capable of socialization. This feeling of solidarity which has its roots in the dim consciousness of mutual interdependence begets the clan, and, strengthened by the consciousness of common ancestry, the (cognatic, based on blood relationship) family. Among breeders of cattle and tillers of the soil, whose common toil leads them to dwell together, the family develops into the house community, which is usually also called family. Out of the union of genetic associations, clans, families, house communities, grows the tribe, and, in course of time, the nation.

---

1. *Geschlecht, Gens, Sippe*：氏族（*Geschlecht* 是氏族，现代用语，*Gens* 指古罗马时期的氏族，*Sippe* 更强调血统）
2. *Urform*：〈德〉初源形态

In lower stages of development, the social order of mankind rests exclusively upon the genetic associations and their union into tribe and nation. These associations therefore fulfil a number of functions. The clan, the house commurdty, the family, is an association economic, religious, military, and legal; it is a community of language, ethical custom, and social life. But in more advanced societies, these functions are gradually severing from the genetic associations; groups of a different kind arise, which add to their new functions by taking over the original functions of the genetic associations. These are: the commune, the state, the religious communion, the society, the political party, the social coterie, the social club, the economic association in agriculture, shop, and factory, the cooperative society[1], the association of the members of a calling, all the associations connected with the transportation of persons or goods. Among the peoples of the highest degree of civilization, a man becomes a member of an almost incalculable number of associations of the most diverse kinds; his life becomes richer, more varied, more complex. And in consequence, the once powerful genetic associations languish and, in part, fall into decay. Only the house community of the nearest blood relatives, who dwell under the same roof, the family in the narrowest sense of the word, has been able to maintain itself in full vigor down to our day; the wider family has largely faded out, and of the clan only a few scarcely perceptible traces remain, and these are to be found exclusively among the higher nobility and among the peasantry.

All later associations are in a relation of pronounced contrast to the genetic associations. With few exceptions every man belongs to a genetic association; there is no such necessity as to the other associations. One is born into the genetic associations; but membership in the other associations is a matter of voluntary joining and reception.

---

1. cooperative society：合作社

The genetic association owes its existence to unconscious impulses; the later associations are the result of conscious human activity. And this contrast is heightened with every advance in civilization. One hundred years ago, a man's occupation or his profession, his religious fellowship, his political affiliations, and his social connections, were determined to a much greater extent than they are today, by his descent, i.e. by the genetic association to which he belonged. All these things were determined by free choice to a much lesser extent than they are today.

Though we know very little of the law of the early times of the peoples from whom the civilized nations of Europe have sprung, there can be no doubt that of what today is mostly, and sometimes even exclusively, called law, i.e. of the fixed rule of law, formulated in words, which issues from a power superior to the individual, and which is imposed upon the latter from without, only a few negligible traces can be found among them. Their law is chiefly the order of the clans, families, houses. It determines the prerequisites and the consequences of a valid marriage, the mutual relation of the spouses, of parents and children, and the mutual relations of the other members of the clan, family, and household. Each association creates this order for itself quite independently. It is not bound by the order which exists in other associations for the same relations. And if the orders in associations of the same kind differ very little from each other, this must be attributed to the similarity of the conditions of life; often to borrowing; but by no means to a uniform order in some manner prescribed for them from without. In the language of German scholarship, there may possibly be a general law (*allgemeines Recht*)[1] in these associations, but not a common law (*getneines Recht*)[2].

As soon as ownership of land becomes established, law arises

1. general law (*allgemeines Recht*)：一般法
2. common law (*getneines Recht*)：共同法

concerning it, but without any general rules of law. Each settlement creates its own land law; each landlord imposes it independently upon his villeins[1]; each royal grant, quite independently of all others, makes provision for the legal status of the estate it grants. There are concrete legal relations in the various communes, settlements, and manors, but no law of ownership in land such as is found in the *corpus iuris*[2] or in modern statute-books.

The same holds true for the contract. The law of contracts is based solely upon the content of the contracts that are being entered into. There are no general legal propositions governing contracts. There is an utter absence of all those rules of compulsion, of eking out, and of interpretation with which the *corpus iuris* and modern statute books abound. Where the contract is silent, there is no law; and the literal, narrow interpretation of contracts, which is so characteristic of the older law, is not based upon formalism, which is usually imputed to primitive times, but which in reality is quite foreign to them, but upon the fact that, outside of the language of the contract, there is nothing to stand on.

General rules of law are found first of all, perhaps, in the law of inheritance. In the most ancient times, only the members of the household of the deceased take by inheritance; and these general rules concern only the rights of distant relatives. Even the Twelve Tables[3] say nothing of the *sui heredes*[4], but do speak of the agnates[5] and the gentiles[6]; and we encounter the same situation in the ancient Germanic folk laws and in the Slavic law[7] books. This shows that these

1. villeins：农奴
2. *corpus iuris*：〈拉〉《国法大全》
3. Twelve Tables：《十二铜表法》
4. *sui heredes*：〈拉〉自家继承人
5. agnates：父系
6. gentiles：氏族
7. Slavic law：斯拉夫法律

rules belong to a later stratum. The disposition by the members of a household of the goods of one of their own number who had died was determined independently, even in historical times, by each and every house and clan. It was only for the event that there were no members of the household in existence that general precepts arose at a comparatively early time.

The earliest state is based exclusively upon the agreement entered into by the noble clans that found it; and over and above this agreement there is nothing that might determine the position, rights, and duties of the individual organs of the state. After kingship for life, and, at a later time hereditary kingship, has begun to replace temporary leadership, everything is dependent upon the personal ity; the weal th; the influence of the king, and upon the number, the bravery, and the loyalty of his retainers. If the king can rely upon his retainers, his power may be very great; if not, he must, in matters of important governmental action, secure the consent of the influential men among the people, possibly of all the people. Accordingly the council of the elders and the popular assembly are not constitutional institutions, but merely means employed by the king to enforce his will. The authority of the royal officials is based on the king's mandate and upon the royal power. Therefore there are no legal propositions concerning it.

The present-day private law of princes is a part of the most ancient legal order of the human race which has been preserved for our day like an antediluvian gnat encased in amber. Von Dungern has conclusively shown that the private law of princes has no material content of any kind. It merely provides that the families of the high nobility may determine their legal relations independently. What that determination shall be lies exclusively within their discretion. This present-day condition of the private law of princes was the condition of all law in time past. The self-determination of the families of the high nobility, however, extends solely to a few questions of the law of the family and of the law of inheritance; whereas in primitive times each and every association and, within the association, each and every legal relation, contract, or parcel of ground had its own law; and, apart from this law of the individual legal relation, there was no law in ancient human society.

This legal order is reflected in the Homeric poems[1], the Scandinavian sagas[2], and the *Germania* of Tacitus[3]. The legal traditions of the Twelve Tables and of the most ancient Germanic legal records, indeed, to a certain extent, present a later development. The latter contain general legal propositions relating to the system of penalties, to penal procedure, and to a few matters of public and private law. These are in part, it is true, merely borrowings from Roman law[4]; in part, they have originated under the influence of Roman law; but for the most part, they bear witness to a more advanced stage of legal development. The Slavic legal sources bear a similar relation to Byzantine law[5].

But even the highly developed Roman law of historical times contains untold survivals which point to an older condition such as has been described. The whole of human life and all relations within the Roman house and clan are based on the autonomy of each house and clan. In the earlier stratum of Roman contracts, the words of the contracts det ermine all righ ts and duties arising therefrom. This is an inevitable consequence of the lack of general rules concerning the presuppositions and consequences of contractual duties. From the earliest times, the right and law of inheritance of the *sui heredes* was never governed by any regulations. This is shown by the sovereign power of disposition of the testament as well as by the lack of all

---

1. Homeric poems：荷马史诗
2. Scandinavian sagas：斯堪的纳维亚传奇
3. *Germania* of Tacitus：塔西佗的《日耳曼尼亚志》
4. Roman law：罗马法
5. Byzantine law：拜占庭法

regulations governing settlenients made by the heirs of the body in the *actio familiae herciscundae*[1]. According to clear evidence, the right of inheritance of the gentiles was regulated quite independently by each *gens*. And what in actual fact is Roman *Staatsrecht* (public law in the narrow sense)? Barring the content of the small number of *leges* that contain *Staatsrecht*, everything that Mommsen sets forth under this head is merely a presentation of the practice of the organs of the Roman state during the existence of the Empire. Mommsen does, indeed, arrive at general legal propositions at every point; but with very few exceptions these were the product of his own intellectual labor; they were abstracted by him from the facts; they never were the rules that regulated the facts. Indeed one may call this Roman public law in the narrow sense, but it certainly is not a constitution of the Roman state. Since Oriental aristocrats[2] have begun to travel in Europe and have been receiving a European education, there is no lack of statutes in the Orient, occasionally even of written constitutions; but these are mere toys, not without significance for the far distant future perhaps, but utterly ineffectual at the present time. If one would become acquainted with the actual public law in the narrow sense of an Oriental state, one must try to understand the activity of the individual organs of the state from actual observation, which is more than a substitute for the *Corpus Inscriptionum Latinarum*[3]. The methodological significance of Von Dungern work on the public law in the narrow sense of Egypt rests on his appreciation of this fact.

In the primitive stage, the whole legal order consists in the inner order of the human associations, of which, indeed, the state is one. Each association creates this order for itself, even though it is true that an association often copies an order existing in other associations,

---

1. *actio familiae herciscundae*：〈拉〉遗产分割之诉
2. Oriental aristocrats：东方贵族
3. *Corpus Inscriptionum Latinarum*：〈拉〉《拉丁铭文大全》

or in case of a splitting up of an association, takes over an order and continues it. Because of these facts, to which must be added the similarities caused by the similarity of the relations, common features will not be lacking. To an observer from the outside these common features might appear to constitute a common law of the nation. But this is only a generalization made by the observer himself on the basis of what he has seen and heard. Tacitus makes a number of statements about the legal relations of the ancient Germans, but a cursory glance at his account suffices to show that it contains no legal propositions, but only statements about what the Germans customarily did and left undone. Society, if one may use the term with reference to those times, maintained its balance not by means of rules of law, but by means of the inner order of its associations.

Passing over a great number of generations of men, we reach the feudal state. It has been extremely difficult for the modern man to understand the feudal state, for the reason that, for a long time, he had been trying to find a constitution of the feudal state; whereas the chief characteristic of the feudal state is the fact that it has no constitution, but only agreements. The relation between the king and the great lords to whom he has granted fiefs is a contractual one. Likewise the relation between the great lords and those whom they have enfeoffed; likewise the relation between the latter and those whom they, in turn, have enfeoffed. On the lowest rung of the ladder are the serfs. Of course, one or more rungs may be omitted, and the feudal lords may have serfs at any level in this scale. In order to write an exhaustive description. of the feudal st ate, one must be able to state the content of all the agreements entered into between the lords and their liegemen and of the relation between the lords and the villeins, which often is merely contractual. The agreements and the relation between the lord and the villeins may be very much alike in a certain district and among a certain people. But this similarity also is based upon the similarity of the attendant circumstances, upon direct imitation or borrowing, not upon a general rule. What is called "feudal law" is primarily a scientific elaboration of the common element in the individual agreements, which at a later period is transformed into a general rule of law which ekes out the content of the agreements.

It is true, in the more developed feudal law[1], assemblies of the feudal tenants of the individual feudal lords are not unknown. Occasionally these are assemblies not only of the immediate tenants of the feudal lord, but also of the tenants of the intermediate feudatories[2]. Sometimes there are assemblies of villeins. These assemblies adopt common resolutions. But before the idea of law had made its way, these resolutions did not contain legal propositions[3] in the modern sense of the term. They are merely expressions of the common will, and their legal significance is based upon the fact that they are being accepted by the feudal lord, and thereby become collective agreements with the feudal lord. Collective agreements in this sense of the term were: the most ancient resolutions of the German Imperial Diet[4], the Magna Charta Libertatum[5], which to the present day has remained the foundation of the English constitution, and on the whole, the law of the German manorial rights[6] and of the corresponding services.

But the feudal constitution was far from being the whole content of the social order of the feudal state. Within the feudal st ate, the clan, the family, the house continued; but the clan was weakened considerably. Side by side with it, new local associations arose, which took over a considerable number of social functions. Among the local associations, the &ty soon became very important, and achieved

---

1. feudal law：封建法，欧洲中世纪关于封建土地保有制、不动产等方面的一整套法律制度。
2. feudatories：封臣
3. legal propositions：法律命题
4. German Imperial Diet：德意志神圣罗马帝国议会
5. Magna Charta Libertatum：《自由大宪章》
6. manorial rights：领地权利

a considerable measure of independence, which in effect placed it outside of the feudal constitution. The feudal constitution, in fact, has always remained a constitution of the open country. Within the walls of the city, a vast number of social associations, which were unknown elsewhere and an active legal life developed. Here for the first time fully developed legal institutions were expressed in a number of legal propositions: the law of real property[1], of pledge[2], of contract, of inheritance.

But these legal propositions constitute an infinitesimal[3] part of the legal order. In the feudal state as well as elsewhere, the great bulk of the legal order is not based upon the legal propositions, but upon the inner order of the social associations, of the older ones (the clan, the family, the house community), as well as of those of more recent origin — the feudal association, the manor, the mark community, the urban community, the guilds and trade unions, the corporations and foundations. If one would obtain a knowledge of the law of mediaeval society[4], one must not confine oneself to a study of the legal propositions, but must study it in the deeds of grant, the charters, the land registers, the records of the guilds, the city books, the regulations of the guilds. Even at this period, the center of gravity of the law lies in the inner order of the human associations.

If one compares the law of the present with that of past centuries, one cannot but be struck at the first glance by the great importance which in the course of centuries has attached to the legal proposition, authoritatively pronounced and formulated. With the sole exception of Great Britain, the *Staatsrecht* (public law in the narrow sense) of all European states has been put into this form, as well as the law

---

1. real property：不动产
2. pledge：担保法
3. infinitesimal：微量的
4. mediaeval society：中世纪社会

of the state magistracies[1], administrative law, procedural law[2], and, apparently, the whole body of private law and of penal law. For this reason the idea that the law is nothing but a body of legal propositions dominates legal thinking today.

This idea, however, contains so many contradictory elements that it refutes itself. This inner inconsistency is least apparent in *Staatsrecht* (public law in the narrow sense), in administrative law, and in the law of procedure. But modern investigation of the normative significance of the factual, of the *Konventionalregel*[3], and of the practice of administrative boards has shown that this branch of the law too does not consist exclusively of legal propositions. On the other hand, the legal rules barely touch the surface of the modern order of the family. The law of corporations and of foundations is based in the main upon the articles of association. In spite of the detailed provisions of the law of contracts, the content of the contract is of greater importance in the individual case than the rules of law governing contracts. Testamentary declarations of will, nuptial agreements[4], contracts of inheritance, agreements among heirs, are of much greater impor tance in the law of inheritance than the rules of law concerning it. Every judge, every administrative official, knows that, comparatively speaking, he rarely renders a decision based solely on legal propositions. By far the greatest number of decisions are based upon documents, testimony of witnesses or experts, contracts, articles of association, last wills and testaments, and other declarations. In other words, in the language of jurists, in a much greater number of instances judgment is being rendered upon questions of fact than upon questions of law. And the fact is a matter of the inner order of the human associations, as to

1. state magistracies：地方执法官
2. procedural law：程序法
3. *Konventionalregel*：〈德〉传统规则与法律
4. nuptial agreements：婚姻协议

which the judge obtains information from the testimony of witnesses and experts, from contracts, agreements among heirs, declarations by last will and testament. Even today, just as in primitive times, the fate of man is determined to a much greater extent by the inner order of the associations than by legal propositions.

This truth is hidden from the eye of the jurist by the fact that to him an adjudication upon a question of fact merely amounts to a subsumption[1] of the ascertained facts under a legal proposition. But this is due solely to a juristic habit of thought. The state existed before the constitution; the family is older than the order of the family; possession antedates ownership; there were contracts before there was a law of contracts; and even the testamen where it is of native origin, is much older than the law of last wills and testaments. If the jurists think that before a binding contract was entered into, before a valid testament was made, there must have been in existence a legal proposition according to which agreements or testaments are binding, they are placing the abstract before the concrete. Perhaps it seems more readily understandable to a jurist that a legal proposition concerning the law of contracts or the law of wills might be binding than that a contract or a will might be binding without a legal proposition. But the mental processes of nations and of men, excepting the jurists among them, do not function in this fashion. It can be shown that the idea that prevailed among men in the past was that their right had arisen from a contract or from a grant; the idea that it had arisen from a legal proposition was altogether foreign to them. And at the present time, unless legal theory exerts its influence, men generally assume that their rights arise not from legal propositions but from the relations of man to man, from marriage, contract, last will and testament. That anyone might owe his rights to a legal

1. subsumption：涵摄

proposition, is a notion that even today is current only among jurists. Social phenomena, however, can be explained not by construing them juristically but by inferring from facts the modes of thought that underlie them.

Up to this point, I have been confining this presentation intentionally to the nations of Europe; but its application is not limited to these. Among primitive races, the law is generally identical with the inner order of their associations. At this stage of development there are no legal propositions at all. At a somewhat higher st age, they appear in the form of religious commands. And it seems that until man has reached a very high stage of development, he cannot fully conceive the idea that the abstract rules of law can force their will upon life. It is true, the German folk laws of the early Middle Ages contain very detailed legal propositions, but probably they were applied only in those parts of the country in which there was a Roman population sufficiently large to bring about the continuation of Roman modes of thought even in a Germanic society. How small the influence of legislation was, even in the Middle Ages, is sufficiently well known. Travelers in backward countries, in the Orient, in parts of eastern and southern Europe, are struck by the general disorder. This disorder is caused by the fact that general legal propositions, even if there are such, are not being followed. There is a strange contrast between this lack of order in public life and the strictness with which the traditional order of the small association, of the household, of the family, of the clan, is followed.

The great master of comparative legal science, Sir Henry Sumner Maine[1], has pointed this out in another connection. He was the first to state that at all times the oldest law has been the procedural law. Taken literally, this statement, of course, is absurd . A society, be

1. Sir Henry Sumner Maine：亨利·萨姆纳·梅因爵士（1822—1888），英国法学家，历史法学派的集大成者。

it never so simple and primitive, whose whole order is based upon procedural law is unthinkable. Even legal disputes are nowhere decided solely on the basis of procedural norms. It is true, often a complaint is dismissed because of a mistake of form on the part of the plaintiff, or a complaint is permitted to succeed because of a mistake of form on the part of the defendant; but in every case where defects of form did not enter into consideration, the decision had to be rendered on the basis of the material law[1]. This would have been impossible if there had been no material law. But although the procedural law was not, indeed, the oldest law, Maine's doctrine is correct in so far as the oldest legal propositions were those of procedural law; perhaps the propositions connected with provisions for penalties. Undoubtedly the material law was already in existence, even though it had not yet been formula ted in legal propositions.

The inner order of the associations of human beings is not only the original, but also, down to the present time, the basic form of law. The legal proposition not only comes into being at a much later time, but is largely derived from the inner order of the associations. In order to explain the beginnings, the development, and the nature of law, one must first of all inquire into the order of the associations. All attempts that have been made until now to comprehend the nature of law have failed because the investigation was not based on the order of the associations but on the legal propositions.

The inner order of the associations is determined by legal norms[2]. Legal norms must not be confused with legal propositions. The legal proposition is the precise, universally binding formulation of the legal precept in a book of statutes or in a law book. The legal norm is the legal command, reduced to practice, as it obtains in a definite association, perhaps of very small size, even without any formulation

1. material law：实体法，与形式法相对。
2. legal norms：法律规范

in words. As soon as there are legal propositions within an association that have actually become effective, they give rise to legal norms. But in every society there is a much greater number of legal norms than of legal propositions; for there always is much more law that is applicable to individual cases than is applicable to all relations of a similar kind; much more law than the contemporary jurists who have attempted to formulate it in words have realized. Every modern legal historian knows how small a portion of the law that was valid at the time is contained in the Twelve Tables or in the *Lex Salica*[1]. Modern codes[2] are in the same case. In the past centuries, all legal norms that were determinative of the inner order of the associations were based upon custom, upon contracts, and upon articles of association of corporations. In the main, this is the situation today.

---

1. *Lex Salica*：《萨利克法典》，现存最古老的日耳曼法典。
2. Modern codes：当代法典

III THE SOCIAL ASSOCIATIONS AND THE SOCIAL NORMS

A social association is a plurality of human beings who, in their relations with one another, recognize certain rules of conduct as binding, and, generally at least, actually regulate their conduct according to them. These rules are of various kinds, and have various names: rules of law, of morals, of religion, of ethical custom, of honor, of decorum, of tact, of etiquette, of fashion. To these may be added some of lesser importance, e.g. rules of games, the rule that one must wait one's turn, for instance at the ticket window or in the waiting room of a busy physician. These rules are social facts, the resultants of the forces that are operative in society, and can no more be considered separate and apart from society, in which they are operative, than the motion of the waves can be computed without considering the element in which they move. As to form and content, they are norms, abstract commands and prohibitions, concerning the social life within the association and directed to the members of the association. In addition to rules of conduct of this kind, there are rules that are not norms because they do not refer to the social life of human beings: e.g. the rules of language, of taste, or of hygiene.

The legal norm, therefore, is merely one of the rules of conduct, of the same nature as all other rules of conduct. For reasons readily understood, the prevailing school of juristic science does not stress this fact, but, for practical reasons, emphasizes the antithesis between law and the other norms, especially the ethical norms, in order to urge upon the judge at every turn as impressively as possible that he must render his decisions solely according to law and never according to other rules. Where the state has not obtained a complete monopoly of lawmaking, this antithesis[1] is not emphasized very much. In Rome, where the law has been defined as the *ars aequi et boni*[2], it was hardly ever heard of; and among the present-day English, it is not stressed nearly so forcibly. In those fields of law in which juristic science does not subserve[3] the practical purposes of judicial decision, in international law, in *Staatsrecht* (public law in the narrow sense), in administrative law, law is by no means so carefully distinguished from morals, ethical custom, decorum, and tact, from the so-called *Konventionalregeln* (conventional rules), and even from considerations of expediency, as is the case, in theory at least, in private and penal law.

Every human relation within the association, whether transient or permanent, is sustained exclusively by the rules of conduct. If the rules cease to be operative, the community disintegrates; the weaker they become, the less firmly knit the organization becomes. The religious communion dissolves if the precepts of religion lose their validity. The family breaks up if the members of the family no longer consider themselves bound by the order of the family. Among the northern Slavs of Austria, the last vestiges of the greater family have completely disappeared in the last fifty years because the more distant members of the family no longer recognize the rules of the communal family life as binding.

Not all human associations are being regulated by legal norms, but manifestly only those associations are parts of the legal order whose order is based upon legal norms. The sociology of law deals exclusively with these; the others are the subject matter of other branches of sociology. Among the legal associations there are some that are

---

1. antithesis：对立性
2. *ars aequi et boni*：〈拉〉法是善良和公正的艺术。
3. subserve：促进

readily recognizable by external criteria, i.e. those that jurists style juristic persons, corporations, institutions, foundations, and, first and foremost, the state. But even in public law, there are numerous legal associations that have no legal personality[1]; such as administrative boards, public institutions, the people, the army, the various classes, ranks, and professions. Much more of this is to be found in private law.

In all legal associations the legal norm constitutes the backbone of the inner order; it is the strongest support of their organization. By organization we mean that rule in the association which assigns to each member his relative position in the association (whether of domination or of subjection) and his function. This rule may deal not only with the relation of man to man, but also with the relation of man to things. Indirectly it deals with the relation of man to man even in the latter case. For the owner of articles of consumption determines what performance is to be rendered in return by those at whose disposal he places the goods; the owner of the factory det ermines the order in the factory and its management; the creditor determines the fate of the subjectmatter of the obligation, and often of the debtor; just as often, however, it is the debtor that determines the fate of the subject matter of the obligation and of the creditor, for, being the possessor of the thing, he has a great deal of legal power over it. But only those rules of law have a share in the creation of the legal order of the association that have actually become rules of conduct in the association, i.e. that are being recognized and followed by men, in a general way at least. Rules of law that have remained mere norms for decision, that become effective only in the very rare cases of legal controversy, do not take part in the ordering of the associations.

This may be said, *a fortiori*[2], of those legal propositions, in reality quite numerous, that do not affect life at all. The same holds true

---

1. legal personality：法律人格
2. a *fortiori*：〈拉〉更有理由

for the norms of morality, ethical custom, and religion. It is always necessary therefore to ask not only how much of what has been promulgated by the lawgiver, proclaimed by the founder of a religion, or taught by the philosopher has been applied by the courts, preached from the pulpits, or taught in books or schools, but how much has actually been practiced and lived. Only that which becomes part and parcel of life becomes a living norm; everything else is mere doctrine, norm for decision, dogma, or theory. Norms of ethical custom, of honor, of decorum, of tact, of etiquette, of fashion are only rules of human conduct; and though a new code of honor (rules for the duel) should appear at every moment, it would remain absolutely without any significance whatever if it did not actually become part and parcel of life.

The first and most important function of the sociological science of law, therefore, is to separate those portions of the law that regulate, order, and determine society from the mere norms for decision, and to demonstrate their organizing power. This was recognized first of all in *Staatsrecht* (public law in the narrow sense) and in administrative law. Indeed hardly anyone doubts today that *Staatsrecht* is an ordering of the st ate, whose purpose is not to decide legal disputes, but to determine the positions and the functions of the organs of the state, as well as the duties and functions of the authorities of the state. But the st ate is above all a social association; the forces that are operative in the state are social forces; everything that proceeds from the state, the activity of the authorities of the state and particularly legislation by the state, is something that is done by society through the association created for that purpose, i.e. the state. The same classes, orders, and interests that control society prevail in the state; and if the state makes war on any one of these, we know that the state has passed under the control of one of the others. *Staatsrecht* (public law in the narrow sense) therefore comprises both a state and a social ordering.

The rich life of a great scholar has been consumed to a great extent by the labor of demonstrating the organizing power of the law of corporations and the contributions which the corporations and their law have been making and are still making today to civilization, particularly to the civilization of Germany. Every page of history teaches the significance of the corporations as associations for the organization of political, intellectual, religious; economic, and social life; and any English or American work on corporations and trusts can complete this picture. It would be needless for the purposes of this book to add anything to these statements.

Gierke contrasts the law of the state and of the corporations of public and private law, which he styles social law[1], with the entire remaining private law, which he styles individual law[2]. But this antithesis is unwarranted. There is no individual law. All law is social law. Life knows not man as an utterly detached, individual, and isolated being, nor does the law know such a being. The law always sees in man solely a member of one of the countless associations in which life has placed him. These associations, inasmuch as they bear a legal stamp[3], are being ordered and regulated by law and the other social norms; it is the norms that assign to each individual his position of domination or of subjection and his function. It is true, membership in the association occasionally, but by no means always, gives rise to individual rights and duties of the individual, but this is not its purpose, is not its essential content.

In the prevailing system of private law, however, the association is given very inadequate expression. Thanks to the analytical method of the juristic science of private law, the great majority of associations have been taken to pieces for the purpose of placing their component

1. social law：社会法
2. individual law：个人法
3. legal stamp：法律特征

parts under the magnifying glass[1] and studying them separately as subjects or objects of rights, as real or personal rights[2]. This may be necessary for practical purposes, but it is unscientific at all events, just as the alphabetical order of the dictionary is unscientific though necessary for practical purposes. The sociological science of law, not being bound by any practical considerations, must reunite the severed parts into a whole. Even when viewed solely from without, the juristic persons of private law, the societies that are not juristic persons, the partnerships, and other communities, and the family self-evidently are clearly seen to be associations. But in actual fact the entire private law is a law of associations. For the private law is preponderantly, and, apart from family law, exclusively, the law of economic life, and economic life goes on exclusively in associations.

Economic life comprises production of goods, exchange of goods, and consumption of goods. Accordingly the economic associations subserve these three functions. Just at this point, however, there is an enormous contrast between the economic undertakings of today and those of a not far distant past. In antiquity and in the Middle Ages, the economically self-suficing[3] household of the free farmer and the *Oikenwirtschaft*[4] (self-sufficing economic establishment) of the royal court and of the seigniorial manor[5] were the prevailing forms. These manifestly were economic associations, and their legal order was apparent. Today economically self-sufficing households are to be found in Europe perhaps only in some secluded region. Until the present day, among the peasantry at least, and, where work is done at home, in rare cases also among handicraftsmen, the family has remained a laboring

1. magnifying glass：放大镜
2. real or personal rights：不动产与动产权
3. self-sufficing：自给自足
4. *Oikenwirtschaft*：〈德〉自给自足经济体
5. seigniorial manor：领主庄园

association which produces goods; but it is no longer self-sufficing, and even among the peasantry it performs its labors only in part for its own needs. And even among handicraftsmen and among the peasantry, these cases are merely instances of survival of forms of economic management which are disappearing. The family generally no longer is a place where goods are produced, but where they are being consumed; and only the very last part of the preparation of goods that are being consumed takes place in the family. Apart from this, the home and the workshop are definitely separated from each other. The workshop sends the goods that it has produced to the market, from which the home obtains the goods it requires. The manufactured products become merchandise. The course that merchandise must travel from the producing to the consuming economic unit is steadily lengthening, and every lengthening enlarges the sphere of trade, of commerce. It is generally true therefore at the present time that the production of goods takes place in the workshop; the exchange, in commerce; the consumption, in the home. And to this three-fold division the legal order of the economic associations of our day must conform.

In every economic association, three things must be distinguished: the working or consuming group of human beings; the material basis of economic life, i.e. the instruments of production and raw materials; and finally the juristic form in which this group of human beings receives the protection of the courts and of the other tribunals of the state for their entire associational life. This, we might say, is a statement of the basic features of the relation between the economic structure of society and its juristic forms.

On the farm, which the farmer manages with the assistance of his wife and children, his men-servants and women-servants, he raises grain and tubers, cattle and sheep. This is the economic content of this association. Its juristic form is ownership, the real right of usufruct or of usufructuary lease in the farm, the family law which unites the members of the family, the contract of Service which binds the men-servants and women-servants to the farm. In part, the great landed proprietor cultivates his lands himself; in part, he has put them out on lease to lessees or to usufructuaries[1]. This economic organization of the great landed esta te det ermines its juristic forms: ownership lease, real rights of usufruct[2]. The tradesman, together with his journeymen and apprentices, works in a rented workshop with his own materials and his own tools; the right of tenancy in the shop, the ownership of tools and mat erials, the contract for wages with the journeyman, and the contract of apprenticeship constitute both the juristic form and the economic content of the trade. The factories of a share company can throw goods on the market whose value amounts to millions of dollars. The share company with its board of directors and board of supervisors, its members and the meeting of the members, with an army of officers and employees, with its right of ownership, its relations of usufruct and ordinary lease in factories, machinery, sources of power, raw materials, and merchandise — all of these constitute the economic order of the manufacturing establishment, which is reflected in the contract of association, in a multitude of legal relations involving real rights, in countless contractual relations with employers and workmen, with ordinary and usufructuary lessors.

A discussion of the other economic associations, of the commercial establishment, of the bank, of the household as a community of consumers, leads to similar results. The association in the commercial establishment and in the bank, very much like that in the factory, consists of the owner and the employees and servants, who are in a contractual relation with each other. In addition to the contracts for wages, there are many contracts concerning the execution of commissions and the performance of duties of other kinds. The order of the commercial establishment and of the bank, to a much greater

---

1. usufructuaries：用益权人
2. real rights of usufruct：不动产用益权

extent than that of the factory, is arranged with a view to dealings with the outside world. For this reason the contracts for services entered into with the individual employees are connected with various powers of agency such as do not exist in the case of the factory. The material basis here appears in the juristic form of ownership or of right of tenancy in the shop and the warehouses, the ownership of merchandise and of sums of money. In addition to the members, the family and the household, as associations for consumption, include the servants. The mat erial basis is the right of tenancy in the dwelling, and the right of ownership in the articles of consumption that are to be found in kitchen, cellar, and storeroom.

The family law within the family, the contract of service, of wages, and of employment in the factory, in the workshop, in the commercial establishment and in the bank, accomplish the same results everywhere that are accomplished in the corporation by the articles of association; in the state, in the commune, in the church, by the public law relation of service; i.e. they bring about the inner order of the group of human beings that has its being within these economic associations. This applies, however, not only to the contract of service, of wages, and of employment, but also to all other kinds of agreements, especially to the contract of barter, to contracts for supplying things for use (contracts of lease, of usufruct, and of loan for use), and to the contract for the extension of credit (*Kreditvertrag*)[1]. The organizing power of all these contracts appears at once if one considers not merely, as is usually done for purely practical juristic purposes, the two parties that enter into the contract, but the whole group of persons who are brought into relation with one another by means of the regular exchange of goods arranged for by contract. All persons that are in this group constitute an economic association,

1. contract for the extension of credit (*Kreditvertrag*)：信贷契约

which produces the goods and offers the services that are needed, and which thereby supplies its members with the goods and services they require. In this association the sum total of contracts entered into, or to be entered into, assigns to each individual his station, his position of domination or of subjection — the latter, it is true, only in a very rudimentary manner — and his functions. In commercial intercourse, contracts, at least those concerning performances that can be delegated to an assignee, are not being entered into as with definite persons, but as with the whole group of persons who are in a mutual relation of exchange of goods with each other. That is the significance of negotiability[1], of endorsement, of clearance of accounts[2], and, in part, of negotiable paper[3] payable to bearer.

The social nature of the contract appears most clearly in credit transactions. Every credit transaction is conditioned upon the existence of stores of material goods in society. As long as mankind produces only so much as it needs for the moment: as long as it lives from hand to mouth, as it always does in primitive stages of development, there are no credit transactions. Even in the stage of economic development in which only natural produce is exchanged, the farmer cannot help his neighbor out with seed corn unless he has harvested more than he requires for his immediate needs; he must have a supply. In present-day society, supplies appear in the form of money. A person who produces more economic goods than he requires for his own needs disposes of them and receives money in exchange. If he spends the money, he buys other goods in order to use them; if he keeps the money, the value of the goods corresponding to the sum of money must exist unconsumed somewhere in the economic system. Extension of credit by the seller for the sale price implies that for the

1. negotiability：流通性
2. clearance of accounts：账户清算
3. negotiable paper：可转让票据

present he will not secure other goods in the place of those sold, that this value, for the time being, will remain unconsumed in society. Every instance of extension of credit for a sum of money therefore is the exercise of a right and power to determine what disposition is to be made of stores of material goods that are in existence in one economic unit in favor of another economic unit; and every credit transaction imports a decision of the question whether or not there is in existence in society a store of goods corresponding to the presumable intention of the person who asks for credit; the credit transaction, therefore, is always conditioned socially. In the most highly developed national economic systems, everyone carries the money that he does not use immediately to the bank. The greater part of the stores, therefore, which the several economic units are laying by for the purposes of the other economic units is accumulating in the banks in the form of money. And since the banks have the right and power to determine what disposition is to be made of these funds in favor of the individual economic units, they actually obtain control over the production, the exchange, and the consumption of goods in society. Their calculations more and more become the basis for the genesis, the development, and the continued existence of economic operations.

The contract, then, is the juristic form for the distribution and utilization of the goods and personal abilities (services) that are in existence in society. Not only the making of the contract, but also its content, is a result of social interrelations. In connection with any one of the ordinary contracts of daily life, it may suffice to raise the question which part of it is peculiar to this specific contract and which part is determined by the social order and by the organization of economic life and of commercial intercourse, in order to satisfy ourselves of the extent to which the latter elements preponderate[1].

---

1. preponderate：占优势

The fact that we are in a position today to satisfy our needs as to food, clothing, and housing by means of the everyday contracts of sale and lease and the contracts for work and labor, we owe to the other fact that in the community in which we live commerce and production of goods have been regulated sufficiently to make this manner of satisfying one's needs possible. Assuredly five hundred years ago this was not possible anywhere, and there is many a part of the world in which it is not possible today. One cannot rent a dwelling in a mountain village where there are none to let; one cannot provide oneself daily with food and clothing unless they are offered for sale in the vicinity[1]; and one cannot hire a man to perform services which are not being rendered in exchange for wages in the form of money. This applies, self-evidently, not only to the subject matter of the contract but to every individual provision of the contract. If one examines a contract point by point, one can easily find the social reason why it is worded exactly as it is. It may be the fact that one of the parties occupies a position of social or economic advantage over the other, or the condition of the market, or the custom of the particular line of business. A person who has changed his residence will notice at once that he is making contracts of an entirely different nature from those that he made before. And though he be ever so firmly resolved not to change his mode of living in any way, the world round about him has changed, and he must conform to it even in his contractual intent. In England, as a rule, one does not rent an apartment but a whole house; one does not purchase one's daily supply of meat at the butchers, but has it delivered weekly at one's residence. Accordingly rental contracts and contracts for the purchase of meat in England have a quite different content from those on the Continent. The writer has intentionally chosen contracts of the retail trade as illustrations, for in

1. in the vicinity：就近；在附近

these the peculiar features of each individual case appear most clearly It has often been shown to what extent the contracts of the wholesale trade and of industry are merely expressions of the general conditions of the market or of the special needs of the particular economic sphere. Most written contracts are drawn up according to printed forms, the content of which often is not made known to the parties, for it is determined by society quite independently of their individual wills. Nevertheless, it is true that the individualizing data that are written into the form are also a result of social interrelations.

The individual contract is so far from being the resultant of the individual wills of the parties that it was possible for the Austrian school of economists to undertake to compute the most important part of the leading contract involving exchange of goods, i.e. the purchase price, exclusively on the basis of its social and economic presuppositions; and an eminent economist, Walras, has made a successful attempt to reduce it to a mat hematical formula. Perhaps the results of all these investigations are directly applicable to those contracts of exchange in which the counter-performance is to be rendered in money: contracts of labor (*Arbeitsvertrdge*)[1] and of lease (*Mietvertrage*)[2], and contracts for work (*Werkvertrage*)[3]; and though it will never be possible perhaps to reduce the remainder of the content of the contract to a mathematical formula, this must be attributed to the fact that the elements that enter into the computation cannot be evaluated readily rather than to the irresolvability[4] of the problem in principle.

But to speak of the social nature of the contract is merely another way of saying that it must serve the purposes of society. It exists in its innumerable forms for the purpose of regulating the production, the

---

1. contracts of labor (*Arbeitsverträge*)：劳动合同
2. lease (*Mietverträge*)：租赁合同
3. contracts for work (*Werkverträge*)：承揽合同
4. irresolvability：不可解决

exchange, and the consumption of goods in human society, which is based on private ownership of the soil, of the means of production, and of the goods for consumption. On the material basis created by ownership, real rights, and perhaps, agreements to supply things for use (lease, usufruct, loan), the contract creating a partnership or the contract which creates a mercantile association and which is closely related to the former unites several adventurers in a partnership or in a mercantile association; the con tracts of labor and of service keep the army of officials and laborers of a manor and of workmen in a factory together; the various contracts of exchange, as instrumentalities of commerce, direct the products of agriculture and of the various handicrafts to the places where they are needed; the contract for the extension of credit makes it possible for the various economic units to obtain the capital that happens to be available for their purposes. In these vast economic machines, ranged one above the other, i.e. in individual, national, and world-wide economic undertakings, each human being that lives and moves creatively within them amounts to a small spring, a wheel, or a screw; and his position as well as his function within them is being assigned to him, in the main, by the sum total of contracts he enters into.

There is not another branch of the law whose organizing significance legal science has so thoroughly failed to recognize, which it has disfigured so mercilessly, and abused so pitilessly, as the modern Continental law of inheritance[1]. If one reads a juristic exposition, searches a code, or studies a collection of decisions, one is occasionally tempted to believe that the law of inheritance is like a lottery; the part of the orphan boy is played by the sections of the code through whose tortuous sentences a mysterious goddess of fate distributes her gifts to the fortunate ones according to a decree that is past finding

1. Continental law of inheritance：欧陆继承法

out. Indeed the mischief began everywhere at a very early date. The clear lines of the law of inheritance of the Twelve Tables and of the German law-books, from which one can, even today, gather, almost without any effort whatever, the social organization of the time, have lost all sense and meaning, since the societies in which they were valid have vanished. A new order has arisen meanwhile, but, strange to say, has been unable, either in Rome or elsewhere, to find clear-cut and universally valid propositions for a law of inheritance adapted to its needs. At the many points of invasion, it has indeed, on several occasions, wrought grave destruction, but has scarcely anywhere built up anything worth preserving. Accordingly almost everything is left to the foresight of the individual. Declaration by last will and testament, family ordinance, *pactum et procidentia maiorum*[1], marriage contract, parental division of inheritance, transfer of goods during one's lifetime, agreement among the heirs out of court, must step into the breach. Such is the chaos of the present-day law of inheritance; a few decaying fragments remaining from times long since past, on which some incoherent patchwork has been placed quite thoughtlessly. The greater part of the burden must be borne by the art of drafting legal documents, a branch of legal science which has been taken notice of by but few, and appreciated by none, and which has undertaken the difficult but fruitful task of making a pathway through this confusion for the needs of life.

Our task here can only be to sketch with a few strokes of the pen the great ever-present organizing basic problem of the law of inheritance of every legal system. The head of the family, the soul of all its undertakings, who had been furnishing bread and, in part, a sphere of activity to the members of the family, has departed this life. How should his work be continued? What disposition is to be

1. *pactum et providentia maiorum*：〈拉〉前人的约定与安排

made of all those things to which his spirit gave life and which his strong arm maintained? Every economic undertaking, the farm, the factory, the mercantile house, and the mine, is an association within which not only the human beings but also the material things are ordered and regulated. In it, all persons and all things are combined into a unified whole in the manner in which they can best serve the purposes of the economic undertaking. Rent asunder or divided into their "conceptual" parts, they at most retain the value of the material that the fragments consist of, and uncounted wealth is lost for all time not only to the surviving members of the family, but to the whole national economic system. Apart from the jurists, perhaps no one who has given thought to these things has failed to observe that this is a matter of solicitude to every strong and able man who, after a life of achievement, is thinking of death. What is to be done in order to prevent disintegration, to put the right man in the right place in every economic organization which the deceased has created, and to assign the right tasks to him? Unless one has had actual experience in such matters, one can form no conception of what goes on after the death of such a man when his affairs fall into the hands of the lawyers; of the way everything works at cross purposes with him, the whole juristic *πολυπραγματεία*[1] of the codes, the attorneys, the notaries, and the courts; of the sedulous determination with which his intentions are being defeated and weapons are being supplied to folly and malice for a work of destruction. But all this is infinitesimal when compared with the infinitely more thorough work that must be done when there is no last will, or, indeed, when the custody of wards committed to the charge of the authorities gives the latter greater powers. Of course, where the past has exercised forethought, as shown in the law of inheritance of the ruling families, of the nobility, of the peasantry, it is

---

1. *πολυπραγματεία*：〈希〉繁忙活动

true that occasionally, in spite of the violent resistance of the lawyers, in many an instance economic undertakings have been preserved from destruction, or, where destruction has already taken place, have been rebuilt. But these usually are like saplings that have no vitality what soever; much more frequently they are surviving fragments that are past hope. Jurists have become conscious, only vaguely however, of the duty to create a law of inheritance that takes into account the multiform and peculiar requirements of modern life. But at the present time the necessary foundation has not yet been laid by anyone. The beginning would have to be made by juristic science. First of all it would be necessary to investigate all the living law[1] that is contained in testamentary provisions, in parental divisions of inheritance, in transfers of property during the lifetime of the donors, in settlements out of court by the heirs, and to discover its guiding principles. One is most likely to find something of this nature in the Swiss Civil Code.

Inasmuch as the law is an inner order of the social associations, its content is determined with absolute necessity by the structure of these associations and by their method of conducting their economic enterprises. Every social and economic change causes a change in the law, and it is impossible to change the legal bases of society and of economic life without bringing about a corresponding change in the law. If the changes in the law are arbitrary and of such a nature that the economic institutions cannot adapt themselves to them, the order of the latter is destroyed without compensation. The farmer is able to produce on his farm the goods that he requires in order to supply not only himself but also the other classes of society with raw materials only so long as the legal order guarantees to him, in a great measure at least, the returns of his labor. If therefore a class which is all-powerful in the state should force upon the farmer a legal order which compels

1. living law：活法

him to give up all that he has harvested, the farm would be deserted, and the powerful in the state would soon be without the means of preserving the state and of maintaining their own economic position. Even foreign conquerors, therefore, have been content with reducing the free farmers to a state of serfdom or of making them their tenants, but have always left them so much of the returns of their labor as they absolutely needed for the maintenance of their economic activity.

The entire private law therefore, inasmuch as it has an organizing content, is social law in precisely the same sense as the law of the state and the law of corporations. It is always concerned with the human associations: it determines the position of the individual in the group of working human beings and the relation of the group to its tools. Like *Staatsrecht* (public law in the narrow sense) and the law of corporations, private law primarily creates associations, not individual rights and duties; and though individual spheres (*Individualbereiche*)[1] arise for the individual in the organized community, this is a reflex effect of organization, in public law no less than in private law. The fact that in this case the association is not based on a constitution or on. articles of association[2], but on the law of things and of contract and on the order of the family, must not hide this great truth from us, for in this case the law of things and of contract and the order of the family serve the same purpose that is accomplished elsewhere by a constitution or by articles of association. A hermit may have a truly "individual sphere" not only in the juristic but also in the sociological and economic sense, but a man living among men cannot. One may have individual rights in economically insignificant articles of use and consumption, e.g. in clothing, in jewelry, in a portfolio, or in stationery, but even in the matter of the furnishings of a dwelling, except in the case of single men or women, there is the common use by the family.

1. individual spheres (*Individualbereiche*)：私人领域
2. articles of association：章程

And even the true individual rights are social rights[1], to the same extent at least as is the legal claim of the member of the commune to participation in the use of the pasture belonging to the commune or of the member of a reading club to participation in the use of the books and periodicals. In conceding to the individual the possession of these things and permitting him to dispose of them according to his pleasure; society regulates their use and consumption; ownership of the goods which it concedes to the individual is merely a result of this social order. The individual enjoys this ownership as a member of an ordered community which respects private ownership and protects it without, in the case of certain things, concerning itself about the way in which they are being utilized. Society could regulate individual use and consumption in a manner quite different from, and much more detailed than, the manner in which it does this today, and we shall be convinced of this at a much earlier date perhaps than we should like as soon as the exhaustion of the resources of nature, which is even now threatening, shall have drawn much nearer. Whenever society actually accords to the individual an individual sphere, it refrains, on principle, from any and all interference. The inner life of the adult man, for instance, is his individual sphere; it lies within the domain of art, of religion, of philosophy, but not of law or of the extra-legal social norms.

The jural associations of human society therefore are, in the main, the following: the state with its courts and magistracies; the family, and the other bodies, associations, and communities with or without juristic personality; associations created by means of contract and inheritance, and, in particular, national and world-wide economic systems. Possession and ownership, which for the purposes of sociological discussions might be treated as, to a certain extent,

1. social rights：社会权利

convertible terms, real rights and claims based on obligation, create the inner order of these associations. This is the part that law plays in the ordering of the political, intellectual, economic, and social life of present-day society. This by no means exhausts the entire material of the law, but it is the part of the law which has power to regulate and order. Apart from this, there is another part of the law, which does not directly regulate and order the associations, but only protects them against attacks. It is connected with the social associations as a sort of secondary order; it maintains and strengthens them, but does not give them shape or form. This applies to the law of procedure before the courts and other tribunals; for it is merely a part of the order of the tribunals which have been created for the protection of social institutions; it is without direct influence upon society. It applies also to penal law, for the latter creates no social institutions; it merely protects goods that are already in existence in society and institutions that have already been established. And, lastly, it applies also to all those provisions of the material private law that concern only the protection afforded by law; like penal law, they create neither goods nor social institutions; they but regulate the already existing protection afforded by the courts and other tribunals. These norms did not come into being within the social associations themselves as the inner order of the latter, but arose in juristic law or in the law created by the state. All rights of monopoly, especially patent rights and copyrights, are created by the state. They consist in a command, addressed to all who are subjected to the will of the state, except the person who holds the right, to refrain from engaging in any activity in a certain sphere. Norms of similar nature have occasionally arisen in juristic law also.

And now we must point out the significance, but slightly considered hitherto, of the extra-legal norms[1] for the inner ordering of the

1. extra-legal norms：法律外规范

associations. The statement that legal institutions are based exclusively on legal norms is not true. Morality, religion, ethical custom, decorum, tact, even etiquette and fashion, do not order the extra-legal relations only; they also affect the legal sphere at every turn. Not a single one of the jural associations could maintain its existence solely by means of legal norms; all of them, at all times, require the aid of extra-legal norms which increase or eke out their force. Nothing short of the cooperation of the social norms of every description can ofifer a complete picture of the social mechanism.

A glance at what is going on round about us every day will serve to convince us of the truth of these statements. There is no state in which a government would be possible for any length of time which relies solely on the law. Even Macchiavelli[1] urges his *Principe*[2] to observe, outwardly at least, certain precepts of morality, religion, ethical custom and honor, decorum and tact. No administrative tribunal would be able to function if it were guided solely by rules of law; and for a government official it is positively a matter of official duty in his dealings with the public as well as with his colleagues to observe not only the precepts of law[3] but also those of morality, ethical custom, honor, decorum, and tact. Certainly there is no institution of public life in which so many things are regulated by organizing legal norms as the army; and even this highly developed law does not suffice. It is well known how highly the army esteems the organizing value of morality, ethical custom, religion, honor, decorum, tact; nay, even of etiquette and of fashion. Indeed examples taken from the past show that an army which knows only legal norms can become a mob which is beyond the pale of society, and which is controlled solely by

---

1. Macchiavelli：马基雅维利（1469—1527），意大利政治思想家和历史学家，著有《君主论》《论李维》《论战争艺术》《佛罗伦萨史》等作品。
2. *Principe*：〈拉〉君主
3. precepts of law：法律规则

means of barbaric discipline. The term parliamentary courtesy, which undoubtedly is known to all civilized nations, sufficiently demonstrates the role which the extra-legal norms play in public representative bodies. And it is in this connection that they first became the object of scientific investigation as *Konventionalregeln* (rules arising from convention or agreement).

Is it otherwise in family and property law? A family the members of which reciprocally insist upon their legal rights has already disintegrated in most cases as a social and economic association. If they appeal to the judge, they have arrived at the point where they part company. The prohibition of the abusive exercise of legal rights (*Chicane*)[1] shows that even real rights may not be exercised without giving heed to certain extra-legal norms; and where land or dwellings adjoin, there is the further requirement of customary observance of the dictates of morality, ethical custom, decorum, tact, and etiquette. Contracts must be interpreted and performed according to the requirements of good faith[2] and commercial custom. That is to say that many other things must be considered besides the rule of law and the meaning and language of the contract. Nevertheless life demands a great deal more than even the most liberal-minded jurist would concede on the basis of good faith and business custom. There is perhaps no other contractual relation which is so thoroughly stripped of extra-legal content as is the contract of ordinary lease in a large city; nevertheless even in this relation the "good landlord" and "the desirable tenant" are valued highly. These two expressions are in common use in Vienna; the "thing itself" doubtless, is in existence everywhere. In the case of a usufructuary lease[3], however, the personal characteristics of the parties to the contract often are of even greater

---

1. legal rights (*Chicane*)：法律权利（斜体为拉丁文）
2. good faith：诚实信用
3. usufructuary lease：用益权租约

importance than the content of the agreement. No man of experience in business affairs will enter into a usufructuary lease without having made the most searching inquiry concerning the personal characteristics of the other party. He does this in order to make sure that he is justified in assuming that the other party will observe the non-legal norms that are customary in the relation of lessor and lessee. The organizing significance of the extra-legal norms appears with particular clearness in the contract for services and wages. On the part of the entrepreneur or of his authorized representative, a certain firm insistence upon his legal right, together with an instinct for morality, ethical custom, decorum, and tact constitutes the principal part of the aptitude which is usually called a talent for organization; if this is lacking, a contract is without value not only for him but also for the workmen and employees. On the other hand an entrepreneur could not work with people who recognize only the legal point of view. Moreover such people could not get on with one another; the undertaking would be disorganized. The influence of extra-legal norms was recognized first and most clearly in the case of contracts for the extension of credit[1]. They mark the dividing line between morally unexceptionable investment of capital and usury, which is always proscribed morally, and usually also legally. Although it is said that mercantile strictness should always obtain in mercantile intercourse, a merchant who is ever ready to insist on the letter of the law will quickly alienate his customers and those with whom he has business connections. Business custom, business honor, and business decorum constitute elements of commercial legal life. The content of these terms may be described as fair dealing (*Kulanz*)[2]. At a time in which the prevailing sexual morality is being violently attacked even by some choice spirits, it may not be altogether superfluous to call to mind that the existing order of the

---

1. contracts for the extension of credit：信贷契约
2. fair dealing (*Kulanz*)：公平交易

family is based upon it. If there is any ulterior motive behind these often well directed attacks, it can only be the thought that they are preparing the way for an entirely new order of the family. It would be absurd to believe that the family in its present form can be maintained if the present conception of sexual morality, without which it cannot exist, is given up.

We may say therefore that the law is the order of state or political, social, intellectual, and economic life, but it is not the only order. There are many others which are of equal value, and which, taken together, perhaps, are of much greater effectiveness. Indeed life would become a hell if it were regulated by law alone. It is true, the extra-legal norms are not being observed inviolably[1], but this is equally true of the legal norms. The order of the social machine is continually being interfered with. And though it does its work with much creaking and groaning[2], the important thing is that it shall continue to function. To this extent, at least, its norms must be observed; and to this extent they are being observed in every country in which there is a tolerably well ordered life. And lastly, a breach of the existing order often is more than a merely local or temporary disorder; not infrequently it indicates the beginning of a new stage of development.

Let us for a moment compare our present-day society and its legal order with a socialistic society as various socialists have so often pictured it. Both, as it were, may be compared to enormous hoisting machines? by means of which humanity is to be supplied with the goods it requires in order to maintain its life and to develop its powers. In a socialistic society, as well as in our present-day society, there will be farms, mines, and factories, in which goods are being produced; there will be means of transportation like our railroads,

---

1. observed inviolably：始终遵从
2. creaking and groaning：字面意思是“吱吱作响”，比喻一个东西出现问题。

steamboats, and vehicles, which deliver these goods at large magazines and storehouses where they will have to be stored, as is done in our warehouses and shops, until there is a demand for them; finally there will have to be smaller undertakings in which goods are being prepared for immediate consumption, as is being done today in the workshop of the mechanic and also in the kitchen and in housekeeping generally. In a socialistic society, as well as in our present-day society, untold millions of busy hands will be stirring on the farms, in the mines, the factories, the agencies of transportation, the warehouses and storehouses, in order to supply the goods which humanity requires, to transport them to the places where they are needed, and to distribute them. But above them all will hover an all-knowing and all-overseeing[1] official body which makes an advance estimate of the total requirement, orders its production, directs the workman to the places where the work is to be done, and orders the products to be sent where they are needed. Our present-day society indeed has no official body of this kind. But the task which, in a socialistic society, is to be performed by this omnipotent board of superhuman stature[2] is performed in our present-day society by the law acting automatically and with such simple instrumentalities as the family order, possession, contract, and the law and right of inheritance. The owners, as entrepreneurs, provide the establishments at which goods are being produced, the means of transportation, the warehouses, and the salerooms; they assemble the workers by means of contracts of service and wages, and secure the necessary capital by means of contracts for the extension of credit. The merchants estimate in advance how much merchandise the human race will require, and, by means of agreements of exchange, direct it to the places where it is needed. And they accomplish all of this, it is true, not without a considerable amount of error, friction, and opposition,

1. all-knowing and all-overseeing：无所不知与无所不管
2. omnipotent board of superhuman stature：像超人一样的全能机构

but certainly with much less friction and expenditure of energy than the most efficient purely bureaucratic board could accomplish it, Possession, ownership, real rights, contract, inheritance, and, for purpose of consumption, the family accomplish almost automatically in our society those things for which a socialistic society would require a complicated network of bureaucratic boards.

IV SOCIAL AND STATE SANCTION OF THE NORMS

A doctrine which has a great vogue at the present time, and which derives from various sources, seeks to explain the origin of the legal norms and, occasionally, also of the other social norms, especially those of morality, by the power of the dominant groups in society, which have established them, and are enforcing them in their own interest. But power over men can be maintained and exercised permanently only by uniting them in associations and prescribing rules of conduct for them within the association, i.e. by organizing them. In this sense the doctrine referred to would be in harmony with that taught here, according to which the social norms are but the order of the human associations. But the statement that the dominant groups of the associations set up the norms of conduct for the other members of their association solely in their own interest is meaningless or incorrect. Man always acts in his own interest, and he who is able to state exhaustively the interests which motivate human conduct is able to solve not only the question of the sanction of the norms but practically all questions of social science. On the other hand, it is quite incorrect to say that the interests of the dominant groups[1] in the associations conflict with those of the whole association or with those of the other members. To a certain extent the interests of the dominant groups must coincide with the interests of the whole association, or at least with those of the majority of the members of the association;

1. dominant groups：占主导地位的群体

for if this were not so, the other members would not obey the norms established by the dominant group. It is unlikely that one could ever gain the support of a great number of men for any project unless every individual had at least a vague idea that the project, if realized, would redound to[1] the advantage of all. And this idea is never altogether without foundation. The order of an association, abstractly considered, may be a poor one, may perhaps afford undue advantages to its leaders, may impose heavy burdens upon the others, but it is always better than no order at all. And the fact that there is no better order in existence is always a cogent proof that the association, in its given spiritual and moral condition, and in view of the economic supplies it has had at its disposal, has been unable to create a better order.

The question then is by what means do the social associations induce their individual members to obey the norms of the association. There is, certainly, nothing more untenable psychologically than the idea, which has such a vogue, that men refrain from laying violent hands upon other men's property only because they fear the criminal law; that they pay their debts only because they fear that their goods will be levied on. Even at times when penal laws lose their force — as is often the case temporarily in time of war or of domestic disorder — it is always only a very small portion of the population that participates in murder, robbery, theft, and plundering; and in times of tranquillity[2] most men perform the obligations they have assumed without thinking of levy of execution. From this it does not indeed follow that the great majority of men conform to the norms because they are prompted by an inner impulse[3]; but it does follow that fear of punishment or of levy of execution is not the only consideration that prompts them to do so, quite apart from the fact that there is a sufficiently large number of

1. redound to：有益于
2. in times of tranquillity：安定时期
3. inner impulse：内在冲动

social norms which threaten the transgressor neither with punishment nor with levy of execution, but which nevertheless are not ineffectual.

Sanction is not a peculiarity of the legal norms[1]. The norms of ethical custom, morality, religion, tact, decorum, etiquette, and fashion would be quite meaningless if they did not exercise a certain amount of coercion. They too constitute the order of the human associations, and it is their specific function to coerce the individual members of the association to submit to the order[2]. All compulsion exercised by the norms is based upon the fact that the individual is never actually an isolated individual; he is enrolled, placed, embedded, wedged, into so many associations that existence outside of these would be unendurable, often even impossible, to him. We are speaking now of basic facts of the inner, the emotional, life of man. The psychic needs of ordinary common place creatures, who everywhere constitute the compact majority, must indeed be appraised none too highly; nevertheless there is no one to whom country, native land, religious communion, family, friends, social relations, political party, are mere words. Most people perhaps will set little store by[3] one or the other of these, but doubtless there would be very few who do not cling with all their hearts and minds to one group at least. It is within his circle that each man seeks aid in distress, comfort in misfortune, moral support, social life, recognition, respect, honor. In the last analysis it is his group that supplies him with everything that he sets store by in life. But the importance of these associations is not limited to these moral, intangible considerations, for on them depends success in one's profession and business. On the other hand, one's profession and business draw one into a number of professional and business

1. Sanction is not a peculiarity of the legal norms：制裁并非法律规范的特征。
2. submit to the order：遵从秩序
3. set little store by：不重视

associations.

All of us then are living within numberless, more or less compactly, occasionally quite loosely, organized associations, and our fate in life will, in the main, be conditioned by the kind of position we are able to achieve within them. It is clear that in this matter there must be a reciprocity of services rendered. It is impossible for the associations to offer something to each one of its members unless each individual is at the same time a giver. And in fact all these associations — whether they are organized or unorganized, and whether they are called country, home, residence, religious communion, family, circle of friends, social life, political party, industrial association, or good will of a business — make certain demands in exchange for that which they give; and the social norms which prevail in these communities are nothing more than the universally valid precipitate[1] of the claims which the latter make upon the individual. He therefore who is in need of the support of the circle to which he belongs — as who is not? — does wisely if he conforms, at least in a general way, to its norms. He who refuses to conform to them must face the fact that his conduct will loosen the bonds of solidarity with his own circle. He who persistently refuses obedience has himself loosened the bonds which until now have united him with his associates. He will gradually be deserted, avoided, excluded. Here then, in the social association, is the source of the coercive power, the sanction, of all social norms, of law no more than of morality, ethical custom, religion, honor, decorum, etiquette, fashion, at least as far as the outward observance of the precepts is concerned. Especially as to etiquette and fashion, Jhering[2], many years ago, in two articles published in the Berlin *Gegenwart*[3] and entitled,

1. universally valid precipitate：普遍有效的析出物
2. Jhering：耶林（1818—1892），德国著名法学家，新功利主义（目的）法学派创始人。
3. *Gegenwart*：〈德〉风采杂志《当代》

"Das soziale Motiv der Mode[1]" (The Social Motive of Fashion) and "Das soziale Motiv der Tracht[2]" (The Social Motive of Dress), showed that this is their very nature. These articles, with some omissions and changes, were subsequently incorporated in the author's *Zweck im Recht*[3]. Etiquette and fashion are the norms of a privileged social circle; they are the external indicia of belonging. In order to be received and enjoy the advantages of being a member, one must know and observe them.

A man therefore conducts himself according to law, chiefly because this is made imperative by his social relations. In this respect the legal norm does not differ from the other norms. The state is not the only association that exercises coercion; there is an untold number of associations in society that exercise it much more forcibly than the state. One of the most vigorous of these associations is the family. Modern legislation more and more does away with the possibility of execution of a decree for the restitution of conjugal relations[4]. But even if the family law were abolished in its entirety, families would not bear an aspect much different from that which they bear to day; for fortunately the family law requires state sanction only in rare instances. If the workman, the employee, the office-holder, the military officer, do not perform their contractual and official duties from a sense of duty, they do so because they wish to keep their positions, perhaps because they wish to rise to better ones. The physician, the attorney, the mechanic, the merchant, are interested in exact performance of their contracts because they wish to satisfy their patients, clients, and customers and to increase the number of the latter; at any rate, because they wish to establish or strengthen

1. *Das soziale Motiv der Mode*：〈德〉时尚的社会动机
2. *Das soziale Motiv der Tracht*：〈德〉着装的社会动机
3. *Zweck im Recht*：〈德〉法律的目的
4. restitution of conjugal relations：恢复婚姻关系

their credit. Penalty and levy of execution is the last thing that enters their minds. There are large mercantile houses which, as a matter of principle, do not bring suit on a mat ter arising in their commercial relations, and as a rule do not permit themselves to be sued, but satisfy even an unfounded claim in full. They meet refusal of payment and frivolous demands by severing commercial relations. To this ext ent their own power is sufficient unto them; to this extent they can dispense with the aid of the courts and with legal protection. Likewise persons of superior social position avoid litigation of controversies, e.g. with servants, employees, workmen, mechanics. Their social and economic influence affords sufficient protection from imposition. For decades the English trade unions[1] have declined all recognition by the state, thereby consciously and intentionally foregoing legal protection. Manifestly they did not fare badly by doing so. Modern trusts and cartels[2] have at their disposal a complete system of means of coercion, by which they are enabled, without ever calling upon the power of the state or upon the courts, to enforce their just, as well as their often altogether unjustifiable, demands against everyone who happens to come within their sphere of power. In the course of the investigation of the iron cartel instituted by the Austrian government one of the chiefs of the cartel, Direc tor Kes tranek, made the statement that it was a matter of minor importance to him whether the iron cartel was legally efficacious or not, since the agreements, whether legally valid or not, were being kept as if they were legally valid. He said: "The iron-masters are men who keep agreements, even if they have no legal validity." He might have added that the individual ironmaster can be coerced by means as efficacious as any that are at the disposal of the courts of the state. Likewise legally binding force of trade-union agreements would be without great significance to the workingmen

1. trade unions：工会
2. trusts and cartels：托拉斯与卡特尔，垄断组织形式。

since they are being kept for all that as if they were legally binding, chiefly for the same reasons for which the agreements of the iron magnates are being kept. Both friend and foe admire the compact structure which is seen everywhere in the Catholic Church[1], in its legal order no less than in other respects. Nevertheless the ecclesiastical law[2] is enforced only to a very small extent by the state; and where separation of church and state is in effect, not at all. It rests, as a whole, chiefly on a social basis. In France, since the enactment of the law of separation, church taxes are being paid conscientiously even by non-believing Catholics. Nothnagel, of whose services science was deprived by his untimely death, devoted the highly interesting first-fruits of his juristic labor to the question of enforcement by social *Interessengruppen*[3] (groups having common interests).

There is nothing that is better adapted to throw light upon[4] what has just been said than a brief consideration of modern strikes. For years the factory worker has most conscientiously been performing all obligations arising from the contract for work and wages. What has impelled him to do this? If it is not his sense of duty, it is fear of dismissal and unemployment, the prospect of getting on better in the factory in which he is working, or of the respect of his associates and of his superiors. Compared with this, law-suit and compulsory execution are to him little more than mere words; for he has nothing that he can call his own but the strength of his hands. Now he joins the newly organized union, which passes a resolution that its members must not work with non-union workmen. It is true, the law which is being applied in the courts of the state and in the other tribunals denies to this norm all legal efficacy; but the workman will accept

1. Catholic Church：天主教堂
2. ecclesiastical law：教会法
3. social *Interessengruppen*：社会利益共同体
4. throw light upon：阐明

it without objection, for it was created by an association with which he is most intimately connected. And when his associates lay down their tools in obedience to this resolution, he does not hesitate for one moment to join them, to break the contract which he has faithfully kept for years, and to expose himself and his family to the perils of unemployment. Adversity and destitution, which follow dismissal, have lost all their terrors for him; the force of the contractual norm, which is an enforceable legal norm, has been completely shattered by another norm. The strike has divided the entrepreneurs and the workmen in this branch of industry into two belligerent armies; and in each camp the commands of the leaders are being blindly obeyed although doubtless they are legally unenforceable. Ultimately peace is brought about, i.e. a wage agreement. Whether this can be sued upon is a question that has, as is well known, generally been answered in the negative, and it is unlikely that, according to existing law, a suit on it can be maintained in court. But that is not the important consideration. It will nevertheless be kept in violate by both parties, even by entrepreneurs who are not parties to it as well as by workmen who may enter the employment long after the agreement has been made. For now the wage-scale agreement is the basis for the order of the work in this branch of business. And though the parties may not be satisfied with the agreement, they know that even a bad order is better than continued warfare.

There are two forms of sanction which are preponderantly, though not exclusively, peculiar to the legal norms; to wit[1] penalty and compulsory execution[2]. What is the significance of these two forms? Do they, as is usually assumed, impart to the legal norm such efficacy as it has? If the law were without sanction, or to put it accurately, without the coercion effected by penalty and compulsory execution,

1. to wit：亦即
2. penalty and compulsory execution：刑罚与强制执行

would it really be merely a fire that does not burn as Jhering thinks? (There are, incidentally, many kinds of fire that do not burn.) To answer these questions exhaustively would probably require a detailed study of the coercive effect of penalty and of compulsory execution; but a fleeting glance at life will suffice to convince us that both are of importance in a very limited measure and in certain situations only. If we exclude the cases in which appeal is made to the courts because the question of fact or of law is in dispute, in which it is not a matter of enforcing law and right by coercion but of showing what is law and right in the given case, it will appear that the coercive force of penalty and of compulsory execution, as mass phenomena at least — and only these are of moment here — is effective only in a very limited measure and in so far as, for some reason or other, the other sanctions of the social organizations fail to function.

As to penalty, its true significance is shown by penal statistics. It is true, penal offenses occur in all social circles. But if we disregard persons of inferior social value[1] who are not amenable to social restraints[2]; if we leave out of consideration a few misdeeds as to which social influences are less effective because these misdeeds as such do not affect social position (insult, duel, political crime, and, among a large part of the German peasantry, bodily injury); if we consider not individual cases? but the great bulk of the daily work done by the criminal courts, we shall see that criminal law is directed almost exclusively against those whom descent, economic distress, neglected education or moral degradation has excluded from the human associations. It is only in the case of these outcasts that the widest association, which includes even them, i.e. the state, steps in with its power to punish. The state as an organ of society protects society against those that are outside the pale of society.

1. persons of inferior social value：低社会价值人
2. amenable to social restraints：遵从社会约束

The measure of its success is shown by its experience extending over thousands of years. The conviction is steadily gaining ground that the only serious weapon against crime is the possibility of regaining the criminal for human society and thus again subjecting him to social restraint.

Is the situation otherwise in case of compulsory execution? The writer has already pointed out that in the case of claims arising from contracts of service, wages, and labor it plays a very insignificant part. It is of social significance only in the case of obligations to pay money, i.e. in but a small fraction of legal life. At this point it may suffice to raise the question whether the agreements from which obligations to pay money arise are being entered into with an eye to compulsory execution. For when the creditor extends credit he doubtless takes into consideration everything that might prompt the debtor to make repayment. A single glance, however, at the organization of credit shows of what small significance compulsory execution is in business which is done on credit. We are fully justified in saying that in a developed economic system a person may not safely be granted credit if the creditor has to take into consideration the possibility of the necessity of compulsory execution. Whether or not credit can safely be extended is determined in general by means of a thorough social and psychological investigation of the person who is asking for credit. In a case of ordinary extension of credit the actual basis for the investigation is furnished by experience in the affairs of everyday life; in case of mercantile credit, by a widely ramified organization. If this investigation shows that litigation or compulsory execution might result, the question whether credit can safely be extended is answered in the negative.

The security of credit depends upon the wealth, the social position? the personal relations, and the honesty of the person asking for credit. All of these things must warrant the assumption that he will always bear in mind and fulfil his obligations. The most imperfectly organized form of extension of credit, i.e. the usurious credit[1], which seeks to guard against loss by exacting excessive int erest, is the very one that relies most strongly on the deb tor's being prompted to pay by his sense of duty or by his position in life. All these things indicate the importance of the social associations which credit presupposes. And if, as may happen at any time, credit is extended to a stranger, this can be accounted for only by the fact that somehow the bearing of the borrower has created the impression that his position, his situation, his wealth, warrant the assumption that he is solvent. In Rome, where every sale, because of the liabilities arising from the transaction, was in fact a credit transaction, one did not, as the sources show, readily buy from a person one did not know.

To say then that credit can safely be extended is not to make a prediction as to the result of compulsory execution. It is rather to make a statement as to the social relations upon which the creditor relies when he extends credit. One does not extend credit to a person whose position does not warrant the assumption that the obligation will be performed; one deals with him for cash or in reliance upon security given, e.g. a pledge. Transactions for cash or transactions secured by a pledge[2] however are transfers of possession[3], and therefore not only do not presuppose compulsory execution but do not presuppose so much as a legal order. One would enter into a cash or a pledge transaction even with savages who have never before seen a white man, provided one were protected, by an escort for instance, against violence on the part of the savages. In civilized society, possession is rendered sufficiently secure by the inner order of the associations; and, ultimately, it is protected also by the state, the most inclusive association known to society, as an organ of society. Transactions for

1. usurious credit：高利贷信用
2. pledge：担保
3. transfers of possession：占有转移

cash or secured by a pledge can be entered into with anyone because they are transactions that involve only a transfer of possession, and therefore do not presuppose compulsory execution, but are designed to render the latter superfluous. The right of pledge of the lessor therefore has the beneficial effect that anyone can lease a dwelling without reference to his credit rating. If the lessor does not get his rent, he can take possession of the chattels[1] which the lessee has brought into the house, and is protected by the community in doing so. In England, where the right of pledge of the lessor does not exist, references are required in case of lease which show that credit can safely be extended to the lessee. Only the innkeeper, who has no option as to the customer with whom he will deal, has a legal right of pledge (lien[2]) on all of the goods which the guest has brought into the inn. Here again security based on possession takes the place of the organization of credit in civilized society.

To consider the right of compulsory execution, as jurists often do, as the basis of the legal order involves a tremendous overestimation of its scope. Limited in its effectiveness to a small fraction of legal life, i.e. the obligation to pay money, it is secondary even within this sphere to the force of the social interrelations which urge us to perform our obligations. There can be no doubt that the creditor usually makes a correct calculation as to whether credit may safely be granted to the debtor, i.e. that the considerations which prompt him to extend credit coincide with those that prompt the debtor to meet his obligations. In fact, a person to whom his personal reputation, his social standing, his business relations, in short his credit, mean anything surely will never even think of hazarding a compulsory execution. All these things mean too much to him to endanger them for the sake of a momentary advantage. The gambler pays his unenforceable gambling debts

---

1. chattels：动产
2. lien：留置权

under a merely social compulsion, and the average man is at least as sensitive to social sanction as the average gambler. Even unenforceable debts arising from stock-exchange differences are usually being paid, although in these cases the social and economic consequences of failure to do so are much less than in case of true business debts. The generally known ineffectiveness of the usury laws demonstrates that the persons from whom usury is being exacted can be compelled to pay even without compulsory execution. The reports of mercantile credit associations show that the well known purely economic means of coercion, to wit boycott and black list, are effective even where compulsory execution has remained altogether fruitless. Nothnagel, in the book referred to above, mentions older material, which however is still valuable. Compulsory execution, like penalty, we may therefore say, exists only for those that have come down in the world and for those whom society has cast out. It is effective against the reckless borrower, the cheat, the bankrupt, and against him who has become insolvent through misfortune. However much of a burden these classes of borrowers may be on business life, they are too insignificant to warrant the statement that the value of the legal order depends upon the protection it affords against such elements.

On the whole the effect of the coercive order of the state is limited to protection of one's person, of one's possession, and of claims against those who are outside of the pale of society. Whatsoever else the state may do in order to maintain the law is of much less significance, and one might reasonably maintain that society would not go to pieces even if the state should exercise no coercion whatever. After all, commerce was able to eke out a precarious existence even in the ancient Polish republic; and it pursues its way even in the Orient today, although the corrupt and extermely incompetent administration of justice there scarcely deserves the name. Before the judicial reform of the thirties of the last century, the benefits of the expensive and cumbersome English civil procedure did not extend far beyond the well-to-do upper crust[1] of English society. This however did not prevent the English from becoming a rich and highly civilized nation. Moreover legal protection in Germany and Austria under the older procedure was not much more effective. Under such circumstances one extends credit more sparingly, or protects oneself by carefully thought-out safeguards; the rest must be done by the social associations. Goethe[2], who did not fail to observe that the Imperial Supreme Court had extremely little influence upon the administration of justice, quite correctly pointed out the things that are really important. It is a more serious matter if the administration of criminal justice breaks down also. But Hungary, sou them Italy, and Spain prove that a nation can survive centuries of brigandage[3].

Not only in primitive times, when society as a whole consisted chiefly of small associations, but much later, even at the present time, there is no lack of instances of societies maintained exclusively by the inner order of its associations. Wherever the power of the state is extremely feeble, there is no order but this. And indeed on this order, societies have been built up in Europe even in modern times, e.g. that of the former Polish Republic, of Hungary in the seventeenth and eighteenth centuries, of the kingdom of Naples, of Sicily. This is true, in part, of the Orient also. In the Middle Ages, the weakness of the state brought about special associations for legal protection and caused men to resort to commendation[4]. In modern times similar formations can be found, e.g. the confederations of the former Polish Republic, the Camorra[5] and the Maffia in Naples and Sicily. In conclusion, the

---

1. upper crust：上流社会
2. Goethe：歌德（1749—1832），德国戏剧家、诗人、自然科学家，曾在莱比锡学习法律，后在韦茨拉尔的最高法院工作。
3. brigandage：强盗
4. commendation：领主附庸
5. Camorra：克莫拉，类似黑手党的犯罪组织，于 17 世纪起源于意大利坎帕尼亚地区。

studies of Noeldeke on the Arabs of the sixth century may be referred to in order to prove that the existence of a great nation, nay, what is more, of a large and opulent commercial city, may be maintained solely by the inner strength of its associations. "Here it is important to note that among the Arabs there are no traces of the formation of states. The clan, the tribe, are moral units of great authority, but without any power of coercion. He who refuses to take part in an undertaking of the tribe or of the family may incur derision, even contempt, but there is no means of coercing him. Only the vengeance of blood guarantees a certain measure of security. If any other crime can be punished by any means other than private vengeance, I have no knowledge of that fact. To rob a member of one's tribe or a guest was disgraceful, but the robbed had no other means of redress than to try to get back that of which he had been robbed. This was the prevailing state of affairs not only among the Bedouins[1], but also in the cities; even in Mecca. It is almost incredible that a city whose inhabitants were engaged extensively in commerce, who were very much superior mentally to the Bedouins, and who soon after successfully undertook to conquer and rule one half of the world, had no actual government. But we must always emphasize the fact that the authority of the most prominent citizens offsets this defect fairly well. After the heads of the clan — who exercised only a moral authority over the latter — had agreed upon an undertaking, an individual or an individual family would not be likely to dare to refuse to cooperate; this has happened however." From the last remark of Noeldeke's, it follows that only the extraordinarily close cohesion of the Arabic clans, which continues down to the present time, and the support which each individual found among his own people have made the existence of such a society possible.

---

1. Bedouins：贝多因人，阿拉伯游牧民族。

A study of the beginnings of human society discloses the fact that the force of the legal norm, which at the time is as yet undifferentiated from the norm of religion, of morals, and of ethical custom, is based exclusively or almost exclusively on the influence exerted upon every individual by the members of the narrower association of which he is a member. Generally everyone conforms without making objection to the order of the family or of the clan. True legal or penal coercion is scarcely ever employed against a fellow-member of a narrower association. Obstinate resistance[1] is met with exclusion, from the association, which is considered the greatest misfortune that can befall a man. Note the Homeric words *ἀφρήτωρ, ἀνέστιος, ἀθέμιστος*[2]. Enforcement of one's rights by violence as well as defense by violence are resorted to only against outsiders, as to whom the norms of the association are ineffectual. It is an error to believe that we have advanced far beyond such a state of affairs. Even today, just as in the beginnings of legal development, the force of law is based on the silent, uninterrupted sway of the associations which embrace the individual. From this point of view, the law appears even today to be related, in its essential nature, to the other social norms, i.e. to the norms of religion, morals, ethical custom, decorum, tact, etiquette, fashion. Even today exclusion from the community (the church, the association, society (*aus der Gesellschaft*) in the social as well as in the juristic sense), withdrawal of credit, loss of position or of custom, is the most efficacious means of combating insubordination. Even today punishment and compulsory execution, which the jurist is accustomed to look upon as the basis of all legal order, are merely the extreme means of combat against those that have been excluded from the associations, just as the feud was the extreme means of combat against a member of a strange community.

---

1. Obstinate resistance：顽固抵抗
2. Homeric words *ἀφρήτωρ, ἀνέστιος, ἀθέμιστος*：荷马言：没有手足情，没有家园，没有法律。（斜体为希腊文）

Nevertheless the fact that the force of the social norms is so universally traced to the coercive power of the state requires explanation. Every false doctrine must, in the nature of things, be based on a correct observation of some sort or other. All our perceptions and sensations are always true; only the conclusions we draw from them can be false. In the first place, the validity of only a part of the law is maintained by the coercive power of the state. This part is neither very great nor very important, but it is the part which is of greatest interest to the jurist; because the latter is not concerned until coercion becomes necessary. In the second place there are doubtless many norms which most people would not observe if there were no sanction in the form of penalty or compulsory execution. In this connection the norms of police law (Max Ernst Mayer), which incidentally are applied not only by the judges of the police courts and of the criminal courts, but also by the judges of the civil courts, are of minor importance. Being norms for decision and having been created by the sovereign power of the state, they are foreign to the life of society, and often do not become known except through the decisions rendered in accordance with them, and they become rules of conduct only through these decisions. These decisions then appear to be the real promulgation of the law, and the rule *ignorantia legis nocet*[1] appears in its true significance. It is a fact of greater importance that the entire military system and the entire tax system of the modern state, that is to say, the very thing which customarily is considered the basis of the life of the state, could not exist for a single moment without coercion exercised by the state. All this however merely amounts to saying that the state and a considerable portion of society have consciously become antagonistic to each other. In consequence of this antagonism, the military and the tax system of the state have remained so unrelated

1. *ignorantia legis nocet*：〈拉〉不知法不免责。

to society that they have become state institutions exclusively. History will probably show that this is merely a transition stage. It was not the case in antiquity. The whole military system and that part of the services required by the state which had to be rendered by the commonalty were socially organized. This is true even today in small states.

The conception of law as a coercive order[1] therefore is based upon the fact that its exponents have one-sidedly taken into consideration only those portions of the law that derive their force solely from the state. But that is not the whole story. To a considerable extent, this conception has been derived from a consideration not merely of law, but of social life as a whole. It is being observed that there is an enormous contrast in society between the rich and the poor; that the entire burden of the work of society rests upon the poor; that in exchange they receive little more than the bare necessaries of life; that the legal order compels them to render valuable services to society in exchange for services of much less value. That this state of affairs is endured by those to whom it causes such losses can be understood only if one assumes that it is being forcibly maintained by the sovereign power[2] of the state. This thought has been followed through to its logical conclusion in the socialist philosophy of history. The latter begins with a discussion of the older economic organization of mankind, of the ordering of the clan and of the family, of the household as a self-sufficing economic unit[3], of industry carried on by organized crafts, whereby an equal division of the fruits of labor among all who participated therein was secured (Engels, Rodbertus); and shows that this state of affairs, under the influence of capitalism, is continually shifting, to the disadvantage of an ever increasing

1. law as a coercive order：法律作为强制秩序
2. sovereign power：主权权力
3. self-sufficing economic unit：自给自足的经济单位

majority of those who have not and to the advantage of an ever decreasing number of those who have (Marx). The older economic order, it is contended, was sustained by the great majority, who found it to be to their advantage to do so; the later capitalistic order is being maintained exclusively by the state, which is a powerful, elaborate organization of those who have for the protection of the legal order, which is based on property, contract, and the law of inheritance. The socialists therefore quite consistently urge those who have not to oppose to the organization of those who have the organization of the masses in order to bring about a legal order which is more favorable to the latter.

If it were true that the legal order of the present day cannot be maintained without the help of the state and that the latter is nothing but an organization of the small and ever decreasing minority of those who have against the great mass of those who have not, the legal order and the state were condemned already. But the present inquiry has shown that the resources of the state for the protection of the legal order are, in actual fact, not being employed against the great masses of the people but only against the small minority of those who have been cast out, who are cut off from all social relations. There is no need for any exertion on the part of the state to subdue the great mass of the people; the latter submit to the legal order willingly because they realize that the legal order is their order, the order of the economic and social associations, of which each one of them is a member. It cannot be true therefore that a small minority makes use of these associations for the purpose of exploiting the great majority. To say that this can be done for a long period of time without eruptions of violence is to contradict all historical experience and all mass psychology[1]. Every great strike which is accompanied by a breach of agreement

---

1. mass psychology：大众心理

demonstrates that the means at the disposal of the state are insufficient to enforce legal claims against hundreds or thousands of resisting human beings. If therefore the great majority of human beings — and this includes, as can readily be seen, the whole working class — render obedience to the legal order, they undoubtedly must be actuated by a very strong conviction, though not perhaps a clear understanding, that it is necessary to do this — necessary in order to secure their own interests. This same conviction is clearly manifested in every revolt the object of which is not political but economic revolution. By far the greater number will be found on the side of the sovereign power of the state, and a revolutionary movement of this sort has never been successful even to the extent of being able to maintain itself permanently in a state of any considerable magnitude.

In fact, since the present legal order is at the same time an organization of production and exchange of goods it is not possible to abolish it without, at the same time, depriving the great majority as well as the small minorities of the means of subsistence. It is necessary, therefore, if civilization is to continue, that the existing legal order should not be abolished, unless it can at once be replaced by another, a socialistic order. That this can be accomplished at any time without further ado is no longer contended by anyone competent to judge, even a socialist. Intelligent socialists have long since been speaking only of a gradual development of the capitalistic economy into a socialistic one. Incidentally, I believe that I have shown elsewhere (Südd. Monatshefte, 3 Jahrg.) that even this cannot be accomplished within a calculable period of time. If therefore the present-day social order, in spite of the great sacrifices it exacts from the majority of the people, exhibits a tolerably firm structure, this is due to the fact that, for the moment, there is no other order available that could do more, or even as much, not only for those who have, but also for those who have not. The question of the ultimate goal (*Endziel*) may safely be passed over. As a practical mat ter, even the socialistic working class of Europe is concerned only about such an improvement of the present legal order as secures to it a modest, but attainable, social advancement.

In view of the coercion by means of which the social associations enforce observance of the norms, it may be said that the individual manifestly is at all times both active and passive; every member of the association takes part in bringing pressure to bear, and every individual, in turn, must submit to pressure. The coercive power of the norms — a fact of mass psychology — posits at the same time the observance of the latter a fact of individual psychology. It would be a mistake, nevertheless, to lay too much stress upon this particular fact. With the great mass of men who throughout their whole lives perm it themselves, without objection, to be fitted into the vast social mechanism, it is not a matter of conscious thinking, but of unconsciously habituating themselves to the emotions and thoughts of their surroundings, which are with them from the cradle to the grave. The most important norms function only through suggestion. They come to man in the form of commands or of prohibitions; they are addressed to him without a statement of the reason on which they are based; and he obeys them without a moment's reflection. They have not subdued man but have educated him. They are being impressed upon his mind in his childhood; an "It is not done," "It is not proper," "Thus hath God commanded[1]" follows him through his whole life. And he submits with a willingness which is the greater the more emphatically experience brings home to him the advantages of obedience and the disadvantages of disobedience. The advantages and disadvantages are not only social but also individual; for he who obeys a command is spared the arduous labor of doing his own thinking, and the still more arduous labor of making his own decision. Liberty and independence are ideals of the poet, the artist, and the thinker

1. Thus hath God commanded：这是上帝的命令。

only. The average man is a Philistine[1], without much appreciation of these things. He loves that to which he has become habituated, the instinctive, and hates nothing more than intellectual exertion. That is the reason why women become enthusiastic over men of strong will. The latter make their decisions for them, and do not even give the thought of resistance opportunity to arise. For all the trouble and pains that they are thereby freed from they are sincerely grateful to their husbands.

In this way, obedience to norms ultimately impresses its stamp upon the whole man. It makes not only the individual act, but the man himself, just, moral, faithful, tenacious of ethical custom, dignified, tactful, honorable, well-mannered, modern. He submits to the norms from conviction, and this imparts stability to his conduct. After the social pressure which is brought to bear upon the individual in each case by the habit of obedience to the norms has fashioned the character of the individual, it can no longer be effectively counteracted by other influences. The social norms give shape and form to the individuality of man.

It might not be amiss for everyone who is investigating the origin and the effects of the legal norms to make an attempt to answer the much simpler question why he does not meet a man in the street wearing conventional civilian clothes without a cravat. It cannot be a matter of mere fastidiousness[2]; for undoubtedly there is a great number of men who are quite indifferent to matters of dress, who nevertheless would never appear in public without a cravat. In order to facilitate the inevitable historical investigation, I will say that this in itself rather superfluous article of dress, which, incidentally, is not of impeccable taste, is descended from the garb of the Croatian regiments in Paris in the days of Louis XIV, from whom, by the bye, it got its Austrian

1. Philistine：俗人
2. fastidiousness：过分讲究

and French name (cravat). And for the very reason that at the present time it is not readily seen that the social norm requiring every civilized European man who has any self-respect to wear a cravat fulfils any function in the creation or preservation of the social order, a detailed study of it would yield a great amount of information to the jurist.

Accordingly social norms, whether they are legal norms or norms of another kind, always have their origin in an association; they impose an obligation only on the members of this association; and this obligation is binding upon them only in their dealings with members of the association. They have no effect upon anyone outside of the association. If these propositions had been enunciated in classical antiquity they would not have required further proof, for they would have been accepted as self-evident truths. At that time, no one doubted that law, religion, morality, ethical custom, were in existence only for one's own people, and that one's own people occasionally did not even include all those that dwelt within the walls of the city; at any rate, that it never extended beyond the closest tribal or lingual relationship. Beyond this, there was no bond that was not established by treaty of guest-friendship, of friendship, or of commerce. This is the situation even today among all peoples that are outside the pale of European civilization. It is true, in most cases the person of the guest is sacred, but the moment the guest crosses the threshold he becomes a member of the household; and often enough the protection extended ceases the moment he leaves the house.

At the present time, it is true, this is no longer the case to the same extent. It is clear however that the norms of ethical custom, decorum, tact, etiquette, fashion, have no validity beyond a certain circle. But the legal norms, in part at least, impose an obligation on everyone; and this obligation is binding upon everyone in his dealings with every other human being. Three or four world-religions proclaim their truths to all mankind. Modern morality likewise no longer recognizes the ancient limitation that its norms order the relations of those only that belong to the same people. The question is, what is the meaning of all this?

The religions, to begin with, both in their doctrines and in their ritual norms, appeal only to those that profess the faith. The fact that they proclaim themselves world-religions means simply that their doors are open to everyone that accepts their truths. In this respect they differ from the religions of antiquity, which were limited to their respective peoples, but this difference lies in a different sphere.

As to modern ethics, however, the situation is quite different, irrespective of whether its basis is religious or philosophical. Its object is to impose the moral commandment[1] upon all men and to make it binding upon them in their dealings with every being that bears a human countenance. It must be emphatically denied, however, that this has ever amounted to more than a preachment or a teaching, that this morality has in fact become a rule of conduct for the great masses of mankind. Even today commandments of morality are actually being obeyed with any degree of exactness only in the intimate circle of the family, at most among friends. Outside this circle the effectiveness of the moral command decreases steadily; and as to the st ranger, the average man recognizes no teaching of morality which obligates him to do anything more than to extend courtesies which require no effort; and hatred of the enemy of one's country is considered as praiseworthy today as it was in the most remote antiquity. A glance at the atrocities occasionally perpetrated in the colonies of this or that great power shows the depths to which the morality of modern man may sink where there are no associational bonds; and these atrocities are only a small fraction of the atrocities which the nationals of the most highly civilized nations of the earth believe they have a right to perpetrate upon defenseless natives.

---

1. moral commandment：道德戒律

It is true there is a series of legal norms that are valid in favor of everyone and bind everyone. Eut these are either a part of the law created by the state or they are but norms for decision, not rules of conduct. Even the so-called private international law and criminal law contain only norms for decision, are addressed to the authorities and not to the people. The living law, even where it is created by the state, is preponderantly, as to its content, limited to an association. The rights and duties arising from *Staatsrecht* (public law in the narrow sense) presuppose the right of citizenship in the state; the law of the family presupposes membership in the family; the law of corporations presupposes membership in the corporation; the law of contract presupposes a contract; the law of inheritance presupposes membership in the family or the acceptance of a testamentary gift (of which the mere non-repudiation, according to some laws, is an equivalent). Other rights and duties arise from the position of an official, of a servant of the state. It is only as to the claim to life, liberty, and property that a different rule obtains at the present time; for this claim is being recognized, at least within the territory in which European civilization holds undisputed sway, as a valid claim of everyone, irrespective of nationality. This is a relatively modern achievement. As late as the sixteenth century, the life and the property of the alien were by no means secure in Europe. Even today it is not an indispensable element of civilization, as is shown by the history of colonies everywhere and by the fate of the Negroes in America. The anti-slavery legislation of the nineteenth century shows how difficult it was to instil into the most highly civilized nations of the earth respect for the life and the liberty of the defenseless Negro. But with these temporal and local limitations[1], respect for the life, the liberty, and the property of every man is today not merely a norm for decision and

1. temporal and local limitations：时域与地域限制

a policy of the state, but has actually become a principle of the living law. To this modest extent, the whole human race has already become a vast legal association. This cannot be said, however, of other legal relations, especially of the law of contract. The uncertainty of credit relations in far distant countries a standing phrase in trade reports-bears eloquent witness to this fact.

Nevertheless the fact remains that at the present time there is in existence a religious and philosophical system of ethics which does not limit its morality to an individual human association. This fact requires explanation. Its import is that, at least among the select spirits of the world, there exists a conception of a morality which embraces all men, a conception of law not confined within any boundaries. Although it is at the present time nothing more than a dream of the noblest and best which promises a better future, it has been realized in the living law to the extent of securing, in the seats of the highest civilization, life, liberty, and property to every man.

V THE FACTS OF THE LAW

The modern jurist is accustomed to seeing a world ruled by law and legal coercion. To this world, which is his world, he owes his *Weltanschauung* (world-view, philosophy of life)[1], which assumes that law and legal coercion have been in existence from the beginning of time. He can not conceive of human communal life without them. A family that is not held together, or at least supervised, by the constituted authorities, property that is not protec ted by the courts, a contract that cannot be sued upon, or that may not, to say the least, be set up as a defense, an inheritance that cannot be obtained by legal means, are to him things that are altogether outside of the legal sphere, that are without legal significance. In this way, legal order, court, and legal sanction become a unit in his mode of thinking, and he will unhesitatingly speak of law or legal relation only where he finds a court and legal coercion, or perhaps an administrative tribunal and administrative coercion.

In this narrow world of ideas the purely juristic concept of the sources of law had its origin. Manifestly it could only be a matter of explaining the origin of the rules according to which legal coercion is being exercised by courts and administrative tribunals. Following this path, the prevailing juristic science[2] arrived at the well known theory of the two sources — a theory which derives all law from statute or custom. It is manifestly based on the precepts of the *corpus iuris civilis*

1. *Weltanschauung* (world-view, philosophy of life)：〈德〉世界观、生活哲学
2. prevailing juristic science：主流法学

and of the *corpus iuris canonic* which recognize only the *leges*[1] and, in addition thereto, *consuetudo*[2] as sources of law. Its epistemological basis[3] might well be the logical theorem of the excluded middle[4]. Since all law which is not statute law must needs be customary law, the question as to the concept of customary law resolves itself into the question: What must be the nature of law that is not statute law? We are not told why there can be no sources of law other than statute and customary law. No suggestion is being made that a scientific inquiry into the nature of law should be instituted. Whatsoever is said about customary law moves within a circle of commonplaces. In the last analysis the Romans proceeded in a much more scientific manner inasmuch as they were content with simply enumerating the six or eight methods according to which, in their system of law, legal rules that were binding on the judge arose. Nevertheless not one of the attempts to add as much as a third source to the two that have been recognized until now has met with success, i.e. the addition of science or judicial usage or the rule established by agreement or customary dealings between the parties (*Konvenlionalreget*) or, as has been attempted by writers on commercial law, commercial usage (*usance*)[5].

The saddest part of the matter perhaps is the fact that those who are struggling with the concepts of statute and customary law are not looking for the difficulty in the quarter in which it may be found. In the matter of the sources of law, it is not a question of how the rules of law which the judge or the administrative official must apply assume the form in which they are binding on him. The law does not consist of legal propositions, but of legal institutions. In order to be able to

---

1. *leges*：〈拉〉法律
2. *consuetudo*：〈拉〉习惯
3. epistemological basis：认识论基础
4. logical theorem of the excluded middle：排中律
5. commercial usage (*usance*)：商业惯例

state the sources of law one must be able to tell how the state, the church, the commune, the family, the contract, and inheritance came into being, how they change and develop. The function of a theory of the sources of law is to discover the vital forces that bring about the development of legal institutions. It is not sufficient to state the forms in which legal propositions, *or,* to be more exact, legal propositions of a certain kind, are to be found. Law and legal relation is a matter of intellectual concept which does not exist in the sphere of tangible reality, but in the minds of men. There would be no law if there were not men who bear the concept of law in their consciousness. But here, as everywhere else, our concepts are fashioned from the material which we take from tangible reality. They are always based on facts which we have observed. These facts must have been in existence before the concept of law and legal relation began to dawn in the human brain. And at the present time certain facts at least must be in existence before we can speak of law and legal relation. It is here that we must look for the workshop of the law. The first question of juristic science, the question as to the origin of law, accordingly becomes the question: Which are the factual institutions that become legal relations in the course of legal development, and which are the social processes through which this comes about?

A group of human beings becomes an association through organization. Organization is the rule which assigns to each individual his position and his functions. We are chiefly concerned therefore with determining the facts with which the human mind associates such rules. These facts, though apparently very heterogeneous, may be traced back to a very small number. They are — if we may be permitted to state the results of our inquiry in advance the following: usage, domination, possession, declaration of will. Usage here does not mean "customary law." We are not speaking of the customary application of legal propositions. Usage here means: The custom of the past shall be the norm for the future. Usage determines the position of the head as well as of the members of the association, the relation of superiority and of inferiority, and the functions of each individual member. Usage creates the order of all genetic associations: of the clan, the family, the household. In the family and in the home this is true perhaps even up to the present time. In a primitive stage, usage is still essentially normative in all local associations and in the state. But even in a highly developed commonwealth, like the Roman republic or present-day Great Britain, the constitutional law position of the organs of the state rests on usage. As to Rome, one need only page through Mommsen[1]'s *"Römisches Staatsrecht"*[2] in order to convince oneself of the truth of this statement. The small number of Roman statutes that have a public law (*staatsrechtlich*) content refer exclusively to the *comitia*[3]. Moreover down to the days of the Empire even Mommsen knows of no other means whereby to determine the rights and duties of a Roman magistrate than to state what his duties were according to traditional usage, and what he actually did do. And in order to make a presentation of British public law, one must proceed in the same way. The King, the Parliament, the ministers, the highest officials, all the organs of the state, regulate their course of con™ duct chiefly according to usage, or, in English terminology, according to precedents. The dominant associations of antiquity and of the Middle Ages likewise maintained their order through usage.

The majority of present-day associations have an order which is based on agreement, articles of association, legal proposition, and constitution. Nevertheless even in these, usage has by no means lost all significance. Wherever agreement, articles of association, legal proposition, or constitution has left a doubt or has failed to make

---

1. Mommsen：蒙森（1817—1903），德国学者，作家，获 1902 年诺贝尔文学奖，著有《罗马史》《罗马公法》等作品。
2. *Römisches Staatsrecht*：〈德〉《罗马公法》
3. *comitia*：〈拉〉公民会议，全体罗马市民均有资格参加的会议。

provision as to the position and duties of an individual, usage governs. Even in a constitutional state, therefore, usage is of the utmost importance (*Konventionalregel*); and in labor unions (in the factory) it is the indispensable basis of associational life.

Usage, to use Jellinek's phrase, is effective through the "normative power of the factual." Its ordering and regulative power in the association is based on the fact that it reflects the equilibration of the forces existing within the association. The interest which all members have in the associational life, their interest in the proper utilization of every force which is operative in the association, in placing every one of its members where he can render most service, in assigning to him rights and duties according to the needs of the whole, are counterbalanced by the aspirations of the individual to live his own life, to assert his own personality, to pursue his own interests. Usage always reflects the final equilibration of the forces. In general, a usage which produces norms for the future arises when a person who has been placed in a certain position claims a certain right without encountering opposition; when a person to whom a task has been assigned undertakes its performance without a protest; or when a protest that has arisen is overcome. In genetic associations, the decisive factors are physical strength, mental power, experience, personal prestige, age. In other associations they are wealth, birth, personal relations. The rights and duties connected by usage with a certain position usually pass from the holder to his successor; but if the distribution of power is changed by the succession, usage at once adapts itself to the changed situation.

The only association whose order, even today, depends chiefly upon usage is the house community of the family, not only as a moral and social, but also as an economic association. Among the peasantry it is an association for the purpose of production and consumption; among the urban middle classes, for consumption only; among a part of the working classes, almost exclusively for dwelling together. There is a great difference, economically, between the middle-class family and the working-class family, even where the latter is also an association for consumption; for the former is usually maintained exclusively by the earnings of the head of the family, while the latter is maintained by the earnings of all the able-bodied members of the family. A glance at these three kinds of families shows that each one of them has its own law not merely as to personal subordination but also as to property and earnings, and that the contents of the documents that are drawn up concerning family affairs (nuptial agreements, wills) differ to such an extent according to the station of the maker that it is possible without more ado to determine the station of the latter from the documents. The absolute supremacy of the peasant within his household becomes a mere general guidance among the middle classes, and among the working classes it is attenuated to what amounts, at most, to a moral influence. Among the peasantry, property and consumption is in common; among the middle classes there is individual ownership of property, but consumption is in common; among the working classes everything is separate; each member of the family owns his share and contributes his quota to defray the common expenses. Similarly in all other associations the content of usage and the order which is created thereby is determined by the economic bases of the associational life.

A careful distinction must be observed between the relation of superiority and inferiority, which exists in every organized association, and which is the expression of the inner order of the association, and the relation of domination and subjection. A command issued by a person occupying a position of superiority in an organized association is quite different from a command issued by a person who has the power of domination. The former is issued in behalf of the association, the latter in behalf of the person who issues it. A person who is in a position of superiority as well as a person who is in a position of inferiority acts in the consciousness of serving the association, but a person who is in a relation of subjection to another is conscious primarily of serving the person to whom he is subjected, and only occasionally of serving the association at the same time. The association remains unitary in spite of the relation of superiority and inferiority, which is necessarily produced by its organization; but relations of domination and subjection divide it into ruler and ruled. In an association thus organized, the rulers, and often the ruled, too, form associations of their own, or associations within the association.

We must distinguish two kinds of relations of domination and subjection[1], to wit those relations that flow from the family relationship — the subjection of children to the power of the father, of the wife to that of the husband — and relations of subjection of a purely social origin, slavery and serfdom. The idea presents itself most naturally to refer to legal precepts all the manifold and variously gradated relationships of domination and subjection, which are found in all stages of social development, down to the very latest, down to that which has been attained only by the most advanced nations of Europe and America. In fact the prevailing idea is that it is the legal proposition which subjects the wife to the husband, the children to the father, the ward to the guardian, the slave and the serf to the master. But the relations of domination and subjection were actually in existence everywhere before there was a legal proposition which regulated them as constituent parts of the legal order. Domination in every instance is merely the counterpart of the defenselessness and helplessness of the person subjected. The latter is subjected to domination because he enjoys no legal protection (*Rechtssckutz*); and he receives no protection because he is not a member of an as so ciation which might protect him, or because the association to which he belongs is too weak to protect him.

The situation of the slave and of the serf, and perhaps that of the guest and of the ward, it is true, is seemingly quite different from

---

1. domination and subjection：支配与服从

that of the women and the children. The former do not belong to the association of the rulers, but are strangers who have come within their sphere of power. Women and children however are members of the same association as the rulers. Recent study of the relation of the sexes and of the various groups of people of the same age in the most ancient society has shown that in primitive society the two sexes and the several groups of people of the same age everywhere form separate associations. To a certain extent this is true even at the present time. Even today we see women and men combining in groups for the protection of their separate interests, and even today there are traces of opposition between the groups of people of the same age. The latter is a common phenomenon in secondary schools, likewise between journeymen and apprentices[1] in a trade. Both surely are survivals of stages of development which have long since had their day rather than the beginning of a new development.

In the most ancient societies an association is formed at the outset by the efficient (*yollwertig*) members, who in case of need would be able to repel an attack single-handed and who could extend to others the same measure of assistance that they ask of the latter. The woman, the child, the youth who as yet is unable to bear arms, cannot do this, for they, by themselves, cannot form an association capable of self-defense. The stranger living in isolation cannot do this, for he has no association to take his part; the member of a vanquished tribe or nation cannot do it, for the community of which he is a member has just been crushed; the poor oppressed man cannot do it in unsettled times, for the protection which the association to which he belongs might possibly extend to him is ineffectual against the arbitrary dealings of the powerful. All of these, the woman, the child, the stranger, the vanquished, therefore are subjected to the domination of the man who is inclined to protect them, i.e. the husband, the father, the

1. journeymen and apprentices：熟练工与学徒

guest-friend, the victor. Every other person who lacks confidence in his own strength voluntarily places himself under the protection of another. If the defenseless one fails to find a protector, he becomes the prey of anyone who seizes him and spares his life; he becomes a slave of the latter. The weak person who has a master is no longer defenseless, for every attack upon him is now an attack on the master.

But all of these protective relationships presuppose that the protected is in position to offer some advantage to the protector. The relationship of ruler and ruled exists for the benefit of the ruler and not of the ruled. A man who with the utmost exertion can produce no more than he himself requires for a bare existence, as for instance a very poor hunter or shepherd, has no lord and master. The lord would derive no benefit from his lordship. A captured enemy therefore is not reduced to slavery, but is slaughtered, or, in exceptional cases, received into the conquering tribe. Only the woman is of value even at this stage of development, for she is the object not only of economic, but also of sexual exploitation. For this reason her life is spared, and she is compelled to do work which the man disdains either because he deems it beneath his dignity, or because it requires too much exertion.

Defenselessness alone cannot serve as the basis of a legal relation. It abandons the defenseless person like an ownerless chattel or beast to him who reduces him to possession, but it does not give him an owner. It does not give anyone a right in him. Domination however is more than mere possession of a person and exploitation of his labor, for it is a legally regulated relation between the person who has the power and the person who is subjected to the latter. The fact of personal subjection is based on the economic productivity of his labor, but it becomes a part of the legal order only in a case where the labor of the subjugated person[1] is of decisive significance for the economic order

---

1. subjugated person：受支配的人

of society. The unfree person may be a laborer on a farm or a groom of the chamber at the court of a king; he may, together with thousands of fellow-sufferers, toil on plantations or in mines; he may together with his wife and children live in a cottage on the land of his lord as a tenant-farmer paying rent to the latter, or he may till the soil on his own account as a serf for a moderate return on the plot of ground allotted to him; he may become a teacher or a manager in the service of his lord or he may render knight's service to the latter or he may engage independently in a trade or a business in the city. Whether he is one or the other of these is determined not by the arbitrary will of the mast er, but by the economic constitution of the country as a whole and by the qualities of the human beings that constitute the mass of the unfree population. Doubtless it was impossible in the days of the early Roman Empire to conduct an agricultural establishment on the basis of a system of villeinage[1]; likewise it was impossible in mediaeval Germany to raise cane sugar and tobacco on plantations. The legal position of the unfree man depends upon his position in the economic system. The farm-hand, the slave on the plantation, the groom of the chamber, the tenant-farmer, the villein, the man rendering knight's service, the civil official, the tradesman, are in totally different situations as unfree persons, in fact as well as in law. In Roman slavery this fact did not meet the eye except to a very limited extent. This however is due to the fact that the Roman jurists, who concern themselves only with the law that is applied by law courts, tell us nothing of the inner order of the household. A presentation of the Roman law of slavery which is not limited to the legal sources but which takes into account inscriptions and documents would most emphatically set forth the differences in the legal relations, of which the legal sources merely give slight intimations. A legal system which

---

1. system of villeinage：农奴制

is less enamored of abstractions than is the Roman will give outward form and expression to the differences in the legal situations of the unfree as determined by their economic functions. Accordingly from the very beginning of the Middle Ages the several types of serfdom of the Continental law have corresponded to differences in the economic constitution. The two later types, *Grundherrschaft*[1] and *Gutsherrschaft*[2], correspond to differences in economic management as well as in legal treatment of the unfree. In my book entitled *Rechtsfühigkeit*[3] (in Franz Kobler's collection entitled *"Das Recht*[4]"), I have shown in detail that the legal capacity of the individual and his position in the economic order are always interrelated.

Perhaps originally all domination, viewed as a legal institution, was a property interest in the person subjected to domination. Serfdom undoubtedly began with man-stealing; marriage, possibly, with woman-stealing; and the parental power is possibly based on the possession of the children as long as they are quite small. But domination can be permanently maintained as possession only in very rare instances, perhaps in the case of slaves on a plantation, who are kept under uninterrupted surveillance and are locked up at night. In general, domination presupposes something more, something different, a certain state of mind, a certain placing and fitting oneself into the relation of domination and subjection. Domination without this state of mind could be maintained only by uninterrupted surveillance and in most cases would be perfectly worthless to the lord and master.

For the process of economic utilization of a thing, the legal relations respecting the thing doubtless are immaterial. The field will bear cabbage even if the husbandman who has planted it has acquired the

---

1. *Grundherrschaft*：〈德〉领主所有制
2. *Gutsherrschaft*：〈德〉地主所有者
3. *Rechtsfähigkeit*：〈德〉权利能力
4. *Das Recht*：〈德〉法律

field by an invalid will; the loom weaves the thread into cloth without inquiring how the manufacturers acquired it; and a slice of bread appeases the hunger even of a person who has stolen it. The important thing in the process of economic utilization is possession. Goethe has expressed this thought very clearly in the famous passage in *Dichtung und Wahrheit*[1] in which he sums up his reflections on the Imperial Supreme Court sitting at Wetzlar. It is perhaps the best thing that has ever been written on the reason for protecting possession. We are not indeed concerned here with possession in the sense of any doctrinal formulation, but, to speak in the words of the famous master of the doctrine of possession, with possession "as the possibility of actual control over the thing; and the extent of this control is the extent to which our will to control is, as a matter of experience, habitually deferred to. Whether this is the case, is a question of actual life, which must be answered according to the diversity of the relations, especially of those of the object, according to the means at the disposal of the subject for carrying out his will, according to the state of public safety, of public morals, and of economic development." (Randa.)

Whether possession is recognized or not, then, is a "question of actual life." The important thing is not the legal precept of positive law[2], but the rule of conduct which governs life. The possession of the lessee, the borrower, the depositary, "as a matter of experience, was habitually respected" in the Continental common law by the other party to the contract even after Savigny had shown that according to Roman law they were not entitled to this. Again the Continental common law doubtless did not "as a matter of experience habitually" respect the possession of the thief or of the robber in spite of what the Roman law said on this point. When a third person found property that had been taken by theft or robbery in the possession of a thief or

1. *Dichtung und Wahrheit*：〈德〉《诗与真》，歌德自传作品。
2. legal precept of positive law：实证法的法律规定

robber, he did not hesitate, because of these precepts, to take it forcibly if possible, and to deliver it to the person injured or to the authorities. Was the law otherwise in Rome? One would have to imagine a strange case indeed in which a thief or a robber whose possession had been interfered with would have applied for the *interdictum unde vi*[1] or *utrubi*[2]. An actual case of this kind cannot, to my knowledge, be found in the sources.

Possession is a fact of the law in the sense that it is the possessor who employs and utilizes the thing according to its economic purpose. Every system of law protects the possessor in the economic use of the thing. It is a matter of indifference whether the protection is secured by means of independent legal remedies, as in Roman law, by means of private delictual actions (trespass), as in English law, or chiefly by means of the criminal law, as in Scandinavian law. Even as it is, protection of possession is everywhere; to a great ext ent, a matter for the criminal courts and the police. In the case of movable things, the protection afforded by the criminal law is sufficient at the present time to protect against theft and embezzlement; the independent remedies are used very little. The French Civil Code[3] therefore has abolished the independent protection of possession of movables. True, the action of ownership may be used, just as under the German Civil Code, by any possessor against anyone except the person who has just been deprived of the thing by theft or loss. Accordingly it serves the purpose of a possessory action as well. In the case of immovables specific protection of possession is indispensable in Roman law and in the Continental legal systems derived from the latter because the protection afforded by the criminal law as well as that of the law of delicts is altogether

---

1. *interdictum unde vi*：〈拉〉制止暴力剥夺令。恢复占有令状的一种。
2. *utrubi*：〈拉〉动产占有保持令。该禁令目的是保护动产占有。
3. French Civil Code：《法国民法典》

too ineffectual. Since in the *Code de Procedure Civile*[1] the action for interference with possession, *la complainte*, presupposes uninterrupted proprietary possession for one year, and thus has become a petitory action, and since there is no true possessory action, the French administration of justice has invented a means of protecting possession which is purely a police remedy, *la reintegrande*[2], which requires neither proprietary nor uninterrupted possession: *attendu que les voies de fait ne peuvent pas être tolerees dans une societe civilisée et que si cette action n'existail pas il faudrait l'inventer*[3].

Possession, as a purely economic relation to a thing, is distinguished from ownership and the other real rights. Economically the owner as such has no dealings with the thing; he remains the owner even though he does not concern himself about the thing for years, even though he knows nothing about it. This proves at all events that the concept of ownership was formulated, in part at least, by influences other than economic. To carry out the distinction between possession on the one hand and ownership as an independent concept on the other to its logical conclusion is to say that the law completely disregards the economic order? which takes form and shape in possession, and recognizes only the order based on ownership and real rights. The sharp distinction made in Roman law between ownership and possession might indeed lead to this view. This is the view of the juristic literature also inasmuch as it manifestly assumes that it is not the protection of ownership but that of possession that requires justification. The primary thing however is not ownership, but possession. A glance at mediaeval German law presents a legal order

1. *Code de Procédure Civile*：〈法〉《法国民事诉讼法》
2. *la réintegrande*：〈法〉恢复占有之诉
3. *attendu que les voies de fait ... pas il faudrait l'inventer.*：〈法〉鉴于在文明社会中不能容忍这种攻击，因此，如果不存在这种诉讼救济，则有必要创设。

which is predominantly based on *Gewere*[1] (i.e. the right of possession) and not on ownership. The vital energy of this thought has been demonstrated by its subsequent history; it has not only made its way against all opposition in the Continental common law, but has attained full development in England, and there meets the requirements of one of the greatest mercantile nations of the whole world; it prevails in the modern codes, the French Civil Code, the German Civil Code and the Swiss Civil Code. A comparison of the results of the entire legal development with Roman law shows that in all questions that are of significance for life, the latter strives for the same goal as German law, i.e. to make the order of ownership conform as closely as possible to the economic order, which is embodied in possession.

The person who makes use of a thing according to its economic purpose is entitled to Gewere. In the case of immovable things, at least, the latter conforms perfectly to the economic order; for everyone who has a share in the ret urns yielded by a thing, or derives any economic advantage from it has Gewere in it, and yields only to him who has shown a better right. Until this happens, his share in the economic yield is a mat ter of right, he has the power of disposition over the thing, and is entitled to the true Gewere as soon as the person who has a better right has lost it through failure to assert it. Gewere therefore actually presents a pretty complete picture of the economic constitution for the time being, to the extent that it has its roots in the law of things. If it were possible to describe the kind and extent of all the *Gewere* (rights of possession) that exist in all the things within a certain legal sphere, the result would be, barring the shifts conditioned upon purely obligatory rights, a fairly faithful picture of the economic situation in that sphere of law. English law has developed this basic idea of German law inasmuch as it actually

1. *Gewere*：〈德〉占有权

grants to the possessor all the rights of an owner until he has been deprived of *Gewere* (possession) by a person who has a better right. He receives the frtdts of the thing (he that sows shall reap), he controls the thing with full legal effect, but he is unable to give a better right to the transferee than he himself has. The transferee, like the transferor, yields to the person who has a better right, and must surrender all profits received (*mesne* profits) to the latter, but is preferred to every third party whose right is inferior to that of his transferor. Since English law does not recognize any absolute right of ownership, but invariably lets the decision hinge upon the question which of the two persons entitled has the bet ter right, English jurists can say now and then that every possessor is an owner until he is deprived of the thing by litigation. And finally the right of the possessor becomes the best right as soon as the period of prescription has run against the claim of the person who had the better right. Where the law is couched in these terms there can, of course, be no usucapion[1]. In Roman law, in consequence of the concept of absolute ownership, the economic point of view apparently recedes into the background. In actual fact however the Roman law merely denies to the possessor the use of a certain action, the *rei vindication*[2] and in its stead grants him the *actio Publiciana*[3] and, to the fullest extent, the possessory actions. In Roman law also the possessor may keep the thing and utilize it economically until he is deprived of it by litigation; and in the litigation as to ownership he occupies a favored position. He acquires the fruits of the thing provisionally at least, and — here Roman law goes further than English law — after he has consumed them in good faith, definitely and without making compensation. If he has utilized it in his trade or business in good faith, he acquires ownership. This is the meaning

1. usucapion：取得时效
2. *rei vindicatio*：〈拉〉返还所有物之诉
3. *actio Publiciana*：〈拉〉善意占有之诉

of the Roman provisions as to specification. Since the validity of an agreement entered into with reference to the thing does not depend on the ownership of the thing, and since the *actio Publiciana* which follows the terms of the agreement is regularly available to the goodfaith transferee, the possessor also has the power of disposition over the thing to this extent. Finally, according to Roman law, the economic relationship becomes ownership through usucapion; through the running of the period of prescription, it becomes the "best right." In all these things, the modern Continental law follows the Roman law. Only, in case of movables that were found or stolenit has made provision to prevent the possessor from utilizing the thing; and this chiefly in order to protect the owner against injury.

Roman law goes beyond German and English law; possibly, too, beyond practical necessity, inasmuch as it protects the possession of the thief and the robber, which has been acquired in an uneconomic manner, although doubtless in actual life such possession is not considered a legal relation. It does not go so far as the above-named legal systems inasmuch as it does not treat the economic relationship to the thing that is based solely upon relations of the law of obligation, e.g. relationship of lease, both ordinary and usufructuary, as possession. It does however, with a few insignificant exceptions, placethe good-faith possessor in the position of an owner to the same extent at least as do German and English law, and since good-faith possession alone is of significance for the economic constitution, we can say that manifestly, even in Roman law, the economic point of view prevails over the legal concept of ownership. The modern Continental legal systems have, in general, adopted these basic ideas of the Roman law of possession, albeit with a few historically conditioned concessions to Germanic law.

It is only on one point that the right of the owner rather than that of the possessor has become the rule of conduct, i.e. inasmuch as only the owner can. validly transfer ownership, or the "best right." This principle, which is binding in Roman and English law with reference to all things? is limited in the law of the Continent to immovables[1]. Where this principle governs, the transferee must needs make inquiry as to the right of the transferor or protect himself against loss by means of a contractual warranty. The security of the buyer is based on the warranty of the seller, i.e., as in Roman law, on his credit; and every sale becomes a credit transaction. In England? in case of immovables, there is the liability of the attorney who draws up the contract and undertakes to investigate the title of the seller (investigation of title). In the case of movables[2], on the other hand, the possession of the seller is generally sufficient on the Continent to transfer title to a good-faith purchaser. It is extremely interesting to observe how the effect which has been given to possession has made its way in the course of the last century even where no effect had been given to it before that time; how, on the Continent, it developed into the related principle of the "public assurance"[3] of the land register, into "the reliance on collateral states of fact" (Wellspacher); how the French hypothec registers gradually became land registers; how the land registers are gaining in importance even in England; how in England the maxim "*Hand muss Hand wahren*[4]" which until quite recently had been limited to purchases made in the open market (and in part also in a retailer's shop), is, thanks to modern legislation, steadily gaining ground.

The law of possession, therefore, is the true law of the economic order and is most closely related to the living law of economics. For this very reason it is one of the most fluid fields of the law. Every

---

1. immovables：不动产
2. movables：动产
3. principle of the "public assurance"：公信原则
4. *Hand muss Hand wahren*：〈德〉以手护手原则。"以手护手"原则是古日耳曼法中的原则，用以规范物的无权处分人与物的真正所有权人之间的关系，其意为后手为前手权利的唯一保障。

economic change at once results in a change in the law of possession. On questions of possession the statements of the Roman jurist very often are conflicting. This must be attributed, in part at least, to changes of opinion. On no other point has German law offered such unyielding resistance to Roman law, and still it has itself been changing continually. The English action of trespass, too, bears a different aspect in every century. The law of possession as found in the codes of the nineteenth century is out of date at the present time; both Austrian and French judicial decision must resort to legal material not contained in the codes.

In this sense the legal relations of possession were at all times nothing but the legal side of the economic system of landholding. What does one mean when one speaks of nations of hunters and of shepherds? Clearly, that in general these peoples do not know of ownership in land, that they merely assert a claim to a tribal sovereignty over the territory they occupy a sovereignty which grants to each member of the tribe the right of hunt and pasture. The earliest form of agriculture, however, the raising of field grass, implies possession of the cultivated land — a possession which is protected at least by legal self-help. Fixed relationships arise when the two and three-field system comes into vogue: unrestricted ownership of the *Hofstätte*[1], partition of the *Feldmark*[2] among the individual families that had settled in the *Höfe*, ownership in the arable land in *Gemenglage*[3] limited by *Flurzwang*[4] and *Nachbarrechte*[5] common ownership of the *Allmende*[6], of woodland, and of meadowland. A more intensive system

---

1. *Hofstätte*：〈德〉丈夫的个人财产
2. *Feldmark*：〈德〉空闲土地
3. *Gemenglage*：〈德〉混合地带
4. *Flurzwang*：〈德〉耕地轮作制，一种以德国人命名的广泛应用于欧洲各地的种植方式。
5. *Nachbarrechte*：〈德〉相邻权
6. *Allmende*：〈德〉未分割公地

of agriculture, especially the *Fruchtwechsel*[1] leads to freeing the soil from feudal burdens, and, in part, to the arising — not until the most recent times, it is true of individual rights in the common mark. And lastly, the financial and credit systems transform the parcel of ground into an object of commerce and create the modern land law.

It is true, because of the free ownership of Roman law and of the modern legal system, the immediate connection between the legal order of possession and the economic order, between land law and the possessory order, does not appear at once. Free ownership is apparently the same in every tract of land, whether there be on it a forest, a mine, arable land, or a house subject to ground rent. The explanation of this lies in the fact that the Roman as well as the modern immovable is a result of the process of freeing the soil from the burdens that had been resting upon it — a process which created the free Italic soil in Rome at a time prior to the beginning of historical tradition that cannot be definitely ascertained, and which began to operate in England in the seventeenth century, and on the Continent in the eighteenth and nineteenth centuries. Before the soil has been freed from these burdens, landed property occupies a definite place in a clearly defined economic and social relationship: The *Hof* in the village settlement, the arable field in the *Gemenglage*, woodland and pasture in *the Allmende* — all these are an integral part of the social order of the region. Likewise the claims of the ultimate owner, as well as the burdens and duties of the usufructuary, are conditioned by their position in society, in the state, in the whole economic interrelationship. Thus the extent and the content of the right of ownership in each immovable is determined, either positively or negatively, by law, i.e. the nature of the right of ownership in a certain immovable cannot be derived from the concept of ownership. As to the arable field in the *Gewann,* as to woodland

1. *Fruchtwechsel*：〈德〉轮流种植

and pasture in the *Allmende,* as to the *Hof* of every husbandman in the village, and as to every knight's estate, (*Rittergut*), the extent and manner of usage, everything that a neighbor can demand or is under obligation to permit, everything that the ultimate owner has a right to demand and that the usufruc tuary owner must render, is fixed in each individual case. These restrictions and limitations, which at a very early period had existed in ancient Rome as well as, though perhaps not to the same extent as, in the Middle Ages, disappeared when the soil was freed from its burdens.

As soon as the soil is freed from its burdens, it is no longer necessary to say anything about the content of ownership; the owner no longer has to consider neighbor or inferior. He can do or leave undone what he pleases. This of course does not mean that the content of ownership is no longer conditioned by the whole economic order. It means primarily something negative; i.e. that one kind of constraint which has prevailed until now has been done away with by the change of the economic constitution. Ownership must now create its new legal order for itself in accordance with the economic order. It does this in the sphere of the law of the family and of the law of slavery as well as by means of free agreement with owners of adjacent land (*Nachbarrecht,* i.e. law and right of neighbors) and with hired workmen. The legal order is busily at work fashioning, by means of a series of economic precepts, a law of ownership that is adapted to the thing itself as well as to its economic purpose. These precepts however are usually being treated as parts of administrative law and therefore, from the juristic point of view, ostensibly no longer affect the law of ownership. This results in the conceptually absolute, unconditioned "Roman" right of ownership, which permits not merely a certain, but any conceivable, use of the object of ownership. "Roman" ownership is ownership which, by means of juristic intellectual labor, has been wrested out of its social and economic connection.

But after all, this ownership is merely a kind of juristic fiction. The doctrine of the "absolute power of control over the thing" is usually presented today as if it constituted the entire content of the concept of ownership, as if there were no *Forstrecht* (law of forests), *Wasserrecht* (law of water), *Bergrecht* (mining law), no *Agrarrecht* (agrarian law), no *Bauordnungen* (building-regulations), and no *Gewerbeordnungen* (trade-regulations), as if there were no "conceptual" difference between ownership of a tract of woodland and ownership of a pocketbook. This was not correct even in the case of *the fundus* of the *solum Italicum*[1], which, to the fullest extent possible, was kept free from all burdens and restrictions, and which forms the only empirical basis for the modern concept of ownership; for Roman law, too, knew of *Forst, Wasser Agrarrecht,* as well as of *B auordnungen* and *Gewer be ordnungen* even though the greater part of all this has not been handed down to us, and though, in part, it must be gleaned from inscriptions, scattered legal sources, and other records. Ownership (including the real right of usufruct, the right of a usufructuary lessee, at any rate of the ordinary lessee) of woodland, of water, of a mine, of arable land, of a building, are from inner necessity quite different things, both economically and legally. Likewise ownership of, and the real right of usufruct or of usufructuary lease in, the objects that constitute the aggregate of things employed in an industrial undertaking may have a totally dissimilar content according to the kind of undertaking. This is not referable to diversity in the precepts of the lawmaker. In this field, even more than elsewhere, the legal precepts are nothing more than a precipitate of that which has actually been practiced at all times. It is referable to the fact that it is impossible to exercise the rights of ownership in things of totally dissimilar natures according to identical principles. The economic nature of a thing determines the relation between the owner and a neighbor; it determines the

1. the *fundus* of the *solum Italicum*：意大利的土地

inner organization of the undertaking which it subserves and the position of the latter in commerce. Inasmuch as the agreements through which ownership is utilized form part of the exercise of the right of ownership, the content of these agreements det ermines the content of the right of ownership. Accordingly ownership of a factory is a different thing from ownership of a mine; for the contract of employment entered into with a miner is quite different from a contract with a factory worker; and ownership of a railroad, for the same reason, is different from ownership of a tract of woodland, for the railroad freight contract is different from a contract for removing stumps. For the precepts governing the agreements upon which the order of property rights in things that serve a particular economic purpose is based constitute the essential content of the particular law that exists for these things, e.g. the law of mines, of forests, of railroads.

Possession everywhere becomes a legal relation in virtue of its being fitted into the economic order. Man subjects the natural world surrounding him to his will by means of his economic activity. In this sense possession is merely the factual side of the economic order. The objects of possession increase in number as soon as their usefulness is understood.

Wild animal taming is contemporaneous with the beginnings of cattle-breeding; land-taking, with the beginnings of agriculture. But methodical management presupposes not only possession, but also protection of possession. For it is possible to provide for the future by gathering supplies and producing goods only in case possession is protected to some extent; not until possession is protected can a possessor count on actually retaining the proceeds of the labor he bestows upon preserving, augmenting, and utilizing his possession; and therefore in an established economic order, relations of possession must become legally protected relations of possession. In every instance therefore the order of possession is a reflection of the economic order.

There can therefore be no doubt as to the reason for the protection of possession. It lies in the fact that agriculture, trade, industry, commerce, would be unthinkable without security. The difficulty which the concept of possession caused to the jurists who had been trained in Roman law lay in the fact that they were always striving to define possession without reference to the economic order — an impossible undertaking. It is much more difficult to explain the reason for the existence of ownership, except in so far as it closely follows the order which is based on possession. Here complicated social relations are contributing factors, and the whole question belongs to the subject matter of another field of inquiry.

From this discussion it follows that the sociology of law must, to a certain extent, treat possession and ownership as interchangeable terms. The necessity of doing this is accentuated by the fact that both statutes and juristic science as a rule do not differentiate between the two. Let anyone attempt to make a clear-cut distinction between these two concepts in the law of finance, mines, water, forest, or agriculture. Whatsoever is stated in these departments of law as to ownership, with rare exceptions, applies also to possession, and vice versa. This is the case also in everyday life, which at every moment finds it necessary to treat possession as ownership. Only in those parts of the law of possession that deal specifically with possession and ownership is a clear-cut distinction made between the two. In these exceptional cases the sociology of law will also observe the distinction. In such case, ownership, as distinguished from possession, implies the sum total of legal remedies that are available to a non-possessor in order to acquire proprietary possession of a thing.

We have now arrived at the point where we must enter upon the discussion of the legal declaration of will as a fact of the law. It is neither necessary nor possible at this point to investigate the factual bases of the legal declaration of will and of the legal disposition in all its ramifications. There are only two classes that are of significance in the legal history of the world, to wit agreement (*Vertrag*) and disposition by last will and testament. The articles of association of the law of corporations were originally a statement of the existing usage or a form of agreement, and therefore are not of independent significance as a fact of the law.

At this point, our discussion will deal in the first place only with the agreement. Just as a distinction was made between possession on the one hand and ownership and real right on the other, so a distinction must be made between the mere fact of understanding and the *Vertrag* (agreement). Germanistic legal science, spinning out a thought first expressed by Brinz, has worked out the distinction between *Schuld*[1] (debt, obligation) and *Haftung*[2] (liability) with extraordinary precision, and by doing so has laid the foundation not only for the historical but also for the sociological discussion of the contract. *Schuld* is the *Sollen* of the debtor[3]; it is that which according to the experience of life is considered the content of the obligation; liability (*Haftung*) is the right of the creditor to enforce his claim, a right which secures satisfaction even against the will of the debtor. And the understanding is converted from a bare fact into a fact of the law and thereby into a *Vertrag* (agreement), even though no liabilHies (*Haftungen*) arise, but merely a debt, or obligation (*Schuld*). The Roman *contractus* gives rise to obligation (*Schuld*) and liability (*Haftung*); the *pactum* (pact) brings about no liability (*Haftung*), but as a rule brings about an obligation (*Schuld*). The *pactum* (pact) therefore usually amounts to a *Vertrag;* the *contractus,* always. The traditional juristic science, which, following the Romans, devoted sufficient attention to the distinction between possession and real right, does not know how to deal with a parallel phenomenon in

1. *Schuld*：〈德〉债务
2. *Haftung*：〈德〉责任
3. *Schuld* is the *Sollen* of the debtor：债务是债务人应履行的义务（*Schuld* 和 *Sollen* 为德语）。

the sphere of the law of contracts, although the Romans have done some preparatory work also in this sphere, by means of their concept of *naturalis obligation*[1] which Windscheid in his day estimated at its true value as merely an obligation according to the *Verkehrsauffassung*[2] (the view of commercial custom).

One root of the law of contracts is the present exchange of goods, or barter. This did not arise from friendly intercourse between neighbors. Within the clan, in his own village, man in the lower stages of development was as little given to making contracts as he is given to doing so today in his own family group. Interchange of goods was brought about by means of taking booty or by means of gifts exchanged between a guest and his host. The oldest merchant is the pirate at a more advanced stage of development, who has become convinced that it is of greater advantage to himself to trade with a stranger than to rob him. And the oldest known forms of trading are closely related to robbery. Shortly before the harvest, the pygmies of Africa make raids into the fields of the negroes, carry off the bananas, peanuts, and maize which grow there, and by way of exchange leave behind dried meat, the chief product of their economic activity. The silent trading that Herodotus and Pliny[3] tell of belongs to a more advanced stage. "The oldest agreement is the agreement for the exchange of goods; it can be entered into without any personal, verbal relations; the chronicles tell of silent trading between Russians and strangers, neither party understanding the language of the other." This is Budanow-Wladimirski's introduction to the history of the contract in his history of Russian law.

The second root of the law of contracts is subjection to the

---

1. *naturalis obligatio*：〈拉〉自然债务
2. *Verkehrsauffassung*：〈德〉商业惯例的角度
3. Herodotus and Pliny：希罗多德（公元前 484—前 425）和普林尼（23—79），都是古罗马时代伟大的历史学家。

domination of another. An instance of this is the sale of one's own person. The man who is in need of seed corn for his economic activity or who has lost more at gambling than he can pay surrenders himself as a slave to the wealthy lord, who takes the man into custody for the advance and lets the latter work for him. Another instance is the enfeoffment with a knight's fee, which obligated the feoffee to render military and knight's services; another, the enfeoffment for rent and services, which imposed on the feoffee the payment of rent and the performance of services; another, the agreement of commendation, whereby a freeman places his person and his property under the dominion of a more powerful man, who in exchange for services and rent promises protection against attack.

In the contract of barter as well as in the contract of submission, there is a granting of possession; in the former, possession of the thing; in the latter, of the person. But there are certain subsidiary agreements which are connected with the transfer of possession, e.g. in the case of a contract of barter, the warranty that the thing has not been stolen; in the case of a contract of submission, an understanding about mutual performances, the promise of the creditor to release the debtor as soon as the debt has been paid or worked out. In this case the obligation or debt incurred is greater than the liability (*Haflung*); for there is no liability in case of subsidiary agreements of this nature.

But a debt can be secured by means of the possession of a person other than that of the debtor, or of a thing other than that which was the subject of the contractual agreement. This happens when a debtor gives a third person to the creditor as a hostage, or delivers a pledge to him. Until now the liability (*Haflung*) consisted in the creditor's keeping the debtor or the thing that was owed in his own possession until he had been paid. At this stage however the contractual obligation is severed from the possession of the person or of the thing which constitutes the subject or object of the contract. The liability (*Haftung*) becomes self-existent, and the extent, content, and duration of the liability (*Haftung*) is determined by the extent, content, and duration of the obligation; in the last analysis, by the contract. The creditor who refuses to release a hostage or to return a pledge although the debt has been extinguished is guilty of man-stealing or of theft, and this at quite an early time constituted the basis of a claim which could be prosecuted by appeal to the courts. In the early stages, perhaps, the penalty for such conduct was death. Limited to the duty to return the person or thing, the widely entertained view may be correct that contractual obligation became enforceable by legal action because of the fact that the person obligated who had not performed was treated as liable to punishment. Apart from that, the idea that a person who performs his obligations poorly or not at all is liable for the resulting damage arose at a very late time, much later than the immediate liability (*Haftung*) based on the contract.

All further development of contractual liability (*Vertragshaflung*) is a progressive severance of liability (*Haftung*) from possession of the object of the liability (*Haftung*) and a progressive reception of the content of the obligation, or debt (*Schuld*), into the liability (*Haftung*). The immediate sale by the debtor of his person and the giving of hostages is superseded by a conditional sale and by the finding of a surety or sureties. The debtor sells his person to the creditor only in case he fails to make payment (the *Treugelöbnis*[1] of the Germans, the *nexum*[2] of the Romans, numerous examples in ancient Russian law), or he finds a surety against this event. The pledge becomes a wager, i.e. a thing of no value or of lesser value is given as a symbol. In this way the contracts of subjection and of pledge gradually become *real* contracts. At a later time the contract of barter ceases to be a contract of present exchange and becomes a *real* contract, i.e. the very fact that one party has accepted the performance of the other obligates the former to

---

1. *Treugelöbnis*：〈德〉信用保证
2. *nexum*：〈拉〉债务口约，一种契约形式。

render a counter-performance. At a later period, the acceptance of part performance is sufficient, and finally even the acceptance of an apparent performance (*Arrha*, earnest-money). This brings about the liability (*Haftung*) for the promised performance not only of the giver but also of the taker. Whether, apart from this, the promise under oath, whereby the debtor had called down upon himself the vengeance of the gods if he should fail to keep his promise, was, at this early stage, of decisive importance for the development of law as a formal contract cannot be ascertained at the present state of our knowledge. Originally the formal promise served merely to confirm the compromise providing for payment of *wergild*[1] or penalty.

This imports chiefly that the liability (*Haflung*) no longer results from possession but from the contract. The creditor obtains a right of enforcement against the person or property of the debtor which is independent of possession, and whose nature and extent are determined by the content of the contractual debt, or obligation (*Vertragsschuld*). This whole development has been placed beyond all doubt as to Germanic law by modern research; and Roman law, although it has become known to us in a much later stage of development, has preserved numerous traces of it. I think that most probably the few words that Festus has handed down to us from the *foedus Latinum*[2] under the key-word *nandtor* refer to the right of the creditor to take possession of the property of the debtor. The oldest Roman action, the *legis actio per manus iniectionem*[3], even in historical times, is a living vestige of the creditor's right against the person of the debtor. The creditor seizes the debtor wheresoever he finds him, and leads him away into custody. This is not man-stealing but legal self-

---

1. *wergild*：〈拉〉赎罪赔偿金
2. *foedus Latinum*：〈拉〉与拉丁人达成的盟约。该盟约以罗马人与拉丁人形成的所有协议是有效力为前提，盟约本身只规范与之相关的裁制事宜。
3. *legis actio per manus iniectionem*：〈拉〉拘禁之诉

help, and therefore does not give rise to a feud. Anyone who would defend the debtor must go to the praetor[1] with the creditor. The prevailing view that the creditor did not perform the *manus iniectio*[2] until he got into court is manifestly erroneous. We find the *legis actio per manus iniectionem* among the southern Slavs as late as the end of the Middle Ages under the name Udawa. It has been described very vividly by Novakovic, together with the mitigation which it underwent in the course of time, in a treatise published by the Serbian Academy of Sciences, chiefly on the basis of Ragusan sources.

It was not until liability (*Haftung*) was completely severed from possession and the extent of the liability (*Haftung*) coincided with the content of the obligation (*Sckuld*), at least in principle, that the road was cleared for the credit contract. The credit contract however brings about a complete change in the nature of the contract. The contracts of barter and of subjection thereby lose their original peculiar nature, so that it becomes possible to extend credit to the debtor, or obligor, for the counterperformance for which he is liable. The sale of his person by the debtor becomes a loan of money or of things, the enfeoffment for services and rent becomes a contract of ordinary and usufructuary lease, to which all personal subjection and the obligation to labor are foreign (although this was not fully carried out in Roman law); so that in more advanced stages of development only the contract for services and wages and the mandate (*Auftrag*)[3] remind one of the fact that, at some time in the past, the contract could bring about personal subjection. The extension of credit converts the contract of barter into a consensual contract.

Tracing the development of the understanding into a fact of

---

1. praetor：裁判官
2. *manus iniectio*：〈拉〉拘禁
3. mandate (*Auftrag*)：委任契约

the law, one must distinguish the following stages: the *Barvertrag*[1] (contract for present exchange), the *Schuldvertrag*[2] (contract creating a debt or obligation), the *Haftungsvertrag*[3] (contract creating a liability), and the *Kreditvertrag*[4] (credit contract). The *Barvertrag* (contract for present exchange) merely effects the acquisition of possession of the subject mat ter of the con tract. The fact of the law here is not the contract, but the possession; all the legal consequences that ensue are consequences of the transfer of possession, not of the contract. As soon as promises are connected with the transfer of possession, and obligation (*Schuld*) is attached to these, the contract, in addition to the exchange of possession, effectuates an obligation (*Schuld*), and thereby becomes a self-existent fact of the law. It is through the *Haftungsvertrag* (contract creating liability), which gives to the creditor the right to proceed against the person or property of the debtor which he has in his possession, that the contract, as a fact of the law which creates liability (*Haflung*), is gradually being emancipated from all connection with possession.

The principle of the Continental common law that informal contracts are actionable implies that every contract, on principle, brings about debt or obligation (*Schuld*) as well as liability (*Haflung*), and that the extent of the liability is determined by the extent of the debt, or obligation. This fact has made it difficult for the common-law jurist to perceive that today, as well as in the hoary past, in addition to *contractus* there are *pacta* (pacts); that in addition to contracts creating liability there are contracts creating merely an obligation.

We must therefore emphasize so much the more vigorously that the important thing for the economic life is not the liability (*Haflung*) but

1. *Barvertrag*：〈德〉现场交易契约
2. *Schuldvertrag*：〈德〉债务契约
3. *Haftungsvertrag*：〈德〉责任契约
4. *Kreditvertrag*：〈德〉借贷契约

the debt, or obligation (*Schuld*); that in the great majority of cases it is immaterial whet her a contract is actionable or not, provided only that according to the rule of conduct which governs life one can count upon its being performed. In view of the fact that contracts are actionable on principle, it seems very natural to suppose that in actual life contracts are being performed only because they are actionable; not only legal history, however, but also a glance at modern life shows that, on the contrary, contracts have become actionable because, as a rule, they are being performed in life. Even today, the contract which cannot be sued upon, and which effects merely an obligation (*Schuld*), plays an important role in economic and social life. A very important part of industry is based on child labor, and most of the contracts for work and labor that were made with children undoubtedly were absolutely invalid down to the time of the legislation for the protection of working-men, and many are invalid today. But that has not prevented exploitation of children from being at all times a most profitable business. For a century at least, a large part of the business transacted at the Exchange has been beyond the bounds of the legally enforcible, and, in part, beyond the bounds of the legally permissible. Particularly, the social struggles and the economic movements have brought about a whole series of contracts that are not enforcible; numerous cartel agreements of entrepreneurs, many wage agreements among working-men, and most agreements between representatives of labor and of employers (*Tarifaerträge*[1]) probably are not legally enforcible.

It is necessary therefore to bear in mind that, not only in history but also in the law that is valid today, in addition to understandings that are altogether outside of the legal sphere, there are agreements that import an obligation (*Schuld*) but no liability (*Haftung*); that import a rule according to which men regulate their conduct in life, but not

1. *Tarifverträge*：〈德〉劳动集体合同

a rule according to which the authorities proceed; and that these contracts are as significant for the economic life as legally enforceable contracts. Juristic science must not overlook this. And it must go further. It must bear in mind that the enforcible contract does not rule the world to the extent that it is being enforced by the authorities, but to the extent that it has become a rule of conduct.

Legal history shows us that whenever the contract becomes a fact of the law, this does not amount to a recognition of the sovereignty of the human will, but of the role actually played by the contract in social and in economic life. To the law the contract is nothing more than an instrument of the social and economic order. But the contract becomes a fact of the law, though only to the extent to which there is a social and economic need therefor; and it disappears from life as soon as the need which brought it about has disappeared. Ent ering into a relation of protection or into a contract of enfeoffment would be as impossible today as it would have been to secure a loan by a hypothec in the Germany of Tacitus. The law of contracts, too, is nothing more than the legal form of the social and economic order.

Up to this point it has been possible to base our discussion upon generally recognized results of comparative legal science and upon the history of law. The same cannot be said of the law of inheritance. The prevailing doctrine derives the law of inheritance from the common ownership of the family; even where the latter no longer exists, it still produces after-effects according to the prevailing view inasmuch as it gives to certain kinsmen who in time past had been members of the family community an inchoate right of inheritance. If this were true, the law of inheritance would be a development from another legal relation and we should find it necessary to investigate, not the facts that have led to the law of inheritance, but those that have led to the inchoate rights of kinsmen.

Sir Henry Sumner Maine, however, in his day, expressed doubts as to the correctness of this doctrine. It has been refuted, it seems to me, by Ficker, at least as to the Germanic peoples, to whom it was originally attributed. Ficker has, as I believe, conclusively shown that the law of inheritance is older, even among the Germans, than the inchoate right of the members of the house commuidty, that the owner may, at a time at which there exists a fully developed right of inheritance of the kinsmen, dispose of his property freely without concerning himself about the claims of his children, to say nothing of the claims of more distant kinsmen.

The early history of the law of inheritance must begin with the house community. The law of inheritance has its roots in the house. We are concerned here with two questions. First of all, to whom did the estate belong if the deceased lived in a house community; and, secondly, to whom did it belong if he lived alone, perhaps surrounded only by unfree persons or servants? The latter case manifestly occurs very rarely in primitive society, perhaps never; but it does occur with increasing frequency at a later period in a well ordered state, which makes it possible for a person to live alone. It is easily understood that the property of the deceased that was not put into the grave with him became the property of the members of his house community who had dwelt and worked together with him in the household. This indeed applies only to his movable possessions[1], for this order obtains even among hunters and cat tie-breeders, and is therefore older than ownership of land. The members of the house community of the deceased need not take possession of the goods of the latter, for they are in possession at the moment of his death, and they are in position to resist interference by a third person with the same means as during the lifetime of the deceased. The members of the household remain in possession of the goods the latter left behind, and carry on as they always did; the situation has changed very little; the number of persons

1. movable possessions：动产

in the house has merely been decreased by one. The fact of the law, then, at this stage, is possession. But the primitive law of inheritance has not progressed much beyond this remaining in possession on the part of the members of the house community. Accordingly if the deceased has not lived in a house community, his estate becomes ownerless. Among the Romans and the Germanic peoples clear traces of this state of affairs remain even in historical times. The most important traces however are to be found among the Slavic people, whose oldest legal monuments present a most interesting, very early stage of development, which the other people of Europe had passed through long before their legal tradition was recorded in writing. To the Russians, the Poles, the Masovians, the Czechs, the Moravians, and perhaps the Serbs, of the eighteenth century, the right of inheritance of the collateral kindred is still an unknown thing; in the case of a death without an heir, the estate is *"leer"*, and escheats to the ruler, or, in case of an unfree person, to the lord.

As to the limited recognition by the Slavic codes of the fourteenth century (the statute of Wislica[1], and the code of Tsar Duschan[2]) of the right of inheritance of the collateral kindred, the very wording shows that it is an innovation. Among the Slavic peoples, the princes, whose power had developed very rapidly, manifestly acting in their own interest, retarded the right of inheritance of the collateral relatives for a long time because it curtailed the right of escheat. Among the Bohemians and the Poles, the right of escheat of the princes may be traceable to German influences; among the Russians and the Serbs, to Byzantine influences.

It has been shown that the declaration by last will and testament

1. the statute of Wislica：《韦斯理卡法典》，波兰法典。
2. the code of Tsar Duschan：《杜尚法典》1394 年塞尔维亚沙皇斯特凡・杜尚在拜占庭法律和塞尔维亚习惯法的基础上制定。

did not become an effective *post mortem*[1] disposition until a very late date. Before that time all that could be done was to receive a stranger into the house: and this had the effect that the goods of the head of the house would pass to the person so received equally with the other member of the house community.

A little later the gift *mortis causa*[2] with present delivery, but with legal effect postponed until the death of the donor, made its appearance; then the *Treuhand* transaction[3], whose importance for universal legal history was shown in the truly pioneering work of Robert Caillemer. In the Roman law of inheritance the *Treuhänder*[4] appears twice: as *familiae emptor*[5] and as a fiduciary. The English uses and trusts also have their roots in the *Treuhander* transaction. Here too, therefore, the law of inheritance shows no independent characteristic features; it follows the order of possession and makes use of the contract. The effect of receiving a person into the house (*arrogatio, adoptio, adfatomie*)[6] is that the person received has immediate possession of the goods of the deceased; the gift *mortis causa* and the *Tretthand* transaction are effective in conjunction with transfer of possession. The disposition did not become a self-existent fact of the law of inhe rit ance until the testament came into use.

The economic significance of the law of inheritance does not appear so clearly as that of the other legal institutions, for in this department several currents frequently cross and interfere with each other. The chief concern is the continuation of the economic undertaking. This appears quite clearly in the case of the peasant family household. In

---

1. *post mortem*：〈拉〉死后
2. *mortis causa*：〈拉〉死因
3. *Treuhand* transaction：信托交易
4. *Treuhänder*：〈德〉信托人
5. *familiae emptor*：〈拉〉家产买受人，通过拟制买卖形式取得遗产的遗嘱执行人。
6. *arrogatio, adoptio, adfatomie*：〈拉〉古代日耳曼法中 3 种不同的收养类型

this case the economic undertaking is continued without much ado by the survivors; but this is not, properly speaking, a law of inheritance, for the family household is immortal. If there are no survivors, the economic association collapses, for there is no one to continue the undertaking. This is simply another way of saying that the estate is ownerless, or that the ruler, supported by the military power of the state, takes possession of it. Before long however endeavor is being made to preserve the inheritance for the former members of the household or for the kinsmen. The purpose of the law of inheritance thereafter is to serve not an economic but a purely social association, the family. Undoubtedly there is the secondary thought that the kinsmen[1] will continue the economic undertaking of the deceased, but a glance at the actual state of the law of inheritance shows to what extent in this very matter of the succession of the kindred the economic point of view has been thrust into the background by the social. It is self-evident that only where, as in English law, the right of inheritance of the firstborn prevails, has precaution been taken against the destruction of the economic undertaking through the collapse occasioned by the succession; but the motive in this case, too, was consideration for the family, and the whole institution was not thought out on economic lines. Hence the strong and significant endeavor to preserve the economic undertaking by means of adoption or of dispositions *mortis causa*[2]. Where the law of inheritance is non-economic in an especially high degree like the later Roman or the modern Continental law, making a last will and testament[3] is considered a duty; and dying intestate[4] is a great misfortune. Even where there is a declaration of will by last will and testament, non-

1. kinsmen：近亲
2. dispositions *mortis causa*：临终处分
3. making a last will and testament：立遗嘱
4. intestate：未留遗嘱

economic influences are brought into play; such as consideration for the family, which is often protected against loss of the inheritance by means of a testamentary disposition; consideration for the church; consideration for institutions for the public welfare; and finally reverence for the dead. These were purely social forces, but they gave effect to declarations by last will and testament long before the latter were recognized by the authorities.

Without doubt it would be a great mistake to consider the economic phenomena and fail to take the other social phenomena into consideration. The state, the church, education, art, science, social life, entertainment, play a role in the life of society no less than economic labor. We have therefore pointed out the significance of non-economic influences, particularly in the discussion of the human associations and of the law of inheritance. It is self-evident that they assert themselves at every moment in the relations of domination and subjection and in the law of possession and of contract. We must not forget in this connection that the economic situation is the presupposition for every form of noneconomic activity. The state can be maintained, the church can be served, education can be provided, art and science can be fostered, time and means for social life and entertainment can exist, only to the extent that the national economy produces returns that are greater than the amount required to satisfy the needs of the workers. For this reason an understanding of the economic order is the basis for an understanding of the other parts of the social order, especially of the legal order of society.

If we fix our attention on the facts of the law in the very beginnings of social life, we shall see that all of them can be traced back to two, to wit the human association, which is kept together and regulated by usage, as the subject, and possession, the social relation which becomes a legal relation within the association, as the object. In the beginning all domination seems to have been based on possession of the subjected person in an association. The contract consists in unilateral or reciprocal transfer of possession or in self-surrender into the possession of another; the law of inheritance consists in this, that the kindred of a deceased keep for themselves that which hitherto they have possessed in common with the latter, and that they divide among themselves that which the latter possessed for himself in the common household. All law then arises from the fact that within the association there is added to respect for the person of the members respect for his possessions, and that this becomes the basis of the general order and the general rule of conduct. At a later stage, the possession of a human being becomes the right in the human being (relations of domination and family relations), and finally the right to demand a performance from a human being (personal liability[1]); possession of a thing becomes a right in the thing or the right to various emoluments of the thing (ownership and real rights[2]); and finally possession of the thing on the basis of a contract becomes a right in the thing based on a declaration of the previous possessor. From this time forth all development of law consists in the slow development of the norms which command respect for the person of the member of the association and for his possessions and in the development of the latter into norms for the peaceful exchange and transportation of goods, in. the extension and the differentiation of the human associations into an increasingly comprehensive, intricate, and diversified organization of the human family.

We may perhaps be permitted to spin this thought out a little further. In the simple associations of the peoples on the lowest level of development known to us, there is neither possession of things nor contracts. The order of the association is based chiefly on usage, and perhaps on domination over women and minors. The fact of this domination is sufficiently explained by the fact that the peoples who

---

1. personal liability：个体责任
2. real rights：物权

are found on the lowest level of development known to us have, after all, reached a certain stage of development at which differences of sex and of age give rise to associations within the associations. In the oldest associations, which have long since disappeared, usage, most probably, was the sole ordering element. And also in the original association of our present-day society, in the community of the family household, possession and contract are very far from being looked upon as facts of the law. Here too the whole order is based on usage; the more so, the better and more intimately the family life is organized. Contracts that are made with reference to family relationships (especially contracts concerning matrimonial property) are made solely for the purpose of regulating the situation in case of dissolution of the community of the household. So long as the family is not disrupted, and its members get along well with one another, usually no one gives thought to contracts, much less to possession. Among all the facts of the law, therefore, usage is the sole primitive one. Possession and contract become facts of the law only in the higher associations, which are composed of several simple associations, and they are not found at all where there are no composite associations of this kind. As to these two facts of the law, possession is evidently older and more primitive than the contract. Where possession does not govern the relations within the associations, the latter either have not yet been combined into an association, of a higher order or they have already dissolved the latter; in either case they are at war with each other. Even today possession det ermines the reciprocal relations of people who, being associated in a but loosely knit association[1], wish to get along peaceably with one another. One may instance the occupying of seats and chairs in a railway coach and on a ship, and the monopolizing of newspapers in a cafe; the rules as to standing in

1. loosely knit association：松散联合体，联合体内部的各主体之间处于较为分散的状态。

line at a ticket-window or waiting one's turn in a waiting room are also related to the rules of possession. The contract presupposes a much closer relationship; the closer, the more completely it is severed from the bare transfer of possession. A contract that involves more than a present exchange, even an understanding that has absolutely no binding force, is usually made only with acquaintances, persons of the same social class, business friends, or business men, in foreign countries perhaps with fellow-countrymen.

The whole economic and social order of the human race is based upon the following small number of facts: usage, domination, possession, disposition (usually by contract or by testamentary disposition). These facts by their very existence determine the rules of conduct for the human associations that are comprised in human society. These rules, self-evidently, are not exclusively legal norms. They are the elements into which the infinite diversity of the phenomena of our legal world, and in part of the world of the other norms, resolves itself. Every small human society creates its own order self-actively and where the smaller associations combine, or are combined, into larger associations the combined association must indeed, in its relations with its component parts, create a new order, but must needs also, substantially, take over the order which has already been in existence in the original cells, and in general leave it in the form into which it had developed there. Indeed it is very simple, but extremely superficial, to believe that, at the present time, the state creates the order everywhere. In spite of the state law of the family, which allegedly is the same everywhere, there are no two families exactly alike; in spite of the state law of communes, there are no two communes exactly alike; in spite of the law of societies, there are no two societies exactly alike; in spite of identical laws of property, of contract, and of trades, there are no two agricultural establishments, workshops, factories, and, self-evidently, contracts, that are exactly alike. The differences appear much more distinctly if one considers not only the wording of the regulation and of the contract (a superficial proceeding), but also the way in which these are being applied and habitually entered into in the individual associations. The center of gravity everywhere lies in the order which the associations create for themselves, and life in the state and in society depends more upon the order of the associations than upon the order which proceeds from the state and from society.

But this great diversity must not cause us to overlook the uniformities. The latter are based on the fact that the conditions of the economic and of the social life of the various associations are to a great extent, both as to time and place, and in part too, independently of time and place, so uniform that a great number of identical rules necessarily result from this uniformity. In addition, there are direct borrowings. For as to content norms do not arise anew with every new association. In every society there is in existence a great store of legal and extra-legal norms which live in the consciousness of men. In the course of millennia it has been accumulating within the associations which came into being in the far distant past. And men who unite to form a new association bring this store of norms with them, having inherited it, or having acquired it by study. Each new generation has begun with that which the primitive ages, lying far behind us, have created in their as yet very simple associations. It has taken over the greater part of it unaltered; that which has become unsuitable it has discarded; other parts it has moulded over into special forms for special purposes; some parts, especially in case of organizations of a legal nature, it has posited expressly by means of statute or contract. Each new family, in essentials, reflects the existing family order; each new economic undertaking, in its characteristic features, follows the legal as well as the extra-legal constitution of undertakings of a similar nature; every newly made contract derives the greater part of its content from the traditional content of contracts of the same kind. And every new development which arises for new purposes, and which stands the test of time, is added to the treasure of social norms, and serves to guide later associations. There is an endless and uninterrupted process of adaptation to new needs and situations, in which is embodied, at the same time, the development of the human race and of its norms. It may suffice to instance the great number of new norms, not only of law, but also of morals, ethical custom, honor, good manners, *tact,* and perhaps, at least in a certain sense, etiquette and fashion, which have come into existence in the course of the last decades in consequence of the social movement in the various associations which it has occasioned or for which it has created a new order.

A fact which is an isolated occurrence in society is not a social fact; it cannot bring about social norms, and it will remain unnoticed by society. It cannot be considered a component part of the social order until it has become a common phenomenon. When a group of human beings of a certain kind, let us say a particular form of family life, a new church, a new political tendency, a relation of subjection, a form of possession, a content of a contract, becomes an important and permanent phenomenon because of common occurrence[1], then, and not until then, society must take cognizance of it. It must either reject it, if need be, combat it, or it must receive it into the general social and economic order as a suit able means for the satisfaction of social and economic needs. After this has been done, it becomes a new form for the organization of society, and thereby a social relation; under certain circumstances, a legal relation.

---

1. common occurrence：经常发生

VI THE NORMS FOR DECISION

Courts do not come into being as organs of the state, but of society. Their function originally was merely to determine, upon authority given by clans or families which had entered into a close rela tionship with one another, whet her a quarrel between the members of different associations could be composed by payment of a penalty or whether it could be expiated only in blood, and eventually to determine the amount of the penalty. It is not until a much later date that courts are being erected by the state for matters that directly concern the state, e.g. attempts on the life of the king, trading with the enemy, violation of the military order. At a later time, the state gains control also over the courts of the former class; but the distinction between administration of justice by the state and by society continues today in the distinction between the jurisdiction of criminal and of civil causes, in spite of the extensive encroachments of the criminal courts upon the one-time purely social sphere. But the courts were never completely converted into state institutions[1]. Society has always had, and has kept to the present day, courts of its own that are independent of the state; and courts of this kind come into existence from time to time even today. Though the prevailing juristic science applies the term courts only to the state organs for the administration of justice, with which it must concern itself professionally, the sociology of law, when it defines the term court, is concerned only with the question whether or not the institution involved performs the general functions

---

1. state institutions：国家机构

of a court. Considered functionally, the court is a person or a group of persons who are not parties to the controversy and whose function is to establish peace by the opinion which they express about the subject matter of the controversy. This opinion has no binding force even when pronounced by a state court of primitive times; it is a mere opinion. He who refuses to submit may resort to self help, to a feud, but he puts himself in the wrong, and loses the purely social advantage of having a just quarrel. At the beginning the court, even the state court, has no means whereby to coerce a contumacious person[1] who refuses to appear though he has been summoned, or who flouts its decision, other than exclusion from the community (exile), whereby the person excluded becomes an outlaw, and must wander about, seeking rest and finding none, until he is either killed, or reduced to slavery, or received into another community. At this stage the death penalty, which is found at a very early time, is merely a sacrifice to the gods, among the classical peoples, to the gods of the nether world, the victim for which is the outlawed person.

If we consider only the functions of the court, we must include among the courts quite a number of variously named institutions for the social administration of justice, whose relation to the state is a more or less distant one: courts of honor, courts of discipline[2], courts of arbitration, courts of societies, courts of conciliation[3]. For the social jurisdiction of English clubs a special body of law and a special technique have been developed. The decisions of these tribunals are subject to attack in the courts of the state and to review by the latter. Nothnagel discusses all these phenomena in the work already referred to, entitled *Exekidion durch soziale Interessengruppen*[4]. The judgments

1. contumacious person：不服从的人
2. courts of discipline：纪律法庭
3. courts of conciliation：调解法庭
4. *Exekution durch soziale Interessengruppen*：〈德〉《社会共同利益体的裁判执行》

of all of these courts, like those of the courts in primitive times, are limited to exclusion from the group. On the other hand administrative tribunals created by the state, especially the police and in part the presiding officers of bodies of representatives of the public, doubtless exercise a judicial function. Courts, of whatsoever description they may be, must not render their judgments arbitrarily or without giving reasons, but must base them on general principles. The norms for decision upon which the latter are based invariably appear as the result of an inspiration of higher power and wisdom; nay, indeed, at a lower stage, as the result of an illumination by the godhead. The norm for decision, like all social norms, is primarily a rule of conduct, but only for the courts. It is not, primarily at least, a rule for the men who are the doers in life, but for the men who sit in judgment upon the doers. In so far as the norm for decision is a legal norm, it appears to be a legal norm of a special kind, different from the legal norms that contain general rules of conduct.

Whence do the courts draw their norms for decision? To render a decision in case of a quarrel means to delimit the spheres that are in dispute[1], above all things to delimit them just as they had been delimited before the quarrel arose. This delimitation is indicated, in the first instance, by the inner order of the associations as it existed at the beginning of the quarrel. Every norm for decision therefore is based primarily upon this inner order, i.e. the facts of the law, which create the order, upon the usages, which assign to each individual his position and his function in the association, upon relations of domination and possession, contracts, articles of association, testamentary dispositions[2]. In every quarrel the point involved is that a norm which is based on these facts has been violated, and in all litigation, in order to be able to render a decision, the judge must

---

1. delimit the spheres that are in dispute：划定争端范围
2. testamentary dispositions：遗嘱处分

ascertain these facts either from his own knowledge or from the evidence. All these facts constitute the basis of the decision just as they have developed and taken shape in the concrete association before the quarrel arose.

In the past there has frequently been a toying[1], especially among exponents of the natural law theory, with the thought that the whole law must be susceptible of being summed up in a few clear propositions that are obvious to unaided human reason. They evidently had an idea, quite vague indeed, that the existing usages, relations of possession, contracts, articles of association, testamentary dispositions, were sufficient for the rendering of judicial decisions, and required only a few additional rules to complement them. But he who adopts this view fails to see that the norm for decision is always something more than and distinct from the inner order of the association. Even where the norm for decision is based directly upon an order of an association that is formula ted in express words, even where it goes back to a bylaw[2] of a society, to a contract, or to a last will and testament, it is always a thing quite distinct from the inner order of the association; for a relation as to which there is a dispute is something different from the same relation at peace. That which before had been adaptable and flexible has become rigid, immovable; vague outlines have become clear and sharply drawn, and often a meaning must be read into the words that the parties had never been clearly conscious of. But the judge in a law-suit has duties to perform with reference to the relation submitted to him for decision which involve more than this relation, which have remained altogether foreign to the experience of the associations so long as they were left to themselves; and as to these duties he can learn nothing from the inner order of the associations. For such cases, he must have at his disposal norms for

1. toying：随意对待
2. bylaw：社、团制定的规章制度

decision which are independent of this latter order.

We must consider chiefly the requirements of the administration of justice as such. Every social association is, to be accurate, a special case that cannot be duplicated anywhere in the world. There are no two families in which the position of the father, the mother, the children, the servants, is exactly the same; no two parts of the world in which the identical relations as to landholding obtain; no two contracts, by-laws of corporations, testamentary declarations, that do not differ from each other; in addition to the differences in words and phrasing, there are differences in the relations of persons and things. It is self-evident that one sees these differences becoming greater and greater as one considers wider spheres; in different communes, provinces, nations, the associations present different pictures. The administration of justice cannot function where there is such a medley; for technical reasons, if for no others, it must reduce the same to simple formulae. This is done by means of universalization and reduction to unity. Social relations are judged according to the form of relations of this kind that prevails in a given locality, or the social relations of a whole country are judged indiscriminately by the form of these relations that prevails in a certain part of the country or in a certain social class. If it is customary in a given locality for the husband to have absolute power of disposition over the property of his wife, a disposition actually made by a husband is held binding on the wife with utter disregard of the question whether or not this was the custom in the given family.

If it is a general custom of the country that everything that the lessee has inseparably attached to the soil becomes the property of the owner of the land, this custom is treated as the common law of the country, and an action by the lessee for such expenditures is dismissed everywhere even though this custom can not be shown to exist in this or that part of the country. This is the process called universalization. But courts go further than this. An order which is in conflict with the general norm is held invalid even though its existence is clearly proved. By this means the law is made unitary. This results in general and unitary norms for decision, but not in a general and unit ary living law; and individual as well as local differences may well continue to exist beneath the crust of external uniformity.

But the associations themselves require norms for decision for their own completion and perfection. In their normal state, they are supplied with norms for those situations only which the parties involved have anticipated; every new situation, which has not been anticipated, confronts them with the necessity of finding new rules of conduct. This indispensable task of completing the structure of the associations is usually performed from within. If a father contracts a second marriage, the relations of the members of the family to each other are dislocated at once; the family must try to create a new order for itself; a few norms that have prevailed hitherto are given up, and new ones are received. If leased property is employed in a new form of economic enterprise as to which nothing is said in the contract of lease, the parties must arrange their relations accordingly. In many cases an unconscious adaptation takes place; in others a new contract is entered into. But it is the difficulties created by such an unanticipated event that most frequently cause the parties to appeal to the judge. The judge cannot find the solution in the inner order of the association; for the latter has at this very juncture proved unable to create an order. He must have special norms for the decision of the case at hand.

In addition it must be remembered that in every case when a quarrel or controversy arises, the associations have usually got out of their established order into a state of disorder. It would be foolish thereafter to try to make the norms of the association the basis of a decision, for the latter have lost their ordering power in the association. Special norms are required, not for the peaceful relation but for the legal dispute. And these will often differ from the former even as to content.

The compilers of the Civil Code for the German Empire were ill-advised when they made the *Verwaltungsgemeinsckaft*[1] the normal statutory matrimonial regime. As long as the spouses get on well with each other, the marriage will automatically establish the *Verwaltungsgemeinschaft* of the Civil Code as its order; the wife will entrust her husband with the management of her property even though there be no statutory provision, will not exercise a special supervision or demand a det ailed accounting. The spouses who get on well with each other have no need of a judge, and it was a superfluous thing to establish *Verwaltungsgemeinschafl* by statutory enactment where it was already in existence. But if the marriage relation has become inharmonious, the love and confidence which hitherto has induced the wife to live with her husband in *Verwaltungsgemeinschaft* has disappeared. The statute ought to have selected the regime of separation of goods; for this regime alone can protect the wife, in the case of an ill-starred marriage[2], against abuse of the husband's power. No one has failed to see this in the case of ordinary community of property. It is just barely conceivable that an able and honest business man might enter into a partnership with an utterly incapable and indiscreet man, and in such case it would be a good arrangement if the former should by contractual agreement take away from the latter the right to inspect books, letters, and accounts. But such a prohibition is effective only as long as the partnership relation is peaceful, as long as the other party submits to it, in order to maintain the partnership perhaps, but it is not effective as a norm for decision. If the partnership relation should give rise to litigation, the courts must not be bound by this prohibition.

The legal dispute also has its peculiar needs. Certain questions do not arise until the quarrel has begun. How they are to be solved cannot

---

1. *Verwaltungsgemeinschaft*：〈德〉管理共同体，共同管理。这一术语涉及德国制定法所规定的婚姻制度。
2. ill-starred marriage：不幸的婚姻

be determined by the inner order of the association; for the latter is not an order of war, but of peace. In the very earliest beginnings of administration of justice, in the most common case that came before him, the judge had to find norms for decision that went beyond the inner order of the associations themselves. If it was a question of homicide, it was incumbent upon him to decide not only whether the complainant was entitled, on the basis of the inner order of his clan, to demand a penalty, and whether the defendants, were liable according to the order of the clan, perhaps as members of the clan, but over and above that, what the amount of the penalty was to be. On these points, he can not find anything in the inner order. This is true to a still greater degree in the more difficult and more complicated relations of later times. It will not suffice to award the parcel of land to its owner with all the powers and privileges which ownership gives in the experience of life. What is to be done about the crops which the previous owner has planted, about the work and labor he has done and the expenditures he has made? It will not suffice to enforce the contract as it was made; the judge must render judgment on things that the parties never thought of. What happens if the thing the debtor was obligated to deliver has perished before performance could be rendered? What if it is of a nature qtdte different from that which has been presupposed? The person who renders the decision can answer questions of this kind creatively only if he is guided by the form which the relations of life have assumed, not in peaceful development, but during the course of the litigation. To this group belongs the whole law of damages[1], of compensation for unjust enrichment[2], the right of avoidance (*actio Pauliana*)[3], the provision of the material law[4]

1. law of damages：损害赔偿法
2. unjust enrichment：不当得利
3. the right of avoidance (*actio Pauliana*)：撤销权
4. material law：实体法。与程序法对应。

concerning the protection of legal rights, the principles concerning the duty of allegation and proof, and the legal effect of a judgment. We are here presupposing throughout, not a living order, but litigation about an order that is dead.

The last group consists of those norms for decision that have arisen from the clash of the spheres of influence of several associations. In our present-day society, every human being primarily is a member of the state; the spheres of the various other associations to which he belongs are largely intertwined, and all are within the sphere of power of the state. The forces inherent in the associations which cross and embrace one another are variously distributed, and the struggle among them is usually carried on within several spheres at the same time. This struggle, to a very great extent, is about the norms according to which the courts render their decisions. An extreme measure of parental or maritai authority may be proportionate to the distribution of power within a certain family or within the family in a certain class or locality; but it is in conflict with the general order of the family in the state and in society, which have impressed their stamp upon the prevailing norms of law of morality, of ethical custom, of etiquette. The state and society therefore will not tolerate it, and will attempt to bring about an order which is more in harmony with the views that prevail generally, at least when appeal is made to its courts for the settling of disputes. Every wage contract, however disadvantageous to the working-man, will reflect quite accurately the relation of power that obtained between the employer and the employe at the time the contract was made. But if the working class obtains a greater measure of influence in society, it will attempt to shape the wage con tract according to its ideas; a movement will arise within society which will stigmatize one or the other provision of the contracts of wages as contrary to morality and decency, and which, perhaps, will attain power enough to influence even the norms for decision applicable to wage contracts.

The courts decide on the basis of their norms for decision whether a social norm has been transgressed or not. The prevailing juristic science takes for granted that it must be a legal norm that has been transgressed, that the object for which courts have been erected is not the protection of non-legal norms. But it is evident that this can apply only to the organs of the state for the administration of justice. And even as to these it is true only if we call every norm according to which a court renders a decision a legal norm. Eut if we do that, the question becomes a mere question of terminology. If we consider the inner content of the norms according to which the courts must render their decisions — and that is the only fair way to proceed — we shall be convinced that the non-legal norms play an important role even in the courts of the state.

In a primitive stage of development, there is so little differentiation between law on the one hand and morality, religion, ethical custom, decorum, on the other, that the administration of justice utilizes them all indiscriminately. The Roman *prudentes*[1] and the German *Schöffen*[2] appeal without hesitation to morality, ethical custom and decorum; the English judge, who at the present time is perhaps the only heir of the traditions of the ancient judicial office, does the same thing. But all of these are bound by the ever recurring limitation that non-legal norms may be used only to eke out the positive law, to act as stop-gaps; the judge therefore is not authorized to disregard the legal norms in favor of the non-legal ones. The principle is extremely elastic, and occasionally the limitation which it imposes upon the discretion of the judges can scarcely be felt; nevertheless it is of very great importance. It imports that the bases of our social order that have been expressed in legal norms may not be disturbed by other social orderings and rules. It does not apply therefore when the state itself intervenes in the

---

1. *prudentes*：〈拉〉法学家
2. *Schöffen*：〈德〉法官助理

administration of justice. The Roman praetor, the king in the Frankish and in the German kingdom, the English chancellor, render decisions according to fairness or according to morals, i.e. according to non-legal norms, and occasionally even contrary to the established law. From these decisions, it is true, legal propositions subsequently evolve. Although the praetorian law and English equity[1] grew chiefly out of norms of morality, ethical custom, and decorum, they became separate and distinct legal systems in the course of time. This however merely shows that the chief difference between law and non-legal norms of this kind is a matter of stability, certainty, and the general conviction as to their social importance, not of content.

Even in the courts of the Continent, however, which had been completely transformed into state courts, which had become exclusively organs of the administration of justice, the principle that the courts must base their decisions exclusively upon the law was never more than a matter of seeming. The rule of law itself continually refers them to other social norms; it will tolerate no abuse of the law which violates morality, ethical custom; or decorum; it forbids immoral contracts; commands performance of contracts[2] according to good faith and the custom of everyday life; provides penalties for insults, for violation of the proprieties and for gross mischief. It entrusts the decision to the free discretion of the judge; and that often means to a discretion based on other than purely legal considerations. But the administration of justice actually goes much further than the law. The fact that the judge was rigidly confined to the law in every respect has hitherto merely prevented the judges from openly making non-legal norms the bases of their decisions, but not from doing so in various, sometimes very transparent, disguises. The holding of the French courts that the owner of a building may not let a shop

1. English equity：英国衡平法
2. performance of contracts：合同履行

to a competitor of his tenant in the same building, on the ground that according to the statute he has impliedly given to the latter a warranty *de tout trouble*[1], amounts to a recognition of a principle of propriety which the wording of the statute does not express even approximately. Generally speaking, the non-legal norms of morality, ethical custom, and decorum become legal norms so readily that in most cases a differentiation is altogether impossible. In Lot mar's book *Der unmoralische Vertrag*[2] (The Immoral Contract), the basic features of this process are presented with reference to a single instance in an incontrovertible manner, although in other respects the ideas we have presented here are quite foreign to this book.

All of this, of course, does not mean that the courts should, without more ado[3], render their decisions according to non-legal norms. All legal propositions are not suitable for norms for decisions; *a fortiori*[4] all non-legal norms, taken indiscriminately, are still less so. To make a proper selection is a task of enormous difficulty — a task which makes much higher demands upon the powers of the judge than the mere application of law. The strong tendency on the Continent to make the judge merely a ministerial servant[5] of the statute who has no right to exercise any discretion whatever arises, I am convinced, from a suspicion that he is not equal to so difficult a task. The Roman *prudentes,* the English, and, in part, the French judges, have proved their ability in this matter; and the *Oberappellationsgericht*[6] at Lubeck as well as the *Oberhandelsgericht*[7] at Leipzig have demonstrated that the German judge, too, possesses the necessary ability. And, lastly,

---

1. warranty *de tout trouble*：免于干扰的保证（斜体为拉丁文）
2. *Der unmoralische Vertrag*：〈德〉不道德契约
3. without more ado：毫不迟延
4. *fortiori*：〈拉〉更何况
5. ministerial servant：执事
6. *Oberappellationsgericht*：〈德〉高等上诉法院
7. *Oberhandelsgericht*：〈德〉商事高等上诉法院

the work must be done at all events, and it is being done today. And if it must be admitted that, as a result of the imperfect regulation of the administration of justice, it is being done in a most exceptionable manner, we may nevertheless say that one cannot solve a difficulty of this nature by closing one's eyes to it.

As to courts other than those that are organs of the state for the administration of justice, the contention is no longer made that they arrive at their decisions on the basis of legal propositions. The administrative tribunals of the state, the police, the courts of discipline, the presiding officers of bodies of representatives of the people, must very often render judgments based on the norms of morality, ethical custom, honor, decorum, tact, etiquette. This applies to an even higher degree to the non-state courts, the various courts of arbitration, courts of societies, courts of honor, courts of cartels, courts of trusts, courts of tradeunions, courts of clubs. In ecclesiastical courts, religious norms also play an important role. The police imposing a penalty for a violation of decency; the presiding officer of the *Abgeordnetenhaus*[1] reprimanding a member for violation of parliamentary custom; the court of honor compelling an officer to resign because of a breach of the code of honor; the disciplinary court condemning an official for injuring the reputation of the class (by failure to exercise sufficient tact); the court of a club excluding a member for non-payment of a gaming debt; the court of a cartel ordering a boycott against an entrepreneur for furnishing goods to an entrepreneur against whom a boycott had been declared; the court of a union declaring that a member is not in good standing for having worked during a strike — all of these are courts which are erected and maintained by society itself, and which, on the basis of norms which are preponderantly extralegal, display a fruitful and ever increasing

1. *Abgeordnetenhaus*：〈德〉下议院

activity, and, in part, have means of compulsion at their disposal which are of greater effectiveness than those of the state tribunals. In the book of Nothnagel, to which I have referred repeatedly, much material has been gathered on this point, which, though somewhat out of date, is nevertheless useful at all times.

The norm for decision contains the general proposition on which the decision is based, and thereby sets up the pretension that it is a truth which is valid, not only for the specific case under discussion but for every like or similar case. A judgment decreeing that the *wergild* is to be paid to the brother of the slain man by the brother of the slayer establishes a rule that, in the clan of the slain man at least, a brother always has the right to assert the claim; that, in the clan of the slayer, a brother is always liable. A judgment allowing recovery against the defendant on the basis of a contract implies that under the circumstances of the case an enforceable claim arises from a contract of the kind in question. Even a decision of the question by casting lots, as is often done on a lower level of development, amounts to a general acknowledgment that in cases like the one in dispute the party in whose favor the lot is cast wins.

This is the law of the stability of legal norms, which is of such vast importance for the creation of law. It is based, in the first place, on social psychology. Rendering contrary decisions in like or in similar cases would not be law and right, but arbitrariness or caprice. It is based also on a certain sound economic quality of thinking. The expenditure of intellectual labor which undoubtedly is always involved in seeking norms for decision can often be avoided by rendering a decision according to a norm which has already been found. Moreover there is a great social need of stable norms for decision, which make it possible in a limited measure to foresee and predict the decisions and thereby to put a man in position to make his arrangements accordingly.

The law of the stability of the norms for decision functions chiefly in time. The court will not, without good cause, depart from a norm which it has applied in the decision of a case as long as the norm is remembered, and often special measures are being taken to prevent its being forgotten. But it functions in space also; for the norms for decision which, have been found by one court will readily be applied by other courts which exist in the same sphere of influence, if for no other reason, in order to avoid the labor incident to finding norms. Since the courts, in a more advanced stage of development, at least inasmuch as they are the organs of the state for the administration of justice, are given a local competence, their norms for decision also become competent and fixed for this territory, and where several courts enter into reciprocal relations, for the territory of all of these courts.

The sovereignty of the state in the field of law, which is so significant for modern law, is based on the stability of the legal norms. The prevailing modern belief that *Rechtsgebiet*[1] and *Staatsgebiet*[2] are identical arises from the fact that the courts within the territory of a certain state consistently follow certain norms of decision. The stability of the norms for decision receives a special significance because of the fact that it extends not merely to like or similar cases but also to cases that are only approximately similar. This makes it possible to apply a norm to cases as to which it is not a decision at all, on the sole ground that the latter are similar to the decided cases. Every such decision, indeed, is based on a new norm for decision, but the content of this new norm is merely this: that the existing norm is applicable to the case. The new norm has extended the sphere of application of the original norm and enriched its content; and every such extension and enrichment in turn functions according to the law of the stability of the norms for decision. Juristic lawmaking is based chiefly on this continued

1. *Rechtsgebiet*：〈德〉法律实施范围
2. *Staatsgebiet*：〈德〉国土范围

projection, as Wurzel has called it, of the norm to new cases. Thanks to this law of stability, the norms acquire an extremely tenacious life and an enormous extensibility. Every reception of foreign law is an instance of the operation of the law of the st ability of the norms. Many a norm which, possibly, the Roman *pontifices*[1] have thought out, continues to function today. One might raise the question here: If it is true that the norms grow out of the situations themselves for the decision concerning which they are to constitute the basis, how does it come about that a norm can still be applicable so long after it was created and under a totally different social and economic order; that the present-day German law contains norms which as to content are identical with those of the *corpus iuris,* nay, with those of the Twelve Tables and the Decalogue[2]; that the French Civil Code can be valid for two so dissimilar societies as the French and the Roumanian?

The answer is this: The norms, especially those that have been derived from Roman law, have become so general and so abstract, by the uninterrupted process of extension and of enrichment of their content in the course of the millennia, that they are adaptable to the most diverse situations. This shows however that after all the law of the stability of the norms is based on a superficial view of things. In actual fact it is not the same norm at all; it has remained unchanged in appearance only; it has received an entirely new inner content.

The great contrasts between the law of the past and the law of the present, the differences between the laws of the various countries and nations, are based on the facts of the law, in every instance, rather than on the legal norms. The usages, relations of domination and subjection, relations of possession, contracts, testamentary dispositions, change to a much greater extent than the norms, and react upon the latter even though the wording of the latter has remained unchanged.

1. Roman *pontifices*：罗曼祭司法。该法过去曾垄断法律解释。
2. Decalogue：《摩西十诫》

In the *Eigentumsklage*[1], the principles of compensation for fruits[2] or expenditures may be worded, in the main, just as they were among the Romans, but it is by no means immaterial whether they are applied to a Roman fundus or to a modern knight's estate or to securities amounting to millions. One need only bear in mind what is meant by the terms *fruits* and *expenditures* in each of these three cases to see at once what changes the norms have undergone meanwhile. The Roman law of obligations has, in a certain sense, manifested an astonishing power of resistance. But in Rome both the creditor and the debtor were *patres familiae*, heads of families the membership of each of which often comprised more than half of a hundred persons. Today the creditor and the debtor are, formally at least, individuals. In view of this vast difference, what is the significance of the fact that today the liability of the individual for fault and accident is similar to that of the liability of the *pater familias*[3] in time past in Rome? If one strikes glass or iron with the same hammer, there will be a different sound in each case.

Nevertheless one must not assume that this pouring of a new content into the norms obviates all difficulties involved in the law of the stability of the norms. The bulk of the complaints about unsatisfactory laws amounts to this: that the norms, because of their stability, function in situations for which they were not created, and to which therefore they are not adapted. But the evil effects are limited considerably by the fact that these norms are not norms of conduct but of decision. If the stability of the Roman norms should actually compel us to live according to Roman law, e.g. in the enlarged family of the Romans with its *manus* marriage[4] or its free marriage arbitrarily

1. *Eigentumsklage*：〈德〉所有权确权之诉
2. fruits：孳息
3. *pater familias*：〈拉〉家父
4. *manus* marriage：夫权或父权婚姻（*manus* 为拉丁文，是古罗马法律中规定的“对他人之权”）

dissoluble, if it should actually compel us to adapt our system of landholding to the Roman *fundus,* the resulting situation would be unendurable. In actual fact, all that it comes to is that occasionally a law-suit is decided according to Roman law. The part of our daily life that appears in the courts is by far too insignificant to make it impossible for us to endure the most unjust decisions. Much though we may suffer under this state of affairs, we submit to the inevitable; for stability of the norms, as a basis for judicial decision and for juristic science, is inevitable.

The stability of the norms for decision causes them to lose their original form and to become legal propositions. One of the most important results achieved by Jung in his book, *The Problem of Natural Law,* is that "the power of the *Praejudiz*[1] (which rests on the stability of the norms for decision) is part of the conceptual presuppositions for the formation of legal propositions." Before we can discuss the norm for decision in the form of the legal proposition, however, we must consider another form of law in general, the law created by the state.

1. *Praejudiz*：〈拉〉先例

VII THE STATE AND THE LAW

A clear-cut distinction must be made between state law and statute. State law is created by the state, not indeed as to its form, but as to its content; it is law that came into being solely through the state, and that could not exist without the state. The form in which it arises is immaterial. Not every statutory precept contains state law. There are statutes whose sole function is to create the inner order for a legal relation, e.g. articles of association, regulations for the conduct of a commercial enterprise; moreover the state can enter into a contract by enacting a statute. Articles of association, regulation of commercial enterprises, contract do not become state law because they have been put into statutory form; they remain what they were, the inner order of a legal relation. In the same way, jurist-made law can be put into statutory form, i.e. the legislator may confine himself, in the manner of the jurist, to universalizing, reducing to unity, to finding norms according to what seems to him to be justice. The resolutions of many mediaeval corporate bodies of the state, especially of the German Diet[1] and of the English Parliament, normally were *Weistumer*[2], i.e. they were juristic law not only in content but also in form. On the other hand state law can come into existence not only in the form of statutes, but also in the form of administrative or police regulation, of magisterial law, of judge-made law. The Roman praetor was essentially a *Gerichtsherr*[3]; his praetorian edict therefore contains mostly

---

1. German Diet：议会
2. *Weistümer*：〈德〉法律的宣布
3. *Gerichtsherr*：〈德〉最高司法权威

magisterial law (*Amtsrechf*)[1], occasionally when his object was merely to resolve doubts and difficulties, judge-made law; but the *edictum de posito et suspense* or *de calumniatoribus*[2] is state law, police regulation, and criminal law. The English judges, acting as organs of the state, have created the most important parts of the English criminal law of the state in their legal decisions. English equity also contains much state law.

Most jurists would be slightly astonished if they were asked how it happens that the state, which they are accustomed to look upon as the source of all law, concerns itself about law at all. But the question is not altogether unjustified. In its origin the state is a military association, whose relation to the affairs of the legal order is very loose; and, with the exception of a few modern states, established in the former and the present English colonies in North America and in other parts of the world, it has remained an essentially military association to the present day. It is possible to place the origin of the state in the far distant past, but one must not look for it in the clan or in the community of the household. The earliest formation which is at all historically connected with the present state is the confederation of the warlike nobility of several tribes related by language, who, followed by the remaining freemen, choose a military leader, not only for the special emergency, but as a permanent leader. The state has never denied its military origin; at every stage of its development military interests were in the foreground; and with the exception of the English colonies referred to above and a few minor European states, this is true everywhere today.

To the purely military functions of the young state two others were added at an early date, which however are closely connected with the former. First of all, it is the function of the state to supply the king,

---

1. magisterial law (*Amtsrechf*)：裁判法
2. *edictum de posito et suspenso* or *de calumniatoribus*：〈拉〉关于搁置物与悬挂物的告示或关于控告者的告示。

the permanent military leader, and his followers with the necessary material means. This is done in the earliest times by means of urgent demands for gifts — a method which later, especially in the Orient, becomes out and out extortion. The Romans, in their provinces, appear to have been the first to develop an orderly system of taxation. In addition, the state at an early period developed a crude police activity, especially in cases of insurrection and rebellion. The great territorial states of the Orient did not develop beyond this stage until the middle of the nineteenth century. This stage is followed, after a long interval, in small territorial and in city states at first, later also in large territorial states, in the Roman Empire, in the Carolingian Empire[1], in England, by a well ordered system of administration of justice by the state; and much later, in the same states, by legislation. A true administration by the state, even approximately comparable in the diversity of its purposes with that of the present day, did not arise until the seventeenth century in France. Prior to this time, there is nothing like it except in city states. In the Orient scarcely anything like it is to be found down to the most recent period, or in the old Republic of Poland, or in England down to the nineteenth century. We might therefore speak with Adolf Wagner of a law of an ever increasing, and more than that, of an ever more rapidly increasing, activity of the state, if it were not for the fact that the culminating point either has already been passed or will have been passed in the near future.

There are, manifestly, four things that cause the state to appear, in such an eminent degree, to be the source of law. These are the following. First its participation in lawmaking through legislation; secondly, its participation in the administration of law through the state courts and in part through other tribunals; thirdly, its power and control over the state tribunals, by which it is enabled to give effect

1. Carolingian Empire：加洛林帝国

to its statutes; lastly, the idea that the preservation of a factual sit nation corresponding to the law can be effected primarily, or at least ultimately, through the state's power of compulsion. This last point however is of no importance here since it is without influence upon the creation and development of state law.

The history of law has shown that originally both legislation and administration of law were beyond the sphere and province of the state. The administration of justice does not derive from the state; it has its roots in the time before the existence of the state. Its oldest form appears quite clearly in the judgment scene on the shield of Achilleus[1], for the only possible interpretation of which we are indebted to Hoffmeister. Two men are quarreling over the *wergild* for a man who was slain. One boasted that he would pay all; the other disputed this, saying he would not accept anything. In other words, the kinsman of the slain man insists on the vengeance of blood, and the wise judges are called upon to decide whether he shall prevail, or whether he is obligated to accept the penalty. The court has not been commissioned by the state, and the judgment is not made effective by compulsion exercised by the state. If the other party refuses to submit, he may have his vengeance in spite of the judgment. The only consequence of doing so is the loss of the purely social advantages of a just feud. Traces of this stage in the development of the administration of justice can readily be found in the criminal law of the sagas of Iceland, as it has recently been set forth with such vividness by Andreas Heusler, the younger. It is easily recognizable not only in the legal procedure in the pre-Carolingian period[2] but also in the much more highly developed procedure of the Roman Twelve Tables. At this stage, penalties in fixed amounts have already been prescribed, but the injured party is

1. the shield of Achilleus：阿喀琉斯之盾。据《伊利亚特》第 18 卷描述，该盾牌上刻有丰富的叙事场景。
2. pre-Carolingian period：前加洛林王朝时期

not yet obligated to accept them; the judgment delivers up the party who has done the injury to the injured party unless an agreement is reached (*ni cum eo pacit*[1]). The procedure is rigid and formal, as indeed it must be between deadly enemies; the competence of the court is limited, in the main, to cases demanding the death penalty (homicide, man-stealing, bodily injury, theft).

Zallinger has pointed out that this procedure could not possibly have been the only procedure in the primitive period of the history of the Germanic peoples. Surely even in primitive times quarrels arose not only between deadly enemies but also between members of a close association; and some of these most likely because of minor wrong-doings. In actual fact it can easily be shown that provision had been made everywhere for the composition of quarrels of this nature, but the reports that we have concerning them are meagre since the jurists, for obvious reasons, are not interested in them. We find the jurisdiction of the head of the clan, of the head of the house, of the elder of the village. We find family courts and village courts. The procedure is quite informal. The legal principles according to which the decisions are arrived at are unsettled and uncertain; the judgment is a sort of amicable settlement unless it pronounces exclusion from the community. The head of the household in Rome did indeed have the *ius vitae ac necis*[2]. But things of this kind are rare in antiquity as the Romans themselves point out and cannot readily be found in other courts of a close association. (Can it be shown to have existed among the ancient Russians?) It probably arose after politically organized states had come into existence.

The work of Pachman, *Russian Customary Private Law* (*Obytschnoje graschdanskoje prawo w Rosii*)[3], contains a full discussion of this kind

1. *ni cum eo pacit*：〈拉〉达成协议
2. *ius vitae ac necis*：〈拉〉生杀权
3. *Russian Customary Private Law* (*Obytschnoje graschdanskoje prawo w Rosii*)：《俄罗斯习惯私法》

of administration of justice. In Russia communal courts, which perhaps are rooted in a very early period, and which are devoted to the administration of the affairs of the peasantry, have maintained their existence down to the present day. Legislation has merely circumscribed their jurisdiction, but has left their freedom unrestricted down to the most recent times. In the sixties and seven ties their activity was investiga ted by a government commission, which published a six-volume report of its findings. The work of Pachman is based on this report (with the exception of the article on *Artele*[1]). The results are, as Nalyschew and Kowalewsky point out, extremely open to attack, for the courts at the present time are in a state of the utmost disintegration. Nevertheless the work of Pachman is not without value. The sole legal proposition which is met with in all parts of Russia in communal administration of justice is extremely significant. It is *Grech po polu*[2] (the damage is equally divided between the parties). If the court cannot make up its mind what decision it is to render, it divides the damage equally between the parties.

But there is a third class of courts. These are exclusively of state origin; they arise from the military leader's power and control over his followers. The military leader self-evidently acts as soon as the commonwealth is endangered, especially in case of treason, or of trading with the enemy. But he does not confine himself to these cases. The military leader must maintain discipline among his troops and, particularly, prevent feuds: he cannot permit vengeance of blood to become prevalent while he is face to face with the enemy. For this reason a certain jurisdiction over private affairs is inevitable at an early time. At a more advanced stage, the king has it as a matter of course. The sovereign power which the king attains in time of peace enables him to administer justice in times of peace also. This however

1. *Artele*：〈德〉合作社
2. *Grech po polu*：平等分配损失（斜体是拉丁文表示的俄语语音）

is done according to principles, and according to a procedure, quite different from those of other courts and, at all events, not according to the sole discretion of the king, but according to that of the counsel of his advisers.

The next step in the development is that, in consequence of the loosening of the bonds of the old associations, the composition of quarrels among people in a close relationship loses most of its importance, and that, consequently, the disputes between persons within close relationships are also brought into the regularly established courts. Since the latter henceforth are no longer limited to sitting in judgment in cases involving the death penalty, it becomes their task not only to compose quarrels, but to render decisions. The second step is the organization of these courts by the state. This has been done in various ways. Either the power to institute proceedings is put into the hands of a state official, as was done in Rome, or the state supplies the courts with a presiding officer, as was done in the kingdom of the Franks by Charles the Great, and in England after the conquest. At the same time the royal administration of justice as a function of the state continues. This is followed by the third step, the development of the king's jurisdiction. The king's advisers become self-dependent judges and actually displace all the old established courts in virtue of their special privileges, or perhaps because of the superior quality of their administration of justice (as in England), or they are converted into courts of appeal (the Parliaments in France, the *Hofgericht*[1] of the German kingdom). The personal jurisdiction of the king however is not yet abolished by any means. Finally the lay assessors (*Beisitzer*)[2], who are chosen from among the populace, are eliminated from the regularly constituted courts, and the latter become purely state courts manned by state officials. Perhaps there is a later stage of development,

---

1. *Hofgericht*：〈德〉国王法院
2. lay assessors (*Beisitzer*)：陪审员

at which popular elements are again employed in the administration of justice. This was done in England as early as the days of Henry II in the assizes: and at a somewhat later date in the trial by jury. On the Continent this tendency, which did not appear until after the French Revolution and which was at first limited to criminal causes, has been extended more and more to certain kinds of private-law causes.

This conversion of the administration of justice into a function of the state is limited to Europe however. The Orient, where it has remained untouched by European influences, to the present day knows nothing of state administration of justice. The Kadi[1] is appointed by a spiritual authority, and is independent of the state. Likewise, in Mohammedan countries justice is administered either by temporal or by spiritual local authorities which are neither appointed nor commissioned by the state. Turkey alone established state courts, when it began to adopt European ways after the Crimean war, but it has preserved the jurisdiction of spiritual courts for a great number of causes.

State law appears in history at a much later date than state administration of justice. The state, in the first place, creates its own order, *Staatsrecht* and when it creates tribunals of any kind whatsoever, it prescribes their competence, their order of conducting business, and occasionally also their procedure. At an early date, statements of law are being drawn up by private individuals at the behest of the state, or are being recognized by the state, which are collections of the norms according to which the courts conduct their business or render their decisions. These collections, however, are not state law even though additions and modifications have been added to the traditional element. Such additions are found in collections of this kind that are of an altogether private nature, and this fact merely demonstrates that man has ever been unable and unwilling, both then and at a later

1. Kadi：〈德〉（伊斯兰教国家的）法官

period, to observe the distinction between stating law and positing law, just as the medicine man who was closely related to the jurist found it necessary not only to know but also to discover his remedies.

The presuppositions under which state law can arise are conditioned upon the nature of the latter as a command addressed to the courts and other tribunals and directing them how to proceed. It can proceed only from a person who has control over the courts and the other tribunals. Before the state can create law in this manner, the administration of the affairs of the state and the order of the administration of justice must be unitary, to a certain extent. The powers of the state must have reached a degree of development sufficient to compel the performance of the commands of the central power throughout the whole territory of the state. This includes a certain military development and a police department of some sort. Lastly, the law of the state is conditioned upon certain factors of popular psychology. The state must find material from which it can select pliant judges and officials. In this matter, the ability to read and write is of great importance. It must be reserved for the as yet unwritten history of legislation by the state to show how legislation everywhere followed the development of the administration of the affairs of the state. We can imagine of what value a study of the laws of Hammurabi[1] and of other Assyrian law[2] would be as long as we know nothing of the nature of the Assyrian state. The mere thought that the state can create law which is as effective as the law that arises from long continued custom, i.e. in the words of the gloss to the *Sachsenspiegel*[3] that "the will of the country is to be treated like law" presupposes an enormous power of abstraction which man possesses only in an advanced stage of development. Since the German lay

1. Hammurabi：《汉谟拉比法典》
2. Assyrian law：《亚述法》
3. *Sachsenspiegel*：〈德〉《萨克森法典》

judges (*Schöffen*)[1] of the early Middle Ages were not endowed with the latter, there could be no true legislation in the Empire. It is well known that the small number of German imperial statutes that had been enacted by the time of the thirteenth century, imitations of Roman models, have received scant attention. For this reason statutes are, in general, unknown in the Orient down to the present time. When Turkey began to promulgate statutes, it had to create entirely new courts. If the Sultan had sent a copy of the commercial code to a Kadi, the latter, most likely, would not have known what to do with it. Furthermore there can be no legislation by the state without an administration of law that is subservient to the state. This too was lacking in the Middle Ages. After the French Parliaments had, to a limited extent, emancipated themselves from state control, they offered resistance even to the statutes of an absolute king. The German territories undoubtedly would not have attained a system of state law as early as the sixteenth and seventeenth centuries if the universities had not supplied them with excellent material for judges and officials who were in a situation of complete dependence upon the state. Finally there must be effective means of publishing state regulations, and the populace must have some understanding and appreciation of the content and purpose of a statute. If, nevertheless, statutes are frequently met with in a country where all of these presuppositions are nonexistent, we are likely to find that they are utterly ineffectual imitations of foreign models. The Frankish kings imitated the Roman Caesars; Tsar Duschan of Serbia, the Byzantine emperors; and in modern times many an Oriental state strives to imitate the Europeans, e.g. Siam[2], which had a Frenchman draw up a civil code.

State law is found only where the administration of justice and of the affairs of the state is directed from a central point and is based

1. lay judges (*Schöffen*)：非职业法官
2. Siam：暹罗，泰国旧称。

on a strong military and police power. At first these conditions exist only in states of small territorial extent; in antiquity, in Egypt with its unusually powerful state, and especially in the city states, Athens and Rome; in the Middle Ages, in the city states of Italy and Germany. The Roman citizen and the Roman official did indeed carry the concept of state law into every part of the enormous Empire; but it did not begin to prevail until the later days of the Empire, after the *constitutio Antonina*[1]. Modern investigation has shown that there was much of seeming and little of actuality in this. The Germanic states that arose on the wreckage of the Roman Empire did have state law, as the Capitulary legislation[2] shows, but this can be explained by the fact that they had taken over a great deal of Roman civilization and of the Roman bureaucratic institutions. It is very difficult to determine whether and to what ext ent these stat utes really were valid, whether they were actually applied. On this very point doubts have been raised in recent days, especially by Dopsch, whose work, I regret to state, I have not been in position to avail myself of. The greater the distance bet ween the Germanic states and the Roman Empire, both in time and in space, the more their legislation fades out. Jenks, the English legal historian, has appended to his book, *Law and Politics in the Middle Ages,* a table of the sources of the mediaeval law in Italy, Germany, France, England, Scotland, Spain, and Scandinavia. It is very instructive. The columns devoted to Italy and to the kingdom of the Franks are filled for the period from the sixth to the ninth century; there is an occasional entry concerning Spain. True, these entries are chiefly declarations of the existing law, but these statements, as is well known, contain legislative innovations; moreover, they also contain true state law. In the column devoted to England a few statements of law appear and these as of the sixth century only. In the tenth

1. *constitutio Antonina*：安东尼敕令
2. Capitulary legislation：教会立法

and eleventh centuries, legislation in all these states is at a standstill. Statements of law are found in England and Scotland. In the eleventh century, the systems of law in the cities of Italy are beginning to attract attention. True statutes, Schupfer informs us, are found first in Milan (as of the dates 1026, 1061, 1065). As to this point nothing appears in Jenks' table[1]. At a somewhat later date the *Landfrieden*[2] appear in Germany, which however, it seems, first developed from ecclesiastical commands and voluntary agreements into statutes in the eleventh century. To these the laws of the cities are added in the twelfth century.

This discussion of externals does not teach us very much. There are two questions that are of much greater importance than the question whether the will of the state has been proclaimed as law anywhere — perhaps under foreign influence or by some accident. These questions are: first, when the idea that the state has a call, and is able, to create law independently was first seriously entertained, and how it took root; and secondly, when the idea that only the state can create law begins to gain ground. Neither of these questions has been investigated. In Greece, outside of Athens, there are few traces of state law. In Sparta[3], the utter absence, in earlier times, of the concept of state law later developed into a prohibition forbidding any change in the old customary law, the so-called legislation of Lycurgus[4]. The idea of a state monopoly of law remained foreign even to the Romans until the last days of the Empire. It is clearly expressed for the first time by Constantinus[5]. Until that time only the *ius publicum*[6] is

1. Jenks' table：爱德华·甄克斯在《中世纪的法律与政治》一书中所附的关于中世纪法渊源的表格。
2. Landfrieden：国家安宁；公众安宁。类似于英格兰的国王安宁。
3. Sparta：斯巴达
4. Lycurgus：莱库格斯，古希腊时代斯巴达的立法者，他所建立的莱库格斯法确立了贵族寡头政制，实行国民军事教育等制度。
5. Constantinus：君士坦丁一世（272—337），西罗马帝国皇帝。
6. *ius publicum*：〈拉〉公法

considered a creation of the state. And, as I have shown in my *Beitrage zur Theorie der Rechtsquellen*[1], in addition to *Staatsrecht* (public law), the Romans consider the positive law, i.e. the *leges, senates consulta*[2], *edicta magistratuum*[3], *constitutiones*[4], a part of the *ius publicum*; but not the law which has not been posited, the *ius quod sine scripto venit compositum a prudentibus,* the *ius civile*[5] in the technical sense, which together with the *ius gentium*[6] and the *ius naturale*[7] they subsume under the head of *ius privatum*[8]. It is impossible to determine when the Romans began to create law by means of statutes. But even in historical times, they hesitated to modify the *ius civile*[9], the traditional customary law, by means of statutes. This is shown by the fact that their older *leges,* which are directed against abuses, do not abolish these abuses by directly doing away with the legal propositions upon which the abuse is based, but by giving the injured party a right to demand restitution. They are all *leges imperfectae*[10] (*lex Plaetoria*[11], *lex Furia testamentaria*[12], *lex Marcia*[13], *lex Cincia*[14]); and Gaius, in his day, still speaks of the matter as if the old *ius civile* were still in existence side by side with the *leges* which had

---

1. *Beiträge zur Theorie der Rechtsquellen*：〈德〉《法源理论的贡献》
2. *senatus consulta*：〈拉〉元老院决议
3. *edicta magistratuum*：〈拉〉执法官告示
4. *constitutiones*：〈拉〉皇帝敕令
5. *ius quod sine scripto venit compositum a prudentibus*, the *ius civile*：〈拉〉技术意义上的市民法
6. *ius gentium*：〈拉〉万民法
7. *ius naturale*：〈拉〉自然法
8. *ius privatum*：〈拉〉私法
9. *ius civile*：〈拉〉市民法
10. *leges imperfectae*：〈拉〉不完善的法律
11. *lex Plaetoria*：〈拉〉《普莱多里法》，公元前 3 世纪制定的保护未成年人免受欺诈的法律。
12. *lex Furia testamentaria*：〈拉〉《关于遗嘱的富里法》
13. *lex Marcia*：〈拉〉《马尔其法》。公元前 311 年罗马制定的赋予人民选举军事裁判机构的权利。
14. *lex Cincia*：〈拉〉《琴里亚法》。公元前 204 年罗马通过的旨在改革罗马共和国法律体系的法律。

abolished it. In the Middle Ages, from about the time of the collapse of the Carolingian Empire, the idea that the state can create law or modify it is altogether non-existent. At the diet of Stela, in the reign of Otto *I*, in the year 942, the right of grandsons to inherit from their grandfather is not determined by a statute but is established by the *Gottesurteil* (judgment of God)[1] of the legal combat. No trace of this idea is found in the *Sachsenspiegel*. And surely the two-sword theory does not refer to it. It expressly denies to the pope, the bearer of the spiritual sword, the right to modify the law of the land and of feudal tenancy. The gloss to the *Sachsenspiegel* concedes that *Willkür*[2] is to be treated as law, but only within very narrow limits. The *Weistum*[3] of the Parliament of Merton (1235–1236) is famous: *Ac rogaverunt omnes episcopi Magnates, ut consentirent, quod nati ante matrimonium essent legitimi, sicut illi qui nati sunt post matrimonium quantum ad successionem hereditariam, quia ecclesia tales habet pro legitimis, et omnes Comites et Barones una voce responderunt, quod nolunt leges Angliae mutare, quae usitatae sunt et approbatae.*[4] This attitude of the Comites and Barones is by no means to be explained as caused by a disinclination to accept the principle of legitimation — for there were illegitimate children at that time in England as well as elsewhere — but by the absence of the idea that law can be created or modified by resolution of Parliament.

And when a statute is enacted, it is by no means "the will of the State." Its oldest form seems to have been that of contract. This may have been the case among the Romans. The Roman *leges sacratae*[5] may

1. *Gottesurteil* (judgment of God)：〈德〉上帝裁判
2. *Willkür*：〈德〉自由意志
3. *Weistum*：〈德〉颁布法律
4. *Ac rogaverunt omnes ... sunt et approbatae.*：〈拉〉大意为：英格兰主教们要求英格兰贵族（包括小贵族、地主、伯爵和男爵）允许婚前出生的非婚生子女享有与婚生子女同等的遗产继承权。但是贵族们的回答是一致的：他们不希望改变已经习惯的和大家都认同的英格兰法。
5. *leges sacratae*：〈拉〉神圣约法，早起罗马社会的平民在圣山上指定的法律。

originally have been an agreement sworn to by all citizens whom they concerned. Similar situations are found in ancient Greece. There is no doubt that this applies to the oldest statutes of the German kingdom, the *Landfrieden*[1]. They had to be sworn to and had validity only for those who had sworn to them. They derived their power not from the will of the state, but from the oath, although the individual often took the oath under compulsion. Even in England, a statute was agreed upon between King and Parliament like a contract. Another form is the "Privilege." *Privilegia*[2], granted to cities by the lords of cities, are in the first place the city charters in Germany and Italy as well as the confirmation of city statutes. Very often the statute is disguised as a *Weistum* (declaration of law). Jenks says of the English Parliament that it is a law-declaring rather than a law-making body. It has been said of the Magna Charta[3], one of the most famous sources of state law in the history of mankind, that "the form of this solemn instrument is that of a deed of grant" (Maitland) . With such difficulty, and so gradually, the idea of state law, which indeed is anything but easily comprehensible, has made its way even among the most advanced nations of the human race. The fact that the concept of law as created by the state is found among the glossators[4] and later also among the postglossators and the canonists[5] in the early Middle Ages with reference to the church is not in conflict with this view. For the latter reflect not their own ideas, but the doctrines of the *corpus iuris* of the Byzantine age[6]. We may disregard the question how much of this can be traced to political, especially Ghibelline[7], ambitions.

---

1. *Landfrieden*：〈德〉国家安宁法
2. *Privilegia*：〈拉〉法律创设的特权形式。
3. *Magna Charta*：《英国大宪章》
4. glossators：注释法学者
5. canonists：宗教法学者
6. *corpus iuris* of the Byzantine age：拜占庭时期的《国法大全》
7. Ghibelline：保皇党人

In the Orient, traces of state law are as few and far between as traces of state administration of justice. Whatsoever is called statute in extra-European states is either a declaration of law like the law of Moses or of Zarathustra or of Manu[1], or it is a regulation issued by the sovereign power of the state, without any general significance beyond the special case for which it was issued. We may disregard imitations of European models made without serious intent.

As to content, state law originally contained only norms for decision. It is merely a direction to the courts, which by this time have become state courts, directing them how to adjudge legal disputes. The government of the state, as developed first of all in France after the collapse of Rome, was concerned only with collecting taxes and with military affairs (the *intendants*) . It knows of state law, therefore, only as to these things. The financial and military authorities receive special directions for individual cases; later, directions couched in quite general terms to act in certain clearly defined cases; and finally detailed directions issued by the central power instructing them how to proceed. This constitutes the basis of a new kind of state law, the law governing state action, i.e. state administrative law. From France, this law spreads over the whole continent of Europe. Where there are no state administrative authorities, as in the ancient German kingdom, in England, in Poland, in Hungary, there is no effective administrative legislation. Occasionally the state resorts to charging the autonomous administrative bodies of the lesser associations, especially of the communes (*fiemeinde*), the districts (*Bezirk*), the counties with the execution of the stat utes; in England it also commissions the justices of the peace. But these means are as a rule poorly adapted to this purpose. If the will of the state is to be carried out effectively, special agencies must be constituted for this purpose. When the English, therefore, enacted legislation for relief of the poor,

---

1. the law of Moses or of Zarathustra or of Manu：摩西法，查拉图斯特拉法，摩奴法

they created a board for this purpose, and when they enacted legislation for the protection of factory workers, they created a board of factory inspectors. These institutions have frequently served as models for similar purposes elsewhere.

Now, what is the propulsive force in this whole development? What prompts the state to take over, to an ever increasing extent, the administration of justice and the creation of law, which originally belong to the lesser associations of which society is composed, and finally to assert, in theory at least, supreme power over all these things? If we consider the state by itself, quite apart from society, this conduct is incomprehensible; we cannot understand it as long as we think of the estate as an institution suspended in mid-air. We must think of it as an organ of society. The cause of it is the steadily progressing unification of society; the quickened consciousness that the lesser associations in society, which in part include one another, in part intersect one another, in part are interlaced with one another, are merely the buildingstones of a greater association, of which they become parts. The structure of every association is conditioned by the constitution of the individual associations of which it is composed. The interdependence of all social associations upon one another and the dependence of the whole upon its component parts constitute the *consensus universel* of Comte[1] and the social consensus of Herbert Spencer[2], without which the concept of society is incomprehensible, and a science of society is unthinkable.

An association which is absolutely unconditioned by anything other than itself, e.g. a clan on a distant island or in the desert, could, of course, create an order for itself quite independently. What it considers marriage, is marriage; and what it considers ownership, is ownership. This applies also to the smaller associations that constitute society

1. *consensus universel* of Comte：孔德的普遍民意（斜体为拉丁文）
2. social consensus of Herbert Spencer：斯宾塞的社会同意

to the extent that they live independently of one another. But as the associations coalesce and become members of society, the situation changes accordingly. Each association in society, and society itself, becomes more and more sensitive to everything that goes on within the associations that compose the whole. And they thereby sense something that really exists, i.e. that their existence as a whole is conditioned by the state of the parts. Doubtless a society is possible in which marriage is replaced by a much looser union of the sexes; but it would be something quite different from our present-day society. Not only the marriage relation but numberless other things will also have to undergo a radical transformation if society is to regain its equilibrium on this changed basis. The production of goods, especially in agriculture, is based to a considerable extent, and the consumption of goods is based practically altogether, upon the marriage relation and on the family, the latter of which is also based on the marriage relation; for the greater part of mankind, as is well known, still dwells, and makes provision for its sustenance, in the home. The rearing of children, the educational system, morality — all of these things would have to be provided for according to quite new principles if the demands of the various innovators in the sphere of marriage were to be acceded to. The difficulties which would be created for society by these changes cannot be estimated today. The Cyclopean wall[1] which has outlasted thousands of years is shaken if but one stone is moved out of its place. Society has rigid forms for matrimony and the family, as to which not even non-essentials may be changed lightly. At each and every innovation society trembles for the whole, and carefully eliminates everything that is found to be out of harmony with the existing situation.

This explains the endeavor of society to effect a unit ary inner order of the associations according to its needs, and upon this endeavor the

---

1. Cyclopean wall：独眼巨人墙。阿尔戈斯赫拉神庙的支撑结构。由于建造它的石块巨大，一般认为只有巨人的神力才能办到。

various kinds of general social norms are based. One may contend that each and every, even the smallest, social association, every family, every house, every village, every commune, every country, every nation, has its own law, its own religion, its morality, its ethical custom, its code of decorum, of tact, of fashion. Accordingly a person who has an accurate knowledge of the circumstances often is able to tell at the hrst glance where a certain individual belongs. Side by side with these, however, there is a law, a religion, a code of morality, of ethical custom, of tact, of decorum, of fashion, which have their origin in the larger association, and which, the latter imposes upon the smaller ones that it is composed of; and in the end norms of this kind proceed from society as a whole. Accordingly each society has legal norms of general validity through which it acts upon the inner order of the associations of which it is composed. We find everywhere not only individuals who are placed under a disadvantage by society, but also associations which are being slighted, outlawed, persecuted, e.g. marital relations; certain kinds of families; peoples; religious communities; political parties, to whom society makes life a burden; contracts which are not considered binding even by society. These norms are made effective through the same kinds of social pressure that are employed by the smaller associations in enforcing their norms against the individual. These norms, however, and especially the legal norms, do not constitute the inner order of the associations, but the inner order of society, which imposes them upon the smaller associations as an external order. This order, to a much greater extent than the inner order of the associations, bears the stamp of an order of domination, of conflict. To a great extent, it is the expression of the relation of the associations that rule in society to those that are being ruled and of the struggle of the associations that constitute organized society with those that refuse to be fitted into the organization. And a whole series of social norms by no means serves the purpose of directly creating an order in the associations, but merely of carrying the order which is created by society into the associations. They are secondary norms therefore. As long as the administration of justice has not yet been taken over by the state, the administration of justice as a whole, the procedure of the courts, which as yet are purely social, is based on such purely social secondary norms. But we meet this phenomenon even today in so far as there are social courts which are independent of the state, to wit courts of honor, courts of societies, courts of clubs, courts of arbitration. Their jurisdiction and procedure are regulated solely by social norms of the second rank. The enormous importance of the state for the law is based upon the fact that society avails itself of the state as its organ in order to give effectual support to the law that arises in society. It is not impossible to conceive a state which is independent of society. This concept has long since been expressed theoretically in the doctrine of the "social kingdom[1]." It would be a state which is composed exclusively of the sovereign, an army, and a class of civil officials — a state in which the sovereign is an absolute ruler, in which the army is blindly devoted to the latter, in which all of these are altogether out of touch with the remainder of the population, withdrawn from the influence of each and every social tendency. This is conceivable, of course, only in the case of an army of mercenaries, commanded by foreign officers, and a class of officials which is self-perpetuating and the members of which will marry only within their class. The not infrequent marriage regulations for officials and for officers of the army or of the navy are evidently prompted by the desire to make the latter independent of society, at least of certain strata of society. It would be difficult to adduce historical examples of states altogether dissevered from society. An approximation perhaps is a state which consciously places itself into opposition to society even though it be only as to one point, e.g. the government of the Emperor

1. social kingdom：社会王国理论。该理论认为国家由主权者、军队和官员构成。

Joseph II in Austria, Frederick the Great in Prussia, Peter the Great in Russia, Napoleon III in France, and perhaps the activity of Stein and Hardenberg in Prussia, of Struensee in Denmark. But even under the most favorable circumstances governmental systems of this kind have been unable to maintain themselves anywhere for any length of time; they collapsed, at the very latest, at the death of the ruler. If the ideas which they tried to realize were taken up again at a later time, this was brought about by the fact that meanwhile society had undergone such changes that at that time society itself demanded those things which formerly it would have been necessary to do against its will.

Apart from these exceptions, the state is, from almost every point of view, and particularly in matters of law, merely an organ of society. But even in an absolutist state, the sovereign, the army, the civil officials, are connected in so many ways with the influential classes and strata of society that they generally do only those things which the latter demand. If resistance to society or even an attempt to act in opposition to society should appear in the state at any point, society would find innumerable means to make its will effective. Social forces are elemental forces, against which the will of man cannot prevail, not for any length of time at least. The whole question of the constitution of the state, as Montesquieu understood it in his day, and as it has been mooted again and again since then, concerns the technical task of fashioning the state so that it may carry out the will of society with as little resistance and friction as possible. In a free state, the head of the state and the judiciary are still, in theory, independent of society; in actual fact, however, they are so restricted by the constitution and the legislature, so exposed to the influences of power, that they cannot possibly resist the trends that prevail in society.

Society utilizes the state as its organ to impose its order upon the associations belonging to it. A considerable part of the law created by the state does indeed contain norms of the first rank, which are being posited by the state as an organ of society. Norms of this kind are: the constitution of the state, the purely state norms for decision, the precepts established by the state for various departments of social and economic life (e.g. education, trades, finance). But another very important part of state law is designed exclusively for the protection of social or state law by means of norms of the second rank; this is the law of crimes and the law of procedure, since these have become state law; furthermore the *Gefährdungsverbote*[1], police precepts. Law of crimes, law of procedure and police law, therefore, contain norms of the second rank exclusively; they do not order life directly, but are designed merely to maintain the order established by other means.

It is readily understood, therefore, that state law, in all essentials, merely follows the social development. If society wishes to get rid of, exploit, or suppress a certain association, e.g. a people, a religious communion, a social rank, a class, a political party, the state with its agencies, its courts, in so far as they are dependent upon the state, and especially with its legal propositions of the second rank, the law of crimes, the law of procedure, the police law, espouses the cause of the persecutors. It dissolves societies, forbids assemblies, attacks religions, political parties, scientific doctrines, and provides a legal basis for these things through legislation. The rare exceptions, a few of which have just been mentioned, merely confirm the rule. But society will shift its position if it appears that the persons attacked cannot be overcome. It is then faced with the necessity of receiving the new cell into the old structure as well as possible. This involves an adaptation to society on the part of the association which hitherto has been the subject of attack by society; and at the same time, an adaptation on the part of society to the association. Society must recover its equilibrium. The greater part of the process therefore takes place within society itself. Another part of the task must be performed by juristic science.

---

1. *Gefährdungsverbote*：〈德〉禁止危害生命、健康与财产的法令

New legal propositions must be created for the new relation. Roman juristic science has often enough performed this duty in a splendid manner. The juristic science of the Continental common law as well as juristic science in England and France have likewise rendered outstanding services in this sphere. Lastly, the constitution of the state, the method of administrative procedure, and the state law in its entire ty must be adapted to the new order. But if the distribution of power in society is changed to such an extent that they who hitherto have been the oppressed party obtain control of the state — a thing that does not happen, of course, where there is a mere military, or palace, revolution in which case the social structure remains untouched, but only where there is a social revolution — the law of the state and the agencies of the state espouse the cause of the victors; and often enough the persecutors have become the persecuted.

In reality, therefore, the historical fact that state law is manifestly gaining ground is merely the expression of the intensified solidarity of society. As the conviction grows stronger that everything that is in society concerns society, the idea appears that it would be a great advantage if the state should prescribe a unitary legal basis for each and every independent association in society. I may be permitted to elucidate this idea by means of a few illustrations.

Let us consider the legal situation of the Roman household. Where, as here, about thirty or forty adult free persons were living together, subjected to the power of a superior, there could, self-evidently, be neither complete anarchy nor purely arbitrary rule by the head of the household. The Romans possessed too much administrative efficiency to permit either one or the other. Indeed what we do know about the Roman household shows that a firm legal order obtained therein. There were family laws which could be asserted even against the *pater familias*[1]. We know, at any rate, that the marital rights of a married

---

1. *pater familias*：〈拉〉家父。一般指对家庭中任何其他人享有家长权的人。

son of the house and of a married daughter of the house were always respected by the parents and that the *manus* belonged to the son of the house, not to the *pater familias*. The persons who were subjected to the *potestas* had their own property, which had been bestowed upon them by the holder of the *potestas*[1] or which they had acquired by their own efforts, e.g. land, cattle, business undertakings; obligatory rights existed among them; and we are told of a family court. From the point of view of Roman society, these relations, in. the beginning at any rate, were not legal relations; for society, on principle, did not concern itself about what went on within the household. Roman society knew only one kind of law the law which regulated the relation of household to household, and which was administered by the magistrate and by the court. In the course of time this situation underwent a change; for the son of the house became a business man and the goods in the house that belonged to him, his *peculium*, became the foundation of his credit. In this way, the son of the house began to assume a position in the world that lay outside of the household, and his legal position within the household became a matter of importance for trade and commerce. To this extent the inner order of the household became a part of the social law: the praetor publishes regulations concerning it in his edict, and the jurists discuss it in their writings. Finally the legislation of Imperial times directly intervenes in the relation between the bearer of the *potestas* and those *in potestate*[2], protects the son of the house against abuse of the parental power; grants to him the right to own property, which the *pater familias* cannot take away from him. The Roman law of slavery developed in a manner somewhat different but very similar in principle.

In the mediaeval system of landholding, a similar process goes on,

1. *potestas*：〈拉〉支配权
2. the bearer of the *potestas* and those *in potestate*：支配者与受支配者（斜体为拉丁文）

albeit on a much grander scale. The unfree tenants by custom of the Middle Ages surely had definite rules regulating their relations to each other and to the lord. These rules were recorded at an early day and in this way the Continental *Hof und Dienstrechte*[1], the byrlowes[2], by-laws, customs of the English manor arose. These regulations doubtless were law and they are treated as such by modern legal history. But they were law only within the association; for at the outset, seigniory[3] in mediaeval times, like the Roman house, constituted a world of its own, whose inner order was of no concern to the outside world; and as late as the seventeenth century, Coke, the English jurist, refers to the relation between the lord and the copyholder as "a little commonwealth," although in Coke's day only vestiges of this situation had remained. In the later Middle Ages, seigniory gradually merges into society generally, and, in consequence, that which originally has been law solely within the inner association of the manor, henceforth becomes a law recognized outside of the manor, and is recognized as such by mediaeval society as a whole. In this way, that which had belonged to the copyholder solely by the custom of the manor became property that was protected by the common law both in Germany and in England. A very famous passage by Lit tie ton, who about the middle of the fifteenth century wrote a work on landholding (Upon Tenures) indicates the transition by the fact that his first sentence on tenants by custom flatly contradicts what he says in the second. The passage reads as follows: "It is said that if the lord do oust them, they have no other remedy but to sue to their lords by petition, for if they should have any other remedy they should not be said to be tenants at the will of the lord, according to the custom of the manor. Tenant by the custom is as well inheritor to have his land according to the custom

1. Continental *Hof und Dienstrechte*：庄园与劳役习俗（斜体为德语）
2. byrlowes：地方法
3. seigniory：领主权

as he which hath a freehold at the common law." The second sentence, moreover, is said to be not by Littleton, but to be a later interpolation. The further development is this: ultimately the relations governed by the custom of the manor are completely merged into the law of society, the association of the manor disintegrates, and the several tenants by the custom enter into a direct relation to society.

A third example is the development of the state itself. Every great territorial state, at the beginning, consists of commonwealths which have created their own order. Up to the time of the social war, Roman Italy was merely an international law alliance of Italic city states with the city state of Rome; the modern centralized states of Europe, at first, were associations of cities and provinces, which in turn were composed of communes; and each of these city states, each province, each commune, had its traditional or its posited order which, with the exception of possible *privilegia* and city charters, had arisen and developed quite independently of the state. In Roman Italy, the change was first brought about by the creation of the *municipia*. From that time on, the order of the city was based on a Roman statute. And since the rise of the modern centralized state, the provinces are being put on a legal basis by the state, or are being completely fused with the latter, as e.g. in France and Italy; and the law of the communes is being regulated by state ordinances for the government of cities and communes. It has often been said that this did not, as a matter of fact, necessarily bring about a thoroughgoing change of law, for the Roman municipal constitution did not differ much from the constitution which had obtained until then in the Italic city states, and the modern ordinances for the government of provinces and communes, too, have often been following tradition. But it did bring about an enormous revolution in principle inasmuch as the original order of all these commonweal ths, which had been independent of the state, was replaced by an order derived from the state. Every province, every city, every commune was thereby converted from an independent living organism into a mere administrative unit of the state. The federal states of the German Empire however, down to the present day, have constitutions which have not been derived from that of the German Empire.

Now these facts are the standard according to which the prevailing concept of the nature of law is to be judged. This concept is, in the main, that a norm is a legal norm only if it has been posited by the state as a legal norm. This view has, I think, been refuted by our present discussion, for we have seen that only a small part of the law, i.e. st ate law, is, in actual fact, created by the state. As a rule, however, when writers attribute the creation of all law to the state, they mean only that a norm, whatsoever may have been its origin, becomes a legal norm only when the state recognizes it as a legal norm, and surrounds it with norms of the second rank, penal provisions, procedure, administrative regulations. If this is really a constituent element of the concept "legal norm" the formations which we have discussed hitherto, i.e. the order of the Roman household, of the mediaeval manor, of the primitive community (unless one looks upon the latter as states) are not parts of the law. One might indeed contend that the Roman son of the house (*filius familias*[1]), except in those cases in which he could, at a later time, assert his claims in court, had no *Recht*[2] (law and right). It is well known that that was not the view of the Romans, for the sources clearly show that the *manus* is in the *filius familias* and not in the bearer of the *potestas,* that the *peculium* was the property of the *filius familias* (eventually of the slaves), that *obligationes naturales*[3] could subsist between the bearer of the *potestas* and the person subject to the *potestas,* even though all of these relations were not protected by the courts — the possible protection given by the censor, which was

---

1. *filius familias*：〈拉〉家子，与家父相对的概念。
2. *Recht*：〈德〉权利
3. *obligationes naturales*：〈拉〉自然债务

not a legal protection, cannot of course, be considered here — and though legal remedies against third persons were given only to the *pater familias*. As well deny the validity of the German *Hofrechte*[1], the English manorial customs, for the tenant could not appeal to them in any court of the state. But the most accurate students of the law of the Middle Ages have expressed a different opinion, to wit: "Then as to the case between lord and tenant, the tenant cannot sue the lord in the lord's court; the tenant in villeinage[2] ejected by the lord has no remedy anywhere. But is this, we may ask, a denial of legal right? The king disseises[3] the Earl of Gloucester; the earl has no remedy anywhere; yet we do not deny that the honor of Gloucester is the earFs by law or that in disseising him the king will break the law." (Maitland.) And another, whose knowledge certainly is not inferior to that of Maitland, says: "The concept that that which the lord is under obligation to give to the man is owed to the latter in the legal sense is immanent in all Germanic law of associations. Enforcible duties however arose from this situation only in case a higher power in the association was authorized to intervene for the protection of the rights of the members of the association. Nevertheless in all cases the conduct of the bearer of the power who refuses to grant to the person subjected to the power that which the latter is entitled to or demands something that he is not authorized to demand is considered a violation of law (*Unrechi*)." (Gierke.)

The view that law is created by the state therefore will not bear the test of historical analysis. And we may therefore say that it has been refuted; for if it be essential to the concept of law that it be created by the state, how could it have been in existence without the state throughout long epochs of history? The only remaining question is

1. *Hofrechte*：〈德〉领主法
2. villeinage：农奴土地保有
3. disseises：强夺

whether the concept which we associate with the term law is of such a nature that the view that the law is created by the state can be justified. It seems necessary therefore to form a clear idea of its significance in every detail.

In all spheres of life we find relations which in every respect are like those which the state recognizes, regulates, protects, and to which the state is by no means opposed, but for whose protection it has provided no legal remedy. Among these are numerous economic, social, and religious associations, political bodies, and many a contract. In addition there are similar phenomena in the law of things and in the law of inheritance. In a limited measure, this is true, in the German civil law, of an association that does not possess legal capacity. The so-called "freedom of coalition" of the working classes in the second half of the nineteenth century was based on the same idea. The state by no means disapproves, nay, perhaps it actually approves, of the idea that men as a matter of justice and law proceed according to a certain order, but its will is that they should do this voluntarily or solely under social pressure. Very often it is merely a matter of the technical difficulty of finding an adequate juristic rule and an adequate form for the legal protection; the relation is not "juristically" construable. This is frequently true in the case of rights, particularly of special rights of the members of juristic persons, of the rights of the beneficiaries of a given foundation or institution. The German jurists, for example, were unable to fit the duty to supply beets, which is incumbent upon the shareholders in a beetsugar factory, into their legal system; and the Austrian jurists are unable, even today, to fit the South Slavic Sadruga[1] into their legal system. Similar technical difficulties are standing in the way of recognition of the *Tarifvertrag*[2]. Moreover it happens occasionally that people intentionally decline the legal protection of

---

1. Sadruga：家长制公社
2. *Tarifvertrag*：〈德〉集体劳动合同

institutions which they have created although they might enjoy it. This was done for a long time in the case of the English trade unions, and is being done in the case of the Roman Catholic church in France today. Writers who have expert knowledge of the sit nation in France say that this attitude strengthens the church considerably, e.g. Bureau, in his book *La séparation de l'Eglise et de l'Etat*[1]. In the case of cartels and trusts it seems that both sides object to legal protection by the state. And contracts are occasionally entered into, and testamentary provisions made, in such a way that, according to the declared will of the person making the disposition, no legally enforceable claim can arise therefrom.

Still more important is the fact that the greater part of legal life goes on in a sphere far removed from the state, the state tribunals, and state law. What is the important consideration here? It is clear, to begin with, that the confused mass of statutes cannot possibly cover the variegated diversity of legal life. New communities, new relations of possession, new contracts, new regula tions as to inheritance, all as yet unknown to the statutes, are continually coming into existence even today, just as they did in the hoary past. Must these relations wait until they receive mention in a statute before they can become legal relations, in spite of the fact that the basic institutions of our society furnished the order for the affairs of mankind for thousands of years without this aid? And what of the enforceability of these claims by courts or by other tribunals? In the long run it is only a very few of the incalculable number of the relations of human life that attract the attention of the courts and of other tribunals. There are millions of human beings who enter into untold legal relations, and who are fortunate enough never to find it necessary to appeal for aid to a tribunal of any sort. Since the relation which has never

---

1. *La séparation de l'Eglise et de l'État*：〈法〉《教会与国家的分离》

come into contact with legislation and judicial adjudication, after all, is the normal relation, it follows that in the very cases that constitute the rule, everything would be lacking that is necessary to det ermine whether we are dealing with a legal relation or not. Moreover the line of demarcation between that which the courts and the other tribunals are able to do and that which they think they must leave undone is continually shifting; and this shifting is brought about not only by legislation, but also by actual usage. Should every change of this nature, should every variation, imperceptible though it be, react upon all the relations which have never been and never should be brought to the attention of the courts?

After all, even today there are two legal systems which are absolutely independent of the state, or, to be more accurate, independent of state legislation, state adjudication, and state administration. These are ecclesiastical law and international law. A person to whom law always means state law could not regard ecclesiastical law as law unless it is state ecclesiastical law. But this is in conflict with the general view which, as we know, is the strongest support of the prevailing doctrine. Ecclesiastical law is law, irrespective of what the attitude of the state may be, for the reason that it is the legal order of the church. And ecclesiastical law has lost nothing of its legal quality through a complete separation of the church from the state, such as obtains in France. Likewise the opposition to the recognition of the legal nature of international law has been silenced altogether. It was based, from the very beginning, not upon a scientific investigation of the nature of law in general and of international law in particular but exclusively upon the fact that the latter did not fit into a readymade pattern.

If the ideal of the most advanced state socialist should be realized; if all goods were produced by the state in state-owned workshops through its employes, and furthermore if these goods were distributed by the state through its employes among those entitled to consume them, then indeed we should have a system of law which is state law in the fullest sense of the term, not merely a few legal propositions which have been created by the state. In that case, state legal institutions will have taken the place of ownership and contract as well as of private production and private exchange of goods. A picture of a commonwealth whose law is exclusively state law is presented by Bellamy, the American writer, in his utopian *Looking Backward*[1]. Whether we should be happier in such a state, we shall not discuss here. At any rate the present discussion has shown that as yet we are far from a state of that description.

The view, therefore, that all law is state law is scientifically untenable. It is based, in part, upon the fact that, by means of certain utterly impermissible artifices, its proponents refer every legal norm, whatsoever may be its nature, and from whatsoever source it may be derived, and by whatsoever means it may preserve its existence, to the state, and upon the fact that, in part, they forcibly close their eyes to the great mass of law that has come into being independently of the state and exists independently of the state. But the highly one-sided concept of law which has come into existence thereby has exerted a fateful influence upon true scientific study as well as upon practical juristic science and upon the teaching of law, not only inasmuch as it is false in itself, but inasmuch as it has deprived the investigator of the law of a field of investigation which is highly stimulating and extremely fruitful By confining the attention of the investigator to the state, to tribunals, to statutes, and to procedure, this concept of law has condemned the science of law to the poverty under which it has been suffering most terribly down to the present day. Its further development presupposes liberation from these shackles and a study of the legal norm not only in its connection with the state but also in its social connection.

Wherever the legal norm attracted the attention of the sociologist,

1. utopian *Looking Backward*：乌托邦小说《回顾》，美国作家贝拉米（1850—1898）的作品。

irrespective of whether it was a matter of tracing its origin, of determining the concept, of examining its social function, it has always been found in the company of other social norms. Nevertheless there can be no doubt that there is an unmistakable difference between it and the non-legal norms. It is as impossible to deny the existence of this difference as it is difficult, in view of the present state of the science of law, to indicate precisely wherein it consists; and the object of the discussion that follows is rather to define the problem than to offer a solution. This problem is not peculiar to the law; for indeed one is also under the necessity of instituting inquiry as to how ethics differs from religion and ethical custom, how the latter differs from decorum and tact, how decorum and tact differ from honor or etiquette, how etiquette differs from fashion. On the other hand the lines of demarcation between the various kinds of norms are undoubtedly somewhat arbitrary. Here as everywhere else the concepts do not lie in the nature of things, and every sharp line of distinction is imported into things by man. Within the various species of norms there are sub-species which constitute the transition from one group to the other, and in the case of many a phenomenon it is scarcely possible to determine accurately to which group it belongs.

Difficult though it may be to draw the line with scientific exactitude between the legal norm and other kinds of norms, practically this difficulty exists but rarely. In general anyone will be in position to tell without hesitation whether a given nonn is a legal norm or whether it belongs to the sphere of religion, ethical custom, morality, decorum, tact, fashion, or etiquette. This fact must be made the basis of the discussion. The question as to the difference between the legal and the non-legal norm is a question not of social science but of social psychology. The various classes of norms release various overtones of feeling[1], and we react to the transgression of different norms with

1. various overtones of feeling：不同的情感反应

different feelings. Compare the feeling of revolt that follows a violation of law with the indignation at a violation of a law of morality, with the feeling of disgust occasioned by an indecency, with the disapproval of tactlessness, the ridiculousness of an offense against etiquette, and lastly with the critical feeling of superiority with which a votary of fashion looks down upon those who have not attained the heights which he has scaled. Peculiar to the legal norm is the reaction for which the jurists of the Continental common law have coined the term *opinio necessitatis*[1]. This is the characteristic feature which enables one to identify the legal norm.

But the question arises at once what has caused the variety of overtones of feeling as reactions to violations of the various species of norms? We find that norms with apparently identical content, at different times, in different countries, in different classes and ranks of society, manifestly belong to different groups, and that they readily pass from one group to another. In the course of the millennia the prohibition of marriage outside of one's own rank has been a norm of law, of religion, of morality, of ethical custom, of decorum, and today, perhaps, it is merely a norm of tact, of etiquette, or even of fashion. At the present time, judging from the overtones of feeling that are released, it is based among the Polish nobility upon the code of morals prevailing there; among the Austrian nobility upon the conceptions of decorum; among the French nobility upon their ideas of etiquette. It prevails, perhaps, in the same locality at the same time with widely divergent effects. A marriage of the young farmer to his maidservant may be looked upon as an offense against morality; that of the merchant prince to his servant-girl, as a violation of the rules of etiquette. How can we account for these different reactions? In the first place by the different structure of the various social classes in question,

---

1. *opinio necessitatis*：〈拉〉法律确信，是一种认为某行为是法律义务的信念。

and the different structure of the same social classes at different times and in different countries. But the assumption is obvious that where there is a difference in the structure of the community in which the norm is valid, the norm, though it retains its wording unchanged, nevertheless serves a different purpose and accordingly has a changed content.

On the other hand, it is easy to convince oneself that, though a norm of the same wording can indeed belong to two different groups, it has a different content in each case. The agreement in wording therefore is a purely external thing. The proposition, "Honor thy father and thy mother," can be considered a command of law, of morality, of religion, of ethical custom, of decorum, of tact, of etiquette, and of fashion. As a legal norm it commands a child to honor his parents by means of certain outward demonstrations; as a norm of morality, in general, by means of conduct evincing honor and respect. Religion, unless it simply repeats the command of morality, prescribes religious duties in addition, espedaily prayers for one's father and one's mother. Ethical custom demands that one show such respect for one's parents as is customary in good families. As a norm of decorum it forbids such omission of manifestations of respect as would be offensive to others; as a norm of tact it disapproves of much less serious offenses which might release a feeling of displeasure among those that happen to be present. Etiquette refers solely to deportment toward one's father and mother in society. If respectful demeanor toward one's parents were fashionable at a given time in fashionable circles, a person moving in these circles who should omit it would be guilty of an offense against fashion.

At any rate one must not state the difference between law and morals, as is frequently done today, as consisting in this, that law is heteronomous; morals, autonomous; that law is imposed from without; morals comes from within. All norms as rules of conduct — and they are to be considered here only as such — are autonomous and heteronomous at the same time. They are heteronomous, for they originate in the associations; they are autonomous, for their basis is the attitude of the individuals of whom the association is composed. The norms are autonomous also in the sense that obedience to the norms is considered of full value only when its proceeds from a conviction which has been given shape by the norms. This is the true kernel of Bierling's *Anerkennungslehre* (doctrine of recognition)[1]. A norm, whether it be a legal norm or a norm of some other kind, must be *recognized* in the sense that men actually regulate their conduct according to it. A system of law or of ethics that no one gives heed to is like a fashion that no one follows. Only we must bear in mind that what has been said about the rule of conduct must not be applied to the norm for decision; for courts may at any time draw forth a legal proposition which has been slumbering for centuries and make it the basis of their decisions. And we must not conceive of this doctrine as Bierling did, as implying that the norm must be recognized by each individual. The norms operate through the social force which recognition by a social association imparts to them, not through recognition by the individual members of the association. Even the moral anarchist[2], if he is well advised, will conform to the norms which prevail in the community; perhaps, as indeed happens occasionally, with gnashing of teeth and vociferous imprecations upon the hypocrisy of society, prompted, nevertheless, by consideration of his own interest; if for no other reason, because he does not wish to lose the advantages which he gains by doing so, because lie wishes to avoid the disadvantages incident to rebellion.

The sociological science of law, therefore, will not be able to state the difference between law and morals in a brief simple formula in the manner of the juristic science that has hitherto been current. Only a thorough examination of the psychic and social facts, which at the present time have not even been gathered, can shed light upon

1. *Anerkennungslehre* (doctrine of recognition)：〈德〉认可原则
2. anarchist：无政府主义者

this difficult question. Though we are well aware of the great degree of caution made imperative by the present state of juristic science, we may perhaps be permitted to assume, at this time, the following essential characteristics of law. The legal norm regulates a matter which, at least in the opinion of the group within which it has its origin, is of great importance, of basic significance. The individual act which is commanded by the legal proposition may not be of great weight, as for instance in the case of statutes regulating foods, or concerning prevention of fires or infectious diseases of cattle, but we must always consider the consequences if violations of these statutes should assume the dimension of a mass phenomenon. Only matters of lesser significance are left to other social norms. Therefore the proposition, "Thou shalt honor thy father and thy mother" is considered a legal proposition only where the organization of the state and of society is based chiefly on the order of the family. A community which conceives of God as being in an immediate relation to its affairs will be inclined to elevate religious norms to the rank of legal norms. On the other hand, the legal norm, as contrasted with the other norms, can always be stated in clear definite terms. It thereby gives a certain stability to the associations that are based on legal norms, whereas associations not based on legal norms, e. g. political parties, religious communions, groups of relatives, social relations, are characterized by a looseness, a lack of stability, until they assume a legal form. Norms of morality, too, of ethical custom, of decorum, often become legal norms as soon as they lose their universal character, and, couched in clear precise terms, assume basic significance for the legal order of society. In this way, the Roman *prudentes* and the praetor often succeeded in introducing them into the legal system; in this way, equity[1] arose in England, which is today a system of law as fully developed

1. equity：衡平法

as the common law. It may well be possible therefore that the normal precept of good faith in contractual relations may, in the course of time, be compressed into a series of definite and clear legal propositions.

Correct observation therefore underlies the habit of speaking of the heteronomy of law and of the autonomy of morals[1]. This is not a matter of essential characteristics but of differences of degree. In the case of legal norms, society devotes much more thought to the matter of formulating than in the case of norms of morals and of the other non-legal norms; in view of the importance it attaches to law it is anxious to have not merely a general direction, but a detailed precept. Everyone ought to be able to know from the mere wording of the legal norm how he is to regulate his conduct in a given case; whereas the non-legal norms, couched as they are, in general terms, are little more than general guides; and on this basis, everyone must make his own rules of conduct in the individual case. It is true therefore that, in case of norms of morality, it is to a much greater extent a matter of the inner attitude of mind than in the case of law. A man without any inner sense of law knows how to perform his duties as a citizen of the state, knows that he must perform his contracts, respect the property right of others; but in order to be able to conduct himself correctly from the point of view of morals, religion, ethical custom, decorum, etiquette, and fashion, he requires a sense of morality, religion, ethical custom, decorum, tact, etiquette, and fashion. Without this sense, he cannot hit upon the correct thing. For this reason, when non-legal norms are involved, the center of gravity is inwardly within a man's self to a much greater extent than when legal norms are involved.

If we bear these characteristics in mind, it may be possible to give a more exact definition of the legal norm. Legal norms are those norms

1. heteronomy of law and of the autonomy of morals：法律他律与道德自律

that flow from the facts of the law, to wit from usages, which assign to each member of the social association his position and function, from the relations of domination and subjection, from the relations arising from possession, from articles of association, from contracts, from testamentary and other dispositions; furthermore, those norms are legal norms that arise from the legal propositions of state and of juristic law. The *opinio necessitatis* is found only in connection with these, and therefore we may say there are no legal norms other than these. But this proposition is not convertible. Not all norms that arise in this way are legal norms. In the first place legal propositions contain much that is not norm but "*unverbindlicher Gesetzesinhalt*[1]," Again there are norms that flow from legal propositions and from facts of the law, which however do not belong to the sphere of law, but of ethics, of ethical custom (regulations as to clothing), of honor (compulsory dueling among officers). Even religious dogmas have been posited by statute. These characteristics therefore do not furnish a positive delimitation of legal norms from other norms. Such delimitation would require first of all a thorough study of the nature of the non-legal norms.

Whether we can consider a norm which is socially valid but which violates a prohibition issued by the state a legal norm in the sociological sense, is a question of social power. The decisive question in this connection is whet her or not it releases the overtones of feeling which are peculiar to the legal norm, the *opinio necessitatis* of the common law jurists. It is precisely in this matter that the juristic science of the Continental common law, in a manner deserving our deepest gratitude, has prepared the ground for the work of the sociology of law through its doctrine of the so-called abrogative power of customary law; it has assumed and demonstrated that

1. *unverbindlicher Gesetzesinhalt*：〈德〉非义务性法律内容

legal propositions that are in conflict with the legal consciousness may languish and die. Let me cite as illustrations the fate of many a penal provision of the *Carolina*, the Prussian order in cabinet cited by Adickes, which provided the death penalty for handing a petition to the king in person; the order of the Austrian council of ministers, which declared that the possession and the acquisition of money tokens of the revolutionary propaganda, e.g. of Mazzini ducats[1], Kossuth dollar notes[2], which one can now purchase as curiosities in the shops of Vienna, was high treason. In general, a legal relation entered into in spite of a legal prohibition, a forbidden society, a forbidden contract, a forbidden marriage, a forbidden testamentary gift, a forbidden club, will not be considered legal institutions. Compulsory dueling also is not considered such even among officers of the army or navy. It is otherwise when a transaction which the state has not prohibited but merely treats as ineffective becomes common in society generally, e.g. marriage entered into by church ceremony only, the unrecorded transfer of land, the *Treuhandgeschäft*[3], as a form of testamentary disposition. These, as experience has shown, can readily compel recognition by society as legal institutions; and, in the course of time, by the courts and the state.

1. Mazzini ducats：马志尼硬币
2. Kossuth dollar notes：科苏特纸币
3. *Treuhandgeschäft*：〈德〉信托

VIII THE CREATION OF THE LEGAL PROPOSITION

The most diversified content may be clothed in the form of a legal proposition, in particular, in the form of a statute. There are therefore legal propositions without any normative content whatsoever, with a non-obligatory legal content, statutes in a purely formal sense. And there are legal propositions from which no legal norms can be derived, but only social norms of some other kind. We shall not discuss either of these species, but only legal propositions which contain legal norms. Their purpose is to serve as the basis for judicial decisions or for direct administrative action.

Every legal proposition which is to serve as the basis for judicial decisions is itself a norm for decision, formulated in words, and published in an authoritative manner, asserting claim to universal validity, but without reference to the case that may have occasioned it. The prevailing school of juristic science treats the judicial decision as a logical syllogism[1] in which a legal proposition is the major premise[2]; the matter litigated[3], the minor; and the judgment of the court, the conclusion. This idea presupposes that every judgment is preceded in time by a legal proposition. Historically this is quite incorrect. The judge who, in the beginnings of the administration of justice, awards a penalty to the plaintiff has found the existence of a concrete

1. logical syllogism：逻辑上的三段论
2. a legal proposition is the major premise：法律命题是大前提。
3. the matter litigated, the minor：诉讼事项是小前提。

relation of domination and subjection, a relation of possession, a usage, or a contract, and a violation thereof, and thereupon has independently found the norm fixing the penalty. Perhaps in each of these decisions the thought is germinating that in a similar situation, a like or a similar decision ought to be arrived at; but this germ at this time is buried deep in the subliminal consciousness[1] of the judge. If we assume that the judge in primitive times protected possession or contract only because he had assumed the existence of a legal proposition according to which possession or contract ought to be protected by law, we are attributing our own conception to him. He thinks only of the concrete, not of the abstract. The legal historian, who is trying to gather the law of the past from such judgments, may at most read out of them that which was universal, the universal usage, but not that which was universally valid. Nevertheless, in spite of the lack of legal propositions, the norm for decision was not a matter of pure caprice. The judge always drew it from the facts of the law, which had been established either on the basis of his own knowledge or of evidence, i.e. from usages, from relations of domination and of possession, from declarations of will, and, chiefly, from contracts. Given these facts, the norm was given; it was impossible to separate the question of fact from the question of law.

Today we have the identical situation when there is no legal proposition in existence for the case that is to be decided. The judge can only ascertain the existence of the usages, of the relations of domination, of the legal relations, of the contract, of the articles of association, of the testamentary disposition involved in the litigation, and on this basis find a legal norm independently. Neither the ascertainment of the facts nor the free finding of the norm for decision appears as a subsumption of the case in litigation under a proposition

1. subliminal consciousness：潜意识

relating to possession. All attempts to construe, all artificial heaping up of paragraph upon paragraph of a code, can deceive only a biassed mind as to the truth that a decision according to a legal proposition is possible only where there is a legal proposition already in existence.

It is true, according to juristic terminology the question to be determined in a case of this kind is one of fact and not of law. But the judicial decision was rendered not only on the basis of the facts ascertained but also on the basis of a norm for decision which the judge had drawn from the facts. This norm for decision, indeed, is not as yet a legal proposition. It lacks the formulation in words, the claim to universal validity, the authoritative publication, but it is a part of the valid law, for if this were not true the judge would have no authority to decide the litigation according to it. Even in this case therefore the question of fact cannot be separated from the question of law.

But even where a legal proposition has been found which covers the instant case, the legal proposition does not yield the decision without more ado. The legal proposition is always couched in general terms; it can never be as concrete as the case itself. It may define the term "accessories (*Zubehör*)[1]" never so minutely, the question still remains whether the subject of the litigation falls within this definition or not. Here too the judge must ascertain the facts; here too he must decide independently whether the ascertained facts correspond to the definition of "accessories" contained in the legal proposition. Whether the judge answers this question in the affirmative or in the negative, the judgment is always rendered on the basis of a norm for decision which he has found independently, and which decides the question whether or not the subject mat ter of the litigation is part of the "accessories." Even where this norm for decision merely individualizes the content of the legal proposition in concrete form, it is nevertheless not identical with the

1. accessories (*Zubehör*)：从物

norm found in the legal proposition; for the question what constitutes "accessories" is something differen t from the question whet her a certain object is a part of the "accessories." In such a case, the prevailing tendency in juristic science invariably assumes that we have a decision as to a question of law; one speaks of a question of fact only where the subsumption under the legal proposition is not controverted or is incontrovertible. But it is clear that in this case, as in the earlier cases, the question of fact, the ascertained facts, cannot be dissociated from the question of law, the norm for decision which the judge has found at this very moment. This concrete norm for decision, which the judge has deduced from the facts, is introduced between the legal proposition which contains the general norm for decision and the ascertainment of the facts by the judge.

Whether the judge, therefore arrives at his decision independently of a legal proposition or on the basis of a legal proposition, he must find a norm for decision; only, in the latter case, the judicial norm for decision is determined by the norm contained in the legal proposition, whereas in the former case it will be found quite independently. The more concrete the legal proposition, the more precisely the judicial norm of decision will be determined by the norm of the legal proposition; the more general the legal proposition, the more independently and the more freely the judicial norm will be found. But there are legal propositions which grant an unlimited discretion to the judge. Examples of this kind in private law are the legal propositions on abuse of a legal right[1], on *großes und leichtes Verschulden*[2], on good faith, on unjust enrichment. In criminal law and in administrative law they also play an important part. In these cases, the legal proposition does indeed appear to contain a norm for decision; actually, however, it is merely a direction to the judge to find a norm for decision independently. It is as if the legal norm

1. abuse of a legal right：权利滥用
2. *großes und leichtes Verschulden*：〈德〉涉及重大与轻微过失的行为

left the decision to the free discretion of the judge. These cases seem to belong to the second group. This however is a matter of appearance only; in reality they belong to the former, where the judge finds the decision freely. The upshot of all of this is that the difference between a decision according to a legal proposition and one not according to a legal proposition is a difference of degree merely. The judge is never delivered up to the legal proposition, bound hand and foot, without any will of his own, and the more general the legal proposition, the greater the freedom of the judge.

Every norm for decision contains the germ of a legal proposition. Reduced to that part of its content that is basic principle, couched in words, proclaimed authoritatively with a claim to universal validity, the norm for decision becomes a legal proposition. This is true even where it is merely a concrete individualization of the concept contained in the legal proposition. Let us say, for example, that the norm has declared that a certain object is subsumed under the legal concept of "accessories"; there lies in this declaration the germ of the legal proposition that objects of this kind are always "accessories." Considering the matter historically, we may say that most legal propositions arose out of norms for decision. As to the greater part of our codes we can show positively how the legal propositions were extracted from the decisions contained in the *corpus iuris*; and where the *corpus iuris* does not state decisions, but legal propositions, these, with rare exceptions, undoubtedly have had their origin in norms for decision which were first enunciated by a jurist when a dispute was submitted to him for decision.

It is possible that now and then legal propositions were thought out by jurists without reference to a definite decision. The rule of the Prussian law about the "*Erbschatz*[1]" perhaps arose in this way; for,

---

1. *Erbschatz*：〈德〉一种共同生活期间共用的财产

according to credible reports, an "*Erbschatz*" has never been met with, either before or after; the same may be said of the so-called *Schulfälle*[1] (moot cases). Of course these can be only very insignificant legal propositions. We can also say that a legal proposition is prior in time to the norms for decision where a statute regulates an institution in order to introduce it, particularly where the latter is imported from a foreign country, as, for instance, the statute concerning companies with limited liability or the statute containing the *Höferecht*[2] of the Austrian peasants. But apart from these exceptions the concrete, as is usual, is prior to the abstract; the norm for decision, to the legal proposition.

The creation of a legal proposition out of the norms for decision requires that further intellectual effort be applied to the latter; for we must extract from them that which is universally valid and state it in a proper manner. This intellectual labor, whosoever it may be that is able to do it, is called juristic science. The Historical School of jurisprudence has taken infinite pains to show how "customary law," or, to put it more accurately, legal propositions of "customary law," arise immedia tely in the popular consciousness. It is a vain endeavor. Lambert has shown conclusively that with the exception perhaps of legal maxims, legal propositions do not arise in the popular consciousness itself. Legal propositions are created by jurists, preponderantly on the basis of norms for decision found in the judgments of courts. The judge therefore who, when he gives the reasons for his decision, states the norm for decision in the form in which it is to be binding in future cases, may be said to be engaged in juristic labor. Judge-made law is always merely a subdivision of juristic law. Juristic science is created by the writer or teacher, an Eyke von Repgow or a Bratton, who endeavors to extract the law of his day from the judicial decisions; and he does this even where, as

1. *Schulfälle*：〈德〉模拟法庭案件
2. *Höferecht*：〈德〉农村继承法

editor of a collection of decisions, he states the legal propositions that are derived from the decision in the form of a head note, or where, as editor of a statute, he adds them to the various sections in the form of annotations. And *a fortiori*[1] we may speak of juristic science when a juristic writer or teacher, in his writings or in his teaching, states the legal propositions which in his opinion are applicable to the cases he is discussing. And lastly the legislator who puts the norms for decision into statutory form is also engaged in scientific juristic labor, provided they contain more than mere state law. And every such legal proposition, wheresoever it may have had its origin, lays claim to universal validity. This is self-evident; for it would be a senseless procedure to write down, teach, or publish as a statute a legal proposition without the intent that it should be valid in all cases to which it is applicable. To be sure, as a rule, only the legislator has the power to make his will prevail. In the case of a judge or a writer the value of the performance is decisive of the success of his intellectual labor. If the legal proposition is good and practical, its chances of gaining recognition are as fair as the chances of a good and practical idea in any other sphere, perhaps as fair as the chances of a good and practical invention. The few words of Pomponius[2] on the *disputatio fori*[3] illustrate a process which may be considered fairly typical. The legal proposition is accepted not *ratione imperii*[4] but *imperio rationis*[5].

After all, as daily experience shows, the success of a thought in every field of human activity does not depend exclusively upon its inner value but also upon certain out ward circumstances, particularly upon the weight generally attached to the words of the person who has given

---

1. *a fortiori*：〈拉〉更有理由
2. Pomponius：彭波尼（130—180），罗马法学家，其大量作品收录入《学说汇编》。
3. *disputatio fori*：〈拉〉当庭辩论
4. *ratione imperii*：〈拉〉权力压制
5. *imperio rationis*：〈拉〉理性权威

utterance to the thought. This weight very often increases with the power of the author of the legal proposition in the state, his position, and his personal reputation. In several countries a definite usage has developed as to this matter. Occasionally this usage is well set tied; usually it is rather uncertain. This side of the question was discussed exhaustively by Lambert with an admirable knowledge of the literature on the question in his work *La fonction du droit civil comparé*[1]; I have done this as to the Romans in my *Beitrage zur Theorie der Rechtsquellen.* Under different names and under very different attendant circumstances; four kinds of persons have attained to prominent positions in history. They are: the judge, the juristic writer and teacher, the legislator, and the official who has been ent rusted with this matter by the state. In order that the norm may become a legal proposition, it must pass through the alembic of juristic science, judicial, literary, legislative, or magisterial.

The prevailing Continental doctrine, at the present time at least, denies, it is true, that the judge has the right to call new legal propositions into being. It contends that new law can originate only in the popular consciousness in the form of customary law and in legislation; that the function of the judge is merely to apply the statute; that judicial decisions are merely juristic literature, interpretations of existing law, to be rejected wherever they purport to do more than this. Indeed the Continental commonlaw juristic science of the Historical School has quite consistently dealt with judicial decision in this way. Its older representatives, Savigny, Puchta, Vangerow, and Brinz, paid no attention to it at all; the later ones, particularly Windscheid, as a rule merely inquired whether the decisions are in accord with the *corpus iuris,* and which of the points of view represented in juristic literature they follow. Over and above this, they regarded them merely

1. *La fonction du droit civil comparé*：〈法〉《比较民法的功能》

as evidence of the customary law. Even Seuffert's *Archiv*[1] in its first volumes reprints chiefly the literary discussions contained in the decisions. But all of this was mere theory; in actual fact one always felt that judicial decisions are something more than, and different from, juristic literature. Demand was always being made that the administration of law should be stable, a demand which is quite incomprehensible from the point of view of the prevailing trend in jurisprudence. If the judge is to follow the statutes and the customary law exclusively, he cannot, at the same time, follow principles which have not been laid down by statute or by customary law, but by another judge. If we demand that the judge should not depart from previous decisions, in order that the administration of justice may be stable, the decisions are more than literature, more than non-obligatory literary views on the interpretation of a statute or the construction of a case at law; they are judge-made law.

The case of scientific law is different. It is a matter of elementary truth that science can only know that which is, and cannot command what should be, that science therefore creates no norms, but merely investigates, presents, and teaches. The question as to creative juristic science must therefore be formulated in a way quite different from that in which this is usually done. The question is not whether new law arises from the knowledge of law, but whether the jurist, as a person versed in the law, claims the right to create new law. It is self-evident that this question can be answered historically only, and the answer will be in the afirrmative wherever juristic science is not content to be limited to making a most faithful and unprejudiced presentation of that which is law, but strives, over and above this, to create norms independently which shall be binding upon the judges for all cases for which none can be found in the other sources of law.

1. *Archiv*：〈德〉档案

Among the Romans, juristic science was a science of this kind, i.e. a science which is always creative, even when it is not conscious of it. It came into vogue in all common law countries when the Roman law was received. As late as its last classical period, which indeed was limited to Germany, the juristic science of the common law produced an abundance of new legal material, of which the German Civil Code affords an approximate idea. It is strange that hitherto no one has undertaken the grateful task of sifting the content of the Code historically and of showing the contribution that was made by the juristic science of the Continental common law. The juristic science of the Orientals (Islamic, Hindu) and at least the older science of the Scandinavians (the *Rechtsprecher*[1]) may perhaps be of this kind, as Lambert has shown. On the whole it is very rarely limited altogether to receiving and stating law. In the main it is such only among the present-day English; less so; it seems, among the Americans.

Great differences, indeed, appear in details. It is self-evident that the importance of science is in an inverse ratio[2] to that of the statute and that of the judge; the higher the position of the judge the greater the jealousy with which he guards his independence; the more omnipotent and comprehensive[3] legislation, the more limited the sphere it is willing to concede to the jurist. For this reason juristic science declines whenever a codification has been made and does not awaken to a new life until the people become aware of defects and gaps in the latter. The jurist tries to influence the judge through his opinions, his teaching, and his writings, and through his criticism of judicial decisions; he either finds norms for the decision of the individual case or seeks to set up general principles, in the manner of the traditional juristic technique, which may serve as guides for the

1. *Rechtsprecher*：〈德〉法律的裁制者
2. in an inverse ratio：成反比
3. omnipotent and comprehensive：无所不能与全面的

judge in the decision of individual cases. All these forms occur in the course of history. In Rome the influence of the jurists was based at first solely perhaps on their activity as *prudentes*, giving *responsa* as to individual cases[1]; thereafter also on their activity as teachers of law; in later Imperial times, preponderantly on their literary works. The importance of the Continental common law juristic science consisted chiefly in the literary process of extracting general principles which were to guide the judge in the decision of individual cases. In most recent times, jurists have regained an established position as critics through the annotations which they have appended to the judicial decisions in the great collections of reported cases. These critics, the *arrêtistes*[2], have made the study of French judicial decision their life's work; in their annotations they are attempting to give, in addition to a detailed scientific critique, a history of the course of decision on the question as to which the judicial decision has been rendered. The originator of this tendency is Labbe, one-time professor of Roman Law at the University of Paris. A most attractive history of the *arretistes* is given by Meynial in the *Livre de Centenaire du Code Civil*[3].

It is self-evident that where scientific or judge-made law prevails there must be valid traditional or established criteria governing the evaluation of judicial or juristic decisions. Of course it could never have been the understanding that in general every judicial decision and every opinion of a jurist should be binding as such. In the case of judge-made law perhaps the official position of the judge is decisive, as a rule; in the case of juristic law there is very often no external criterion; the question is decided by the value of the work, or — a circumstance that often has no bearing on the value — the reputation

1. giving *responsa* as to individual cases：对个案的解答
2. *arrêtistes*：〈法〉判例评注汇编者
3. *Livre de Centenaire du Code Civil*：〈法〉《民法典百年文集》

of the author. The statements of Pomponius in the *Enchiridion*[1] afford an insight into the manner in which a jurist of the Republican era achieved the reputation which a *conditor iuris*[2] was required to have until the matter was finally settled in the days of the emperors. In England there is a definitely fixed regulation as to the binding quality of judicial decisions. In general the decision of a higher court prevails over that of a lower court, but the "great judges" whose names have become historical are being cited with an incomparably greater measure of reverence than the great multitude of the others.

A limitation exists, however, beyond which the judge and the legal writer must not go. Their decisions must be in harmony with the principles of the existing valid law and of juristic science. Its function is therefore often, though not always, conceived to be this: It is not to create new law, but to discover the principles and rules of justice already existing in the law. Flexible and elastic though this limitation may appear, it must not be overlooked; for it, as well as the limitation of the statute, is an expression of the strong conviction that the judge and the jurist are qualified to build on the foundation of the existing legal order, but not to shake it or substitute another for it. The remark is often found in French juristic literature that the famous article 1382 of the French Civil Code would suffice for the solution of the social question. Now the enormous power which this article entrusted to the French judge was used by him to create a judge-made law of damages which, in its basic outlines, is perfectly clear and consistent, and which is essentially new, although formally at least it is based on the existing law. But no attempt was ever made to utilize it for the solution of the social problem or for the introduction of any revolutionary innovation into the legal system. And one may safely set one's mind at rest, for such an attempt will never be made. It will not be made

---

1. *Enchiridion*：罗马法《教本》
2. *conditor iuris*：〈拉〉法的建设者

for the same reason that an attempt of this kind has never been made under normal circumstances. The introduction of the English common law into Ireland through a judicial decision (case Gavelkind[1]) is even today regarded as a daring Cossack *coup de main*[2]; and in that case a people which had been crushed by defeat was involved; furthermore it was done at the command of the victor, who has often enough had occasion to regret it. A similar attempt in Bengal[3] failed; the judge and the sovereign power of the state had to yield in the face of a general uprising. The power of the judge is not sufficient to overcome the enormous powers of resistance inherent in society which would rise up in opposition to an attempt to place society on a new foundation by means of a judicial pronouncement; and a judge requires knowledge of the world sufficient to be able correctly to estimate these powers of resistance as well as his own power. The judge has often, it is true, disregarded the law in the service of an unscrupulous sovereign power; occasionally, supported by the law, he has been able to offer successful resistance to a strong sovereign power; but he has never risked a conbat with the state, society, and traditional law. Much less has juristic science, with its limited powers, ever done this.

Both judicial and scientific law are always subject to the critical inquiry whether they have remained within the limitations with which they are hedged about — a criticism which has given the quietus to many an attempted innovation. Great though the power of the Roman jurists may have been, it would never have sufficed to abolish the Praetorian law of succession[4] or the *fideicommissa*[5], perhaps not even the *actio de effusis et deiectis*[6]; and Pollock says of the English judge:

1. case Gavelkind：肯特郡土地保有习惯案
2. Cossack *coup de main*：哥萨克突袭（斜体为拉丁文）
3. Bengal：孟加拉国
4. Praetorian law of succession：继承的裁判官法
5. *fideicommissa*：〈拉〉遗产信托
6. *actio de effusis et deiectis*：〈拉〉坠落物或投掷物致害之诉

"Failing a specific rule already ascertained and fitting the case in hand, the king's judges must find and apply the most reasonable rule they can, so that it be not inconsistent with any established principle." The freedom of the Continental administration and science of law, at this moment, is still more narrowly limited. So juristic and judge-made law are always exposed to the danger of being crushed by the mass of the traditional element. The thought of a remedy through legislation does not suggest itself nearly so readily to man on a lower stage of development as it does today. The legislative machinery operates slowly and haltingly as yet, and the thought that it might alter the customary law has not yet occurred to anyone. One need but read Gaius and note how circumspectly he discusses the *senatusconsulta*[1] and the *leges* of the Empire[2] which were in conflict with the ancient *ius civile*.

These might be the historical presuppositions for magisterial law. Like judge-made law, the latter is posited by persons to whom certain functions have been assigned in the administration of justice in the course of the performance of these functions. It is not being posited however on the basis of the usual judicial authority and powers, but on the basis of authority and powers granted by the state that far transcend these. It has happened twice in the history of law that a state official acted when it became necessary to end the sway of norms for decision that had become rigid and antiquated. The Roman praetor and the English chancellor fulfilled their historic mission by opposing an altogether new legal system to the traditional system. Since the Middle Ages, magisterial law has no longer been able to gain a footing on the Continent. The royal courts of the Frankish and of the German kingdom failed to achieve a stable administration of justice; the capitularies[3] of the Frankish kings were not magisterial law, but an

1. *senatusconsulta*：元老院决议
2. *leges* of the Empire：帝国法
3. capitularies：法令汇编

echo of the legislative power of the Roman Caesars. In Rome as well as in England, the magisterial law became a fixed, fully developed system of legal rules, which confers upon the person entrusted with its application no greater freedom than do the other parts of the law.

Norms for decision found in statutes are juristic law if they are the product of the same kind of intellectual labor as the norms for decision of the judge-made and of the literary juristic law. As to the nature of a legal proposition, it is manifestly quite immaterial whether it is found in the reasons given for a judgment, in the discussions of a writer, or in the paragraphs of a code, though this may be quite important where its effectiveness is in question. As it is, a large part of the juristic law contained in statutes has been taken from the juristic law existing at the time. But if the legislator has not prescribed a new norm for decision but has merely stated it, it is none the less juristic law, in spite of the fact that that which might have been said in a judicial opinion or in a treatise has been said in a statute. This statutory juristic law[1] is just as susceptible of expansion and development as law that has been created in any other way. On this principle, the adoption of foreign statutes is based. State law, too, can surely be adopted from foreign countries, but only by the will of the state, i.e. by a statute, an ordinance, or any other enactment of the sovereign power of the state. It is manifest that universal compulsory military service, income tax, or regulation of self-defense could not by any manner of means be adopted from foreign law in any other way than by an act of the sovereign power of the state. But juristic law, even in the form of a statute, may migrate from one country into another like a scientific doctrine or like a practical invention. It makes its way into the literature, and thereby, or perhaps independently, into the judicial decisions. Even apart from the reception of Roman law, there are

---

1. statutory juristic law：制定法中的法学家法

numerous examples of this phenomenon. The Austrian Civil Code at the present time actually is valid law in Hungary; indeed it is being taught by the law faculties, although it may not be cited in judicial decisions. The French Civil Code has gained recognition in Russia, the German Commercial Code in Switzerland and in the Scandinavian countries; and at the present time the German Civil Code is gaining a footing in the Scandinavian countries.

Norms for decision in statutory form, whether taken from juristic law or created by the legislator, are a precarious[1] matter. It is much more difficult for the legislator to formulate a correct general rule than for the judge to decide an individual case; and it is a much more hazardous thing for him to posit an absolutely binding dogma for all time to come than it is for a jurist, who is proceeding scientifically, to enunciate propositions which are continually being examined and re-examined. The norm for decision becomes an entirely different thing when published in a statute from what it was before. Hitherto merely a presentation of what appears to be the proper rule, it now becomes a precept as to what ought to be the rule. It loses the pliability which had enabled it to adapt itself to every better insight and to every development. How often has a juristic doctrine been thrown overboard, and another substituted for it, although behind the pretense of a better insight there lay hidden the need of taking a new development into account. A method of procedure that is permissible where a legal doctrine is involved might not be permissible at all, or at least only with greater difficulty, when one is dealing with a statute. The legislator therefore ought to attempt to mould life according to his own ideas only where this is absolutely necessary; and where he can let life take care of itself, let him refrain from unnecessary interference. This doubtless was the leading, though unexpressed, thought in the

---

1. precarious：不稳定的

fight which Savigny, for a time, waged against legislation, not merely against codification as is often mistakenly asserted today. Every superfluous statute is a bad statute.

Nevertheless it would be childish to give up altogether the thought of expressing juristic law in statutory form. Scientific and judge-made law everywhere surpasses statute law in wealth of material, adaptability, and mobility; but in more advanced stages of development mankind is brought face to face with a number of problems of legal life that can be satisfactorily dealt with only by the state.

The experience of thousands of years has shown that only moderate local needs can be satisfied when the creation of law is split up locally; legal development can take place on a grand scale only when it takes place in a vast area and originates in a single central point. In order to attain a rich development it requires an abundance of stimuli, which are given only by the variegated manifoldness[1] of legal relations that may be found in a country of considerable size, and a central point where all these stimuli converge. Such a central point however can be created only by the state. This of course presupposes a thoroughgoing legislative activity. Legislation has not served this purpose in the two grandest legal systems of the world. The Roman and the English law did not arrive at the perfection which they have attained through legislation. In Rome the jurists were working at it with the immense intellectual resources of a vast empire; in England the judges, sitting in London, who for centuries had had to find the law for a great, economically developed, and politically advanced country. The common law is chiefly the product of the labors of the courts in London. Only the third world system of law, the French, owes its success to legislation. A highly developed legal system then may arise without legislation by the state, but surely not independently of the

1. variegated manifoldness：多彩多样

state. As a rule, however, statutes are indispensable for the purpose of getting rid of antiquated law and of quickly bringing about necessary innovations; for the rule that juristic science and administration of justice must not get into conflict with the law that has already been posited is an insuperable limitation upon their creative activity. With the exception of magisterial law, which down to the present day has had only two opportunities for free development, and which itself soon hardened into an inflexible rigidity, it may be said that it has always been the statutory law that was able to come to the assistance of the process of legal development when the latter had arrived at a dead center. This is the reason why one can say that the state, which in times of economic or political disturbance always is both an effect and a cause, may be called the most important lever of social progress. This is the reason why revolutionary parties which are violently attacking the state, from which legislative action proceeds, have often demanded legislative intervention, while conservative groups, which support the state, are filled with silent mistrust of its labors. But also in times when the course of events was undisturbed, legislation has proved an indispensable instrument for the removal of antiquated institutions and the advancement of legitimate interests which are struggling for recognition.

In addition to the norms for decision of the juristic law, modern codes contain *Kautelarjurisprudenz*[1] in the form of the so-called *Reglementierungsbedingungen*[2]; occasionally, at least according to the intent of the legislator, in the form of *nackgiebiges* (noncompulsive)[3], contract law or of precepts concerning testamentary dispositions. The legislator by means of subsidiary law requires the inclusion of those provisions that, in his opinion, the prudent draftsman ought to include

---

1. *Kautelarjurisprudenz*：〈德〉意指涉及预防性规则的法学家活动。
2. *Reglementierungsbedingungen*：〈德〉预防性规则
3. *nachgiebiges* (noncompulsive)：〈德〉非强制性

in the document. These statutes likewise are, essentially, juristic law. Moreover, they also contain state law, e.g. the provisions concerning entry in a book of record and concerning the supervision to be exercised in the matter.

At the present time the magisterial law[1] has become silent in England also. Since equity has been elaborated into a fixed system of law, its decisions contain judge-made law, not magisterial law. When the Continental common law withdrew into the background in Germany, the literary juristic law[2] went with it; the teacher of law confines himself to the teaching of existing law, and the discussions in the works of juristic literature are no longer treated as legal propositions but merely as suggestions for judicial decision and legislation. At the present time juristic law flourishes only in the form of judge-made and statute law.

A glance at a modern edition of a code "with annotations taken from the judicial decisions" shows the relation between judgemade law and the law contained in statutes. To the various provisions the editor has appended legal propositions drawn from judicial decisions. These purport merely to individualize concretely that which is laid down in the statute; actually however they are of equal value with the juristic law of the statute, both as to content and as to purpose. And as a matter of fact the element of concreteness lies in the cases on which they are based. When the statute is restated, as was done, for example, in the case of the German Commercial Code[3], these annotations are received into the statute. Occasionally the decisions are in conflict with one another. This however proves only that the juristic law is still uncertain. If they are in agreement it is as difficult to prevail against them as against the actual words of the statute.

---

1. magisterial law：行政执法官法
2. literary juristic law：文献法学
3. German Commercial Code：《德国商法典》

It would seem to follow from this discussion that there is no occasion for decisions that are found freely. But a more careful examination of the annotations shows that their connection with the provisions of the statute is quite external; that actually they are quite independent of them. The French editions of the Civil Code[1] append the decisions on unjust enrichment[2] to the provisions as to management of another's affairs without authority[3]. The French jurists do not doubt that they have nothing to do with this subject-matter. In this case, therefore, we may say that the decisions have created the juristic law as to unjust enrichment quite independently.

The situation is the same where the statutory provision is so general as to amount to no more than a direction to the judge to find the norm for decision himself. In such case, the legal propositions extracted from these norms for decision do not elaborate the statute, they add new law to it. What is meant in German law by abusive exercise of a legal right, when the performance of an obligation is a violation of good faith, when a contract is immoral (*den guten Sitten widerspricht*[4]), we do not know as yet, for the German Civil Code contains no provisions on these subjects, and we probably shall not know from judicial decisions until a century has elapsed. And these decisions will be so far from being based on the Civil Code that a judge in any other jurisdiction may adopt the norms contained therein, without any hesitation, e.g. for the concept of an immoral contract, or of abusive exercise of a right, unless the statutes of his jurisdiction contain divergen t provisions.

In my book on the declaration of the will by silence, I have shown that among the Romans this term meant only a declaration made

---

1. The French editions of the Civil Code：法国民法典
2. unjust enrichment：不当得利
3. management of another's affairs without authority：无因管理，指在无法达成约定的情况下，为避免他人利益受损，自愿管理他人事务或为他人提供服务的行为。
4. *den guten Sitten widerspricht*：〈德〉与良好的教养相背；不道德

in a manner other than by means of words and the meaning of the declaration as discovered by means of an interpretation based on the experience of the ordinary intercourse of life. The decisions of the German, Austrian, and French courts take it to include, in addition, the following: the acceptance of an offer by performance or by acts of appropriation; the binding force of a declaration which imposes an obligation on one of the parties only, e.g. of *Verbürgung*[1] (becoming surety) or of *Verpfändung*[2] (giving a pledge), or of *Verzicht*[3] (disclaimer) without any acceptance by the other party ("*stillschweigende Annahme*[4]") (acceptance by silence); the extinguishment of an obligation by long continued failure to exercise one's rights (" *stillschweigender Verzicht*[5]," properly speaking, a hidden prescription) (disclaimer by silence); expiration of the right to make a transaction effectual after a lapse of time by approval or confirmation ("*stillschweigender Verzicht*") properly, a hidden limitation as to time) (relinquishment by silence); the power of the contents of an invoice to bind the person receiving the same where the latter had not provided against this ("*Stillschweigende Annahme*") (acceptance by silence). Delivery by silence ("*stillschweigende Ubergabe*[6]") in the case of the *societas omnium bonorum*[7] and of the fruits to the usufructuary lessee[8] means that, by way of exception, ownership is transferred without transfer of possession, i.e. solely on the basis of the agreement. It is impossible to regard all of these merely as concrete individualizations; all of these, undoubtedly, are special, independent legal propositions of juristic law, connected in a purely external way

---

1. *Verbürgung*：〈德〉成为保证人
2. *Verpfändung*：〈德〉做保证
3. *Verzicht*：〈德〉弃权
4. *stillschweigende Annahme*：〈德〉默示承诺
5. *stillschweigender Verzicht*：〈德〉通过默示方式放弃自己权利
6. *stillschweigende Übergabe*：〈德〉默示交付
7. *societas omnium bonorum*：〈拉〉共同合伙
8. fruits to the usufructuary lessee：用益权承租人的孳息

with the Roman norm for decision concerning declaration of the will by silence.

The borderline between state law and juristic law is not easily determinable. In the first place juristic law consists of the norms for decision which the jurist has created by universalization. State law consists of commands directed by the state to its tribunals. The jurists cannot issue commands, they can only find law. The state does not find law, it can only command. Norms directing administrative action therefore are always state law. But as to many a statutory norm for decision one may well be in doubt as to whether it contains a statement of grounds for decision based on juristic law or a command by the state directing the judge how to decide the litigation. The principles governing the passing of the risk in case of a sale doubtless are juristic law. The norms for decision found in the German Civil Code on the prerequisites to the acquisition of legal capacity by organizations undoubtedly are state law. But between these there are a number of borderline cases, as to which it is not clear where they are to be counted.

External criteria however are not lacking. The jurist draws his law from the social relations; juristic law therefore does not extend beyond the relations from which it was taken. All true juristic law therefore is limited to the persons and the things that are connected with the relations for which the jurist has made his law. Juristic law is dominated by the personal principle as was the whole law at the time when there was no law but juristic law. The Roman *ius civile*[1] and the Germanic popular laws[2] were personal and real[3], as is the Mohammedan law today. The state, on the contrary, enacts its statutes for a given territory, and all true state law therefore is territorial law.

---

1. The Roman *ius civile*：罗马市民法
2. the Germanic popular laws：德国民间法
3. personal and real：动产与不动产

The Roman *leges*[1], therefore, with the exception of the *leges de iure chili*[2] and the Frankish capitularies[3], were territorial law. In the modern law this criterion has disappeared outwardly; but if one examines the principles of private international law[4], which somehow or other have come into vogue between the time of the theory of the "statutaries" and Zitelmann, one will find that, nevertheless, it makes its way everywhere. That part of modern law which is juristic law is effective as personal or as real law beyond the territory of the state; but state law is effective only within the territory of the state. The most precise formulation of this principle is found in the national theory of private international law which has been received into the Italian Civil Code, and according to which the law of a citizen of a state follows him everywhere, with the exception of the *lois d'ordre public*[5], whose validity is always territorial.

The two kinds of legal propositions also differ in force and effectiveness. This is not a question of the distinction between compulsive (*zwingendes Recht*[6]) and non-compulsive law, which, as I have shown in my book on the compulsive law, is of significance only in so far as it refers to the legal consequences of transactions which in part can be excluded by the will of the parties, and in part take effect unconditionally. In this sense, there is also a compulsive juristic law; and state law occasionally, though not often, is non-compulsive. But certain kinds of legal propositions are always juristic law rules of interpretation, subsidiary lawwhereas only state law can confer advantages, which the person advantaged cannot relinquish, and can impose disadvantages as to which there is no dispensation. On the

---

1. The Roman *leges*：罗马法
2. *leges de iure civili*：〈拉〉有关市民法的法
3. Frankish capitularies：《法兰克墨洛温王朝法令集》
4. private international law：国际私法
5. *lois d'ordre public*：〈拉〉治安法
6. *zwingendes Recht*：〈德〉强行法

other hand, st ate law, as the *corpus iuris* shows, has much less power of resistance to the changes of time than juristic law; almost all of the juristic law, but very little of the state law, contained in the *corpus iuris* has been received into the Continental common law.

The legal propositions which are contained in the legal commands of the state directed to courts and administrative tribunals are based on the will of the person who has power and control over the courts and the administrative tribunals; but their content does not always proceed from the state. The distinction between *Gesetzesbefehl*[1] (command contained in a statute) and *Gesetzesinhalt*[2] (content of a statute) which prevails today is based on sound sociological discernment. But the answer to the question by whom the command must be issued is a matter which in no wise depends upon the constitution of the state but upon the questions: in whose hands do the military and the police powers of the state lie, is the person in whose hands these powers lie thereby enabled to exercise control over courts and administrative tribunals, will he be able to induce judges and administrative officials to do his bidding? If he has the seat of the administration of justice and of the civil administration in his power, even the content of a statute that has been enacted in a constitutional manner is powerless against him, and he can give effect to state law even though it be unconstitutional. It is well known that the legislation of the Roman emperors down to the days of Diocletian[3] was based on the possession of power of the kind described, and each of a number of rival Caesars had the power to legislate within his particular sphere of power. Accordingly the Prussian government was in position to impose the constitution which it granted; the Russian, to change the election laws; the Danish, to carry out a reform of the military system by royal

1. *Gesetzesbefehl*：〈德〉制定法包含的命令
2. *Gesetzesinhalt*：〈德〉制定法内容
3. Diocletian：戴克里先（244—312），罗马皇帝，284—305 年在位。

decree. The constitutionality of the Austrian so-called paragraph 14 decrees, as is well known, is being disputed by many; but their validity, in view of the character of the Austrian officials and judges, is being denied by no one. The force of these facts is so overwhelming that even a govern ment which denies the legality of a preceding one will, as a rule, acknowledge the validity of legislation that was enacted meanwhile. Accordingly the Stuarts recognized the legislation enacted during the Usurpation; the Bourbons: the legislation of the French Revolution and of the Empire.

IX THE STRUCTURE OF THE LEGAL PROPOSITION

The immediate basis of the legal order of human society is the facts of the law: usage, relations of domination, relations of possession, declarations of will, particularly in their most important forms, to wit: articles of association, contract, and testamentary disposition. From these facts the rules of conduct which determine the conduct of man in society derive. These facts alone, therefore, and not the legal propositions, according to which the courts render decisions, and according to which the administrative tribunals of the state proceed[1], are of authoritative significance for the legal order in human society. Nevertheless the legal propositions gain significance for the latter inasmuch as the decisions of the courts and the measures taken by the administrative agencies affect the facts of the law and thus bring about changes in the existing usages, relations of domination, relations of possession, articles of association, contracts, and testamentary dispositions, i.e. on this presupposition the decisions of the courts and the measures taken by the administrative agencies, which are based on the legal propositions, in turn produce norms which regulate the social conduct of human beings. New facts of the law therefore can be established not only, as in past centuries, by the application of force, or, as is usual in our days, by the silent, unobserved sway of social forces, i.e. particularly by new kinds of associations, new

1. administrative tribunals of the state proceed：国家行政裁判

kinds of agreements, and testamentary dispositions[1], but also, at least indirectly, by means of legal propositions. For this purpose however it is not sufficient that the legal proposition should have formal validity, or that it should be applied in isolated cases; for an isolated fact is not a social fact. It is necessary for this purpose that men regulate their conduct according to the legal proposition. A legal proposition which dictates to the courts and administrative tribunals the course of action which they are to follow contains what amounts to a legal norm for the courts and administrative tribunals as soon as these bodies actually carry it out; it becomes a rule of conduct only when the social relations are actually being ordered thereby.

The legal norms which are deriving from the legal propositions, therefore, always have reference to social relations, but the nature of this reference varies. The sum total of the legal norms which have validity for courts and other tribunals has never been identical with the sum total of social law; there have always been a number of social legal relations which have been free from all intrusion from this quarter. This appears more clearly in Roman law than in any other legal system, for no jurists ever had a clearer conception of the extent of their legal propositions than did the Roman jurists as to their *ius civile* and *ius honorarium*[2]. There is a kind of official Roman family law; but side by side with it there were family relationships which were recognized socially only and which were regulated by no norms for decision, or almost none. These are concubinage and the matrimonial relation[3] of a Roman with a person who did not have *connubium*[4] — a relation which has been called by modern writers *matrimonium iuris gentium*[5] and the issue of these relationships which in their nature are

1. testamentary dispositions：遗嘱处分
2. *ius honorarium*：裁制官法
3. concubinage and the matrimonial relation：非法同居关系与婚姻关系
4. *connubium*：〈拉〉通婚权
5. *matrimonium iuris gentium*：〈拉〉万民法婚姻

very like marriage. The Romans have, at all times, exercised a peculiar kind of control over their freedmen concerning which a few precepts arose at a very late date in the Praetorian law[1]. Up to that time it was enforced preponderantly by social means. The *precarium*[2] is a typical instance of a possessory relation which was protected only by social law. The praetor began to extend a certain measure of protection to it, at least against third parties, by means of the *interdictum de precario*[3], but this was not done until the last days of the republic. For the longest time, the relations of possession of the *ager publicus*[4] were of the same nature. The contradistinction between the *pacta,* which have only social validity, and the *contractus,* which are enforceable in the courts, is found throughout the whole course of Roman legal history. Express statements have been handed down to the effect that all testamentary declarations of the will, the *donatio mortis causa*[5], the *testamentum per aes et libram*[6], the *fideicommissum*[7], originally were transactions about which the state and the courts did not concern themselves. It is self-evident that this enumeration by no means purports to be exhaustive. A reference may suffice to the *statu liberie*[8] to the position occupied by those freedmen who had not been formally manumitted before the praetor began to protect them in the enjoyment of their freedom, to the *fiducia*[9], to the oldest form of *locatio conductio*[10], to the *clientela*[11],

---

1. Praetorian law：裁判官法
2. *precarium*：〈拉〉临时让与
3. *interdictum de precario*：〈拉〉针对临时让与的禁令
4. *ager publicus*：〈拉〉公田
5. *donatio mortis causa*：〈拉〉死因赠与
6. *testamentum per aes et libram*：〈拉〉铜衡遗嘱，它采用的是所有权要式转移的方式进行的虚拟卖买。
7. *fideicommissum*：〈拉〉遗产信托
8. *statu liberi*：〈拉〉半自由人
9. *fiducia*：〈拉〉信托
10. *locatio conductio*：〈拉〉租赁
11. *clientela*：〈拉〉受保护的身份；受保护的地位

which, even at the latest times, existed solely as a social institution.

We meet this relation between the norm for decision and the social law elsewhere. In the thirteenth century, Brae ton, employing the phrases of Institutes[1] i, 3, 18, says concerning the English law of contracts: *Conventionalis (stipulatio) quae ex conventione utriusque partis concipitur, nec iussu iudicis vel praetoris; et quarum totidem sunt genera quot paene rerum contrahendartm, de quibus omnibus omnino se curia regis non immiscet, nisi aliquando de gratia.*[2]

By way of illustration from modern law we may be permit ted to mention the important role played by the religious marriage in many parts of Italy where a civil marriage is required by law; the various free associations which are not covered by the law of associations and on which, until a very recent date, the system of associations in France was based; the family community[3] (Sadruga), which is still in existence among the southern Slavs of Austria but unknown to the positive law of Austria; the agreements found everywhere which are unenforceable legally and enjoy social recognition only; the testamentary gifts given in trust, by means of which religious associations which, until the most recent legislation on the subject, had not been recognized in France had accumulated property worth untold millions.

In my book, *Das zwingende und nichtzwingende Recht im burgerlichen Gesetzbuch fiir das Deutsche Reich*[4] I have discussed the nature of the legal proposition and its relation to the sit nations of fact which it regulates. Referring the reader to this book, I shall introduce here only so much as is indispensable for the present discussion. Every legal proposition

---

1. Institutes：〈拉〉《法学阶梯》
2. *Conventionalis (stipulatio) quae ... aliquando de gratia*：〈拉〉协议是基于双方的约定，不是基于承审员与裁判官的命令。协议标的与种类是正比成本的。
3. the family community (Sadruga)：家庭社区（“Sadruga”为斯拉夫语音译）
4. *Das zwingende und ... das Deutsche Reich*：〈德〉德意志帝国民法典中的强行法与非强行法

that contains a norm attaches a command or a prohibition to a given state of facts as the legal consequence of the latter. The state of facts which conditions the norm, the command, or the prohibition, is a fact of the law, i.e. a usage, a relation of domination or of possession, or a declaration of the wilt In the case of a legal proposition which functions as a norm, we are always concerned, therefore, with the relation of the command or the prohibition which has been converted into a norm to one of the above named facts of the law. We must accordingly distinguish three classes of legal propositions.

In the first place there are legal propositions that accord the protection of the courts and other tribunals to the facts of the law as they exist in society. They do this either unconditionally or under certain conditions by recognizing the usages of the associations as being legally effective, protecting relations of domination and of possession, enforcing contracts and testamentary directions. In all these instances the norms of the legal proposition conform as a matter of logical necessity to the norms which derive directly from the facts of the law, i.e. from usage, domination, possession, declaration of the will. These are the norms that result "from the concept," "from the nature of the thing." "This is the proper place in law for the logical element, and logical necessity is raised to a sort of mathematical precision in so far as the concept of value enters in; for value, in fact, partakes of the nature of the mathematical: it is an equation. This juristic mathematics, "an arithmetic of concepts," therefore is found in the law of claims for damages and unjust enrichment; in the law of claims arising from contracts in which value is given for value, from contracts of barter, and from contracts for furnishing things for use (*Gebrauchsbeschaffungsverträge*)[1]. Distinguished from legal propositions of this kind are those that negate existing facts of the law or that self-actively create

1. contracts for furnishing things for use (*Gebrauchsbeschaffungsverträge*)：利用物的契约

facts of the law. On the basis of legal propositions courts and other state tribunals artificially create or dissolve associations, establish or abolish relations of domination, give, take away, or transfer possession, rescind articles of association, contracts, testamentary declarations of the will, or occasionally create them by compulsion. Under this head are found chiefly the legal propositions that decree expropriation or forfeiture of things; that declare certain relations invalid, null, voidable, or punishable. Modern statutes undertake to coerce parties into performance of legal acts employing chiefly for this purpose a device called "*Reglementieren*[1]," i.e. they prescribe a definite content for articles of associations and contracts, and supervise the observance of these regulations through state officials (registers).

It is self-evident that a social relation that is void, invalid, or punishable is some thing quite different from a relation that the courts and other state tribunals regard as lying outside of the legal sphere; a void marriage is something different from a relation that is no marriage at all; a society, membership in which subjects a man to punishment, is something different from a free association which lies outside of the scope of the law of societies; a prohibited contract is some thing different from a contract on which neither a complaint nor a defense can be based. They are denied the protection of the courts and other state tribunals, not on the ground that the law does not make provision for them but on the ground that they are to be banished from society. Of course, if courts and other tribunals tolerate them, or permit them to continue, in spite of the prohibition, then, from the point of view of the sociology of law, they do not constitute relations which are excluded from society by the legal propositions, but merely relations to which legal protection is denied; for the sociology of law is concerned, not with interpretations of legal precepts, but with

---

1. *Reglementieren*：〈德〉（通过规章）规制

the attitude of society toward them. We can see every day that void, forbidden, punishable marriages, societies, relations of domination and possession, contracts, gifts *mortis causa*[1], are actually being sustained; that even slavery, thinly disguised, flourishes, in spite of abolition and amenability to punishment, in South America, in the Congo Free State, in Russia.

A third species of legal propositions attaches legal consequences to facts of the law, quite independently of the norms that result from the usages, the relations of domination and of possession, and the dispositions created by these facts. Let us bear in mind certain rights and duties connected with ownership, *i.e.Bannrechte*[2] and trade rights, the obligation to pay taxes, the duty to insure in connection with certain contracts, the duty of the owner of poisons and explosives to give notice.

The norms prescribed by the legal proposition therefore can either secure absolute enforcement for the norms that flow from the facts of the law or they can hinder them or invalidate them; and, lastly, they can attach legal consequences to them that bear no relation whatsoever to the legal consequences that flow from the facts. Accordingly the legal order which society self-actively creates for itself in the facts of the law, in the existing usages, relations of domination, and of possession, articles of association, contracts, testamentary dispositions, is brought face to face with a legal order which is created by means of legal propositions, and enforced solely by means of the activity of the courts and the other tribunals of the state. And norms, rules of conduct, flow from this second legal order no less than from the former, to the extent that it protects, gives form and shape to, modifies, or perhaps abolishes the facts of the law. And only those norms that are contained in these

1. gifts *mortis causa*：死因赠与（斜体为拉丁文）
2. *Bannrechte*：〈德〉限制权。例如要求某地或某一层级的居民提供某种必需品或劳动的特别法。

two legal orders constitute the whole law of society. The important thing for the norms of the second legal order is not the distribution of interests in the individual social associations, but the distribution in society as a whole, which comprises all the associations within a certain territory. The second legal order then is an order which has been imposed by society upon the associations.

The juristic writer, the teacher of law, and the legislator, who formulate the legal proposition, always act as persons commissioned by society, whether it be in virtue of the confidence which society places in them, as in the case of the Roman and of the common law jurists up to the time of the recent codifications, or in virtue of social or official position, *or*, as in the case of the legislator, upon the authority of the constitution of the state. The form and the content of a legal proposition are the result of the joint labors of society and of the individual jurist, and the sociology of law will have to distinguish the contribution of the former clearly from that of the latter.

The impulses to create law which result from the distribution of power in society have their source in society. The frequently used word *Machtverhältnisse*[1] (distribution of power) indeed is not available as a scientific term because of its indefiniteness; we are using it here as referring to the distribution of power which is based on position in the state, on economic or on social position. Furthermore the legal proposition does not owe its existence to any consideration of the interests of individual classes or ranks, but of those of all social strata; and it is immaterial whether actual general interests are involved or merely imagined ones, as in the case of the superstitious belief in the existence of witches. Under this head comes the defense against external enemies and elemental forces. In the last analysis, at least in the judgment of those that act, the interests of individual strata of the

1. *Machtverhältnisse*：〈德〉权力分配

population are general interests when popular opinion does not regard the interests of the other strata as worth taking into account, e.g. the interests of the slaves in Rome; up to the nineteenth century, quite generally, the interests of the unfree peasantry; in the Polish republic, and in ancient Hungary, usually, the interests of those who were not members of the nobility; and until late in the nineteenth century, the interests of the non-propertied classes[1]. And for most modern men and women the interest of the utterly neglected (*Verwahrlosten*)[2] and submerged (*Verlorenen*)[3] perhaps is but little more than something to be protected against. In their opinion, the general interest includes protection of the social order against individuals who are beyond the pale of society. This protection may be effected by means of a part of the criminal law, police law, and procedural law. In reality all of this is a matter of the distribution of power. A decision rendered for the protection of the general interest may be said to be a decision based solely upon considerations of expedience. Wherever there is no doubt as to where the power lies in a state, or where the voice of popular consciousness speaks in no uncertain tones, the task of the jurist is a merely technical one. The content of the legal proposition is given by society. His function is merely to provide the wording of it and to find the means whereby the interests which are to be secured can be secured most effectively. This technical function however must not be underrated. The clumsiness of procedure and the limited capacity for expression of the material law often cause enormous difficulty in this matter. They are the cause of all formalism in law. Formalism is not an admirable quality of law, but a technical defect which must be overcome. A glance at Roman and English legal history reveals the difficulty which in time past was caused by the clumsiness of

---

1. non-propertied classes：无产阶级
2. utterly neglected (*Verwahrlosten*)：完全忽视
3. submerged (*Verlorenen*)：淹没

procedure. The state of our doctrine as to statement of the cause of complaint, as to proof, and as to content of the judgment shows that it is still troubling us. The invention of the *bonae fidei indicia*[1] by the Romans may be counted among the greatest achievements of the human mind in the field of law. Their work was continued in a splendid manner by the French courts; and, in Germany, by the Hanseatic courts[2], by the Niirnberg Court of Commercial Appeals, and by the Imperial Supreme Court of Commerce. Unfortunately the achievements of the German Commercial Courts have already been forgotten in part. The investigations that have been instituted in the field of the history of legal doctrine can give us an idea, as to Roman law at least, of the labor that had to be expended before the action of theft became an action *in rem*[3], before the liability of the possessor for pretended possession or for possession surrendered, for the destruction of the thing (*Sache*[4]), for fruits and for damage done, was established and defined. The present most unsatisfactory state of many legal institutions is attributable, in a measure, to the fact that we have not as yet been able to establish technically perfect legal propositions concerning them.

The decision as to the interests involved in a dispute is entrusted by the state to the jurist when it is clearly indicated neither by the general interest nor by the distribution of power in society as a whole. This situation may be brought about by various causes. In the first place very often the parties to the dispute are quite unaware of the great social interests involved in the decision; very often the latter are distributed among the various classes and ranks in such a manner

---

1. *bonae fidei iudicia*：〈拉〉诚信审判。指裁制官在审理合同案件时需考虑双方行为是否诚信。
2. Hanseatic courts：汉萨同盟法庭
3. action *in rem*：对物诉讼（斜体为拉丁文）
4. *Sache*：〈德〉物

as to place them above the struggles of class and rank; in many cases these social in teres ts are too inconsiderable and insignificant to become involved in the dispute. Very often, too, the possessors of power, who are called upon to render the decision, are not at all involved in the conflict of interests. The most important cause however is the fact that the powers that are engaged in the struggle in behalf of the different interests counterbalance one another or that the influences that proceed from the groups that are most powerful politically, economically, or socially, are checked or thwarted by other social tendencies, which are based on religious, ethical, scientific, or other ideological convictions.

When the jurist is asked to draw the line between the conflicting interests independently, he is asked, by implication, to do it according to justice. This implies, in the first place, something negative. He is asked to arrive at a decision without any consideration of expediency and uninfluenced by the distribution of power. In recent times, it is true, it has often been said that justice, too, is a matter involving questions of power. If the writer means to say that the idea of justice, on which the decision is based, must have attained a certain power in the body social at the time when it influences the judicial finding of norms or the activity of the state, he is indeed stating a truth, but it is a selfevident truth; and a self-evident truth does not require statement. But if he means to say that, under the cloak of justice, effect is always being given to the influence of political, social, or economic position, the statement is manifestly incorrect. A legal norm whose origin can be traced to such influences is usually stigmatized by that very fact as something unjust. Justice has always weighted the scales solely in favor of the weak and the persecuted. A just decision is a decision based on grounds which appeal to a disinterested person; it is a decision which is rendered by a person who is not involved in the conflict of interests, or which, even though it be rendered by a person involved in this conflict, nevertheless is such as a disinterested person would render or approve of. It is never based on taking advantage of a position of power. When a person who is in a position of power acts justly, he acts against his own interest, at any rate against his immediate interest, prompted by religious, ethical, scientific, or other ideological considerations; perhaps merely by considerations of prudent policy. The parties of political and social justice, e.g. the doctrinaire liberals[1], the English Fabians[2], the German Socialpolitical or National-Socialist parties[3], the French Solidarists[4], find their adherents chiefly among ideologists who are not personally interested in the poetical and social conflicts of interests. In this fact lies their strength and also their weakness.

But all of these are negative characteristics. Which are the positive characteristics of justice? The catch phrase about balancing of interests which is so successful at the present time is not an answer to this question; for the very question is: What is it that gives weight to the interests that are to be balanced? Manifestly it is not the balancing jurist, writer or teacher, judge or legislator, but society itself. The function of the jurist is merely to balance them. There are trends caused by the interests that flourish in society which ultimately influence even persons that are not involved in these conflicting interests. The judge who decides according to justice follows the tendency that he himself is dominated by. Justice therefore does not proceed from the individual, but arises in society.

The role of the person rendering the decision is of importance

---

1. doctrinaire liberals：教条自由主义者。他们机械地适用自由主义机制，不考虑具体情况。
2. English Fabians：英国费边主义者。费边主义是近现代社会主义流派之一，英国社会改良主义团体费社的思想体系。
3. German Socialpolitical or National-Socialist parties：德国社会政治或民族社会主义政党。这些党派以民族社会主义为其政治主张。
4. French Solidarists：法国社会连带主义者。社会连带主义是以实证主义哲学为基础的社会学理论流派，在政治学、法学领域有较大影响。

only inasmuch as, within certain limitations, he can select the solution which corresponds most nearly to his personal feelings. But in doing this, he cannot disregard the social basis of the decision. If a Spartacus[1], favored by fortune, had abolished slavery in antiquity, or if the socialists should abolish private property, let us say in a beleaguered city, as was done in Paris during the days of the Commune[2], these facts would have nothing to do with justice. And a judge who, in a decision which he renders, recognizes private property in means of production in spite of the fact that he is a socialist, or who admits the defense that the debt sued upon in a stock-exchange transaction is a gaming debt although in his opinion the setting-up of this plea is a breach of good faith, does not thereby contradict himself. In doing these things he is merely being guided by social tendencies against his own individual feeling in the matter. A rebellious slave, the government of a beleaguered city, like that of Paris during the Commune, can indeed proceed according to their individual feelings, but they can do so only because they have been removed from social influences by the force of circumstances. Justice is a power wielded over the minds of men by society.

It is the function of juristic science, in the first place, to record the trends of justice that are found in society, and to ascertain what they are, whence they come, and whither they lead; but it can not possibly determine which of these is the only just one. In the forum of science, they are all equally valid. What men consider just depends upon the ideas they have concerning the end of human endeavor in this world of ours, but it is not the function of science to dictate the final ends of human endeavor on earth. That is the function of the founder of a religion, of the preacher, of the prophet, of the preacher of ethics,

1. Spartacus：斯巴达克斯
2. days of the Commune：巴黎公社时期

of the practical jurist, of the judge, of the politician. Science can be concerned only with those things that are susceptible of scientific demonstration. That a certain thing is just is no more scientifically demonstrable than is the beauty of a Gothic cat hedral or of a Beethoven symphony to a person who is insensible to it. All of these are questions of the emotional life. Science can ascertain the effects of a legal proposition, but it cannot make these effects appear either desirable or loathsome to man. Justice is a social force, and it is always a question whether it is potent enough to influence the disinterested persons whose function it is to create juristic and statute law.

But although science can teach us nothing concerning the ends, once the end is determined, it can enlighten us as to the means to that end. The practical technical rules that perform this function are based on the results of pure science. There is no science that teaches men that they ought to be healthy, but practical medical science teaches men who desire to be healthy what they can do, according to the present state of the natural sciences, to bring about that result. Practical juristic science is concerned with the manner in which the ends may be attained that men are endeavoring to attain through law, but it must utilize the results of the sociology of law for this purpose. The legal proposition is not only the result, it is also a lever, of social development; it is an instrumentality in the hands of society whereby society shapes things within its sphere of influence according to its will. Through the legal proposition man acquires a power, limited though it be, over the facts of the law; in the legal proposition a willed legal order is brought face to face with the legal order which has arisen self-actively in society.

The idea that society must be governed by laws (legal propositions) is found among the ancient Greeks. It plays an important role among the Romans, appears again in the sixteenth century, and since that time has been the basic idea in all the great political and social trends in Europe down to the beginning of the twentieth century, especially in the absolute *Wohlfahrtsstaat*[1] (state promoting the public welfare), in the mercantilistic[2], natural-law, and social-political movements. For the modern development of law it has attained an enormous, a fateful significance.

What can the sociology of law offer to juristic science in this sphere? The ultimate ends of our pilgrimage on this earth doubtless shall ever remain hidden from our eyes, but we can, at any rate, overlook a small part of the way. The highest aim of all science is to vouchsafe to us a glimpse of the future; the investigator gradually becomes a seer. As the physicist endeavors to determine the course of a cannon-ball in advance, so the disciples of the social sciences endeavor to calculate in advance the unifying regularities in the course of the future development of social happenings. They can point to many great successes, particularly in the general sphere of economics, and every advance in sociological study will bring new successes.

Sociology teaches us the laws governing the development of human society and the effects of the legal propositions. It teaches juristic science how the legal propositions may be adapted to the laws of social development in accordance with their effects. Sociology indeed is just as far from teaching us that we must regulate our lives according to these scientific laws in the matter of our legal propositions and our conduct generally as the natural sciences are from telling us that we must be healthy. But men usually wish to do that which is expedient, just as, with very rare exceptions, they desire to be well. Accordingly on the basis of the results of the steady progress of the science of sociology, juristic science will be in a correspondingly better position to tell the judge and the legislator when they are performing useful labors, and when, inasmuch as they are resisting the laws of development and failing to understand the effects of the legal

---

1. *Wohlfahrtsstaat* (state promoting the public welfare)：〈德〉福利国家
2. mercantilistic：重商主义的

propositions, they are bootlessly frittering social forces away. If there is such a thing as *richtiges Recht*[1] or to be more exact *richtige Rechtssätze*[2], they are those that advance the human race in the direction of its future development. It is true that inexpedient conduct can never be prevented altogether, for doubtless it has its function somewhere in the universal scheme of things, but solely in the nature of a hindrance, of a resistance of the means employed.

The sociologist, therefore, who on the basis of his scientific knowledge is endeavoring to draw a picture of the social order as it will exist in the future, and of a legal system that, even in the present, shall be adapted to the future, is by no means engaged in an unscientific undertaking. Marx's attempt to show the necessity of socialism by showing that social development must needs lead to socialism is not unscientific, at least no more so than the weather predictions of the meteorologist for the guidance of tillers of the soil, or the writings of geologists on the future of gold for the benefit of those engaged in directing monetary policy. It is true, unfortunately, that in investigations of this kind very much that is untenable sails under the flag of science, but the blame for this must not be attributed to the subject but to the newness and incompleteness of this whole field of knowledge. And the query why every sociologist presents that which seems to him to be the end of the development as the end of all development beyond which mankind will never be able to go is, possibly, based on a misapprehension. The astronomer who is examining the uttermost nebulae that his telescope can reach, the microscopist who shows us the smallest particles that his instrument can lay hold on, do not deny that behind these worlds there are other worlds; behind these minute particles there lie things that are still more minute. So every sociologist knows that behind the horizon

1. *richtiges Recht*：〈德〉正确、正义的法律
2. *richtige Rechtssätze*：〈德〉正确、正义的法律命题

which limits his vision at the time there lie other horizons, which are withdrawn from his view, but he is content with that which is attainable. All these matters that have been presented up to this point, the relation of the legal proposition to society and its being conditioned by the social development, were clearly discerned by the founders of the Historical School; for what they call the legal consciousness of the people is but the trends of justice in society. It is true they were in error as to the scope of their doctrine, for the latter did not give an explanation of the law but only of the legal proposition; and not of every legal proposition, but only of the proposition that is based on justice; but even admitting this limitation we must say that their work of more than a century ago was a mighty deed. To what heights they towered above their successors appears from the fact that there has not been found among the latter a man able to continue building on the foundation which they had laid.

Perhaps the task which science must perform with reference to justice can best be shown by discussing a question which at the present time is violently agitating the colonial politicians of France. The nomadic tribe of Arabs on the rim of the desert in Algiers and in Tunis[1], who are owners of immense herds of sheep, camels, and horses, require not only extensive pastures for their herds but also long str etches of roadway in order to be able to drive their cattle from one place of pasture to another at the time of the changes of the seasons. Doing this, they cannot avoid entering upon land that is being tilled. Thereby agriculture on a large scale becomes impossible. Now is agriculture to continue in this wretched state in order that a few hundred Arabs may be able to find food for their herds? By way of reply one may put the counter question: Should several hundred thousand sheep as well as a great number of horses and camels be

1. in Algiers and in Tunis：在阿尔及尔与突尼斯

sacrificed for the benefit of agriculture on the rim of the desert, extremely precarious as it is in view of the "desperate uncertainty of rain," and incapable of development, since only ten thousand hectares are involved at most? A similar battle was raging in Switzerland about the middle of the nineteenth century bet ween the t illers of the soil and the breeders of cattle (*Grossvieli*) on one side and the breeders of small cattle (*Kleinvieh*) on the other. The agriculturalists were on the side of the breeders of cattle because agriculture could expand only at the expense of the pasture for small cattle not of that for large cattle. It is said that there is a similar conflict of interests awaiting adjustment at the present time in Norway and Sweden between the Lapps[1], who are breeding reindeer, and the farmers, who are crowding them out of their pastures. Everyone who has concerned himself with Spanish national economics knows of the vast importance of the role played in Spain today by the pastures for Merino sheep[2], which make agriculture impossible in many parts of the country.

Questions of this nature and scope confront the jurist every day. Whether it be a question of defining the limit up to which a person engaged in an industrial enterprise may inconvenience a neighbor by noises and odors; of determining the extent to which the life, the health, the mental and the physical development of the workman must be considered in the case of a labor contract; of determining the standard according to which the usufructuary, after the usufruct has terminated, must make compensation for deterioration or may demand reimbursement for expenses incurred; of laying down a rule fixing the extent to which the clause concerning competition may limit an employee in the free exercise of his power to work; or of drawing up in statutory form the regulations according to which society should guarantee to the non-propertied classes a certain standard of

1. Lapps：拉普人，亦称“萨米人”，北欧地区的原住民。
2. Merino sheep：美利奴绵羊

living by means of a minimum wage, provision for illness, old age, unemployment, for widows and orphans: the just decision should always protect the higher interest where the interests are in conflict. But which is the higher interest?

If a decision were rendered, or a statute enacted, according to the wishes of the breeders of cattle or of the agriculturalists, of the persons engaged in industrial undertakings or of their neighbors, of the owners of land or of the usufructuaries, of the employers or of the employees, of the propertied or of the non-propertied classes, the decision would not be according to justice but according to power. If justice is to govern, the decisive factor must not be the wishes of one party or the other, but the question which of the conflicting interests are of greater importance to society, i.e. the interests of cattle-raising or of agriculture; of industry or of the sanitary condition of the neighborhood; of the owner of land or of the usufructuary; of the employer or of the employee; of commerce or of free exercise of one's powers; of increase of wealth in the hands of the propertied classes or of the welfare of the non-propertied classes. And he who is called upon to render a decision must take into account not only the present moment, but also the coming generations; not only the economic needs, but also the political, ethical, and cultural significance of cattle-raising and of agriculture, of industry and of public hygiene, of great landed estates and of rights of usufruct, of employer and of employee, of commerce and of free activity, of property and of the welfare of the non-propertied classes.

To render a decision of this kind is one of the greatest and most difficult tasks, and one most heavily freighted with responsibility. To answer questions of this kind means to be able to read the signs of the development of the future in the society of today, to sense its needs in advance, and to determine its order in advance. If we shall ever be able to attempt this on the basis of scientific knowledge — and in a most modest measure it is being done today — it will be found that only an intellect equipped with the full armament of science can be called upon to perform this task. Meanwhile our sense of justice is merely one of those great indefinite divinings of hidden interrelations in the vast scheme of things, which, like religion, ethics, and perhaps art, lead mankind to distant unknown goals. In these paths the genius is the born leader of mankind. Even in the most primitive days, the legislator and the judge stand in the thoughts of men by the side of the founder of a religion, the prophet, the poet. The genius is the more highly developed man in the midst of a human race that has remained far behind him; the man of the future, born, by a mysterious coincidence, into the present, who today thinks and feels as some day the whole race will think and feel. Therein lies his tragic fate, for he is lonely; and his sole compensation lies in this, that he shows the way to others. The divinings which conjure up the picture before the mental eye of the genius bestow upon him such a masterful insight into hidden interrelations as ordinarily might be expected only as a result of the most perfect knowledge. In his speech in the English House of Lords for the protection of laborers who were working at machines, Byron[1] developed ideas of justice which did not penetrate into the consciousness of men who were trying to bring about social justice for at least fifty years; in his speech on the Irish question, he gave expression to a concept of justice that was first embodied in a bill by Gladstone[2]; at the beginning of the nineteenth century he assisted in the renascence of Greece, which we all are marveling at today. For though justice is based on social trends, it requires the personal activity of an individual to make it effective. In this it is most like art. The artist, too, as we know today, does not produce his work of art from his inner self; he can but give shape to that which society

1. Byron：诗人拜伦
2. Gladstone：即威廉·尤尔特·格莱斯顿（1809—1898），英国自由党政治家。

furnishes him with. But just as the work of art, although it is a result of social forces, requires an artist to clothe it in a visible form, so justice requires a prophet to proclaim it. And again like a work of art, which, though shaped out of social materials, nevertheless receives from the artist the stamp of his whole individual personality, justice owes to society only its rough content, but owes its individual form to the artist in justice who has created it. There is no such thing as one justice only, as there is no such thing as one beauty only, but in every work of justice there is justice, just as beauty speaks to mankind in every true work of art. Justice, as it has been given individual form in statutes, judicial decisions, works of literature, is, in its highest manifestations, the resultant of an inspired synthesis of opposites like every other grand creation of the human mind.

The mind of man is so manifold, the stratification of society[1] is so variegated, that it is impossible to state the concept of justice in a single formula. Perhaps none has met with so much success as the formula which Bentham[2] borrowed from Beccaria[3], to wit the greatest happiness of the greatest number. But it has never been "demonstrated," and it cannot be numbered among those truths that are evident without demonstration.

In the first place Bentham's formula will by no means convince everyone. Not the religious ascetic to whom earthly happiness in general appears as of no value whatever; not the member of the aristocracy according to whose ideas the "greatest number" [4] has not been created for happiness but for labor and obedience; not the aesthete, to whom a Michelangelo or a Napoleon outweighs millions

1. stratification of society：社会分层
2. Bentham：边沁（1748—1832），英国法理学家，功利主义哲学创始人。
3. Beccaria：贝卡利亚（1738—1794），意大利法理学家，代表作《论犯罪与刑罚》，近代资产阶级法学开创者。
4. the "greatest number"：最大多数

of the all-too-many; not the patriot, who is much more concerned with the power and greatness of his country than with the happiness of the individuals that constitute its citizens; not the energist, to whom striving and making his efforts effective is of much greater importance than happiness. This formula will gain adherents only among those who are convinced of it from the outset — those who consciously are democrats. It is a democratic catchword[1], and saying this we have said by implication that it expresses the thoughts and feelings of a small minority only. For democracy is an aristocratic thought. There are no true democrats other than those who are aristocrats in their intellectual natures; among those who are aristocrats by birth only those are democrats who have inherited this distinctive feature with their rank. The plebeian is never a democrat. He demands equality only with those who are above him, never with those that are below him. There is something of the highest quality of nobility, a consciousness of enormous power, an unconquered defiance, in not only refraining from demanding privileges but also rejecting them when they are offered.

And what did all these democrats among aristocrats and aristocrats among democrats take the words "greatest number" to mean? To the Gracchi[2] they were several hundred thousand proletarians among the Roman commonalty; to Ulrich von Hutten, the German order of knights, which certainly was not more numerous; to Bentham himself, the middle classes of the urban bourgeoisie; to Marx, the millions of the laboring classes. If one had demanded of the Gracchi that they should grant to the non-Italic peregrine equal rights with the citizens, or of Hutten that he should grant to the peasants equal rights with the knights of the Empire, they would have considered such a proposal most unjust. Bentham contented himself with the cold comfort that

1. catchword：口号；流行语
2. the Gracchi：格拉古兄弟，指提比略 · 格拉古好和盖约 · 格拉古，他们是公元前 2 世纪罗马共和国著名的政治家、平民派领袖。

it is possible even for the lowest working-man to rise into the middle classes — perhaps for one among ten thousand. Is that the "greatest number" ? The idea of offering some sort of assistance to factory workers by means of a very moderate social policy first occurred to Bentham's greatest disciple, John Stuart Mill[1]. From the standpoint of pure arithmetic, Marx surely was right. But in his whole book there is not a single line on the question how the socialization of the means of production can be made to benefit those who are beyond the pale of society. And if one considers the population of the whole world, the latter surely are the "greatest number." And in a socialistic Utopia published, prefaced, and recommended by Kautsky, one of his most faithful disciples, we find the doctrine that the socialistic society will secure tropical fruits and other products through enforced negro labor, for "the negro will not work voluntarily."

And finally, what is the meaning of the "greatest happiness" ? To Bentham and his disciples these words meant, in a general way, the economic well-being of the middle classes and the greatest possible scope for the free exercise of the powers of the individual. But is it not true that they who have the deepest insight into human nature have pointed out that the "greatest number" are happiest when they are led by strong men who forge their fates for them? When their individuality is merged in a community, or even when they serve a master who provides for the day, and in the evening protects them from privation and misery? Is it not true that a perhaps equally "great number" experience the greatest happiness when they live in contemplative laziness, at the expense of someone else, albeit suffering great privations withal? Bentham's conception of the greatest happiness is that of a certain class, in a certain country, at a certain time, to wit the middle classes in England at the beginning of the last century.

---

1. John Stuart Mill：约翰·斯图亚特·密尔（1806—1873），英国著名哲学家、经济学家。

Carlyle submitted a concept which was diametrically opposed to this, and which was equally good for a different social stratum of the same country at the same time. Happiness is a meaningless word in general, which does not correspond to any actuality. It would be hard to find a man to whom it means anything definite; perhaps no two men to whom it means the same thing. And in general happiness has nothing to do with legislation and the administration of justice. Nevertheless Bentham was right and carried his point; for he put into the form of a clear juristic demand that which in his day had been the vague ideal of a powerful trend of justice. But his doctrine is of no significance beyond the class, the time, and the place.

There is no formula in which the idea of justice is summed up and fully expressed; it is a term that expresses a way and a goal — a goal which lies in the sunlit distance, which the human mind can divine, but not know, and a way which man must tread with faltering and uncertain steps. He who shall be able to speak the last word on the subject of justice will thereby have found the law of the development of the human race, perhaps of the universe. Meanwhile science must rest content to contemplate the line of development which has been graven into the past and to divine that which the near future will trace out for it.

It is a long way that leads from the inner order of the associations to the legal propositions of our codes and juristic handbooks. In primitive times only the legal propositions governing procedure and the regulations concerning penalties are being created; and they are being created solely according to considerations of expediency. The norms that are contained in these propositions belong to those that constitute the second order of society, for they do not order and regulate the associations directly but are designed merely to ward off dangers. The norms of the first order, which are required by the exigencies of litigation, do not as yet exist in the form of legal propositions; they derive from the inner order of the associations through universalization and reduction to unity, or they are being obtained by a process of free finding, and are not being developed into universally valid legal propositions until a later time. At the same time the legal propositions of the second order grow in number and power, an ever richer procedural law develops, the regulations as to penalties are being converted, in part, into a law of damages, and: in part, into a law of crimes. Finally state law arises as the norm for the decisions of the courts, and as the basis for action by the state.

At each of these stages, society is as active as the jurist. Every legal proposition is shaped out of materials furnished by society, but the shaping is done by the jurist. It is indeed the norms that are already prevailing in society that, universalized and reduced to unity, become legal propositions; but in the last analysis the jurist decides what is to be universalized and reduced to unity, which of the various orders of the family that come within his sphere he is to treat as the model order according to which he decides the controversies that arise in the others, which of the various contents of contracts that occur furnishes the standard for the decision of controversies arising from all like contracts. The purpose of the free finding of norms is merely to eke out and to take the place of the inner order of the associations where the latter fails in the adjudication of litigation; and the whole "second order[1]" is destined, from the very beginning, to surround the inner order of the associations, as it is being created anew every moment by usage, relations of domination and of possession, with a wall of defense against attack and danger. The law governing interference by society and the state with the inner order of the associations also proceeds at all times from a larger social or state association, which is endeavoring to exert influence over the smaller associations of which it is composed. However great the extent to which these norms arise

1. second order：次级秩序

from the relations already existing in society, the jurist who transforms them into legal propositions must supply not only the wording but also a great deal of the content. But the jurist who in this manner places the stamp of his personality upon the legal proposition in turn is subjected to the influence of society. Its distribution of power, its ideas of the general interest, its trends of justice dictate to him what he is to universalize and reduce to unity, what norms he is to find for the relation that is in dispute, what is to be protected against attack and danger, what is to be surrendered to the latter, where the selfcreated order of the associations is to be modified or abolished. Only a small part of the legal proposition therefore is the expression of the personality of its author to such an extent that one might assume that it would not have been worded as it is had it been created by a different person. And even at this point we must not fail to observe to what extent every man, even the most individual genius, is a resultant of the influences of his environment, that every man can be born and work only in a given society, that everywhere else he would be impossible and would make shipwreck.

The prevailing school of jurisprudence, which sees in every legal proposition only the expression of the "will of the lawgiver," altogether fails to recognize the important part of society in its creation. The teachers of the Natural Law School, in their day, had a much deeper insight into the matter inasmuch as they endeavored to base the law upon the sense of justice, i.e. upon the social trends of justice; Savigny and Puchta with their doctrine of the popular consciousness of right and law as the basis of legal development merely restated thoughts of the natural law in terms of a social point of view. Bentham, by his principle of utility[1], with which Jhering's *Zweck im Rechte*[2] coincides in the main, for the first time, in a comprehensive manner, directed

1. principle of utility：效益原则
2. *Zweck im Rechte*：〈德〉《法的目的》

attention to the general interest, which, it is true, he often enough confused with the interest of a single class, the bourgeois middle class. The materialistic interpretation of history went much further than the natural law doctrine, than the Historical School, than Bentham and Jhering. It pointed out to what extent the law, and therefore also the legal propositions, are a superstructure erected on the foundation of the economic order, and also to what extent the legal propositions are being fashioned and created under the pressure of the distribution of power in society. But in doing this it became biassed, for it intentionally excluded from its consideration the element of human personality, the trends of justice as well as all non-economic influences which it always, and occasionally in an extremely arbitrary manner, traced back to economic ones, and usually, though quite unintentionally, all consideration of the general interest. The sociology of law must not overlook any of these things; it must consider everything that takes part in the creation of the legal proposition.

X THE VARYING CONTENT OF THE CONCEPT OF JUSTICE

The creation of the legal proposition takes place everywhere under the influence of the concept of justice. On the basis of this concept, the judge finds the norms for his decision when there is no legal proposition to guide him. A statute, a judicial decision, an administrative action by the state, is judged according to its inherent justice. Every political party has chosen justice, at least according to its alleged conviction, as its goal. In all these cases, what is the concrete content of the concept of justice? And since, in the case of the norm for decision, of the legal proposition, of criticism, of political parties, in general in the case of all law, we are dealing with interests which are to be protected, or to be given effect to by law, we must put the question thus: Which are the interests that are considered just? Hedemann has investigated this question in a wider connection, limiting his investigation however to the private law legislation of Germany, Austria, and Switzerland in the nineteenth century, and has solved it in a manner that meets the most rigorous demands of science. Here however we must disregard the usual classification of law. We are not concerned with the influence of justice upon private law, criminal law, administrative law, procedural law, but with interests which are to be protected by private law, criminal law, administrative law, and procedural law, according to justice.

The legal history of the primitive period of the nations of Europe presents a picture of an administration of justice by the state which is limited altogether to things that immediately concern the state:

attempts on the life of the king, trading with the enemy, violation of military discipline. Apart from these things, legal protection is a matter for the primitive or genetic associations, the clan, the family, the household, which are being held together by the strong conviction of each individual member that he can maintain his existence in this world, filled with violence and outrage as it is, only by the closest possible union with his own. These genetic associations create the courts, regulate procedure, create the first legal propositions. We are fairly well informed on these matters through a series of statements of law which date from the earliest times. As to the law of Europe, it is chiefly the Twelve Tables of the Romans, the Germanic popular laws, which came into existence at about the same stage of development, the Scandinavian sagas, and a few Slavic sources of law that are to be considered. From these we gather that in the society in which this law was in force the most vital concern was to repel violence directed against the state, the person, life, and possession. These ancient regulations refer almost exclusively to murder, homicide, wounding, robbery, theft, and despoiling of inheritances. The legal precepts contained therein are engrossed with concern for the state, for the life of the people, for the peace of the domestic hearth, of possession, and of the workshop. These are the only interests that are considered worth protecting, and legal protection is extended by means of self-help, vengeance of blood, outlawry, and finally by means of a money penalty. These legal propositions, which according to the modern conception should be included in criminal law, are the prototype of all those upon which, down to the present day, the legal security of the st ate, of the person, and of possession are based.

It is a remarkable fact that everywhere, after the first codifications, tradition is silent for a long time. Among the Romans as well as among the Germans the dark centuries begin. Very little information has been handed down to us concerning the creation of law during this time. As soon as the sources begin to flow more plentifully, we see a picture that is quite different. This took place in Rome about the end of the Republic; among the Germanic peoples about the thirteenth century; in England the darkness was dissolved at a somewhat earlier date; among the Scandinavians, in the fifteenth century.

The interests that are considered worth protecting are the same as in earlier days, i.e. the state, the human body and human life, possession; but the means are considerably more ample and diversified. First of all the state acts much more frequently, exercising its power to punish not only when the state itself is concerned but also, and with increasing frequency, when the security of the bodies, of the lives, and of the possessions of the people is concerned. Furthermore the state has secured control of the social courts to a great extent, and through these affords a much more effective protection than society was able to afford at an earlier time. At the same time that the state administration of justice undertook the protection, by means of deterrence, against violence, crafty and thievish interference[1], the conversion of the penalty into payment of damages for damage done made it possible to grant satisfaction for the wrong done not only in case of violent, crafty, thievish interference, but also in case of interference of other kinds. And lastly we find the action for the vindication of a right in the narrowest sense of the term, the object of which is to secure for the person entitled the very subject matter of his right, i.e. the thing of which he claims ownership or possession, or which the defendant owes.

The prevailing school of jurisprudence has precluded itself from an understanding of this development by assuming a basic difference between a claim for damages and a claim which asserts a right[2]. It deals with the claim for damages in the law of obligations[3]; the claims in the nature of a vindication of a right it deals with in connection with

---

1. crafty and thievish interference：诡计多端的干涉
2. a claim which asserts a right：主张权利的请求权
3. claim for damages in the law of obligations：债法中的损害赔偿请求权

the various rights to which they refer, e.g. in the case of a property claim, in connection with the doctrine of ownership. But Mauczka has correctly pointed out that the rights of personality[1], the rights in one's life, body, honor, good name, cannot be protected, even against violation without culpability, except through a claim for damages. These claims therefore are not a part, analytically, of the law of obligations, but of the law of persons. The same is true of the other claims that assert rights. The action *in rem* based on loss of possession — incidentally the action brought for protection against interference with a relation of domination has the same origin — arose from the action for deprivation of possession either by thieves or robbers. It is therefore intimately related to the action for damages because of robbery and theft. The claim for damages therefore, even today, takes the place of an action *in rem,* whenever the recovery of possession is impossible, occasionally even when it is not desirable. In modern English law and to a certain extent in classical Roman law the claim to a thing (*dinglicher Anspruch*)[2] can be effectively asserted only in the form of a claim for damages. The claim for damages in these cases therefore is, in part, the necessary, and in part the historically given, form of the action for deprivation of ownership and possession, a certain form of the action based on ownership and possession. Likewise the action for damages because of damage done to a thing of which the plaintiff was owner or which he had in his possession always remains an action based on ownership and possession. As in the case of the action brought because of deprivation, so in the case of this action for damages, ownership or possession is the basis of the action. In fact, since the *actio negatoria* is today no longer conceived of, as was the case among the Romans, as an action involving a question of servitude but as an action based on ownership inasmuch as, though the object of the

1. rights of personality：人格权
2. the claim to a thing (*dinglicher Anspruch*)：物上请求权

action is the protection of one's property against an asserted servitude, its basis is ownership, we shall have to consider the *actio legis Aquiliae*[1], not according to its object but according to its basis, as an action based on ownership.

The actions which are based on unjust enrichment are also actions based on ownership or on possession. They are actions by the owner or by the possessor for compensation, up to the amount of enrichment of the other party, for the loss which he has suffered by being deprived of his ownership or his possession for the benefit of another. When a creditor sues to have a transfer of the debtor's property set aside, the basis of the action is the loss of his security. It is therefore in reality an action based on the law of obligations. In the Roman law the claim for the return of unjust enrichment has attained a rich development: *condictiones sine causa*[2], *actio negotiorum gestorum*[3], *actio de in rem verso*[4], *actio Pauliana*[5] as the action of the creditor to set aside the transaction. It was elaborated to a much greater degree of refinement by the Continental common law, especially under the influence of Windscheid. Since the French Civil Code contains provisions only for the repayment of money paid that was not owed, the development of the claim based on unjust enrichment in French law took place almost exclusively through legal decisions which, in point of form, as a rule were based on the *actio in rem verso*. Planiol contented himself with basing it on the principle *neminem cum alterius detrimento et iniuria fieri locupletiorem*: "C'est une des rates regies de droit naturel, qui dominent toutes les lois, alors meme que le legislateurn'a pas pris specialement le

---

1. *actio legis Aquiliae*：〈拉〉阿奎利亚法律诉讼，由《阿奎利亚法》所创设的诉讼。
2. *condictiones sine causa*：〈拉〉无债因请求返还之诉
3. *actio negotiorum gestorum*：〈拉〉无因管理之诉
4. *actio de in rem verso*：〈拉〉转化物之诉
5. *actio Pauliana*：〈拉〉保利安之诉

soin de les formuler.[1]" At the present time in the view of the German as well as of the French law, all gain which is not based on the will of the parties, and for which compensation is not given to him at whose expense it was made, will serve as the basis for an action based on this unjust enrichment. In English law the relation between the claim for unjust enrichment and the claim of ownership or possession, is marked much more clearly because the usual act ions for the enforcement of both claims (*trover*[2] and *indebitatus assumpsit*[3]) originally were actions for interference with possession (trespass). Trover, which originally was an action for things found, now covers all cases in which the defendant has converted to his own use things that belonged to the plaintiff or of which the plaintiff had possession, or has unjustly deprived the latter of their possession and use. *Indebitatus assumpsit* usually covers cases of the same kind as trover where money is involved.

The actions that assert rights, or demand damages, or ask for restitution of unjust enrichment, together with the criminal law that is applicable, are merely various forms of protection of the person, of the relation of domination, of possession. Justice demands that the person, the relations of domination, and possession be protected. Justice also demands that the protection be extended and improved; but in every case the technical question remains to be solved: In what manner shall the requirements of justice be met? Justice must be patient so long as norms for decision and legal remedies sufficient to carry out its demands have not yet been found. The development of the law of damages offers a good illustration of this. The owner of a thing that was stolen or lost can demand its surrender even from an innocent

---

1. *neminem cum alterius ... de les formuler*：〈拉〉这是一个自然法规则，适用于一切法律，因此立法者没有做出专门规定。
2. *trover*：〈拉〉追索非法占用之诉
3. *indebitatus assumpsit*：〈拉〉债务人承诺偿还或履行，普通法的一种诉讼方式。

purchaser, but he can demand damages from a person who injures the thing only in case he is able to show that the latter is culpable.

This more lenient manner of dealing with the person who injures the thing is not a requirement of justice. The reason for it is historical to begin with. The action for the vindication of a right against a third person in possession of the article that had been stolen or acquired in some other wrongful manner had grown out of the action of theft at quite an early date. Eut the original action for damage done, which was looking toward the payment of a penalty, which is in the nature of a punishment, has, in every system of law that has reached a more advanced stage of development, presupposed culpability in the person doing the damage. Because of this historical connection with the ancient action for a penalty, the action for damage done had to be based on culpability even at a time when the penalty had become compensation for damage done. In order to subject it to a development parallel to that which led from the action of theft to an action based on ownership, one would have to find a legal proposition that can make a clear-cut distinction between damage caused without fault and damage that is the result of pure accident. Neither the Romans nor the modern jurists down to the present day have been able to do this, and because of this technical difficulty we still cling, as a matter of principle, to the legal propositions, which, in very many cases, are felt to be unjust, to wit *casum sentit dominus*[1], loss from accident must lie where it falls. Roman law and our older law knew a few exceptions to this. In the nineteenth century at least a few undertakings that can be prosecuted only with great danger to others have, by statute, been made liable for the damage caused by them, but hitherto only the French judicial decisions have given wider application to the principle of liability for damage caused without fault. But it has been possible only in part to

1. *casum sentit dominus*：〈拉〉损失归所有人承担

deduce clear legal propositions from their norms for decision.

The oldest contract involves transfer of possession. In the contract of barter possession of goods is being transferred; when a person voluntarily surrenders himself into bondage for a debt, i.e. in the case of all contracts that obligate a person to render services and performances (in the contracts of subjection), possession of one's own person is being transferred. In the beginning the contract is ineffectual without such transfer of possession; and we may say accordingly that the courts do not protect the contract itself but merely protect the possession which has been transferred to the recipient against deprivation through robbery, theft, or deceit. The situation is not changed when a pledge is substituted for the subject matter of the contract, or when a third person is substituted, as a hostage, for self-delivery into bondage. The creditor can now rely on the possession of the pledge or the hostage, and is protected in this possession in the same way in which he is ordinarily protec ted in the possession of a thing; he has no other rights as yet that he can enforce at law against the other party.

A true law of contracts does not come into existence until the *Haflung*[1] (liability) arising from the debtor's word is greater than the liability arising from that which he has transferred to his creditor. For a long time stress was laid upon the relation in thought between the symbols which were delivered to the creditor, i.e. the *arrha*[2], or earnest-money, the part performance, and the giving of security by means of delivery of the subject matter of the contract or of the debtor into the possession of the creditor; but this relation evaporates more and more, until finally the promise as such, in an ever increasing measure, creates the *Haflung* (liability).

Originally legal protection of the contract always meant only the

---

1. *Haftung*：〈德〉责任
2. *arrha*：〈拉〉定金

legal protection of the disposition that was made in connection with the contract either of a thing or a person, either one's own or another's, at any rate the legal protection of the disposition of one's own person for the purpose of rendering services or of furnishing goods. If the disposition is not carried out at once, it creates at first merely an obligation (*Schuld*)[1] owed by the person making the disposition; to this obligation is added the *Haflung* (liability) arising from the word of the party making the disposition as soon as the courts compel him actually to carry out the disposition. The law has taken these steps hesitatingly and in a certain sense reluctantly — always as a concession to the most urgent and imperative demands of life. *Haflung* (liability) makes its earliest appearance in the case of the compromise as to the payment of a penalty and in the case of the contract to extend credit in connection with the symbolic self-sale of the debtor; the *Haftung* (liability), which, in the case of a sale, is based on the warranty (that the thing has not been stolen): arises at a later time. True *Erfüllungshaftung*[2] (liability for the performance) of the promise connected with the contract of barter presupposes a great amount of commercial intercourse and of division of labor in society. Roman law has not yet reached the stage at which the seller is compelled to perform his promise. It merely compels him to transfer possession and to assume the *Haftung* (liability) for the promise that the buyer shall be permitted to keep the thing. The *locatio conductio* and the other contracts of exchange, the so-called innominate contracts, have not reached even this stage. They give rise, essentially, to an obligation, not *to Haftung* (liability). The modern *Übereignungsvertrag*[3] (contract to convey title) was the first to create the duty to transfer the property. But it is only the French consensual contract and the English deed that produce the effect of

1. obligation (*Schuld*)：债务（斜体为德文）
2. *Erfüllungshaftung*：〈德〉履行责任
3. *Übereignungsvertrag*：〈德〉所有权转让契约

the disposition, i.e. the complete transfer of ownership at the very moment the contract is entered into. It may be said therefore that the development of the idea of justice everywhere strives to make the word (promise of the parties) the all-efficient source, in the contract, of legal effects enforceable at law. But primarily the contract appears as nothing more than the exercise of the right of disposition over one's person or one's possessions. Manifestly the basic thought is merely this: Just as the owner may burn the thing he owns, or cast it into the sea, so he can also transfer it to someone else. Just as the will of the owner is authoritative in general as to anything that is subject to it, so it is also in case the will is declared in a contractual disposition. The contract, from this angle, is a means of utilizing one's property.

Herein lies the germ of another thought sequence. Since the power of disposition over one's property by means of a contract is a means of utilizing the property, that which is to be effected by utilizing the property is part of the content of the contract. In the contracts which are of the greatest importance for commerce the object is to acquire, in exchange for the disposition of one's property, a counter-performance from the other party, which in tum consists in a disposition of property. At a very early date therefore, at first in contracts of exchange, later, to an ever increasing extent, in other bilateral contracts also, performance by one side became the basis of a judicially recognized claim to counterperformance[1] by the other side. But the contract comprises two dispositions which not only condition each other, but which are in an intimate relation with each other and which are intertwined with each other, and a legal system which concerns itself exclusively with the two dispositions contained in the contract without considering their mutual relations, gives expression only to a part of the content of the contract, not to the whole content.

1. counterperformance：对待给付

The book of Zitelmann, *Rechtsgeschäft und Irrtum*[1] (Legal Transaction and Error), contains a model analysis of the psychological processes that go on when a disposition is made. Since every contract contains dispositions, both the point of departure and the result of Zitelmaan's book are absolutely correct. But Zitelmann stops with the disposition. He divides the contract into two independent dispositions. To him a contract still is two dispositions, not the intertwining of two dispositions. Inasmuch as this intertwining is a part of the psychological process in the making of the contract, it is not appreciated at its full value by him. The abundant modern literature of the Continental common law and of the law of the German Civil Code first paid attention to this point.

Incomparably more profound studies of it are contained in the doctrine of value in economics. As is well known, the adherents of the English classical school have written on this subject, as well as the economists of the school which is usually called the Austrian school because its chief exponents were Austrians, although among its founders must be numbered, in addition to the Austrian Karl Menger, the Englishman Jevons, and the Frenchman Walras, and although it has many adherents and out standing exponen ts not only in Austria but also in France and England, and especially in Italy and America. Apparently the classical school and the Austrian school have reached highly divergent results; actually, however, it seems, they have thrown light upon the identical problem, albeit from different angles.

The concept of value of the classical[2] is as truly justified as is that of the Austrian school. But for the question we are now discussing, the concept of value of the Austrian school alone is important.

We are concerned with the contract that has been entered into according to economic principles. "In every concrete economic

1. *Rechtsgeschäft und Irrtum*：〈德〉《法律行为与错误》
2. the classical：古典学派

unit, innumerable tendencies are conceivable in the conduct of the economically active subjects; it is true however that, disregarding economically irrelevant divergencies, but one way of conducting economic undertakings can be the expedient, the economic one; or, in other words, there are innumerable uneconomical ways of conducting every economic undertaking, but, disregarding economically irrelevant divergencies, in every case only one, a strictly determined, strictly circumscribed, way of conducting it along economic lines is conceivable." (Karl Menger.) The economic contract is a contract in which equal values are exchanged.

The investigations of the Austrian school were confined chiefly to sale and barter; and in these spheres, to the subject mat ter of the mutual performances, especially to the price. In most recent times, Kleinwachter has included the urban contract of lease[1] (*Bodenrente*). It is self-evident that investigations of this kind might be instituted with reference to contracts of all kinds, even those that are altogether unilateral, and that do not involve any exchange at all, also to contracts that have no economic content, especially contracts of family or of public law. In every case the contract is based on a psychological process which can be analyzed just like the process which underlies the contract of exchange. In this respect the English doctrine of consideration[2] yields valuable results, as Pollock has shown in his work on contracts. An investigation can not be said to be complete or exhaustive which does not take into account every single understanding arrived at in the contract as well as all *Haftungen* (liabilities), conditions, periods of time, limitations of time; for the economic situation is determined not only by the subject matter and the price, but by the whole content. Until now however BohmBawerk has considered only the influence of time, i.e. the periods of time / in

1. contract of lease：租赁契约
2. doctrine of consideration：对价原则

his work on *Kapitalzins* (simple interest).

The ideal of a perfectly just contract is one that is based throughout on the principles of sound economics. If the norms for decision were to follow this ideal, they would necessarily be altogether inapplicable to an uneconomic contract or they could give effect to it only as it ought to have been made according to the principles of economics. This ideal however cannot be attained by practical juristic science. In the first place the principle that a contract must be based on the principles of economics perhaps cannot be expressed in a general juristic formula, much less in a legal proposition; furthermore the jurist lacks the requisite procedural devices, especially in the matter of proof. Juristic science therefore must set itself a much more modest task. On the one hand it must reject the most glaring instances of uneconomic action; on the other hand it must, in proper cases, correct details of the con tent of the contract according to sound economic principle. Legal history shows that the norms for decision in the law of contracts are in fact developing in this direction under the influence of the idea of justice.

The causes that bring about uneconomic contracts are carelessness, error, necessitous situation, duress. The legal propositions that make against taking advantage of these things in entering into contracts are among the oldest everywhere on the whole earth; in particular, the oldest statutes are directed against it. These are the statutes against usury and fraud. Statutes against usury and fraud are found in Greece, in Rome, in the Middle Ages in Europe; they are the expression of the earliest development of penal law beyond its primitive stage, and they are gaining ground more and more even today.

Beyond this point the law of contracts moves very slowly. In the view of all the older legal systems, of the Roman, of the mediaeval, and even in the more recent Roman law in the view of the legal propositions as to *stipulatio*[1] and the other contracts which give rise to *actiones stricti*

1. *stipulatio*：〈拉〉要式口约

juris[1], in the view of the older Continental common law, and in many respects even of the modern English law, the contract, is, essentially, nothing but a disposition. This point of view appears to have been overcome, to a limited extent, only in the later Roman law, in the later Continental common law; and in the latest Continental law.

But neither the Roman nor the modern law has arrived at a final conclusion. The root of the difficulty is the law of error in the making of the contract, and the law governing the interpretation of contracts. To direct the judge to decide according to business usage and *bona fides*[2], according to good faith and *boni mores*[3], as was done by the Romans and much more frequently by moderns, is by no means a solution of the difficulty. This is not a legal proposition that contains norms for decision but a direction to the judge to find norms for decision according to justice, i.e. according to the principles of sound economics — norms which will give the fullest possible effect to all those considerations on which each party based its calculation of value, and, on the other hand, will deny legal protection to the incurably uneconomic, especially to the incurably immoral, contract. These judge-made norms for decision however are susceptible of universalization, and can, therefore, at a subsequent time, be converted into legal propositions. A large part of the Roman law of contracts is based on universalization of decisions rendered on the basis of *bona fidesy* and the moderns have developed additional legal propositions from the decisions reported in the Roman sources. In my book *Die stillschweigende Willenserklärung*[4] I believe I have given an intimation of the wealth of legal propositions on the law of contracts that is found

---

1. *actiones stricti juris*：〈拉〉严法诉讼。判决主要依赖于审判员对程序和法律形式的严格遵守，诉讼内容却遭到忽视。
2. *bona fides*：〈拉〉诚信
3. *boni mores*：〈拉〉善良风俗
4. *Die stillschweigende Willenserklärung*：〈德〉《默示的意图表示》

in modern judicial decisions. It is selfevident that legal propositions of this kind should not be included in a code; they are juristic science in the narrowest sense of the term.

Among the legal propositions that have been derived from the principle of good faith[1] (*Treu und Glauben*) in this manner, there is one that merits a more careful consideration. It is the proposition that each party is held responsible for the truth of the statements he makes when the contract is entered into. If the other party has made his calculations of value in reliance upon these statements, the norms for decision give effect to the contract in accordance with this calculation. The so-called declaration theory[2] has understood this correctly. This legal proposition can be *applied* to a third party. Whenever a third party by his conduct has induced this calculation of value, he is bound by the contract as it was made in consequence of his conduct. This is the principle of "reliance on collateral facts[3]" (*Vertrauen auf äussere Tatbestände*), as Welspacher has named it. An application of it is the legal proposition *"Hand muss Hand wahren."* It means that a contract which was made in good faith with a possessor is valid against the owner who had ent rusted the thing to the possessor and in this way had created the collateral state of facts, in reliance upon which the good-faith purchaser made his calculation. Another application of the principle is found in the case of public records. The records supply the parties with official information on which the latter can base their calculations. A person who by his conduct has caused the register to be false or incomplete cannot prosecute his right against a person who made this false or incomplete record the basis of his calculation; at best he can proceed against the person who has profited thereby. A few legal propositions carry the principle of reliance upon collateral

1. principle of good faith：诚信原则
2. declaration theory：公示理论
3. reliance on collateral facts (*Vertrauen auf äussere Tatbestände*)：外部事实信赖

states of fact considerably further than this limit; these however are not based on good faith but on practical considerations, security of business transactions and of credit, the social importance of the public record.

It is interesting to note that the English law of contracts in its norms for decision adheres to the older conception of the contract as a disposition to a much greater extent than the Continental law. Until recently it knew of no public land records. They were introduced tentatively only a few years ago. Until recently, with the exception of a few instances, e.g. the doctrine of market overt[1], it did not know the principle "*Hand muss Hand wahren*," which was first laid down in a series of statutes of the years 1823 to 1877, in the so-called Factors' Acts[2], and then only for commercial purposes, and it holds the parties bound by their declarations to a much greater extent irrespective of whether they correspond to the presuppositions of upright business dealings.

It is impossible to extend these investigations to contracts other than those of the law of property, especially to the contracts of family law and public law. Although the canon law as to the grounds of invalidity of marriage, which is a result of the experience of a thousand years and of deep insight into human nature, is out of date, self-evidently, in a few particulars today, it may serve as a sample of what the human mind can accomplish in a field of such difficulty. This achievement has not been equaled in any other legal system, not even in the modern law of marriage, nor in the modern law of the contract concerning property.

We have shown what role justice plays in the law of contracts. It progresses, one may say, along the path of penal law protection of faithful performance of contractual duty by means of penalties for

---

1. doctrine of market overt：公开市场原则
2. Factors' Acts：代销商法

usury and fraud from Zitelmann's conception of the contract to the conception of the Austrian school of economists, from the contract conceived of as a mere disposition to the contract which serves the purpose of acquiring a counter-performance by means of this disposition. In the early law, the contract is merely a means of utilizing one's possessions. The more the law develops, the more it sees in the contract an instrumentality of honest commercial intercourse. It is self-evident that: at every stage, the contract was not only the former but also the latter, i.e. both a means of utilizing one's possessions and, at the same time, an instrumentality of honest commercial intercourse. But the question is not what the nature of the contract is, but how the norms for decision give effect to it. For the purpose of giving effect to the contract as an instrumentality of upright commercial intercourse, even irrespective of questions of the material law, a refinement of procedure was required such as the Romans did not have before the praetorian procedure with its *exceptiones* and *bonae fidei indicia* came into use. The mere *denegalio actionis*[1], even though it did actually serve this purpose, surely was not sufficient to accomplish it. And even today the goal has scarcely been approximated.

Because of the great influence of purely military considerations upon the development of the law of inheritance, it is not easy to recognize the part played by the idea of social justice in the development of the latter. The law and right of inheritance began everywhere contemporaneously with the house community. The part of the property of the deceased that was not given to him to take with him on his last journey remained to the members of the household. The further development is based in the first place upon a fiction of membership in the household, except in so far as military considerations were given weight. If there are no members of the

1. *denegatio actionis*:〈拉〉诉权

household, the inheritance, which would have been without an heir, is offered to those who had been members of the household of the deceased, or would have been had there not been a division of goods. This is the basic idea of the agnatic law of inheritance[1]. An agnate is an actual or a fictitious member of the household, a person who would be a member if he or his ancestor had not withdrawn from it. When the Romans say that an agnate is anyone who is under the same *patria potestas*[2] as the deceased, or would be if the ancestor were still alive, this is merely another mode of expressing the same thought, for the *patria potestas* is the power of the head of the household over the members.

The agnatic law and right of inheritance, therefore, is not a law and right of inheritance by relatives. It must be immediately apparent to everyone that its basis is the house community as long as the greater part of the people live in house communities, and inheritances actually go to present or former members of the household. But it becomes increasingly less apparent the more the rule becomes the exception, the rarer house communities, excepting those of parents and offspring, become. Finally, the whole relation between agnatic law and right of inheritance and house community is forgotten, so that the agnatic law and right of inheritance appears as a species of capricious and irrational law and right of inheritance in the relatives limited to the male line. This was the conception of the Romans as early as the days of the Republic, and it is the conception of the modern English. Now justice demands that these utterly incomprehensible caprices and accidental features of the law of inheritance should be abolished, and that simply the nearest relatives, i.e. those that are not exeluded for some particular reason, should be entitled to the inheritance. In this way the agnatic law and right of inheritance becomes a law and right of inheritance in the family. The justice of the family Tight of

---

1. agnatic law of inheritance：父系继承法
2. *patria potestas*：〈拉〉父权

inheritance is obvious especially at a time when the deceased himself has, in most cases, inherited the property which he leaves, i.e. has acquired it from the family. A special development of this right has found expression in the maxim *paterna paternis*[1], *materna maternis*[2]. All inherited property, according to this maxim, should revert to the side from which it came.

Ficker's investigations have shown that the fictitious house community and the family community are of no significance for the original law of inheritance of the Germanic peoples. In so far as the free man was not prevented by actual members of the household, he could dispose of his property *inter vivos*[3] as he saw fit; after his death it was without an heir unless it escheated to the state or to the commune. The same situation obtains among the Romans and the Slavs. The right of the agnates or of the relatives (*Beispruchsrecht*), that their consent must be obtained before land can be sold, belongs to a later order everywhere. And the fact that there are no legally effective testamentary dispositions in primitive times is attributable to the lack of legal remedies to enforce them; but the *Treuhandgeschäft* (trust transaction)[4], the contractual gift *inter vivos* coupled with a postponement of legal effect until after death, is not made impossible thereby. The great importance of the trust transaction was set forth in the excellent book of Robert Caillemer on the basis of a great wealth of material. The *Treuhandgeschaft* (trust transaction) is a contract, and the element of justice in this transaction is identical with the element of justice in the contract: the power of disposition of the owner over his property. And this remains the basic idea of the law and right of inheritance by testamentary disposition even after the *Treuhandgeschaft*

1. *paterna paternis*：〈拉〉由父系后嗣继承的父系财产
2. *materna maternis*：〈拉〉由母系后嗣继承的母系财产
3. *inter vivos*：〈拉〉在世时
4. *Treuhandgeschäft* (trust transaction)：〈德〉信托交易

has become a unilateral testamentary declaration. The will of the owner, as in the case of contract, controls the disposition of his property, in this case, even beyond the grave. The more the agnatically fashioned *rechte Erbrecht* (true law of inheritance)[1] — to rehabilitate this fine term which Puchta had suggested as a substitute for *gesetzliches Erbrecht* (statutory law of inheritance)[2], which is very likely to be misunderstood — appears to be out of harmony with the family order which prevails in society today, the more the disposition by last will and testament grows in importance. Before long it has come to be considered a misfortune to die intestate. This was the case in Rome and in the early Middle Ages. Since the middle of the twelfth century, actuated by self-interest, the church has prepared the way for the last will and testament. Thereafter the endeavor to provide for one's family, for pious and public uses, for the economic undertaking that one has been engaged in, looms large in the minds of men.

These clear trends of justice in the law of inheritance are being crossed by a series of thoughts that belong to entirely different orders. In the ancient city states, the parcels of ground owned by countrymen and by city dwellers are at the same time warriors' portions. These were not to be diminished in number by the death of the possessors, and, on the other hand, they were not to be weakened by the division of inheritances to such an extent as to make it impossible for the possessor to gain his livelihood from them. The right of inheritance of the freeman among the Germanic peoples seems to have been influenced by the same considerations. This accounts for the limitations on the right of women to take by inheritance. These military points of view are most strongly expressed in the law relating to the right of the *Erbtochter*[3] to take. The purpose of the whole feudal

---

1. *rechte Erbrecht* (true law of inheritance)：〈德〉真正的继承法
2. *gesetzliches Erbrecht* (statutory law of inheritance)：〈德〉制定法上的继承法
3. *Erbtochter*：〈德〉最后一个男继承人的女儿

law was to provide an expensively equipped horseman for the army of the feudal lord, and the feudal law of inheritance is designed to effectuate this purpose. As to the right of inheritance of the villeins the constitution of the manor and the will of the lord are decisive. The latter's concern is undiminished revenues and services; his endeavor is to establish a law and right of inheritance according to which every parcel of ground will have an owner able to render the required services. Again there is the desire to assign the various parts of the inheritance to those to whom they would be of benefit: the arms to the men; the *Gerade* (i.e. the paraphernalia)[1] to the women. Again in the higher ranks of the nobility there is the rooted idea to establish the law and right of inheritance in the interest of the glory of the family. Among the free peasants the principle of the house community survives here and there; to wit one of the sons takes possession of the farm, the other heirs are provided for as servants. Elsewhere the elder sons are portioned off, and the youngest son, who has remained with the father, gets the farm (ultimogeniture, borough-English).

The English law of inheritance has, preponderantly, been under the sway of such trends ever since the influence of the London courts in the fifteenth century caused the feudal law of succession, which had been confined to the holders of knight's fees, to be extended to all classes. The immovable property descends to the first-born son according to feudal law; in default of a first-born son, to the first-born male child among the children of the nearest relative (with a rather complicated computation of the degrees of relationship); while as to movables, the right of succession of relatives together with the right of the surviving spouse has been making its way for two centuries. In the seventeenth century an unlimited freedom of testamentary disposition prevails, which is not even limited by a law providing for

1. *Gerade* (the paraphernalia)：私人物品

a *Pflichtteil* (duty part, or compulsory portion)[1]. The attachment of the English to their law of inheritance is not easily understood by a Continental. They have made only minor changes during the course of the nineteenth century.

In the most recent development of the law of inheritance, only a few leading thoughts are discernible. In the law of testamentary disposition, the tendency is toward untrammeled power of disposition, limited only by the law creating a duty part, or compulsory portion, in favor of the descendants and the ancestors of the testator, occasionally also in favor of the surviving spouse. The duty part, or compulsory portion, is thought of as making provision for those persons for whom the testator is under a duty to provide. The *rechte Erbrecht* (*supra*)[2] is characterized by a state of extreme perplexity. It almost seems as if the idea were this:

Someone must take the property after the death of the owner; who takes, and what the taker does with it after he has it, is a matter of indifference to the law provided only that it remain in the family. In Germany and Austria a contrary tendency has set in, but only in the peasants[5] law of inheritance, i.e. the tendency to preserve the farm in such condition and extent as will insure adequate husbandry. The Swiss Civil Code contains an interesting attempt to arrive at a profounder understanding of the problems of the law of inheritance.

In spite of all this, the leading ideas of justice in the historical development of the law of inheritance can easily be traced. Remaining in possession of the goods that were left, by a process of extension, became a right of inheritance in the fictitious members of the household, the agnates, and this is transformed into a right of inheritance in the members of the family. To this is added the trust

1. *Pflichtteil* (duty part, or compulsory portion)：〈德〉特留份
2. *rechte Erbrecht* (*supra*)：〈德〉真正继承权

(*Treuhandgeschdft*) in the form of a contract *mortis causa*[1], and out of this grows the testamentary disposition as soon as the necessary juristic technique has been developed. The law and right of inheritance by last will and testament is limited in part — only by the right of the members of the household and of the nearest relatives to take by inheritance, and in England not even by that. Secondary trends lead to a law and right of inheritance in the interest of the preservation of the glory of the family, of husbandry, of economic undertakings, to gifts to the church and other public institutions, especially in testamentary dispositions. In the beginning the criminal law affords no protection, even against theft and robbery; for the inheritance is considered ownerless in case there are no members of the household. Later however state regulations appear for the safeguarding of the rights of the heirs (sealing of the inheritance, permission to take possession of the goods of a deceased person granted only after a court proceeding).

An idea of justice that has become widespread is that labor should be placed on a par with property as wealth that is entitled to protection. It has been recognized in the word of Scripture[2], "The laborer is worthy of his hire[3]"; and in the socialist assertion of a claim to the fruits of one's labor it has been given a clearly defined expression, which, of course, as long as the present social order continues, does not demand that it be realized by means of legal propositions. But the norms for decision do not even make provision for it to the extent to which it could easily be received into the framework of the present-day social order; and, to a great extent at least, the cause of this is the difficulty of adequately formulating the legal proposition. Accordingly a cause of action which is similar to the cause of action for unjust enrichment through the property of

1. contract *mortis causa*：死因契约（斜体为拉丁文）
2. Scripture：《圣经》
3. The laborer is worthy of his hire：做工的人应得其报酬。

another lies only in the rarest of cases against the person who has unjustly enriched himself through the labor of others. It is only in one field, the field of creative intellectual labor, that the difficulties, which in this sphere were enormous, have been overcome by the combined labors of the jurists of almost all civilized peoples, and a considerable part of the problem has been adequately solved. To it we owe our law protecting literary and artistic creation and the criminal law protection of intellectual property. It is true, much remains yet to be done. So in France the idea is being agitated to secure for the artist whose works have been sold at a ridiculously low figure a share of the increase in value of these works after he has become famous. The justice of this idea is not being disputed, but it is impossible to find the technical solution of the problem. The means proposed, to wit to assure to the artist and to the members of his family after him as a matter of law two per cent of the price obtained at a public auction as an inalienable right, clearly is utterly ineffectual. The correct thing would be to grant him a right of preemption in respect of his work, but even here the closer one approaches the problem, the more the difficulties accumulate.

The ideas of justice therefore give rise to legal propositions that supply society with increasingly rich and varied means of defense against attacks upon its order. In all these cases, it is always a question of developing materials rather than of transforming those already existing. Personality, domination, possession are protected by the inner order of society. They are protected in the first place by means of a threat of punishment, by giving causes of action for damages, and lastly, especially in the case of possession; by giving causes of action for the assertion of rights and for unjust enrichment. The causes of action arising from contract are realizing, more and more perfectly, the original peculiar purpose of the contract, i.e. to utilize the power of disposition over one's possessions in order to acquire a counterperformance, and, in the case of the *Kreditauslausch* (exchange of credit)[1] and of the contract for furnishing things for use, to obtain equal value. Judicial and state protection of the right of inheritance likewise, in so far as it is based on justice, carries out a series of thoughts which are already in existence in life. They are the following. The inheritance, to begin with, is the store from which the members of the household and the nearest relatives of the deceased derive the means of sustenance. Over and above this, it belongs to the family of the deceased; the dispositions made by the deceased are effective beyond the grave. The fact that the protection of intellectual labor by means of legal propositions and legal remedies was effected only in the last centuries must be attributed to the fact that intellectual labor did not come into its own before that time. Thus far then the whole law, which is based on justice, is nothing more than an expression of the existing facts of the law, an expression of social statics. In contrast to, and distinct from, this justice there is another justice, which is an expression of social dynamics. In the latter the idea prevails not only that the legal proposition is able to preserve the *status quo*[2], but that it is a means whereby society can order the relations within the various associations in its interest. The powerful impelling forces of this dynamics are individualism and collectivism. It is believed that, through judicial decisions and administrative action, the existing facts of the law can be modified or abolished and that by this means the progress of society can be guided into certain channels.

The significance of individualism and of collectivism for the development of the law I have discussed with so much detail in my book on legal capacity (*Rechtsfähigkeit*)[3] that I may be permitted to limit my present discussion of this point to a reference to this book. In the present connection, the important thing is their effect upon the

1. *Kreditaustausch* (exchange of credit)：〈德〉信用交易
2. *status quo*：〈拉〉现状
3. legal capacity (*Rechtsfähigkeit*)：权利能力

norms for decision. The culmination of individualism is the principle that every man is an end unto himself and is not subject to any power that would use him for its own ends: neither to a domination that would subject him to the individual will of another nor to a domination that would subject him to the will of an association in which he does not serve himself but only the whole. The ideal of justice of individualism[1] is the individual and his property, the individual who has an untrammeled power of disposition over his property, who recognizes no superior but the state, and is not bound by anything but the contracts he has freely entered into. Individualism therefore dissolves all relations of dependence established by custom, i.e. slavery, domination, and subjection, and abolishes, or at least weakens, the family law powers. The power of the husband falls into disuse under its influence; marriage itself is loosened to a considerable extent by more easily obtainable divorce; the paternal power, guardianship, and curatorship gradually cease to be selfserving rights of a master, and become an office, the duties of which are being performed for the benefit of the person subjected to it. This development, which reached its culmination in the Austrian Code at the beginning, in the Swiss Code at the end, of the nineteenth century, is destined to reach its culmination in France in the revision of the Civil Code. Only a modest beginning is to be found in the German Civil Code. After the associations, into which the individuals appear to have been placed as members by society, have been dissolved and destroyed, the only connecting links that remain between the individual and society are ownership, contract, and the state, to which even individualism concedes the unlimited right to use the individual as a means to an end. Between the state and the individual are only those associations which the state creates as its institutions or endeavors to treat as such

1. The ideal of justice of individualism：个人主义正义的理想

(commune, country, church), and those that the individual enters voluntarily either by joining or through contract (clubs, societies). All the rights that the individual is entitled to are transmuted by norms for decision into individual rights, real rights or obligatory rights. This may be said even of the time-honored community of ownership in the family: the right to maintenance becomes a claim for maintenance. The German Civil Code puts the matter in a form that indicates the true situation: maintenance shall regularly be paid in the form of a money annuity. This precept, as such, which has been derided a great deal, is quite proper in the system of the Code; for whenever maintenance is to be awarded in a judicial proceeding — and this is preponderantly the case in the individualistic private law — it will regularly be done in the form of a money annuity. In general duties are imposed upon an individual by norms for decision only in a case where the individual has undertaken a duty contractually or has brought it upon himself through fault (*Schuld*)[1].

The individualistic law of things[2] is st riving for a liberty of property which shall set the latter free from all relations with, and considerations for, the community. The individualistic law of contracts demands liberty of contract, with the limitation indeed that the individual shall not have power of disposition over his own person inasmuch as the individualist has always considered the person inviolable. The individualistic law of inheritance culminates in the endeavor to accord the fullest practicable equality of treatment to the heirs that are entitled to take, and to provide society with the greatest possible number of individuals that are endowed with property and freedom of contract. The individualistic law of the state places the individual in a direct relation to the st ate: its ultimate mode of expression is the right of suffrage. Every form of limited suffrage

1. fault (*Schuld*)：义务
2. law of things：物权法

hitherto has always been found to be a veiled right of suffrage[1] in the householder or in the head of the family. This disappears where the right of suffrage is universal; the state appears as consisting of individual human beings. Woman's suffrage, it would seem, presents the public law dissolution of the household and of the family into individuals as its component parts as well-nigh completed. Thus, severed from all relations, judged, essentially, according to identical norms for decision, human beings are equal before the law.

The world-historical significance of individualism lies in this, that it has done more than merely to create legal propositions, that it has, through the legal propositions, directly affected the facts of the law. It has done away with the usages in the associations by abolishing the associations; it has changed them by changing the structure of the associations, especially by loosening the structure of the family and by bringing the state into an entirely new relation to the individual; and, in particular, it has given a deathblow to the power of domination in the family and in the ruling associations among civilized peoples. Through the establishment of liberty of property and the liberation of land from all burdens and charges, which followed in the train of liberty of property, it has utterly changed the relations of possession; through liberty of contract it has freed trade and commerce from untold fetters; and through liberty of industrial activity it has shifted the center of gravity in the acquisition of wealth to movable property. But the very greatness of the revolution most effectively bears witness to the fact that the legal propositions have brought about these effects solely through the elemental social forces, to which they in turn owed their very existence.

In the nineteenth century collectivism appeared as a reaction from individualism. Inasmuch as it found expression in socialism or

---

1. right of suffrage：选举权

communism it has no place in this discussion; for in this form it has had no influence upon the present-day development of law. Other, more moderate, forms of the idea, however, particularly in the last decades, have come to be of great significance in all departmerits of the law.

Collectivism expresses the opposite of the idea of isolation (*Einzelgedanke*[1]) of which individualism is the protagonist. According to the individualistic idea of isolation, it is the duty of each individual to look out for himself, utilizing his property and his work as advantageously as he can. But individualism, even in the days of its greatest power and influence, was not able to prevent communities from coming into existence, and continuing to exist, in which at least certain claims of the members were satisfied by the whole body according to quite different principles. In the house community of the family, in the corporations, in the societies for the promotion of the public welfare, in the state in so far as it is a military community or a community of officials, or a welfare community, there are no performances and counterperformances nicely calculated according to property and contract. The individuals render services according to their powers and abilities, and receive according to their needs. Although collectivism, unlike socialism and communism in this, does not endeavor to erect the whole social structure on the basis of principles of this nature, it does attempt to introduce into society some of the principles which appear fully realized in the existing communities. For the free utilization of property through contract there is to be substituted an order under which the individual, at least in emergencies, would render services to the whole according to his powers and abilities, and the whole would provide for the needs of the individual — at least in emergencies.

---

1. *Einzelgedanke*：〈德〉个体思维

The point of departure is the great inner contradiction with which individualism is afflicted. In spite of the endeavor to treat all men alike, it permits some of the greatest inequalities to remain, especially the inequality in wealth, which the equality before the law merely serves to accentuate. The more the rich and the poor are dealt with according to the same legal propositions, the more the advantage of the rich is increased. In contrast to socialism, the social movement that is based upon collectivism does not attempt to abolish the inequalities, but merely to mitigate them. Its aim is to counterbalance the advantage in fact which the rich enjoy by means of social institutions and legal propositions which impose limitations upon the rich and prevent them from availing themselves of these advantages in too great a measure.

In spite of the apparent conflict between them, both individualism and collectivism are after all nothing but the expression of a tendency running counter to the legal order which is founded on ownership of property. The latter gives to the possessor the exclusive power of control over the economically profitable forces of nature, and this is the sense not only of the law and right of ownership but also of almost all the other legal institutions. According to its inner nature, every contract, even the contract of labor, is a utilization of one's property by the exercise of the power of disposition over it; and although the workman is not exercising this power of disposition over his property in the narrower sense of the term, but over his physical and mental powers, he does it for the sole purpose of enabling the owner of the means of production to acquire the working power of the workman, and thereby make his property productive. Whether the family serves the purpose both of production and of consumption of goods, as it did in the past, and as the family of the peasant still does even today, or whether it serves only the purpose of consumption as is the case preponderantly today, it is being kept together by the owner of property and receives its content from the ownership of property. The state and the public corporations are the organs of a society which is based on property; other associations exist for the administration and utilization of property which is held in common for common purposes. These purposes, of course, may possibly be ideal purposes. In the days when society consisted of slaveholders, in the feudal society in Europe down to the days of its last offshoots in the nineteenth century, and in the family down to the nineteenth century, property was invested with certain rights of domination which were exercised by the owner either directly or through the state and through the public corporations, and by the owner of means of production through the guilds. It was at this point that individualism made its attack. When it demanded liberty of property and contract, it meant merely that no rights of domination should be connected with property. Since vestiges of these can be found today only in the state and in the family, the historic mission of individualism has well-nigh been fulfilled. Collectivism goes deeper than this. It is not directed against the direct right of domination but against the indirect right and power of domination in the owner, particularly against the personal subjection which appears as the consequence of exclusive right and power of disposition over the resources of nature. Collectivism seeks to counteract this right and power of domination by endeavoring to bring about the creation by the state or by society of new communities or the development by the state or by society of those that are already in existence. This, it is hoped, will aid and support the individual in his struggle for existence (right of combination, trade-unionism, organizations for the common welfare). On the other hand, it is urged that this be done by direct action of the state, this greatest, this all-inclusive association, which, it is urged, should interfere more vigorously than it has done hitherto through legislation and through its agencies in the interest of those who are laboring under a handicap because of the property system. The state limits the rights of the owner in so far as they might become dangerous to the person or the property of another (extension of liability for damage done, usually up to but not including damage done by *vis maior*[1]), and imposes special duties toward the workmen and other employees (legislation for the protection of workmen in the narrower sense). Just as the old usury legislation tried to prevent the owner of money and consumable goods from availing himself of his ownership for the purpose of exploitation in the contract for the extension of credit, so the state today forbids the owner of the means of production (*Arbeitsmittel*[2]) to resort to certain kinds of exploitation in the contract of labor (limitation of the labor of women and children, of the working day, Sunday rest, prohibition of payment in kind (*TruGksystem*). It compels the owner of the means of production (*Arbeitsmitiet*) to permit the workman to receive a greater share of the fruits of his labor (wage policy, minimum wage in England, Australia, and New Zealand). It expends a part of the produce of the national economy for the benefit of the non-propertied classes (old age pensions, social insurance, state institutions for the public welfare, the public welfare law of inheritance of the project for the Swiss code, state housing policy). The state takes over a part of the production of goods in order that the fruits and profits arising from it may accrue to all strata of the population (movement toward state ownership and control). Similar action by the communes is of similar significance (municipal socialism). In the case of collectivism, too, it appears that the world is not ruled by legal propositions. It produces its effects only by creating associations, imposing charges on property, limiting the liberty of contract, i.e. by creating facts of the law.

The social idea of justice therefore has not destroyed the individualistic idea of justice; it has fulfilled it. However much the idea of individualism and that of collectivism may clash, in the course of history the spheres within which each of them is justified are

1. *vis maior*：〈拉〉不可抗力
2. *Arbeitsmittel*：〈德〉生产资料

gradually being delimited. Individualism, too, must concede to the state whatsoever it requires for the purpose of doing justice to each individual, and collectivism, too, must be in position to justify its existence by promising to the individual a better present, or at least a better future, than he could obtain as an individual.

Individualism and collectivism are not confined to the legal sphere. They have made their influence felt in art and literature; in philosophy and ethics; perhaps in every sphere of human activity. And in the legal sphere, they undoubtedly have been active at all times. The "individualism" of the Roman law and the "social trends" of the mediaeval German law but recently were fashionable terms, although surely there was no dearth of social trends in Roman law and none of individualistic trends in German law, and although the outward impression that one receives is determined by the stage of development that the person who is forming a judgment on these two systems of law has in mind. Every article on the *artele* bears witness to the influence of collectivism in Russian law. Whenever several Russians embark on a common undertaking, even though it be merely a hunting expedition, they form an *artel,* an association. But for two centuries, at first individualism, then collectivism, have consciously been the motive power in the creation of law. They have not only brought about legal propositions, but have powerfully influenced human conduct, and have given rise to much new law. There is much in the work of individualism that has called forth just criticism, nor have all the results of collectivism stood the test. It seems that we are again facing an individualistic tendency, which undoubtedly will be followed by a tendency of the opposite kind. Like the thread of a screw, these two ideas of justice alternately have been drawing the human race upward.

Among all of the ideas of justice that have been described until now there is not one that has failed to encounter an antagonist in the course of historical development who, in the deepest chest-tones of genuine conviction, would proclaim the opposite as that which alone is just. This affords a deep insight into the nature of justice. It would be difficult to find a principle that is so widely recognized as being just as the "sacredness" of property[1]. One need not point to the jibe of the socialists at the sacredness of property, "of which they prate most to whom nothing else is sacred." It may suffice to call attention to the fact that expropriation for the benefit of the public is held to be fully as just as property itself. This of course, by itself, would not be convincing. But a more searching investigation of the modern development of law reveals the fact that the expropriations by the state which are generally being demanded and which are actually taking place either quite openly or most thinly veiled, have become so numerous and so extensive that the principle seems to have been converted into its opposite, and that every instance of interference with property by the state is felt to be just, provided only that it seem somehow covered by a reference to the public interest. This is by no means a new phenomenon; for even a man with the highly developed sense of justice of an Adam Smith has justified the incredible confiscations perpetrated under the Navigation Acts[2] on the ground that they were being perpetrated in the interest of British naval power. This applies also to the contract. It is just that every man should be bound by the contract as he has made it, but demands are continually being made in the name of justice for new limitations of the liberty of contract in the interest of public morals, of personal liberty, of social policy, of honesty in daily life. Anton Menger says of the reliance upon collateral states of fact in matters covered by the maxim "*Hand muss Hand wahren*" that, in the interest of the security of commercial transactions, the whole national wealth is thereby subjected to an expropriation, which indeed is limited, but which is operating without interruption. Anton Menger also combats individualism in the law of the family. He says that in

---

1. "sacredness" of property：财产"神圣"
2. Navigation Acts：航海法

modern society the family is practically the only place where love and devotion are being cultivated, and that it is to the interest of the non-propertied classes that it be maintained and strengthened. Nothing seems to most people to be more just than that all the children of the deceased should inherit equally, and the legislation of the French Revolution seems to have been altogether unable to persuade itself that it had sufficiently given effect to this idea. Nevertheless I am convinced that the German peasantry of Austria regard the law and right of the single heir (*Anerbe*) which prevails among them as just. According to this law all the children, with the exception of the single heir (*Anerbe*)[1], are limited to a very niggardly duty part, or compulsory portion (*Pflichtteil*)[2]. Not even those children that are being disadvantaged make any complaint about it. In this whole matter it is by no means a question of subjecting a universally valid principle to salutary limitations in one detail or another. The point is that often enough, at the same time, opposing principles are conceived to be just, sometimes in different strata of society, in circles that are remote from each other, but just as frequently by people who are in a very close relationship to each other. Both the two parties to a law-suit are usually convinced of the justice of their cause, and perhaps they may well be; for each is appealing to a different idea of justice.

But a searching consideration of the facts of legal history permits us to pick out a clear line of development everywhere in the variegated diversity of the phenomena. Among the conflicting ideas of justice[3] there always has been one that gained the victory at the time, and the victories were gained not because of historical accident but in accordance with an inner unifying regularity. As everywhere else in the universe, so also in society, the yesterday is contained in the today,

---

1. single heir (*Anerbe*)：单一继承人
2. compulsory portion (*Pflichtteil*)：特留份
3. conflicting ideas of justice：冲突的正义观念

and the today in the tomorrow. In the sphere of law, justice is the idea of today which has grown out of the idea of yesterday and the idea of tomorrow which is growing out of the idea of today. In order to become a legal proposition, the legal today and the legal tomorrow, born in society, must be given form and shape by a personality who thinks and senses what the future will bring. This is the basis of all practical juristic science, of all legislative policy, of all the systems of legal philosophy that have hitherto come into existence. It is true, we are in no better case than the herbalists of past centuries, to whom thousands of years of experience of the human race had given a vague idea of the virtues that are inherent in the various plants. The jurist and the legislator will gradually become more and more like the modern scientifically trained physician in proportion as sociology is able to trace and present the laws of the development of human society。 At the present time there are a few modest beginnings in, and only in, the science of economics.

XI JURISTIC SCIENCE IN ROME

Everyone who has compared a statute with a book that has been written about it has observed that the bulk of the book is many times greater than that of the statute, occasionally as much as several hundred times greater. The idea suggests itself to inquire into the cause of this phenomenon. How did it come about that so large a volume was written about so brief a statute? To this question the jurists have a very plausible answer at hand. Every statute, be it never so clear and detailed, leaves room for all manner of doubt. To resolve these doubts is the function of juristic literature. Now the doubts must be rather great if they can be resolved only in books that are of so much greater size than the statutes themselves. Under these circumstances, I take it, the further question is justified: Why are the statutes not couched in terms that leave no room for doubt? For nothing is gained under our present-day method if, in order to arrive at a clear understanding of what the statute ordains, one must refer to a book that has been written about it. The statutes therefore ought to be more detailed or juristic literature is superfluous.

Time was when the jurists themselves entertained this idea. They endeavored to draft the statutes in such minute detail as to make doubt as to their meaning altogether impossible. The immediate result was that the statutes became bulkier, but the bulk of the juristic volumes was not decreased thereby. In the course of time jurists began to awaken to the fact that each word that is added to a statute gives rise to further doubt. Today almost all jurists of true insight incline toward the opinion that the briefer, the more chary of words, the statute is, the better it is. The current answer, therefore, to the question why that which is written in the books is not contained in the statute cannot possibly be satisfactory.

Further inquiry will convince one that the difference between a statute and a book that discusses the statute is not quantitative but qualitative. The juristic books do not offer something additional but some thing different. For they contain the juristic technique, practical juristic science. Technique is out of place in a statute. If it is put into the statute, as has been attempted by those that demand that everything be found in the statute, it at once loses its characteristic nature and becomes a hybrid, which not only does not aid the development of the technique, but disfigures the statute, and not infrequently interferes with its operation.

Practical juristic science, which is to be the sole subject matter of our discussion at this point, is the art of making law subserve the legal needs of daily life[1]. It is therefore something quite different from the science of law. Although there might be as many kinds of practical juristic science as there are kinds of legal needs in daily life, only two branches of this technique have become important. These are, first, judicial technique, which arises from the need of adjudication of legal controversies, secondly *Kautelarjurisprudenz*[2], the art of drawing up legal documents. A clean-cut line of demarcation between the two cannot be drawn; for in drawing up legal documents one must consider the question how a legal dispute arising from the document would have to be adjudicated, and on the other hand judicial juristic technique must continually consider the question how legal disputes which involve documents must be dealt with. Judicial juristic technique always was the leading one and is often considered the only one. It is indeed the older of the two; for the art of drawing up legal documents does not

1. making law subserve the legal needs of daily life：使法律促进日常生活的法律需要
2. *Kautelarjurisprudenz*：〈德〉起草法律文件的艺术

come into being until a relatively more advanced stage of development has been reached. Judicial juristic technique therefore must needs be the point of departure for a scientific presentation of practical juristic science.

Practical juristic science did not arise from the need of applying existing law according to rules of art, but from the need of fashioning a legal system so that it might be practically applicable. The law as a rule of conduct, the law in the sense of a social order, is as old, indeed, as society itself; but the law never arises spontaneously in such a form as to be immediately available for use as a norm for decision, and does not suffice for the decision of all causes that may arise. The earliest function of the jurist, then, is to fashion the social law into norms for decision, and, furthermore, to find the norms required for the adjudication of the legal controversy. Legislation, or creation of law by the state, is not found at this stage, and for a long time to come will not be found to an extent worth considering. The jurist is not yet an organ of the state, but of society. He fulfils his task as law-finder not in virtue of a commission from the state but in virtue of the reputation and the confidence he enjoys in society, just like the soothsayer and the medicine man. The fact that as a rule (it seems, not always) he is a priest does not argue a close relation between law and religion; for the other arts and sciences, too, were fostered chiefly by the priesthood, e.g. the arts of healing, music, and poetry. In a stage of development in which society is as yet altogether unorganized, the priesthood is the bearer of all intellectual life.

A practical juristic science of this kind must needs exist in every society that has attained even the lowest degree of civilization. On a soil that is especially adapted such as never existed in Greece, but did exist in Rome and in Iceland in the greatest conceivable measure — it can develop most luxuriantly. In the more advanced stages of legal and social development, a few additional functions are being added to the earlier ones of juristic science: a knowledge of the existing law;

a deeper insight into human nature, which is developing more and more, and into human relations, which are continually becoming more and more complicated; the ability to formulate the existing law in a legal proposition that will meet the present need; the ability to find the proper solution in case a practical need arises, and to make use of legal knowledge for the solution of practical problems. In the course of historical development, one or the other of these qualities comes to the fore. But let it be said most emphatically that it is the Continental idea of the last two or three centuries only that would limit practical juristic science to a knowledge of the existing law, and to the solution of practical problems. The wise men in the court scene on the shield of Achilles are not expected to proceed according to established rules, but, on the basis of their deeper insight into human nature, to find a judgment which will compose the quarrel about the penalty which is to be paid for the man that was slain. The ten men who composed the Twelve Tables, or those other four men who proclaimed the *lex Salica per ires malleos*[1], had been asked to make a comprehensive statement of that part of the law which had already penetrated into the consciousness of men in the form of clear legal propositions, and where such propositions were lacking, to eke out the law suitably and in conformity with the rules of juristic technique. This was also the function of the Scandinavian *Rechtsprecher* (declarer of the law)[2] and of every other codifier of the law in time past. In those days the scientific training was lacking which is necessary in order to enable one sharply and clearly to draw the line of demarcation between codification of laws and the creation of law, and which is presupposed today in, and only in, the juristic faculties of universities. Accordingly, juristic science, historically speaking, comprises all of the following: knowledge of the law, application of the law, and creation of law; and, essentially,

---

1. *lex Salica per tres malleos*：〈拉〉萨利卡法
2. *Rechtsprecher* (declarer of the law)：〈德〉法律宣告者

this has remained true to the present day.

The position of practical juristic science in the development of law in its great historical continuity has never been made the subject of investigation. Only the work of Lambert, which has repeatedly been mentioned, *La fonction de droit civil comparé*[1] contains an attempt of this sort. The object of this book however is the clarification of a different problem. Hitherto practical juristic science has always developed only in connection with a certain legal system; and, as a mat ter of fact, there are as many practical juristic techniques as there are legal systems. An understanding of the significance of practical juristic science for mankind could be gained only from a comparative history of the juristic science of the civilized peoples at least. Self-evidently however the solution of a problem of this kind is not to be thought of at this point. Nevertheless there is a practical juristic science which has become of world-historical significance, i.e. the legal science of the Romans, and that of the Continental common law, which has grown out of it. We shall deal chiefly with these hereafter. Anglo-American juristic science[2] will be presented but very briefly, and that of the Scandinavian legal system will be merely touched upon. Since that of the Continental common law has in many ways served as a model for the other important juristic sciences, except the Mohammedan[3], a more detailed presentation of its nature will be conducive to an understanding of the others.

Before we shall enter upon a discussion of the practical juristic science of the Roman law and that of the Cont ine nt al common law, let us but glance at the statements of German law and at the German law-books; for they belong to a much more primitive stage of legal development than our tradition of the Roman law. It is true,

---

1. *La fonction de droit civil comparé*：〈法〉民法比较法的功能
2. Anglo-American juristic science：英美法学
3. Mohammedan：伊斯兰教的

the German popular laws[1] are not an original source of law. Drawn up in territory that at one time had been Roman and had enjoyed a high degree of legal development, influenced by the latter, and also by the church, they contain much that is not native to the soil, particularly much state law; and much that surely never had been law, and that never did become law at a later time. If we eliminate these borrowings, which belong, in the main, to the field of public law, there are left, as the content of these laws, chiefly precepts as to legal procedure, criminal law, law of damages, and as to the law and right of inheritance of collateral relations[2], and a few private law regulations, the majority of which had manifestly got in quite accidentally and had been received merely because they had been applied shortly before in the adjudication of litigation. But it is not only the narrowness of the legal material that is striking, but also the dearth of legal propositions. A few centuries later, in the Middle Ages, the number of legal propositions has indeed increased considerably, in several regions at least; particularly the laws of the cities contain an incomparably greater number of them than the *leges barbarorum*[3]. But the number of divisions of the law to which they refer is not greater than it was in Frankish times, to wit procedure, criminal law, criminal procedure, law of damages, and law of inheritance; we might add a part of the law of suretyship, pledge, warranty in sales. Perhaps in addition to the rules that may be found in the collections a few other rules were in use here and there about the form of certain classes of contracts. At any rate there were not many of them.

We can positively assume, then, that practically the whole store of rules of law that the contemporaries knew of at the time the popular laws

1. German popular laws：德国民间法
2. right of inheritance of collateral relations：旁系亲属继承权
3. *leges barbarorum*：〈拉〉蛮族法

or the city laws were collected has been handed down to us. But they could not possibly have contained a sufficient legal order; not even from the point of view of the requirements of the administration of justice. Where then did the judges and the *Schoeffen*[1] get the norms for decision which they required? To answer this question by referring to their sense of fairness and justice would be inexact. For tradition shows that, in the majority of the cases, the inner order of the individual legal relation which was the subject matter of the particular controversy served as the source of the norms for decision. Long before norms for decision couched in general terms were in existence in sufficient numbers, such norms were taken from the content of the subjective rights as they severally appeared. In mediaeval German law every tract of land may properly be said to be an individual. It has its own law which arises from custom or from the document of grant or from the contracts that were entered into concerning it or from its location in the mark[2]. All this, and nothing but this, is conclusive as to the extent of the rights of the landowner, the rights of property and the rights to emoluments[3], the relations between neighbors, ground rents and other returns, and the permanent charges on land. Likewise there is no general law of corporations. The corporations make their own law or they receive it from the king or from some landowner. Every man belongs to some one or more legal group or groups; and the legal group, in the main, determines the legal status of its members independently. Moreover most of the free families, especially the noble families, have created their own law through ordinance, agreement, or tradition. This law governs the rights of personality, family, and inheritance of its members. The most subjective law however is the material law of contract, which is based almost exclusively upon the content of the various contracts. The

1. *Schoeffen*：即 lay judges，〈德〉非专业法官
2. the mark：马克尔公社，中世纪日耳曼人的一种村落组织。
3. rights to emoluments：报酬请求权

declarations of law and the judgments that have been handed down to us show that the basis for the adjudication of a legal controversy was the law, as ascertained in each case, of the parcel of ground, of the corporation, of the family, of the noble house, or the content of a contract, i.e. the inner order of the relations, which clearly appeared from tradition, the documents submitted, or commercial custom.

All of this, as is well known, did not prevent the mediaeval writer from writing the *Sachsenspiegel*[1], in which, no doubt, he stated a much greater number of legal propositions than he found in existence at the time. It is known today, to a certain extent, how he came to do this. In the public law parts he worked with an ideal conception of the ancient glory of the Empire. This we shall not discuss here. But if we examine the private law, the part we are most concerned with here, we shall see that he is vigorously and consciously universalizing the form of the subjective legal relations within the borders of his narrower homeland, with which he had had opportunity to familiarize himself while acting as *Schoeffe* (lay member of a court), and that, most likely, he has invented more or less of it. In spite of the great diversity in the orderings of the family, the relations of possession, the contents of contracts, and the relations of the various ranks and classes, there have developed in certain districts under the influence of economic uniformity, of the system of legal documents, and also through direct imitation and borrowing, certain common features in the law of real property, of rank, of the family, and of contract. They attracted the attention of Eike von Repgow, doubtless a man of wide experience and keen powers of observation, who made a systematic presentation of these features in his book. Since he was not writing a code but a book of law, he was chiefly concerned with preserving that which was common to legal relations of the same kind, without

1. *Sachsenspiegel*：〈德〉《萨克森法典》

expressing disapproval of that which was divergent or peculiar. The latter was not to be done away with; for it was just as much entitled to continue as that which is general. But the effect was a different one; for posterity did not treat the *Sachsenspiegel* as a book of law, but as a code. The divergent and peculiar was greatly disadvantaged by these universalizations, which he had laid down andin part, had laid down quite arbitrarily; for in every instance it had the burden of proving that it was permissible. Success in this matter was a matter of comparatively rare occurrence, much rarer than it had been before the general had been laid down. We must assume that it was successful only when the parties concerned had already become aware of it, especially when it had been recorded in writing either in a collection of laws or in a document containing a grant. Accordingly the mere fact of universalization in the *Sachsenspiegel* became a self-active, law-creating force; the general became a rule; the divergent and peculiar, an exception. In this way, the *Sachsenspiegel* has become a universal norm for decision even beyond the boundaries of the German Empire; of course not in the form of a universalization but as a precept, as a norm in the sense that now the decision based on the universalization of the *Sachsenspiegel* has been substituted for the decision based on the subjective nature of the individual legal relation, at least in all cases where the divergence and peculiarity was not clearly and unmistakably manifest. It is well known that this development has often gained legal force for the doctrines of the *Spiegler*, even when the latter did not contain universalizations but free inventions. This highly remarkable peculiarity of juristic science, the conversion of its forms of thought, of its legal theorems, into norms, this great antinomy of juristic science, is the basis upon which its worldhistorical position rests.

The *Schwabenspiegel*[1] and the smaller *Kaiserrecht*[2] arose in the same

1. *Schwabenspiegel*：〈德〉《施瓦布法典》
2. *Kaiserrecht*：〈德〉王室法

way and have attained a similar importance. In France the same thing occurred in the case of several books of law, especially the *Grand Coutumier de Normandie*[1] the *Etablissements de Saint Louis*[2], the *Somme rural*[3], and, although not until long after the death of the author, the *Beaumanoir*[4], in England, in the case of Bracton, much more so, in the case of Littleton and Coke. We may pass by the Swedish, Norwegian, and Icelandic books of law, since they are closely connected with the peculiar *Gesetzsprecheramt* (office of declarer of law); the Danish law-books however do not differ much from the works named above. The same may be said of the records of the feudal law, the Assizes of Jerusalem[5], the *Libri feudorum*[6], the feudal law of the *Sachsenspiegel.* In this way the great work of Hugo Grotius has created the modern law of nations.

The significance of the books of law lies not only in the fact that they universalize but in the fact that this process of universalization leads to reduction to unity. He who universalizes merely states that which is universally valid; but reduction to unity always imports a precept to the effect that the particular should conform to the universal. Universalization in itself is merely a logical process without which scientific and practical thinking is impossible. But in juristic science it is norms that are being subjected to this process, not the unifying regularity of phenomena, as in the other practical sciences and in the true sciences. And in consequence it is not more nearly universal unifying regularities that result from the logical process, as is usual in cases of universalization, but universal norms. The great antinomy of

1. *Grand Coutumier de Normandie*：〈法〉《诺曼底大习惯法》
2. *Etablissements de Saint Louis*：〈法〉《圣路易汇编》
3. *Somme rural*：〈法〉《乡村合集》
4. *Beaumanoir*：〈法〉《博马努瓦习惯法汇编》，由中世纪法国法学家博马努瓦汇编。
5. Assizes of Jerusalem：《耶路撒冷法律和论文集》
6. *Libri feudorum*：〈拉〉《封土之争》

juristic science[1] which, I presume, the latter has in common with all other practical sciences that deal with norms, but not with the other practical sciences and with the true sciences, lies in this, that its modes of thought and its doctrines are being converted into norms.

To begin with, it would be most amateurish forthwith to draw inferences as to Roman legal development from mediaeval, especially Germanic, legal development. In the days of the Republic, the Roman law was valid, in the main, only in a very small area, and a legal system of this kind is something quite different from a legal system that is valid in a vast area like the German. On the other hand one cannot compare it with the Italian or the German city laws; for in the latter the city population, which is engaged in commercial and industrial pursuits, was the important consideration, while the Roman law of the more ancient times dealt preponderantly with the nobility and the peasantry of the adjacent open country. In the days of the Empire it was being transformed, rapidly and positively, into a system of law adapted to the needs of an empire. The development was supervised and in par t direc ted from a single center, and in this respect can be compared only with the English law, as to which the London courts have been fulfilling a similar function from the days of Henry II. But the Roman Empire was much larger than England, so far as the London courts are concerned, ever has been, and the provinces enjoyed a much greater measure of independence in the matter of law than the various parts of England; perhaps more than is generally believed today. A comparison with France, at least up to the time of the Revolution, would be much more fitting were it not for the fact that the French provinces, in spite of their subjection to the Parliaments, were so much more independent

1. The great antinomy of juristic science：法学的巨大矛盾

in their creation of law than the Roman, at least so far as the law pertaining to Roman citizens is concerned. Moreover, we must take into account the condition of the Roman tradition. As to the time of the Republic it is extremely fragmentary, and as to the days of the Empire it presents only that in which the jurists of the capital were interested, and it presents this with a marked metropolitan coloring that dominates the whole presentation. In addition to the discussion of the law concerning the peasantry and the rural nobility, which undoubtedly constitutes a heritage from the days of the Republic, there is a presentation only of the law concerning the magistrates of the capital and the official class; commerce and industry receive scant attention.

If one bears in mind these extraordinarily important differences, one has eliminated the most important sources of error in the comparison of the development of the mediaeval law with that of the Roman law. In the first place this comparison shows the historical position of the law of the Twelve Tables. We must concede to Pais and Lambert that throughout historical times there has been no authentic tradition of its text. This is proved by the comparatively modern language, by the fact that its text varies in different quotations, by the many interpolations that date from a later time, e.g. the statement as to the division of the *nomina*[1] and the *aes alienum*[2] among the heirs, or the proposition that the title to the thing sold does not pass to the buyer until the price has been paid. But I think that there is abundant testimony that the Romans had a codification, perhaps an official one, albeit one poorly transmitted, of the old customary law, which goes back in substance to the fifth or fourth century before our era. So far as one can judge from the content that has been handed down, it parallels the Germanic folk laws throughout. In the main, it contained precepts as

---

1. *nomina*：〈拉〉任命
2. *aes alienum*：〈拉〉信托让与

to procedure, penal law, law of damages, right of collateral relations to inherit, rights of neighbors, *ius sacrum*[1]. Over and above this there are a few propositions about forms of contracts and testaments. The former perhaps are interpolations; the latter, perhaps, originally had a meaning quite different from that which was attributed to them at a later time.

If this is correct, it follows that, at the time the Twelve Tables originated, the store of legal propositions was in a general way comparable to that which existed among the Germanic peoples in the sixth or in the eighth century. The chief significance of this fact is that by that time the Roman of those days had become aware of only a very small part of the law of society. As in mediaeval German law, the majority of the norms for decision had to be derived, in each individual case, from the subjective nature of the various legal relations. The fact that we find no trace of the great diversity which we meet with in the history of the German Empire and of German law can be explained by the fact that the territory in which the Roman law of the Twelve Tables, as well as that of the period immediately following, was valid was a very minute one in comparison with that in which the German law prevailed; but, in proportion to the extent of territory, the Roman legal institutions of the time of the Twelve Tables surely were not more unitary than those of the kingdom of the Franks or of mediaeval Germany. The idea that there ever was a unitary law of the Roman *gentes*[2] is out of the question. Each *gens* had its own law, which was based on tradition, perhaps upon precept, surely not upon legislation. An abundance of vestiges of this law of the individual *gentes* may be found in historical times. Surely there were common features which permitted of a comprehensive presentation such as was perhaps contained in the lost pages of Gaius. Nor must it be thought that the

1. *ius sacrum*：〈拉〉奉祀礼仪法
2. *gentes*：〈拉〉宗族法

law of the Roman household, as we know it, was quite generally the inner order of the Roman house. In my book on Legal Capacity, I have shown that the family law that has been handed down by tradition referred only to the relations of the family to the outer world. The inner order of the family must have been subject to very great variations according to rank, calling, wealth, place, descent, *gens,* and also as to time, from century to century. It is quite unthinkable that the Roman artisan or the small merchant or even the proletarian ever was a member of the larger family as we know it, or that the foreigner who had acquired Roman citizenship at once began to regulate his life and that of his family according to the precepts of the Roman jurists. The sources are silent on this subject because that which goes on in the bosom of the family is no concern of theirs. What does concern them is the fact that the *pater familias*, and he only, represents the household in court, and that he alone has the power of disposition over its wealth. But before this outer order had been established, the Roman family, just like the Roman *gens* down to Imperial times, had no law other than its inner order, which, just like the *gens,* it had, in the main, established itself. That the divergencies in the order of clans and families influenced the law of inheritance in the far distant past is, to say the least, very probable, in spite of the fact that the law of inheritance was the first to be regulated by general propositions. Even in Cicero's day inheritance among the patrician *Claudii*[1] was regulated differently from inheritance among the plebeian *Claudii*.[2] As to Roman land law, there is today a growing recognition of the fact that we know it only in the form into which it was put when the original constitution was abolished. That this was brought about by the Twelve Tables is the more improbable the earlier the time into which one places them. In

1. the patrician *Claudii*：克劳狄名门氏族
2. the plebeian *Claudii*：克劳狄平民氏族

the fifth century, the *fundus*[1] was not yet *res mancipi*[2]. Accordingly the *mancipatio*[3] of the law of the Twelve Tables, if it dates from that time, could not possibly have been applicable to the *fundus*. Moreover, before the village organization and the district organization were abolished every parcel of Roman land was an individual in the same sense as the German parcel of the Middle Ages. The law that governed it was not determined by legal propositions; the latter had to be ascertained in each individual case on the basis of tradition, contracts, document of grant, location in the village mark, relations between neighbors. The Roman law of agreements, even in historical times, was by no means laced so tightly within formulae as modern presentations would lead us to believe. Of course one would have to give up at the outset the preconceived notion that the classes and the contents of agreements that the Romans were familiar with can, in some way or other, be gathered from the classes and contents of their *contractus*. So far as we can decipher the Roman law of agreements, we conclude that an agreement had to be of considerable importance in daily life before a contract action could be brought on it. The prior in time was the agreement, not the action. This was the situation in primitive times, and it was the situation in Imperial times also; there always were more agreements than *contractus*. And if one had to, or wanted to, enter into an agreement on which an action could not be brought, one would rely on *iuramentum, satisdatio, pignus*[4]. The Catonian formulae, even though one should refer them exclusively to legally enforceable agreements (and this can hardly be correct), constitute the best evidence that assurance that the agreement would be performed was not sought for in the right to sue but in the security that was given. The sources

---

1. *fundus*：〈拉〉土地
2. *res mancipi*：〈拉〉要式物，需通过要式买卖等特定方式转让。
3. *mancipatio*：〈拉〉要式买卖
4. *iuramentum, satisdatio, pignus*：〈拉〉宣誓、担保、质押

show that in other relations, too, the Romans did not set great store by the right to sue. The great significance of *fides*[1] appears from the role that was played as late as the days of the Empire by the *fiducia*, on which an action could not be based until a very late period. The same phenomena may be observed in the case of the *fideicommissa*. The *iuramentum liberti*[2], too, was in vogue for a long time before an action could be brought on it. For a few contractual claims for *ceria pecunia* or *ceria res*[3], it is true, an action lay, the *condictio*[4], which did not go out of use until a later period; it is possible, as many believe today, that after the adoption of the formulary procedure an *actio in factum*[5] was given in these cases. The further we penetrate into tlie past, the more of contract law is found to be outside of the *ius cioile*, and there were relatively fewer universally valid rules governing them.

This, it is true, is flatly contradictory to the prevailing view that the rigidity and the strict adherence to forms which characterized the older law was not relaxed until a comparatively late date, and then only gradually. The latter view, however, is based, perhaps, on several misunderstandings. It is not true that life and intercourse among men were bound by rigid forms; but appeal to the courts was permitted only under very strict conditions. In general, one must get rid of the idea that the courts were open to everyone in primitive times, as they are today, just because one's right had been violated. In order to appeal to the courts, one had to be a man of power, and such a person engaged in litigation only with his equals. The appeal to law took the place of the feud. Even in historical times, instances can be found on every page of legal history that show the importance of having a powerful patron

1. *fides*：〈拉〉信任
2. *iuramentum liberti*：〈拉〉宣誓解放自由人
3. contractual claims for *certa pecunia or certa res*：金钱或某物的契约请求权（斜体为拉丁文）
4. condictio：请求返还之诉
5. *actio in factum*：〈拉〉事实之诉

in litigation. In the typical action against a poor man, the *legis actio per manus iniectionem,* the decisive question was whether the defendant could find a man of rank and wealth, an *assiduus*[1], to take his part. The rigid, staccato forms of the court procedure correspond to the relation bet ween two mortal enemies as they stand before the judge; they are of the same coinage as the rules of single combat.

But the prerequisites to resort to law have nothing to do with the forms and formalities of legal life. Originally the basis for a cause of action could consist only in an accusation that the accused had perpetrated a misdeed. The *malo ordine tenes*[2] of Frankish times was, as is now admitted, the basis of the *rei vindicatio* also. As to this basis of a cause of action the formalities of commercial intercourse are altogether immaterial. The claim arising from contract, the only one as to which rigid forms could be decisive, is one of those that did not become justiciable until a very late period of time. Since the oldest form of legal protection provided for the contract consists merely in the protection of the possession which was transferred by means of the contract, it is self-evident that the contract is enjoying legal protection only inasmuch as it is accompanied by transfer of possession. But the fact that the contract was protected only where it was accompanied by transfer of possession does not make transfer of possession a formality of the contract. In the gradual severance of the obligation of the contract[3] from the transaction of transfer of possession, the gradual strengthening of the idea of the independent contract may be seen. Not until then did symbols of possession become a matter of form. The calling of witnesses to assure the buyer that the thing sold had not been stolen, or of relatives whose consent was necessary to make the alienation binding — these things are not formalities. And it is just as

1. *assiduus*：〈拉〉有固定住所的人
2. *malo ordine tenes*：〈拉〉非法占取
3. gradual severance of the obligation of the contract：契约债务逐渐分离

improper to conceive of the crudeness and the clumsiness of the oldest form of procedure, which made a straightforward presentation of the state of facts, a more careful elaboration of the claim, and the effective assertion of defenses, impossible, as strictness of form. These things were merely defects of technique, not formalism. Primitive times know of awkward and naive, but not of rigid, forms. Wherever the latter arise, in religion, in art, and in law, the order of development, as history teaches us wherever we can trace it far enough, is a hardening of forms that originally had been soft and flexible, not the reverse. It is true, a time comes when they become an unendurable fetter, which occasionally is thrown off all of a sudden, but we must not on that account believe that the fetter lies at the beginning of all development. Wherever we are enabled to survey a longer period of time, as in Germany, France, and England, we become convinced that the law has always developed from freedom to rigidity. At any rate we may be permitted to quote the words of Maitland concerning English law, which ever since the fifteenth century had been stifling more and more in a veritable bog of formalism until it regained a fair measure of freedom through the influence of Bentham in the nineteenth century. Says Maitland: "It is a mistake to suppose that our common law starts with rigid, narrow rules — knows only a few precisely defined forms of gift, and rejects everything that deviates by a hair's-breadth from the established models. On the contrary, in the thirteenth century it is elastic and liberal, loose and vague." Accordingly Roman juristic science found itself, at the beginning of its career; probably in the fourth century B.C., face to face with the same task that confronted the writer of the *Sachsenspiegel* when he began writing his book. There were only a few universal legal propositions in a comparatively small number of branches of private law. In other cases, the norms had to be found by observing life; one had to ascertain what custom was in vogue in the *gens* or in the family on the point in question, what agreement the parties had reached and entered into, what was commercial or trade usage in a given region or class. If we take a look at the fragments of the juristic science of the Republic, or at Labeo, or at Sabinus, we shall discover that the Roman law has traveled a long way in the course of fewer centuries by far than separate the *lex Salica* from the *Sachsenspiegel.* In this extremely fragmentary tradition we find a wealth of legal propositions, which, in part, have been elaborated to a marvelous degree of refinement. In spite of the great amount of labor that has been bestowed upon the study of the history of Roman law, no satisfactory answer has been found to the question whence the Romans got their legal material. In time past the belief was universal that they had obtained it by a process of interpretation from the statutes and from the edict. But this answer would merely shift the question somewhat, for we should then be constrained to ask whence the statutes and the edict got their legal mat erials. But we may now regard this doctrine as generally abandoned. At the present time, we have sufficient knowledge of the Twelve Tables, of the later private law statutes, and of the edict to know that this great wealth could not possibly have been obtained there. At most, they have made contributions of consequence only to the law of unlawful acts and of intestate succession. Perhaps I may claim for myself the credit of having shown in my *Beitrage zur Theorie der Rechtsquellen*[1] that Roman juristic science has created its material independently of any other source of law. The main root of the Roman law is the *proprium ius civile*[2], i.e. the juristic law which the jurists themselves have created. According to the words of Pomponius, it is the *ius quod sine scripto venit compositum a prudentibus, ius quod sola prudentium interpretatione consistit, or according to Boethius' probatae cilium iudiciis creditaeque sentenciae.*[3]

---

1. *Beitrage zur Theorie der Rechtsquellen*：《法源理论的贡献》
2. *proprium ius civile*：〈拉〉自有的市民法
3. *ius quod sine scripto ... creditaeque sentenciae*：〈拉〉没有书写成文，而是通过法学家的解释来构建的法。或按波伊丢斯的话，它是为城邦的法官所批准以及判决所赞同的法。

Although in form an inteipretation of the Twelve Tables, this *ius civile* was an absolutely independent creation of the Roman jurists. For a further discussion I must refer the reader to the book mentioned above, the conclusions of which have quite generally been accepted.

Even though it has been established that juristic science in Rome has itself furnished its material, the question where the jurists got it remains unanswered. On this point, the writings of the Roman jurists contain a great amount of information which has not yet been made accessible, and which I may possibly turn to account at some future time in a second volume of *Beitrdge zur Theorie der Rechtsquellen.* Moreover there are some scattered references on this point in the literature of recent date. The *veteres*[1], including Labeo and Sabinus, employed the same met hods that were employed by the author of the *Sachsenspiegel* (the later writers, to a great ext ent, merely continue working on the basis of the tradition), i.e. they have consciously, forcefully, and intelligently universalized that which they had observed within a narrow sphere, the inner order of the relations, of which they had a lively understanding from actual observation. They did not, however, select a certain place or a single class, rank, or profession as their point of departure — a proceeding which would be most unlikely at all events. Their point of view was changing continually according to the legal institution they were dealing with, partly because, at the time when juristic science began to consider the question, the views of a certain class, profession, rank, or perhaps of a certain locality were dominant; partly because certain legal institutions appeared chiefly in certain social strata. But a point of view once adopted is usually maintained quite consistently throughout. The basis of the Roman family law is the constitution of the family of the Roman peasant-proprietor[2]; and this state of affairs continued after the latter

1. *veteres*：〈拉〉过去的学者
2. Roman peasant-proprietor：罗马自耕农

had disappeared from Roman society. The enormous revaluation of all human life at the end of the Republic and in Imperial times had surely revolutionized the inner order of the family, but this fact found incredibly little of corresponding expression in the norms concerning the capacity to appear in court, the inheritance and the contract of the *filii familias* — the *senatus consultum Macedonianum*[1], a little mitigation of the old precepts as to the incapacity of the *filii familias* to appear in court and to acquire property or rights, a few slight changes in the law of inheritance, and nothing more. Only the law and right of *dos*[2] in the free marriage and perhaps the free marriage itself as we find it at a later time arose among the nobility and the well-to-do middle classes. The Roman testament, too, seems to have arisen among, and to have been concerned primarily with the interests of, the peasantry. The Roman law of sales is concerned chiefly with parcels of ground, slaves, cattle — in brief, with the individual transactions of the dealings of peasants and small men; a few principles of the law of the market were universalized at a later time so as to cover other sales also. Scarcely a trace can be found of consideration of wholesale trade and industry. The *mandatum*[3] manifestly is of aristocratic origin; it arose from the relations between the great lord and his *clientes*[4] and stewards. The roots of the law of partnership have been traced; they lie in the household of the peasant family, later in occasional associations for purposes of gain or speculation, and lastly in permanent associations for the purpose of conducting joint enterprises. *Sachmiete* (letting and hiring of a thing)[5] involves almost exclusively law pertaining to great landed estates and tenement houses. Studies of this kind yield

---

1. *senatus consultum Macedonianum*：〈拉〉马切多尼安元老院决议
2. *dos*：〈拉〉嫁资
3. *mandatum*：〈拉〉委任
4. *clientes*：〈拉〉门客
5. *Sachmiete* (letting and hiring of a thing)：〈德〉租赁物

some information as to the time at which the law governing these institutions arose.

What the mutual relations between the two parts of the Roman law, the *ius civile* and the *ius gentium*[1], were while these developments were taking place is of little importance for the question we are discussing here. It is possible that the Romans in their universalizations also took the general commercial law of the nations of the Mediterranean littoral into account, but, according to what has just been stated, this does not seem probable; at any rate, they did this only to a limited extent. Moreover, transactions that manifestly were parts of the *ius gentium*, like sale, ordinary and usufructuary lease, were a basis for juristic law only in the form in which they were in use among Roman citizens. This self-evidently applies, even to a greater extent, to the *mandatum* and to the *societas*. This is the only way one can account for the fact that the law of sales remained the law chiefly of the traffic in land, slaves, and cattle and that so little is said of the subject matter and the forms of wholesale trade and other commerce, in which foreigners took part also. We must not forget that the *ius gentium* applied to Roman citizens only so far as it had become juristic law, and that to this extent, as I have shown in my book, the Romans, when they spoke of the *ius civile*, included the *ius gentium*.

The juristic universalizations[2], as I have said a propos of the *Sachsenspiegel*are one thing as to their purpose, another as to their effect. They purport to be statements of that only which is universally valid, and their effect is that everything that has been stated becomes a norm according to which everything is judged that has not been able to maintain itself as something of a distinct and particular nature. Here the great antinomy appears again to which, in every instance, juristic science owes its position in the history of the world. Universalization in

1. the *ius civile* and the *ius gentium*：市民法与万民法（斜体为拉丁文）
2. The juristic universalizations：法律的普遍化

its nature is a logical process through which the human mind extracts the universal from the diversity of things which would otherwise be beyond comprehension. But in juristic science the universal becomes a norm, a precept; the particular, an exception, which must justify its existence in each and every case. What the relation was between the universalizations of the Roman jurists and life cannot readily be shown in detail; but this much is certain: the latter did not follow the former in everything. It has already been pointed out that the inner order of the family of the later times did not correspond to that which the jurists had borrowed from the family of the peasant-proprietor. Another example of this is the sale, which became a contract of transfer not because of the juristic law but in spite of it. But the universalizations demonstrated their enormous power in their function as norms for decision for the courts. They were unreservedly recognized as such in Rome; and in the last analysis, even today, controversies that are covered by the law of family, of the matrimonial regime, of things, of obligations, of inheritance, and, occasionally, even of corporations are being decided according to universalizations at which the Roman jurists arrived through observation and study of indigenous relations, and which have passed over into modern law.

It is with these universalizations that have become norms for decision that is connected the boundless wealth of norms for decision which the Romans found solely for the purpose of satisfying the requirements of litigation because they believed them to be appropriate means to the ends sought and to be meeting the demands of justice. They include first of all the highly ramified subsidiary and non-compulsory law of contracts[1], in addition, the rules relating to liability for *dolus, culpa,* and *mora*[2], to bearing the risk, to the legal consequences of mistake, to the point of time at which a legal right is

---

1. subsidiary and non-compulsory law of contracts：补充与非强行的契约法
2. dolus, culpa, and mora：故意、过失与延迟

acquired or lost, to claims for compensation for unjust enrichment, to the extent and the content of the procedural claim, to *Rechtskraft* (force of law)[1], to conflict of claims. Of all of this nothing, or very little, is to be found both in the *Sachsenspiegel* and in other law-books so far as they are independent of Roman law. Even the modern English law, which in many respects is more richly elaborated than any other legal system in the world, has remained far behind the Roman law in the mat ter of legal propositions of this kind. For various reasons, but especially because they can most easily be transplanted to foreign soil, I am inclined to believe that it was the great store of norms for decision, clear, well thought out, and well adapted to the purpose intended, that qualified the Roman law to become a world system of law.

In spite of their fragmentary condition, the sources make a deep insight into the workshop of Roman law possible. The system of actions which prevailed in Roman law at the time that is of the greatest importance for legal development indicates that there is a distinct procedure for each claim. The parties must express their desires and requests in clear and definite terms, and at the same time perform certain acts, and all of this is definitely prescribed in the forms for each *actio*[2]. The system of actions grew out of the procedure of primitive times. Originally an appeal to the court lay only in case of certain misdeeds, and in making his appeal the plaintiff had to state in advance not only the misdeed but also the sum which he demanded by way of penalty. Out of the complaints, which varied according to the misdeed, there arose, at a later time, actions which varied according as the claims varied. In the Roman *rei vindicatio*[3] the connection with the old action for theft still appears quite clearly. Since it manifestly was a matter of extreme difficulty to obtain a new *actio* for a claim,

1. *Rechtskraft* (force of law)：〈德〉既判力
2. the forms for each *actio*：每个诉讼的形式
3. *rei vindicatio*：〈拉〉返还所有物之诉

the existing forms had to be worked over continually in order that the system of actions might meet the needs of life. This required great legal knowledge and technical ability. The forms had to be drawn up so that they might readily conform to the claims, and also that the very greatest possible number of claims might be asserted by means of each form. The draftsman required a keen eye for the various relations of life out of which the claims arose, and for that which was common to the great number of claims for which he was drawing up a new *actio.* All of this was of decisive importance for the art of drawing up legal documents. Because of the comparatively great rigidity and inflexibility of the *actiones* it was important to draw up a document so that an existing *actio* would fit it, or to protect the parties so fully by means of securities that they could dispense with the *actio.*

Under this system the process of universalization in a certain sense took place mechanically. Every lawyer would, as far as possible, squeeze the legal relation for which he was about to draw up a document into one of the existing documentary forms, and the claim which he was about to assert, into one of the existing litigious forms; and for each claim the *actio* yielded not only the procedure but also, in connection with the appropriate document, a large part of the material law. The claims based on the same documentary forms and drafted according to the same litigious forms, therefore, had a series of rules of law in common. Once the document and the *actio* for a contract of *dos*[1] have been established, a universal law of *dos* has been established, for everyone would draw up the contract according to the existing document in order to be enabled to avail himself of the recognized *actio.* The endeavor to economize in the use of forms led to combining quite heterogeneous relations into a common *actio,* e.g. to subsuming the contract of labor under the category of the contract of letting and

1. *actio* for a contract of dos：嫁资契约诉讼

hiring; or the claim of the guardian or of the curator under the category of *negotiorum gestio*[1]. It often therefore led to very unnatural juristic constructions and to a very unsatisfactory distortion of the material law. The Romans called the art of drawing up documents *cavere*[2], the drawing up of the forms for litigation, *agere*[3]; in addition there is the *respondere*[4], the giving of juristic opinions, which self-evidently also became a lever for universalization. There is a good deal of Roman law that we shall never understand until at least a small portion of the industry that has been expended upon the reconstruction of the praetorian edict is devoted to the practice of the lawyers who drew up legal documents. Difficult though it is to find traces of the Roman forms for contracts in our tradition, in many ways much more could be done than has been done until now. Further study will make many things clear that until now have been incomprehensible to us. By the time the freer procedure according to written formulae replaced the older spoken formulae, the technique of the jurist had become fixed to such a degree that this innovation remained without any influence whatever on it.

In my book on the theory of the sources of the law (*Theorie der Rechtsquellen*[5]), I have dealt with the question how the opinions of the jurists became a part of the law that was binding in the law courts, i.e. of the *ius civile*. From the fragment of the Enchiridion of Pomponius, which unfortunately is very incomplete, we can gather only that in the days of the Republic the only requisite was that they should emerge victoriously from the *disputatio fori*[6]. According to a remark of Suetonius, Caesar was anxious to regulate the matter (*ius civile*

---

1. *negotioruw gestio*：〈拉〉无因管理
2. *cavere*：〈拉〉撰约
3. *agere*：〈拉〉行动
4. *respondere*：〈拉〉解答
5. *Theorie der Rechtsquellen*：〈德〉《法源理论》
6. *disputatio fori*：〈拉〉法庭辩论

ad cerium modum redigere[1]); perhaps Augustus merely carried out this intention when he regulated the *ius respondendi*. But the jurists were not creating law solely by giving opinions; their influence as teachers and writers must have been much more effective. A glance at the juristic literature that has come down to us will show what method they pursued. The jurist usually introduces his opinion with extreme modesty, e.g. *et puto, magis arbitror, sed magis sentio, aequius est, magis est*[2]; but occasionally a more forcible expression like *existimo constituentdum*[3] is found. At this point the *disputatio* begins, no longer in the forum but in the literature, employing phrases like the following: *et magis placuit, sed magis visum est, et magis putat Pomponius, et ego puto, secundum Scaevolae sententiam quam puto ver dm, et magis admittit* (*Marcellus*) *tenere eum, el est aequissimum, or* a phrase of rejection: *quae sententia era non est et a multis notata est, nec utimur Servii sententia*; until finally the rule is established: *maiores constituerunt, Cassii sententia utimtir, Labeo scribit eoque iure, et hoc et Julianus admittit eogue iure utimurhaec Quintus Mucius refert er vera sunt, abolita est enim quorundam veterum sententia.*[4] Until one could say of a rule which had been stated by a jurist, *eoque iure utimur*[5], it had not finally won its way to victory.

It seems that the praetorian law did not begin its powerful and independent development until the formulary procedure had been

1. *ius civile ad certum modum redigere*：〈拉〉以某种形式编辑市民法
2. *et puto, magis arbitror, sed magis sentio, aequius est, magis est*：〈拉〉我认为，我进一步裁断的意见是，我进一步的观点是，我认为更加公正的是，我认为进一步需要考虑的是
3. *existimo constituendum*：〈拉〉我判决决定。
4. *et magis placuit, sed magis ... est enim quorundam veterum sententia.*〈拉〉更令人满意的是；看起来更佳的是；彭波尼认为更佳的是；我认为；依据谢沃拉的观点；马克卢斯认为最好采纳的观点是；根据被认为是正确的观点来判断。或是使用反驳的用语：正确的判断不是这样；正如许多人知道的那样，萨维的观点不正确。直到最终建立起如下规则：多数人认为；凯西最后认为；莱波认为法应该是这样；朱利安努斯最后认为法的规制应该是；昆塔斯·穆修斯认为正确的应该是；在这一问题上，先前的观点被否认。
5. *eoque iure utimur*：〈拉〉依据法律

introduced. Doubtless the creative activity of the praetor has been overestimated for a long time. Lenel's reconstruction of the edict shows sufficiently how small the contribution of the praetor to the whole proud structure of the Roman law was. The edict con tains legal propositions of very diverse kinds: procedural law, penal law, police regulation. So far as it contains civil law, it is, for the greater part, juristic law, and, what is more, judgemade juristic law. It was found by the praetor in the course of his judicial activity. His norms closely follow the norms of juristic law, the procedural forms of which the praetor availed himself, often with very insignificant changes, for his purposes; and there can scarcely be any doubt that the same jurists who were perfecting the *ius civile* inspired the thoughts which the praetor embodied in his edict. And so his finding of norms, just like that of juristic law, is based upon universalization of the concrete nature of the various relations of life, and in part upon the same principles of justice and fairness that the jurists follow. It is true, the praetor was limited by the *leges* and the *ius civile*, and perhaps had to render obedience to the commands of the senate; in any case, however, relying on his *imperium*[1] he could proceed much more boldly and with much more determination than the jurists. It is difficult to determine at the present time where the line was drawn for him; perhaps it varied with the time and the personality of the praetor.

But the purely practical activity of the jurist does not explain everything. A legal system that is the out come of a purely practical legal activity leads only to a series of legal propositions loosely strung together, like the mediaeval German law and, in many respects, the modern English law. The fact that the Roman law, as early as the days of the jurists of the later Republic, seems to be a well ordered and perfect structure, containing a great number of universal legal

---

1. *imperium*：〈拉〉治权。管理事务的权力。

propositions, must be attributed to the fact that the Roman jurists were not only practicing lawyers, but also writers and teachers. Of course, had they been writers and teachers only, their word would have had no greater weight than that which is given to it by their reasoning; they must needs, like the English writers of text-books, have been confining their activities to collecting the results of the judicial decisions, occasionally embroidering them with a modest criticism, and here and there timidly drawing an inference which no one as yet had dared to draw. Before long, however, it became the customary practice to concede the same importance to the literary utterances of the jurists that the utterances indisputably had which they made in the exercise of their practical calling. And so they dared to undertake, even in their capacity as writers, not only to tell him who sought advice in their books what had been customary in the past, but also, anticipating possibilities that had been overlooked until that time, to make additional universalizations and to create new norms for decision. Of still greater consequence is the fact. that they were teachers. It is a characteristic peculiar to the teacher to exhaust the content of a legal proposition altogether, to reveal everything that it contains. A teacher, it is true, does not desire to create law, but he desires to develop it. When a practicing lawyer is dealing with a breach of contract he will confine himself to the points upon which the decision must hinge. When a writer deals with it he will chiefly consider the contingencies that might give rise to a legal controversy. But the teacher will be anxious to say everything, that is: who has the right; against whom it can be asserted; when and where the correlative duty must be fulfilled; what its content is and what content it can possibly have; what are the consequences of delay, and of non-fulfilment. The Roman law owes its great systematic completeness and perfection of form to the teaching activity of the jurists.

If one would, to some extent, justly appreciate the work which juristic science has done in Rome in this manner; if one would be convinced that Roman law has become what it is through the labors of the jurists and not because of any inexplicable innate juristic gift of the Romans, one should compare the *ius civile* with any one of the departments of their law that customarily was not influenced by their juristic science — among others, the legal relations concerning the *ager publicus*[1], public law, and a large part of administrative law, criminal law, which did not become the subject matter of juristic activity until a late period, and then only in a limited measure and only inasmuch as it was regulated by the *leges iudiciorum*[2]. Here one finds nothing of that which appears so admirable elsewhere in Roman law. As to the *ager publicus* there were scarcely any universal principles; every single usufructuary lease was a distinct legal relation, and the Roman magistrate, like the German *Schoeffe,* had to derive his decision from the particular form of the legal relation. In criminal law, a universal theory is sought for in vain; on all questions of principle there is an embarrassed stammering; norms for decision are found exclusively by means of interpretation of the statutes. This surely is not inherent in the material, but is caused by the lack of a great juristic tradition; for *iniuria*[3] is not treated in a less intelligent manner than any other subject matter of private law. Whether the juristic science of Roman public and administrative law ever amounted to more than an orderly collection of statutes and ordinances and of the results of the course of the judicial decisions cannot be determined from the tradition with any degree of certainty.

Still the very history of juristic science in Rome discloses that essentially; like juristic science everywhere, it was a preserving rather than a propelling force. Hesitatingly, unwillingly, and dispiritedly, it yields to the imperative exigencies of life, and never goes further than

---

1. *ager publicus*：〈拉〉公田
2. *leges iudiciorum*：〈拉〉法庭
3. *iniuria*：〈拉〉侵辱

is absolutely necessary. And even that which is absolutely necessary it prefers to do unobservedly, disguising the new as something old, doing this by means of impossible interpretations, fictions, and constructions. Innovations that are very useful but somewhat daring are rejected even by the classical jurists. It is certain that the jurists were bound by that which was existing valid law. Over and above this, the limit of their power was a sense of that which might be permissible rather than a clearly defined line. Had their power to find law been quite unlimited, there would have been no need either of private law legislation (*leges de iure civili*[1]) or of a praetorian edict; juristic science would have been able to satisfy every need of new law. The way in which Roman juristic science in its endeavor (which moreover it has in common with the juristic science of every other system of law) to make that which it has at hand suffice, sought to go not one step beyond that which is necessary — the economy of the law, as von Jhering has called it — has in many ways served as a model for the juristic science of the Continental common law.

1. *leges de iure civili*：〈拉〉私法立法

XII JURISTIC SCIENCE IN ENGLAND

In the last analysis it is an extraordinary piece of good luck for the sociology of law that from the early Middle Ages the English jurists (more Roman than the Romanists, says Maitland) steadfastly closed their minds to the Roman law. To this fact must be attributed the other fact that among the nations of European civilization, in addition to the Roman or Continental common law, another legal system, the Anglo-American, has attained a high and altogether independent development. If it is the function of all scientific study to demonstrate the unifying regularity of the phenomena, sociology could never fulfil this task if no other legal system besides that of the Roman law and that of its offspring, the Continental common law, had attained to a more advanced stage of development. For the other legal systems of the globe, which have remained uninfluenced by Roman law, have continued in so undeveloped a condition that they cannot be adduced for purposes of comparison except with earlier stages of our law. A comparison of the whole course of development of Roman and English law is outside of the scope of the present inquiry, which is limited to a study of legal science in England with continual reference to that of Rome and of the Continent. It is impossible to appraise legal science in England justly without a fleeting glance at the development of English procedure.

The oldest English procedure does not differ from the original procedure of the other Germanic peoples. We may assume therefore that it coincides in its essential features with the prehistoric procedure of Roman law. This view, which perhaps appears strange to many, is based on the fact that all those things in Roman procedure in historical times that appear to be striking peculiarities, the two stages, a preliminary proceeding followed by the *Beweisverfahren*[1] (the proceeding in which proof is made) and the division effected by the *litis contestatio*[2], manifestly are survivals from, an earlier stage of the development of procedure, and, unless indications are deceiving, are found in essentials among all Germanic peoples. The formula of the later Roman procedure is none other in form and content than the conditional *Beweisurteil*, which is followed among the Romans as well as among the Germans by the *Beweisverfahren*. Since there is absolutely reliable evidence that the two-fold division of the trial existed in the procedure by *legis actio*[3] also, inasmuch as the *litis contestatio* in this form of procedure effects a division just as it does in the formulary procedure, there is no doubt that in the *litis contestatio* of the *legis actio* procedure an alternative *Beweisurteil* was rendered which, though perhaps it was not drawn up in writing, was very similar to the formula both in form and in content.

The actual development of English law and English procedure begins with Henry II, in the twelfth century. This king was perhaps one of the greatest juristic geniuses that ever sat on a throne, and although, as Maitland puts it, he sold his labor, inasmuch as he demanded heavy payments therefor from the parties, he has achieved bet ter results than any other vendor of justice ever has. First of all we wish to present, at this place, a brief sketch of his legal reform. But we wish to preface this with the statement that he converted his *curia regis*[4] into a permanent court of justice, over which he, a jurist in heart and soul, used to preside.

Perhaps the most important of his procedural innovations is the

---

1. *Beweisverfahren*：〈德〉举证程序
2. *litis contestatio*：〈拉〉争讼程序
3. *legis actio*：〈拉〉法定诉讼
4. *curia regis*：〈拉〉御前会议

assisa novae disseisinae[1], which seems to have been invented under the influence of the canon law *actio spolii*[2], and which granted to everyone who had been disseised[3] the right to obtain a writ which directed the sheriff to form an *assisa*[4] consisting of twelve men of the neighborhood (*duodecim liberos el legales homines de visneto*) who, as soon as the royal justices should arrive in the vicinage, should make answer to the justice whether or not a disseisin had t aken place. This *assisa novae disseisinae* was followed at a later time by other assizes, the basic features of which were: summons by royal writ to appear before the justice and judgment based on a verdict of men of the neighborhood. In addition the king had granted to everyone who desired to assert a claim to land the privilege of taking the mat ter out of the local communal court by means of a royal writ and of bringing it before the *curia regis*. These innovations offered many advantages to the parties, especially since the *curia regis* enjoyed a much greater measure of confidence than the local courts, employed a procedure that was much more expeditious and technically on a much higher plane than the clumsy ancient Germanic procedure, and had substituted for traditional, highly imperfect means of proof, such as trial by combat and oath with oath-helpers, the testimony of the men of the neighborhood.

We are dealing here with the first germs of the English jury. As Brunner has shown — and the results of his investigations have been generally accepted in England — this procedure originated in Normandy. Henry II, who at the same time was the Duke of Normandy, most probably had become familiar with it in his native country. But it was adapted to new needs in a manner so magnificent that his innovation may be called one of the greatest legislative acts of

---

1. *assisa novae disseisinae*：〈拉〉恢复新近被占土地之令状
2. *actio spolii*：〈拉〉侵夺之诉
3. disseised：被强占地产的
4. *assisa*：〈拉〉令状

all time. The assize[1], it is true, is not yet the English jury. The latter grew out of the assize at a much later time. In the case of the assize the *homines liberi et legales*[2] are called together by the summons, but the *jurata*[3] presupposes a submission to the verdict of the neighborhood by mutual consent. *Thejurata* arose later, when the parties, in order to avoid the unwelcome methods of proof, the trial by combat, and the oath with oath-helpers, agreed, without demanding an assize, to submit their controversy to the verdict of the men of the neighborhood. But even when there was an assize, the parties often agreed to ask men of the neighborhood to render a verdict on matters not mentioned in the writ. The mediaeval English jurists say: *assisa vertitur in iuratam*[4].

Because of the technical superiority of the procedure of the king's courts, because of the greater assurance of a just judgment, and because of their impartiality, the ancient Germanic mode of trial gradually disappears altogether, and is replaced by divers new modes of trial patterned after the *assisa novae disseisinae.* The complainant applies to the king's chancellor, and, upon payment of a fee, obtains a writ which summons his opponent to appear in the king's court. Each kind of claim has an appropriate writ[5], stating the claim and prescribing the procedure. Some of these writs are writs of course, but for a claim not falling within one of these writs, a new writ, more expensive and presupposing some influence with the king's courts, must be drawn up. In the later actions the jury displaces the assize altogether. The difference between the two is this: The jury is no longer summoned by the writ but at the request of the parties, and the question as to which the jury are to give their verdict is no longer

---

1. assize：咨审团
2. *homines liberi et legales*：〈拉〉咨审团成员全部
3. *jurata*：〈拉〉合意咨审制
4. *assisa vertitur in iuratam*：〈拉〉状召咨审团存在于宣誓之中
5. writ：令状

stated in the writ but is to appear from the proceeding.

Every Romanist who reads this description is at once reminded of the Roman formulary procedure and of the praetorian *album*[1], on which all the formulae that were in current use were recorded. From these the plaintiff had to select the one that was appropriate, while if there was no appropriate formula the plaintiff had to have one made especially for his purpose or secure one from the praetor. In fact English legal historians very often compare the procedure which prevailed in England down to the Judicature Acts[2] of the nineteenth century to the Roman formulary procedure. The comparison however is based upon a very superficial study of the situation. The common element is this, that the writ and the formula (the latter, at least according to the prevailing view) were written documents, and that each contained the plaintiff's claim. But the formula concludes the proceeding before the court; the writs open it. The formula is a *Beweisurteil*[3]; the writ, a summons. Upon a closer investigation, one will not compare the older English procedure with the formulary procedure but with the Roman procedure by *legis actio*. The fact that the latter was begun by a private summons, the *in ins vocatio*[4], the English proceeding, by an official summons, may be considered an immaterial difference. But as in Rome, so in England, both the plaintiff and the defendant were required to state their proposals in definitely fixed terms, following the statements of the royal writ and in accordance with the legal basis of the action. As in Rome, so in England, the formal law and right was also the material law and right. Each kind of claim had its appropriate procedure, and the law of procedure determined the material legal bases of the claim. As in Rome, so in

---

1. praetorian *album*：裁判官布告栏
2. Judicature Acts：司法组织法
3. *Beweisurteil*：〈德〉证据判决
4. *in ius vocatio*：〈拉〉传唤受审

England, the material law was chiefly the law of the several actions (*actiones*). Each action has its own precedents, and English jurists write their text-books on the several actions. "To a considerable degree the substantive law administered in a given form of action has grown up independently of the law administered in other forms." (Maitland.) The oldest English law, then, like the Roman law, was a law of actions. In comparison with this great number of analogies, I presume, the differences become insignificant, but we shall not pass over them altogether in silence. The English judge directs the whole proceeding in the presence of the jury; in the more developed procedure he no longer pronounces a conditional judgment like the Roman judge, but permits the parties to formulate the question of fact — frame the issue — upon the determination of which they are willing to let the outcome depend, submits this question to the jury, and pronounces his final judgment according to the verdict of the jury. The jury has nothing to do with the question of law. The latter is a matter for the judge.

The English system of *legis actiones* was not replaced by a system essentially similar to that of the Roman formulary procedure until the Judicature Acts were passed, which abolished the old formulae, and permit ted the parties to submit their written proposals to the court in a manner that seemed good to themselves. This proceeding, too, is divided into two parts just like that of the Roman formulary procedure (in chambers and in court), with this difference: The proceeding before the judge, i.e. the proceeding *in iure*[1], follows the preliminary procedure; furthermore the proceeding before the judge includes the proof.

The personal interest which the judges had in the law-suits that came before them, because of the large fees they received, constitutes an extraordinarily important element in the development of English

1. *in iure*：〈拉〉法律审。与事实审相对。

procedure. It explains their persistent endeavor to enlarge their jurisdiction and to adapt the forms of action most practically to the needs of the parties in order that their activity might increase. Strangely enough they have shown no interest in a more expeditious and more simple procedure. Perhaps they feared that they might reduce their perquisites.

In order to justify these extensions of jurisdiction, the English jurists resorted to the use of fictions. There were three king's courts of major importance, all of them sitting in London: Common Pleas, King's Bench, and Exchequer[1]. The true civil court was the court of Common Pleas. The jurisdiction of the court of King's Bench, which would ordinarily be of rare occurrence in an action bet ween private persons, was based on a fiction that the defendant was *in custodia Mareschalli*[2], held in confinement for the king, and therefore subject to the jurisdiction of the court of the King's Bench. The court of Exchequer, which in fact was a fiscal board, based its jurisdiction upon the fiction that the plaintiff was in arrears in the payment of his taxes to the king, and was unable to pay them because he could not collect his money from the defendant.

The functioning of the court is conditioned upon the plaintiff's securing a proper writ for the cause of action. If he does not secure the proper writ, he loses the law-suit. In the early Middle Ages, it is true, writs were readily issued for any claim that appeared justified, and so Bracton could write: *Tot erunt formulae brevium quot sunt genera actionum*[3]. But in the course of time this matter becomes more difficult. Only writs of course (*de cursu*) are being issued without more ado.

1. Common Pleas, King's Bench, and Exchequer：英格兰皇家民事法庭、王座法庭和财税法庭
2. *in custodia Mareschalli*：〈拉〉最高指挥官庇护下
3. *Tot erunt formulae brevium quot sunt genera actionum*：〈拉〉有多少种讼诉，就有多少种令状格式。

The barons, assembled at Oxford (1258), pass a resolution: *Ke il ne enselera nul breffors bref de curs sanz le commencement le rei e de sun conseil ke serra present* (*ut praetores ex edictis suis perpetuis ius dicerent*)[1]. But the statute of Westminster (1258) permitted the *clerici de cancellaria*[2] when they were unanimous, to issue a writ *ne contingat de cetero quod curia diu deficiat querentibus in iustitia perquirenda*[3]. If the *clerici* can not agree, let them report to Parliament. Nevertheless since the beginning of the fourteenth century it becomes increasingly difficult to obtain a new writ, especially since the judges became jealous of the chancellor and began to quash new writs. Bracton's proposition was converted into its converse: *Tot erunt actiones quot sunt formulae brevium.*[4]

Only one writ constitutes an exception: the writ of trespass. Originally a criminal action for breach of the King's Peace *vi et ar mis*[5] trespass became a civil action about the sixteenth century, [1] and all the actions that were in use in the eighteenth and nineteenth centuries were derived from it. Its three oldest forms are: assault and battery (bodily injury)[6], *de bonis asportatis* (depriving one of the possession of chattels)[7], and *quare clausum fregit* (interference with one's possession or

[1] But see Maitland, Equity and the Forms of Action, pp. 348 fol.

---

1. *Ke il ne enselera nul bref fors bref de curs sanz le commendement le rei e de sun conseil ke serra present* (*ut praetores ex edictis suis perpetuis ius dicerent*)：除当然令状外，若无国王的命令和王座参事在场，则御前大臣将不盖大臣之印于任何令状，以便裁判官根据其永久告示执法。
2. *clerici de cancellaria*：〈拉〉御前会议事务官
3. *ne contingat de cetero quod curia diu deficiat querentibus in iustitia perquirenda*：〈拉〉防止国王的法庭未来不能向起诉者提供有效的正义支持。
4. *Tot erunt actiones quot sunt formulae brevium*：〈拉〉有多少种令状格式，就有多少种诉讼。
5. *vi et armis*：〈拉〉武力
6. battery (bodily injury)：身体伤害
7. *de bonis asportatis* (depriving one of the possession of chattels)：〈拉〉剥夺他人的动产占有

depriving one of possession of immovables)[1].

Trespass became very popular, and exhibits a series of new forms, which during the course of the seventeenth and eighteenth centuries practically superseded all the older forms of action. As early as the beginning of the sixteenth century, it came into close contact with ejectment, which thereafter took the place of the real action for immovables. On the basis of the provision of the Statute of the second Parliament of Westminster in *consimili casu*[2], case branched off from trespass. From case, the chief difference between which and trespass is that the plaintiff did not have to allege *vi et ar mis,* several importa nt actions developed in turn. Chief of these is assumpsit, which branched off at the beginning of the sixteenth century. The defendant has undertaken by contract to deal with the plaintiff's goods in a certain way, e.g. to perform some labor in relation to them, and in doing so has caused damage to the plaintiff. This action of assumpsit subsequently becomes an action on the promise, a contractual action which takes the place of the old action of debt. In Slade's case (1602) it was held that "Every contract executory imports in itself an assumpsit, for when one agrees to pay money or to deliver anything, thereby he assumes or promises to pay or deliver it." This is *indebitatus assumpsit,* which later became in part an action for unjust enrichment, "in which the element of contract is purely fictitious." About the middle of the sixteenth century trover begins to germinate within the sphere of trespass on the case. The accused has found a chattel which the plaintiff had lost, and though demand has been made, refuses to return it; he has converted it to his own use (conversion). Subsequently trover lies against a third person; loss and finding is feigned; the only essential thing is the detention and the conversion to the defendant's

1. *quare clausum fregit* (interference with one's possession or depriving one of possession of immovables)：〈拉〉妨碍或剥夺他人对不动产的占有
2. *consimili casu*：〈拉〉收回土地令状

own use. Trover becomes a general action *in rem* for movables and, at the same time, a very convenient action for unjust enrichment (conversion of another's goods to one's own use). According as these actions are used to demand either the thing itself or compensation, or both, they are real [1] actions, personal actions, or mixed. Ejectment[1] is a real action; assumpsit and trover are personal actions, for in the case of movables and of contractual relations the plaintiff in an action at law can recover only damages (it is otherwise in equity). For this reason the English call movables and obligations personal property.

Trespass owes its enormous success to various causes. In the first place it was a proceeding that was more vigorous and more expeditious than the older forms. Its origin as a penal action for breach of the King's Peace accounts for the practice of beginning the action with provisional arrest of the defendant. The matter of proof, too, was regulated much better. In the case of the old actions *in rem* (writ of right, detinue) and of contractual actions (debt), oath with oath-helpers (wager of law) was still available. In the assizes the sworn triers had to be called at the time the original writ was issued, and were permitted to make answer only to the question that was put in the writ itself. In trespass there was a jury; it was summoned during the course of the proceeding, and was required to answer the questions that arose from the pleadings of the parties. The influence of the attorneys was of importance also. Trespass was reserved to the King's Bench. In the court of Common Pleas a certain class of attorneys, the sergeants-at-law, who were appointed by royal writ, were enjoying a monopoly. All other attorneys therefore had an interest in

[1] Ehrlich uses the English words here. For a full discussion of the classification see Maitland, Lectures on the Forms of Action, in Equity and the Forms of Action, chaps. I, V, and VII.

---

1. ejectment：逐出租地之诉

getting suits into the court of King's Bench, in which they themselves could appear as attorneys, and therefore also in increasing the number of causes over which this court had jurisdiction.

The extension of the various actions to new situations was brought about in part by the judges holding that a certain action lay in a given case. Thereafter there was no more difficulty. In this way Slade's case made assumpsit a general contractual action. Still more important is the system of fictions. The most famous is the fiction in the action of ejectment, the *actio in rem* for the determination of ownership in later English law. Ejectment originally was an action of trespass by the lessee against any third party who deprived him of possession. At the beginning the owner, John Rogers, availed himself of this action in the following manner: Basing his claim on title, which he asserted to be in himself, he made actual entry, and then made a lease to Richard Smith, who was thereafter ejected by William Stiles and brought suit against the latter. William Stiles, the casual ejector, thereafter gave notice of the suit to the present tenant, George Saunders.

In the suit against the present tenant the lessee at first had to prove the following: 1. That the demandant was entitled to lease the land to him, i.e. that the demandant was the owner; 2. That the latter had actually leased it to him; 3. That he, the lessee, had actually taken possession of the land; 4. That he had been ejected by the casual ejector. This procedure however was simplified considerably by means of a number of fictions which were invented by Chief Justice Rolle during the Commonwealth. The lease, the entry, and the ejection by William Stiles now are purely fictitious. The latter, the fictitious casual ejector, simply gives notice of the pendency of the action to the tenant, George Saunders. If the tenant George Saunders remains silent, the land is awarded to the lessee (in behalf of the actual plaintiff); for the casual ejector has no intention to defend his right. If the tenant chooses to defend, he is permitted to do so only upon condition that he admit the lease of the land by John Rogers to Richard Smith, the entry by the latter and his ejection by Stiles. Thereafter the suit is confined to the question of the right of John Rogers to lease the land to Richard Smith, in other words, to the question whet her John Rogers has title.

The question obtrudes itself why this roundabout way was selected for the purpose of giving to the owner the remedy of the lessee instead of creating a direct remedy for him. Maitland thinks it was impossible to do this inasmuch as the owner had the real action, the writ of right, and the possessory action (the assizes); that it was impossible to leap over this obstruction. And since trespass with its fictions, after all, served the purpose best, there was no need of a change. Since there was no disadvantage involved, the law contented itself with discussing the legal relation between the actual plaintiff and the actual defendant in a suit in which the formal issue was an interference with the possession of a fictitious lessee by a fictitious ejector who gave notice to the defendant. By a series of Judicature Acts in the nineteenth century this system of *legis actiones* was abolished and replaced by a free formulary procedure, which will be discussed later.

In the twelfth and thirteen th centuries the English law as it was applied in the royal courts was extraordinarily fluid and flexible. But in the fourteenth and fifteenth centuries it became rigid and formal, chiefly because of the great difficulty experienced in obtaining new writs. This state of affairs prompted the chancellor to take a considerable part of the development of the law into his own hands. From ancient times the parties had been accustomed to apply to the king for relief from a wrong they had suffered. This is a part of the ancient jurisdiction of the king, upon which, in the last analysis, the whole jurisdiction of the king's courts, which are gradually replacing the older courts, is based. Especially after the chancellor refuses to issue new writs as a matter of course, the number of such appeals to the king is increasing at an extraordinarily rapid rate. These appeals are petitions praying for relief either in a case where relief cannot be had at the hands of the courts because of the lack of a suitable writ or in a case where relief is sought from an unjust judgment rendered by the courts. The king refers the parties to the chancellor, who investigates the matter, and, if he has satisfied him self that an injustice has been done to one of the parties, interferes, and sees to it that the latter obtains justice. This procedure is in a general way modeled upon the procedure of the ecclesiastical courts. It is a very natural thing for the chancellor to take his procedure from the ecclesiastical courts; for, as a rule, he is a cleric. It is self-evident that this does not make an end of the activity of the courts or render it superfluous. The chancellor is not permitted to interfere directly with the administration of justice. But, in his capacity as a royal official, he has at his disposal remedies by means of which he exercises his power, which in turn he derives from the fullness of the king's power. In virtue of this delegated royal power he has the power, in the first place, to enjoin the parties in a given case both from appealing to the courts and from availing themselves of a judgment already obtained in a court; and finally he has the power to enforce his decree through his own officials.

Accordingly, the chancellor actually has the power, on petition by one of the parties, to withdraw any litigation, whether it has already been adjudicated or not, from the jurisdiction of the courts and to take it into his own hands. The commands and prohibitions directed to the parties are called injunctions. They can be enforced by the chancellor by means either of imprisonment or of fines. They are being issued *sub poena*[1]. They can of course refer not only to a matter submitted to the courts by one of the parties to a controversy but also to the greatest possible variety of other matters.

The courts did not submit to these interferences by the chancellor without some show of resistance, especially since, although only in rare

1. *sub poena*：〈拉〉禁止令

cases, the injunctions applied even to the courts as such. Resistance to the chancellor began in the reign of Edward IV, and, in the reign of James I, led to a conflict between Justice Coke and the chancellor, Lord Ellesmere. The chancellor contended that his decrees were not addressed to the courts but to the parties; that "Injunctions did not interfere with the common law. The judgment stood. All that the chancellor was concerned with, was the conduct of the parties to the case in which the judgment had been given." On this basis James I, following an opinion of Bacon, at that time attorney-general, decided the quarrel in favor of the chancellor. Thanks to the recognition of the validity of the injunctions, the chancellor definitively prevailed. During the seventeenth and eighteenth centuries the courts made repeated attempts to put the matter to the test again, but without success. Thereby the chancellor, entrusted with a jurisdiction of his own, was enabled to create a legal system which, in many respects, is a perfect analogy to the praetorian law of Rome.

It would of course be a very superficial procedure, if, relying upon a few similarities in external matters, one should permit oneself to be misled into placing the chancellor and the praetor side by side. Not external details, but the whole inner structure of the legal systems created by them, justifies one in seeing the same historical phenomenon in the two officials. This view, it is true, does not appear to any appreciable extent in English books, for the English take little interest in a conceptual understanding of their law. But a reading of the presentation of the matter by Professor Langdell, an American scholar, resolves all doubts. From LangdelFs book, entitled "Survey of Equity Jurisdiction[1]" (Cambridge in the United States 1905), I quote the following:

"As legal rights have in them no element of equity, so equit able

1. Survey of Equity Jurisdiction：《衡平法院管辖研究》

rights have in them no element of law. ... As law is a creature of the State, so equity was originally a creature of the supreme executive of the State, i.e. the king. What then was the power of the king which enabled him to create eqidty? It may be answered that he had in him the sole judicial authority as well as the sole executive power, but none of the legislative power, i.e. he could not alone exercise any portion of the latter. By virtue of his judicial power he had entire control over procedure, so long as the legislature did not interfere; and this it was that enabled him to create equity. As he had no legislative power, he could not impart to his decisions in equity any legal effect or operation, but when he had by the exercise of his judicial authority rendered a decision in equity in favor of a plaintiff, he could enforce it by exerting his executive power against the person of the defendant, i.e. he could compel him to do or to refrain from doing what ever he had by his decision directed him to do or to refrain from doing...".

A Romanist need not be told that only a slight change in the wording of this statement will make it equally applicable to the praetor.

Moreover the inner similarity between the praetorian law and equity appears also in a series of details, first of all in the fact that the latter is directly connected with the *ius civile,* the common law. It is not an independent system, but can be understood only as an appendix to the common law. Without equity the latter would indeed be a hard, rigid system of law, ill adapted to the requirements of life, but after all it would be a system of law. Equity without the common law simply could not exist. Just as the work of the praetor constituted an appendix to the *ius civile* in content as well as in form, just as he created praetorian institutions on the model of those of the civil law, created remedies by means of *actiones fictitiae* and *utiles*[1], which were analogous to those of the civil law, and created a praetorian law of

1. *actiones fictitiae* and *utiles*：〈拉〉拟制诉讼与扩用诉讼

inheritance to follow and supplement the civil law of inheritance, so the chancellor imitates the common law. A principle of equity is: *aequitas sequitur legem*[1]. For almost every common law rule which is not simply a procedural rule there is a corresponding rule of equity. And the praetor's success in creating legal institutions quite independently, e.g. the praetorian property law or the praetorian law of inheritance, is paralleled, and perhaps surpassed, by the success of English equity in the same sphere of endeavor.

Nevertheless the basic differences between the praetorian law and equity must not be overlooked. The Roman *index* was subordinate to the praetor, who could therefore issue directions which the former had to obey. The English judge is quite independent of the chancellor. All the latter can do is to enjoin the parties not to appeal to the courts or not to avail themselves of a judgment rendered by the law court. He can summon the parties to appear before him, and can issue a decree which he can enforce by means of his own. In consequence, equity is much more independent of the common law than is the praetorian law of the *ius civile.* Equity is not, like the praetorian law, a component part of the whole legal system, but is a separate legal system side by side with the other. And in the course of time equity becomes just as fixed and inflexible as the common law. The chancellor no longer creates new legal remedies, but develops those that are already in existence, just as the judges develop the institutions of the common law. The chancellor enunciates no new legal principles, but develops his precedents in precisely the same manner as the judges develop theirs. Equity has become the legal system according to which the chancellor proceeds, just as law is the legal system according to which the courts render their decisions. There are differences in procedure; chiefly this, that there is no jury in the court of chancery. There is a difference

1. *aequitas sequitur legem*：〈拉〉意为：衡平法是遵循普通法的法律规则，不与普通法相违背。

too in the legal consequences (*Rechtsfolgen*[1]). But in the last analysis the chancellor is a judge just like the others. Whether equity or the common law shall apply ultimately depends upon whether the parties appeal to the chancellor or to the courts, and whether the chancellor or the courts to which the party applies is the tribunal competent to render judgment in the matter. If a person asks for an intervention of a nature for which equity has made no provision, the chancellor refers him to the courts.

Since the Judicature Acts, equity has become a division of the Supreme Court of Judicature. It is a court in name also. In case of a conflict bet ween equity and law, the principles of equity prevail. Certain legal remedies, it is true, can be applied only in chancery; others, in the other divisions of the Supreme Court. But once the jurisdiction of the division has been determined, chancery as well as the courts, wherever the case may be pending, can apply either law or equity. Only the procedure still varies. Although every English barrister may practice both in chancery and in the courts, it is customary for those barristers that have their offices in Lincoln's Inn to practice in chancery. Equity comprises, in the main, the law of trusts, a considerable portion of the law of pledge, a few legal remedies of the law of inheritance, specific performance (the right in case of contractual obligation to demand performance of the promise, not merely damages), finally the injunctions, i.e. the preliminary prohibitions directed to one party where the party applying for the injunction antici pates irreparable damage. Equity therefore covers only a small number of legal institutions and remedies. But among them is one which in itself constitutes a distinct legal system — the trust.

Trusts can be traced back to the fourteenth century. The original

1. *Rechtsfolgen*：〈德〉法律后果

term was use (from *ad opus*). The trust is a transaction, which was well known on the Continent in the Middle Ages, and which was named the *Treuhandergeschaft* (fiduciary transaction). The fiduciary is called the trustee; the person for whose benefit the transaction is entered into, the *cestui que* trust[1]. In Germany and France, as well as in England, in the later Middle Ages, the fiduciary transaction was a substitute for the last will and testament. Whenever anyone wished to leave a thing to the church or to someone else, he delivered it to the trustee with directions how to deal with it. The chancellor assumed jurisdiction over this matter and compelled the trustee by the application of the means of power (*Machtmittel*) at his disposal, just as the Roman emperor compelled the fiduciary, to perform the last will of the deceased. Before long transactions of this kind were entered into *inter vivos,* and a thing that had been delivered to the trustee was treated as belonging in equity to the beneficiary from the moment of delivery. The great extent of these transactions was brought about chiefly by the feudal system with its numerous limitations on freedom of action and the ever present danger of escheat to the feudal lord, which made circumventions of this sort necessary. The great feudal lords were vitally interested in the use. It is true the vassal was thereby enabled to prevent many an estate from escheating to the lords, to the great detriment of the latter, by enfeoffing a feoffee[2] to uses who was to hold for the vassal himself; for a person who enfeoffed a feoffee could impose a condition that the trustee should hold for the feoffor. But the great feudal lords themselves were feudatories, the greatest among them holding directly from the king, and they in turn derived advantages from the trust over against their own feudal lord, the king. Their influence for a long time was sufficiently great to cause the chancellor to extend vigorous protection to trusts. But Henry VIII,

---

1. *cestui que* trust：信托受益人（斜体为拉丁文）
2. enfeoffing a feoffee：授予封地

who had everything to lose and nothing to gain by the use, wrung from an unwilling Parliament a law according to which every use gave to the beneficiary a legal estate, i.e. the corresponding common law right. The statute had scarcely been enacted, when it was interpreted away by an interpretation which limited its application in a manner that took away all its practical significance. It has not hindered the development of the trust.

The law of trusts is not an isolated trust relation but a whole legal system. It comprises first of all the law of corporations. A considerable portion of the ecclesiastical law of the numerous English religious denominations and of the Catholic church, the whole English law of societies, is based upon this proposition: The trustees hold the property in trust for the believers, for the members of the societies. A special law of things has arisen within the law of trusts. As soon as the subject matter has been transferred to the trustee, the beneficiary at once acquires all rights of use, consumption, and disposition which were intended for him and which he can transfer except in so far as he is limited by the trust. The trustee indeed retains the legal title, but solely as a *nudum ius*[1]. Only a purchaser who has bought the legal estate *bona fide* for value and without notice can deprive the beneficiary of his interest. Since the courts, at least where land is involved, treat the least negligence in the investigation of title as construetive notice, this case could arise only where the documents had been forged very skillfully. The law of the assignment of obligatory rights, as a whole, is a part of the law of trusts. [1] Not until a most recent date was it regulated, in part, by statute.

The English law of family property also developed within the law of

[1] This sentence is probably based on a statement in an early edition of Stephen's Commentaries on the Laws of England.

---

1. *nudum ius*：〈拉〉裸权

trusts. The family settlements provided that the family property was to be held by the trustee for the benefit of the wife, the children born or not yet born. In this way the wife, at a time when the matrimonial community of goods prevailed at common law, was placed in a position of complete independence of her husband in the mat ter of property law and right, because that which had been given to her in equity was not touched by the community of goods. At the present time this equitable right has been established by statute as the general matrimonial regime. In part, the English law of the declaration of the will by last will and testament is also based on the law of trusts. Historically speaking it was here that the law of trusts had its beginning.

Of no less importance was the influence of the chancellor on the English law of pledge[1]. The pledge law of the common law, the mortgage, corresponds to the oldest form of the Roman *fiducia.* The pledgee obtains full legal ownership of the thing pledged as soon as the debt is due and unpaid. But the chancellor compels him to return the thing pledged to the debtor in case the debt is paid at a later time, and thus enables the pledgor who, indeed, has already aliened the property, to create additional pledge rights in the thing, which of course could only be equitable rights.

Here the Romanist self-evidently is reminded of the two-fold ownership in Roman law. Indeed even the external similarity is extremely striking. Just as the praetor had developed the transfer of possession into a real contract, so the chancellor utilized a contract for the benefit of a third party — and that is what the trust is in the last analysis — in the same way. And even though Maitland in his work on equity most emphatically denies that the trust is a right *in rem*, this applies only to the juristic construction of the whole legal relation.

---

1. law of pledge：担保法

The ext ent to which the whole inner structure of the equitable right and the praetorian rights correspond is pointed out by Langdell's presentation:

"As equity wields only physical power, it seems to be impossible that it should actually create anything. It seems moreover to be impossible that there should be any other actual rights than those that are created by the State, i.e. legal rights. So, too, if equity could create actual rights, the existence of rights so created would have to be recognised by every court of justice within the State; and yet no other court than a court of equity will admit the existence of any rights created by equity. It seems therefore that equitable rights exist only in contemplation of equity, i.e. that they are a fiction invented by equity for the promotion of justice. Still as in contemplation of equity such rights do exist, equity must reason upon them and deal with them as if they had an actual existence."

And at another place Langdell, again speaking of the chancellor, says:

"Through his physical power he could imprison men's bodies and control the possession of their property, but neither his orders and decrees nor any acts as such done in pursuance of them had any legal effect or operation; and hence he could not affect the title of property except through the acts of its owners. Even when he made a decree for changing the possession of property, it took the shape of a command to the defendant in possession to convey to the plaintiff, and it was only as a last resort that the chancellor issued a writ to his executive officer, commanding him to dispossess the defendant and put the plaintiff in possession."

This presentation shows that the norms for decision in English as well as in Roman law are preponderantly juristic law. The statutes, it is true, seem to be of greater significance than in Rome; but this may be attributed to the fact that we have altogether too low an opinion of the productivity of the Roman legislative machine in the days of the Republic. The original body of English norms for decision however does not derive its origin from statutes. We may consider the assizes of Henry II as a part of the law created by the st ate, although they do contain much that is juristic law; but the *formulae*, to which, as all English jurists admit, a considerable part of the English substantive law, the material law, owes its existence, doubtless belong to the category of juristic law. We know the authors of a few of these *formulae*. The writ *quare ejecit infra terminum*[1] was an invention of Bratton's teacher William Raleigh; Lord Chief Justice Rolle refined and improved the writ of ejectment. The sit nation is not altered by the existence of the fictions, which are in no wise different from the fictions of the praetor and of the juristic science of the Continental common law. On the whole it is admittedly an error, based on the mistaken idea that all creation of law is within the sphere and province of the legislator, to believe that fictions must not be origin a ted by jurists. It is true, the Roman jurists did not employ them, but the older juristic science of the Continental common law and of the French law made extensive use of them. It would be a difficult matter to state wherein the constructions of the Roman and of the Continental common law differ from fictions — as a rule only in the mode of expression.

Now where did the English judges get the norms according to which they decided the law-suits that were brought before them? How did the English common law develop from them in the course of the centuries? Undoubtedly it developed in the same way as the Roman *ius civile*. The basis of the decisions here also is the inner nature of the legal relation, agreement, articles of association, last will, custom, commercial usage, which, universalized, yield a unitary norm for decision in other situations. Since the history of the older English law

1. *quare ejecit infra terminum*：〈拉〉期前被逐出租地

is better known than the history of Roman and of German law we are in a better position to trace the process of reduction to unity and of universalization. We see how the courts evolve the law of things by universalizing feudal law; how the husband's sole ownership of the property which the wife brought into the marriage relation is gradually being adopted by the courts; how they gradually substitute the right of the first-born to inherit for the right of all children to take equally, which had been the law until that time. Everywhere the endeavor appears to be to make the law unit ary by extending the legal principles that prevail among the upper classes to the whole people. In a similar way the law of commerce is created as late as the eighteenth century by a process of universalization and reduction to unity. Furthermore, from the very beginning the English judge thought himself empowered to find norms for decision according to justice and fairness.

It is self-evident that the development of equity in a still greater measure takes place in the light of history. Sir George Jessel, Master of the Rolls, one of the greatest of equity judges, says on this point:

"It must not be forgotten that the rules of equity are not, like the rules of the common law, supposed to have been established from time immemorial. It is perfectly well known that they have been established from time to time, altered, improved, and refined from time to time. In many cases we know the name of the Chancellor who invented them. Take such things as these: the separate use of the married woman, the restraint on alien ation. the modern rule against perpetuities, and the rules of equitable waste. We can name the Chancellors who first invented them, and state the date when they were first introduced into equity jurisprudence, and therefore in cases of this kind the older precedents are of little value. The doctrines are progressive, refined and improved, and if we want to know what the rules of equity are, we must look, of course, rather to the more modern than the more ancient cases." (Quoted by Holdsworth, History of English Law, from an opinion.)

Equity has been created in the same way in which all other juristic law has been created. The law of trusts and family settlements and of the equit able mortgage is based chiefly upon universalization of the traditional content of agreements. The remainder of the law of equity, as Sir George Jessel has put it, consists essentially of norms for decision, freely found by the chancellors, in finding which they consider themselves far less bound by previous decisions than do the common law judges.

The thing that may seem most striking to the Continental jurist in English judge-made law is the importance attached to the personality of the individual judge. A lawyer citing a case refers to the judge by name. If the decision is rendered by the whole bench, each judge states the reason for his decision separately, and thereafter these norms are cited under his name. It is true, each one of the high courts as such has weight and influence, but what that weight and influence is depends not upon the court but upon the judge. There are judges who were epoch-making in the history of English law and whose names are spoken of with reverence centuries after their death; the rank and file have long since passed into the great silence. Each one of the great judges has a pronounced personality, which is described in the history of law very much in the manner in which that of the great poets and artists is described in the history of literature and of art. The following are mentioned as the most famous: Coke, Hardwick, Mansfield, Stowall, Grant, Willes, Jessel, Cairns, Bowen, Parke; and among American judges perhaps: Marshal, Kent, Story, Shaw, O. W. Holmes, Jr. In a book of Maitland's, I find the following significant words: "*I* have mentioned this case, because we may say that when the court of Appeal overruled Jessel, M. R., the case was very near the border line."

Juristic science in England also comprises the business of drawing up documents, and in this respect, too, it has become a perfect art, chiefly in the matter of documents concerning land and marriage contracts (family settlements). Its basis is the established custom of the attorneys, which however closely follows legislation and decided cases. The judicial decisions that deal with documents are being carefully recorded and taken into account. Frequently the judges say that they cannot depart from the decided cases although they consider them wrongly decided, on the ground that the conveyancers may possibly have been following them in the preparation of legal documents.

The nature of English juristic law was stated by Sir James Parke, later Lord Wensleydale, in a case that was argued before the House of Lords in the following words:

"Our common law system consists in applying to new combinations of circumstances those rules of law which we derive from legal principles and judicial precedents; and for the sake of attaining uniformity, consistency and certainty, we must apply those rules, where they are not plainly unreasonable and inconvenient, to all cases which arise; and we are not at liberty to reject them, and to abandon all analogy to them, in those to which they have not yet been judicially applied, because we think that the rules are not as convenient and reasonable as we ourselves could have devised."

On this occasion I may be permitted to correct an erroneous opinion that is very widespread on the Continent, i.e. the opinion that the free finding of law in England in some way is in a causal connection with the fact that the law of England has not been codified. For the free finding of law is a valid method even when applied to statutes. Here too the judge, by a free finding of law, determines the meaning where there is an ambiguity, and supplies the omitted words where there is a gap; and these decisions are as binding upon the court for the future as those that deal with the common law. Only where the meaning is plain, the court is not bound by previous decisions. On the other hand, where an erroneous interpretation is very old the courts may not lightly disregard it (Hardcastle, The Construction and Effect of Statute Law,

Third Edition, p. 93 et seq.). Consequently the glorious freedom of action which the English judge enjoys would be preserved even if the English law were codified. In an article in the Law Quarterly Review (Vol. 19, p. 15) on the Codification of Mercantile Law, Chalmers quotes the following words from a report of the Royal Commissioners on the Criminal Code Bill, which had been prepared by the judges Lord Blackburn, Lord Justice Lush, Sir James Stephen, and Mr. Justice Barry:

"The great richness of the law of England in principles and rules embodied in judicial decisions, no doubt, involves the consequence that a code adequately representing it must be elaborate and detailed, but such a code would not, except in a few cases in which the law at present is obscure, limit any discretion now possessed by the judges. It would simply change the form of the rules by which they are bound."

English and British juristic literature, on the other hand, has created law only in a very limited measure. Holdsworth in his History of English Law mentions only five juristic writers who have become figures of outstanding importance in the history of English law. They are: Glanvill, Brae ton, Littleton, Coke, and Blackstone. But it is impossible to show that the *Tractatus de legibus*[1], which is usually attributed to Glanvill, the chief justiciar of Henry II (died about 1190), and the work of Henry de Bratton (usually called Bracton) exerted any influence upon the development of English law. Blackstone's book is a presentation of the existing law, not a work of practical juristic science in the sense of a literary development of law, and but few of his doctrines have gained general recognition. Only Littleton (?–1481) and Coke (1552–1628) remain. Pollock mentions Sir Michael Forster's Treatise on Crown Law, the first edition of which was published in 1762, as "the latest book to which authority in the exact sense can be

---

1. *Tractatus de legibus*：〈拉〉《英格兰法律与习惯论》

ascribed."

Moreover the juristic writers of England make no attempt to find norms independently in the manner of the Continental writers. They content themselves with collecting the decisions. Furthermore there is an utter absence of commentaries on the statutes in the Continental sense, for a statute can be interpreted only by judicial decisions. "English text-books are almost entirely a collection of cases with comments interspersed. Sometimes a general rule is stated which may go a trifle further than the cases do; sometimes an opinion is thrown out on a point not covered by authority. Still the cases are the gist of the book," says Bryce. It is only in recent times that books that contain independent inquiries and attempt deeper study, like the works of Sir Frederic Pollock or of the American writers Langdell and O. W. Holmes, Jr., are beginning to appear.

The English common law is the law not only of England, Ireland, and Wales, but to a great extent of Scotland, also of the United States, of almost all the English colonies except perhaps where aborigines are concerned, and even in dealings with them it is usually applied as subsidiary law. The Indian codifications as a rule preserve the common law unchanged. One may well say that it is valid law in states and nations that are counted among the wealthiest and most advanced of the whole world. And since it does not presuppose particular laws which it must supplement, its influence is much more direct and effective than that of the Continental common law. Moreover it comprises not only private law, but also criminal law, mercantile law, and — purely historically — procedural law. It is true, it has never attained the finish, the perfection, and the fine elaboration in detail which is characteristic of the Continental common law, but it surpasses the latter by far in wealth of legal propositions, in variety of legal institutions. The juristic science of a legal system such as this must not be ignored in the development of legal science. It can be traced back in its beginnings to the time of Henry II, i.e. to the middle of the twelfth century. One of its first achievements, the assize of novel disseisin, dates from the year 1166. In point of venerable age indeed it is surpassed by the Continental common law juristic science, but this is counterbalanced to a great degree not only by the enormous extent of the territory in which it is valid and in consequence by the great diversity of situations with which the English jurists are called upon to deal, but also by the early and great development of commerce and industry as well as of the social and political relations of the peoples concerned. All of this has provided an invaluable amount of stimulation.

Since the movement toward free finding of law has directed the attention of Continental jurists to English juristic science and the English method of finding law, the statement is often made on the Continent that the English are satisfied neither with the results of their juristic science nor with their method of finding the law. May I therefore in conclusion be permitted to quote the words of two eminent English jurists, who moreover are considered experts in Continental affairs. Both of them, it is true, are not speaking directly of the free finding of law but of case law; the legal system based upon it; but inasmuch as this presupposes free finding of law, their opinion must be referable to both. One of these is the aged author of the American Commonweal th, James Bryce, who in his youth sat at the feet of Vangerow in Heidelberg and dedicated his first work to the Holy Roman Empire of the German Nation. What he says about case law sounds almost like a *hymnus,* which he prefaces with the following words: "It is an abiding honor to our lawyers and judges, to have worked it out with a completeness and success unknown to any other country." (Studies in History and Jurisprudence, Vol. II, p. 289 et seq.)

Let him who would be informed as to what so distinguished an English jurist thinks of the grandeur of the English legal system, as compared with the Continental system, read the three pages following the words quoted from the work cited above. They seem so much more persuasive since Bryce, as is well known, is an unbiassed observer of foreign institutions and is by no means blind to the disadvantages of the English method.

Perhaps the following remark of Pollock's, quoted from the book already referred to, will be found more persuasive than all of this. Says Pollock: "Where the two systems have come into competition as they have done in the Province of Quebec, the Cape Colony, and other British possessions originally settled under Continental systems of law; the method ascribing exclusive authority to judicial decisions has invariably, so far as I know, been accepted." In other words, wherever the English case law system, which is founded upon the free finding of law, comes into contact with the Continental methods of applying law, the latter are inevitably thrust aside. Anyone who knows the conservative turn of mind of the jurist can judge from this how obvious the superiority of the English method of finding law must be. In this connection one must not fail to note that both in Canada and in South Africa many a feature of the English organization of the administration of justice which is usually pointed out is absent, e.g. the extraordinary centralization of the courts and the high position of the judge, although even as it is, the position of the judge in these countries might be higher than it is in central Europe.

In conclusion I would quote the words of Holmes, an American jurist. He says of the common law that it is "a far more developed, more rational and mightier body of law than the Roman."

The complaints that are being heard in England about case law refer exclusively to its terrible lack of systematic arrangement. In fact, scattered throughout thou sands of volumes, it is like a tropical primeval forest, where the wanderer who has lost his way is threatened with new surprises and dangers at every tree that he sees. But this fault does not lie at the door of the free finding of law, but at that of the absolute binding force of all judicial decisions, which continues at least until such time as they are reversed by a higher tribunal.

But even though the free finding of law gives rise to the idea that the law that has been found should not readily be given up, the evils that have arisen from it in England as consequences of the historical development do not, by any means, have to be taken into the bargain. They can easily be avoided.

Juristic science in England differs from juristic science in Rome chiefly in this, that it is not preponderantly literary as was the latter, at least in the days of the Empire, but almost exclusively judicial. In spite of this, as our inquiries have shown, the two systems have developed on parallel lines throughout. Procedure passes through the same stages as in ancient Rome, the judges create the common law by employing the same methods of universalization and of finding norms that the *prudentes* employed in creating the *ius civile,* and the English magisterial law[1] presents the same essential characteristics as the Roman, not in a few externals merely, but in its whole inner structure. Is there need of further proof to show that we are face to face with a natural unifying regularity of events?

1. magisterial law：治安官法

XIII THE JURISTIC SCIENCE OF THE OLDER CONTINENTAL COMMON LAW

The reception of Roman law in the Middle Ages and in modern times may properly be considered here, for it undoubtedly created a new and unique phase of juristic science. It is clear in the first place that the kind of juristic activity which occupies the foreground in every indigenous legal development, i.e. the creation of norms for decision through universalization and free finding of law, thereafter necessarily had to be thrust into the background by the wealth of norms for decision which the Roman law books offered ready for use. This appeared so much more clearly inasmuch as the Roman universalizations in part lost the characteristic quality of universalizations when Roman law was received. On the soil on which it had its origin, a universalization must be felt as what it actually is, i.e. as a universalization. Transplanted to a soil on which the phenomena that have been universalized do not occur, it ceases to be a universalization, it becomes a rule, occasionally appearing to be quite arbitrary, which knows neither universal nor particular, and according to which legal disputes are being decided. The whole Roman law, which had been given the force of law in this way, became a collection of juristic norms for decision. Whereas in Rome it had grown directly out of life, it now faced life as a fixed, immovable standard. Legal life no longer was the subject matter of juristic science, as it is to a certain degree in an indigenous legal development, but its object. And thereby juristic science became something quite different from what it had been before that time. It now faced life as something approaching from without. It undertook to force rules upon society which it had not invented itself but which it had taken over from elsewhere, without any thought of whether society desired them or not, without any concern as to how society fared under them, simply because they were in existence. And in a great measure it has been successful. The great antinomy of juristic science, in the hands of which all modes of thought become forces that have the power to create norms, has again demonstrated its historic significance.

Although the reception of Roman law relieved the jurist of the burden of dealing with life by continally creating the law which the latter requires, it brought him face to face with another, perhaps a greater, difficulty, i.e. the difficulty of adapting the new law to legal relations that were altogether foreign to it. How could the jurists, in the years immediately following the reception, get the idea into their heads that the Roman sources were dealing with the same institutions that they themselves had to deal with? Was it so obvious that the peculiar mediaeval rights in land or the contracts, which in part were of a totally different nature, must be adjudged according to Roman law? The mere fact of the reception is sufficient to establish the basic presupposition of the sociological science of law that there are legal institutions that exist independently of the positive law; at any rate it proves that among all the peoples by whom the Roman law was received there were legal institutions which they had in common with the Romans, at least to such an extent that the application of the Roman law did not appear to be altogether impossible.

This must be attributed in part to the state of the Roman law into which Roman juristic science had put it. With inimitable mastery the latter had selected those elements that are universally human, and that must exist in every society. The concepts of corporation, family law powers, ownership and real rights, the various agreements, inheritance, — all of these and many other basic concepts of juristic science in general, not only of juristic science as it exists among a certain people, it had developed and set forth, and had found the proper norms for the decision of the most important questions that might arise in a legal controversy. But mediaeval society was so totally different from Roman society because it was in a stage of development so far removed from that of Roman society that, at the time of the reception, the number of legal institutions as to which one could be certain at the outset that they were identical with those of Roman law must have been exceedingly small. It was the case perhaps only as to this or that family relation, a small number of agreements, let us say, as to sales and loans. Apart from these, though there were many external similarities, the differences must have preponderated.

The situation that the jurists of the time of the reception found themselves in can perhaps be illustrated best by means of a comparison. Let us suppose that by a miracle, the law of England should, at this very moment, become the valid law of some part or other of the European continent. Let us suppose further that the Continental jurist consults the Stephen-Jenks commentaries on the Laws of England (incidentally the only work on English law that can be compared with the comprehensive presentations that are in vogue on the Continent). He would be surprised to find that the basic concept of his whole legal thinking up to the present time — the concept of ownership — is not being discussed at all. To begin with there is no concept of ownership which comprises the law both as to movables and immovables. A concept that corresponds to ownership of immovables is there called a freehold, and is defined as "an estate, either of inheritance or for life held by free tenure." Here almost every word is unintelligible to a Continental jurist, and the concept itself is still more so. For "freehold[1]" refers, in the first place, to immovables only. It is a sort of real right which includes usufruct, heritable lease,

1. freehold：（房地产）自由保有

and heritable building right[1], and which excludes the free ownership of land of the Continental law inasmuch as it presupposes tenure. He would find it necessary in the first place to resolve all doubts as to the question whether the free ownership of the Continental law, since it is not a feudal fee, is covered by this concept. This question the Continental jurist, whether he likes it or not, will find himself constrained to answer in the affirmative, for the reason that tenure in modern English law is a pure fiction, and for the further reason that, if this were not so, there would be no legal regulation at all, not only of ownership but also of usufruct, of heritable lease, and of heritable building right, all of which are conditioned upon acquisition from an owner. And apart from this, the difficulty of working with a concept of property which comprises also usufruct, heritable lease, and heritable building right, and among the sub-divisions of which are found the base fee[2] (property to which most strange resolutory conditions are attached) and the fee tail[3] (inalienable property which passes to certain definite heirs, our Continental *fideicommissum,* and, after all, not a *fideicommissum* at all). What does all of this refer to?

The famous decretal of Pope Alexander III, which regulated the passing of the advowson[4] to the *firmarius*[5], proves that this imagined and impossible illustration quite faithfully reflects all the difficulties that necessarily had to arise from the reception of Roman law in the Middle Ages. A vast literature rich in disputes and teeming with false conclusions and misunderstandings concerned itself for centuries with the question to whom, as persons having a *real* right[6], the advowson

1. usufruct, heritable lease, and heritable building right：用益权、可继承租赁权与可继承建筑权
2. base fee：附条件地产权
3. the fee tail：限嗣继承地产权
4. advowson：（教会法）圣职推荐权
5. *firmarius*：〈拉〉出租土地者
6. *real* right：物权

passes, since it was impossible to decide which kind of Continental *real* rights corresponds to the English *firma.* In a thorough historical and doctrinal inquiry, Wach has indeed presented an exhaustive discussion of the nature of the *firma;* but he has not solved the practical question, i.e. which Contmental institution must be regarded as a *firma,* for the simple reason that it cannot be solved. There is nothing on the Continent that could be said to be a *firma.* The question cannot be answered; it would have to be decided.

At the time of the reception, irresoluble questions of this kind cried out to the Continental jurists from every line of the *corpus iuris.* Had they been men of scientific training, let us say of the Historical School of Savigny or of the modem sociological school, they surely would never have undertaken this task, which cannot be performed scientifically. They would have said to themselves at the outset: The kind of ownership that the sources speak of does not exist among us (in the Middle Ages, not even the name; much less the concept); the unfree person that we are dealing with is not the Roman slave. Institutions like the *stipulation* the *cautio indiscreta,* the *mandatum,* or the *locatio conductio operis* or *operarum*[1] do not exist today, just as there is no *legatum per praeceptionem* or *peculium profectitium*[2]. Doubtless there are phenomena of legal life which present a certain similarity to the above-named Roman institutions, but the divergencies are so great at every point that it would be a highly unscientific procedure to deal with them according to identical principles. What prevented the juristic science of the Romanist jurists from bleeding to death was the fact that it never undertook the scientific task which Savigny in

1. the *stipulation*, the *cautio indiscreta*, the *mandatum*, or the *locatio conductio operis* or *operarum*：要式口约、不可分割的保证、委托、承揽租赁或雇佣租赁（斜体为拉丁文）
2. *legatum per praeceptionem* or *peculium profectitium*：先取遗赠或父子特有产（斜体为拉丁文）

his day suggested to it. The jurists of the time of the reception had law cases in hand and they searched the *corpus iuris* for decisions that might fit them. And the decisions did fit whenever there was a certain amount of similarity bet ween them and the cases. Scientific exactitude was not sought after. The function which their juristic activity subserved was not a scientific one but the eternal, practical one of all juristic science, to wit to make the law subserve the requirements of life.

This practical labor however was made considerably easier for all the generations of jurists since the Middle Ages by the fact that it had already been done, in part at least, by the glossators under most extraordinarily favorable conditions. For in the tenth and eleventh centuries, when the glossators began their work, the relations with Roman antiquity were extremely close, at least in the parts of Italy where the glossators lived and in southern France. Many Roman legal institutions, though distorted during the course of the centuries, may still have been in existence at the time, at least to an extent sufficient to establish the connection in a certain measure. A still more important factor was the part played by the language alone. At that time, Latin still was a spoken language, and in its own way interpreted the Roman world to the person who used it, without however laying any claim to historical accuracy. The Roman *miles*[1] surely was something quite different from the mediaeval knight; but since the knight was called a *miles,* the doctrine of the *peculium castrense*[2] was applied without more ado to the knightly *filius familias.*

In spite of all this there were many difficulties that stood in the way of applying Roman law to the existing legal relations. And these difficulties were the cradle of the jurisprudence of conceptions. Everywhere, even in an indigenous legal system, there must be some

---

1. Roman *miles*：罗马兵士
2. *peculium castrense*：〈拉〉军营特有产

sort of relation between the legal norm and the legal relations, but in by far the greatest number of cases actual observation of life is sufficient for this purpose. The great objection that one could make to the definition of a railroad given by the Supreme Court of the Empire is the fact that it is so altogether superfluous. Do we not know without this definition what a railroad is? At any rate we shall find that, after innumerable readings of the definition given by the Supreme Court, we have not added to our knowledge. A few borderline cases may indeed be doubtful, but what are they among the vast number of cases that are being decided quite clearly and unmistakably by actual observation for everyone that has ever seen a railroad and who is there today that has not seen a railroad? And actual observation taught the Roman, with the same certainty, what a *delegatio*[1] and a *mandatum in rem suam*[2] was; and the Salic Franks what a *chrenechruda* was. But in the Middle Ages often enough there was no actual observation to aid the jurist in his attempts to gain an understanding of the Roman law, and this lack the jurisprudence of conceptions was designed to make up for.

For practical juristic science the important problem was how to apply Roman law. It does not loom very large in the work of the glossators, for with them the scientific interest outweighed the practical. They are occupied more with ascertaining the con tent of the *corpus iuris* than with the manner of its application. The *corpus iuris* was a new code to them, and their attitude toward it was very much like that of jurists toward any new code, even that of the present-day German jurists toward the German Civil Code. Their first concern was to find out what it contained. Accordingly the glossators were chiefly engaged in interpreting the *corpus iuris,* not in developing a practical juristic science. But they could not escape the questions of practical application altogether, for although they were not practical jurists,

---

1. *delegatio*：〈拉〉职权的委托
2. *mandatum in rem suam*：〈拉〉为自己利益委托

they wanted to become teachers of practical jurists. And therefore they found it necessary, in all cases in which actual observation or the language failed to give them information, true or false, to study the sources themselves for the purpose of getting a clear knowledge of what their precepts actually referred to. Accordingly we find that even the glossators engaged in investigations of concepts, for instance, of the concept *res publica*[1], in order to determine whether in legal contemplation, in addition to the Roman Empire, there was another community in the nature of a state, of the concepts *universitas, delegation possessio chilis,* and *naturalis.*[2]

This purely practical side of the work in turn involved great practical difficulties. The pure concepts of the sources of the Roman law, the universalizations of the facts of Roman legal life as such, which the Roman jurists had but rarely formulated in words, and even more rarely had formulated correctly (*omnis definitio periculosa*[3]), would be just as unavailable to the jurists of the Middle Ages as the concepts of freehold or of *firma* of the English law would be to the Continental jurist. In order that the Roman concepts might be available, they had to be extended so as to include the phenomena not only of the Roman law but also those of the mediaeval law. For this purpose everything had to be eliminated from the concept that did not fit into the present, that is, everything that was given by the particular social and economic relation out of which the concept had arisen in Rome. The more empirical content is taken out of a concept, the more abstract it becomes; and so the Roman universalizations became abstractions in the Middle Ages. The mediaeval and modern abstractions are Roman universalizations which to a considerable extent have been emptied of

---

1. *res publica*：〈拉〉公有物
2. *universitas, delegatio, possessio civilis,* and *naturalis*：集合体、委托、民法占有以及自然（斜体为拉丁文）
3. *omnis definitio periculosa*：〈拉〉定义均属危险

their content.

It would be unfair to take this to mean that in their abstractions the jurists had given up all connection with economic and social life. A juristic concept without any relation to life, and therefore without empirical content, is simply unthinkable. But here the situation was the following. The practical purpose which the legal relation subserved in Rome did not exist in modern society. At the same time there was a different practical purpose in modern society for which, at any rate, the Roman precepts could be utilized. The thing to do therefore was to receive only so much empirical content into the concept as was necessary in order not to interfere with the utilization of it in mediaeval society. The correality of the sources of Roman law, like every joint liability, has arisen out of relations of community between the co-obligors, especially out of family communities, partnership relations, and relations of suretyship. Undoubtedly the nature of these community relations has had a bearing upon the nature of the joint obligation. The correality of husband and wife, of brothers holding goods in joint ownership, was something different, even in Rome, from the correality of persons engaged in a joint adventure. The Roman jurists did not fail to take account of these differences; although this fact does not appear very clearly since with them it was always a freely chosen correality. The community relations however out of which joint obligation arose in the Middle Ages and in modern times were so totally different from the Roman relations that the Roman law of joint obligation would have been unavailable for the modern relations if in defining joint obligation the Roman community relations which constituted its basis had been taken into account, and the classes of joint obligation had been dealt with separately according to the differences in the character of these community relations. Therefore an abstract concept of joint obligation was formed. Its whole economic content is limited to the fact that the creditor can demand the whole performance from each joint debtor. The relation of the joint debtors to the creditor and to each other, which would vary according to the kind of community relation that subsisted between the joint debtors, is left out of account in this abstract joint obligation. And so Roman law remains applicable although it manifestly presupposes community relations of a kind quite different from those that were in existence in the Middle Ages. It was intended at the outset that this abstraction should be utilized only for the purposes of litigation. In actual life there are no abstract joint debtors. Each class of joint obligations has an economic basis of some sort, and according to the various kinds of economic bases there are different classes of joint obligations. The brothers who are holding their goods in common, the joint adventurers, the sure ties who assume this relation as principal debtors, become abstract joint deb tors, and so it became possible to utilize the rules which had arisen in Rome for the regulation of these relations indiscriminately for the modern abstract joint debtor whether he be a joint debtor because of a matrimonial community of goods, a joint making of a bill of exchange, suretyship, mercantile association, joint adventure, or civil law partnership. The well known difficulties which have sicklied o'er the Romanist doctrine of correality and solidarity[1] have their origin in the concept of abstract joint obligation[2].

The adaptation of Roman law to the needs of a society that was altogether foreign to it was facilitated by the form which the basic concept of every legal system, the concept of ownership, had received as early as the days of the Republic. It certainly is not true that ownership in Roman law was an abstract ownership. At Roman law, ownership was just as truly an economic mat ter as ownership necessarily must be anywhere else. But this Roman economic ownership of the *Italic fundus,* of which alone the jurists are speaking, was of such a nature, because of

---

1. doctrine of correality and solidarity：连带责任
2. abstract joint obligation：抽象连带债务

the Italic system of ownership of land, that at the time of the reception it inevitably led to an abstract concept of ownership.

Had the Roman jurists been dealing with land in its original village community, with all its relations to neighbors and the relations of subjection to the lord of the manor, which inevitably result from situations of this kind, it would scarcely have been possible to adapt such a law of real property to the needs of mediaeval society; the reception of Roman law would have been as impracticable perhaps as the reception of the English law of real property would be on the Continent today. But since the Romans, as is well known, had abolished their original village community at a time prior to that of the historical tradition, Roman law knows nothing of the village, but knows only the individual farm (*Hof*). Confronted with the task of creating a new land law for *the fundus,* which had been severed from all its former relations, the Roman jurists created it in the likeness of the ownership of movables. They simply dealt with the owner of land according to the same rules according to which they dealt with the owner of a movable thing. That is to say: The *fundus* is a *res mancipi* like the slave, like the head of cattle. Were it not for the fact that a few remnants of the older order had been retained, such as the servitudes, especially the *servitutes praediorum rusticorum*[1], the *actio damni infecti*[2], the *operis novi nuntiatio*[3], the *actio aquae pluviae arcendae*[4], there would be practically no peculiarities in the classical Roman law, at least as to the *ager privatus*[5]. Indeed it is very doubtful whether this was the whole of Roman land law, whether there was not, in addition to this, much local and economic law, which varied according to the use to which

1. *servitutes praediorum rusticorum*：〈拉〉城市地役权
2. *actio damni infecti*：〈拉〉损害赔偿之诉
3. *operis novi nuntiatio*：〈拉〉新施工告令
4. *actio aquae pluviae arcendae*：〈拉〉排放雨水之诉
5. *ager privatus*：〈拉〉私有土地

the land was being put and of which we no longer have any knowledge; at least some law regulating the right to build and some mining law can be found even in the sources of the classical period. But all of this seems to have been outside of the sphere of interest of the jurists. We must point out most emphatically however that even this juristic law of ownership and possession was the law of a certain economic order of possession, the economic order of the possession of the *ager privatus* in Italy, and that it did not extend beyond this order. It applied neither to the *ager publicus*[1] in Italy nor to the *solum provinciate*[2]. But of all of these divergent orders of possession only a few scanty provisions about the *ager vectigalis*[3] and the *emphyteusis*[4] found their way into the sources. In the Middle Ages only the church was able to utilize these.

If we treat land like a movable thing, the relation of the ownership of land to society is eliminated from the concept of ownership, and there remains only one question that has any bearing on the right of ownership and the right of possession connected therewith, to wit the question of the act ions claiming ownership or possession. The Roman jurists who, in the case of land, can disregard its economic relations and the economic constitution of Italy are concerned chiefly with the actions claiming ownership or possession. Practically everything therefore that the Roman jurists have to say about ownership of land clusters around the various forms of the actions claiming ownership or possession. The acquisition and the loss of ownership and of possession, considered chiefly as the presuppositions for the actions, the parties to an action for the protection of ownership and to the interdicts, the problem of proof: this is practically all that we can learn from the Roman jurists.

---

1. *ager publicus*：〈拉〉公有地
2. *solum provinciale*：〈拉〉外省地
3. *ager vectigalis*：〈拉〉赋税田
4. *emphyteusis*：〈拉〉永佃权

The law of ownership and of possession of the Roman jurists then was a legal order based on the Italic system of landholding, and the fact that it contained chiefly regulations concerning actions claiming ownership or possession must be attributed to the fact that because of the peculiar nature of the Italic system of landholding, it was only these actions that required regulation. But even in the code of Justinian it had taken on an altogether different significance. And this was due not only to the fact that the Italic system of landholding meanwhile had undergone a complete change but also to the fact that the Roman land law meanwhile had become the law of the Empire, and was to be the law of the provinces also, the system of landholding in which was altogether different from the Italic system. This new land law was stated, albeit in a very incomplete and imperfect form, in the Imperial constitutions, which are found in the Code and in the Novels[1]. Perhaps for the greater part there were no regulations at all, and the civil service as well as the administration of justice had to make shift as well as it could. At the same time the law of property and of possession of the classical jurists was received into the Institutes and into the Digest, and was thereby engrafted upon the new system of landholding. In this connection however it no longer was the law for a certain system of landholding but a law which contained a few precepts, chiefly concerning actions claiming ownership or possession by way of supplement to a regulation of the system of landholding which was laid down in the Code and in the Novels. In this form it was admirably fitted for the reception. The jurists of the countries which received it of course did not, and self-evidently could not, entertain the idea of receiving the Roman system of landholding when they received the Roman law. Neither the ancient Italic system of landholding, which the classical jurists presupposed, nor the later

1. in the Code and in the Novels：在《法典》与《新律》中

system of the Imperial *constitutiones*[1] became valid law in the Middle Ages, which had developed a possessory order based on the feudal system. They conceived of the Roman law of property and possession as a legal order which, disregarding all actual systems of landholding, regulated merely actions claiming ownership or possession. As a law which regulated merely actions claiming ownership or possession it was not incompatible with any system of landholding, not even with the mediaeval system. The abstract Roman concept of ownership is therefore, properly speaking, not an achievement of the Roman law but of the reception. It is a law of ownership, whose whole economic content is the action claiming ownership, which does not regulate the economic possessory order but presupposes it.

Accordingly the creation of abstract concepts was merely an altogether indispensable juristic device for the adaptation of the Roman norms to the requirements of a different society. The result on the whole was the same in every case as in the case of joint obligation and ownership. The indigenous social order remained in existence as one freely chosen, based on customary law, on particular law; to it, usually in a quite arbitrary manner and only for the purposes of procedure, the Roman norms were added so far as it was possible to comprehend them in a legal concept which had been emptied of its peculiarly Roman content. But this process was permissible only to the ext ent to which the concepts which had been created in this manner could be applied to mediaeval and modern situations. A limitation therefore was imposed upon the jurisprudence of conceptions at the point at which it became impossible, even though the greatest possible measure of abstraction be employed, to subsume legal relations which belonged exclusively to mediaeval or modem law under the Roman legal concepts. The jurists of the early days of the reception both in

1. Imperial *constitutiones*：皇帝谕令（斜体为拉丁文）

Italy and in Germany avoid these difficulties with a marvelous lack of embarrassment. The glossators pay very little attention to this matter. It is their business to interpret the Roman law, not to apply it. To which of the relations of their day that are foreign to the Romans the Roman law should not be applied is discussed by them, on principle, only once as far as I know, i.e. in the gloss to 1.32. D. leg. 1, 3: *de quibus scriplis legibus non utimur: in feudis*[1]. Nowhere in the gloss is there a hint as to how, for example, the mediaeval community relations, bearer papers, which are met with in Italy as early as the eleventh century, and the *commenda*[2], which can be traced into antiquity, are to be dealt with juristically, although the glossators must have been familiar with all of these things. From their whole attitude one can infer that they believed Roman law to be applicable only to those relations which were regulated therein. Whatsoever had been ordained by other statutes, ordinances, customs, was outside of the sphere of Roman law; they therefore without more ado recognized the ordinances of the Italian cities as valid side by side with the Roman law. Perhaps the gloss to I.7 C de agr. 11, 47 is a typical case; there decisions based on the passage from the Code appear side by side with decisions based on *communis consuetudo*[3]. There is a close connection between this attitude of the gloss and the fact that it reflects the state of affairs in the early years of the reception of the Roman law. Roman law is being applied only where its application is, in a sense, a matter of course. It is a significant fact that Zasius, who in point of time occupies the same relative position to the reception in Germany as the later glossators to the reception in Italy, preserved the independence of the institutions

1. *de quibus scriptis legibus non utimur: in feudis*：〈拉〉成文法律没有价值，最终靠盟友。
2. *commenda*：〈拉〉康孟达组织。中世纪后期兴起于意大利的分担商业风险的商业合伙形式。
3. *communis consuetudo*：〈拉〉共同习惯法

based on German law with the same lack of embarrassment.

But when in the days of the postglossators as well as in Germany in the seventeenth century, the Romanist jurists obtained control over the practical application of law as well, the principle came into vogue that every case must be adjudged according to Roman law unless a different norm has been established for its decision. Thereafter the jurisprudence of conceptions could no longer avail; for the Roman concepts, at least the concepts of the sources that have been transmitted to us, were not adequate to the requirements of the much richer and much more complex modern life. Apart from this, it was inevitable that most unsatisfactory results should be brought about when the institutions of two such *toto caelo*[1] dissimilar societies as the Roman on one hand and the mediaeval and modem on the other were to be jumbled together and to be judged by the same norms for decision, regardless of the gulf that was fixed bet ween them in point of time as well as of economic and of social development. There were several ways of escaping from these difficulties. One could distort the Roman concept in such a manner as to adapt it to the foreign institutions; one could combine the heterogeneous institutions of Roman law in such a manner that the norms for decision that resulted from this combination would meet the requirements of the case in hand; one could falsify the Roman norms for decision so thoroughly that they yielded the desired result. In fact, all of these methods were employed at different times according to the requirements of the individual case. We have now reached the jurisprudence of constructions.

The exigencies of the system of actions caused the Romans themselves to resort to a jurisprudence of constructions whenever it became necessary to meet new requirements of life with such legal

1. *toto caelo*：〈拉〉完全，全然

means as were at hand. It is true, the praetor and the jurist could find new legal propositions for new legal institutions; but this power doubtless was hedged in by traditional limitations, of which we have no detailed knowledge. On the other hand, proceeding by means of constructions offered the advantage that one could, to a certain degree, work with the law that had already been established, and could thus avoid the many dangers involved in a new finding of law. This method does not include the use of fictions; for only the legislator and the praetor could avail themselves of the latter as finders of law, and not, as in England, the jurists. True juristic constructions are the following: the construction of suretyship as *mandatum pecuniae credendae*[1], of assignment as a *mandatum in rem suam*, of the payment of a debt by the surety as a purchase of the obligation, of the dormant commercial partnership as a *depositum irregulare*[2]. These Roman constructions however did not yield binding rules of law; to the Romans they were merely technical remedies. The Roman jurists did not hesitate to reject such inferences from their constructions as did not suit their purposes; and so the surety who had paid was not entitled, like the purchaser of an obligation, to demand a warranty from the creditor, or to demand more from the debtor than he had paid to the creditor.

The glossators likewise resort to construction and they by no means do this in a very modest measure. The proposition of Roman law, *alteri stipulari nemo potest*[3], they limit by holding that though a third party does not, indeed, get the right to bring the *actio directa*[4], he may be permitted to sue directly by means of the *actiouiilis*[5] without obtaining an assignment, which the sources presuppose. They construe the

1. *mandatum pecuniae credendae*：〈拉〉委托借贷
2. *depositum irregulare*：〈拉〉非常寄托
3. *alteri stipulari nemo potest*：〈拉〉无论何人不得为他人为约定。
4. *actio directa*：〈拉〉直接诉讼
5. *actioutilis*：〈拉〉扩用诉讼

constitutum possessorium[1] as abstractly as possible in order to weaken the requirement of deliveryin a case of transfer of ownership. They distort the Roman *dominium*[2], perhaps unconsciously, by making a distinction between *dominium directum* and *dominium utile*[3], and thereby obtain appropriate norms for decision applicable to the mediaeval rights to take fruits and profits (*Nutzungsrechte*). In order to give to corporations the power to adopt resolutions of the whole body, they misinterpret the Roman proposition 1. I, § 2, *D.* 42, *2 municipes per se nihil possidere possunt, quia universi conseniire non possunt*[4], by adding an arbitrary gloss: Gloss V° *non possunt: subaudi hic facile vel commode.* They distort the concept, consciously I am sure, of the *servus publicus*[5] by calling the notary of their day, the *iabellio,* a *servus publicus* in order that he might be able to enter into contracts in behalf of his mandants as their representative. *Quia publice servit, non quia servus est*[6], says Accursius.

Bartolus and his pupils however gave an incomparably greater impetus to juristic construction. They gave direction to the Continental common law technique for many centuries. The most famous of these constructions are the following: (1) The whole theory of the territorial validity of statutes, almost without any basis in the *corpus iuris,* the only point of contact, and a purely external one at that, *being I. 1.* C. *de summa Trin.* 1, 1. (2). The *aequitas Bartolina*[7], the obligation, established by Bartolus, of the *ecclesia* as owner of a parcel of ground held under a perpetual lease (*emphyteusis*) to let the land,

---

1. *constitutum possessorium*：〈拉〉占有转移协议
2. *dominium*：〈拉〉所有权
3. *dominium directum* and *dominium utile*：〈拉〉直接所有权与扩用所有权
4. *municipes per se nihil ... non possunt*：〈拉〉城邦的公民不能占有任何东西，因为无法获得所有人同意。
5. *servus publicus*：〈拉〉公奴隶
6. *Quia publice servit, non quia servus est*：〈拉〉为公共服务的人不是奴隶。
7. *aequitas Bartolina*：〈拉〉衡平

after the direct line of descent of the *emphyteuta* has become extinct, to the collateral relatives of the latter by heritable usufructury lease. This is based on 1. 1, § 43. D. *de aqua quot. et aest.* 43, 20. All that Ulpian says in this passage is that the purchaser of a parcel of ground has a legal right to have the right to draw water from a public aqueduct restored to him if he can show that the right had been gran ted to the land and not only to the person of his predecessor — a case that is in no wise connected with the grant of an *emphyteusis* to the collateral relatives of the *emphyteuta*. (3) The doctrine that a servitude can be established by the mere appointment of the *pater familias,* which also owes its origin to Bartolus, who based it on a very unsatisfactory interpretation of the sources. (4) The denial, by Cinnus and Baldus on the basis of C 4, 28, 5, of the *exceptio*[1] of the *senatusconsullum Macedonianum*[2] against the *filius familias* in mercantile matters. (5) The construction by Baldus, of the bill of exchange as a purchase in order to circumvent the law prohibiting usury. (6) The construction, by later commentators, of the power of a general partner of an unlimited mercantile partnership to enter into a contract with a third person in behalf of the partnership as a mutual *praepositio institoria*[3]; of the assets of the unlimited mercantile partnership as a *corpus mysticum ex pluribus nominibus conflatum*[4]; of insurance against risk as *emptio venditio periculi*[5].

Outwardly the jurisprudence of conceptions and the jurisprudence of constructions[6] manifestly are the very antithesis of the method of

1. *exceptio*：〈拉〉抗辩
2. *senatusconsultum Macedonianum*：〈拉〉马其顿决议
3. *praepositio institoria*：〈拉〉设置经管人
4. *corpus mysticum ex pluribus nominibus conflatum*：〈拉〉一显名合伙人加多个隐名合伙人组成的团体
5. *emptio venditio periculi*：〈拉〉风险买卖
6. the jurisprudence of conceptions and the jurisprudence of constructions：概念法学与建构法学

the Roman jurists. The latter sought to investigate the various legal relations, as they occurred in daily life, by a searching study of life. They universalized the results of these investigations, and thereby either found, through immediate observation, the norms for decision which naturally flow from the economic and social connections of the legal relation, or invented norms that were adapted to the nature of the legal relation. Both the jurisprudence of concept ions and the jurisprudence of constructions however do not seek to get first-hand knowledge of the affairs and happenings of daily life. They purport to establish the concept of the legal relation just as the Roman jurists had it, for the sole purpose of subsuming all the legal relations of their own time with which they had to deal under the Roman concepts and of then applying the Roman norms for decision to them. For the greater part, however, this is seeming only and not reality. The jurisprudence of conceptions and of constructions would amount to pure logical operations, to an arithmetic of conceptions if, and only if, it had brought about the application of the Roman norms for decision to modern situations without any consideration of the question whether the result is appropriate to them or not. But it is easy to demonstrate that this was not the case. Without a certain first-hand observation of the legal relations of life there can be no juristic science. The Romanist jurists must understand the relations of the life of their own time in order to be able to subsume them under the Roman concepts. Like the jurists of all times they therefore sought to understand the legal relation that was submitted to them for decision. Accordingly, proceeding on the basis of the records, the documents, the testimony of witnesses, on the basis of what they knew from other sources as to custom and business usage, they ascertained in every single case the rights of the parcel of land, of the family, of the human beings, of the content of the agreement in question. This knowledge of life furnished the basis for the formation of concepts and for the constructions which we find in the writings of the glossators and of the postglossators.

It was life, and life only, that could teach the glossators what is the content of the real rights to take fruits and profits which they construe as *dominium utile*[1]; life only could tell the commentators something about insurance against risk, which they tried to reach by means of the concept *emptio venditio periculi*. The concepts of the modern legal relations which the Italians developed in this manner they do not naively subsume under the Roman concepts, but they take the results of this operation into account in advance. They did not utilize the Roman concepts for the purposes of juristic science in the form in which they found them in the sources, but first of all refashioned them according to the rules of the craft by means of abstraction and construction so as to produce a result that was suitable for the new universalization, or at least not altogether too objectionable. If the Roman norms for decision were absolutely inapplicable, they made no use of them. Accordingly they never attempted to apply the Roman law of slavery to the serfs of the Middle Ages, except in a case where temporarily, as was the case for instance in Prussia in the seventeenth and eighteenth centuries, the serf lived in a state of oppression so great that the existing modern relations suggested the application of the Roman norms. This characteristic of juristic science appears much more clearly in the case of construction than in the case of mere creation of concepts. In this case the jurist has not only acquired a first-hand knowledge of the legal relation but has also found the norms which he intends to apply by means of universalization and free finding of law. All that he is now looking for is texts in the sources that will provide him with the norms he desires. Since he proceeds with the greatest conceivable measure of arbitrariness, rejects everything that stands in his way, does not stick at falsifications and distortions, there can be no doubt about his success. There can be nothing that

1. *dominium utile*：〈拉〉所有权收益

more exactly describes the nature of the juristic construction than the well known story that Bartolus would first find the solution of a legal problem that was submitted to him, and would then direct his pupils to gather texts from the sources to support his solution. Bartolus surely was not the only one who had the solution before he had the texts.

Lastly the jurisprudence of conceptions and the jurisprudence of constructions caused the juristic concepts of the sources, which, ina great measure, had lost their original content, to be filled with an entirely new content. The gloss, in the discussion of the *universitas personarum*[1], could not avoid, as Gierke's presentation has shown, expressing an opinion about the phenomena of the life of its time which, in its view, were *universitates,* i.e. about the empire, about cities, villages, guilds, about churches in charge of a *collegium* of clerics and convents, about churches at which only one cleric was employed; it began to distinguish between different kinds of property of the *universitas,* between the *res in palrimonio universitatis*[2] and the *res universitatis*[3], and, in the arrangement of the inner affairs of the latter, to keep separate and distinct the various amounts of goods belonging to each — each of which was governed by legal principles peculiar to itself. The *miles* of the sources, who has capacity for the acquisition of a *peculium castrense*[4], becomes the mediaeval knight in the writings of the glossators, as Fitting shows; it was required that he should not be a trader; that he have passed the squire's examination, that he have taken the oath of knighthood; that he have been girt with a sword; that he have received the *nota publica,* which the gloss does not refer to the accolade, but to the knot, which the knight wore on his sleeve until some prince or some lady of high noble rank took it off; and

1. *universitas personarum*：〈拉〉人的集合体
2. *res in patrimonio universitatis*：〈拉〉财产集合体中的物
3. *res universitatis*：〈拉〉团体物
4. *peculium castrense*：〈拉〉军营特有产

that his name have been entered in the list. On an equal footing with this *militia armata*[1], with reference to the *peculium quasi casirense*[2], was the *militia inermis*[3], which was sub-divided into a *caelestis* for the clerics and a *litterata* for the jurists. In a similar fashion the postglossators utilized the concepts of Roman law for the purpose of construing the absolutely modern concepts of the bill of exchange, of the mercantile partnership with unlimited liability, of the assets of a corporation, and of insurance.

Accordingly the new juristic science is based, to precisely the same ext ent as was juristic science among the Romans and in the *Sachsenspiegel,* on the individual legal relation, out of which the norms for the decision of the individual legal controversies arise. As at all times, so also in the days of the glossators and the post-glossators, the great mass of decisions was rendered on the basis of the nature of the individual relations, knowledge of which had been gained in the manner indicated, on the basis of actual observation, on the basis of what is found in the records, on the basis of the documents and of the testimony of witnesses. To state this in modern parlance, in most legal controversies the question of fact, not the question of law, was being adjudged. Whenever the question of fact was of general significance, or admitted of, and actually occasioned, a universalization, it became a legal proposition. These new legal propositions served the purpose of pouring a new content, adapted to the needs of the time, into the concepts of the *corpus iuris.* This was done in the guise of formation of concepts and of constructions. The juristic science of this period therefore is only to a limited extent that which it purports to be, i.e. a presentation and explanation of the content of the sources. To a much greater ext ent, it is a new juristic science, which, in the new period, is

1. *militia armata*：〈拉〉作战武器
2. *peculium quasi castrense*：〈拉〉准军营特有产
3. *militia inermis*：〈拉〉无防御的军队

fulfilling the eternal task of all juristic science, i.e. the task of making the law subserve the needs of life.

Creation of concepts and construction have remained the tried household remedies of Romanistic juristic science wherever the latter has made its way, espedaily of its, historically and scientifically, most important branch, German juristic science, from the sixteenth century onward. The attempt of Zasius to place the German villein on a level not with the Roman slave but with the Roman freedman is first of all an attempt — abortive, it is true — to create an abstract concept of freedman. If Zasius had been at all willing to consider the economic and social relations of the two statuses, he would, self-evidently, have realized that Germanic villeinage[1] is much more like Roman slavery than like the condition of the freedman; for in both villeinage and slavery, we are dealing with a status acquired at birth. The villein becomes a freedman, as Zasius himself observes, through manumission. But Zasius altogether disregards the economic and social relation, considers only the provisions of the Roman law about freedmen which seem to correspond, to a certain extent, to the condition of the Germanic villein, and utilizes it for the creation of the concept, according to which he judges Germanic villeinage. In order to be able to do this, it was necessary to have a clear understanding of the concept of villeinage, and this he owes to a searching and deep study of life.

There is nothing that can give us a better idea of the way the Continental common law originated than this attempt of Zasius. Had Zasius been successful, his attempt would have brought into existence a general concept of "villein" on the basis of the Roman concept of freedman. The norms of the Roman law concerning freedmen that are applicable to the ordinary villein would have become a part of the Continental common law; the others would have been rejected. Over

---

1. villeinage：农奴身份

and above this, self-evidently, everything would have remained in force, as a matter of local law, that had been established concerning them according to custom, customary law, regulation, contracts, statutes. The Continental common law of ownership, of pledge, of obligations and of inheritance have all been created and elaborated in this fashion. But Zasius's attempt to create this concept failed. It seemed altogether too much like a *tour-de-force*[1]. And as a result of this failure, the legal situation of the villein was determined exclusively by contracts, local regulations, custom, customary law, and statute. One hundred years after Zasius, Mevius admitted this unreservedly in his book entitled *Von dem Zustande der Abfor derung und der vermederten A bfolge der Bauers-Leute,* which contains the words, quoted by Stintzing: "*Worinn aber ihre Dienstbarkeit und Freiheit soviet sie beyder theilhaft sein, bestehe, lässet sich in universum nicht wol beschreiben. Angesehen ein jedwedes Land und Territorium seine eigne Weisen, Gewohnheiten und Gebrauche hat ... Darumb dieselbe wol erforschen und beleuchten muss wer von der Bauern Zustand, Gebühr und Recht urtheilen will.*" [1] [2]

The first achievement of German juristic science, the creation of the concept of Gattung (*genus*)[2] and of *fungible*[3] goods by Zasius, was also brought about in this manner, i.e. by first-hand observation of the contract for supplying goods (*Lieferungsvertrag*), which became a thing of practical importance in the sixteenth century, but was

[1] "Wherein however their subjection and their freedom, in so far as they have both, consist cannot well be described *in univer sum.* In view of the fact that each country and territory has its own manners, customs and usages. ... Therefore he who would judge of the condition, duty and right of the peasant must investigate and study them well."

[2] I.e. goods not owned by the seller at the time the contract is entered into.

1. *tour-de-force*：〈法〉绝活
2. Gattung：〈德〉种类；种属
3. fungible goods：可替代物

unknown to the Roman jurists. In this way, the things that had been done by the glossators and the postglossators were being repeated everywhere. The concepts that were taken over from the Romans were being filled with a new content. The individual legal relation as it is reflected in the documents, in the testimony of witnesses, in records, in custom and business usage, provides the material, which is being universalized, and then judged according to the statements of the sources. But in many cases this has been preceded by a working over of the matter by local law. It is well known to what extent the famous German Romanists of the seventeenth and eighteenth centuries were endeavoring to present, not Roman law, but the law of their native country in Roman garb. Each one of them is being referred to as of the part of the country to which his life's work belongs. So Carpzov and Struve are being referred to as of Saxony; Mevius, as of North Germany; Lauterbach, as of Wiirttemberg; Stryck, as of the Mark. For the investigation of the legal relations of their native country they made use of judgments, opinions of faculties, records of trials, as well as of the positive law of the territory in which they were working and for which they were writing. Here too then the first-hand observation of the individual legal relation constitutes the beginning.

By the reception of the Roman law therefore the jurists were not spared the necessity of observing life, or of universalizing its facts. But the center of gravity has been shifted somewhat. So far as the Roman norms were simply taken over, the jurists could limit themselves to a mere presentation and explanation of Roman law. Apart from this, the original free procedure, as it was customary among the Romans and among the German *Schoeffen*, was replaced by the highly artificial but essentially similar procedure by creation of concepts and construction. The use of such unscientific means as the distortion of concepts and falsification of norms — a thing that was done consciously to a very great extent — would have been reprehensible only if they had been under an obligation to work scientifically. But they had no scientific aims; but only the eternal, constant aim of practical juristic science to make the law subserve the needs of life.

XIV THE HISTORICAL TREND IN THE JURISTIC SCIENCE OF THE CONTINENTAL COMMON LAW

Since the middle of the sixteenth century Romanistic juristic science is under the steadily growing influence of the historical trend. The aim of all history of law is to discover the original meaning of the legal propositions and the original significance of the legal relations. These are purely scientific endeavors, which, as such, have nothing to do with practical, juristic science, and which we need not therefore discuss at this point. In so far only as the historical jurists are working in the interest of the application of law, they are concerned, not with pure science, but with practical juristic science. I have not been able to ascertain as a fact that the French and Dutch legal historians anywhere asserted in plain words that the results of their investigations should be authoritative for the practical application of law, but this may be attributable to the fact they do not recognize any science of law other than the historical science. Such an assertion could have only one meaning, to wit that the historical, theoretical science of law is also practical juristic science. At any rate the Historical School of the nineteenth century in Germany has been entertaining this thought, and has been acting according to it. This can be inferred not so much from the faltering and uncertain statements of their programs, several of which, by Savigny, indeed can scarcely be interpreted in any other way, as from their other writings. Especially Savigny's *De possessione*[1],

1. *De possessione*：〈拉〉《论占有》

which has practically become a model for the writing of monographs in the Historical School, proclaims this thought to the world with all the force at its command. Six hundred and ten of its six hundred and fifty-four pages are devoted exclusively to Roman law, without deigning the modern development worthy of as much as a single word. As soon as the meaning which a statement of the sources bore in the mouth of a Roman has been ascertained, the practical question is disposed of also. There is nothing in it that might be of any further interest to Savigny. A meager section of thirty-five pages hastily disposes of the "modifications of the Roman law." He examines them to ascertain whether or not they can be harmonized in principle with that which was law among the Romans. If it can be shown that this is possible, one may accept them. If not, they are to be turned aside with a contemptuous gesture. At a later time, in his *System*[1], Savigny preached quite different principles of dogmatic treatment of the law, but until that time the *De possessions* alone was authoritative as to method. It would be a difficult matter to find a book of equal influence in the monographic literature not only of Germany but of the whole Continental common law. I have gained the conviction on my travels that in the literature of the world there is not another monograph the name of which and, in part, the content of which is so well known to the jurists of each and every legal system as Savigny's *De possessione*. It is the true *Programmschrift* (program book) of the Historical School for practical juristic science.

It is not therefore the guiding principle of the historical jurists that a scientific understanding of any legal system can be gained only from history. That is a scientific axiom without any practical significance. The guiding principle is, rather, that this scientific understanding must suffice for practical juristic science. And this thought received its specific

---

1. *System*：〈拉〉《当代罗马法体系》

coloring from the fact that in the basic conception of law of all legal historians of the Romanistic tendency since the days of Cuiaccius — a conception which they never expressed, but according to which they always acted — law does not consist of legal relations but of legal propositions, so that all that is necessary for a scientific understanding of law is to ascertain the meaning which the legal propositions bore in the mouth of those who first enunciated them. As a practical matter, therefore, the historical conception amounted to this, that the practical application of law must attribute only that meaning to a legal proposition which was intended by its originator. Here again the historically significant antinomy of juristic science which converts its modes of thought, even against its own will, into norms becomes operative.

Only this limitation of the "historical view of law," as Savigny has called it, to the legal propositions can explain the attitude and the conduct of the legal historians. Since the days of Jhering, the founders of the Historical School have often been called romanticists in Germany. But this is unjust; for neither the founders of the Historical School nor any of their adherents among the Romanists actually were romanticists. The yearning, which is characteristic of the romanticist, to turn life back into the past was utterly foreign to them. They surely have never evinced any desire that the *patria potestas* should be revived, or that contracts should be made in the form of the *stipulatio*. And if Savigny has spoken bitter words in a book-review of the modern system of land registration, he surely did not mean to urge the adoption of the Roman law of pledge. Since the law, in the eyes of legal historians everywhere, was not the legal relations but the legal propositions, they have not been concerning themselves about the form which the legal relations assume in actual life. They let life take its course; but they did insist that the courts should adjudge the legal relations according to the Roman legal propositions in the form in which they have been ascertained by scientific investigation. But as to this, they could not but make shipwreck. Had life, under the influence of the Historical School, again become Roman, the application of Roman law would have followed as a matter of course. But since life remained modern and necessarily had to remain modern, it was impossible to apply Roman law to legal relations that in part were unknown to the Romans and in part were totally different from those that had existed among them.

Accordingly the legal historians again found themselves face to face with the problem of applying Roman law. And they sinned most grievously as to this difficulty by not seeing it. They did not even investigate it, although, from their point of view, it would have been their first duty to do this rather than to throw light upon a few dark points in the history of Roman law. They never inquired how the glossators, the postglossators, and the German Romanists of the sixteenth century performed the adaptation of Roman law. Savigny's history of Roman law in the Middle Ages was a history of juristic literature. Apart from this, in the hands of the legal historians, the legal history of the time following the reception is almost exclusively a history of legal doctrine. Wherever their glance touched upon jurists of past centuries, they were interested in the way in which the latter understood Roman law, not in their attitude toward the law of their own day. To the present day, we have no presentation of the law of the gloss, of the postglossators, or of the German *usus modernus*. Indeed, even the number of treatises on the history of legal doctrine that treat of the way in which the glossators, the commentators, and the *usus modernus*[1] dealt with individual legal institutions is extremely small.

But you cannot do away with a difficulty by ignoring it. The question

---

1. *usus modernus*：〈拉〉《学说汇编》的现代应用

of the adaptation of Roman law must be solved daily by judicial decisions. A juristic science that ignores the adaptation of law of the past to the legal relations of the present does not offer practical law but historical law. This judgment does not condemn the Historical School of the French and of the Netherlanders very severely; for, it seems, their aim was to teach law and to let the administration of law get along with it as best it could. But the German legal historians did not profess to teach Roman law but law that was applicable in Germany, and therefore it was incumbent upon them, will he nill he[1], to consider both the Roman law and its adaptation. Their method of procedure usually was simply to take over the results of the adaptation as it had been performed by their predecessors. They applied the legal propositions of Roman law to the same modern relations to which they had already been applied by the glossators, the postglossators, and the teachers of the *usus modernus* in Germany. The pandects of the Historical School differ from the older works chiefly in this, that they no longer discuss the adaptation but presuppose its results. In all essential respects they present merely those results that the Continental common law jurists attained as early as the eighteenth century. But they have persistently refused to quote the writings of the latter; for in spite of the fact that they were deeply indebted to them, they despised them unspeakably with all their hearts. And, therefore, thanks to these legal historians, we have lost all knowledge of the historical connection between the adaptation of the nineteenth and that of the earlier centuries. But resort to this device failed when questions were involved that had not arisen before the nineteenth century. Inasmuch as the Historical School provided no new means of solving these problems, the old ones that had stood the test of experience had to suffice. Jurists proceeded, just as they had done before, by immediate

---

1. will he nill he：不管其愿意否

observation and universalization, concealing their met hods according to approved models under the guise of construction and creation of concepts.

As an illustration let us take the vast Continental common law literature on the making of contracts where the parties are not in the presence of each other. It discusses questions which have arisen thanks to the modern development of the postal and telegraph systems, and about which of course nothing is to be found in the Roman sources. The solution therefore had to be found quite independently. The basis was observation and the universalization of experience; subsequently however the solutions which had been arrived at in this manner were read into the sources. This happened also in the case of Jhering's doctrine of *culpa in contrahendo*[1] and of the negative interest in a contract. More important are Einert's and Liebe's works on the bill of exchange[2]. After the law of bills of exchange has been developed, it is being pressed into the Romanist formulae of the "literal contract" and of the *stipulatio*. Bahr's work was done solely on the basis of observation; the derivation from the sources is mere external adornment.

All that we can say of the upshot of the endeavors of the legal historians for practical juristic science is that construction by means of conscious distortion and falsification has been limited to a considerable extent. They insist that the legal propositions should everywhere be employed according to their original meaning. Though this may appear to be a rather insignificant result, the effect of the historical trend in practical juristic science was an enormous one. By making the ascertainment of the meaning of the legal propositions at the time of their origin the sole function of juristic science, they intentionally shifted the center of gravity of the juristic interest into

---

1. *culpa in contrahendo*：〈拉〉缔约过失
2. bill of exchange：汇票

the past. They excluded the present from juristic science, and actually transmuted a creative art into a manner of science, but only into a kind of philology, which did not concern itself with the knowledge of things but with the knowledge of what has been said about things. They took no further interest in the whole development from the time when the proposition had been stated in the form in which it is binding today down to the present; they refused to go beyond Sabinus or beyond Papinian, or if Justinian had inserted an interpolation into the text, beyond that. The practical effect of thrusting creative juristic science into the background has been the doctrine that the solution of all problems must be reached by interpretation of the sources. The doctrine of the legislator who foresees everything that may arise and of the perfection of the legal system, which existed, in the germ, in the writings of the postglossators, has received its scientific consecration at the hands of the legal historians, especially of those of the German school.

But precisely for the reason that the legal historians actually rejected the thought of any and all conscious creative development of the law beyond the content of the sources, they were compelled to continue the development of juristic methods. All the arbitrary proceedings, the naive misunderstandings and conscious falsifications, of former schools of jurists had served the purpose of adapting the law to new needs, and of enriching it by means of norms that the present time required. But the zeal of the legal historians to go back to the original content of the sources brushed aside, if not all of this most valuable legal material, certainly a considerable portion of it, and by so doing impoverished the law. The gulf that was fixed between the traditional law and the present time had continually been becoming wider and wider, and had to be bridged somehow. This was done chiefly by converting the creation of juristic concepts and juristic construction into a mathematics of concepts and into a constructive systematism (*Systematik*).

The nature of the juristic mathematics of concepts can be shown by means of a comparison of juristic with mathematical concepts. Juristic concepts are empirical. They are a synthesis of the norms that govern an empirically given legal relation, and that are so essential to it that they distinguish the given legal relation from other similar relations. By means of formal logic therefore no other norms can be derived from a concept than those that have been utilized in creating the concept, for formal logic cannot, by any means, provide new thought material; it can only unfold such material as is already in existence and analyze it.

Mat hematical concepts on the other hand are arb itrary, or as the famous French mathematician Poincare has called them, conventional. Properties or necessary characteristics are being attributed to the concept, quite without any concern as to the question whether they are actually conceivable or not. Take for instance the imaginary number[1], infinity[2], Riemann's plane[3]. And it is not required that the deductions that may be made from the concept should in any way harmonize with reality; all that is required is that they should not be self-contradictory. This disregard of reality by mathematics is absolutely justifiable; for the mathematician does not lay claim to any ability to exercise control over the world of reality by means of his concepts. Mathematical thinking is a source of purest delight to some natures which are especially adapted to it; to others it is, in part, inaccessible; upon others, among whom, unfortunately, I must be numbered, its effect is positively repellant.

But it is not impossible to treat empirical concepts as if they were mathematical concepts, to attribute properties to them arbitrarily, and to make deductions from them that are foreign to reality. Natural

1. imaginary number：虚数
2. infinity：无穷大
3. Riemann's plane：黎曼平面

philosophy in past centuries has followed this path often enough. A procedure of this kind suggests itself to juristic science with an exceptional degree of force because of the fact that there actually is in its concepts something arbitrary, conventional. The legal institutions, the norms for decision, the statutory provisions, from which it draws the essential characteristics of its concepts, the inner empirical necessity of which often is not apparent to us, are the product of the labor of the human mind, and that which is being adduced on the basis of this material often makes the impression that, at the pleasure of the originator, it might just as well have been arranged otherwise. It surely was purely a matter of convention that the Roman jurists of the Empire made the order of the family of the peasant proprietor of the days of the Punic war[1], which had long since disappeared, the basis for the concepts of the law of the family; that the French Civil Code made community of movables, and the German Civil Code community of administration, the statutory regime. And how many other things connected with each of these legal institutions might be regulated in a way quite different from the way it was actually done! The similarity bet ween juristic and mathematical concepts indeed is merely an outward one; for the concept itself was not created arbitrarily, its empiric basis alone rests — and this, too, is only seemingly true — on human volition. Nevertheless this superficial similarity has been sufficient to produce a juristic method which is closely related to the mathematical met hod. But this alone does not suffice to explain the enormous importance of the juristic mathematics of concepts.

We must add the remarkable fact that juristic science, although it is basically different from mat hematics, has at all times had a strange power to charm mat hematical minds. A juristic mathematician is not endeavoring by means of juristic science to satisfy the needs for which

1. Punic war：迦太基战争。罗马共和国与古迦太基之间于公元前 264—前 146 年间发生的一系列战争。

the latter really exists, but to secure the high intellectual enjoyment which analytical mathematics or the theory of numbers could afford in a much less questionable manner. Like the mathematician, he creates juristic concepts which, in part at least, he creates arbitrarily; but unlike the mathematician, since the great antinomy of juristic science at once asserts itself, he demands that the conclusions, which he arrives at by unfolding the concept, be at once realized; that they be recognized as norms; that the judge render his decisions, and the legislator legislate, in accordance with them. In his judgment the solemnity and dignity of the art to which he has dedicated his life lies in this very thing, that it bestows entity upon the figments of his imagination.

The juristic mathematician may be found in all latitudes, occasionally even among the Romans, where he flourishes most luxuriantly perhaps in the doctrine of the *ius accrescendi*[1] in case of legacies, and among the present-day French and English; but the Continental common law was an extraordinarily favorable soil. For the universalizations, the historic basis of which had long since been forgotten; the norms for decision, the social justice of which belonged to a distant past, which, in the main, we cannot understand; the statutes, the expediency of which, as in the case of the *lex Falcidia*[2], is a mystery to us today: all of these things could very easily — here more than elsewhere — give rise to the idea that a considerable portion, or the greater portion, of the law is arbitrary and conventional. The Historical School, which ought to have fostered an understanding of the economic and social relations out of which the legal propositions, as is well known, arose in Rome, has always been antiquarian rather than historical, and was not equal to a task of this magnitude. Inasmuch as the Historical School accentuated

1. *ius accrescendi*：〈拉〉取得权利
2. *lex Falcidia*：〈拉〉法尔其第法

the practical necessity of going beyond Roman law, it is easily understood that the mathematics of concepts had never flourished so abundantly as under the domination of the historical school in Germany. Its most outstanding representatives were preponderantly mathematicians, to wit Puchta, Vangerow, Windscheid, Brinz, and, in his earlier days, Jhering. It may suffice to point out the things that once upon a time were "conceptually" impossible, to wit assignment of an obligatory right[1], testamentary creation of a foundation which was to be established by the testament itself (*Staedelscher Erbfalt*); the maxim *Kauf bricht nicht Miele*[2], the servitude of a shareholder in a parcel of land belonging to the share company. On the other hand it was "conceptually" necessary that a swindler who sold a cargo of coal which was on the high sea to several people should be permitted to recover the whole purchase price from each buyer in case it sank at a later time, because of the maxim that *the buyer bears the risk*[3]. I wonder whether a Roman would ever have rested content with a formula of this kind, and whether he would not have freely found a suitable norm.

A typical instance of the mathematics of concepts is the concept of ownership of the Historical School. Its empirical basis comprises the following: ownership of movable things, which as a consequence of its economic purpose, as a rule, permits every possible use and consumption; the Roman ownership of the *fundus Italicus*[4] and the modern ownership of land which have arisen out of the removal of all burdens and charges from the land, both of which, because of the Roman and of the present-day system of landholding, permit of extensive rights of taking fruits and profits; the right of the lord in land which is held in feudal tenure. Now these, I take it, are legal

1. assignment of an obligatory right：债权转让
2. *Kauf bricht nicht Miete*：〈德〉买卖不破租赁
3. *the buyer bears the risk*：买受人承担风险
4. *fundus Italicus*：〈拉〉意大利土地

relations which economically are so unrelated that it is scarcely possible to create an empirical concept common to all of them, for this empirical concept must needs be expressed in economic terms. The Romans were able to get along without a concept of ownership in the *ager publicus* or in the *solum provinciale,* and the English of today can quite well dispense with a universally valid concept of ownership; the older Continental common law juristic science, too, did not have it, but made a distinction bet ween *dominium directum* and *utile.* The Historical School was not willing to dispense with an omnipresent ownership. Searching for a concept which should cover the most heterogeneous relations, they inevitably had to arrive at a concept that was altogether uneconomic. The most acceptable formulation, perhaps, is that of Windscheid. The latter defines it as follows: Ownership is the right which in itself makes the will of the person entitled decisive as to the thing in the totality of its relations. Manifestly, this concept is absolutely arbitrary. If one compares it with an economic juristic concept, e.g. the law and right of pledge, of usufruct, of sale, one will perceive at once that, as contrasted with these, it does not import any economic relation at all, but is merely a formula, designed to give a common name to a man's manifold economic relations. Nevertheless a number of inferences were drawn from it, to wit that there can be only one ownership of a corporeal thing; that a *real* right in a thing that one owns is impossible; that the extinction of a *real* right frees the thing from the limitations imposed by the *real* right; that in the *actio negatoria* the owner need prove no more than that he is the owner. Do these norms really flow from the concept of ownership as Windscheid has formulated it? The words, indeed, are so indefinite that they can mean not only this but many other things besides. But could one not speak of ownership even if these four elements were not present? It is certain that, in various legal systems, the owner may have the right to hunt, the water right, the mining right in a thing which he owns; that if another has the real right to hunt and to mine, and this right is destroyed, the right of the owner is not by this very fact at once extended so as to include these rights; that the owner remains owner even if in the *actio negatoria* the burden of proof is regulated differently. On the other hand one might say of the usufructuary that he can have no right in the thing as to which he has the right of usufruct; that the destruction of a *real* right frees his right from the limitation that had been resting upon it, and that it is sufficient if, in an *actio negatoria*, he establishes his right. After this, not much remains of the concept of ownership. But the norms, which are said to flow from the concept, in actual fact originated in Roman law; they are therefore empirical, and it is undoubtedly quite arbitrary to say that since they arise from the concept, they are valid even where their validity cannot be established empirically. The allocation of the burden of proof in the *actio negatoria* is a part of the latest development of juristic law, and is so far from being conceptually necessary that it has failed to gain universal recognition.

A second typical example of Savigny's mathematics of conceptions is his doctrine of essential error. According to Savigny the legal transaction is, conceptually, a declaration of the will. Consequently, there is no legal transaction where, because of essential error, the will and the declaration do not coincide, whether or not there be fault (*Verschulden*) on the part of the person in error. Since the contract is only a species of legal transaction, he says, the above statement applies also to the contract, even though the other party be not, and could not be, aware of the error. In so far as the legal transaction, empirically, is nothing more than a declaration of the will, this doctrine is correct, i.e. it is correct as to gifts, and other transactions imposing a unilateral obligation (suretyship, acknowledgment/ ratification), declarations by last will and testament, agreements of family law, perhaps also most compromises. But as applied to mercantile contracts it is manifestly incorrect. It is so far from being concep tually necessary that the courts, as my investigations of the course of decisions of the last century have shown, have only rarely, and then solely on doctrinal grounds, rendered decisions according to Savigny's theory. Where an agent without fraudulent intent meant to enter into a contract in the name of the principal, and the other party had no means of knowing this, no attention has ever been paid thereto, although this is perhaps the most common instance of error *in persona*.

These two examples afford a deep insight into the nature of the mathematics of concepts. The concept of ownership which the Historical School has created and Savigny's concept of the legal transaction have arisen from observation of actual life and are therefore empirical. We know the individual legal relations which constitute the basis of these concepts; the norms which purport to result from the concept belong, in part, to the existing law. But these concepts were not abstracted carefully from the facts of experience like those of the natural sciences, nor were they created, like the concepts of practical juristic science, with a view to the requirements of the application of law. They are universalizations of reality; they are not scientific, however, but superficial, unprofessional, containing a series of quite arbitrary admixtures, like those of the older natural philosophy or of Shelling's philosophy, by which, as is well known, Savigny and Puchta were influenced. Nor are they practical, for all consideration of expediency is foreign to them to begin with. The fact that formal logic deduces norms from them is due to the fact that these ide nt ical norms were utilized in the creation of these concepts. Formal logic, at all times, can derive those norms from a concept which it has first put into it. In so far as norms have been created empirically, they are *richtig* (correct), but if they are not based on reality, they are independent creations of juristic science. They differ from the other parts of juristic law in this, that, seemingly at least, they were created independently of social influences, distribution of power, considerations of expediency, or trends of justice. But to this very fact the success of the mathematics of concepts may, in a great measure, be attributed. The latter attained its fullest development at a time when it was believed that all creation of law should be reserved to the. legislator. Whenever the administration of law found that which was offered by the Roman and also by the modern legislator insufficient for its purposes, that which men were least unwilling to place at its disposal was a juristic technique which was altogether divorced from society, and which purported to be derived exclusively from concepts. It can be shown that when Savigny and Puchta presented their doctrine of a scientific law they had this kind of creation of law in mind. Others, it is true, would have none of it. To speak of juristic science as a source of law, according to Windscheid, is to confuse the woman in childbed with the midwife.

A finding of norms which is absolutely divorced from social influences, and which consists in logical inferences from given concepts, can scarcely be called a creation of law, and a juristic science which is confined to it can scarcely be considered a source of law. The mathematics of concepts, however, as a matter of fact never attained its goal. Artificially created as they were, these concepts were always susceptible of transformation wherever the distribution of power, considerations of expediency, and trends of justice demanded it. Whether the transaction which was entered into by an agent is treated as having come into existence by the will of the agent or of the principal depends upon which construction yields the more satisfactory result. And admitting this, we have again recognized the social influences. Moreover on countless occasions the mathematics of concepts has been used as a means of warping justice.

The last building stone employed by the Continental commonlaw juristic science is its *Systematik* (systematism). The origin of the latter does not lie in the requirements of the practice of law. It is true, books that are merely practical, that are designed exclusively for the practice of law, must needs have a certain orderly arrangement; but this arrangement is designed merely to facilitate quick orientation; like the alphabetical arrangement of dictionaries, it has no effect whatever upon the content. The systematism of juristic science grew out of the necessities of teaching. It is the function of teaching to present the material to the learner in an orderly, lucidly organized arrangement. A learner will remember a few comprehensive truths more easily than a great number of unrelated details. While it is important for practical purposes to state at each point everything that refers to that point, a teacher will strive to formulate as many general principles as possible, and derive particulars from them. Hence the endeavor to group the legal phenomena as to which general statements can be made, and to discuss the legal relations to which the same rules are applicable, in the same chapter. It is true, these are external considerations, but probably the legal relations which have been grouped because the same rules, let us say, of procedure apply in case resort is had to law to enforce them are related internally as well. The division of rights into *real* and obligatory rights, which is connected with the important distinction bet ween *actiones in rem* and *in personam*[1], the orderly statement of the rules concerning *real* rights and concerning the law of inheritance on one hand and concerning contracts, damages, and other obligatory rights on the other, have originated here. Accordingly *Systematik* begins at Rome in the text-books. The system of Gaius, which surely was derived from an older source, dominates the teaching of law down to the time of Justinian and is found in the Institutes of the latter. In the Middle Ages and in modern times, the elucidation of Justinian's Institutes serves the purpose of an introduction to the study of law, and since the seventeenth century numerous books have been making their appearance in Germany which contain the whole body of legal material, arranged according to the system of the Institutes. It is followed by the French Civil Code and the Austrian Civil Code,

---

1. *actiones in rem* and *in personam*：〈拉〉对物诉讼与对人诉讼

and, with a few exceptions that touch the surface only, by the pandect system[1] of the nineteenth century, which begins with Hugo and Heise, and by the German Civil Code.

At first jurists were not conscious, to any considerable extent, of the inner interrelationship of the legal institutions which was being expressed quite undesignedly by these systematic presentations. But in the course of time it became more conspicuous, and occupies the foreground in the systematic endeavors of the Ramists and of Donellus. Later the legal relations which were being dealt with together appeared as variations of the same legal relation. The periods of life appear as species of status; ownership and the other *real* rights, as classes of *real* rights. The more comprehensive legal relation receives a distinct name and a universal definition is being sought for it. The next step is, that all legal precepts which contain identical provisions for several related legal relations are no longer referred to these individual legal relations but to the legal concept which embraces them all; and in the end, unless there are particular reasons against doing so, everything that is predicated as to one of these relations is considered valid as to all of them. The achievement of *Systematik*, then, is the consistent continuation of the process of universalization. Accordingly we find that even the Romans had universalized a number of norms solely in the interest of systematic presentation, e.g. the norms about *actiones in rem* and *actiones in personam,* about *obligationes naturales,* about liability for fault and for delay in contractual relations. An admirable modern example of systematic universalization is Windscheid's doctrine of claims based on unjust enrichment. Systematic universalization is very closely related to juristic construction. The Romans very often employ universalization for purposes of pure construction. When they subsumed the agreements for work, labor, and services under

1. pandect system：潘德克顿体系。19 世纪德国法学家以罗马法文本为基础，构建的关于民法学的体系。

the *locatio conductio* (contract for letting and hiring), their object was to make them actionable *contractus*. The attempt to make barter actionable in the same way has, it is true, failed.

The German Historical School, however, went one step beyond this universalization. Even the *jurisprudence of constructions* was able to utilize for its purposes the fact that identical facts and identical legal effects occur in distinct legal relations. When the Romans construed the payment of an obligation by the surety as a purchase of the obligation, they did this on the basis of the observation of the fact that both in the payment of an obligation and in the purchase there is a counting out of money. They gave the same effect to the counting out of money in a case of payment that it would have in a case of purchase. In this case the counting out of money is lifted out of its connection, and is treated as an independent legal transaction, the effect of which is the right to demand the transfer of the obligation. Likewise the construction of the *offene Handelsgesellschaft* (unlimited mercantile partnership)[1] as a partnership contract with *mutua praepositio*[2] of the partners is based upon the separation of a legal effect of the *praepositio,* of the power of agency, from the *praepositio*, and upon a combination of it with the partnership contract, which in its nature is quite foreign to the *praepositio*. The characteristic feature of this kind of construetion is that a certain fact or a certain legal effect which is found only within the sphere of a legal relation as a whole is singled out and used as a building stone in the construction of another legal relation.

According to this method the German legal historians have been building the "general part" of the whole system of private law and of the law of obligations. It is based upon the conscious endeavor to utilize constructively certain facts and legal effects, which occur

1. *offene Handelsgesellschaft* (unlimited mercantile partnership)：〈德〉无限商事合伙
2. *mutua praepositio*：〈拉〉相互监督

again and again in the most diverse legal relations. On the same basis rest the doctrines of conditions, of qualification as to time, of error, of duress, and of fraud, of representation, alternative obligations, contracts for the benefit of third parties, of plurality of creditors and debtors, of payment, and of many other things. In connection with these, another universalization was introduced. A precept as to one of these elements which was found in the sources in connection with a certain legal relation was referred to this element as such in whatever legal relation it might be found. A typical illustration is the way in which the Continental common law juristic science dealt with the retroactive force of the condition. A series of decisions recorded in the sources, which referred exclusively to certain individual legal relations in which a condition occurred, or perhaps only to one individual case of that kind, was applied quite indiscriminately to every condition, whether it was contained in a testament, a marriage con tract, a gift, a purchase, or the giving and taking of a pledge. The way the doctrine of mistake in a legal transaction was dealt with is stranger still. Interesting specimens of this method are also found in the doctrines of representation and of the protection of legal rights.

Systematik was of much greater importance for the notion of a perfect legal system than was the mathematics of conceptions. A system indeed is nothing more than an arrangement of that which is in existence, but in addition it always gives rise to a conception of the whole. Before long the legal system was treated as if it comprised not only the legal material in hand but the whole law. The concepts, whose content no longer was individual legal relations but whole classes of legal relations, became so comprehensive that they took on the appearance of logical categories, which comprised the whole world of legal phenomena. If there was something that was not subsumed under the concept of contract of a certain kind, it was a contract *simpliciter*[1];

1. contract *simplicter*：绝对契约

if it was not a contract, it was a legal transaction; and if it was not a legal transaction, it was a juristic fact, to say the least. A private right was either a right of family law, a *real* right, or an obligatory right. Much skill was employed to determine whether proscriptive rights and perpetual charges upon land belonged under the former or the latter head, or whether possibly they were to be placed under a third. Copyright and the right to one's name seemed to defy classification under any of these heads. Accordingly the right to one's name became a right of personality, the *real* rights became absolute rights, which included among other things the law of copyright. The important thing was that a place was found for everything in the legal system, and that norms for decision, too, were to be found at each of these places. As it was, the Continental common law possessed a vast wealth of norms, but this procedure of making every norm for decision which had been created for a given legal relation or for a given case applicable to all kinds of legal relations, related and unrelated, increased the number of norms a thousand-fold. The lifework of Schlossmann was directed chiefly against this kind of finding of norms.

Manifestly this method of dealing with the law presented something labeled *Systematik* that no longer was *Systematik* at all. Its object was not a presentation of the material of the sources in an appropriate arrangement but instead an attempt to present an. entirely new content. It surely is not one and the same thing that a norm which decides a case of mistake in a transaction of purchase be limited to a transaction of purchase and that its scope be extended to every contract, nay, what is more, to every legal transaction. Moreover these jurists were not drawing inferences from analogy. Every analogy must be justified by a similarity of legal situation. But the jurists were proceeding here as if all of these norms for decision had been laid down as principles in the *corpus iuris,* and as if the individual decisions of the sources were merely applications of a principle applicable to all of the legal situations that had been collected. This was indeed a gain in the number of norms, but to a great degree it was a questionable gain, for in the last analysis the important thing is the kind and nature of the norms. A decision that might be quite satisfactory for an individual case will often be ill adapted to the legal relation as a whole. In most cases it will be absolutely impossible to find a norm that will be equally applicable everywhere, e.g. in the law of the family, of things, of obligations, and of inheritance. In fact the doctrines of conditions, of plurality of creditors and debtors, of conflict of claims, contain more controversial questions than legal propositions. Every jurist knows how to deal with a contract of insurance or of assumption of an obligation; but what if these two contracts, which are in no wise related to each other, are submitted to him as contracts for the benefit of third persons? In consequence of all this, the Continental common law juristic science of the nineteenth century consists of two quite distinct groups of material. The law of persons, things, contracts, and the family deals with formations that are imbued with life; the general part of the system and the general part of the law of obligations is a playground for bloodless abstractions that scarcely touch the earth with their toes. In the *Systematik* of the historical school, the great antinomy of juristic science, which is continually at work transmuting forms of thought into norms, is celebrating its last, its most fateful triumph.

But we must not undervalue *Systematik* on this account. It can render only those services for which it exists. *Systematik* is not juristic science, and therefore its function is not to put the law into condition to meet the requirements of the administration of justice. If it is misused for this purpose, as was done by the Continental common law juristic science, it is in fact a construction, but a construction undertaken according to points of view quite other than those of juristic science, a construction in which the economic and social relations in which the legal institutions appear are being given expression to, at most, by sheer accident only. Undoubtedly a great deal of juristic scholasticism must be attributed to the Continental common law systematic constructions.

We must not however overlook an important difference between the most important, who are also the most numerous, adherents of the Historical School, on one hand and the jurists of other schools on the other. No other jurists were as indifferent as they to the question whether or not the results of their constructions or of their systematic finding of norms were in harmony with their sense of justice. This must be attributed in part to their conception of the function of juristic science. Inasmuch as it was primarily incumbent upon them to ascertain the intention of the originator of the legal proposition, they were in a position to decline to assume personal responsibility for the decision. Again, the fact that the jurists who have attained a great reputation in the Historical School were scholars rather than men of affairs, as one might expect in view of the preponderantly scientific trend of this school, may have been of still greater importance. A professor of anatomy used to ask a student, who, while dissecting a corpse was trying to rectify a false cut by following it up with a right one, whether he would also rectify his false cuts in the case of an operation on a patient. For there is a difference between developing one's manual skill and one's acumen on a *corpus vile* and on living human flesh.

This discussion has led us to a point where we can survey the work of the Continental common law juristic science in its totality. Of course, for a long time no thinking person has failed to realize the obvious truth that the Continental common law is not the law of Rome nor even that of Justinian. If one should eliminate from the *Manuel* of Girard everything that refers to the ante-Justinianian law, one would by no means have a textbook of pandect law. The text-books of Puchta or of Arndt, even though they utterly ignore post-Roman creation of law, and confine their presen tat ions to Roman legal material, are something quite different from dogmatic presentations of Justinianian law. A further question is wherein these differences consist; as far as I can see, it is in creation of concepts, in constructions, and in *Systematik*.

There can be no doubt that the pandectists[1] of the Historical School were honestly convinced that they were defining the legal concepts according to the law of Justinian. But in actual fact they did not do this. Every one of their concepts had to be formulated at the outset so as to include not only the Roman but also the modern phenomena. The definition of ownership indeed was suitable for the *fundus optumus maxumus*[2], which was being discussed by the jurists of a time as late as the days of the Republic, but it had to cover not only this but also the ownership of the feudal lord and of the holder of shares of stock. Even if the same words had been used by Labeo and Sabinus, they would have meant something different in the mouths of the latter from what they would mean in the mouths of Vangerow and Windscheid. In the case of more concrete concepts, especially those of the law of pledge or of the law of obligations (for an example, let us say, *delegatio*) this fact is apparent at once. No doubt the pandectists of the Historical School endeavor to state every legal proposition in the form in which it was to be valid according to the law of Justinian. But their very statement was a construction of it. Every word they employed was not used with reference to the Roman situations but was adapted to the modern German relations. In all these respects they were children of their time, and — a fact that is still more significant — they were the heirs of the practitioners from the eleventh to the eighteenth century. The fact that their *Systematik* was not that of the Roman jurists would have made no difference. Every legal historian creates a system for his presentation which in his opinion is most appropriate to the matter he is presenting. But their system was not a system of an historical presentation of the law of Justinian, but a picture, clumsy, schematic, and imperfect

---

1. pandectists：潘德克顿派
2. *fundus optumus maxumus*：〈拉〉最优土地。即没有法律负担的土地。

though it was, of the legal organization of a modern society。 At the same time, thanks to their *Systematik* they arrived at a system of doctrine that was utterly foreign to the doctrine of the Romans; and this fact is of so much greater importance in view of the fact that many, e.g. Savigny, Puchta, Unger, consider the dogmatic fruitfulness of the system the chief element of value in the science of law.

The day of the Continental common law juristic science is done. The Civil Code for the German Empire has driven it out of its last place of refuge, and no power in the world will be able to restore its glory that has passed away. Whatsoever of value its labors of more than two thousand years have produced must be preserved for the future by the sociological science of law. But the latter will not be a juristic science. The deathless function of all juristic science, however, i.e. to make the law subserve the ever changing, ever new needs of life, will remain. No code will be able to destroy it. For this task there will always have to be a juristic science, though it may be of a nature different from that of the present, though it may employ other instrumentalities, and have other aims. That it will be different from that of the present is self-evident; for every age has not only its own art, its own science, religion, and philosophy, but also its own juristic science. The Roman jurists, too, presented something different in each century. Justinian presented something different from that which the classical jurists presented; and the Romanists of the Middle Ages and of modern times do not present the Roman law of Justinian.

In the same way, the juristic science of the future, though organically connected with the traditional mat erials, will find that it must refashion these materials in order to satisfy the new requirements. It is true that the sociological science of law must needs furnish the scientific basis; but it can take root only in a soil which has been furrowed and plowed by the Continentai common law juristic science. There will be a repetition of the process that has been going on wherever sciences have grown out of practical activities. The natural sciences have repaid all their borrowings from medicine with compound interest. The juristic science of the future, I believe, will discard for good and always all the mummery of creation of abstract concepts and of construction. But it must be admitted that these things always only served the sole purpose of concealing a necessary social process from the eyes of busybodies. Free finding of law is not, as some have thought, a finding of law that disregards the statute, but a finding of law that is untrammeled by useless and superfluous confinement in abstraction and construction.

In the years last past many a bitter word has been spoken concerning "pandectology[1]" and although these words were not spoken by me, I will not deny that they were spoken, for I know that I bear a great deal of responsibility in the matter. In the heat of battle, this was justified, and perhaps it was necessary. I therefore feel it incumbent upon myself to point out the great achievements of "pandectology." I would remain true espedaily to the memory of Bernhard Windscheid. In my youth I studied his writings with great enthusiasm, and if I and those who are pressing forward with me have gone beyond him, we are indebted to his teachings for it. Time has done the rest. Before long the eyes of the last of the German jurists that have seen a living Continental common law will have been closed in death; the last voice that has taught a living Continental common law will have been silenced. Let them see to it that the valuable creations of the labors of two thousand years, separated like wheat from the chaff, are handed down to the coming generation. What they do not save will be lost forever. But the three volumes of Windscheid's Pandects will remain as a link between a great past and an unknown future. And therefore we shall be grateful to Kipp for keeping this treasure abreast of the times with a tireless diligence that is worthy of its great creator.

---

1. pandectology：潘德克顿法学

XV THE FUNCTION OF JURISTIC SCIENCE

The role of juristic science in history is quite different from everything that men have from time to time thought to be its function, just as our notions of the meaning of our activities can give us no information about their true significance. Juristic science has never been what, at the present time, it is generally thought to be, i.e. a presentation of that which has been delivered to us by tradition as law, nor has it ever been a set of rules directing us how to proceed on the basis of the rules that have been delivered to us as law. A juristic literature which has no other aims, such as the English text-books and in part our own *Lehrbücher*[1], is not juristic science, and no legal system could subsist on intellectual juristic labor that does not do more than that. There must always be a creative juristic science. But in order to appreciate its labors from every point of view, we must consider separately the three elements that are comprised in it, i.e. the element relating to the function of the attorney; the element relating to the legal transaction; and the element relating to the judicial function.

Let us begin with the function of the attorney. The forms of the procedure at law, in a sense, are the weapons which society, or the state in the name of society, has placed at the disposal of conflicting interests. The means that society has provided for this purpose are limited in number; for society could not possibly provide aid for all interests that are being contested or attacked. It must select those that are most important and most worthy of assistance. But no society

1. *Lehrbücher*：〈德〉教科书

could at the outset state once for all which interests it will protect; for in every developing, progressive society new interests are continually gaining importance, and those that have already been recognized are continually being subjected to new attacks. Whether society will or will not protect an interest is determined by the courts. It is the function of the attorney to persuade the court that society has provided a remedy for the interest which he represents. This is the art of *Klagebegründung*[1] (establishing the basis for an action). Secondly, he must show the court that the interest in question is worthy of protection. This is the art of *Beweisführung* (making proof). If the attorney has persuaded the court, he has secured protection for an interest to which it had been denied until then, or he has secured protection against an attack to which the interest had been exposed until then. This, doubtless, is a step forward in legal development, which he has brought about by his individual activity.

The proceeding at law originally merely served the purpose of preventing feuds or of mitigating and regulating them. By skillfully developing the art of establishing the bases for actions, the inventive genius of the attorneys has brought it about that the legal proceeding also grants satisfaction for injury suffered, and that it finally becomes a universal remedy for the establishment of justice without a feud. The book of Declaireil, entitled *Les preuves judiciaires en droit franc*[2], which in general affords the most profound insight into the nature of the most ancient form of legal proceeding, has shown that the law of proof owes its origin, growth, and development to the activity of the parties; that it was not created by the judges prescribing the mode of proof to the parties, but by the parties continually seeking and finding new ways of persuading the courts of the justice of their respective causes. The forms established for the pursuit of one's right, for the making

1. *Klagebegründung*：〈德〉诉求表达
2. *Les preuves judiciaires en droit franc*：〈拉〉《法兰克时期的司法证据》

of proof, for compulsory execution, are given at all times by the traditional organization of the courts, by the content and the nature of the means at the disposal of the courts for giving effect to their powers, by the form of the proceeding at law. But it is the business of the attorney to adapt these over and over again and again to the attainment of new ends. The attorney who for the first time brought the action *de arboribus succisis*[1] when he brought suit for cutting down vines would have obtained the same protection for the interest in vines that had already been secured for the interest in trees if he had not made the mistake as to form that Gaius speaks of. A similar service was rendered by the German attorney who, according to Hedemann's report, brought action in order to have the defendant enjoined from defaming a woman, and by that other attorney who brought about the well-known *Freskenurteil*[2] of the Imperial Court (*Reichsgericht*).

The branch of juristic science that deals with the legal transaction is chiefly concerned with the legal document, although it is also concerned, of course, with the oral transaction. The legal document, like the legal transaction in general, does not exist exclusively for use in the proceeding at law. Its chief function is to provide the order of the legal relation. It is the task of the draftsman of the legal document to organize the relation that the parties are about to establish, to find the legal means whereby their objects can be realized, to state their duties and obligations in correct legal terms. This order, which is based on the document, is in itself a product of creative juristic science. That which the parties vaguely had in mind is given a fixed, definite, tangible form by the jurist, without which it could not exist. As a result each one of the parties concerned knows exactly what he is to do and not to do. It is well established that the jurists who were drawing

1. *de arboribus succisis*：〈拉〉关于修剪树权的诉讼
2. *Freskenurteil*：〈德〉赛壬壁画案，德国帝国法院要求房屋的主人将损害的壁画恢复原状，不能侵犯壁画的著作权。

up legal documents have created the *Kommenda*, and the economic community, i.e. the right of the single heir *{Anerbenrechi*) among the German-Austrian peasantry. But it is immaterial whether the legal relation is a new one in its entirety; the insertion of a clause into a well-known contractual form may be a creative act.

But the branch of juristic science that deals with legal transactions must not content itself with merely organizing; it must make provision for the protection of the products of its labor against attack and violation. We are not concerned exclusively, nor even primarily, with the case in which recourse is had to law. The forms handed down by Cato refer both to actionable and, with a single exception, non-actionable agreements, but it is certain that *iuramentum, satisdatio, pignus*[1] are of much greater importance than *actio* and *exceptio*[2]. The branch of juristic science that deals with legal transactions has made extensive contributions particularly to the development, if not to the invention, of security without resort to litigation, from the Roman *fiducia* and the ordinance of German city law down to the modern *Vinkulationsgeschdft*[3]. The more imperfect the administration of justice, the more seriously people will endeavor to put the transaction in a form that makes resort to law unnecessary. Descriptions of commerce in the Orient show to what lengths people will go in order to attain this end. Nevertheless the chief function of the branch of juristic science that deals with legal transactions is to put the relation into such form as will enable it to prevail even if resort is had to litigation, and the parties are interested not only in having a legally enforceable cause of action but chiefly in a proceeding that is free from difficulties and delays and does not involve much expense. Up to this point, then, the aims of the branch of juristic science that deals with legal

1. *iuramentum, satisdatio, pignus*：〈拉〉宣誓、诉讼担保、质押
2. *actio* and *exceptio*：〈拉〉诉权与抗辩
3. *Vinkulationsgeschäft*：〈德〉凭单借贷

transactions are not essentially different from those of the branch that deals with the function of the attorney. The object of this branch like that of the other is to utilize the means that are at hand for the best possible protection of the interests in question. Like the branch that deals with the function of the attorney, it does creative work for interests that without it would either be not protected at all or, at best, very imperfectly, that are indebted to it either for all the protection they receive or, at least, for the fact that the protection they receive is effective. And often enough it is a protection that the existing law was inclined to deny to them. The pledge in the form of a sale with right of repurchase, the forbidden loan at interest as the *Kommenda,* unenforceable obligations made effectual by means of contractual penal ties or bills of exchange, are so many triumphs of this branch of juristic science over backward or undeveloped administration of law.

The work of the attorney-at-law and of the lawyer who draws up legal documents, therefore, is a technical one. They must, in the first place, get a clear understanding, through first-hand observation and study, of the interests that are entrusted to them in order that they may be enabled to make them comprehensible to the courts, and, by making proof, induce the courts to take cognizance of them. The imperfection of human nature, limited means and limited understanding, with which the courts are afflicted like all other creations of the human mind, render a technique of this sort indispensable. It would be superfluous if the courts were omnipotent and omniscient, just as we could dispense with the telescope and the microscope if our eyes were so much more efficient. Therefore every improvement of the tools of the profession renders a considerable amount of juristic technique superfluous. Such improvements are the transition from the procedure by *legis actio* to the procedure by formula both in Rome and in England, the substitution of the direct procedure for the indirect one on the Continent, which was brought about by permitting a free evaluation of proof in the place of a restricted one.

The attorney and the lawyer who draws up legal documents attain their purpose only if they succeed in persuading the judge to adopt their views. Their labor is in vain unless the judge considers the remedy a suitable one, the proof admissible and sufficient, and — most important of all — recognizes the interest which is seeking protection as worthy of it. The judicial decision therefore is a decision of two questions. In the first place, it decides the technical question whether society is able and willing to grant protection to the interest that is being asserted, and whether the existence of the latter has been demonstrated to the satisfaction of the court; and in the second place it renders an independent decision on the question whether the interest merits protection. And if it is true that the attorney and the draftsman can not possibly limit their activity to representing interests that have already been recognized by the courts, but that they must be ready at all times to bring about the recognition of interests that are newly arising, it follows that they must again and again raise the technical question as well as the question whether the interest is worth protecting, and thereby again and again confront the judge with a new task.

The norm according to which the judge renders his decision is the outcome of a most complex proceeding. It was necessary for the attorney or the draftsman to have knowledge based on actual observation of the relation of life within which the conflict of interests had arisen, to put it into a form suitable for protection by law, and to demonstrate its existence to the judge from his own knowledge as far as possible, through the testimony of witnesses and experts, and by means of documents (in ancient days perhaps also by means of oracles, judgment of God, and the casting of lots). This is followed by a balancing of interests on the part of the judge, the determination of the question whether the interest merits protection. This in turn leads to universalization, reduction to unity, and finding of norms. Of course it is a matter of little importance whether the balancing of interests is done independently or on the basis of norms that are already in existence.

We have been considering the contributions made by the attorney, the draftsman, and the judge separately for the sake of a better understanding of the nature of the process as a whole. Ultimately, however, the contributions which the attorney, the draftsman, and the judge have made to the norm for decision must be fused into a unit in the norm itself. In fact often enough the judge, for lack of an attorney or of a draftsman, undertakes the technical problem himself. And he often enough solves it in a way quite different from the way the latter would have solved it. Just as all of these elements enter into the norm for decision, so they must also enter into the legal proposition, which contains a norm for decision; for the latter is merely a more developed form of the norm for decision. And in the legal propositions of judgemade law, which are to be found in the reasons given for the decisions, we find all these elements side by side, to wit observation, putting into proper form, proof, balancing of interests by means of universalization, reduction to unity, and finding of norms. But in the legal propositions presented in juristic literature or in legislation, these elements have become intermingled and it is often difficult to separate them. The composition of the legal proposition appears historically only when the latter is traced back to its inception. I shall attempt to do this in the following discussion.

When the four men promulgated the law to the Salic Franks (*per ires malleos*), they most probably were sincerely convinced that they had not overlooked anything that was essential Today every young jurist who is preparing himself for his examination finds out to his sorrow how greatly they were in error, how much more he must know about the law of the Salic Franks, merely in order to pass his examination, how small a portion of the whole was embodied in the *lex*.

For each homicide the *lex Salica* provided a wergild, graduated according to the rank of the person slain. These provisions are stated in a few, readily understood propositions. But in the background there is the whole of Frankish society, organized according to rank and other considerations. Who may demand the wergild? Who other than the guilty person, is obligated to pay it? What is the manner of payment? What happens if it is not paid? The number of such questions concerning the provisions about the wergild is infinite. On the basis of proof and of his own knowledge, the judge must find additional norms; and, on the basis of these norms, the judgment determines whether the plaintiffs are entitled to the wergild, whether the defendants are liable, whether or not it has been paid according to law. Of all of these questions, not a trace is to be found in the *lex Salica;* manifestly, because they had not yet been brought to the attention of the authors of the *lex;* because, unlike the very provisions about the wergild, they had not yet been made the subject matter of the juristic science of the Salic Franks.

A legal proposition about a penalty to be paid by a thief to the person from whom the thing was stolen presupposes a rather definitely fixed right of ownership in movables. It follows therefore that there must have been rules about acquisition, loss, and forfeiture of the right of ownership, some notion as to the difference between a person who acquires property lawfully and a thief or a robber. The provisions as to a penalty to be paid by the abductor, in the case of abduction of a woman, to her father or to her relatives are manifestly based upon a certain order of the family in virtue of which the woman is under the power (*potestas*) of her male relatives, who also have the right to give her in marriage. The content of all of the norms for decision, therefore, that have been developed into legal propositions about wergild, theft, abduction of women is being eked out by norms for decision that have reference to the inner order of the clan, of ownership, of the family, and that have not yet been expressed in legal propositions.

This is the beginning of juristic science. It is concerned at the outset solely with a series of norms for decision that can be made the bases of judicial decisions. These norms indeed are connected with other norms for decision which are given by the relations of human life. But these are as yet unknown to juristic science; they lie beyond its horizon, and the judge acquires them unconsciously from observation of the relations of life. But the more the science of law develops, the greater is its sphere, the deeper it penetrates, and the greater are its efforts to prepare for immediate use in the administration of justice not only the ultimate norms for decision but also those that these latter presuppose and those that the last named presuppose in turn. As a result, the legal propositions are becoming more numerous and detailed. All of this is done partly by means of universalization and reduction to unity of the inner order of the relations of life, partly by means of finding new norms, according to the distribution of power that obtains in society and according to the ideals of justice that rule the hearts of men. In this way Roman law and English law have developed, and in this way the Continental common law has been re ju vena ted time and again, and in this way law is developing at the present time.

These norms for decision which have been transformed by the jurists into legal propositions can be distinguished, even by their outward form, from those that constitute the inner order of human relations and, in general, the rules of human conduct, and that, self-evidently, also find their way into the works of the jurists. One can know them by their fine dialectic formulation, the formally correct delimitation of justice and injustice. There is no possibility that men could ever regulate their lives according to such juristic subtleties.

In the terminology of modern juristic usage one might say that all development of juristic science consists in the conversion of a question of fact into a question of law. The only difficulty is that today "question of fact" has two distinct meanings. On one hand it refers to the inner order of the relations of human life brought about by usage, regulation, contract, inheritance, last will. On the other hand it refers to a violation of this inner order, which leads to a law-suit or to a criminal proceeding. But "question of fact" in the first sense is a constituent part of "question of fact" in the second sense of the term. In order to know to which one of the *Claudii*[1] the inheritance of a freedman belongs, a judge must know the order of inheritance in the *gens Claudia*; in order to determine whet her or not the maternal uncle of the slain man is entitled to the wergild, he must have information about the order of the family of the slain man; in order to ascertain whether a contract has been broken, the content of the contract must be shown.

The question of fact becomes a question of law through universalization, reduction to unity, and free finding of norms. Until this has been done, there is no antithesis between "question of fact" and "question of law." The jurist of the hoary past dealt exclusively with questions of fact, for there were no juristically formulated norms for decision in existence. The law that he required for the decision of the cases that came before him was supplied by custom, witnesses, and documents. All of these were questions of fact. The principles that resulted from the decisions as to questions of fact, after they had been recognized and universalized, were the first legal propos it ions. Ever since t hat time, every day has added new ones to those that were already in existence. This is going on today. Although a paragraph of the code is cited in every judicial decision, as a matter of fact, by far the greater number of judicial decisions is rendered, not on questions of law, but on questions of fact. But in all these decisions on questions of fact, general legal principles are lying imbedded, which practical juristic science brings forth into the light of day, as a rule in the headings of the collections of decisions, and also in the annotations to the codes — unpretentious as they are. Thereafter juristic literature

1. *Claudii*：克劳狄乌斯家族

and doctrine take possession of them; and finally they are added to the mass of existing legal mat erial and appear in the codes themselves.

A very graphic picture of this method of procedure employed by legal science is presented by the development of the law of the contract of current accounts (*Kontokorrentvertrag*[1]). The first step was that the practical jurists who dealt with mercantile affairs became aware of the fact that they were dealing with a peculiar contract as to which there were no legal propositions in existence. A few judicial decisions were rendered on this contract, and the judges whose duty it was to render them found it incumbent upon themselves to make a statement as to the nature and content of the contract, which was based in part on their own knowledge and in part on opinions of merchants, on the testimony of witnesses and of experts. At that time all of this was a question of fact. The decisions were rendered on this question of fact, i.e. the nature of the relation resulting from the current accounts (*Kontkorrentverhaltnis*) that had been submitted to them for decision. Before very long, however, jurists began to realize that this form of contract was in great vogue in mercantile circles, and that it was as well worth considering as the contracts of sale and lease. They thereupon began to universalize the contents of the contracts of current accounts, and by this process obtained a general law of the contract of current accounts. This work of universalization was done chiefly in juristic literature, especially in the book of Griinhut and in the book of Levy, translated by Riesser. These were followed by a few treatises, text-books, and handbooks, and finally the results were embodied in the new Commercial Code. Indeed treating the contract of current accounts as a contract of mutual granting of credit or as a novation of the individual obligations was a superfluous and not very happy construction, for when applied to the contract of current accounts

1. *Kontokorrentvertrag*：〈德〉经常账户合同

the legal propositions concerning granting of credit and novation underwent a radical change. The whole process however was typical, i.e. observation of the legal relation in actual life, a few decisions on the basis of this observation, universalization of the results in juristic literature, superfluous construction, and finally codification. The law of the contract for services has been created before our very eyes by the same process. A century ago not a trace of it was in existence. The *locatio conductio* of the Roman law was absolutely inapplicable to our relations; the modern codes were silent on the subject, the French Civil Code contained two articles, one of which has been rescinded since that time. In Germany — not in France — there was a small number of legal propositions concerning a few sub-varieties, particularly concerning the contract for domestic service. Now on what basis did the judge render his decisions as to suits arising from a contract for domestic service? On the basis of the content of the given contract, i.e. on the basis of proof by testimony of witnesses and by documents, and of custom, as to which, if he did not know what it was, he heard the testimony of witnesses who did know; and all of this he would eke out according to justice and fairness. Out of these elements a fixed judicial custom arose in France, which provided a detailed regulation of the contract for services; and in Germany there grew up at least a general consciousness of right and law, which however did give rise to a series of legal propositions that are now embodied in the German Civil Code.

This appears very clearly wherever, because of procedural institutions, the question of fact and the question of law are treated separately. As it is usually understood, the separation is meaningless indeed, for there is no question of fact that is not, at the same time, a question of law. The question of proof itself is a question of law. In the mat ter of proof, we are concerned not only with the question whether the facts are established but also, in every case, with the question whether a legal relation arises from these facts and whether this legal relation has been violated by the conduct of either party. Accordingly there lies within the sphere of the question of fact the proof, not only of the existence of a contract, of a section of the articles of association, of a last will and testament, but of the whole inner order of the relations, of all rights and duties which are actually expressed in the words of the articles of association, the contract, the last will and testament, and, where a question of unlawful conduct is involved, the proof whether an interference with a right of another has taken place. The question of law thus becomes a matter of universalization, of reduction to unity, and of finding of norms. We may disregard the doctrine, for which Wlassak has gained general recognition, that the *formula in ius concepta*[1] arose from the formula *in factum* among the Romans, for the reason that, though it is not improbable, it is too doubtful, and that it is probable that the Roman jurists quite frequently created a formula *in ius concepta* without the intervention of the formula *in factum*[2]. But even if we disregard the question of the development, the distinction is quite in harmony with what is being presented here; for the *factum* comprises the whole inner order of the relation, e.g. duties arising from contract and from the *patronatus*[3], i.e. the relation between an owner and his manumitted slave, and the violation of these duties; the *ius* comprises the universalization, the reduction to unity, and the finding of norms. In the development of English law, of which we have a more comprehensive knowledge, all these things are obvious with an almost plastic clearness.

When the English discuss the advantages of the jury, they are in the habit of saying among other things that a jury can decide a case "without making bad law." This means: Had the judge decided the case, the decision would have given rise to a new legal proposition of

1. *formula in ius concepta*：〈拉〉权利诉讼程式
2. *in factum*：〈拉〉事实诉讼程式
3. *patronatus*：〈拉〉庇主权

judge-made law, possibly a bad one, but the verdict of the jury does not do this. This affords a deep insight into the origin of all juristic law, not only of that of English law. The jury purports to decide the question of fact; the judge, the question of law; but if the judge had rendered the decision instead of the jury, a legal proposition would have resulted. This, I take it, clearly indicates the nature of the distinction between the question of fact and the question of law. All law has arisen from the universalization of that which had originally been a question of fact in the individual case, or from the finding of norms on the basis of this universalization; and the reason why no law arises from the decision of the jury is that universalizing of this nature, if it is to contain a legal proposition which shall be binding for the future, must be done, not by the jury, but by the judge. But unless the judgment rendered by the judge on the basis of the verdict of the jury happens to be merely an application of an already existing legal proposition to the case in hand, it always creates new law according to the Anglo-American view; for, except in the case of a mere application of law, the judge has always created a new norm by universalizing the facts established by the verdict of the jury, or he has found a new norm on the basis of this universalization.

The famous justice of the Supreme Court of the United States, O. W. Holmes, Jr., has stated the application of this doctrine to liability for culpability with great acumen. The jury passes on the question of fact; the court, on the question whether the facts constitute culpability, which gives rise to liability in damages. The second question involves a standard. Did the defendant exercise the measure of care which is required of a man in the conduc t of the affairs of life? Who is to decide whether this measure of care has been exercised or not? Holmes thinks that this second question is a question of law. Says Holmes: "It is that the court derives the rule to be applied from daily experience, as it has been agreed that the great body of the law of tort has been derived," "and in this way the law is gradually enriching itself from daily life as it should." Whether therefore the facts established by the jury constitute culpability on the part of the defendant is a question to be decided by the judge. And out of these decisions the whole law of damages has grown. Now doubtless there are cases in which it is perfectly clear that they fall on this side of the line or on that. In such case, the judge renders the decision as to liability in damages quite independently, on the basis of the facts established by the jury. Why the judge? In these clear cases, a fixed rule of law as to the standard to be applied is already in existence. There are other cases however in which there is doubt. In those cases the jury passes not only on the facts but also on the question whether there is culpability; for in those cases the judge does not have a rule of law at hand concerning the standard to be applied to determine the question whether there is culpability. As soon as a rule has arisen, the question as to the existence of culpability is a question for the judge. In other words, it is a question of fact whether the defendant by his conduct has violated the legal relation in a blameworthy manner; but the question whether this conduct, judged according to an already established standard, obligates him to pay damages is a question of law. The difficulty in the law of damages, says Holmes, is this, that certain cases of negligence occur too rarely "to enable any given judge to profit by long experience with juries to lay down rules, and that the elements are so complex that courts are glad to leave the whole mat ter in a lump for the jury's determination?"

And in fact in one case it is actually possible to show historically how a whole legal system has been developed from such adjudications of individual cases by the jury, based solely upon the concrete nature of the legal relation in question as a question of fact. It is the English commercial law, the law merchant, the creator of which, in the opinion of the English, is Lord Justice Mansfield of the middle of the eighteenth century. He became the creator of this law inasmuch as he universalized the facts which were the basis of the individual decisions into legal propositions. I am quoting from the book of Carter, entitled A History of English Legal Institutions, the words of Justice Buller, taken from his opinion in a case decided in the year 1787, in which he describes the development graphically, almost as if he had been an eyewitness:

"Before that period (i.e. about 1750) we find that in courts of law all the evidence in mercantile cases was thrown together; they were left generally to a jury (i.e. the rules were treated as a matter of usage to be proved by evidence, without distinction of law and fact), and they produced no established principle. From that time we all know the great study has been to find some certain general principles which shall be known to all mankind, not only to rule the particular case then under consideration, but to serve as a guide for the future. Most of us have heard these principles stated, reasoned upon, enlarged, and explained, till we have been lost in admiration at the strength and stretch of the human understanding." (Lickbarrow v. Mason, per Buller J., 2 T.R. 63.)

Without this constructive activity of the jurists, without their universalizing and reducing to unity, general legal propositions cannot arise from the inner order of human associations. The inner order as such remains a legal norm; to be exact, a norm for decision. An example, which extends down to our own time, is found in the private law of princes. Dungern has rendered the great service of showing that, materially, the latter consists exclusively of those rules which the individual princely houses have laid down as their inner order with reference to the questions that fall within the sphere of their autonomy. Not one of these regulations has attained the significance of a legal proposition that is binding upon anyone outside of the family that has set it up. Indeed, for centuries attempts to create a universal private law of princes have not been lacking; but the jurists that made these attempts evidently were not sufficiently influential among the higher nobility, in whose power this matter lies, to prevail.

In the numerous cases in which the jurist must draw his norms for decision from the inner order of the relations, actual experience of life must supply him with the necessary materials. How did the Roman know that in a marriage with *manus* all of the wife's property became the property of the husband, and that in case of the freer marriage she retained it? He knew it because he knew the inner order of the Roman family. How did Thol know, when he wrote the second edition of his *Handelsrecht* (mercantile law), that each partner in a mercantile partnership with unlimited liability was entitled to the "*rechtmassige Gebrauch der Firma*" (rightful use of the firm name)[1], so that each partner in virtue thereof could bind the remaining partners? He knew it because he knew the organization of commerce. In primitive very simple and transparent relations, an unconscious mental working over of the happenings of the day suffices to give to the jurist who has some sense of reality the required knowledge of the affairs of life round about him; in the manifold, highly complex, and, in part, confused situations of our day, very often long, searching investigation is required. In every case, however, it is mere knowledge, not authoritative regulation, that we are concerned with.

This presentation alone is sufficient to show that the current teaching that it is the function of juristic science to range states of fact under established legal concepts is a fatal error. The inner order of human relations which results from the traditional constitution of the family, the corporation (*Körperschaft*), the association (*Genossenschaft*), from the relation between serf and feudal lord, from the content of contracts, articles of association, and last wills and testaments, from usage — this inner order, from which the judicial decision derives the greater number of its norms for decision, which juristic science universalizes, subsumes under the juristic concepts, or construes with

1. *rechtmässige Gebrauch der Firma*：〈德〉有权使用公司名称

the help of the latter, is not a part of the world of fact, like an eclipse of the sun, or the chemical composition of water, but is in itself a part of the law. Not facts are being adjudged but legal relations. Juristic science creates legal propositions only on the basis of legal relations. Family, corporations, ownership, real rights, purchase, usufructuary lease, ordinary lease, loan, were legal relations before the Roman jurist had made his first universalization; likewise in the Middle Ages they were legal relations before they were being adjudged according to Roman law. And after the reception, in so far as the Romanistic art and science of drafting legal documents did not interfere, they remained what they had been before, even as to content. The only difference was that thereafter they were adjudged according to Roman Law. Likewise, if English law should be introduced anywhere on the continent of Europe, the family, the corporations, ownership, the real rights, and the contracts would remain what they had been until then; and even though they should be adjudged according to English law, they would not become English legal relations. Legal relations are created by society, not by legal propositions.

Now let us consider the work of juristic science since the reception of Roman law. First of all we must put aside everything that served only the purpose of setting forth most faithfully the content of the sources; for this merely served to transmit that which had itself been transmitted, it did not continue the development of the art and the doctrine. The new material however that was added to that which had been transmitted was always based on what had been gained from actual observation of the legal relations and had been universalized. In this respect the method of the modern jurists does not differ from that of the Romans. There is a difference only in this, that they did not, like the Romans, derive the norms for decision directly from the universalizations or find them freely, but that they fitted the results of their labor into the Roman system of concepts, and, in appearance at least, attempted to utilize the Roman norms for decision for this purpose. But since they did not approach their task without preconceived notions, but had arrived at their decisions in advance, to which they subsequently adapted their concepts and constructions, their method, in fact, was a rather free finding of law on the basis of reasons that were adduced afterwards.

For the norms which are taken directly from the organizations, the term "*Natur der Sache*[1]" (nature of the thing) has become current in the German juristic science of the Continental common law, particularly since the beginning of the nineteenth century. The "nature of the thing" is derivable from the forms of the associations of the state and of society and of economic associations which life has created self-actively. This is the *naturalis ratio*[2] of the Romans; this is hidden behind so many of their *sed aequius est, sed melius esl, sed humanior est eorum sententia*[3], and this, too, is one of the active forces of the natural law movement, down to its last offshoot, the "*Lehre von dem richtigen Recht*[4]" (theory of the true or just law). German common law juristic science as a rule summed up in concepts that which itself or the legislator had learned from direct observation of the associations which life had created, and then deduced the norms from the nature of the thing, i.e. "from the concept." The latter was merely another technical term for the "nature of the thing." No jurist, not even a jurist of the last century, has ever been able, in spite of the positivist tendency, to dispense altogether with considerations based on "the nature of the thing," even when, like Windscheid, he apparently rejected them. They have been recognized expressly — to name only a few of the greatest names — by Savigny, Puchta, Wachter, Unger, Goldschmidt, Bähr.

---

1. *Natur der Sache*：〈德〉事物的本质
2. *naturalis ratio*：〈拉〉自然之理
3. *sed aequius est, sed melius est, sed humanior est eorum sententia*：〈拉〉如果这符合平衡，如果这符合善良，如果这符合人道的要求。
4. *Lehre von dem richtigen Recht*：〈德〉正义法理论

Adickes devoted his first book to them.

The norms "derived from the nature of the thing" or "deduced from the concept" are the rules of conduct that govern a legal relation in life; they are a product of the labor of life, not of that of a legislator or of any other power that has authority to posit norms, and they can be the subject matter of scientific knowledge, but they can not be ordained or prescribed. Therefore, however they may have been formulated, even though it be in a statute, their scientific content can be examined into. One can always ask the question, not only whet her the definition of *Erbleihe* (freehold) or of usufructuary lease[1], as contained in the statute, but also whet her the norms which the stat ute merely derives from the concept, correspond to that which is considered valid in everyday life as to these legal relations. Therefore it is justly denied that definitions, and — this ought to be added — the norms that derive from them, "from the nature of the thing," should ever be put into a statute; for, if they are correct, they are superfluous when put into the statute; they would be in existence even if there were no statute; if they are incorrect, they constitute what has often been called the *"unverbindlicher Gesetzesinhalt*[2]" (nonobligatory content of the statute), and must needs cause mischief; for men are not readily given to ignore even the non-obligatory content of a statute. The Roman maxim, *omnis definitio in iure periculosa*[3], indeed appears to go beyond this; for *ius civile* does not mean statute but juristic science — a fact which can be explained by the further fact that Roman juristic science could posit binding juristic law. It does however contain merely the monition that it is easier for a jurist to infer a single norm from the order of the social associations than to combine all the norms that constitute the framework of a living association in a definition.

---

1. usufructuary lease：附用益权租约
2. *unverbindlicher Gesetzesinhalt*：〈德〉制定法上无强制性的内容
3. *omnis definitio in iure periculosa*：〈拉〉民法上的任何定义都是危险的

All of this self-evidently refers only to the juristic definitions of the institutions that are created by actual life itself. The *Tatbestand* (constitutive facts)[1] to which, according to the precept contained in the statute, a statutory norm for decision or any other statutory command is to be applied is also frequently called a definition (*Begriffsbestimmung*). The empirical content which has been included in this *Tatbestand* indeed indicates the relation of life that is to be protected against interference. The existence and the qualities of the latter are independent of the legal proposition; for example bodily injury is as far from being the work of the legislator as extra-marital paternity. But the legal proposition alone determines the circumstances under which a relation of life should receive legal protection, and when the established legal consequences should ensue, e.g. what kind of bodily injury is to be punishable, when extra-marital paternity obligates a person to provide support and maintenance. The author of a legal proposition then is, if not absolutely free in determining the *Tatbestand* of social institutions, at any rate freer than in defining them. The *Tatbestand* is a part of the content of the statute and cannot be said to be either superfluous or incorrect. It may be stated too narrowly or too broadly with reference to the intent of the legislator or with reference to the purpose which the statute was designed to accomplish, and the judicial decision may disregard the wording of the statute. But in so doing it does not emend the statute; it interprets it or ekes out its meaning. The constitutional rights and duties of a citizen of a state and the rights, powers, and privileges of an owner are quite independent of the statutory definition (*Bestimmung*) of state and of ownership; nothing is to be punished as theft but what is included in the *Tatbestand* of theft; and no legal transaction can be set aside by means of the *actio Pauliana* except those which the statute governing

1. *Tatbestand* (constitutive facts)：〈德〉构成要件事实

avoidance has declared to be voidable (*anfechlbar*). In the case of the state and of ownership the question is one of the form of organization; in the case of theft and in the case of the *actio Pauliana*[1] it is a question of the *Tatbestand* contained in a norm for decision. The present discussion establishes a palpably clear contradistinction between these two situations.

With rare exceptions, practical juristic science creates the legal proposition on the basis of observation of the facts of legal life, on the basis of universalization of the results of such observation. Its method presents an unmistakable similarity to the methods of the pure sciences, which also are regularly based on observation and universalization of that which has been observed. This similarity quite readily accounts for the fact that juristic science is often being conceived of not as a practical science but as a pure science, and that demand is frankly being made in its behalf for a method like that of the natural sciences. Though the method of pure science and that of juristic science appear to be very similar to each other, they are, as Rumpf has convincingly demonstrated, very dissimilar. The object of the former is knowledge; that of the latter, finding of norms. The observation and universalization of the jurist does not proceed without bias, in the spirit of pure science but, from the outset is dominated by consideration of the distribution of power, of expediency, and of ideals of justice, which give direction to the process of finding of norms. And therefore juristic observation and universalization is directed to diff ere nt objects from the beginning, and attains resul ts different from those of pure science. On the basis of scientific proceeding, the Roman jurists would never have treated the family order of the free peasant proprietor as the only order of the Roman family, the English judges would never have

---

1. *actio Pauliana*：〈拉〉撤销转让行为之诉

universalized the law of inheritance of the knights into a law for all classes, and the authors of the German Civil Code could not possibly have made community of administration the general regime. All of this becomes explicable only if we bear in mind that they were not bent upon ascertaining facts in a scientific manner but upon establishing practical precepts for the future.

The course of decisions as to rights of personality[1] which is going on at the present moment is an instructive illustration of this. Its points of departure are two statutory provisions. One is the recognition in the Austrian Civil Code of the "innate rights, whose existence is made manifest by the light of reason"; the other is the action permitted by the Swiss Civil Code for "an injunction against interference" in a case of unauthorized violation of personal relations. The fact that the juristic science of the Continent required such crutches for the development of the rights of personality is an indication of the sad plight it is in today. It is not likely that the Roman jurists would have resorted to this method in order to find the *bonae fidei contractus*[2]. In France, too, the rights of personality were protected to a great extent without the aid of statutes. Since the course of judicial decisions, except in France, has not been playing a prominent role, the development of the doctrine is chiefly literary. The leading works are those of Specker in Switzerland and of Mauczka in Austria. It is extremely instructive to observe the manner in which these writers developed a detailed law of personality. The statute affords no help for this purpose; for legal precepts which are so utterly lacking content as those of the Austrian and Swiss codes mentioned above leave the development of the law where they found it. What Specker and Mauczka say about the rights of personality is so absolutely independent of the statute that it would be applicable without more ado within the sphere of the German Civil

1. rights of personality：人格权
2. *bonae fidei contractus*：〈拉〉诚信契约

Code, which does not mention rights of personality at all other than the right to a name, if only the Germans could make up their minds to recognize the creative power of juristic literature.

It is true, Specker and Mauczka include many a thing in the law of personality, which might more properly be included in a revised copyright law, or a more advanced law of possession, or of neighbors' rights (prohibition of the publication of private letters or of a photograph of a private dwelling, protection against noises or unpleasant odors). If these things are excluded, the law of personality may be defined as the social and judicial protection of the interests of the individual which arise from his position in his social association (his family, his household, his social life) or in society as a whole. The point in question, in the words of Jung, is "the fact that since we are living together in this world, each of us demands a certain amount of consideration from the other." The measure of consideration is always determined by the position which the usage of the association assigns to the individual. For this reason, the norms which safeguard the rights of personality are based upon usage. And in an association in which the position of an individual has been reduced to a mere nothing by the usage of the association, as was the position of the Roman slave or of the *filius familias*[1] in the household, there is no right to life. And what is the extent, even among the civilized nations of our times, of the right to physical inviolability and liberty in women and children? But the recognition, in a general way, of the right of every human being to life, physical inviolability, and liberty merely proves that the idea of the equal value of all human beings has made its way to this extent in the usage of society. In the same sense every person nowadays is entitled to the protection of his honor, a right which formerly was conceded only to members of the privileged classes. The other rights of personality

1. *filius familias*：〈拉〉家子

that are being recognized today, such as the right to one's picture, to privacy, to protection of one's emotional and aesthetic life, are merely extensions, granted because of the recognition of the heightened inner life of our time, of the protection which the associations in time past had granted to their members from the protection of the sensibilities of their bodies to protection of the sensibilities of their souls. No innovation in principle is involved. Of course it is apparent without argument that the right to one's name, seal, and coat-of-arms merely serves to protect the interest of the position which is indicated thereby. The social norms, moreover, that protect the interests of personality at the present time are a part of the law to a very limited extent only; they are preponderantly norms of morality, ethical custom, decorum, and tact. They are being converted into legal norms by an extremely gradual process.

At the present time, legal protection of the interests of personality is given chiefly by criminal law, and therefore only against the grossest attacks. The movement for the recognition of the rights of personality is striving to gain the much more effective protection of private law for these interests. If its objects were of a purely scientific nature, it would necessarily confine itself to the observation of the usage in the household, in the family, in business life, in social life, and gather therefrom what interests of personality are to be found there, and to what extent they are being protected by social norms. But inasmuch as it is a *Kunstlehre* (practical science) it poses its problem quite differently. It is concerned with the creation of clearly formulated legal propositions, which are to determine under what presuppositions, by means of what legal remedies and of what kinds of compulsion, the rights of personality, which arise from social usage, should be protected. But this investigation must be preceded by observation and universalization of the interests of this nature that are in existence in society, and their significance must be determined. But this process of observation and universalization not only ceases when there is nothing left of practical importance, but culminates in a most unscientific procedure, to wit in the balancing of interests as the basis of the finding of norms. It is true, juristic science would be in a much better case if instead of instituting observations and universalizations for its purposes it could draw on an already existing store of scientific knowledge, as can be done today in the case of medicine perhaps, and in the technical practical sciences. But for the present, since there is no sociology of law which could do the preliminary work for practical juristic science in this manner, the jurist must rely on his own experience for the knowledge of the relations of actual life which he requires in order to be enabled to create norms for decision on its basis. Apart from this, the statutes and the various branches of the social sciences will serve as sources of knowledge. But however great the amount of information he may receive elsewhere, in view of the inexhaustible and enormous diversity of the affairs of life it cannot possibly suffice. It must be supplemented at all times by the fullness of his own observation and his own experience. From this discussion it is apparent that a young man is not qualified for a seat on the bench who has merely demonstrated that he is able to master the most important statutes and a number of text-books. The best that a judge can give must be drawn from his inner self; the sections of the statute book and the textbooks are like an imperfect sketch for a picture; and only the observations and experiences of a full and rich life can give form and color to it.

The legally binding force of juristic law, it is true, is an enigma. The legal norm is always a command, and we ask, "How can the discussion of a jurist contain commands?" The question cannot be disposed of but can only be touched upon here. First of all we must point out that this is not an isolated occurrence. The writer on ethics formulates ethical norms, and the norms of outward decorum, of honor, of etiquette, of fashion, of games, must likewise be originated by someone. When one is in doubt, one refers to a book, e.g. to a book on decorum, a code of honor, a book of etiquette, a journal of fashions, a collection of rules for games.

Whatever is printed in the books is accepted as binding, and very often there is no other reason for this than that it is assumed — and very often the assumption is not justified — that the man who wrote the book somehow was authorized to laydown such rules.

In general the psychological basis of juristic law is the same. It is true the basic function of the jurist is to give information about the norms that are already in existence; but how shall one teach what it is that has validity as a norm unless the content of that which is taught in turn becomes a norm? Whom should we ask for instruction on the question what norms are valid but him who teaches the norms? The line of demarca tion between *Normenlehre* (the science of norms)[1] and *Lehrnormen* (norms that are being taught)[2] manifestly is so tenuous that it must needs be overlooked in actual life; and in this way the great antinomy of law arises, which continually converts doctrine into norms, but veils the process itself from the eyes of those who are taking part in the process.

But in the case of legal norms, unlike the case of a norm of decorum, etiquette, fashion, or of a game, it is not sufficient that they are being taught by someone. They must become established, they must prevail in the struggle. This often happens in society, without anyone's taking notice of the fact, when society automatically accepts that which is suitable and rejects that which is unsuitable. Perhaps no one has ever stated this better than the authority followed by Boethius. In his view juristic law (*ius civile*) is *probatae civium creditaeque sententiae*[3]. Occasionally this struggle of the norms for existence takes place according to an orderly process, e.g. the *disputatio fori* of the Romans

1. *Normenlehre* (the science of norms)：〈德〉规范科学
2. *Lehrnormen* (norms that are being taught)：〈德〉教授的规范
3. *probatae civium creditaeque sententiae*：〈拉〉市民合理观点的认可

and the citation of the Continental common law writers. And in this struggle the reputation of the originator is usually decisive. Most norms draw their vitality from the reputation of the man who has enunciated them. It is only very rarely however that the intellectual greatness of the person is the sole decisive factor, as in the case of the elder jurists of the Roman Republic, of the authors of the German and French books of law in the Middle Ages, and perhaps of the Islamic jurists. Practically in every case a high official position is an additional requisite. The Roman jurists of the Empire became *iuris conditores* in virtue of the *ius respondendi*[1]; even the Nordic declarer of the law is a public official; since the days of the glossators, the university professorship is the decisive thing among the Continental common law jurists. As late as the nineteenth century the jurists who exercised any great influence in the matter of creating law in Germany, with few exceptions (Bahr, Liebe, Einert; perhaps Salpius), were academic teachers. In England and in America high judicial office is required. But even in these countries judges are not "fungible" personalities in virtue of their office. Even though judge-made law is binding as such, it is by no means a matter of indifference by whom the proposition which one cites in court has been enunciated. Decisions of courts are, it is true, cited by attorneys in great numbers, but only a few have abiding value. The great jurists who have been actively engaged in the development of the law are always numbered among the greatest men of the human race. Their names are being mentioned and their works are being read centuries after they have departed this life.

1. *ius respondendi*：〈拉〉法的解答

XVI THE LAW CREATED BY THE STATE

Unlike the legal norms that have arisen in society, norms that have been created by the state are rarely being enforced by purely social compulsion. The state has need of its own peculiar means of power (*Machtmittel*) for this purpose, i.e. of its courts and other tribunals. And for this reason, the most important question is whether the state has suitable agencies that can give effect to these norms. The question then whether there is state law in any given state is not only a constitutional question but also an administrative one. The significance of the statutes of a state cannot be understood until one knows the agencies whose function it is to put them into effect. Everything depends upon their educational and cultural endowment, honesty, skill, and industry. For this reason a legal proposition will be given widely divergent interpretations in various sections of human society. After large portions of English, French, and Belgian constitutional and procedural law had been transplanted into foreign soil in the nineteenth century, men became convinced that they had effects quite different from those they would have at home. Transplantation has been most successful in the sphere of commercial law; for commerce is regulated essentially alike everywhere in Europe and the agencies of the state have little to do with it.

Permit me to adduce an example. Austrian jurists who, about twenty years ago, had come to Brussels in order to take part, as invited guests, in the dedication of the palace of justice heard with great astonishment that the Emperor Josef II had introduced the oral trial procedure in Belgium. The statute that achieved this miracle was the *Allgemeine Gerichtsordnung* (General Code of Judicial

Procedure)[1], the much maligned *Josephina*, which had been in effect in Austria for more than a century without being credited by anyone with the power to bring about an oral procedure. It is true, the Code of Procedure did provide that, in the country (i.e. everywhere outside of the provincial capitals), the proceedings should be oral. In Austria the oral procedure consisted in this, that the writings were not filed, but were drawn up in the form of protocols and were handed to the judge. Occasionally, it is true, it did happen that the statements of the parties were reduced to writing on the day in court (*Tagfahrt*). The law-suit however was decided in every case solely on the basis of the protocols, and as a rule by a judge who had not participated in the preliminary proceedings. In the Netherlands, which at that time belonged to Austria, the oral procedure was taken seriously. The proceedings in court were conducted orally; at the end, the discussion was embodied in a protocol; and the judge who had conducted the proceedings at the day in court decided the case, with the aid of the protocol, it is true, but chiefly on the basis of the impression received at the oral proceedings. So the ide nt ical statute brought about a written, indirect procedure in Austria, and an oral, direct one in the Netherlands.

But even the best state agencies are neither omnipotent nor omnipresent. If a statute is being obeyed only where the agencies of the state compel the people to do so, not much more has been achieved than the noisy creaking of the official mill. The art of regulating rivers does not consist in digging a new bed for the river all the way down to its mouth, but in directing the current so that it self-actively creates a new bed for itself. Likewise statutes fulfil their functions only where the great majority of the people obey them in obedience to the promptings of an inner impulse.

There are two ways in which a state can act through its law. One is

1. *Allgemeine Gerichtsordnung* (General Code of Judicial Procedure)：〈德〉一般司法程序法

through the norms for decision. The state issues directions to its courts and other tribunals as to the manner in which they should decide the cases that are being submitted to them by the parties. The majority of norms for decision, it is true, have been taken from juristic law; they are state law only when they have arisen independently of juristic law and are designed to subserve the purposes of the state. The other form of state law are *Eingriffsnormen* (norms directing state agencies to proceed)[1].

They direct the authorities to act irrespectively of whether they have been appealed to or not. Although the state norms for decision and the norms directing state agencies to act are not, indeed, in all instances, based upon statutes, we are concerned chiefly with instances where this is the case. Whether a legal proposition brings about direct action or whether it is but a norm for decision does not depend exclusively upon the intent of the legislator or the wording of the statute, but is determined by actual usage. In civil affairs they are preponderantly norms for decision. Exceptions are: matters relating to matrimony, to guardianship, to corporations, to records (land register, commercial register, register for matters of the matrimonial regime), and the state proceeding in the matter of the estate of a deceased person where such proceeding is required. In these cases, in part at least, direct action actually takes place. Originally criminal law consisted exclusively of norms for decision. The injured party himself had to bring the matter before the court. And even today criminal law consists in part of norms that are mere norms for decision even where the action is to be brought by officials of the state, for it is the custom of the authorities to wait for a notice or some other move by the parties. In case of an offense against the state, however, of murder, arson, and other crimes that are considered dangerous to the common welfare or to the state,

1. *Eingriffsnormen* (norms directing state agencies to proceed):〈德〉指令国家机构行动的规范

the state calls upon its agencies to hale the guilty person into court. The same relation between direct action and decision is found in administrative law.

The effect of state norms for decision is usually very much overestimated. The whole matter hinges upon action by the parties, who very often fail to act altogether. Often the statute remains unknown to a considerable part of the population; again the parties for whose benefit it was enacted often lack the material means to enforce their claim, or, because of the actual distribution of power, they lack self-confidence or confidence in the authorities. For this reason legislation for the protection of working-men, so far as it contains only norms for decision, as a rule remains ineffectual. A few years ago I instituted an inquiry which dealt with the question to what extent the Austrian Civil Code, which by this time has been in force for a century, had actually become part and parcel of everyday life. It produced remarkable results. Of the law of warranty, a part of the law which apparently is of extremely great practical importance, only a few regulations concerning defects in cattle are actually effective today — and these, perhaps because they had made their way into the statute from daily life. In case of immovables, warranty is usually excluded by contract; in case of movables, rules obtain which have no connection whatsoever with the Civil Code. But even apart from this, one would not believe to what extent the ineffectual law overbalances the effectual law. A conjecture to the effect that the number of sections of the Austrian Civil Code that have had no influence whatever upon life amounts to about one-third is not too high an estimate. Among them there are some that contain provisions of very wide scope, provisions that might become applicable at any moment but that have not been cited once in the more than 20,000 decisions reported in the Glaser-Unger collection of the decisions of the Supreme Court. It is self-evident that the situation is not altered by the fac1lhat a given legal proposition has been applied here and there. That is far from proving that it has actually become part and parcel of, and regulates, daily life.

Perhaps I may be permitted to illustrate this statement by an example which I have adduced in another connection. The family law of the Austrian Civil Code, as is well known, is extremely individualistic, perhaps the most individualistic in present-day Europe. The relation of the wife to the husband and of the children to the parents, in general, is one of complete independence, almost as if they were strangers to one another. A child may have property of his or her own, and his or her power of disposition over it is as free and untrammeled as that of the parents over their property. Whatsoever the child acquires, accrues to the benefit of the child not of the parents. The child has full power of self-determination and can utilize his or her earning power freely for his or her own purposes. Only so long as the child is a minor is it under the power of his or her father; but the father, the bearer of this power, is not much more than a guardian. His chief function is to see to it that the child suffers no injury in consequence of inexperience, lack of discretion, or weakness. Only in this sense does the father have the right of disposition over the property, the earning power, and the destiny of the child. And even in this, he is under the supervision of the Supreme Court of Guardians, which will adjudge a complaint of a child against a father.

In Bukowina, however, although it is a part of Austria, and although the Civil Code is in force there as well as in the other parts of Austria, the power of the father is an extremely serious matter. The Roumanian peasant, perhaps the only true Roman of our day, exercises a *patria potestas,* which seems strikingly familiar to the student of Roman law. There the children act uaJly belong to the fat her, although not all their lives, nevertheless until they attain their majority at the age of twentyfour; and though this ownership is not as absolute as it was in Rome, it is an ownership of body, property, and earning power, not only so long as they live in their father's house, but even while they are among strangers. If such a *filius* or *filia familias* is in service, the father or the mother appears punctually every month at the employer's residence or place of business and, quite as a matter of course, carries the wages home. And the parents dispose just as freely of the property and the income from the property of the child. And if one asks why the children submit so docilely, the answer is that resistance is something unheard of.

Ever since I directed attention to this phenomenon in an article in Harden's *Zukunft*[1], I have again and again received the reply that those things that are in conflict with the Civil Code are ethical custom, not law. This reply is based on the same old idea, to wit that we are here dealing with a question of terminology, i.e. with the question just what is to be called law. But we are here dealing with something quite different from this, i.e. with the fact that the Austrian Civil Code has not been able to root out this custom, which is in such decided conflict with the Code — irrespective of whether we call it law or ethical custom. It is true that since I first mentioned this custom about ten years ago I have noticed that it has markedly been beginning to fall into disuse; but this must be attributed to the breaking up of the old family order which is being brought about by modern social relations and by modern modes of thought, and which is very clearly perceptible in this country in other ways also, rather than to the influence of the Civil Code, which, we must admit, did not become effective until now, i.e. after the lapse of a whole century. If the jurists were more in the habit of observing life at first hand, they would discover a great number of instances of this kind. The famous investigation of the South Slavic customary law, which Bogisic had instituted, revealed that among all the southern Slavs within the territory in which the Austrian Civil Code is in effect, the well known South Slavic family community, the *Sadruga*, is in existence; this is altogether unknown

1. *Zukunft*：〈德〉未来

to the Civil Code and absolutely irreconcilable with its principles. Moreover on almost every page of the book in which he summed up the results of his investigation we find the remark, with reference to the most diverse subjects, particularly with reference to the law of inheritance and of the family, that the people know that the precepts of the statute have a content quite different from their customary usage, but that they do not follow the statute. In his book, *Das Gewohnheitsrecht und die sozialen Verbande*[1], Dniestrzanski tells of a sort of primitive mercantile partnership which complies neither with the provisions of the Austrian Commercial Code nor with those of the Civil Code. I myself am continually meeting with phenomena of this nature and hope to be able to discuss them in a det ailed juristic exposition. All of this shows to what extent the effectiveness of state law is being interfered with by other social forces.

Direct action by the state is much more effective than a norm for decision. This is convincingly demonstrated by the history of legislation for the protection of working-men. These statutes were originally enacted in order that they might serve as norms for the decision of disputes arising from contracts for wages and from bodily injuries. This applies also to the French statute relating to the twelve-hour day and to the German statute relating to liability in case of accident. These statutes were altogether ineffectual. The office of industrial inspector, as a state agency for the enforcement of the legislation for the protection of workingmen, first breathed some life into them by means of direct official action.

It is self-evident of course that a direct command of the statute directing the authorities of the state to proceed in a certain manner is not always sufficient to bring about such action. The French statute of the year 1806 relating to the cessation of labor on Sunday was never

---

1. *Das Gewohnheitsrecht und die sozialen Verbände*：〈德〉习惯法与社会联合体

enforced. "*Il ne se trouvait presque jamais un commissaire de police ou un garde champetre qui osat dresser un proces-verbal contre les coupables*[1]," de Rousiers says on this subject.

So even state law often fails completely. Often the measures taken by the state for supervision and enforcement are unequal to the task of converting the rule laid down by the state into a rule of conduct. Often it fails because of the unwillingness, the weakness, or the incapacity of the authorities; the indictment which should be brough t as a mat ter of official duty often waits notice from the parties involved. The law of the state regulating corporations and societies is evaded by means of free associations, e.g. in France and, in part, in Austria; partnerships and agreements are withdrawn from state supervision through failure to have them registered; contracts which are prohibited by the state are being entered into and voluntarily performed by the parties; invalid testaments are not being submit ted to the obligatory proceedings for the distribution of the estates of deceased persons and the inheritances are being distributed by free partitioning. In such cases the other social associations have proved more powerful than the great social association, which has created the state as the instrument for carrying out its will. But as soon as the measures taken by the state for the purpose of supervision and enforcement fail in case of a statute that is to be enforced by direct action of the agencies of the st ate, the statu te is reduced to the status of a norm for decision, which is able to manifest a trace of life only in case the whole apparatus is set in motion by the parties concerned.

The effectiveness of the law of the state is in direct ratio to the force which the state provides for its enforcement, and in inverse ratio to the resistance which the state must overcome. The fact that a considerable

---

1. *Il ne se trouvait ... contre les coupables*：〈拉〉敢于对违法者提起口头程序的专职人员几乎从未存在。

part of social activity has found its focus in legislation, administration of justice, and civil administration has not done away with the forces which are operative in society apart from these things. The church, economic life, art, science, public opinion, the family and personal associations, after all, have maintained their independence over against the state either altogether or to a great degree. They are, indeed, *foci* of development of purely social forces with which legislation, administration of justice, and civil administration by the state must cope at every moment. It is an error to think, as often happens, that all the modem state need do is simply to employ the means of power at its disposal in order to overcome every thing that comes in its way. It is trae that no one can offer legally justifiable resistance to the modern sta te as one could to the feudal st ate, to which the great feudal lord was bound solely by agreement. But the forces which the state has at its absolute disposal, the army, the police, and, supported by these, the civil officials, in the nature of things, are equipped for conflict with society only inasmuch as they are called upon to overcome a forcible insurrection, to attain a success which can be gained by a single effort. In the course of time they finally grow weary and their energies flag, and they themselves are too much exposed to social influences to follow the power of the state wherever it would lead them. History shows that the military and semi-military organization of the st ate, in spite of the great impetus which it can develop, and which can, at a given moment, overcome all resistance, is not a match for the uninterrupted sway of elemental forces which have their life and being in the social associations. They operate with less force at the beginning perhaps, but they operate steadily, decisively, and without faltering. Sufficiently developed, the religious, economic, political, and ethical trends created by them sooner or later gain influence, and, under favorable circumstances, gain control over the legislative and magisterial machinery of the state. The French express the thought that the state cannot permanently base its right upon might in the very expressive words: *On pent tout faire avec les baionettes, excepte asseoir*[1]. Even state law must, therefore, continually take the social forces into account.

And to begin with, the state cannot destroy the economic presuppositions of its own existence. The state is conditioned upon the production of economic goods within society in sufficient quantities to supply it with nourishment. It can, of course, find the means for the erection of its own structure by committing depredations upon the national economic system, and it is doing this even today to a terrific extent; for the ruin which will come after the lapse of decades or centuries need not worry the persons that are in power at the present time. But it cannot destroy the national economic system, for it must derive its sustenance from the surpluses of the latter.

Stammler says a fully developed despotism[2] is a legal order which consists of but one paragraph, to wit: The legal relations among those that are subject to the law shall be adjudged and given effect solely according to the concrete decision of the ruler in the individual case. If the ruler had a band of foreign mercenaries at his beck and call, such a legal order would not, in itself, be inconceivable. But how long could it endure? If no one were secure in the possession of his property because a concrete decision of the ruler could deprive him of it at any time, if no one could act in reliance upon a contract because a similar decision might rescind the contract, agriculture, trade, and commerce would be in such a state of disintegration that before long the ruler would have no one left to rule. The many despots of whom history tells, therefore, were very careful not to supply us with warning examples of an essentially unsound legal order (*unrichtiges Rechi*). They did not hesitate in individual cases to plunder, rob, and pillage as much as

---

1. *On peut tout faire avec les baionettes, excepté s'y asseoir*：〈拉〉刺刀可以做很多事情，但人没法坐在刺刀尖。
2. despotism：专制统治

they thought feasible, and occasionally permitted their creatures to do this, but in general they permitted people to attend to their affairs, and unless they were particularly interested in warping justice they suffered legal disputes to be decided according to law and custom. Their own interest, clearly seen, quite readily taught them the value of a legal order.

This is the reason why it is frequently being said, albeit not by modern jurists but by economists of the classical school, that the power of the state is limited by the laws of economics. The state, which has the power to ruin very many things, which can take very much away from one person and give it to another, is nevertheless unable to make one more blade of grass grow than the economic resources of the nation perm it. The significance of the knowledge of this fact as a means of preservation is enormous, for a revolutionary if he should seize control of the state would no more be able to do this than is the present state. It too could take away from one man and give to another, could ruin many things, but could not cause one more seed-corn to sprout than the economic resources of the nation permit. The best that the state as well as its adversaries can do for the future economic welfare of the nation is to treat the economic system of the present with extreme tenderness.

We shall have to get used to the thought that certain things simply cannot be done by means of a statute, that the intent of the author of a statute is a matter of absolute indifference so far as its effects are concerned. Once in force, it goes its own way. Whether the legal proposition is effective, whether it has the effect that was desired, depends exclusively upon whether it is a means adapted to this purpose. And lastly we must get used to the thought that the effect of a legal proposition is determined not so much by the interpretation which jurists place upon it as by other circumstances, which are of much greater significance in the matter, e.g. the individual peculiarity of the people, the prevailing ethical views, the means of power used to enforce it, the kind of legal procedure employed. A statute is effective not by dint of its mere existence, but by dint of its force.

The commands of the state are most effective when they are exclusively negative, when it is not a matter of compelling people to act but of constraining them to refrain from action, when they are given in order to forbid, to attack, to destroy, to extirpate. In this manner the state has been engaged in innumerable contests with religious trends, societies and other communities, to which for some reason or other it had become opposed. This is the content of the whole penal law of the state, and particularly of the only part that in fact has a certain measure of social influence. This sphere includes chiefly police legislation by the state, i.e. legislation for the public safety and the public health, and for the supervision of trades and occupations. In the economic sphere also action by the state is most effective if carried out by means of prohibitions (tariff legislation). The proscriptive rights[1] and the monopolies of the state are mere prohibitions. The state has hindered the free activity of economic forces, and by doing so perhaps has destroyed incalculable economic values, but perhaps has made possible and fostered a given economic venture at their expense. Copyright laws have the same significance. The state issues a prohibition directed to all men, excepting only the author, forbidding them to engage in any activity of a certain kind. This is the whole content of the law in so far as it is of state origin. The only difference between this right and the proscriptive rights and the monopolies is this, that the object of the former is to stimulate or to reward the inventive genius. And so far as the law of the family and of property is not of social but of state origin, its content is almost exclusively negative, e.g. marriages, societies, contracts, last wills and testaments, that are being forbidden, dissolved, declared void, or voidable;

1. The proscriptive rights：剥夺的权利

property that is being forfeited; heirs that are being excluded.

Wherever the state wishes to constrain men to perform an affirmative act, it must proceed much more cautiously. To guide and direct great multitudes of men is a matter of enormous difficulty under all circumstances. It presupposes a great and rare gift. It is most difficult perhaps when it is to be done on the basis of universal abstract rules. Whenever men consider a task useful and profitable, they will combine on their own initiative in order to perform it; often economic and social pressure will also induce them to do so, and action by the authorities serves rather to disturb, to hinder, and confuse than to promote. For this reason it will, most likely, be impossible to impose the will of another upon a superior number of unwilling men. This is shown by the many attempts made in former days to compel striking workmen with the aid of gendarmes or policemen to return to work. The *lex Julia et Poppaea*[1] perhaps secured many a rich inheritance for the Roman fisc; but whether even one single child owes its existence to it is a mat ter of much less certainty. The Austrian tax on bachelors and childless persons is striving for the same results in behalf of the fisc without the addition of flourishes about increasing the population. In the rare cases in which the state successfully compels affirmative action, especially in the administration of the army and of taxation, a specially trained and skilled technique has been developed on the basis of the experience of millennia, or at least of centuries. Face to face however with a breakdown of discipline which had been caused by special circumstances or with a well thought out refusal to pay taxes, the state, on several occasions, had to admit that it was powerless. Similar results are sometimes encountered in prisons and boarding schools, because of the great helplessness and suggestibility of the persons involved. All other cases in which the law of the state

1. *lex Julia et Poppaea*：〈拉〉《关于婚姻的波皮亚法》

produces an affirmative effect are cases of direct dealings between the authorities and the population in which the latter realizes, at least to a certain extent, that obedience to the law of the state will redound to its advantage. The law of procedure perhaps rests chiefly on this idea. Perhaps the most successful venture of this nature that the state has undertaken in recent years is the matter of social insurance. It is a great misfortune for the state that all its institutions tend to become governmental agencies, even foundations for the advancement of education, of art, science, and the public welfare; even schools, museums, expositions, railroads, state monopoly of tobacco, and hospitals. This causes them to lose not only their adaplability to the changing needs of life but also their adherents among the people, who could make them instruments of social progress.

Now how did the law which had been created by the state succeed in impressing its stamp upon society and what social formations has it brought about in the course of historical development? When a state lays down for itself or for its agencies its or their position and functions, it does not thereby create state law in the proper sense of the term, but law of the state. The state thereby creates its inner order for itself and its agencies, just as every other social association must create an order for itself: the church, the commune, the family, the society. The state does no more than this when it engages in economic ventures of a private nature, railroads, banks, or mines. Its law here is the same in principle as that upon which any other economic venture of a private nature is based.

The state actually creates the people of the state (*Staatsvolk*)[1], and it does this, in part at least, through its law. This, it is true, is something quite different from the people in the national sense, which is exclusively a product of society. Most of the latest efforts to

---

1. people of the state (*Staatsvolk*)：国民

nationalize by action of the state, and that means to unite the various peoples which are united in one state not only into one *Staatsvolk* (people of the state) but also into one people in the national sense, have failed. Hitherto it has not been the state but only society that has been able to nationalize effectually. Nevertheless the *Staatsvolk* is an entity of extremely great importance. The unity of a common constitution, a common army, a common language throughout the state; of a unit ary system of civil administration, though the unity of the latter be outward and partial only; the unity of economic territory, which functions chiefly in the collections of duties, taxes, and fees, and in the establishment of means of communications; the unity of legislation and the resultant unity of juristic science and technique and of judicial decision, and finally the capital, the common center, toward which there is a constant flow of the population, and from which a great number of suggestions emanate — all of these things make the *Staatsvolk* a unique unified entity. They exercise a profound influence upon creation of law by society. To attempt to exclude the *Staatsvolk*as has been done repeatedly in recent times, from consideration in the study of legal development is to misapprehend utterly the weight of these facts.

Furthermore the state creates the peace of the state. It constitutes agencies whose function is to preserve it, the administrative tribunals, the police; it assumes control of the criminal courts and by creating state law, supplies them with a basis for their activity. The norms of state law that we are concerned with here are parts of police law, of procedural law, and of criminal law.

They are norms of secondary rank in every respect; they create neither social nor state institutions; they merely provide state protection for those that are already in existence.

In matters economic, the state wields a decisive influence through state law by establishing economic rights that are not conditioned upon the economic production or exchange of goods. At every stage the state, being a predominantly military association, is, in a certain sense, in opposition to the national economic system. It takes no active part in it; for we may disregard its inconsiderable contributions in its capacity of landowner and of industrial entrepreneur. The economic goods that it requires, it secures indirectly from the returns of other economic undertakings. Therein lies the whole economic cont ent of the st ate law of finance. Through it the state, relying on its means of power, determines how much of the returns of the national economy it claims for itself. Even when the state, in a private economic contract, obligates itself to render some performance, it must draw upon other economic undertakings for this, for it is not engaged in economic activity of its own, except when it acts in the capacity of a great landed proprietor or of an industrial entrepreneur. It is self-evident that we are not denying that what the state offers to the people is, or at least can be, of the greatest possible economic significance; but it is not a result of economic activity. For this reason the state can furnish the basis for economic rights only by distributing economic values that are already in existence in a way dififerent from the distribution that would be effected by the undisturbed operation of economic activity or by taking a value that has already been created or that is about to be created from one economic undertaking and placing it at the disposal of another. In doing these things, the state relies upon the instrumentalities of power that are at its disposal. The state law of ownership, the state law and right of inheri tance of collateral relatives, the state annuities and monopolies, the effect of prohibitions by the state in the law of joint ownership, of things, of contract, and of inheritance are based on such distribution and transfer of economic values.

The order of possession is of social, not of state, origin, and therefore is a creation of society and not of the state. The order of ownership, on the other hand, derives its origin chiefly from juristic science. It comprises the norms for decision which determine which one of the parties to the controversy about possession should win, to which one the courts of the state should grant protection. So far as this protection is granted according to the order of possession, inasmuch as the state does nothing more than to give effect to the order of possession as it has arisen in society, the legal propositions according to which this is done are not state law but social law, and, indeed, juristic law. On the other hand, the greater security which the state provides for the order of possession through criminal law, the police, and the law of procedure is an achievement of the state. Society, juristic science, and the state t herefore have coopera ted in the crea tion of the law and right of possession and of ownership. Possession is the social constitution; ownership is the sum total of the norms for decision of juristic law, according to which one's possession is protected by the courts, is restored if interfered with, and is regained if lost. This greater security is state law.

In Roman law and in the systems derived from it, this relation is obscured by the dichotomy of the protection of possession into protection of ownership and of possession in the narrower sense of the term. The idea underlying this dichotomy is the following: Unconditional protection is given only to a specifically qualified possession, to ownership; over and above this, a preliminary protection, which is preponderantly in the nature of police protection, is gran ted to all possession even to the altogether non-economic possession of the thief and the robber. Moreover all protection is denied to various forms of possession that rest on a sound economic basis, especially the possession of the ordinary and of the usufructuary lessee, both of whom are limited to an action on the contract. According to Roman terminology, which is followed by that of the modern Continental law, ownership is not in a general way, as it is in English and Scandinavian law, all legally protected possession, but only such possession as is protected by special remedies (*actio* and *exceptio* asserting ownership[1]).

1. *actio* and *exceptio* asserting ownership：主张所有权的诉讼与抗辩

But over and above this almost all possession enjoys some measure of protection, and bona fide possession can avail itself of remedies in the nature of the *actio Publiciana in rem* which are modeled upon the remedies of ownership. The private law protection of the economic constitution therefore is extraordinarily well provided with forms, and this fact makes it very difficult to see it in its social interrelations.

We have no information as to the historical reasons for the dichotomy and trichotomy of the Romans. But Jhering in his day has shown with admirable acumen that, among the Romans, possession was merely an outwork of ownership, and that protection of possession was merely an aid to better protection of ownership. If we understand possession to mean the economic constitution, and ownership to mean merely the sum total of the norms for decision through which the economic constitution is preserved and restored, the doctrine that protection of possession is merely an aid to protection of ownership manifestly means only that protection is granted to possession and to ownership for the sake of the economic constitution and that the difference between the two is merely a matter of a few presuppositions and of a few diversities in the effect of legal remedies. Jhering, I think, has found the reason why the possession of the ordinary and of the usufructuary lessee was not protected. It was the fact that these possessors, in fact, were serfs among the Romans. The protection which the non-economic possession of the thief and of the robber enjoyed even against the victim of the theft and the robbery probably never was anything more than a bit of scholastic wisdom. Definitive protection of possession in the form of protection of ownership is granted, at least in the fully developed Roman law, to all economically acquired possession, even though it has been acquired by means of a slight disturbance of the economic order (bonitary[1] ownership); and

1. bonitary：无所有权而有使用权

after a short period of usucapion[1], even against the person whose possession has been interfered with.

Other legal systems, chiefly the Germanic system of the Middle Ages, the modern English and Scandinavian systems, do not differentiate between protection of possession and protection of ownership. Every economic possessor is granted the identical remedies. And in a case of possession of movables this is done also in modern German and French law. This perhaps is the most convincing proof that the Roman dichotomy is based solely on a dichotomy of legal remedies, not upon a difference in the nature of the thing protected. The question has often been raised whether, in view of the expeditiousness of the modern Austrian procedure, the dichotomy is justifiable at the present time.

In addition to this social ownership, which consists solely in the protection of the economic constitution by the state, there is an ownership which is purely a matter of state law, and which arises and exists solely through the will of the state independently of the economic constitution. The state can grant the same protection that it grants to the possessor to a person who has no possession, who has never acquired possession economically, by commissioning its agencies independently of all economic presuppositions, in the first place to secure possession for the person favored in this manner, and thereafter to protect him in this possession and repel attacks that may be made upon it. It will also, of course, instruct its courts in case of litigation to decide in favor of the person whom it has thus made the owner. The most important instance is that of the great landowner and the disencumbrance of land of its burdens and charges.

The ownership of land by the peasants is purely economic, and arose independently of the sta te and out side of the state, and to a

1. usucapion：时效所有权

great extent prior to the state. Ownership of great proprietary estates, however, apart from the rare cases of purchase of peasant lands, which hardly ever occurred in the very distant past, owes its existence to the state. The great proprietary estate, in contrast to the economic ownership of the peasant, is a political ownership of the ruling classes, created by the power of the state. In the last analysis therefore it is merely the expression of political ascendancy. When the *populus Romanus*[1] asserted a claim to the ownership of the *solum provinciale,* when the king of England declared himself owner of all the soil of England, they meant to say that in virtue of the right of conquest they would dispose of the land according to their arbitrary will. The principle, *nulle terresans seigneur*[2], merely reflects the fact that the powers that rule the state, the king, and the nobility, have succeeded in overcoming the resistance of the peasant landowners. Likewise every grant of ownerless or of occupied lands by the king to his grandees was merely an exercise of the power of the state. And it is exactly the same thing when counts and princes in the Middle Ages appropriate rights in forests, rivers, and mines, when they compel their subjects to receive their own lands in feudal tenure. Probably this device of subduing the peasants was never successfully carried out to any appreciable extent without the aid of the state. Occasionally the mere formal declaration of the sovereign power of the state that it had determined to treat a person as the owner of land was sufficient to make that person the owner. One of the most famous cases of this kind is the creation of great proprietary estates in Scotland. When the English, after the battle of Culloden, proceeded to destroy the ancient Gaelic clan organization, they accomplished their purpose by declaring that the chieftains of the clans were the proprietors of the whole clan territory, which had, until then, been held in common. The ownership of great

---

1. *populus Romanus*：〈拉〉罗马人
2. *nulle terre sans seigneur*：〈拉〉凡土地皆有领主。

proprietary estates in Bengal began with an error of the English, who in the eighteenth century mistook the tax on land for rent, and thought that the peasants who were obligated to pay a tax were tenants of the maharajahs[1].

There is no doubt that the great proprietary estates owe their existence to the power of the state. When the state created these estates it was acting as the association of powerful warlike nobles. The individual noble to whom enormous domains had been assured or given in fee found among his fellow-nobles, who, united, constituted the state, a measure of support which might, on occasion, become very useful. But he had to do the actual taking possession himself. Without personal means of power, relying merely on a document of grant, no one would have undertaken to take possession of these estates or have been able to maintain possession. The situation is the same as that which one finds in other spheres when a man secures the aid of those who are associated with him in a smaller association in order to attain his object.

The state-created ownership of great proprietary estates as such has no economic content. The state cannot breathe the breath of life into an economic institution by decrees based merely on the possession of power. What is the effect of a grant of land by the state? Is it anything other than the promise of the state to support the grantee in his attempt to take possession, to repel attacks upon this possession by others, and to aid him in securing income from the land? In the case of a new and feeble state this may not amount to very much; it furnishes a sufficient pretext, however, for the powerful noble to exert his own strength to convert the peasant, who until then has been an owner, into a usufructuary lessee or into a serf in order thereby to secure for himself a share of the returns of the economic activity of the latter, or,

---

1. maharajahs：土邦主

to state the matter technically, to get ground-rent (*Bodenrente*)[1]. Giving uncultivated land amounts to a warrant for the returns that may accrue to the donee from his own economic labor or from any other form of economic activity, e.g. from colonization.

Disencumbrance of the soil is the opposite of the feudal grant. It is the abolition of the right to ground-rent which had b een created by the nobility and the state through the exercise of their own power. Numerous disencumbrances of this nature took place in antiquity; for example, among the Romans perhaps in the fourth century of the city, at least in the immediate vicinity of Rome. In England, an incomplete one took place in the year 1660 (12 Car. II); in France, after several earlier at tempts, a complete disencumbrance in the year 1789; in the rest of Europe everywhere during the course of the nineteenth century.

When the state proceeds to emancipate the peasants and to disencumber the soil, the situation is quite different from that of the time when the land was granted to the nobles. The driving force in modern instances of disencumbrance is a powerful urban citizenry which enters into direct relations with the state. The state is no longer exclusively an organization of the landowning nobility. The urban citizenry takes a lively interest in the emancipation of the peasantry, because this emancipation makes it possible to draw them into the general commercial life, into the economic system of finance and credit, and because the domination of the nobility is held in check thereby. The king becomes independent of the nobility, inasmuch as he has already created a standing army and is therefore no longer limited to the military service of the nobility; he begins to administer the affairs of the state himself through officials who are dependent upon him. The king is desirous, in his own interest, of improving

1. ground-rent (*Bodenrente*)：地租

the economic condition of the country, and the modern science of economics, which was originated and developed by the urban citizenry, shows the way in which it may be done, i.e. by advancing industry and commerce through the liberation of economic forces from feudal fetters. The newly developed science of agriculture teaches that progress in agriculture and feudal landholding are incompatible. The nobility gradually loses interest in continuing the servile state of the peasantry, having become convinced that the returns from unfree labor are inadequate, and in view of the changed economic situation welcomes the substitution of a money payment for the feudal burdens. So the state, in emancipating the peasants, merely does that which the general economic situation seems to demand. We may therefore say that both the state-created ownership of the great landed proprietor and the disencumbrance of the soil are achieved by social forces. Apart from such disencumbrance, landholding on a smaller scale very rarely owes its existence to the state. Instances of this are the sale by the state of confiscated estates during the French Revolution, and here and there colonization by the state.

The right of collateral relations to take by succession probably owes its existence everywhere to norms for decision which the state has received into its law and developed. The whole process of development is little understood, for the reason that historical investigations in the field of law have consistently overlooked the relation between the law of inheritance and the military constitution of the state. The fact that in primitive times the estate of a deceased person who had been living alone without clan or family connection became ownerless, and therefore became the property of anyone who seized it, was a matter of little importance as long as there were few persons who lived alone, and as long as, because of the simplicity of the economic constitution, the destruction of economic values incident to ownerlessness did not import great loss. But as soon as the situation changed, it became necessary for the state to make provision for estates of persons that died without heirs. In the ancient state the citizen was also a warrior; and when a citizen died without heirs, his collateral relatives were called to the inheritance in order that the number of warriors might not be diminished. In the feudal state the vacant feud had to be given to someone, for otherwise the feudal services would not have been rendered. If in addition to this there exists in the feudal state a right of inheritance in the collateral relatives, with a preference given to the male relatives, this is a survival from the days of the universal duty of freemen to render military service, which must now seek to hold its own against the will of the king. Fixed principles determining the question to which collateral relatives the feud should be given were arrived at very slowly. The broad lines of this development in Germany, France, Engand, and Italy are well known.

Accordingly a right of inheritance in the collateral relatives[1], comparable to that which probably had been in existence among the Romans and the Germans in prehistoric times, arose everywhere among the Slavic peoples in the fourteenth century. But it developed chiefly at the expense of the right of escheat[2] of the princes and the noble landowners, which had by that time been fully developed. The transition can be seen quite clearly in the code of Czar Duschan. Article 41 provides: "Whenever a noble landowner dies who has had no child or who has had a child which has died, his inherited lands shall be considered ownerless until someone is found of his house to the third child of a brother. This child shall inherit from him." We shall here merely point out the fact that the very wording of this paragraph shows that it is an innovation. Take also paragraph 48: "When a noble landowner dies, his best horse and his armor shall belong to the Czar, his great festive garment and the golden girdle shall belong to the son, and the Czar shall not take it away from him.

1. right of inheritance in the collateral relatives：旁系亲属继承权
2. escheat：转归领主

If he has no son, it shall belong to his daughter, who shall have the disposal of it."

The payments made by the state to its creditors, the salaries of officials, the pensions of officials and of their families, are *rentes*[1] derived from the state. In the earlier days payments by the state to especially favored persons were also of great importance. Payments out of the treasury of the state were an appropriation to a private person of a share of the returns of the national economy which the state had claimed for itself. In the days when payment was made in kind, the state directed the person entitled to collect directly from the person obligated to pay.

In time past the private monopolies granted by the state were chiefly the proscriptive rights; today they are the rights gran ted for the protection of literary and artistic creation, and in part the income from certain professions that are favored by the state. The state forbids the practice of a certain trade in general terms, and excepts a certain favored person from this prohibition. By doing this, it permits the privileged person to engage in an economic activity, to engage in which he normally would not require the permission of the state; but the prohibition of the state enables him to sell the products of his economic activity or his services at a higher price than their economic value warrants. This overplus is a profit, which accrues to him because of the monopoly, and which he receives at the expense of other economic undertakings. State monopolies therefore are creations of society to the same degree as of the state. Economic undertakings, inventions, do not owe their existence to the state. Only the norms of the second order, the norms of penal law, of police law, of procedure, through which the state excludes competition, proceed from the state.

And lastly the state acts through its courts and agencies by imposing

---

1. *rentes*：岁入

limitations upon free activity. It prohibits certain communities or it dissolves them, especially certain family relations (void and punishable marriages); it takes away, and limits, rights of ownership; it denies recognition by courts and administrative tribunals to dispositions by last will and testament and, if need be, destroys them by its own action; it has, in the past at least, not only maintained existing conditions of serfdom by refusing legal protection, but has also exercised an active influence upon the content of this condition of serfdom by the extent to which it granted or refused legal protection, and in the end has abolished them altogether. In this very matter the state proceeds by means of norms of decision. And it does this in essentially the same manner as does juristic science.

Summarizing the influence of state law upon the state of the law in the course of its historical development down to the present day, we may say the following: By creating constitutional and administrative law, the state has created its own law for its own needs. It has fused the various groups that are occupying its territory into a unified people of the state (*Staatsvolk*) and by doing so has prepared the way for a unitary development of law. Through its courts and administrative tribunals, with the aid of its secondary norms, penal law, police law, procedural law, it has brought about for the state and social institutions an increased measure of security. It has established ownership as distinguished from possession, and made possible the right of succession in the collateral relatives. It has created *rentes* and monopolies. By its prohibitions and limitations it has exerted a powerful influence upon social institutions, upon communal life, relations of domination, ownership, possession, contract, succession.

Thereafter society keeps on building on the foundation laid by the state. Communities, relations of domination and of possession, contracts, articles of association, declarations by last will and testament establish their inner order, in part at least, according to the directions of the authorities, according to the kind and measure of protection which they can expect to receive from the courts, or they make special arrangements to avoid the hindrances and traps put in their way by the latter. So in the last analysis the state of the law is a resultant of the cooperation, the interaction, and the antagonism of state and society. And in this way state law, too, can become juristic law.

As soon as state law has actually become part and parcel of everyday life, and has exerted a moulding influence upon it, jurists will no longer confine their attention to the words of the statute but will be concerned with the forms of life that have come into being under its influence. The universalizations which they arrive at in doing this, the norms which they find, will, of course, be juristic law. This happened in Rome in the case of the *Lex Falcidia* and of the *senatusconsultum Velleianum*[1], and has happened again and again since that time. English commerce is regulated by the Statute of Frauds to such an extent that the English were unwilling to change it although it is quite antiquated, but took it over in part almost verbatim into the Sales of Goods Act[2] of the year 1893. Inasmuch as the German testament is derived from the Roman testament, the *Lex Falcidia* was received into German law together with the latter, and has become a part of the living German law no less than the testament. It is well known and generally understood that the canon law prohibition against usury is in exactly the same case. It has all the hall-marks of state-made law. The church, which promulgated it, was an association partaking of the nature of a state, and was, in this case, as the state is in other cases, an agency of society for the purpose of creating law. Through its own courts and through its influence upon the courts of the state, the church was enabled to give effect to its law as readily as a state.

Accordingly we shall have to call the part played by the st ate in the creation of law a very limited one. Nevertheless we are all under

1. *senatusconsultum Velleianum*：〈拉〉《维利安妇女保护法》
2. Sales of Goods Act：《货物买卖法》

the influence of the notion of the omnipotence of the state; and this conception has undoubtedly given rise to a series of social thought sequences which, though they are conditioned historically, and therefore destined to perish at some time in the future which cannot be determined in advance, nevertheless dominate the thinking of the whole civilized human race at this time. Chief of these is the thought that the power to legislate is the highest power in modern society, and that resistance to it is to be condemned under all circumstances; that there cannot be any law within the territory of the state that is in conflict with statute law; and that a judge who in the administration of law disregards a statute is guilty of gross violation of duty. Since it is the function of the sociological science of law, like that of every other science, to record facts, not to evaluate them, it cannot possibly, as some have believed, tend to establish, at the present stage of human development, a doctrine which might lead the judge to violate his judicial oath. And even though it cannot but state that the judge in the performance of the duties of his office is frequently quite unconsciously, albeit sometimes consciously, guided by non-legal considerations, in making this statement it is merely recording facts, not evaluating them.

But the basic social institutions, the various legal associations, especially marriage, the family, the clan, the commune, the guild, the relations of domination and of possession, inheritance, and legal transactions, have come into being either altogether or to a great extent independently of the state. The center of gravity of legal development therefore from time immemorial has not lain in the activity of the state but in society itself, and must be sought there at the present time. This may be said not only of the legal institutions but also of the norms for decision. From time immemorial the great mass of norms for decision has been abstracted from the social institutions by science and by the administration of justice, or has been freely invented by them; and legislation by the state, too, can generally find them only by following the social institutions and by imitating scientific or judicial methods.

XVII CHANGES IN THE LAW IN THE STATE AND IN SOCIETY

And now may we be permitted to enter upon the discussion of one of the most popular questions of juristic metaphysics[1], to wit the question whether at the present time the law grows through legislation only or through legislation and "customary law"; whether there is such a thing as "customary law" today; and if so, whether it can be rendered superfluous by legislation. All of these questions, rightly understood, automatically become superfluous when the origin and the growth of law are rightly understood, i.e. when they are understood to mean the origin and the transformation of social institutions. There can of course be no doubt that in this sphere as well as elsewhere the state can bring about or prevent many things by direct interference and by decisions of its tribunals. But it cannot be disputed that it is unable either to set the whole course of development in motion or to bring it to a standstill, that in a progressive society at least, new institutions are continually coming into being, and existing ones are developing irrespective of what the state may do about it.

A glance at legal history will show that even at a time when the state had already gained control over legislation, great changes were always taking place in the law that were not brought about by legislation. Slavery disappeared from Europe during the course of the Middle Ages; from the beginning of the sixteen th century the peasant in England was gradually acquiring an ever increasing measure

1. metaphysics：形而上学

of liberty, while in Germany his freedom was being progressively curtailed; and wherever modern large-scale industry has been introduced, it has given rise to countless new kinds of contracts, real rights, rights of neighbors, forms of succession, and has influenced even the family law. In the beautifully developing cities of detached houses of our time a servitude requiring the building of detached houses has arisen. Elec trical works have given rise to new kinds of real rights, among others the rights of transmitting currents, and new kinds of obligatory contracts, among others the contract to supply electrical current. These doubtless are changes in the law, and, in part, such changes as history tells of in tones so loud that no one can fail to hear. Perhaps recalling to memory a few pictures from the days of our own youth will enable us to answer the much mooted question whether new customary law can arise today. The family of today is not the family in which we spent our youth; the marriage of today is not the marriage that we grew enthusiastic about when we were young; commerce and life have changed; contracts of purchase and sale, of ordinary or of usufructuary lease, for services and for wages, of a nature quite different from those of the past, are being made. The relations of master and servant, of employer and employee, of producer and consumer, are quite different from those of former days. Share companies, undertakings for the transportation of persons or goods, associations, banks, stock exchanges, and dealings in futures can scarcely be recognized. But a few decades ago, where were the trusts, cartels, unions, strikes, and *Tarifaertrage* (collective labor agreements)? Surely no period of time has ever made such rapid progress as has our time. Never have father and son stood so alarmingly far apart in thought, sentiment, and conduct as today. These, to be sure, are new forms of life; in part, basically changed forms of our whole social and economic life, i.e. new law.

To all of these the state is not a party. The law changes because men and things change. To use an illustration of Herbert Spencer's, one can heap up cannon balls to form a pyramid or a tetrahedron, but one cannot pile them vertically, one above the other, so that they form a wall; one can build a wall with hard, sharp-edged bricks, but one cannot heap them up like cannon balls to form a pyramid. In this sense the qualities of a composite body are always determined by the qualities of its component parts, and the qualities of a human association by the qualities of its members. No two marriages and no two families will ever be found in which the same order obtains, for the simple reason that in the whole wide world there are no two married couples that are exactly alike, nor two sets of parents and children that are exactly alike. The family law of the Romans or of the Germans of the Frankish period was the general order of the Roman or of the Frankish family — an order which was not a creation of Roman or Frankish law but which arose directly out of the qualities and needs of the human beings who lived in these families. Were the eyes of the jurist trained to observe his own time as those of the legal historian are trained to observe past centuries and millennia, he could not possibly fail to see that our modern family law, too, is primarily an order that is not created by the precepts of the statute-book, but one that grows out of the needs of the human beings that live in families, and that it changes and develops according to these needs. What has been said of the family may self-evidently be said of every other association, of the state, of the commune, of the associations of employers and employees in the workshop and in the factory, of national and world economics, i.e. the form of the whole is always conditioned by the nature of its component parts. When men change in the course of time, their law changes with them. The great error of the jurists, even of those of the Historical School is that they are always inquiring into the development of the legal proposition. Let them get used to observing the development of the legal relations and of the legal institutions, and they will see that the legal propositions have developed with them though not even a comma has been changed.

All historical development of law is based on the fact that men and their relations to each other at any given time are of such marked individuality that they can be what they are at a given time only at that particular time, and that they therefore are subject to ceaseless change in the course of time. Within the short span of human life, the change as a rule is not sufficiently great to attract much attention, although there have always been old people who can tell how different all things were in their youth. But in the course of historical development minute changes grow into vast accumulations. The gulf that is fixed between the legal order of the Middle Ages and that of the modern period, vast though it may seem to us, owes its existence to the accumulation of minute changes, the significance of which probably not one of their contemporaries surmised.

That which is primarily subjected to ceaseless change is the distribution of power among the associations themselves, among the individuals that are members of the same association, and among the various associations that together constitute an association of a higher order. And every change in the relation of power necessarily effects a change in the social norms that obtain in the association. For the associations unite their members for the pursuit of common aims, and the norms that arise within them are, in the first place, merely an expression of that which the community, according to the views and moods that prevail within it, quite without justification perhaps, thinks the interest of the whole justifies it in requiring at the hands of the individuals and groups that it is composed of. But the individual in an association lives his own life, having his own ends in view; and where society has reached a more advanced stage of development, he is a member of several associations which make diverse and perhaps conflicting demands upon him. The norms of the community therefore are not only the sum but also the extreme limit of that which the community may demand of the individual, they constitute a compromise between the demands which the whole makes upon the individual and those which the individual makes upon the whole. And this compromise shifts continually according as the content or the effect of the forces within the association varies.

In my book on legal capacity I have shown that the mere fact that the family household as a self-sufficing economic establishment[1] was gradually disappearing necessarily put the whole family law upon an altogether new basis. As long as the household as an economic unit produces almost everything that the members of the household require, the members of the family remain at home; each member has a sphere of activity corresponding to his ability and his position, and is supplied with most of the things which he requires to keep body and soul together. The dissolution of the household as an economic establishment compels the members to leave the household, to seek their livelihood in the world, and with the returns from their labor to buy what they need to keep body and soul together outside of the home in the open market. For goods are no longer produced in the home but in the factory, in the workshop, in a different agricultural establishment. This emancipation from economic dependence upon the household frees the members of the household from the control of the head of the family; the economic struggle which every individual must now wage outside of the house gives him the economic and the psychological self-dependence which enables him to maintain his independence against the head of the household. This appears with the greatest possible clearness in the rights of the married woman, whose sphere of activity in the organized economy of the household was one of equality with that of the husband, but which she has lost, with the exception of a few insignificant remnants, thanks to the modern division of labor, and the modern economic systems of finance and credit. She therefore seeks a sphere of activity outside of the home,

1. self-sufficing economic establishment：自给自足经济体

and the limitations upon the legal capacity of women, which the German Civil Code has carried over to our time from a time long past, will undoubtedly be smashed by colliding with these simple facts. This was the fate of similar provisions in the French Civil Code, which, it must be admitted, was right in this, inasmuch as it came into existence at a time when the organized family household still possessed a considerable amount of vitality. As is well known, neither the French Civil Code nor the German Civil Code deny legal capacity to the married woman, but in actual fact the statutory matrimonial regime of each country practically reduces the married woman to a state of nonage. Nevertheless the married woman of France is as free and unrestrained in her movements as the married woman of any other country in the world. In his book "*La femme dans le ménage*[1]" Binet says on the subject: "*Les mceurs de notre pays nous offrent depuis longtemps le spectacle de L'épouse vaquant en toute liberté aux diverses opérations du ministére domestíque, sans qu'il vienne a I'esprit de personne de lui demander de justification du consentement marital. Et ce n'est pas là un des moins remarquables exemples de Fantinomie apparente, si souvent signalee chez nous, entre la loi et les mceurs, entre le droit et le fait.*[2]" Binet adds the words of Tissier, which he quotes from a report on the Societe deludes legislatives (Ire annee)[3]: "*I'elui qui, sur le role de la femme marieedans la famille en France, sur ses droits et ses pouvoirs concernant les intérêts pecuniaires du menage, ne connait que les textes de notre loi en a une idee certainement bien fausse, et on peut affirmer que ces textes ne sont plus en harmonie avec notre*

1. La femme dans le ménage：〈法〉《家庭中的妇女》
2. Les moeurs de notre pays ... le droit et le fait.：〈法〉依据我们国家的风俗，长期以来，都是妇女在从事各种家务劳动，然而，这是否合乎婚姻合意是值得质疑的。这是一个典型的法律与风俗、法律与事实相违背的例子。而这种违背，经常发生在我们身边。
3. report on the Société d'études legislatives (Ire année)：《社会立法研究报告》（第一章）

maniere de penser, ni avec notre manière de vivre.[1]" Without doubt the family law of the French Civil Code has been abrogated, in part, by new customary law.

From the law of property we shall adduce only the *Lieferungs und Gattungskauf*.[2] It was not known to the Romans. In the Middle Ages it is not found in Germany, at least in ordinary business dealings. When it first appeared in commercial life can not be readily ascertained; but in view of the peculiar nature of mediaeval commerce, at least in Germany, it is not to be assumed that it happened before the reception of the Roman law. Until that time the goods were regularly examined by the purchaser or his agent before the sale was concluded. At the beginning of the modern age it gained in importance, and Ulrich Zasius devotes one of his best known treatises to it. Since that time it has gradually become the transaction that prevails in business generally. One would look in vain for a precept that has introduced it into the legal system and has established its manifold and extremely complicated forms. This contract, which has impressed its stamp upon our whole legal life, came into use without the aid of a single legal proposition. It owes its existence almost exclusively to the rise of large-scale industry, to the introduction of regular postal service, to improved roads, improved facilities for the transportation of freight; and lastly, it owes its perfection of form to the railroads, to navigation, to the telegraph. Is not that new "customary law"?

All legal development therefore is based upon the development of society, and the development of society consists in this, that men and their relations change in the course of time. Other men will live and

---

1. Celui qui, sur le rôle ... maniere de vivre.:〈法〉我们的法律对已婚妇女在家庭中地位的规定，以及其在夫妻财产关系中的权利以及权力的规定，其观念是根本错误的。我们可以确信的是，这些规定已经不再符合我们的思想，也与我们的生活模式相违背。
2. *Lieferungs und Gattungskauf*:〈德〉指定种类的销售合同

have their being in other legal relations, and since legal relations are to a great extent based on legal transactions, new legal transactions will emerge in the course of time and the older ones will disappear. New associations will be formed, new kinds of contracts will be entered into, new kinds of declarations by last will and testament will be made. All of this must appear most palpably in the content of the legal document. The truth, well understood among legal historians, that the law of a given period must be found in the documents of the period has very rarely penetrated the consciousness of the jurist. The reason for this is the fact that he does not see the law, but only the legal proposition. The legal proposition which says that articles of association, contracts, declarations by last will and testament, are legally binding under certain circumstances has remained unchanged while the content of the contracts, testaments, articles of association, has changed. And for this reason the jurist thinks that the law has not changed. If this were true, only that could be called a change in the law which cannot be explained on the basis of the principle of liberty of contract, of testamentary disposition, and of association. But liberty of contract, of testamentary disposition, and of association are mere blank forms or set patterns. And for the very reason that they are merely blank forms or set patterns, the development of the law goes on, within their compass indeed, but not through them. When the Roman *pontifices*[1] for the first time put the testament into the form of a *mancipatio,* they thought perhaps that they had merely been applying the principle of liberty of contract, did not think that they had made a change in the existing law. As a matter of fact however they introduced a most momentous innovation into the law. They put a new picture into the old frame. It is true, a single arrangement or agreement in a contract, in articles of association, or in a will is not new law; for

1. *pontifices*：〈拉〉祭司

the law deals only with that which has a great vogue and which is a matter of customary practice. But a juristic act is never an individual, an isolated, thing; together with the greater part of its content, it is a part of the prevailing social order. The needs that occasion certain legal transactions, e.g. the creation of corporations, contracts, wills, are general social needs, and the means to satisfy these needs are as general as the needs themselves. Accordingly identical articles of ass ociation, contracts, testamentary declarations of will, occur again and again at a given period of time and in a given region — identical not only in content but also in wording. Nobody knew better than the Romans that the traditional content of the declarations of the parties are a part of the existing law. One glance will convince us that practically the whole contract law of the Digest, including the matrimonial regime and the law of pledge as well as the law of wills, is based upon the agreements and declarations that the parties are in the habit of making.

The situation is the same today. To a person who has any conception of the importance of the usufructuary lease in agriculture, a glance at the few meagre provisions of the Austrian or of the German Civil Code will suffice to convince him that they cannot possibly be sufficient to meet the needs of agriculture in Austria or Germany. It is a very superficially modernized law of the usufructuary lease of the Roman *latifundia*[1]. Shortly after the German Civil Code had become effective, Schumacher repeated Blomeyer's statement, made long before, that the contract of usufructuary lease ought to be drawn up in such form that no legislation would be required for the regulation of the legal relations between the lessor and the lessee. Whether there is any sense in enacting legislation of this kind, to avoid the consequences of which the parties must call in the aid of

1. *latifundia*：〈拉〉大地产

the notary, I shall not discuss here, but I would say that the course which German agriculture was to take had been clearly marked out for it quite independently of legislation. The question as to the form and the content of the contracts of usufructuary lease has been discussed repeatedly, and a small, extremely interesting and valuable literature has grown up on the subject, which, of course, the jurists know nothing of. A study of this literature reveals that the agricultural contract of usufructuary lease is an institution, which was carefully elaborated according to technical rules during the course of a century of development, and which possesses a degree of elasticity that enables it to conform to the existing status of the agricultural production of goods; that there are many forms, widely used in Germany, one of which, the one employed in the administration of the royal Prussian domains, possesses a great reputation, although it must be admitted that this reputation has often been impugned.

The law of agriculture offers another illustration. At the request of the German Agricultural Association, Professor Dr. Otto Gerlach, with the cooperation of Dr. Franz Mendelssohn and *Regierungsbaumeister* (architect to the government) Alfred Blum, has studied the workers' settlements in North Germany, and has published the results of his investigations in the reports of the German Agricultural Association. From it the jurist can learn first of all that there is a labor problem in agriculture, and that the future economic and social structure not only of Germany but of all Europe is conditioned upon its solution; that for more than a century, and to an ever increasing ext ent, with ever increasing methodicalness[1] and clarity of purpose, attempts have been making to solve it, chiefly by inducing workers to settle in the country; that these attempts have brought about various new kinds of agreements, i.e. pure contracts of usufructuary lease, contracts of

1. methodicalness：章法

usufructuary lease in connection with contracts for work and labor, and contracts of purchase and sale with special provisions. Perhaps all of these formations are still too heterogeneous and each kind too individual in its nature; but if they are not yet fully developed law, they are law in the process of becoming. Suppose that one of the many systems suggested and tried should meet all the requirements, and come into general use in all Germany or at least in a part of Germany, can there be any doubt that this, even without any legislative interference, which, as can readily be foreseen, would be quite superfluous, would bring about an enrichment not only of economic life but also of the law?

The reason why the law is in a perpetual state of flux is that men, whose relations the law is designed to regulate, are continually posing new problems for it to solve. The family and the marriage relation are not changing at the rate of one change in a century, as the printed histories of law seem to assume; it is a daily, an hourly change, and the great changes that history records are produced by the vast accumulation of these smaller changes. The concept of ownership, too, has been developing hitherto without ceasing, and continues to develop before our very eyes. Doubtless it is not all one, either economically and socially or legally, whether the owner of large tracts of land grants them to vassals or whether he hires a manager with a staff of assistants; whether he carries on with villeins or lets the estate to lessees well supplied with working capital; whether he conducts his economic undertaking according to the three-field system[1] or establishes sugar factories. Each of these methods of operation is subject to its own law, and whenever agriculture turns from one method to another, the law regulating it changes with it. Whether a waterfall turns the wheels of a modest little water mill or supplies an electric power

1. three-field system：三区轮作制

plant with hundreds of units of horsepower is not without a bearing upon the law and right of ownership thereof. The formal principle of liberty of contract cannot prevent the law and right of contract from changing when the contracts that have been customary until that time are being entered into with a new content which meets the new requirements. And the law of inheritance? Surely it is not immaterial whether one leaves a great proprietary estate or a factory, a mercantile establishment or millions in stocks or other securities. The enormous economic progress of our day, which has not yet run its course by any means, must exert the greatest possible influence not only upon the content of last wills and testaments and upon the division of estates in cases of intestate succession, but also upon the whole process of transfer of property *mortis causa.* The matrimonial regime of personal property under French law, the distinction made by English law between succession in case of real and of personal property, have been deprived altogether of their former significance by the fact that the importance of personal property, especially of the ownership of securities, has increased immeasurably during the course of the last century. This, too, proves that the great revolutionary changes in law do not take place in the legal propositions but in the social relations. Would anyone doubt that customary law can arise even now without the expressed permission of the legislator?

It is clear that as compared with the unceasing development of the social law, the rigid, immobile state law lags behind only too often. The law, whatever its form, is always a manner of rule of the dead over the living — to use Herbert Spencer's translation of Goethe's famous words. It is this, perhaps, that makes every collision with the state or its agencies an experience so painful to every person of refined sensibilities — the more painful, the more intimately the relation with which the state interferes is connected with his emotional life. This unpleasant situation becomes endurable only inasmuch as these collisions do not occur too frequently, and can be avoided as a rule by the exercise of a certain measure of care. Fortunately the great majority of men know the state, its courts, its agencies, and its law only from avoiding them. But there are others who see to it that the latter do not become superfluous altogether, and we must therefore discuss the question how the problem of this conflict is being solved in actual life.

To the extent that the law of society is being fitted into the frame of the traditional, especially the frame of liberty of contract, of association, of testamentary disposition, either directly or with the aid of the art and science of drawing up legal documents, it creates the norms for decision which it requires, and according to which it would be judged. The effect of contracts, of articles of association, and of testamentary dispositions is determined chiefly by their wording. In part this law goes beyond the literal meaning of the words, for, in the course of time, the course of judicial decision has learned to interpret them according to *bona fides, Treu und Glauben* (good faith), and according to business usage. This does not mean, as is usually believed, the unexpressed, surmised intent of the parties but the social and economic relation to which these declarations of will belong. *Bona fides, Treu und Glauben,* and business usage accordingly become not only sources of the living social law, but also sources of norms for decision and finally of legal propositions.

It is otherwise where the change has taken place outside of the forms of the established state law. In that case the law is not touched by the change; its norms of administrative action and for decision remain unaltered. The great never-ending task of juristic science is to resolve the conflict between the changing demands of life and the words of the established law. For this purpose it has developed its own technique in its most important branches, to wit the branch dealing with the art of drafting legal documents, that dealing with the work of the attorney, and that dealing with the work of the judge. It is by no means the same everywhere. It was one thing among the Romans; it is another at the present time on the Continent on one hand, and in the territory of the Anglo-American law on the other. It would be an error to suppose that the means adapted to the accomplishment of this purpose have been found once for all. On the Continent juristic science still operates in part with certain very flexible concepts of traditional law and in part with a still more arbitrary and whimsical construction of the whole content of the code. And the chief cause of the movement toward free finding of law is the susceptibility to attack and the insincerity of these methods, which are always seeking, by stealth, to reach a predetermined, definite, desired result, by interpreting the words of a statute the meaning of which is contrary to the result sought. Wherever state law is applied to cases which the legisla tor did not definitely have in mind, it must needs be subjected to a process of revaluation. It would be superfluous to enter upon a discussion of this whole problem since it has recently been made the subject of a brilliant presentation in Wurzel's book entitled "Das juristische Denken[1]," perhaps the best book that has appeared on the Continental juristic method of the present time. Wurzel calls this process "projection," i.e. application of a juristic concept of the legal proposition as it has been formulated, without any change, to phenomena which were not within the contemplation of the proposition or, at any rate, were not demonstrably so. In public law, Jellinek has treated these phenomena as changes of the com stitution.

Juristic projection in its essence is merely the immediate effect of the inner changes in the life of society upon the norms for decision. Without this process of projection, to which resort must be had by the jurist every day and every hour, administration of justice would be utterly unthinkable under state law; particularly in view of the present absolute sway of the latter. Without it, it would have been altogethei

1. Das juristische Denken：〈德〉《法学思维》

impossible to retain the traditional constitutional law, the state private and administrative law of the stormy movement which is under way in society at the present time, and with which legislation is altogether unable to keep pace. To a great extent, it is true, this retention is apparent only. Large-scale industry, railroads, telegraphs, and telephones have imposed new tasks upon the administration of justice and upon civil administration. Unequal to the unaccustomed labor of free finding of law, they made shift by projecting the traditional norms of state law, as well as they could, upon the new relations. A similar thing is going on before our very eyes today. About a quarter of a century ago large-scale industry gained control over a new source of power, electricity. This, without more, imports new social law, but new state law will not fail to appear. The *arretisles* in France who are writing the commen taries in the great collections of judicial decisions by Dalloz and Sirey are concerned at the present time with the development of the law contained in the judicial decisions, which is essentially a projection of the law upon new facts of life.

Projection is midway between application of law and finding of law. Now it partakes to greater extent of the nature of the former, now of the latter. Apart from the cases in which the judicial activity is something quite different from application of law, even in the cases in which it actually is application of law, it is a creative act on the part of the judge. But a creative act presupposes a creative mind. When the administration of justice is unequal to this task, it becomes a dead weight upon legal life. When the Austrian court of cassation, without stating the legal grounds for its action, as it usually does even in its best decisions, found a man guilty of abduction who had bought a railroad ticket for a woman who was fleeing from the brutalities of her husband, it rendered a decision which is felt by every jurist like a blow in the face. Still all that is lacking in this case is a projection in time and space. In a state of slaveholders a decision of this kind would be quite in order; for everyone would be convinced that it is not permissible to help a slave make good his escape. In fact as long as slavery existed in the southern states of the United States of America, i.e. until the war of abolition, such an act was properly punishable there. The Romans, it is true, although they were a nation of slaveholders entertained milder views than the southern states and our court of cassation. A person who *misericordia ductus*[1] freed a slave who had been chained could not be held liable in an *actio doll,*[2] which was penal in its nature, and condemnation in which subjected the party to infamy, but only in an *actio in factum* for damages.

The sway of social forces brings about a continual shifting of the boundaries between the law of society and the law of the state. Interests which had been protected only by norms of social law obtain the protection of state legal norms as soon as their importance is more perfectly understood. A change of this sort can be brought about by judicial decision; the judge, acting solely in the capacity of a functionary of the state, projects a social norm as a state norm upon legal relations to which it did not originally refer. An instructive case of this kind is the defense of gaming. Originally based upon a social norm for decision, it began to take on the character of state law during the last quarter of the last century; in part this was brought about by state legislation and in part by judicial decision, since the courts avail themselves of this defense in order to curb the activities of persons not entitled to operate on the stock exchange. In my book, *Das twingenie und nicht zwingende Recht im Burgerlichen Gesetzbuch*[3], I have endeavored to show how numerous regulations of the Civil Code which were intended to be social regulations must become state regulations as soon as the public becomes aware of the social interests involved.

---

1. *misericordia ductus*：〈拉〉受同情心支配
2. *actio doli*：〈拉〉欺诈之诉
3. *Das zwingende und nicht zwingende Recht im Bürgerlichen Gesetzbuch*：〈德〉《德国民法典中的强行法与非强行法》

This explains how it came about that many a rule of law was received from the law of society into the law of the state without any external change, purely as the result of moral or social changes. The family law powers which in Rome originally were a matter of private law and right similar to the law and right of ownership lose this characteristic quality, in part, as early as the days of the Empire. This is true especially of guardianship. And in modern law the *patria potestas* is gradually being converted into a public office. A large part of the law of contracts, especially the law of the contract of labor, is being converted into state law before our very eyes. The oldest Roman penal law was state law only inasmuch as it was applicable to *parricidium*[1] and *perduellio*[2] although the private law proceeding could often lead to a punishment as severe as that of public law. But this private penal law was displaced by public law to a great extent in the days of the Republic and to a still greater extent during the days of the Empire. The right of the husband to kill his adulterous spouse and her paramour, which has been recognized indirectly at least by the *Code pénal* (Art. 374 Al. *2,* and cf. Art. 375), is the last trace, perhaps, of private penal law to be found in a modern penal code. It may possibly assert itself much more strongly in judicial decisions, especially in jury trials. A French prosecuting attorney stated only a very short time ago that a wife who had killed her husband's paramour must be found guilty because she had not selected the right victim, the husband.

The assumption of control over civil procedure by the state is of great interest inasmuch as the impulse that was causing this change was not supplied by the legal proposition but by the changing ideas of men concerning the function of the administration of justice by the state. This change is a process that extends over thousands of years. Originally legal procedure was "organized self-help," and it

---

1. *parricidium*：〈拉〉弑亲罪
2. *perduellio*：〈拉〉叛国罪

remained self-help in essence as long as its basic principle was the idea of a transaction between the parties. The state assumed control over penal procedure at an early date. Roman procedural law in the formulary procedure, and still more so in the *cognitiones,* contained a few isolated elements that may be said to be state law. These however disappear at a later time in the procedure of the Continental common law. This seems to indicate that in some respects human society in the last century had not advanced as far as that of the Romans. Since the eighteenth century the thought is making its way more and more, in legal science at least, that procedure is a part of state law. This is the period of the *Preussische Allgemeine Gerichtsordnung*[1], the first departure from the principle of a transaction between the parties, the first great attempt, even though it was undertaken with insufficient means, to convert not only the administration of law and penal procedure but also civil procedure into a matter of state law. The Austrian revision was the first attempt to establish a procedure which in most respects would be a true state law procedure, not merely in respect of administration. It sought definitively to subject the administration of law to the purposes of the state. The resistance that was encountered by the departure from the old idea of a transaction between the parties, an idea that had not a single consideration of expedience to support it, is an echo of the primeval legal ideas of the human race in the midst of the whirl of modern life.

How this inner change takes place within the legal institutions and the norms for decision is a question we can discuss only in a most general way. Doubtless a great deal of it goes on in the subconscious mind. A large part of the social norms has not been formulated in words once for all time, but must continually be abstracted anew from the regular, universally approved, actual course of human conduct.

1. *Preussische Allgemeine Gerichtsordnung*：〈德〉《普鲁士普通法院规则》

This is true without qualification in the case of the norms of morality, ethical custom, good breeding, tact. It is impossible to state any basis for them other than the fact that they have been acted upon with universal approbation. And in the case of the legal norm the situation often is the same. A number of rules of law are based upon precedents. The importance of the *Konventionalregel* in public law has been set forth by the Jellinek school, especially by Hatschek, in a very thorough manner. It seems to me that this rule very frequently is a legal norm, but a norm which has been abstracted from actually approved conduct. Such norms, which are based on the general conception of actual conduct, are not only being confirmed by every new course of actual conduct, but are apparently being supplemented or are experiencing a change of content. The insignificant divergencies involved at first remain unnoticed and the parties concerned imagine that the old rule still obtains; but in the course of time they accumulate to such an extent that the original legal institution is converted into something quite different. So it has happened more than once that, thanks to a slight shift in the norms, slavery became villeinage and villeinage became slavery. So a self-serving guardianship was converted into one requiring care and protection; the trustee transaction, into pledgeright and testament; the bilateral *real* contracts, into consensual contracts; *Vorleisiung* (prior performance)/ into a simulated performance (*Arrha*).

Even the wording itself is affected by the lapse of time. It often happens that norms that have been formulated in words receive not merely a new interpretation but a new wording. This too can be done quite without the knowledge of the person introducing the change; for the language of men involuntarily follows their new lines of thought. Quite properly therefore Girard has shown, by way of reply to Lambert, that from the fact that the wording of the propositions of the Twelve Tables, as transmitted to us by tradition, could not possibly have been in existence at the time of the decemvirs, it does not follow that the Twelve Tables were not in existence at all. In the course of the centuries they may have received not only a new meaning but also a new wording suited to the new meaning. And he directs attention to the fact that many of the *brocards*[1] of Loisel have a wording which is quite different from that of the time of the ancient jurist, and that Lambert himself writes: "La caution n'est pas solvable[2]," although the original wording was "La caution n'est pas bourgeoise[3]."

The conscious act of an individual, may participate in the development of law, even though it is usually forgotten within a very short time. The idea of Tarde's that all human progress is based upon an invention made by an individual and upon the imitation of this invention by the great mass of the people is one of those self-evident things that, once they have been enunciated, constitute important scientific knowledge. If the question is asked why the Romans did not permit representation in legal transactions, the reply must be that it had to be invented at some time or other, just like the locomotive. The Historical School which taught that the law was created by the people doubtless was wrong as to this point. There was always one person who did it first; the others followed. One must not, however, even in this matter of invention, over-estimate that which is individual, for it, too, is conditioned upon social presuppositions. The art of pottery, the bow and arrow, the rowboat, and the sailing-vessel, without doubt, were invented thousands of years ago quite independently in different parts of the world. For just as long a time it has been the desire of men to be able to soar in the air like birds, but this desire was not realized before the present century, and then in several places at the same time. An invention is not the deed of an individual, but a deed of society through an individual. The individual performs it as soon as society has supplied the conditions which make the deed possible. We do not

1. *brocards*：〈法〉法律格言
2. La caution n'est pas solvable：〈法〉保证人没有清偿能力。
3. La caution n'est pas bourgeoise：〈法〉保证人不是有产者。

owe the invention to a man sent by Providence. The inventive thought will spring up in every mind that has received sufficient training as soon as the requisite conditions exist. These conditions are, among others, a certain amount of knowledge of the laws of nature, a certain mastery of technique, a certain degree of economic development, which enables the inventor to provide himself with the necessary aids and appliances. The extended use of an invention, too, is conditioned upon certain presuppositions. The fifteenth century would have been unable to build railroads because the necessary capital was not in existence at the time, and, perhaps, also because they would have been believed to be the work of the devil. Where the social presuppositions are lacking, i.e. the economic development and the general appreciation, an invention must fail, like the invention of the steam engine by Denis Papin. The tragedy of the lot of the inventor lies in this fact, that the social presuppositions for the invention and for the appreciation of it by society very often do not coincide. For quite simple inventions like pottery, the bow and arrow, the rowboat, and the sailing-vessel, all presuppositions were in existence thousands of years ago. For the flying-machine, they were first supplied by our century.

The greater number of juristic inventions probably are found among those the presuppositions for which were in existence at an early time and in many places. They are to be found therefore in all parts of the world, like pottery, the rowboat, and the sailingvessel. But there are some legal transactions, norms for decision, and procedural forms that require a great measure of independent conscious labor such as can be performed only by specially trained minds. They are the creations of jurists of a scientific bent, of judges, attorneys, and practitioners of the art of drafting legal documents. *Multis vigiliis excogitata et inventa*[1],

1. *Multis vigiliis excogitata et inventa*：〈拉〉很多认知与创造性的思考

Bracton says of the *Assisa novae disseisinae*[1], the pioneering feat of Henry II. From this point of view, we may say, it is not an error when the various peoples attribute their laws to a personal lawgiver. They are merely symbolizing the many long-forgotten workmen who took part in their creation. And this fact makes the reception of a foreign legal system possible. A reception actually transfers into foreign countries only norms for decision, model forms for contracts and for articles of association, procedural precepts, which have been invented elsewhere. This is done by means of judicial decision, drafting of legal documents, juristic literature, and, occasionally, legislation. It is a characteristic feature of our time however that a great deal of that which, in the past, was done by the jurist of a scientific bent, by the attorney, by the draftsman of legal documents, is, at the present time, generally assigned to the legislator. It is considered the function of the legislator to create norms for decision, model forms for contracts, for articles of association, for societies and corporations. Indeed all modern procedure is created by legislation. It is difficult to determine what may be the causal relation; at any rate it is by no means a gratifying phenomenon. It brings about a onesidedness and a retardation of legal development, and, to a quite unnecessary degree, delivers the state into the hands of those who at a given time are in power.

It seems however that a change is imminent, that today much less is expected of legislation by the state than a decade ago, that there is much more insistence upon limiting its power and a much greater demand that the state stop and reflect upon itself, its functions, and its duties. This must be attributed to a growing understanding of what can be effected and promoted by the means which the state has at its disposal. But the question as to the present-day extent of the sphere

1. *Assisa novae disseisinae*：〈拉〉恢复新近被占土地之令状

of authority of the state and, incidentally, of the statute, is a quite different one. The presentday conception of the state is that of an omnipotence which is contemplated with a certain religious awe, and against which resistance is as impossible as it is impermissible. It is easily demonstrable that this omnipotence is historically conditioned throughout and is based chiefly on the military powers which the state possesses at the present time. Whenever there is a possibility of the state being confronted by another military power within its own territory, as was the case during the days of feudalism, the state is not conceived of as omnipotent. But even today its irresistible power is limited to such things as can be accomplished by means of military power. As a purely social organization the state is but one of many, and, apart from the military power, has only social powers at its disposal, which are by no means superior at all times to those of the other social associations.

The classical school of economists, basing its teachings upon the doctrines of the physiocrats[1], has subjected the question of the limitations upon the power of the state and of the consequences of state activity, especially of legislation, to a thorough and exhaustive examination. This examination showed that the laws of economics, which, in the view of this school, to a great extent comprise many social processes of a non-economic nature, impose limitations upon the activity of the st ate beyond which the state may not go, and, beyond which, to a certain extent, it cannot go. It cannot go beyond them without obtaining results that are contrary to its intention; it cannot go beyond them without beating the air. They have also successfully demonstrated that he who can issue a command that a certain measure be taken does not thereby have the power to control its effects. These investigations laid a solid foundation for modern

1. physiocrats：重农主义者

social science. For the latter comes into being as soon as that which goes on in society is referred not to the will of the human being who is acting but to the forces which are acting independently of him in society, just as the beginning of the natural sciences is the knowledge that the processes of nature must be explained not as being caused by the will of the gods but by the forces of nature. If these suggestions had been followed, they would have led to an art of legislation resting on a scientific foundation. As it is, the results of these investigations have long since been forgotten. As a result, legislation is characterized by a most naive dilettantism, which is satisfied in its own mind that all that is necessary in order to abolish an existing evil is to forbid it.

XVIII THE CODIFICATION OF JURISTIC LAW

The *Corpus iuris chills* contains a text-book (the *Institutes*), excerpts from juristic writings (the Digests), and constitutions (the Code), i.e. it contains in the first place juristic literature both in the form of a text-book and in the form of excerpts from works on the existing law, and a collection of statutes. But only a very small part of the excerpts from the writings of the Roman jurists purports to limit itself to a presentation of the law contained in the *praetorian* edict, the *leges,* and the *constitutiones*[1]. The greater part establishes legal norms independently. Their content therefore is juristic law, which, in part, has been presented in literary form, and, in part, appears in the form of responses and decisions. The older imperial constitutions are chiefly decisions of law cases, and therefore they also are juristic law; some, the *mandata*[2], are commands addressed to imperial officials, and therefore are administrative regulations. The later ones however are statutes in the narrower sense of the term, i.e. "state law," which provide what is to be law in the future. In addition there are *leges, senatusconsulta, constitutiones*[3], i.e. statutes, which contain state law. They are being cited in all parts of the *corpus iuris.* The praetorian edict, which also constitutes a large part, is either juristic law or state law, the latter containing chiefly police regulations. The work

---

1. the *leges*, and the *constitutiones*：法律与谕令（斜体为拉丁文）
2. *mandata*：〈拉〉训示
3. *leges, senatusconsulta, constitutiones*：〈拉〉法律、元老院决议、谕令

of Justinian therefore comprises juristic literature (text-book and literary presentation), juristic law (in the form of literary presentation, responses of jurists, and judgments of the praetor and of the Emperor), and state law (*leges, senatus consulta, edict, constitutiones*).

According to the prevailing view, all of this has been fused into a unit by the will of Justinian, and has become a code. But the various parts of the *corpus iuris* have met widely different fates in the course of time. The parts which at the outset did not contain legal propositions but legal science, i.e. discussions of the nature of law, sources, divisions, system, definitions, content of rights, have remained what they were from the beginning, i.e. a science of law. In so far as it has proved itself to be scientific doctrine, it has gained recognition even in countries in which it has never been received as the law of the land; it dominates the general theory of law even among the English, the Americans, and the Scandinavians. And the juristic law has become, and has remained, the basis of the common law of most of the civilized nations of the Continent of Europe to the present day. On the other hand that part of it which is state law has, in the main, gradually been eliminated. This applies to those parts of the edict that chiefly contained police regulations and to those imperial constitutions that do not, like many a novel of Justinian, simply modify and replace juristic law.

But though Justinian collected propositions of such diverse descent into a code, he was not thereby enabled to fuse them into a unitary mass. Even within the code they retained the stamp of their origin. Manifestly this fact was of very great influence upon their history. Moreover, a more detailed examination would show how widely they differ in structure and efifect.

To form a correct estimate of a modern code, particularly of one of the private law codes of the territory in which the Continental common law used to be in force, the Prussian Code, the French Civil Code, the Austrian Civil Code, and, lastly, the German Civil Code, one must subject it to the kind of examination that the *corpus iuris* by its very outward form challenges one to subject it to. One must separate its three parts from one another, i.e. science of law, juristic law, and state law. In doing this one must of course not fail to observe that juristic law does not cease to be juristic law, does not become state law, simply because it was modified, made milder, adapted to the existing situations, or even found anew, when it was received into the code; for in doing this, the jurist is not working as a legislator but as a jurist. There is a very palpable difference between the provisions of the German Civil Code on the liability of innkeepers, which have been made more rigorous, and the regulation of associations that do not have legal capacity; between the provisions of the French Civil Code that title shall pass at the time the contract is made (*contra* to the rule of the Continental common law[1]), and the precepts as to civil marriage or civil death (*Ja mort civile*). Moreover juristic science in Germany has, to a certain extent at least, prepared the way for a critical analysis of the content of the codes such as is suggested here. The doctrine of the non-obligatory content of a statute applies particularly to the purely scientific elements in a statute, and it has succeeded in causing them to disappear almost altogether from the German Civil Code. This cannot be said of juristic law and of st ate law, although Savigny has brought out the distinction most clearly. In his *Beruf*[2] he most emphatically directs attention to the "two-fold element in the law," the "political" and the "technical," As an example of the former, he cites the *lex Julia et Papia Poppaea*[3]*;* the latter is the "whole legal store, or capital," that which is law without having been enacted.[3] The further elaboration of this distinction by Savigny shows that it coincides with the distinction

1. *contra* to the rule of the Continental common law：与欧陆共同法的规则相对
2. *Beruf*：〈德〉《论当代立法和法学的使命》
3. *lex Julia et Papia Poppaea*：〈拉〉巴比与波培法

between state law and juristic law.

The sifting of state law from juristic law in the modern codes would be a task not only of great scientific but also of great practical importance. It would not be difficult today; for by this time we have pretty accurate knowledge of the sources from which the codes have drawn their materials. They are the content of the Continental common law as it existed at the time and in the country in which the code originated, the indigenous law of the time and country, and the law of nature.

The chief constituent part of the codes everywhere is the Continental common law. For the most part, the common law, which had been received on the Continent of Europe during the Middle Ages and in the modern period, had remained a mere norm for decision for the courts. But one must not limit the importance of the Continental common law to this. Modern investigations have shown that the legal document, especially the notarial document, which, self-evidently, was based on the Italian formbooks, had adapted itself very readily to the common law in every country. Thereby a great deal of the Continental common law became part and parcel of everyday life, became the living law in the territory in which it was valid. The nations of the Continent of Europe are indebted to the Continental common law for the last will and testament, and it can be shown that it was the lawyers who drew up the legal documents that transmitted it to them in the Roman form. It is true the last will and testament would have come into vogue even if conveyancers had not introduced it, albeit in a somewhat different form. But this cannot be said of the Roman law of contracts. In virtue of the fact, and only in virtue of the fact, that the Roman law of contracts as developed in the Continental common law has been made the basis of the legal document, the Continentai common law system of contracts, the fundamental principles of which are Roman, has attained such a preeminent position in the modern legal consciousness that we are inclined today to look upon the

Roman contracts as understood by the Continental common law as something that is, in a certain sense, self-evident. Nevertheless a glance at the mediaeval German legal sources, especially at the documents dating from the time before the reception, shows that, in Germany and France at least, the law of contracts would have developed along entirely different lines had there been no reception — probably along lines similar to those of the development in England. And lastly, as a consequence of the reception, the fixed and clear juristic terminology and the whole juristic technique of the Continental common law juristic science has become part and parcel of the Continental common law everywhere. All of this has exerted a profound influence upon the codes.

The second const it uent part of the codes are the legal propositions taken from the codifications of the indigenous law. The various *Landrechte* (laws of the various states) and the revisions in the sixteenth century in Germany as well as the official statements of the *coutumes*[1] in France at the end of the fifteenth century have been of great importance for later legislation. They are not merely official statements in writing of the indigenous law of France and of Germany that had been in use until that time. The revisions, it is true, were drawn up, in part at least, by jurists who had a knowledge of the indigenous law; and the laws of the various states and the *cotdumes* were based on information given to the authors by experts in the indigenous law; the official drafting of the French *coutumes,* in particular, was done with extreme care. But only a very small part of this information stated legal propositions that had previously been formula ted, and that the persons who gave the information knew in that form. For the most part they were formulated by these persons on the basis of individual impressions at the moment they gave the information. They are

1. *coutumes*：〈拉〉习惯法

therefore universalizations of actual observation of indigenous legal relations, made by the persons who gave the information at the very moment of giving it. We know furthermore that the persons who drew up the statements, in many instances, modified the law intentionally, mitigated its rigors, supplemented it, and, in particular, attempted to assimilate it to Roman law. Apart from this, many rules were taken directly from Roman law and from other statements of law. The *Constitutiones Saxonicae*[1] professedly purported, not to codify existing law, but to harmonize it with the common law of the Continent. One cannot therefore unqualifiedly say that the codifications of the fifteenth, sixteen th, and seventeenth cent uries were codifications of the then valid German law. If by law we do not mean the legal relations but the legal propositions, it would be more nearly correct to say that practically all the law contained in these works came into existence through the codification. Thereby it became juristic law as to form and content. The revisions in the cities, the laws of the states (*Landrechte*), and the *coutumes* owe their existence in part to universalization, and in part to juristic finding of norms such as undoubtedly can be found elsewhere both in the juristic writings of the Romans and in those of mediaeval German writers.

The third kind of material that entered into the modern codes is the law of nature. It is customary to consider the law of nature as a defense set up by the German legal consciousness against the invading Roman law. This view contains a great deal of truth, but it is not the whole truth. For the teachers of natural law, beginning with Pufendorf at least, were practical and theoretical economists, not jurists, and represented, at first unconsciously perhaps, later consciously, the claims and demands of the urban middle classes. The final expression of the natural law movement is by no means to be found in the

---

1. *Constitutiones Saxonicae*：〈拉〉《萨克森法规集》

writings of the juristic ideologists of Germany and France, but in the writings of the French physiocrats whose demands and doctrines, were, in many instances, anticipated in Germany by Pufendorf and Wolf. The urban middle class is the class which was engaged in the trades and in commerce in the seventeenth and eighteenth centuries, and which was just beginning to turn to industrialism. It was already making political demands albeit they were rather modest in Germany. They demanded a powerful state, participation in the power of the state, and a weakening of the power of the feudal nobility.

These demands explain the absolutist trend of the older, especially of the German, teachers of natural law; but the call for an absolute form of government was merely an outward disguise for a developing tendency of much wider scope. The monarch alone was able at this time to create a powerful state; he alone was able to break the power of the nobility. The middle classes of the population could enter into a direct relation with the state, whose embodiment to them at the time was the monarch, only through absolutism[1]. The absolutist welfare state, of the German natural law teachers in particular, is the state which aids commerce, trade, and industry, increases the population, and by so doing provides workmen for commerce, trade, and industry, forcibly curbs enemies of the latter at home, provides legal security and protection against foreign enemies. As is well known, the later teachers of natural law gave up these ideas and demanded constitutionalism in the English sense, and finally, popular sovereignty. In so far at least as all of this was the case, the teachers of natural law surely were not combating the Roman law but feudalism. In doing this they were not espousing the cause of German law but were striving for a political and legal order different from that which was in effect at the time.

But for legislation the economic demands of the urban middle

1. absolutism：专制政体

classes are much more important than the poUtical ones. It was these that were chiefly making for a reorganization of the private law by means of the codes. The endeavors of the teachers of natural law, along this line also, were directed chiefly against feudalism, which interfered with and hindered trade and commerce in the country, and, to a certain extent, in the city also, by means of proscriptive rights and of restrictions of trade, withdrew the peasant from the sphere of the interests of the middle classes, restricted his working power in the interest of the landowner, and made it impossible to utilize it for the purposes of industry. Over and above this, however, they were bent upon the establishment of a legal order, based on liberty of contract and freedom of commerce, which should overthrow the restrictions placed on free activity, and abolish inequalities before the law between classes and localities.

The efforts of the urban middle classes suggested a legislative policy to the teachers of natural law, as their spokesmen, which indeed was in conflict with the existing order inasmuch as the latter restricted the free activity of the individual. Individualism became the ideal of the teachers of natural law, i.e. a system under which the individual, unhampered by class distinctions (equality before the law), can do with his own as he will, and is bound only by contracts voluntarily entered into. That this ideal entailed new and very great obligations, they did not see as yet, and in fact could not see at that time. But they imagined that this very ideal had been realized in Roman law. In so far as Roman law recognizes oppressive class distinctions — binds and fetters the individual by means of public law, penal criminal law, and family law — it usually was not received. All that remained of Roman law was abstract ownership, a soil free from burdens and divisible, liberty of contract, and an essentially equal right of inheritance. These were also the principles of the natural law legislative policy, which from the very beginning had put on the garb of an individualistic legal philosophy. Within the framework of free ownership and liberty of contract, the urban middle classes were able to create most of the legal institutions which they required for their future development. Wherever therefore the teachers of natural law — by way of exception — make a more detailed statement of their law, they create it by means of abstraction from the existing institutions of the urban middle classes in the manner in which Wolf created his law of bills of exchange, or they formulate it according to the wishes of the urban middle classes. They transform the wishes of the middle classes into legal propositions, somewhat in the manner in which the lawyer who draws up a legal document expresses the wishes of his client in the conditions of the contract.

The law of nature went one step beyond this, for it was actually bent upon creating its own particular legal system, in particular its own private law, based upon an individualist idea of justice. The principles of individualist liberty of ownership and liberty of contract, as expressed in the abstract concept of ownership and in the system of contract of the Continental common law in the service of the as yet very limited traffic in goods of the seventeenth and eighteenth centuries; in addition thereto, the traditional morality of middle-class family life; the idea of the right of the owner to dispose of his property beyond the grave carried out to its logical conclusion by means of last will and testament; and the idea of a right of inheritance, intended for the time being for the nearest relatives, and equal among equally close relatives — these indeed are a basis sufficiently broad for them to develop a system of private law upon, in broad outlines at least, and often with an almost mathematical precision. The attempt of the law of nature school to do this manifestly amounted to a finding of norms, i.e. juristic science. It is true, it was a juristic science which was based, in the main, on the living law, and whose relation to the existing law was one of comparative freedom, but, by no means, of absolute independence; for it presupposed the existing social and economic order which, for the most part, has arisen and taken shape under the influence of the existing law.

Accordingly Roman law was more in harmony with the teachings of the Natural Law School than any other system of law, especially ancient German law, could be. With few exceptions, therefore, among these perhaps Thomasius[1], they did not by any means oppose Roman law; on the contrary, they generally were adherents of it. They never tired of emphasizing that Roman law, in its essence, is natural law, or that it differs from the latter only in unimportant details. It must be admit ted however that in spite of this the content of Roman law did not fully satisfy the needs of society in the seventeenth and eighteenth centuries and that a few changes would have been very welcome indeed. But it is not so much the principles of German law that bring the teachers of natural law into occasional conflict with Roman law as the demands of a new era. Offense was not taken at the content, but at the form, of Roman law. What the teachers of natural law were impugning and desired to modify was this cumbersome, voluminous code in a foreign language, utterly lacking clearness of arrangement, weighted down by a mass of material long since antiquated, trailed by a vast juristic literature and interminable controversial questions, among which no jurist, much less a layman, could find his way. Hotomanus, the actual originator of the idea of codification, in his day demanded a brief code, which meets the requirements of the administration of justice, is drawn up in language that is within the grasp of an ordinary intellect, does away, once for all, with the controversial questions, and offers a clear and fair solution of every case that may arise.

Still the teachers of natural law have been successful in advancing juristic technique by one important step. It was impossible indeed to derive legal propositions of any appreciable utility from the

---

1. Thomasius：托马西乌斯（1655—1728），德国法学家与哲学家。

principles of natural law, which were merely the principles of an individualistic property and contract law; but the tendency to derive law from principles made it easier for them to discern what is basic, in the existing law at least. The teachers of natural law perceived an important truth at the outset which the Continental common law had failed to observe until then, to wit that a considerable part of the sources of Roman law merely contains particular applications of legal norms of a much more general tenor, and that a code could be made much briefer, much more easily comprehensible, by including only the general legal propositions and omitting the particular applications. They took it to be their chief function therefore to find these general legal propositions, which, they believed, the Romans had simply derived from the law of nature; and their theory permitted them simply to exclude from the system of natural law any decision which did not suit them, on the ground that it was a deviation from the law of nature. Their method of proceeding was based indeed on a considerable lack of understanding of the heterogeneous tendencies that necessarily run counter to each other within a legal system and of that which is positive and historically given therein, but it was also based upon the valid, good, and new thought, as its true content, that there are general principles in law upon which the individual decisions are based and that exceptional features are not to be accepted without more ado, but are to be examined as to their bases. This is a reliable criterion according to which they were able to eliminate those elements from the positive law that were merely arbitrary exceptions or survivals which can only be explained historically.

The doctrine of the natural law school therefore is, primarily, a criticism of the form and, secondarily, a criticism of the content of Roman law. The latter is leveled generally and essentially at matters of secondary importance. It became authoritative for the later form of the tiny code, which is divided into brief chapters and lays down general principles only. It did not contain very much positive material, and this was taken, in part, from the German legal consciousness, in part from the institutions of commerce, trade, and large-scale industry, which was coming into existence at that time. In other words it arose from the institutions of the urban middle classes in all these fields.

Lastly the teachers of the law of nature taught out-and-out[1] individualistic juristic law. Not being practical jurists, they did not enter upon a discussion of details. They had a general picture in their minds of what they were demanding, but they were unable to propose a practically applicable system of juristic law as a substitute for the Continental common law. Law of this kind does not spring from discussions of legislative policy, but only from the administration of justice, from the decision of individual practical law cases. Even Wolf, who more than any other teacher of the law of nature concerned himself with detailed problems, does not state true legal propositions, but sets up demands as to economic policy, legislative policy, and social policy; according to the idea of the *Wohlfahrtsstaat* (state promoting the public welfare), which, together with those things that he simply borrowed from the existing law and a critique of Roman law, constitute the principal content of his prolix book.

The building stones, then, which were used in the construction of the codes of the end of the eighteenth and the beginning of the nineteenth century were: *first,* the Continental common law juristic science; *secondly,* the legal propositions of indigenous law which were contained in the law of each of the various states (*Landrechte*[2]), the revisions, and the *coutumes,* and *lastly,* the demands of the teachers of the law of nature. The first two are chiefly juristic law. The law of nature, being juristic law also and, in addition, a critique, from the point of view of legislative policy of the existing feudal law and of juristic law, contained no legal material of its own. It did however

1. out-and-out：彻头彻尾的
2. *Landrechte*：〈德〉国家法

exert a decisive influence upon the external form of the codes.

In these three codes these constituent elements are mixed in varying proportions. The Prussian Code, private law only being considered, contains more Roman law than the others; the French Civil Code, the greatest number of provisions taken from indigenous law (the *coutumes*); the Austrian Civil Code is dominated chiefly by the law of nature. There is very little of actual state law to be found in any of them. The codes, then, in the main, contain juristic law put into statutory form; they are statutory juristic law. This shows wherein lay their chief significance for the development of law. The men who drew them up knew quite well, and Savigny knew, that their function was not to create new law but to organize the existing law and put it into suitable form, to eliminate that which had become antiquated, and here and there to adapt the part that was valid to new needs. In the words of Savigny "the existing law is to be recorded, with such modifications and emendations as may be necessary for political reasons."

Although the German Civil Code was composed a century later, it bears the same stamp as the eighteenth-century codes. The juristic science on which it is based is indeed younger by a century than that of the other codes, but after all it is merely the science of the Continental common law — younger by a century. Apart from this, thanks chiefly to Gierke's influence, it contains much German private law; this, too, in the form of juristic law, as it was fashioned by the Germanists of the last century in their textbooks and handbooks of German private law. For this reason it is much more important to emphasize its relation to the law of nature. In form and content it realizes the demands of the teachers of the law of nature much more completely than any previous code, and the reason why this fact has been overlooked so often is that the demands of the teachers of natural law, meanwhile, have become self-evident commonplaces. Accordingly in the sphere of intellectual endeavor the greatest success comes when the truth becomes a commonplace.

A characteristic of the Roman juristic law which has been handed down in the *corpus iuris* is the fact that it is judicial juristic law exclusively. The Roman art and science of drawing up legal documents seems to have had no influence whatever upon the sources of Justinian, which do indeed concern themselves with the content of documents, not, however, with the question how they are to be drawn up, but how the controversies that arise from them are to be decided. The juristic science of the Continental common law, however, was, in a great measure, a science of legal documents. The latter plays a particularly important role in the writings of the commentators, who are continually putting the question how the document must be drawn up in order to avoid this or that undesirable legal consequence. In the writings of the German and the French jurists of the seventeenth and eighteenth centuries, however, this point of view is being emphatically relegated into the background; they concern themselves, just like the teachers of natural law, chiefly with judicial law. Nevertheless even in the French Civil Code and in the Austrian Civil Code, the idea of a model contract is faintly discernible — in the French Civil Code, chiefly in the provisions regulating the matrimonial regime; in the Austrian Civil Code, in the chap ter on loans and usufruc tuary leases. Such legal conse quences are to be provided for as the parties themselves would have provided for, had they drawn up a detailed document. Since it is almost exclusively subsidiary law, it does not require the parties to adopt a definitely prescribed content of the contract, but it does compel them at least to bear in mind the contractual content for which regulations have been provided by the statute if they are desirous of bringing about other legal consequences than those provided for by the statute. Nevertheless even here the consideration of a possible legal controversy seems to have most weight.

It was not before the nineteenth century that statutes were enacted which, following French and English example, purported, in part at least, to state the content of a legal document. Their object was to introduce certain institutions which until then had been unknown at home; which, perhaps according to the then state of the law had been forbidden, or whose permissibility had been in doubt. The plan was to permit the parties, according to foreign models, to establish these institutions by agreement between themselves either by contract or by articles of association. This implies a determination of the content of the declaration of will — for the most part, by non-obligatory law, to a great extent, however, by obligatory law. The object of these statutes manifestly is to prepare the ground for the legal document which the parties necessarily must draw up with reference to the transaction in such a way as to protect them against being overreached (*Reglementierung*[1]). Institutions of this kind are the legal order of societies, of stock companies, of the Schulze-Delitzsch associations[2], of partnerships with limited liability, of the heritable building right. Very often the state supervises the making of these contracts in order to ascertain whether they are drawn up in such a way as to meet the statutory requirements. This supervision may be exercised, e.g. by state action when the agreement is presented for recording or for approval. All of this however must not obscure the fact that what we are dealing with is essentially the art and science of drawing up legal documents, i.e. with juristic law, which is being found by the legislator. In antiquity, in the Middle Ages, even in modern times, it was the art and science of drawing up legal documents that invented both the new institutions and the necessary forms which economic life required. When it became necessary to make provision for the protection of

1. *Reglementierung*：〈德〉严格控制
2. Schulze-Delitzsch associations：海尔曼·舒尔茨-德里奇合作社。由德国城市信用合作社的倡导者海尔曼·舒尔茨-德里奇于 1850 年创办。

third parties, the courts provided norms for decision which science and judicial decision created out of their own materials. Even today our legal life for the most part is based upon these achievements of the past. It may be admitted that these statutes are more closely related to state law than any other part of private law legislation. In this form the art and science of drafting legal documents got into the German Civil Code (law of societies, matrimonial regime, law of partnership), and, to a still greater extent, into the Commercial Code.

All in all it was the task of the codes to sum up the development of juristic law which had taken place until that time, and in so doing to make the necessary changes which legal technique, being bound in a great measure by tradition, lacked the power to make. For the second task, legislative intervention was actually indispensable. On the other hand a code is far from being the only means whereby the greatest of inconveniences connected with juristic law can be remedied, i.e. its enormous extent, its lack of systematic arrangement, its interminable controversies. This has been accomplished more than once by other means. It was accomplished in part by so mechanical a device as the law of citations of Valentinianus III. At the present time, the English, who have to deal with more than twenty thousand volumes of juristic law, contained in their collections of decisions, make shift by considering it highly improper for a barrister to cite opinions to the court that are more than one hundred to one hundred and fifty years old. This surely is a drastic remedy for this, the greatest of inconveniences connected with juristic law, but it is inescapable. Very often the works of private individuals undertake this task. This is the significance of the *Decretum Gratiani*[1] and of the gloss of Accursius[2]. The Continental common law at all times had some book or other which was looked upon as the summing up of all juristic science. In the

1. *Decretum Gratiani*：〈拉〉《格拉提安教令集》
2. gloss of Accursius：阿库修斯评注

last period of its validity it had Windscheid, and after him, Dernburg. The code therefore is merely one of the many possible means of giving to juristic law a suitable form for the administration of justice.

The immediate efifect of the reduction of juristic law to statute law in the codes is merely this, that the juristic law which has been in existence until now reappears as statute law. This change of form is not without effect upon the state of the law. For until that time juristic science drew its content from society, it created legal propositions on the basis of the social facts under the influence of social trends. Henceforth this is to be changed. Among the various thought sequences that result from the introduction of the codes, perhaps one of the most important and widespread is that juristic science henceforth may work only on the basis of the code. The social material that has passed from the earlier stage of juristic science into the code is to be developed by juristic science in its present stage, which is based on the code; but science is not permit ted to fashion new materials independently. Here as elsewhere the intentions and the effects of legislation are at variance with each other.

Since the codes are primarily juristic law, they, like all juristic law, contain a social morphology[1]. They describe the social relations of a legal nature to the extent to which the legislator has become conscious of them and has thought it necessary to regulate them or at least to mention them. This morphological content of the code, of course, cannot become state law; for state law is not a morphology. The state gives form only to itself, to its own institutions, its army, its tribunals. It does not give form to society. It can only issue commands or prohibitions to the latter. But the question can be raised whether or not, according to the intention of the legislator, the morphology of the code is to be an exhaustive one, whether it is not accompanied by a

1. morphology：形态论

command issued by the state that no institutions should be established except those that are permitted and regulated by the state; whether therefore social associations, family relations, forms of undertakings, contracts, dispositions by last will and testament of a kind not described in the code are permitted.

The state can of course issue a command forbidding certain institutions by omitting any mention of them in the code. This has the same effect as any other prohibition by state legislation. By failing to mention juristic persons, the French Civil Code undoubtedly meant to check, perhaps to prevent, the development of corporations, and it has actually affected French corporations very adversely thereby. Likewise the German Civil Code intended to make the creation of *real* rights other than those regulated by the code impossible, and when new contracts are being entered into the question will often arise whether or not they should be recognized under the code. The Austrian Civil Code has abolished ownership of a story of a building by failing to mention it. The only question is whether the state is able to enforce the prohibition. This is of course extremely doubtful where the latter is enforceable only by resort to private law, and where the prohibition of the new institution merely takes away the protection which lies in the right to sue and defend. Prohibited contracts, societies, testamentary gifts (for example, gifts in mortmain) have been able to hold their own even against the codes.

It is true a jurist of the traditional school is inclined to believe that every legal relation that is not mentioned in the code is forbidden. Even the innocent *fidei commissum eius quod supererit*[1], according to a remark of Pfaff and Hofmann's, is believed by many to be forbidden, although the only reason why it is not mentioned in the Austrian Civil Code is that it was thought unnecessary to state a legal precept for this

1. *fidei commissum eius quod supererit*：〈拉〉超过一定限度的信托

case. As a rule, however, the juristic morphology of social phenomena does not import such a prohibition by the state. The four kinds of contracts of the Roman jurists did not abolish agreements of other kinds, and the Roman testament did not make gifts *mortis causa*, which were not testaments, impossible. Likewise the reception of various legal relations into the code and the description of them therein does not have the effect of excluding from the law everything that does not fit into these relations.

So long as the legal relations as to which no provision has been made in the code do not come into contact with the agencies of the state, the practical jurist has no occasion to concern himself about them. From his point of view they are outside of the legal sphere. The modern development of trusts and cartels and of collective labor agreements, demonstrates to what an enormous extent the social development of law can go on independently of and in conflict with positive law. But the situation changes when a legally recognized basis is to be created for these new legal relations by means of legal documents, when litigation arises, or when, for some other reason, perhaps in the course of supervision by the state, interference by an administrative body becomes unavoidable. Then, and not until then, the question confronts the jurist whether he can find suitable forms and norms for decision in the code, or, as the German common law juristic science used to express it, whether he can construe the relation juristically. This is a question of juristic technique, and must be variously answered according to the stage of development which the technique has attained. The answer must be a different one under the Roman system of legal act ions from what it would be in the juristic science of the Continental common law or in that of Anglo-American law. And under a system of free finding of law it would present an entirely different appearance from that which it presents at the present time.

In every legal system there has been an abundance of cases in which juristic construction seemed impossible. One of the most famous examples of the most recent time is the obligation of the shareholders in a sugar factory to furnish sugar beets. The consequence of this impossibility is that the given relation, since it lacks protection by the courts and administrative tribunals, must rely exclusively upon social forces for recognition, protection, and enforcement, or perish. This is indeed a sad result, especially where there is a great social and economic need for this relation, where neither prohibition by the state nor public interest stands in the way. And it must be stated emphatically that the trouble lies not with the relation but with juristic science, whose technical resources are insufficient for the satisfactory performance of its never-ending task, to wit to make the law subserve the needs of life. The codes inevitably increase the difficulties which new phenomena of legal life cause to legal science. For contemporaneously with the codes the idea arises almost automatically that an authoritative command of the legislator has made an end of the activity of juristic science not only as to the past but also as to the future; that thereafter a jurist must seek the solution of every problem that confronts him exclusively within the code. The precepts of the code as to filling up the gaps are a matter of indifference in view of the fact that the code confronts the legal profession as the embodiment of perfection of the legal system. Henceforth juristic science, judicial as well as literary, has only one task to fulfil, i.e. to judge the phenomena of life according to the code. Its starting point must be the code in every case. If the code were able to prevent economic development from going beyond the code, it would also be able to compel juristic science to stand still; for it would thereby deprive the latter of all new subject matter that it might possibly find new norms for. But it has been shown that the code neither produces nor strives to produce this effect. For the new needs of society there must always be new juristic law. The popular reference to remedy by legislation indicates a failure to understand the nature of the function both of juristic science and of legislation. Difficulties of construetion like the difficulty involved in the obligation to supply sugar beets to the sugar factories arise at every moment. They constitute the daily bread of the practical jurist. The legislator who would keep pace with all of them would indeed be a busy man. Moreover, in that case, who would be able to find his way through the labyrinth of statutes? And lastly it is by no means the intention of the private law codes to bind the social and economic forces of the nation until such time as the legislature acts again or perhaps to destroy them.

Human society, particularly human economic life, imperatively demands new legal forms for new forms of life. In actual fact the three older codifications, the Prussian *Landrecht*[1], the Austrian Civil Code, and the French Civil Code, have not been able to prevent social and economic development from outstripping them. New, and theretofore unknown, associations, new kinds of contracts, new forms of undertakings, new kinds of declarations of will in case of death have come into use, and juristic science has found appropriate norms for decision and appropriate remedies both within the framework of the code and without. The new situation under the new German Civil Code, as is clearly discernible even now, will not be different.

The "*Geschlossenheit des Rechtssystems*[2]" never was anything but purely theoretical pedantry. Juristic science has never been able to offer prolonged resistance to great and justifiable social or economic needs, and jurists have always believed that its most important function is to find forms for new social and economic developments that fit into the frame of the code (the art and science of drawing up legal documents) and to establish norms for decision adapted to these new developments without directly doing violence to the code. Anyone who has observed

1. Prussian *Landrecht*：《普鲁士国家的普通邦法》。普鲁士国王腓特烈 · 威廉二世于 1792 年颁布的法典。(斜体为德语)
2. *Geschlossenheit des Rechtssystems*：〈德〉法律制度的完善

the development of juristic science must admit that the task which daily and hourly confronts the jurist not only can be performed by the jurist but is actually being performed daily and hourly. To cite an important and famous example, permit me to mention the matter of life insurance. It is passed over in silence both by the French Civil Code and by the Austrian Civil Code, not by chance, but with the intent to forbid it. That this is true is shown as to the former by a remark of Portalis, one of its authors, and by a remark of Merlin, a contemporary, in his Repertoire; as to the latter, it was proved by v. Herzfeld by quotations from the source material. Speculation as to the length of human life was considered immoral, and fears were entertained that it might stimulate crime. If a contract ought to be held bad in any case on the ground of the silence of the statute in regard to it, this is such a case. What would this world look like if in this case juristic science had not been mindful of its unending task?

The new law which is imperatively demanded by new relations is drawn by the jurists who are working under a code, as was done by the jurists of all times, from the concrete structure of the legal relations themselves, chiefly from declarations of the will, documents, and business custom; it is enriched by means of universalization and finding of norms, and gauged by the content of the codes. This is the way in which the law of insurance arose from the contracts of insurance during the course of the nineteenth century. The codes facilitate the execution of the juristic tasks, both of the judges and of the lawyers who draw up legal documents, in part unconsciously perhaps, nevertheless very effectively, through the extraordinary flexibility of their provisions. Liberty of association, liberty of contract, liberty of testamentary disposition form an enormously wide frame within which most of the things that life requires can be provided for. Moreover the codes invariably contain a series of concepts which make it possible, for judicial decision at least, to create legal norms that are adapted to the new institutions. These are the concepts of declaration of will by silence, business usage, the principle of *gule Treue* (good faith, *bonne foi*), the principle of *Treu und Glauben* (good faith); in addition there are the old tried and proved home remedies of practical juristic science which have been in use since the days of the glossators, to wit the creation of concepts and construction. Accordingly judicial decision in Austria, in France, and in a modest measure also in the territory of the Prussian Code has in fact succeeded in pouring a new content into the law of the codes just as the juristic science of the Continental common law has ever been able to adapt the law of the *corpus iuris* to the needs of life at the proper time and place. At the present time the French Civil Code and the Austrian Civil Code, the two of the older codes that are still in force, are covered with a crust of new juristic law so thick that the original content can scarcely be discerned, and this in a few places only. One can readily understand that in both countries the call for a revision of the civil law has been heard, the task of which will be identical with that which was performed one hundred years ago, i.e. to receive into the code the substance of the law that has been created meanwhile, and at the same time to take account of many new claims and interests which the existing law has not recognized. The new law must needs be a new morphology of society, must give occasion for the creation of new norms, which self-evidently will be as far from being final as any legislator has ever been from speaking the last word on social development.

One must never overlook the fact that even in a code juristic law is not state law. Even in this form, it cannot, because of its very nature, be a command issued to persons subjected to its power, as is state law, but can only be, as it is everywhere else, a direction and an instruction. Surely no one would attribute the same force and power to the rule about the sale on approval as to the provisions of the German Civil Code about *Sachivucher* (a form of usury)[1]. Juristic

1. *Sachwucher* (a form of usury)：〈德〉一种高利贷形式

law is not being imposed upon the relations; it was abstracted from the content of these relations in the past, and it is to conform to this content in the future. Compare the breadth and flexibility of the precepts of the German Civil Code concerning the legal transaction which violates good morals (*contra bonos mores*[1]) with the rule of state law prohibiting usurious transactions, which is contained in the same section. The presuppositions and the effects of the latter must be found exclusively in the code. But as to the question when a legal transaction is *contra bonos mores,* and what its consequences are, information must be gathered from the whole body of antecedent literature and the antecedent course of judicial decision as well as from the whole body of subsequent literature.

The provisions of Roman law as to liability for *culpa lata* and *culpa levis*[2] are typical universalizations of juristic law. In these provisions the Romans by no means intended to lay down in advance exactly what measure of fault the jurist should assume in each individual legal relation. These provisions of the Roman jurists were merely a description of the practice actually followed in the administration of justice. It was not a "should be" for the future, but merely an "is" as to the present. The principles according to which the judges in Rome actually adjudged fault hardened into the doctrine of the Roman jurists about the care required in everyday life.

Received into the modern codes, these Roman universalizations were, in form, converted into legal propositions which were to bind the judge in the future. There is no doubt however that they actually do not do this. The Austrian Civil Code indeed does provide for liability in all contracts even for slight fault; only the measure of damages depends upon the degree of fault. And now let us compare the case of a man

---

1. *contra bonos mores*：〈拉〉违反善良的道德准则
2. liability for *culpa lata* and *culpa levis*：重过失责任与轻过失责任（斜体为拉丁文）

about to under take a journey who deposits his valuables with a friend, who, as a mat ter of friendship, undertakes to keep them safe, with the case where he delivers them to a professional depositary for hire. That which is considered fault in the case of a professional depositary will of course not be considered fault in the case of a friend who is merely doing a favor. The course of judicial decision in Austria apparently makes the same distinction that the Romans made, i.e. in the former case there is liability for slight fault, or negligence, in the latter only for gross negligence. The only effect of the precepts of the Civil Code was that the judges made no distinction between gross and slight negligence but simply denied that there was fault in a case in which they did not think it proper to hold the party liable. The attempts, therefore, of the Austrian Civil Code to convert a doctrine of juristic law, an essential characteristic of which is adaptability, into a rigid, inflexible norm has failed. And I presume that the same result has been reached wherever the codes have recognized the degrees of *culpa levis* and *culpa lata*.

The codes therefore have had the effect neither of bringing the course of development of law to a complete standstill nor of limiting it exclusively to legislation. The development of the living social law as well as of the art and science of drawing up legal documents and of judicial decision continues the even tenor of its way. The authors of the codes did indeed believe that they would be able to exclude juristic science altogether. It was not only Justinian that entertained this idea but also the Emperor Joseph II, Frederick II, and Napoleon I. It is said that when the last named saw the first commentary, he exclaimed: "*Mon code est perdu*[1]." The reason for this is that, like all men of action, they lived only for the moment, and were bent upon doing away with a future that was independent of their wills.

During the time immediately following the appearance of a

1. *Mon code est perdu*：〈拉〉我的法典不能应对

code, it is true that, to a certain limited extent, there is no need of juristic labor. Since the code has received all the juristic law that was in existence at the time, questions of greater importance at least have been settled for the moment, and when juristic science insists upon participating in the work, the authors of the code are justified in rejecting its overtures as those of an officious and superfluous intermeddler. But before very long, time will bring questions for which no answer, or no satisfactory answer at least, can be found in the code. And at this very moment, juristic science is again brought face to face with its never-ending task of making the law subserve the needs of life; and it fulfils this task by employing the same means that it has used from time immemorial. As soon as life has caught up with the code, juristic science begins to function with renewed vigor. The older a code, the more clearly its work of modifying and eking out becomes apparent. Practically not a single proposition of the *Danske Lov*[1] of the year 1683 is valid today in its original sense. And time has had a powerful effect also upon the French codes of the beginning of the nineteenth century. He who knows only the French Civil Code has only a very imperfect conception of the civil law that is in force in the French courts. One must not seek the law that is actually valid in France in the codes, but in Dalloz and Sirey. And recent though the German Civil Code is, German judicial decision has resorted to legal material not embodied in the code in an untold number of instances, as Hedemann, Jung, and other adherents of the free-finding-of-law movement delight in pointing out.

This then is what has happened in the case of the three older codes. The French Civil Code has produced a result in this connection that is extraordinarily instructive. While juristic science in France was temporarily at a standstill, there appeared in Germany, immediately

---

1. *Danske Lov*：〈丹麦〉《丹麦法典》。1683 年由丹麦国王克里斯琴五世组织汇编。

after the promulgation of the French Civil Code, the famous handbook by Zachariae, which amounts to a professed juristic development of the law of the French Civil Code, and which has been recognized as such by the French. Why did this book appear in Germany and not in France? Because to the French the code was but an orderly statement of the results of their juristic science up to that time, to which, they thought, they had nothing to add, for the moment at least. But to the German it was an altogether different thing from the very outset. It was not the results of the juristic science of his own law that had been expressed in the code, but the results of a juristic science that was based on a totally different social morphology and that created different norms. Zachariae's work was practically of the same nature as that done by any other jurist in case life has outstripped and grown away from the code. He worked into the juristic law of the code the law created by judicial decisions that had been rendered in the society of which he was a part, and which, in part, was very different from French society. In this way his handbook became a model for the later French juristic science, which found it incumbent upon itself to work into the code the law created by the judicial decisions rendered in French society, which, however, had undergone a considerable development meanwhile. The French consider his work a classic, just as they do its French continuations by Aubry and Rau.

XIX THE THEORY OF CUSTOMARY LAW

Mommsen has pointed out quite emphatically that among the Romans "usually and especially in the language of the law books," e. one may say technically, the phrase *ius publicum* did not mean law that concerns the people, but law that is posited by the commune; that *ius publicum* in this sense is that which the older legal language called *lex publica*; that *ius publicum* therefore is not *Staatsrecht*, but law posited by the state. This remark of Mommsen's is borne out by the sources. In my *Beitrage zur Theorie der Rechtsquellen*, I have shown that *ius publicum* is very seldom used in the sense of *Staatsrecht* and never, as is usually believed, in the sense of compulsory law, but regularly in the sense of law that is posited by the state. In the writings of Cicero and of the jurists of the age of the Republic, *ius publicum* is the *leges* and the *plebiscita*[1]; in the writings of the jurists of the Empire, it comprises in addition the *senatusconsulta*, the praetorian edict, and the law of the imperial constitutions. Wherever a given precept is referred to by the jurists as belonging to *ius publicum,* it is based, as can be shown, upon a *lex,* a *plebiscitum*, a *senatusconsultum*, on a provision contained in the edict or in a constitution.

The concept of *ius privatum* is given by the contrast to this sense of *ius publicum,* i.e. it is the law that is based on the other, the non-state, sources of law; it is the Roman customary law, especially the Roman juristic law. The words of Ulpian on this point must be taken literally: *Tripertitum est: collectum etenim est ex naturalibus praeceptis aut gentium aut*

---

1. *plebiscita*：〈拉〉平民法决议

civilibus[1]. These three kinds of *praecepta,* the *praecepta naturalia*, as well as those *iuris gentium* and the *praecepta civilia,* are parts of non-state law.

Ius privatum is a later, purely academic concept occasioned chiefly by the notion that logic somehow required the subsumption of all classes of legal propositions that were not *ius publicum* under one head. The original legal language did not employ the term *ius privatum* but *ius civile*. The oldest meaning of the term *ius civile,* which is found wherever the term is used absolutely without an opposite, like *ius gentium,* for example, from the *auctor ad Herennium*[2] down to the classical jurists, is the juristic law which is applicable in a proceeding in a Roman law court. In Cicero's day the opposite to *ius civile* still was *leges. Legibus et iure civili* is one of his standing phrases. The *leges* which govern court procedure also, chiefly the *leges testamentariae*[3], he calls *leges de iure chili.* The praetorian edict occupies a subordinate position in Cicero's day, and the later sources of the law, *senatusconsulta* and *constitutiones,* are not yet in existence.

Accordingly the Romans in the days of the Republic distinguish but two sources of law, *ius civile,* or, as it is still called by Pomponius, *proprium*[4] *ius civile,* and *leges.* The former is juristic law, which is traced back to juristic interpretation of the Twelve Tables somewhat in the manner in which the Mohammedan jurists trace their vast body of norms to a few hundred passages of the Qoraiij of which only a very small number contains as much as a single legal propositiom It is self-evident that by this time no one takes this derivation of *ius civile* from the Twelve Tables seriously, as is shown by the presentation of Pomponius. At a later time the praetorian edict is added to the *leges*

1. *Tripertitum est: collectum etenim est ex naturalibus praeceptis aut gentium aut civilibus*：〈拉〉私法分为三个部分：自然法的规则、万民法的规则、市民法的规则。
2. *Auctor ad Herennium*：〈拉〉《献给赫伦尼》的作者
3. *leges testamentariae*：〈拉〉遗嘱条款
4. *proprium*：〈拉〉自己的

and the *ius civile*. It cannot be shown that it was, in theory, considered a source of law as early as the days of the Republic; but practically it was a source, as appears from Cicero's writings. The great mass of private law, without doubt, derived from the *ius civile*. The edict and the *leges* dealt with special subjects only, whenever the necessity for new regulation appeared. The two sources that were added in the days of the Empire, the *senatusconsulta* and the imperial constitutions, were not universally recognized until after the Byzantine Empire had been established.

Since I first published this view of the sources of Roman law, it has quite generally been accepted by unbiassed scholars. I should like to add here that since that time I have gathered some material which confirms my opinion. The doubts which critics have expressed refer to the antithesis between *ius civile* and *ius honorarium*. In the book referred to, I made the assertion that, among the Romans, *ius civile* is contradistinguished from praetorian law down to the days of the later Empire in precisely the same manner in which it is contradistinguished from *ius legitimum*[1], the *senatusconsulta,* and the law of the constitutions. And there is much evidence in favor of this view. It is, I admit, in conflict with the well-known fragment of Papinian in the Digest, which divides the whole law into *ius civile* and *ius honorarium*, and which enumerates under the former head, in addition to *auctoritas prudenlium*[2], *leges, plebiscite, senatusconsulta*, and *decreta principum*[3]. We do not know what the passage meant in its original context, but the doctrine which it teaches has not been handed down elsewhere. There is not another passage in which the law is divided into *ius civile* and *ius honorarium* in the sense in which this is done in the passage referred to. In every other text of the sources in which we find a similar division,

1. *ius legitimum*：〈拉〉制定法
2. *auctoritas prudenlium*：〈拉〉法学家观点
3. *decreta principum*：〈拉〉皇帝敕令

the latter refers exclusively to the *actiones* and to the law of inheritance. There are *actiones* that are part of the *ius civile* and there are *actiones* that are part of the *ius honorarium*; there is a *ius civile* law of inheritance and a *ius honorarium* law of inheritance. Beyond this there is no mention of *ius civile* and *ius honorarium*. But before the times of the Severi, even the division of the law of the *actiones* and of inheritance into civil and honorary is never mentioned. In particular, we find no trace of it in Gaius. I have therefore expressed the opinion that the text of Papinian in its original context referred solely to the law of inheritance, and that the doctrine of civil and honorary actions, of civil and honorary law of inheritance, which moreover is based solely on practical considerations and not upon any considerations of the theory of the sources, was invented by the jurists of the time of the Severi. But the basic idea of my book would not be shaken in the least if it could be shown, as is contended chiefly by Girard, that the doctrine of Papinian and of the jurists of the time of the Severi arose at a somewhat earlier period.

This basic idea is the following: the Roman law that was applied by the courts is in its essence and as to its original component parts *ius civile*, juristic law, and remained such until the latest Imperial times. To this original part were added at a later time the *leges*, the *edictum*, the *senatusconsulta*, the *constitutiones*. It is self-evident that I do not mean to say that the words *ius chile* never had any other meaning than juristic law. There is not a single expression of human speech that for centuries had the same meaning at all times. To what degree even the technical terms of the Roman jurists were susceptible of many different interpretations and have changed their meanings in the course of centuries is shown by a glance at the *Vocabularium iurisprudentiae Romanae*[1]. As is well known to every student of language, the meaning

1. *Vocabularium iurisprudentiae Romanae*：〈拉〉罗马法学词汇

of words varies in accordance with the meaning of the words as the opposites of which they are being used. If the term *ius civile* is used as the opposite to *ius gentium,* or *ius militare,* or *ius criminale*, it does not mean juristic law, but the opposite to *ius gentium,* or *ius militare*[1], or *ius criminate*[2]. This I have expounded in my book. And this is the reason why Gaius Inst. I, I, I does not refute my theory, as Mitteis thinks. I have by no means overlooked this passage but have discussed it at length. It is only in those passages in which *ius civile* is used absolutely, without an opposHe, that it invariably, from Cicero to the *auctor* of Boethius, means, as far as I can see, juristic science, juristic law. And I do not believe thal1 have overlooked a single passage. When Paulus says (Sent. IV, 8, 20): "*Idque iure civili Voconiana ratione videtur effectum,*" *iure civili*[3] can only mean "juristic law."

Unless one bears this in mind, one cannot understand the development of Roman law. And this is doubly important since we are not discussing a peculiarity of Roman law. The same phenomena appear in the development of the only other system that has attained to an advanced stage of development — has attained to it without a reception and without marked foreign influences. In English law we find the distinction between common law and statute law, which exactly corresponds to the distinction between *ius civile* and *ius legitimum.* The common law is exclusively juristic law; it is the custom of the realm, established by the judges. And the statute law is merely *ius legistimum* created by the state. Here also a third component part is added at a later time, magisterial law, equity. One can justly say therefore that we are not dealing with an accidental peculiarity of the development of Roman law but with the law of all legal development,

1. *ius militare*：〈拉〉军事法
2. *ius criminale*：〈拉〉刑法
3. *"Idque iure civili Voconiana ratione videtur effectum," iure civili*：〈拉〉这被认为是“在市民法中的沃科尼亚法中的规则所确立的”。

which takes place independently of the power of the state, from within, and independently of any outside influences.

The Roman jurists at the same time speak also of *mores*[1] and of *consuetudo*[2]. These however are not customary law such as courts would have to consider. The norms that arise in Roman society become customary law only by passing through the alembic of juristic law, by becoming *ius civile*. This is seen most clearly in the case of the rule making gifts between husband and wife invalid — a rule which is referred to, in ten different texts at least, as *ius civile*. The discussions of Pernice (*Zeitschrift der Savigny Stiftung*[3] R. A. XX Bd. S. 127) and of Brie (*Die Lehre vom Gervohnheitsrecht* [4]) show that *mores* or *consuetudo* can not become customary law directly without the intervention of the labors of juristic science. These discussions appear the more convincing to me because the point of view of their authors is diametrically opposed to mine.

Customary law other than *ius civile* had not been heard of in Rome down to the end of the classical period. Among the texts of the title of the Digest, *de legibus senatusque consultis et longa consuetudine*[5], and of the title of the Code, *Quae sit longa consuetudo*[6], which were taken from writers of the classical period, there is but one that dealt with Roman customary law, i.e. fr. 1, 3, 36. In this text gifts between husband and wife are being discussed. But this text contains only an academic laudation of this precept. The whole content of these two titles originally did not deal with questions of Roman customary law. The famous passage from Julian (fr. 2 h. t.), in its original context was

1. *mores*：〈拉〉习俗
2. *consuetudo*：〈拉〉习惯
3. *Zeitschrift der Savigny Stiftung*：〈德〉萨维尼基金会杂志
4. *Die Lehre vom Gervohnheitsrecht*：〈德〉《习惯法理论》，西格弗里德·布里（1838—1931）著
5. *de legibus senatusque consultis et longa consuetudine*：〈拉〉关于法律和元老院决议以及长期的习惯
6. *Quae sit longa consuetudo*：〈拉〉那些属于长期习惯的东西

a discussion of the *lex Papia et Poppaea,* probably of the provisions of this statute concerning burdensome communal offices and services. In this connection reference was not made to customary law but to the usage that obtained in the *municipia.* The fact that the two passages from Ulpian, fr. 33 and 34 h.t., as well as the constitution of the Emperor Alexander (C. 1. & 52), were taken from Ulpian's book *De officio proconsulis*[1] indicates that they were not discussing customary law but provincial usage. The texts taken from the *Quaestiones*[2] of Paulus and the *Quaestiones* of Callistratus (fr. 36, 27 h.t.) refer exclusively to the traditional interpretation of statutes. The passage from Paulus, fr. 37 h.t., is taken from the disquisition *Ad legem municipalem*[3]. That it deals only with municipal custom is shown by its very wording: *quo iure civitas retro in eius modi casibus usafuisset*[4]. To sum up: when the classical Roman jurists speak of *ius civile* they mean Roman customary law; but when they quite generally speak of *mores* or *consuetudo,* they do not.

I have taken the preceding paragraph verbatim from my *Rektoratsrede*[5], entitled The Fact of Customary Law. When I had this address printed, I did not know that Puchta had said exactly the same thing, perhaps in a better way, at any rate in a more complete statement, in his book on customary law. I have repeatedly studied this book very carefully, but have always skipped the discussion of Roman customary law because we have made such glorious progress since that time. Then I decided to read it after all, and now I am far from certain that we have advanced very far beyond Puchta. I believe that after all we could still learn something from his work. Puchta's view has met with Savigny's

---

1. *De officio proconsulis*：〈拉〉《论行省总督的职责》
2. *Quaestiones*：〈拉〉《法律问答》
3. *Ad legem municipalem*：〈拉〉《论自治市法》
4. *quo iure civitas retro in eius modi casibus usa fuisset*：〈拉〉在相同情形下城邦先前适用的法律
5. *Rektoratsrede*：〈拉〉就职演说

approval.

Consuetudo was first treated as a source of law by the post-classical jurist Hermogenianus and the later imperial constitutions. At that time the situation was quite different from that of the age of the classical jurists. From the days of the *Constitutio Antonina* the Roman law was law for nations of the most varied charac*ter,* civilization, and descent, whose members had indeed become Roman citizens but had not adopted Roman law and Roman custom even outwardly. They continued to live, as they had done before, according to their ancient law and customs. It was not advisable simply to ignore this fact. Though the emperors were strongly inclined simply to abolish these *consuetudines,* they had to concern themselves with them. Accordingly a post-classical text of the Digest, which was taken from Hermogenianus, expressly states that *quae longa consuetudine comprobala sunt*[1] are binding. The Code contains three imperial constitutions that deal with this question. Justinian, who realized that he could not simply ignore these local laws and customs, took the statements of classical jurists which I have referred to above out of their context, greatly distorting their meaning in the process, construed them to suit his purpose, and added such texts as he could find on the subject in post-classical literature.

The glossators, the postglossators, the canonists, and the common law practitioners of the Continent had a task to perform that was similar to that of the post-classical Roman jurists and legislators. They too were to apply Roman law to peoples of varied character, descent, and civilization, to whom Roman customs and Roman law were foreign, and who had their own law and their own customs. The texts of the Justinianian sources were designed, as it were, to meet this very situation, and could be applied directly. The only question was how

1. *quae longa consuetudine comprobata sunt*：〈拉〉习惯长期支持的规则具有约束力。

much of the customary particular law was to be considered valid, and how to draw the line of demarcation between it and the Continental common law. It is clear that a standard derived from the Continental common law was very welcome; it is equally clear that the jurists who were trained in the Continental common law preferred a narrower policy to a more liberal one. At any rate these texts were anything but a theory of the sources of law in the opinion of those who from the beginning of Romanist juristic science down to the days of the activity of the Historical School were relying upon them. To them they were a statutory provision concerning the validity of particular law and local customs. This situation remained unchanged until it was remedied by the Historical School of jurisprudence, which created a doctrine of such grandeur that it must stir us to unqualified admiration even today, for it has never been surpassed.

In this connection, of course, we are referring exclusively to Savigny and Puchta. Between the basic doctrine of these two pioneers of the historical interpretation of law, especially in the sphere of customary law, and their successors a gulf is fixed that cannot be bridgede Savigny and Puchta may be treated as a unit. And if, occasionally, the doctrine of one differs from that of the other in detail, it does not appear that they were desiring to give expression to a difference of opinion thereby. It is analogous to a variation between the statements of the same writer at an earlier and at a later date. It is true, the views of both have undergone modifications. Savigny's view in the *Beruf* is different from that in the *System*; Puchta's view in the *Gewohnheitsrecht* is different from that of the *Institutionen*[1]; and in the notices and reviews which both have written, one occasionally perceives a modification of view. As to Puchta, we must treat the statement in the second volume of his *Gewohnheitsrecht*[2] and in the review of Georg Beseler's *Volksrecht*

1. *Institutionen*：〈德〉《法理学教程》
2. *Gewohnheitsrecht*：〈德〉习惯法

und Juristenrecht[1] as final; as to Savigny, the *System*. We must not, of course, ignore the other works of Savigny and Puchta, especially their critical works, when these supplement or explain those mentioned above.

In forming an estimate of the doctrines of Savigny and Puchta, one must bear in mind that it was they who first introduced the idea of development into the theory of the sources of law and clearly saw the relation between the development of law and the history of a people as a whole. "This organic relation between law and the nature and character of a people is maintained throughout the passing of time, and as to this point also is to be compared with language. For both there is no moment of standing absolutely still; both are subject to the same progress and development as every other activity of the people; and the development of both law and language are subject to the same law of inner necessity. The law grows with the people, develops with it, and finally dies when the people loses its individuality." (*Beruf.*) This view gave rise to an absolutely new conception of the sources of law: their function no longer is to determine arbitrarily and casually what should be law; they are an expression of a process of becoming and happening which takes place from an inner necessity within the popular consciousness (*Volksbewusstsein*[2]).

And now we see the deeper root of the whole doctrine. Savigny and Puchta's chief endeavor was to establish most emphatically that the development of law goes on immediately within the legal consciousness. Usage is merely the shoot which reaches the surface. "Custom does not create law, it merely makes it possible to gain a knowledge of law," said Puchta in a reply to Beseler. But that is by no means a peculiarity of customary law; it must needs be true of every other source of law. If it is really to create law, it must be

1. *Volksrecht und Juristenrecht*：〈德〉民间法与法学家法
2. *Volksbewusstsein*：〈德〉大众意识

an expression of the general legal conviction of the people. For this reason a statute must be treated exactly like usage. "The common power is the *Geist des Volkes* (spirit of the people), from which legislation, too, derives the content of its pronouncements." It is well known that there is a close harmony between this statement and the doctrines of Savigny from the beginning of his career. In his *Beruf,* he says that the sole function of a code is to state the whole existing law. In the *System*、 he makes the same statement, not only, however, as is generally believed, with reference to the codes, but with reference to all statutes. He says that the already existing popular law (*Volksrecht*) "is the content of the statutes, or, to express the same thought in other words, the statute is the instrumentality of the popular law." A statute, according to Savigny, merely serves the purpose of making the popular law more definite, or perhaps, in the case of progressive development of law, "of shortening the interim of uncertainty in the law." Similarly Puchta says that the activity of legislation is a formal rather than a material one, inasmuch as the legislator is not the possessor of a peculiar legal consciousness, but receives his material directly from the *Voiksgeist* (spirit of the people) and from the jurists. Frequently it exercises an exclusively formal influence upon the law, inasmuch as it states the already existing law, i.e. puts it into statutory form.

The third source of law is juristic science. Savigny in his *Beruf* has called attention to juristic science as a source of law. Puchta devoted a brief section to it in the first volume of his *Gewohnheitsrecht* but made substantial changes in the second volume. Savigny, in his *System*、 follows Puchta, but there is some doubt about this, for the doctrine of neither is quite clear. According to Puchta, juristic science creates law only in case it is not a pure science but a popular one. "In addition to the usage" which is based on a legal proposition scientifically deduced, there is a usage "which expresses the popular consciousness of experts in the law and therefore contains customary law." How these words are to be understood can best be seen from Puchta's statements in his review of Beseler's book: "When we are discussing the common conviction as to the law of bills of exchange, we shall not expect to find this conviction among the peasants; again, when we are discussing the law as to marking off boundaries and as to the servitude of pasture, we shall not consult a banker. But among those in whom we take an actual conviction on the legal proposition in question for granted, we shall assign a prominent place to those whose affairs bring them into more frequent contact with legal questions in general or with a certain kind of legal question. We shall not, for instance, take for granted that all persons of equal mental powers who have the legal capacity to draw bills of exchange have the same strength and ext ent of this consciousness. When dealing with the question of a common popular conviction, we shall select those whose experience in affairs of this kind is most varied as the representatives of the whole class. Imagine a court consisting of persons who have not made the judicial office their profession; will not the opinion of these men, provided they have been called upon repeatedly to serve in this capacity, e.g. of merchants, who have acted as lay judges in commercial courts, *ceteris paribus*[1] be given especial weight among us on a legal question of this kind, even though we are merely seeking to ascertain the popular conviction? Now let us, in our imaginations, substitute for these judges men who do not combine any other profession with their judicial office; let us imagine further that they have received a legal training as a preparation for this office. Do they thereby lose their capacity to represent the popular conviction?"

In this sense therefore customary law and statute and juristic law are shoots from the same slip, i.e. the popular consciousness. Puchta says that ethical custom is the original body of customary law in the same

1. *ceteris paribus*：〈拉〉假使其余情况均相同（或均保持不变）

sense in which the organized system is the peculiar instrumentality of juristic law, and in which the word is the peculiar instrumentality of statute law. The reciprocal relation of these three kinds of law can be most graphically presented by an extract from a notebook of Savigny's of the year 1819, which a kind stroke of fate has permitted me to read. I am quoting this passage verbatim, since it not only is of the greatest interest intrinsically but also seems to show that Savigny is the true originator of the doctrine of customary law formulated by Puchta." "Accordingly the law can be formulated in a scientific manner, first by scientifically trained jurists, secondly through legislation. To fix the essential, invisible, law of the spirit of the people in this manner must therefore be the sole purpose of legislation. Unfortunately, in many instances, legislation has not been carried out in this spirit, and, as a result, the law has suffered grave injury. Let us adopt the view which is the only correct one, and which has stood the test of history, and let us ask how can the law, which, in accord with its true inward nature, has arisen invariably within the consciousness of the people, emerge into an outward visible existence? Our answer is: The language of the law can be provided scientifically (e.g. through books, instruction, etc.); it can also be provided by legislation. In the latter case, the written sources are not originating causes but merely marks and necessary characteristics from which we can draw inferences as to the existing law. Accordingly all statutes serve but this one purpose, i.e. to tell us what the existing law is at the present time, and to preserve it. This is borne out by experience, for most of the existing statutes are the expression of a custom which has been in existence among the people for a long time."

In this way, Savigny and Puchta are endeavoring to place the center of gravity of the development of all law — not only of customary law — into the legal consciousness, "the natural harmony of the conviction of a people, which is a popular universal conception" and to treat its emergence in usage as not essential to the origin of law. People generally, however, fail to realize the profoundness and comprehensiveness of the conception upon which this "spiritualistic" view[1] of these two writers is based. It is presented most clearly perhaps in the following words, quoted from Puchta's review of Beseler's book: "The epoch of German juristic science which subsequently has been called the Historical School found a theory of law in existence, in which the state had been severed from its natural basis, the nation, and had been converted into a purely arbitrary mechanical structure. All law was said to owe its existence to the legislative power, and whatever else insisted that it was a law-creating power — and it would have been necessary forcibly to close one's eyes in order to fail to see that there were legal propositions everywhere that were valid though they had never been promulgated — was somehow brought into connection with legislation, was conceived of as a direct product of the latter, and in this way the absolute supremacy of statute law was maintained — at all events this was accomplished with the aid of the division into written and unwritten law. The Historical School has taken a different path. It based its doctrine on the concept national/ having found in it the natural basis of law and of the state."

It would be difficult to over-estimate the importance of these discussions, particularly in view of the doctrine of evolution, which is their basis throughout. The doctrine of evolution is not merely this or that scientific truth; it is the basis of all modern thinking, one might say a "*Wellanschautmg*" (philosophy). At a time when it was dimly discerned only by a few of the most select minds in the natural sciences, Savigny and Puchta successfully introduced it into the science of law, i.e. into the social sciences. They were successful because they gave an altogether new content to the theory of the sources. Their predecessors were not very much interested in this theory. There was

1. "spiritualistic" view："唯心论" 观点

no doubt in their minds that the question what is to be considered law is decided exclusively by the legislator, and they stated the few rules laid down by the Roman legislator on the question under what conditions customary law should be recognized. At this point Savigny and Puchta are proclaiming their views as to the origin of law. The view is here being proclaimed for the first time that the nation is an organic whole, that it is in a continuous process of development, and that all changes in the law are merely a result of the development of the whole people.

The Historical School, therefore, unlike its predecessors, is no longer interested in laying down rules for the judge as to the application of customary law, but in discovering the law-creating forces in society. The object of the jurists of the Historical School was not to teach how law should be applied, but how it originates; not to give practical directions, but to present a theory of the sources of law which discloses the nature of customary law, explains it, and justifies it. An explanation and justification of this sort they found in the concept "national," and Puchta says expressly: "If customary law is so intimately and necessarily related to the natural concept 'nation,' and if it is the result of the direct activity of the nation with reference to law, the question whether customary law is valid and on what ground it is valid cannot, in fact, arise; for the only answer that can be given is the following: Customary law exists and is valid for the same reason that a popular conviction exists; in the last analysis for the same reason that peoples exist."

Since customary law is based exclusively on the concept "national" there are no other prerequisites to its origination than a common popular conviction. Not even ethical custom can be considered a prerequisite; for the latter is the expression of something that has already come into being, not a prerequisite to its coming into existence. But there are prerequisites to the applicability of customary law by the judge. "But if we take prerequisite to mean something else, e.g. if we take it in the sense of a prerequisite to the application by the judge, to his acceptance of customary law, then that whereof we are speaking no longer is a prerequisite to customary law itself. In this case the question to be answered is: What must the judge take into account when a party litigant appeals to customary law or when for any other reason he is called upon to consult this source of law? What are the presuppositions under which customary law can actually be assumed to exist?" (Puchta). And at another place, "According to the results of the investigations of the nature of customary law, the doctrine of the prerequisites to customary law can mean only this, that it should be ascertained under what presuppositions the fact that a proposition is customarily followed can be a means of cognition of that law for the judge. By no means must one think, in this case, of the prerequisites to the arising of customary law."

This is the sharp distinction which Puchta makes between the question as to the origin of customary law and as to its applicability by the court, which latter of course depends upon the cognoscibility of customary law. It follows therefore that there may be customary law which indeed exists in the conviction of the people, but is not applied by the courts because the prerequisites to its applicability by the court are lacking. Savigny and Puchta make this inference, at least as to the case where the state prohibits customary law. This prohibition, they say, can prevent its recognition by the court but cannot prevent it from arising.

In this discussion, however, a basic difference between customary law and the other sources of law, i.e. statute law and juristic law, has not been sufficiently emphasized. In customary law, as Savigny and Puchta assume, that which has arisen in the legal consciousness of the people is directly converted into ethical custom; the people are not merely conscious of their law, but they live their law, they act and conduct themselves according to it, and this living according to law is not a mere form of manifestation but also a means of cognition of customary law. Customary law therefore is both a rule of conduct and a norm for decision; nay, rather, it always is a rule of conduct in the first place and thereby becomes a norm for decision. This cannot be said of the other sources, and especially of statute law. Both Savigny and Puchta say that it is highly desirable that the statute should also arise in the legal consciousness of the people, but they admit that it is not always the case. Savigny, for instance, in the passage quoted above from his notebook, emphasizes the fact that much legislation has not been enacted in this spirit, and in many ways has done grave injury to the law; and in the *Beruf,* he speaks of the "new" statutes, which "can easily become a fruitless corruption of the law"; and Puchta, too, must admit, after all, that it is not necessary that the "content of a statute should at the time of its enactment have been in existence as law, either in the form of customary law or of usage, inasmuch as a view of the people or of the jurists can be sanctioned that has not yet developed into a firm conviction, into law, or but for the aid of the legislator would never have developed. And therefore legislation is, potentially at least, a true source of law."

The situation is clearer still in the case of juristic law. Let Savigny insist as much as he will that, at a more advanced stage of legal development, the law-creating activity was exercised by the juristic profession as "representatives of the whole"; and Puchta that, by a natural process, the jurists "become the instrumentality through which the common conviction of the people as to law is being expressed and through which the common conviction of the juristic profession is substituted for the conviction of the members of the nation generally." But in the case of customary law, the common conviction of the members of the nation was manifested in this, that the latter as members of the nation acted according to their legal conviction; in the case of juristic law it is manifested, according to Puchta, only by the fact that "it actually was able to assert itself, in part in the conviction of the jurists, in part in the application by the courts." And this, one must admit, is something quite different. Let the jurists have what legal conviction they will, they do not live according to it, as jurists at least; as jurists, they merely apply it. All juristic law therefore appears to be solely a norm for decision, not a rule of conduct. For this reason, the idea expressed by Puchta that in other cases also the legal consciousness usually arises only in a few individual members of the nation is not a very good one; for the bankers actually live the law of bills of exchange, the peasants live the law of bills of exchange, but the jurists merely render decisions according to these laws.

Savigny and Puchta therefore have one thing in mind as the efficient force when they speak of customary law, and another when they speak of statute and juristic law. Customary law arises directly in the legal consciousness of the whole people or of various classes as a rule of conduct; the whole people or the various individual classes regulate their conduct according to it, and in this way customary law becomes ethical custom; in this form it has become cognoscible to the jurist, especially to the judge, and thereafter the jurist, especially the judge, derives the norm for decision from it. Often statutes have come into being in the same way, and this is the only form of legislation that the founders of the Historical School unqualifiedly approve of, to wit declaration of what the law is. But they do not close their eyes to the fact that statutes can arise in other ways. This too Puchta was the first to state. He said it in plain words in his review of Beseler's book. Said Puchta: "A statute is valid because it has been promulgated by the legislator; it is expected to correspond to the actual national will, but its validity is not conditioned upon an investigation of this presupposition; therefore legislation is a formally distinct source of law."

In the light of what has been said this can have only one meaning, to wit: The content of a statute corresponds to the popular consciousness if and only if, it has been drawn from the prevailing rules of conduct; if not, it is foreign to the popular consciousness and does not meet Puchta's requirements; it is binding on the courts, it is true, but only as a norm for decision. It is strange that both Savigny and Puchta fail to observe that the same argument must apply to juristic law, and in a much greater measure than to statute law. For juristic law has never been drawn from the rules of popular conduct; if it were, it would not be juristic law, but customary law. It has not been drawn from the rules of juristic conduct, for the jurists do not, as such, take part in the affairs of everyday life. As Puchta has correctly perceived, it is, to begin with, only the "conviction of the jurists," and is therefore utterly ineffectual as a rule of conduct; or it appears "in the application in the judicial decision" and is a mere norm for decision.

The theory of the sources of law which the founders of the Historical School taught is explicable only on the basis of the strongly felt but not clearly comprehended distinction bet ween rules of conduct and norms for decision in law. On this is based their well known doctrine of the antithesis between the customary law of the beginnings of legal development and the juristic law of a later time. When they assume that in the earlier times law arises immediately in the popular consciousness, their meaning is that at that time law still consists exclusively of the rules of conduct of the entire nation, which therefore constitute the sole basis for the adjudication of legal controversies. And if they contend that at a later time the law-creating activity of the people is confined, for the most part, to the legal profession, they merely mean to say that "for the most part" law no longer arises, as a rule of conduct among the people, but as a norm for decision among the jurists. This idea can be dimly perceived in the writings of Savigny, when he says that "moreover the occasion for juristic activity may be either the communication, by teaching or writing, of the result obtained, or the need of adjudication of a legal controversy"; likewise in the writings of Puchta, when he says: "Thus there appears by the side of customary law, which is based on the common conviction of all the people, law of a different kind which is based on the usage of the experts in the law, the jurists, as the representatives of the people." By the usage of the jurists he can in this connection mean only, as does Savigny, either the theory of decision of legal controversies or the decision itself.

But in order to do some measure of justice to the doctrines of Savigny and Puchta, we must determine what concrete cases of customary law they had in mind when they developed their doctrines? For a single glance at their work will suffice to convince one that it is not a matter of mere abstract philosophizing or of mere deduction from preconceived opinions, or of theories arbitrarily constructed, but of careful induction based upon their own observation. Nevertheless it is not an easy thing to answer this question. Though there can be no doubt that the classical writers on the science of law always had concrete cases of customary law in mind, what they write is so abstract, couched in such general terms, that not much can be inferred from it. Their endeavor is to formulate their doctrines so as to make them applicable to all customary law everywhere; we look in vain for distinctions, for a discussion of details, for an investigation of specific cases. Nevertheless they cannot altogether escape the necessity of giving an indication at least of the actual presuppositions of their doctrines and of illustrating them by a few examples. For this reason it is possible here and there to examine the factual bases of their doctrines.

From the examples adduced by Savigny and Puchta we can gather at least that they consistently conceived of customary law not as a mere norm for decision but as a rule of conduct. Puchta mentions, as modern customary law that was created by legal science, the doctrine that the ancestor of an insane person has the right of substitution to an extent equal to that of pupillary substitution; that the Roman *signatio*[1] of a testament was replaced by the seal of attestation, which was unknown to the Romans; and finally the proposition: *dies interpellat pro homine*[2]. As further examples he mentions the bankers law of bills of exchange, the peasants' law of demarcation of boundaries and of the servitude of pasturage. In several instances he mentions examples of customary law which he has invented himself: "If a man adds his seal to his signature in ... case of a lease of a house, a certain fixed time for the notice to quit is a *naturale negotii*[3]." "The question is whether there is a customary law in a city according to which the lessee of a dwelling newly conditioned is under a duty to return it not in the condition into which it would be put by ordinary use but in the condition in which he has received it, or a customary law according to which the power of the lessor to terminate the lease without the consent of the lessee on the ground that he requires the house for his own purposes has been defined by the recognition of the validity of certain reasons, e.g. the marriage of a son, and has, perhaps, been extended beyond the intent of the Continental common law."

In general however there can be no doubt that they did not arrive at their theory of the sources of law through observation of occurrences of this, at all events unimportant, sort, but through historical study. To them, the standard of primitive law was the law of the Roman regal period and of the early republic, as they conceived of it. In his *Institutionen.* Puchta gives a graphic description of it, and in his *Gewohnheitsrecht* he gives another description — a description which is essentially in agreement with the former. In addition, it can be shown, they had the German law of the Middle Ages in mind. Both among the Romans and among the ancient Germans, the law still consists chiefly of the prevailing rules of conduct; the people participate in the

1. *signatio*：〈拉〉签字
2. *dies interpellat pro homine*：〈拉〉期限代人催告
3. *naturale negotii*：〈拉〉自然之事

administration of justice and their legal consciousness is authoritative for the adjudication of the legal controversy. The jurists as yet have no special legal consciousness of their own; they draw the rules of law from the consciousness of their fellow citizens. Puchta refers expressly to Eyke von Repgow. As to the later period, the founders of the Historical School base their doc trine on the legal situation of the Roman Empire in which the Roman jurists are creating law directly, and their own legal consciousness supplies the basis for the creative activity. This is the empirical basis of their doctrine of juristic law. But a law which arises in this manner is not a rule of conduct but, in its very nature, a mere norm for decision.

Above all things they must come to terms with "the greatest and most remarkable act of universal customary law," i.e. the reception of Roman law in the Middle Ages. Their whole theory is designed to justify the latter. How can one harmonize their theory that the law arises in the legal consciousness of the people with the fact that in the Middle Ages a system of law which was foreign to the legal consciousness of the people became the valid law of Germany? This purpose of theirs is subserved by the theory that the people no longer participate in the creation of law after they have reached a more advanced stage of legal development, that they are being "represented" in this matter by the jurists. Roman law was received in the Middle Ages solely and alone by the jurists, but they acted as the representatives of the people.

This is, in its essence, Savigny and Puchta's theory of the sources of law, stated, as far as possible, in their own words. I have availed myself of the statements of Savigny and Puchta quite indiscriminately for, I am sure, there is no doubt that, in spite of a few minute differences in details, the doctrine as a whole is a unit, a product of their joint labors. And this product of their joint labors is an achievement of the highest rank, which was not understood by the great majority of their contemporaries, and which has not been surpassed in our day.

Moreover they have produced the whole doctrine by their unaided, absolutely independent labors even though certain traces of the influence of Schelling's philosophy or of Burkeys *Reflections on the Revolution in France*[1] may perhaps be found.

Their gravest error has been pointed out repeatedly in this book. It lies in this, that they manifestly conceive of the whole law as consisting exclusively of legal propositions. Legal propositions however do not, at any stage of legal development, arise, fully formed and developed, from the legal consciousness. They are always a product of the labors of the jurists. A few legal relations arise among the people, e.g. corporations and other communities, family relations, ownership and other property rights, contracts, and rights of heirs. This may be the "essential, invisible, spiritual law of the people" that Savigny is speaking of. It is only on the basis of these relations that juristic science and legislation create legal propositions. In order to attain clarity, every theory of the sources of law must carefully distinguish between the question as to the origin of legal institutions, and the question as to the creation of legal propositions.

This first error is the cause of the second, which consists in this, that the jurists of the Historical School make a distinction in principle between the earlier and the later legal development. At a lower stage of development the idea of the development of law immediately within the consciousness of the people presented little difficulty to them, for they took for granted that the whole people was called upon to take part in the administration of justice, and that the legal propositions that it applied resulted directly from the legal consciousness of the whole people. But the history upon which their doctrine was built up was not true. Even when "all the people" judge in the assemblies, it is always parts only of the people that are entitled to take part in the

1. *Reflections on the Revolution in France*：《法国革命反思录》

assemblies, and the legal propositions are formulated and proposed by a few, i.e. by those that are "experts in the law, such as a nation possesses long before it has developed a science of law" (Puchta). It is not these legal propositions that live and have their being within the consciousness of the people, but the legal institutions and the norms of the law of corporations and other communities, of property, and of contract, upon which the institutions are based, and from which the legal propositions are deduced. On the other hand at a higher stage, at which the jurist has already appeared on the scene, legal institutions and norms appertaining to them continue to arise among the people themselves, e.g. (using Puchta's illustrations) the bill of exchange among the bankers, the demarcation of boundaries, and the servitude of pasture among the peasants; only the legal propositions are being formulated by the jurists in their teachings and writings and in statutes. Had Savigny and Puchta distinguished bet ween legal institutions and legal propositions, they would have realized at once that both are being created in an identical manner at a higher as well as a lower stage of development.

Immediately linked with this second defect in principle appears a third defect in the teachings of the jurists of the Historical School, an error more remarkable indeed inasmuch as it prevented them from drawing the obvious inference from their greatest achievement, which was opening up new channels for the science of law, to grasp the full significance of which was reserved for a future generation. I mean the introduction of the idea of evolution into legal history. It is positively amusing to ask Savigny and Puchta what their conception is of the way in which, at least at a more advanced stage of civilization, the consciousness of the people arrives at the legal proposition, and thereby makes its way into the law which is being recognized and applied by the courts, and which according to their conception is the valid law. In this case, they always insist, the immediate influence of the popular consciousness is "negligible." But legislation, too, as they both teach, is of minor significance. Only "in case the development of law must take account of changed customs and views, in case quite new legal institutions become necessary," they say, legislative action may become salutary, aye, indispensable, in order to make an end of the interim of uncertainty, in order to give effect to the equalizing influence of the new law upon other, related legal propositions. Finally, the legislator must act, perhaps, when "stages of development and situations" arise, like those under Constantinus in Rome, which are no longer favorable to the creation of law by the common conviction of the whole people (Savigny). And beyond this legislative action becomes unprofitable.

Legislation therefore is just as negligible as the activity of the totality of the people. All that remains is juristic law. But how do jurists bring about harmony between the progress of their own legal consciousness and the law? It is important to hear Savigny and Puchta themselves on this point. In the first volume of his work on customary law, Puchta says: Scientific law is not customary law; scientific activity is not popular activity; scientific convictions are not those that a man arrives at as one of the people, but such as he arrives at as an individual, therefore the *Volksgeist*[1] (spirit of the people) is not the factor which is directly creative. But the science of law has a subject matter which is national in scope, and the science of law is a true science only if it treats its subject matter as national in scope, i.e. treats it according to its true nature. The jurists therefore must needs act as the representatives of the people if they would exercise the influence on law that has been referred to above. And the people is the original source of this kind of law also, even though it is not created immediately by the people, like customary law, but mediately, through these representatives. A juristic view is law and right whenever there

1. *Volksgeist*：〈德〉民族精神

is a scientific basis for it, i.e. whenever it is true. In order to be true, it must be based on the inner nature of things, and it must be in accord with the *Volksgeist*. That it is in accord with the *Voiksgeist* will appear from the fact that it has made its influence felt in part in the conviction of the jurists, and in part in the application by the court. This is the significance of the authority of the jurists and of the *res iudicatae*[1], which therefore are not sources of law but merely sources — of course, not absolutely infallible ones — of the knowledge of such law as has already come into existence.

In the second volume of his book on customary law, however, Puchta says that under certain circumstances juristic law can be customary law. As the law develops, the mass of legal material increases to such an extent, and the science of law becomes so refined that a comprehensive knowledge and a scientific mastery of the law can be found only among the jurists. Therefore the conviction of all the members of the people is replaced by the conviction of the jurists. "In this connection, it might be a good thing to consider that the jurists do not possess this qualification of natural representation in virtue of their scientific activity, which as such is not a popular one, but in virtue of their preeminent legal knowledge which they have in common with the men learned in the law, who are met with among a people long before the latter has a science of law." Accordingly by the side of customary law which is based upon the common conviction of the people there is another kind of customary law, which is based upon the usage of those learned in the law, of the jurists, as the representatives of the people, provided no proposition is involved for which a scientific basis must be sought, and which is valid only because it is inherently true; and in addition to the customary practice "which is based upon a legal proposition scientifically deduced" there is another customary practice

1. *res iudicatae*：〈拉〉既判力。法院判决对当事人和法院实质上的约束力。

which expresses "the popular legal consciousness of those learned in the law," and which therefore contains "customary law."

Savigny, in his *System*, amplifies Puchta's remarks. Discussing the general nature of the sources of law, he says that one must distinguish between a material and a formal, purely scientific activity of the legal profession. As to the former, he says that the law-creating activity of the people is being withdrawn into the legal profession, and is being practiced by the latter as representatives of the whole people. Later, in the section on the sources of Roman law, he contrasts the theoretical and the practical activity of the jurists. The theoretical activity, according to Savigny, consists in purely scientific investigation, i.e. in establishing and interpreting the text of the sources, working up the results into a legal system, and perfecting the inner organization of the legal system. This activity, he says, does not produce new law; it merely makes possible a purer knowledge of the existing law. By practical activity he means all investigation which has in view the relation between the content of the sources and "the condition of the living law upon which they are to act, i.e. the condition and the requirements of modern times." This activity may be occasioned by the communication, through teaching or writing, of the results obtained, or by the necessity of deciding a law-suit. In either case, the investigation is an instrumental ity of customary law and, at the same time, a part of scientific law.

In the Romanistic practical legal science, Savigny would differentiate between two totally dissimilar component parts. "One part is of a healthy nature, and is based upon the modern requirements that have arisen as a natural result from the completely changed conditions, *inter alia*[1], from the great modifications in judicial procedure, and in part from the great transformation of the whole ethical view of life that

1. *inter alia*：〈拉〉尤其，特别是

has been brought about by the Christian religion. According to the views just stated, we must attribute to this part the power and reality of customary law which has been recognized in a scientific manner. In this connection, it is immaterial that earlier teachers of law made a misguided attempt to derive these propositions from Roman law. These jurists were sincere in their endeavors, and we must, in such cases, consider the investigation of the true Roman law an essential part of our task; not for the purpose of keeping it in force as valid law, but in order to ascertain the true extent of the innovation. The other part has arisen solely from the misguided confusion mentioned above, i.e. from a defective scientific method. It is our task to expose and to dislodge this error, without permitting long undisturbed possession of the field to protect it; especially since, to a great degree, it will be possible to prove that there is imbedded in it an inner contradiction, a basic error in logic." As an illustration he adduces the *Summarissimum* of modern usage.

In concluding this discussion, Savigny adds these words: "The part of the practical law which I have referred to as the sound part is of an importance altogether different from that which I have attributed to the theoretical labor. It is not only effective as an authority which commands respect, but in fact comprises newly created law. Nevertheless we cannot concede even to it a conclusively perfected, immutable existence. It is true, such a proposition of the practical law cannot be deprived of its validity by a purely theoretical examination, by demonstrating its divergence from the law of the sources, for, being true customary law, it has acquired an independent existence. But there can be no doubt that it can lose its validity in the same way in which it got it."

To these words we must add the following remarks of Puchta in his review of Beseler's book: "I find that even though those powers (the powers to interpret the existing law) have been most fully developed, the judicial office requires additional powers without which it would, in very many cases, have no norm for decision at its disposal. In such cases the judge derives the legal proposition which is to be applied from the principles of the existing law. Inasmuch as the law is inherently reasonable, that which follows as a matter of inner necessity from the existing law, must also be valid law."

This can scarcely be called a scientific exposition; it is an embarrassed stammering. The question is, whether the jurists who are working according to a scientific method are authorized to introduce new principles into the law. If they are, let it be stated clearly and unmistakably, and let the methods be stated according to which they can and must do it. It cannot be done by merely developing the principles of the existing law, for they are comprised in the existing law. Puchta is right in insisting in his argument against Beseler that this scientific labor, too, is productive; but its productivity consists in discovering the content of existing law, not in creating new law. And if Savigny alludes to the misguided attempt of earlier teachers of law to derive such propositions from the Roman law, I would say that this method becomes the more hopeless the more our understanding of Roman law, and of existing valid law generally, increases. At all events it would have been the most important task of these great defenders of the creative power of the science of law carefully to develop the methods of original creation of law. But no trace of this can be found in their writings. All that they have to say of the science of law refers exclusively to the means of deriving norms for decision from traditional law, not to a method of finding or inventing new law. And the juristic method which they have in fact developed most successfully, i.e. the historical and systematic method, most flatly contradicts their teachings. A school of jurisprudence whose chief concern is to establish the meaning of legal propositions at the time when they were created is manifestly little qualified for the creation of new law whenever the present time requires it.

In his book, entitled *Volksrecht und Juristenrecht* (1843), Beseler attacked the doctrine of Savigny and Puchta at two points. First of all he denies that direct participation of the people ceases at the more advanced stages of development. He adduces numerous examples from all departments of law — he devotes a whole chapter to *Genossenschaftsrecht*[1] and another to *Standesrecht*[2] — in order to show that the popular law is still alive in the great masses of the people. It is true, he says, the jurists know little of it and the courts pay no attention to it, but the Historical School of jurisprudence teaches that actual usage is not a necessary element of the concept of customary law, but is merely an external characteristic, that all that is of the essence of customary law is that it has arisen directly from the consciousness of the people. Therefore, he insists, it is absolutely immaterial whether this law, which is based directly upon the popular consciousness, is, or is not, known to the jurists, whether it is, or is not, applied by the courts.

Thereupon Beseler attacks the idea that, without more ado, the jurists are to be looked upon as the representatives of the people in the matter of creating law. He expresses the opinion that law might arise, "as to which it is at least a merely accidental matter whether and to what extent it retains its character as popular law." This is the case, above all, when bad laws are enacted in the state, but also "when external influence becomes so powerful from long continuance of its operation upon the state of the law that at last true norms for decision develop therefrom which everyone considers, and must consider, binding." The ultimate basis of the validity of law in this case is custom, "which therefore is no longer a mere external characteristic (*Kennzeichen*[3]) of law but actually participates in its creation, and very often in opposition to the *Volksgeist* (spirit of the people) and to the

1. *Genossenschaftsrecht*：〈德〉社团法
2. *Standesrecht*：〈德〉职业法
3. *Kennzeichen*：〈德〉特征

reason of things (*Vernunft der Dinge*)[1] Customary law therefore, as such, is a thing foreign to the popular consciousness. Its relation to *Volksrecht*, whose origin lies immediately in the popular consciousness, is now one of hostility, now of indifference. It is incorrect therefore, he insists, to say that juristic law necessarily is a continuation of popular law; it may be merely customary law.

It is apparent that Beseler here carried Savigny and Puchta's very own thoughts to their logical conclusion. When they made difficulties about admitting that in their own day the development of law was being continued by the whole people, and were bent upon looking upon the jurists as representatives of the people, they did this solely in order to justify the reception of Roman law, which had been carried out by the jurists and had remained foreign to the popular consciousness. Beseler, who, being a Germanist, was under no obligation to defend the reception, availed himself of this freedom. But inwardly Savigny and Puchta were very close to Beseler — much closer perhaps than they themselves believed.

Beseler devoted a whole section of his book to the question how popular law must be ascertained and recognized. The people in its totality, or in narrower circles, within whose consciousness popular law lives and has its being, he says, has an immediate intuition of it, "which grasps the essential elements of everyday life contained in the circumstances and relations of everyday life, and, at the same time, knows the norms that regulate them and applies them. This may also be said of every individual, within whose consciousness, because of his position and his experience in business and life, the common knowledge of the law is being reflected. ... But if anyone who is a stranger to the life of the people and the views of the people wishes to obtain a knowledge of the law contained therein, he must proceed like

1. reason of things (*Vernunft der Dinge*)：事物的理性

a natural scientist; he must acquire a knowledge of things as they are by means of actual observation." In this case, the sources of knowledge are: inquiry among people that are interested in the matter in hand, mercantile *Pareres*[1] (an institution that might be applied to other relations as well), legal literature, autonomous relations, through which popular law in former days so often expressed itself; in statutes, too, we often find a pure and clear expression of the popular idea of right and law.

If we examine the presuppositions of this presentation, which, as usual, are not expressed, we find that, unlike Savigny and Puchta, when this writer speaks of law he does not mean legal propositions but legal institutions. This is obscured by the fact that, apparently, the basis of the doctrine of both Beseler and the founders of the Historical School is the legal consciousness. But the latter, as to the present time at least, have in mind the legal consciousness of the jurists, who have gained control over the teaching and the administration of law; Beseler has in mind the legal consciousness of the people among whom the legal institutions develop today, just as they did many centuries ago. Savigny and Puchta themselves have put the center of gravity in the legal consciousness, and have treated customary practice as a mere "external characteristic (*Kennzeichen*)." From this Beseler draws the inference that popular law can dispense with the requirement of customary practice altogether in the practical application of law. When Puchta, quite inconsistently with his own point of view, objected to this on the score of the uncertainty of law of this kind, i.e. law without usage as an external characteristic (*Kennzeichen*)." Beseler replied that in the very fact that he had declared that direct observation of the relations of life is of such paramount importance if one would know the popular law, there lay "a direct reference to the habitual customary

1. *Pareres*：〈拉〉专家意见

observance of the norm (usage), which is revealed in the relations of life inasmuch as it controls them." Here the opposing views clash. On one side there is the view that the important thing is the law that is applied by the courts; on the other, the knowledge of the fact that law regulates the relations of life even without the intervention of the courts. The fact that Savigny and Puchta combated the latter view, although they did not consider usage a prerequisite to the arising of customary law, is further evidence of the lack of consistency that characterizes their whole controversy with Beseler. But Beseler has gone much further than Savigny and Puchta inasmuch as he is not content with stating propositions about popular law and juristic law, but is seeking methods for the direct acquisition of knowledge "in the manner of the natural scientist ... by means of observation." The fact that this powerfully stimulating suggestion by the great Germanist remained unheeded is merely another proof that in science, too, it is the distribution of power (*Machstverhältnisse*) rather than the spirit that turns the scale.

The idea of Beseler was realized far from the land of its origin by a pupil of Savigny's, the Croat Bogisic, and by another student of the writings of Savigny, the Spaniard Costa. Both are endeavoring to create a science of popular law, not by establishing legal propositions but by studying legal relations and legal institutions. Bogisic drew up an extensive questionnaire containing more than eight hundred questions, and made the answers which he received from the regions inhabited by southern Slavs the basis of his work (*Zbornik sadašnih pramih običaja južnih Slovena*), and Costa created the foundation of his two-volume work *Derecho consuetudinario y economia popular en Espāna* by direct personal observation and study of the legal relations and institutions he is describing. The second volume, incidentally, also contains works of other writers. The work of Bobcev on Buigarian customary law, *Sbornik na blgarski juriditski obitschai*, employs the method of Bogìšič.

I hope to be able to make a report on all of these books at another place. Several years ago, in an article which appeared in Schmoller's Jahrbuch[1], I emphatically directed attention to the books of Bogìšič which are written in Croatian and which, for that reason, are little known, and I am therefore in every way well armed against the charge that has been leveled at me in Vienna that I have been trying to ignore them by not mentioning them. But I cannot admit, on the other hand, that I owe the basic thoughts of my sociological works to Bogìšič. Since the works of Bogìšič are for the most part inaccessible to West European readers because of the language in which they have been written, everyone cannot convince himself, by a personal examination, of the recklessness with which I have been accused of borrowing. Bogìšič was a veritable genius of the concrete, and his questionnaire is a masterpiece of insight into the legal conceptions of a backward society and the order based upon them. But it would be a vain endeavor to look for general thoughts in his works. The passage from his *Sbornik* which I published in a German translation in the article referred to above is practically all that I have been able to find in his works in the nature of a discussion of principles. He has supplied us with invaluable material but has utterly failed to work out a classification and an organization of this material that I could have availed myself of. Moreover his horizon is extremely narrow; he confines himself to the institutions peculiar to a primitive society, and is not at all interested in the relations existing in a more advanced form of civilization, in a richer life, or in modern business. From this the reader may judge how far I have advanced beyond Bogìšič.

I do however feel constrained to refer to the small volume of Dniestrzanski, entitled *Das Gewohnheitsrecht und die sozialen Verbände*[2] (1905), in which may be found the germs perhaps of a number of

1. Schmoller's Jahrbuch：〈德〉《施穆勒年鉴》
2. *Das Gewohnheitsrecht und die sozialen Verbände*：〈德〉《习惯法与社会联合体》

thoughts that are somewhat like those that I am presenting in the present volume. I first became acquainted with his work while I was writing this book. There can be no thought of a borrowing; for I have expressed these thoughts as early as the year 1903, in an address entitled *Freie Rechtsfindung und freie Rechtswissenschaft.*[1] At the same time it is apparent that the article by Dniestrzanski is absolutely independent of my address.

Moreover it is the extraordinary merit of Bogisic to have written a code which fully meets Savigny's requirements. It is a codification of the property law of Montenegro. It is based upon a very careful and methodical investigation of South Slavic legal custom, not merely of the legal propositions, which are very few in number, but chiefly of the concrete legal relations and legal institutions. These books, the object of which was not historical understanding, which the legislator can quite readily dispense with, but the understanding of that which is in existence, today, have enabled Bogisic to produce a recognized masterpiece.

The barrenness of all theories of customary law that have been advanced hitherto is caused by the fact that their aims are not clearly defined. While the oldest type of juristic science merely sought, under this head, to give directions to the judge in which cases he should recognize local or particular customs in preference to the Continental common law, the Historical School attempts to present the doctrine of the origin of law. But the Historical School never fully realized that the origin of legal institutions and the origin of legal propositions are two quite distinct things; that the former takes place in society, or, according to their terminology, in the popular consciousness, and becomes manifest in the rules of conduct, or in their terminology, in usage, whereas the legal propositions are being created by the jurists.

---

1. *Freie Rechtsfindung und freie Rechtswissenschaft*：〈德〉《法的自由发现与自由法学》

Instead of dealing with these two phenomena separately side by side, they discuss one after the other; and being unaware of the fact that they are dealing with two distinct things, they propound a doctrine which, on the whole, applies only to juristic law, and then apply it to the development of law in society as well. And when Beseler points out that popular law exists even at the present time, that there are legal institutions which arise immediately in society, they do not know what to say in reply to these inferences from their own principles. In a general way, it may be admitted that the doctrines of Savigny and Puchta are correct if limited to juristic law; their continual vacillation and uncertainty is caused by the fact that they have never become aware of the existence of this limitation.

But there is another ambiguity involved. Juristic law, too, has a double function. In the first place its function is to formulate the norms for decision required for the regulation of the legal institutions which have arisen in society by universalizing the social rules of conduct and making them unitary, but over and above this to find norms for decision independently according to the trends of justice that prevail in society. At this point, too, the founders of the Historical School failed to make the necessary distinction. This error however is less palpably felt, for the reason that, to a certain extent, the same rules apply to both kinds of juristic law. Nevertheless let me emphasize the fact that their discussions are applicable chiefly to the second kind of juristic law, albeit, as their doctrine of analogy and of the "nature of the thing" shows, they occasionally have the former in mind also.

At any rate Savigny and Puchta could not fail to realize that it was necessary not only to advance a theory of the sources of law, a science of the origin and development of law, but also to issue directions to the judge concerning the method of testing the binding force of customary law. For this reason they took over from the older juristic science in vogue among the jurists of the Continental common law the doctrine of the prerequisites of customary law, which, however, quite imperceptibly, become means of gaining knowledge of customary law such as is already in existence in the consciousness of the people or of the legal profession. From this point of view, they discuss the met hod, the uniformity, the long continued repetition of the acts, the recognition implied in the judgment, the *opinio necessitatis*, the reasonableness, the publicity, and the effect of error. It is apparent that these wretched *Kautelen* (prerequisites) are not necessary for testing either the legal validity of the institutions that have arisen in society or the binding force of juristic law; but they can serve the purpose for which they were found, for which the practical science of the older jurists of the Continental common law utilized them, i.e. for the ascertainment of the binding force of local and special legal customs in preference to the common law. This was recognized by Savigny, especially when he taught that this narrow point of view "that custom, as the source (*Enstehungsgrund*) of a rule of law must always be resoluble into definite, individual, demonstrable acts" is applicable at most to special (*partikuldre*) customs, of which alone one is in the habit of thinking. "It is not applicable at all to the great and difficult cases of modern customary law, in which the latter is identical with scientific law. The conditions that are usually assumed as conditions precedent to the genesis of customary law, refer throughout to the nature of those acts from which, as we say, it uniformly arises. For this reason they have a merely one-sided applicability to the special (*partikuldre*) customary law, and even as to the latter the various acts must not be looked upon as the sources but rather as the phenomena or characteristics of an existing common legal conviction. As thus modified, the predicate 'truth' may be applied to these conditions, and therefore they must be examined and ascertained separately." He then discusses the conditions in the form in which the Continental common law theory has handed them down. That this is a matter solely of particular customs is confirmed by the English law. The common law, which in its essence is juristic law, throughout follows the rules that Savigny and Puchta have developed for their customary law, which, they say, is chiefly juristic law. In addition, it is true, we find rules like the following: "A custom, in order to be legal and binding must have been used so long that the memory of man runneth not to the contrary; it must be reasonable, it must be continued, not interrupted and peaceably enjoyed; must be reasonable; must be certain; must be compulsory; customs must be consistent with each other; as to the allowance of special customs no custom can, of course, prevail against the express provision of an act of Parliament." The Continental common law jurist must be strongly reminded of home when he reads these words. But all of these things do not refer to customary law but to local and special customs.

The modern Continental common law and the modern German school of legal science mark a step backward from Savigny and Puchta. They are based exclusively on law that is created by the state, and therefore they can have no theory of the non-state, the social, development of law, nor of juristic law. For them the very question becomes all-important that engrossed the attention of juristic science in the days of the Roman Empire and in the days of the Continental common law, i.e. whet her and how a system of law can become valid so as to displace the common law of the state. As a practical matter, this question resolves itself into a question as to the validity of special and local customs. For this reason, the doctrine of Savigny and Puchta was thrust aside and the old doctrine of the prerequisites of customary law was taken up again. Inasmuch as law, in principle, is taken to proceed from the state, permission, approval, or recognition by the sovereign power of the state is demanded in some form or other, either by express words or by silence, and thereby a thought of Justinian's and of the older trend of juristic theory of the Continental common law is being revived. But if, following Savigny and Puchta, modern writers base customary law upon a universal legal conviction as to its binding force, this, in view of the theory that all law proceeds from the state, can mean only that a special prerequisite is being added. The meaning of this doctrine is the following: All law proceeds from the state; under certain conditions, the state permits non-state law; these conditions include among others the universal conviction that the rule in question is law (*Rechtsuberzeugüng*). Zitelmann, however, has conclusively demonstrated that these doctrines are untenable. He himself simply derives the validity of customary law from its validity. It is valid because it is valid. But in this tautology a deeper understanding of the non-state character of customary law, at least, lies hidden. Law can come into existence independently of the state whenever it secures validity in society. Zitelmann did not elaborate his thought. Geny, a Frenchman, however, building on the foundation laid by Savigny and Puchta, and elaborating some ideas of Jhering's, has restored the *libre récherche scientifique*[1], the juristic law of the founders of the Historical School, to its former position of honor. This view is diametrically opposed to the theory, which is also the prevailing theory in France, that the state is the sole source of law.

It is self-evident that the Sociological School of jurisprudence cannot make use of a concept which is composed of such heterogeneous elements as is the traditional concept of customary law. It will analyze it and resolve it into its component parts, and discuss these separately in their proper place and order. These parts are: the origin of legal institutions in society independently of the state, the creation of legal propositions by the jurists, as writers, teachers, judges; and the question to what extent courts and other agencies of the state are bound by non-state law. These are totally distinct fields of knowledge, and fusing them into one can cause nothing but confusion.

But confined to a limited sphere, the concept of customary law is indispensable to the Sociological School of legal science. Where the

1. *libre récherche scientifique*：〈法〉自由的科学探索

creation of juristic law is not regulated by fixed precepts, as it is in England, it is necessarily unsettled and uncertain during the time immediately following its creation. A considerable period of time must elapse before a rule of juristic law gains such general recognition that a judge will no longer consider himself authorized to disregard it even though it conflicts with his own conviction. Thereafter it is something more than juristic law, and it would be quite in keeping with modern theory to call it customary law. Whenever there is a long-continued course of decisions contrary to a statute under circumstances where there can be no error of law, it ought to be made the subject of a special study. The occurrence of such courses of decision is beyond doubt. It has been observed repeatedly in France; and it occasionally blossoms forth even in Austria, a country which in other respects is the paradise of the narrowest sort of worship of the letter. It is often being denied that customary law can arise from such usage. But this only means that the courts, in such cases, can always revert to the statute, and that a judge can not be accused of defeating the ends of the law who decides against the existing judicial usage according to the statute, provided that in doing so he follows his conviction. This phenomenon at all events deserves a more detailed study. As compared with the theory that customary law arises simply from juristic law, it presents numerous peculiarities.

XX THE METHODS OF THE SOCIOLOGY OF LAW

I. Legal History and Juristic Science

There is no antithesis between science and art. Every true work of science is a work of art, and the man who is not an artist is a poor man of science. Production of a work of science requires the same qualifications as production of a work of art; both require a certain receptivity of mind, imagination, and power to give shape to one's material. For this reason every independent investigator must create his own method, just as every creative artist must create his own technique. He who employs another's method, just like the person who employs another's technique, may possibly be a great disciple, but never more than a disciple, who continues the work of the master but does not undertake new work. It is possible therefore to teach one's own or anothet's method or technique, but not to teach scientific method or artistic technique. For the mind which thinks and works independently will ever be seeking new methods and new techniques which correspond to his individuality.

But whatever method or technique it may be, its starting point will always be that which the external world presents to the human mind. For the latter can work only on those impressions that it receives from without. Every deduction is preceded by an induction[1]; all idealizing,

1. Every deduction is preceded by an induction：每一个演绎之前都存在归纳。

by a reception of the outward impression of that which has been idealized. The induetion and the reception however very frequently take place with lightning-like rapidity, unconsciously, without any conscious intention, and only the subsequent process of deduction or of idealizing enters into the consciousness of the scientist or of the artist. This creates the appearance of an inductive science or of an idealistic art.

The social sciences have hitherto been working, and are still doing their work, by means of such unconscious inductions. But when Montesquieu apparently derives a considerable part of his theory of the state by a purely deductive method from his classification of the forms of government; when he bases the despotic form of government upon fear, the monarchical upon honor, the republican upon virtue, the inductions, most superficial and unmethodical as they are, which have preceded the deductions can easily be perceived by anyone. The theory as to despotism is based on the accounts of the Greek city tyrants or the Roman emperors; as to the republic, on the accounts of the small ancient free state and of the Swiss cantons. The wealth of unconscious experience that has been compressed into the theory of value of Ricardo or of Marx, a veritable model of deduction, must be sensed by everyone who has read their presentations understandin gly. And in the preface to his work on *Kapitakins* (interest)[1] Boehm-Bawerk, one of the chief exponents of the Austrian school of economists, which allegedly is purely deductive, says that the facts on which the book is based have been learned by means of simple, informal observation directly from common everyday life as it presents itself to every one of us.

And sociology also, including the sociology of law, must be a science of observation. The man who, a century and a half ago, wrote the

1. *Kapitalzins* (interest)：〈德〉利息

three words *Esprit des Lois*[1] as the title of his book surely was seeking a sociology of law within his own soul even at that early date. And Montesquieu even then was busy for twenty years, indefatigably gathering facts on long journeys, and as an untiring reader. Although his book is not the work of a scholar, but the dilettantish, poorly arranged, desultory work of a grand seigneur, and is planned on a scale altogether too magnificent, it is nevertheless an inexhaustible source of stimulation and instruction, and it would be well worth the effort to avail oneself of the resources of modern science for the purpose of investigating the innumerable problems which he touched upon and disposed of but practically never answered.

We are dealing here not with history of literature nor with methodology but with a method of the sociology of law. The most important question which our time must solve is, what phenomena should the sociologist concern himself with, and how should he gather the facts which he needs in order to understand and explain them? The social phenomena in the legal sphere, which are of importance for a scientific understanding of law, are first of all the facts of the law themselves, i.e. usage, which assigns to each member of the human associations his position and his tasks, the relations of domination and of possession, agreements, articles of association, dispositions by last will and by other means, and succession. To these must be added the legal proposition, considered only as a fact, i.e. with reference to its origin and effect, not with reference to its practical application and interpretation, finally, all social forces, which lead to the creation of law. These are the phenomena that the sociologist must keep in mind, and he must collect the facts that give rise to these phenomena, and explain them.

In the past legal science has dealt with only one of these phenomena

1. *Esprit des Lois*：〈法〉《论法的精神》。孟德斯鸠著名的政治哲学著作，于1748年出版。

in an exhaustive manner, i.e. with the legal proposition. The others it has merely touched upon. And the facts which it adduced for the purpose of getting an understanding of, and explaining, the legal propositions were taken exclusively from history and ethnology. What we have of true, theoretical science of law is either historical or ethnological. Basically however even ethnological science is historical, for it is based on the proposition that the law of all nations has passed through approximately the same stages of development, and that therefore the law of peoples of a lower stage of development, with which the ethnological study of law concerns itself, corresponds, in its main outlines at least, to the past of the law of all other peoples.

Undoubtedly the chief function of the history of law is to supply the subject mat ter for the soci ology of law. But this is not, primarily, a question of the history of the legal proposition, of the history of the sources, or of the history of legal doctrine, but of the history of legal institutions. No serious legal historian believes today that he can present the whole law of a period of time that is past on the basis of the legal propositions that have been handed down, e.g. that he can present the state of the law of Rome at the time of the Twelve Tables on the basis of these Twelve Tables even if they had been preserved in their entirety, or the whole law of the Salic Franks on the basis of the *Lex Salica*, or the law of the Saxon countries on the basis of the *Sachsenspiegel*. He is bent upon gaining a first-hand knowledge of the legal institutions on the basis of a study of the legal document. Yet even the legal document will not enable one to get a perfect picture of the law of the past. It speaks only of contracts, legal relations, and decisions that have been embodied in legal documents; it is silent as to the parol legal transaction and as to the great majority of legal relations, which have been the occasion neither of a document nor of a law-suit. About the legal form of the family, of the system of landholding, of the affairs of everyday life, which would be of vast importance for the understanding of the spirit and of the order of the whole life of the past, we shall not be able to learn much from the legal document. Very often the ability to interpret a picture on an ancient vase would be of much greater value to the legal historian. It is true, in modern times the ability to read between the lines of the traditional material, to spell out of a given word everything that it presupposes, has increased in a most fearsome fashion, but it cannot compensate for the absence of a tradition. The information which could have been obtained only by direct observation is lost to posterity — perhaps forever.

Great though these difficulties may be, the chief function of the history of law, as the founders of the Historical School have pointed out in their day, must be to show that the legal propositions and the legal institutions are growing out of the life of the people, out of the social and economic constitution as a whole. For the sociology of law it is of value only in so far as it is successful in doing this. The various legal propositions as such, the legal institutions divorced from their presuppositions, have no information to convey. If there is a unifying regularity in the phenomena of legal life, to discover and make a presentation of which is the function of sociology, it can be found only in the fact that legal life is conditioned upon the social and economic constitution; if there is a legal development which takes place according to certain laws, it can be recognized and presented only in connection with the whole social and economic development. The sociology of law therefore will not draw its mat erials from legal antiquities but from social and economic history.

The results of practical juristic science are equally important for the sociology of law. Every technique is, at the same time, the beginning of a true science; and this applies to practical juristic science also. In order to acquire dominion over nature, man strives to understand the laws of nature; and in order to gain mastery over life as a jurist, he must know life. The practical jurist of course deals primarily with the norms for decision. But since the latter arise directly from the social formations, or must be referred to the social formations, they cannot enter into his consciousness in any other way, and cannot be presented by him in any other way, than in connection with these formations. It is impossible to teach the law of the family without describing the family; to explain the law of things (*Sachenrecht*) without stating what kinds of rights in things are found in life; to state the law of contracts without stating the content of the contracts that are being entered into. And together with the norms which it states practical juristic science must present a picture of the society in which these norms are to have validity, and this picture is being drawn by men who have devoted their lives to the juristic study of society, and who ought to possess that fine sense of the reality of things which we admire in the ancient Roman jurists, in Bartolus, in many a jurist of the most recent years. In this sense a famous Roman has called jurisprudence *divinarum atque humanarum rerum notitia*[1]. It is the function of law teaching to provide for the *cupida legum inventus*[2], who do not yet know life, a substitute for the study of life at first hand which one must engage in in order to become a jurist, and also to provide them with the results of such observations as they never would institute themselves-observations that will widen their horizon and refine their sensibilities.

Direct actual observation of human relations of a legal nature, universalization of the results of this observation and the appertaining norms for decision these are the scientific elements in juristic science. To this extent, juristic science actually is a morphology of the legal formations of social life. It presents the state in all the ramifications of its activity, the forms of the family, ownership and *real* rights, the contracts and the other forms of the economic distribution of goods, the organization of commerce, of industry, of the trades, of

1. *divinarum atque humanarum rerum notitia*：〈拉〉法学是关于神事和人事的知识。
2. *cupida legum inventus*：〈拉〉立志于法律发现

agriculture, of the mining industry, the fate of property after the death of the owner. The systematism (*Systematic*) of juristic science organizes all of this material, classifies and arranges it, separating the related from the unrelated. The content of the much maligned "general part," too, is scientific in its nature; for by analyzing the composite complicated legal institutions into its constituent parts it reveals their inner structute and creates an accurate and at the same time flexible scientific terminology. The jurists, being under the limitation of practical interests, are concerned with social morphology and with *Systematik* from a point of view altogether different from that of the scientific investigator. The latter however is nevertheless relieved of a great deal of hard work by the fact that all he need do is to arrange the results of the observations of others for his own purposes.

It is true, practical juristic science, in the first place, deals only with legal propositions that belong to a certain system of positive law. And for this very reason, after it has completed the discussion of the legal propositions and has begun the discussion of the relations of life upon which the latter are based, it contents itself with a presentation of the morphology of a society which is governed by a certain system of positive law. But the human relations, upon which a presentation of the law must be based, are independent of the legal propositions. The state and its instrumentalities, persons, ownership, *real* rights, contracts, succession, are found everywhere; and among peoples of an approximately identical civilization and of an approximately identical stage of economic development, they are found in a form which, in addition to some diversities, exhibits a series of common traits. It is quite in order therefore to describe all these legal relations without reference to any system of positive law, as has been done for some time in economics in the case of economic legal relations.

For this reason, I think, it is possible to evolve a general legal science, which is based, just like economics, not on a society governed by a certain positive legal system, but on human society as such. The first and foremost function of the sociological science of law is to present an exposition of the common elements in the legal relations without reference to the positive law that governs them, and to study the elements peculiar to each relation with reference to their causes and effects. In the field of public law, of *Staatsrecht* (public law in the narrow sense), of criminal and of procedural law, much work of this kind has already been done. In the field of private law, little or nothing has been done.

Nevertheless it is particularly in the field of private law that the juristic labors of the jurists of the Continental common law have prepared the way for the sociological study of law. And they have done this in a way that can be fittingly described only by the epithet "magnificent." The juristic science of the Continental common law was itself the heir of a never interrupted, international intellectual activity extending over a period of two thousand years or more. Its basis was the *corpus iuris civilis,* which, in spite of all its defects, was a great achievement. Its roots are to be found in the juristic science of the Roman *pontifices* in prehistoric times. Since that time untold generations of jurists have been bestowing creative labor upon it, the pupil becoming the successor of his teacher both in developing the law and in teaching it. each generation receiving the benefit of the work of its predecessor and continuing to build on the foundation laid by the latter. Accordingly an unbroken chain of oral tradition unites the professors of Constantinople with those of Berytus, the compilers of Justinian's code with each one of the *prudentes* of the days of primitive Rome. It is being understood more and more clearly from day to day that this juristic science of the Roman jurist was, at all times, connected by an unbroken continidty with everything that had been accomplished in this sphere in antiquity, was always ready to appropriate the institutions of other peoples, and in its palmy days, which ext end into the third century of our era, was able to weld these elements into its system as an organic whole. Only that which was received during the decline of the Empire could no longer be assimilated. So in the *corpus iuris civilis,* all the results of a thousand years of ancient legal development, gathered, as it were, in a focus, were transmitted to the Middle Ages. This was followed by the work of the glossators and the postglossators, who in turn were followed by the great French jurists of the sixteenth and seventeenth centuries, by the learned and astute Dutch legal scholars, by the juristic science of the German jurists from the days of Ulrich Zasius. Thus almost all civilized peoples of Europe took part in its creation, and a structure arose which is unique in the history of law and without a peer in other spheres of intellectual life. International participation did not cease until the nineteenth century, when the national codifications brought about a practical juristic science whose sole concern was national law. In Germany, however, the Historical School of jurisprudence is still making the best possible use of the talent entrusted to it, and so the international science of law is enjoying a new, late classical period.

But if the teaching of Bartolus and Baldus was quite different from that of the glossators, that of Stryck and Lauterbach quite different from that of Ulrich Zasius, that of Windscheid and Dernburg quite different from that of Vangerow, the reason for these differences lies in the fact that different times made different demands. The differences are so great that one can almost say that each period was dealing with an entirely different subjectmatter. But if one looks at the connecting links that connect the successive schools, one marvels at the gradual, methodical transition, at the way in which each generation based its teaching directly upon that of the preceding one. It was not theories that suggested the trends and methods to the jurists; the needs created the trend, the method, and the appertaining theory. The necessity of adjusting itself again and again to the changing times gave to the juristic science of the jurists of the Continental common law its extraordinary wealth of ideas, and the fact that it was the law of a considerable part of the civilized world, where its function was to serve the most manifold needs, gave it a remarkable flexibility and expressiveness.

For this reason the juristic science of the Romanist jurists of western and of central Europe never was merely the science of a system of national law, much less of Roman law, but to a certain degree a science of law, a general science of law. It has created the most important presuppositions for a sociology of law which is not bound by the limitations of a given system of law, or of a given people, or by the requirements of customary observance, or usage. It has in the first place created a fixed juristic terminology and, over and above that, a juristic language which is readily understood by every jurist, for the jurists of all civilized peoples learn Roman law from text-books written by the jurists of the Continental common law school. In Germany the Germanists, particularly those of Beseler's school, have contributed much to the development of juristic science. At the same time they have made German law a part of the juristic science of the Romanist school. They have employed its systematism, its technique, its terminology, and thereby they have actually demonstrated that it can subserve not only a Romanist science of law but any science of law. And if one removes from the German common law monographs or from the general works on the pandect law every thing that might look like an interpretation of a text of the sources, there still would remain a scientific achievement which can be made the basis of the study of any system of law, not only of the Continental common law.

The sociology of law therefore must continue its work on the basis of the juristic science of the Continental common law. It must by no means be confused with "*allgemeine Rechtslehre*[1]," or with *Rechtsenzyklopädie*[2], as it is called. It does not present formalistic abstractions from the juristic science of systems of national law, but its

1. *allgemeine Rechtslehre*：〈德〉法的一般原理
2. *Rechtsenzyklopädie*：〈德〉法学概论

living content. Nor does it include true interpretation; the legal basis of juristic science, however, must be shown as well as the form which the institutions have assumed in the course of the administration of justice and of life.

May I be permitted to illustrate by an example the fitness of the juristic science of the Continental common law to constitute the basis for a general science of law? The English doc trine that informal contracts are binding only when supported by consideration is one of the peculiarities of English law that a Continental jurist does not readily understand. Only recently a German work on legal history compared the Roman innominate contracts to the English contracts for good consideration. This: of course, is altogether beside the mark. Consideration and *res* in the sense of Roman law are things of a totally different nature, and the informal contracts of English law are not "*real*" contracts but "consensual" contracts. But an informal contract creates a legal obligation according to English law only when each party has purchased the obligation of the other party by incurring a detriment. If the debtor who owes one hundred pounds pays ten shillings one day before the debt is due at a place other than that provided for in the contract, an informal agreement by the creditor to remit the remainder is binding; for payment before the due day or at another place may be a detriment to him. But if he pays ninety-nine pounds at the time and place provided for, a formal release in writing and under seal is required, for in that case there is no consideration. The situation is different in the case of a loan for use (*commodatum*[1]) or of a bailment (*depositum*[2]), and also in case of a commission (*mandatum*), where the mandatary receives a *res* from the *mandator* for the purpose of executing the commission (e.g. to carry it to some other place). All of these are instances of gratuitous bailment and there is

1. *commodatum*：〈拉〉借贷
2. *depositum*：〈拉〉寄托

no consideration. The recipient is liable for failure to return in an action for damages (*assumpsit*)[1]. But is he liable also for a blameworthy defective performance of his promise or for lack of the care provided for in the contract? In this case the English say that the consideration lies in the detriment which the person who delivers the thing suffers, inasmuch as, by giving possession of the *res* to the recipient at the latter's request, he surrenders direct control over it. But this amounts merely to saying that the *res* takes the place of consideration. The loan for use, the bailment, and the commission (*mandatum*) connected with delivery of possession of a *res* are *"real"* contracts in English law, for the obligation is based on delivering and receiving a *res*. And Pollock in fact admits that where the request is not made by the person receiving the *res* but by the person delivering it, i.e. in the case of the *depositum* and the *mandatum*, an element of the contract, the request, is supplied by a fiction in order to enable the court to find consideration. No greater difficulty than this is involved in stating this refined and diffic ult doc trine in the language and concep ts of the juristic science of the Continental common law.

Where the scientific treatment of law is freed from national limitations, the mere restoration of international activity in the field of law bids fair to yield abundant returns. No science has ever grown great in national seclusion; it requires not only the preparatory work of all preceding generations, but also the cooperation of the whole contemporary generation. One nation, even the greatest and most gifted, is too small to be able to produce a science single-handed and relying solely on its own inner resources, much less a science of law. Consider how the French, the English, and the Italians were lost in the bog of a wretched system of casuistry[2] and exegesis[3] when they limited

1. an action for damages (*assumpsit*)：损害赔偿之诉
2. casuistry：诡辩
3. exegesis：诠释

themselves to their own national law, and on principle rejected all suggestions from without, in spite of the fact that they have thousands of times demonstrated their high and great endowment for scientific activity, particularly in the field of law, and are demonstrating it today by the great progress they have been making in the science of law in recent years, ever since they gave over their national provincialism. Does not the history of juristic science in the countries whose law has been codified preach this doctrine most impressively? Nowhere else is the connection between rise and decline on the one hand, and opening and closing of the border to foreign suggestion on the other, more strikingly apparent.

It is true, the codes brought about the displacement of the international scientific activity of the Continental common law and the rise of a national practical and a national theoretical science of law. This however is a transient phase of development, which is largely being superseded to day. In spite of dissimilarities in legislation, the institutions of civilized nations are so closely related as to permit of a common practical and scientific morphology and creation of norms. And for these, too, the scientific work of the Continental common law constitutes an excellent basis. For the law of the Austrian and Prussian codes a new era began when it came into contact with the scientific work of the Continental common law through the work of Wachter on the private law of Württemberg[1]. Wachter was the first to demonstrate that a local or particular system of law does not necessarily preclude general legal science; for legal science is not primarily concerned with legal propositions but with the formations of life, of which one indeed takes the measure by means of legal propositions, but which one does not arrive at by interpretation of statutes. Unger and Koch have successfully applied this principle to the law of their respective codes,

1. Württemberg：〈德〉符腾堡。德国城市。

while the work of Zachariae has long ago done the preparatory work for its application to the law of the French code. The scientific labor of jurists in connection with the German Civil Code moves along the same lines. It would be absolutely erroneous to attempt to justify this procedure by saying that these codes are based on Roman law. Not Roman law, but the *usus modernus*, constitutes the basis of the Prussian Landrecht, the French Civil Code, and the Austrian Civil Code. The German Civil Code is based chiefly on the pandects of the nineteenth century. The true reason is the fact that for the presentation of the law of the codes a considerable part of the Continental common law morphology and creation of norms could be utilized without more ado; this was not the morphology and creation of norms of a certain legal system but the morphology and creation of norms of the society of the civilized nations of Europe.

When Count Thun undertook to improve the pedantic and antiquated teaching of law in Austria, he devoted one half of the time given to the study of law, the first two years of the whole *quatriennium*[1] to the study of Roman law, of German law, and of ecclesiastical law. The result was an immediate undreamt of advancement of legal science in Austria. It is true, he did not, by his action, cause the historical basis of the Austrian law to be taught, but he opened the door to an invasion by German science. The results of the juristic thinking of the last three centuries in Germany were given academic form and literary expression in the science of the history of Roman and of German law, of the Continental common law, and of German private law; and this German science, which had been driven out of Austria as a result of the codification of the Austrian private law at the beginning of the nineteenth century, victoriously returned to Austria at the time of the reform of legal studies. The lectures on

1. *quatriennium*：〈拉〉四年

legal historical subjects, on the pandects, and on German private law made up for the lack of lectures on legal science for the simple reason that they contained all the science of law that existed in Germany. If Austria was anxious to give to its young jurists something better than the paltry instruction in statute law and in interpretation which before that time had flourished at Austrian universities, if Austria actually desired to give him instruction in legal science, the best it could do was to offer legal history, pandect law, and German private law.

As early as the last century Austin conceived the idea of a general legal science — I would say incidentally that the whole modern theory of norms is contained in his works and he carried it out, only in part however, in his two works (*The Province of Jurisprudence Determined*[1] and *Lectures on Jurisprudence*[2]). His followers, chiefly Thomas Erskine Holland, Amos, and Salmond, attempted complete expositions of legal science which were to be independent of any definite system of law — Holland, in his *Elements of Jurisprudence*; Salmond, in the *Science of Law*. It is significant that both Austin and Amos perceived that the juristic science of the Romanist jurist affords a much more advantageous basis than that of the English jurists; for both made the former their point of departure. John Stuart Mill presents Austin's basic idea in an essay on the latter, and he does it much better than Austin ever did. I quote from his essay:

"The details of different legal systems are different, but there is no reason why the main classifications and heads of arrangement should not be the same. The facts of which law takes cognizance, though far from identical in all civilized societies, are sufficiently analogous to enable them to be arranged in the same cadres. The more general of the terms employed for legal purposes might stand for the same

---

1. *The Province of Jurisprudence Determined*：《法理学的范围》，英国法学家奥斯丁的法学著作，于 1832 年首次出版。
2. *Lectures on Jurisprudence*：《法理学演讲录》

ideas, and be expounded by the same definitions, in systems otherwise different. The same terminology, nomenclature, and principle of arrangement, which would render one system of law definite and (in Bentham's language) cognoscible, would serve, with additions and variations in minor details, to render the same office for another."

This, it is true, is not the whole of sociological legal science. Austin and his followers aie formalists. In all their writings they do not concern themselves with living creations. They purpose to present only a general part in the sense of the German pandectists. And they are interested only in the forms of the legal relations, not in their content, not in the germinative powers of the development of law, nor in its unifying regularity. But it contains a part, at least, of the material which the practical science of law will be able to pass on to the sociological science of law.

XXI THE METHODS OF THE SOCIOLOGY OF LAW

II. The Study of the Living Law

The reason why the dominant school of legal science so greatly prefers the legal proposition to all other legal phenomena as an object of investigation is that it tacitly assumes that the whole law is to be found in the legal propositions. It is assumed furthermore that since, at the present time, all legal propositions are to be found in the statutes, where they are readily accessible to anyone, all that is necessary in order to get a knowledge of the law of the present time is to gather the material from the statutes, to ascertain the content of this material by one's own individual interpretation, and to utilize this interpretation for the purposes of juristic literature and judicial decision. Occasionally one meets with the further idea that legal propositions may arise independently of statute. In Germany the usual belief is that they can be found in juristic literature; in France, in judicial decisions. "Customary law," on the other hand, in the prevailing view, is so unimportant that no effort is being put forth to ascertain its content by scientific methods, much less to create methods for its investigation. Only the teachers of, and writers on, commercial law still concern themselves with usage, in this case, with business custom. This explains why the efforts of those who are carrying on research in law at the present time are bent upon ascertaining the legal propositions of the past, which are not so readily accessible to us as those that are contained in modern statutes. It is believed that the scientific result of the labor expended upon the study of the law of the past consists not only in a knowledge of the development of law, which of course means only the development of legal propositions, but also in an historical understanding of the law of the present; for the law, i.e. according to the tacit assumption the legal propositions of the present time, is rooted in the past. These, I take it, are the lines of thought on which the method of research in the field of law has hitherto been based.

But the statement that the whole law is not contained in the legal propositions applies to a much greater degree to the law that is in force today than to the law of the past. For the men who composed the Twelve Tables, the *Lex Salica*, and the *Sachsenspiegel* actually had a direct personal knowledge of the law of their own time, and their endeavor was to gather up this law with which they dealt, and to formulate it in legal propositions. This however does not apply, even approximately, to the most important part of the legal material with which the jurists of the present day are concerned, i.e. the codes. For in contrast to what once upon a time the jurists had in mind under all circumstances, vaguely at least, the compilers of the modern codes very often did not have the slightest intention whatever of stating the law of their own time and of their own community. They draw their legal material, first, from the compilation of Justinian, from which, self-evidently, they are likely to obtain reliable information on almost any other subject than the law of their own time, i.e. of the eighteenth or of the nineteenth century; secondly, from older statements of law, which, even if they met the requirements of their own time, do not meet those of the time of the legislator; thirdly, from juristic literature, which was chiefly concerned with the interpretation of older laws and of older codes, and, in any case, did not belong to the time of the code in question. The truth of this statement appears most clearly in the case of the German Civil Code, the sources of which have been almost exclusively text-books of pandect law, earlier German statutes and compilations of law, and foreign codifications. Accordingly our codes are uniformly adapted to a time much earlier than their own, and all the juristic technique in the world would be unable to extract the actual law of the present from it, for the simple reason that it is not contained therein. But the territory within which our codes are valid is so vast, the legal relations with which they deal are so incomparably richer, more varied, more subject to changes than they have ever been, that the mere idea of making a complete presentation in a code would be monstrous. To attempt to imprison the law of a time or of a people within the sections of a code is about as reasonable as to attempt to confine a stream within a pond. The water that is put in the pond is no longer a living stream but a stagnant pool, and but little water can be put in the pond. Moreover, if one considers that the living law had already overtaken and grown away from each one of these codes at the very moment the latter were enacted, and is growing away from them more and more every day, one cannot but realize the enormous extent of this as yet unplowed and unfurrowed field of activity which is being pointed out to the modern legal investigator.

It could not be otherwise. The legal propositions are not intended to present a complete picture of the state of the law. The jurist draws them up with a view to existing practical needs, and with a view to what he is interested in for practical reasons. He will not put forth the effort to formulate legal propositions with reference to matters that lie out side of his sphere of interest, perhaps for the sole reason that they are not within the jurisdiction of the courts before which he practices, or because they do not concern his clients. Since commercial law lay out side of the usual sphere of interest of the Roman jurist, we find that the commercial law of the Roman sources is utterly inadequate; and for the very same reason the Romans and, until quite recently, the modern jurists have very little to say about labor law. Even Eyke von Repgow did not deal with the law of cities and with the customs of manors because it lay outside of his immediate sphere of interest.

On the other hand, the attempt to arrive at an understanding of the present through the study of history or of prehistoric times, i.e. of ethnology, is an error in principle. To explain something, according to a saying of Mach's, is to replace a mystery that one is not accustomed to by a mystery that one is accustomed to. Now the present contains fewer mysteries that we are not accustomed to than does the past. The paleontologist[1] will understand the nature and the functions of the organs of a fossil animal only if he understands the nature and the functions of the organs of living animals. But the zoologist cannot learn the physiology of the animals which he is studying from the paleontologist; he will have recourse to paleontology only for the purpose of getting a picture of the development of the present-day animal kingdom. We arrive at an understanding of the past through the present, and not vice versa. Accordingly the history of law and ethnological legal science will not be of value for the understanding of the existing law but only for the study of the development of law.

As a result of the methods employed by modern legal science, the present state of our law is, in a great measure, actually unknown to us. We often know nothing, not only of things that are remote but also of things that happen before our very eyes. Almost every day brings some juristic surprise which we owe to a lucky accident, to a peculiar lawsuit, or to an article in the daily papers. This surprise may concern the peasant tenants in Schwarzenberg, or puzzling heritable building rights in the heart of the city of Vienna, in the Brigittenau, or peculiar relations involving heritable leases in Berhomet, in Bukowina. But he who observes life with careful attentiveness knows that these are not isolated occurrences. We are groping in the dark everywhere. And we cannot plead the excuse that the legal historian can avail himself of, i.e. that a bit of the past has been irrecoverably lost. We need but open

1. paleontologist：古生物学者

our eyes and ears in order to learn everything that is of significance for the law of our time.

In the part of the Austrian code that deals with matrimonial agreements there are four meagre sections, which, according to the marginal heading, deal with the matrimonial regime of community of goods. Anyone who has had opportunity of coming into contact with the German peasantry of Austria knows that they live, almost exclusively, under a matrimonial regime of community of goods. But this matrimonial community of goods, which is the prevailing, freely chosen property regime of the German peasantry in Austria, has nothing in common with the community of goods provided for in the Austrian Civil Code, and the provisions of the Civil Code are never being applied since they are always excluded by a marriage contract formally entered into. What would be the value of a science of law which failed to recognize that the community of goods that the Austrian Civil Code speaks of exists only on paper? What would be the value of a science of law which thinks it is fulfilling its whole task when it ascertains the intent of the lawgiver, which has been expressed in the above four sections, but does not concern itself with the community of goods, which is based on readily accessible legal documents, and according to which practically the entire German peasantry of Austria lives?

Again there is the agricultural usufructuary lease[1]. The few provisions contained in the modern codes on the subject, especially in the Austrian and German codes, were for the most part taken from Roman law, and had arisen on the exhausted soil of Italy in the days of the Roman Empire with its system of extensive *latifundia* and an oppressed peasant class. They would be altogether insufficient today. A glance at life will convince us that they are almost never being applied.

---

1. usufructuary lease：用益权租约

Their operation is almost always being excluded and they are being replaced by the provisions of contracts of usufructuary lease such as are suitable to modern social and economic conditions, and are being entered into between the lessor and the lessee in almost every instance. Though they vary according to the region, the nature of the estate which is being let, and the position of the parties, they have, in spite of this limitation, an ever recurring, typical content. It is apparent, I dare say, in view of this discussion, that a presentation of the law of usufructuary lease of the civil codes, be it never so careful, cannot reflect the actual state of the German or Austrian law of usufructuary lease. To do this, it would be necessary to set forth the typical content of the leases, and for this purpose it would be necessary to search the archives of the offices of notaries and lawyers, and to make inquiries at the time and place.

Or what information can be gathered from juristic literature as to the system of agriculture in Germany or in Austria? Not even the various methods of cultivation of the soil have been formulated from a juristic point of view, and that would be but a small part of the task that has to be fulfilled. All economic cultivation of the soil is linked with other relations which are of the greatest importance to the jurist. In the first place, the neighborly relations between owners of farms operated for economic purposes and of landed estates. They are being regulated in part by custom; in part, by statute. Yet the entire juristic literature has not a single word to say about any of these, except perhaps about the statute. Moreover agriculture, in so far as it is carried on on a scale larger than the very smallest and most insignificant, presupposes a certain organization of labor, which, in the case of great landed estates, becomes a most artistically interlocking and extraordinarily complicated mechanism. To everyone that takes part in it, there is assigned, partly by custom, partly by contract or statute (regulations for servants), the measure of his powers, rights of supervision, privileges and duties, without a knowledge of which this difficult piece of machinery could be understood neither from the economic, or technical, nor from the juristic point of view. In case of similar undertakings all these legal relations occur again and again in their typical form throughout the whole region and often throughout the whole realm; and for this reason it is not a difficult task to study them and set them forth.

Note also the law of the family. The first thing that attracts the attention of the observer is the contrast between the actual order of the family and that which the codes decree. I doubt whether there is a country in Europe in which the relation between husband and wife, parents and children, bet ween the family and the outside world, as it actually takes form in life, corresponds to the norms of the positive law; or in which the members of the family, in which there is a semblance of proper family life, would as much as think of attempting to enforce the rights against one another that the letter of the law grants to them. It is evident therefore that in this case, too, the positive law is far from giving a picture of that which actually takes place in life. So much the less must legal science and doctrine confine itself to giving an exposition of the content of the statutes; it must seek to ascertain the actual forms that the family relations assume, which are essentially uniform and typical although they differ in the various classes of society and in the various parts of the country. We shall not discuss in this connection whether the statute has lost its mastery over life or whet her it never had it; whether life, in the process of growth, has developed beyond the statute and grown away from it or whether it never corresponded to it. In this connection, too, science fulfils its function as the theory of law and right very poorly if it merely presents that which is prescribed by the statute and fails to tell what actually takes place.

The peasant law of inheritance of Germany (*Sering*) and of the German parts of Austria has been investigated more thoroughly and has been juristically evaluated more nearly at its true value than any of the subjects mentioned above. For the other classes, as well as for the non-German peoples and countries of the Austrian monarchy, the work has not yet been done. Juristic literature is content with setting forth the well-nigh unrestricted liberty of testamentary disposition provided for by the civil codes. Ought it not also ask what use is being made of it in the various countries and in the various classes?

The only branch of law the juristic science of which is based not merely incidentally, but throughout, on actual usage is commercial law. The latter has been officially received into juristic science in the form of business custom and "usance." The organization of the great landed estate and of the factory, even of the bank, has, to the present day, remained to the jurist a book sealed with seven seals, but the organization of the commercial house he knows, in its main outlines at least, from the Commercial Code. He knows the position of the principal and of the holder of a general power of procuration[1]; of the holder of a mercantile power of agency and of the mercantile employee, of the mercantile agent, of the commercial traveler; he knows the significance of the mercantile trade name (*Handelsfirma*), of the books of account, and of business correspondence. He has a conception of the significance of all of these things not only from the economic but also from the legal point of view. And the contract law of modern commercial law has not been taken over from the *corpus iuris;* nor is it a product of the diligent reflection of its authors. What the commercial statutes and the commercial codes have to say about buying and selling, about commissions, about forwarding of goods, about the insurance, the freight, and the banking business, is actually being practiced somewhere even though, possibly, not always to the extent set forth therein. Likewise many commercial institutions, particularly the Exchange, have been properly furrowed and plowed by

1. general power of procuration：一般代理权

the jurists. The fact that much hard work remains to be done in every nook and corner is caused less in this sphere than in others by the lack of understanding and appreciation of the actual realities and more by the difficulties inherent in the subject matter and by its extremely rapid development. The gigantic organization of the production of goods which is taking place before our very eyes in trusts and cartels, all the modern achievements of commerce, the numerous new inventions, lead to new formations at every moment, and open new fields of labor for the jurist.

This then is the *living* law in contradistinction to that which is being enforced in the courts and other tribunals. The living law is the law which dominates life itself even though it has not been posited in legal propositions. The source of our knowledge of this law is, first, the modern legal document; secondly, direct observation of life, of commerce, of customs and usages, and of all associations, not only of those that the law has recognized but also of those that it has overlooked and passed by, indeed even of those that it has disapproved.

In our day, doubtless, the most important source of knowledge of the living law is the modern legal document. Even today one of these documents is being studied very extensively, to wit the judicial decision, but not in the sense we have in mind here. It is not being treated as evidence of the living law, but as a work of juristic literature which is to be examined not as to the truth of the legal relations described therein and as to the living law that is to be extracted therefrom, but as to the correctness of the statutory interpretations and of the juristic constructions contained therein. Even the conception of the French *arretisles,* of the jurists who have made it their business to add the explanatory notes on the decisions published in the great collections of Dalloz, Sirey, and in the *Journal du Palais,* is based on a much deeper understanding than this. To them the judicial decision is an expression of the law not as the legislator has pictured it to himself, but as it has developed in the consciousness of the French judges in the course of the century during which the French codes have been in force. In the words of Meynial, who has discussed the work of the *arrétisles* in a brilliant fashion in the memorial volume published in commemoration of the one hundredth anniversary of the introduction of the *code civile* they see in it "*la notion du changement du droit, grace aux inflexions que la jurisprudence fait subir a la loi; celle du consentement general tacite qui fait de la jurisprudence non seulement la servante mais V emule et comme le suppléante de la loir.*[1]"

I myself entertained this idea when about a quarter of a century ago I began to work at my book on the declaration of the will by silence. My intention was to study more than six hundred volumes of decisions of German, Austrian, and French courts, and on the basis of these decisions to present a picture of what judicial decisions had made of the declaration of the will by silence. Before long however my attention was arrested by, and occupied with, what actually took place rat her than by the judicial decision. As a result my book contains, to a great extent at least, a statement of the facts on which the judicial decisions had been rendered, as they actually happened in life, and a statement of the significance of the silent declaration of the will in legal life. In this book, I actually, though unconsciously, applied the sociological method of legal science, for which I subsequently sought to establish a theoretical basis.

At a later time, however, I realized that this method is not quite sufficient. Even the judicial decisions do not give a perfect picture of legal life. Only a tiny bit of real life is brought before the courts and other tribunals; and much is excluded from litigation either on principle or as a mat ter of fact. Moreover the legal relation which is being litigated shows distorted features which are quite different

1. *la notion du changement ... le suppléante de la loi.*：〈拉〉"法"的概念发生了改变：判例不再是制定法的仆人，而是制定法的有力竞争者与替代者。

from, and foreign to, the same relation when it is in repose. Who would judge our family life or the life of our societies by the law-suits that arise in the families or in the societies? The sociological method therefore demands absolutely that the results which are obtained from the judicial decisions be supplemented by direct observation of life.

And for this very purpose the modern business document offers a basis which can become at least as fruitful as the method of past millennia and centuries. A glance at modern legal life shows that it is predominantly con trolled not by stat ute law but by the business document. Non-compulsory law is set aside by the content of the business document. The living law must be sought in marriage contracts, in contracts of purchase, of usufructuary lease, in contracts for building loans, for loans secured by hypothecs, in testaments, and in contracts of inheritance, in articles of association of societies and of business partnerships, and not in the sections of the codes. In all of these contracts, there is, in addition to the individual content which applies only to the particular transaction, a typical, ever recurring content. This typical content is basically the most important thing in the document. If our literary jurists were well advised, they would concern themselves primarily with it, as did the Romans, who, in their commentaries on the edict and in their *libri iuris civilis*[1], wrote long disquisitions on the ever recurring *duplae stipulatio*[2] and the *institutio ex re certa*[3]. In that case we probably should have more monographs on the beer-seller of the breweries, or on the contracts for the processing of sugar beets by the sugar factories, or on the sale of a physician's practice, than on the concept of the juristic person or the construction of a pledge right in one's own *res* (*Sache*). Of course it is a new task for the jurist to make use of a modern document for the purposes of

1. *libri iuris civilis*：〈拉〉《罗马法汇编》
2. *duplae stipulatio*：〈拉〉双倍赔偿的要式口约
3. *institutio ex re certa*：〈拉〉特定物继承人的设立

theoretical and of practical legal science. But the historian, particularly the legal historian, is quite familiar with the study of documents, and the latter might, at the beginning at least, render valuable services both to the theoretical and to the practical jurist. The science of historical documents has developed a technique that is one of the most delicate and difficult things in scientific work, and the industry and labor of a lifetime will scarcely suffice for the mastery of all its refinements. But in the case of the modern document tasks must be fulfilled which in part are quite different from those involved in the case of the historical document and which are by no means lighter.

Above all, we must endeavor to treat the document as a part of the living law, and to derive the living law from it as the Romans did in their law of contracts and of testaments. The titles of the Digest *de contrahenda emptione, de actionibus emti venditi, de evictionibus et duplae stipulatione, pro socio, de stipulatione servorum*[1], and those that deal with the law of testaments and legacies, can still serve as models everywhere. It is a matter of the utmost importance that present-day theoretical and practical science should at last concern itself not with Roman, but with present-day contracts and documents. It would be the first task of modern legal science to examine the documents as to the part of their content that is of general importance, typical, and ever recurring, to treat juristically and to evaluate them from every angle according to their importance from the point of view of society, economics, and legislative policy.

In this way we could at last get a picture of what is taking place among us in the sphere of the document. Although in general the

---

1. The titles of the Digest *de contrahenda emptione, de actionibus emti venditi, de evictionibus et duplae stipulatione, pro socio, de stipulatione servorum*：《学说汇编》关于买卖契约、买卖行为、追夺担保和双倍要式口约、合伙以及奴隶契约的章节。

documents are alike, they differ very much in details according to localities, classes, ranks, races, and creeds. It seems likely that we must perform the function of legal statistics by means of the devices of the science of documents. It will not be possible to do this without new methods, and it surely will not be an easy task to devise such methods. But what splendid results are beckoning to the jurist in this connection, especially if he succeeds in laying bare the historical, economic, or social presuppositions of these diversities.

Still the value of the document would be greatly over-estimated if one should think that one could, without more ado, read the living law from it. It is not at all conclusively established that the document as a whole contains and bears witness to the living law. The living law is not the part of the content of the document that the courts recognize as binding when they decide a legal controversy, but only that part which the parties actually observe in life. The effects of the transactions that are evidenced by documents cannot be learned without more ado from their enforceable legal consequences. Could anyone infer from the articles of association of a society or of a share company that the seemingly plenipotent[1] meetings of the shareholders usually turn out to be utterly insignificant gatherings of yes-men? But the legally operative content of the document gives no reliable information as to the effects not intended by the parties nor yet as to those intended. There is much in the document that is simply traditional; this part is copied from a form book by the person who drafts the document, but it never reaches the consciousness of the parties. They will therefore neither demand nor grant the things provided for therein, and will be very much surprised to hear of them when, in the event of litigation, the document gets into the hands of a lawyer who insists upon them in court. There are other provisions which the parties will permit to be

1. plenipotent：全权的

embodied in the document only in order to be prepared for the worst. It is self-evident that they are not to be mentioned as long as there is no controversy. The other party understands this very well. He accepts the most extreme rigors of a contract of this sort calmlybut haggles most obstinately over all provisions that are intended to be taken seriously. If one reads a contract of usufructuary lease prepared by the administrator of the Prussian crown-lands or of the Greek-Oriental religious foundation of Bukowina, one marvels how it is possible for the lessee to move at all within this barbed-wire fence of paragraphs. Nevertheless the lessee gets on very well. No use is ever being made of all of these contractual penalties, of the clauses appointing stated times, of the short-term notices to quit, of the forfeitures of security, of the right to compensation for damage done, as long as it is possible to get on with the lessee at all. One who is engaged in the practical affairs of life is anxious to deal peaceably with people. He is not interested in carrying on litigation even if he is bound to win.

The standard therefore according to which the Sociological School of jurisprudence must test, not only the legal propositions, but also the legal document, is actual life. Here too it must observe the distinction between the law that is enforced by the courts and the living law. The entire valid content of the document is law that is enforced by the courts (i.e. norm for decision), for, in case the parties resort to litigation, the decision will hinge upon it; but it is living law only in so far as the parties habitually insist upon it even if they do not wish to risk litigation. Failure to observe this heterogeneousness of the component parts of the document embodying the contract results in an erroneous and distorted picture of life itself. But the contrast is of the utmost importance for the administration of justice and for legislation as well. It is questionable whether the latter should lend themselves to permitting those things to be taken seriously which were never intended to be taken seriously.

Of course we can learn only so much of the living law from the document as has been embodied therein. How shall we quarry that part of the living law that has not been embodied in a legal document but which nevertheless is a large and important part thereof? There is no other means but this, to open one's eyes, to inform oneself by observing life attentively, to ask people, and note down their replies. To be sure, to ask a jurist to learn from actual observation and not from sections of a code or from bundles of legal papers is to make an exacting demand upon him; but it is unavoidable, and marvelous results can be achieved in this manner.

From the great number of things that deserve being studied in this manner, I would select only a few. First of all the old law that still survives. The old law, which is popular law and not merely juristic law, lives on under a thin surface of modern statute law, and dominates the conduct and the legal consciousness of the people. The legal historian can not only find many things here as to which his sources are silent, but he can actually observe many things which are generally believed to belong to a time that is long since past. In doing this he can disregard the legal document; for it is well known how often it is but a poor compromise between that which is traditional and the demands of modern law, e.g. in the law of inheritance among the peasants, and in the matrimonial regime. But it is necessary to focus attention to a much grea ter ext ent than has been done hitherto upon those parts of the old law that still exist among the people though they are not embodied in legal documents, expecially since it is doubtful whether it can hold its own much longer against the impact of modern commercial life. Bogisic has discovered the ancient Sadruga, one of the most primitive of human organizations of mankind, within the very territory within which the Austrian Civil Code is in force. In another remote corner of Austria, in eastern Galicia, Dniestrzanski (Customary Law and the Social Associations, Czernowitz, 1905) has found a mercantile partnership comprising the entire Ruthenian tribe of the *Bojken,* and having a remarkable form of organization, which of course is quite foreign to the Austrian statutes. I myself have been able to establish the fact that only about one half of a century ago there were isolated peasant family-communities in existence among the Ruthenians of eastern Galicia and of Bukowina. Today, I suppose, they have disappeared altogether. Mauczka (*Altes Recht im Volksbewusslsein*[1] — Ancient Law in the Popular Consciousness — Wien, 1907 — also in *Gerichtszeitung*[2] Nos. 10 and 11, 1007) has recently shown that there are some survivals of this institution among the German population of Austria as well. And at my suggestion, a Viennese writer, Dr. Kobler, has recorded some observations for my seminar for the study of the living law.

The germs of new law that are viable are probably of greater importance to the jurist than such dying survivals. And here we are confronted by a peculiar fact. It is generally believed that the knowledge that law is in never-ending process of development is an enduring achievement of the historical school, and one would think that this is accepted as true not only as to times long since past but also as to the last century. But science and theory are making a peculiar use of this bit of academic wisdom. So far as the ancient Romans or the Germans down to the fourteenth and fifteenth centuries are concerned, jurists are wide awake to the development of legal institutions, e.g. of the family, of the relations of personal subjection, of ownership of land, of contracts. Statutes, which are of no significance in those days, are scarcely being mentioned. But for the later period, this kind of legal history breaks down altogether, and for the last century, the science of the Historical School resolves itself altogether into a history of legislation. Jurists seem to assume that in this period legal institutions develop only through changes in the paragraphs of the codes. What is the meaning of this? Has the non-

1. *Altes Recht im Volksbewusstsein*：〈德〉公众意识中的《古代法》
2. *Gerichtszeitung*：〈德〉法院报

statutory development of legal institutions ceased altoge ther in the nineteenth century? But today, just as in antiquity and in the Middle Ages, legal history is based not so much upon the emergence and the disappearance of legal propositions that have been formulated in words as upon the emergence of new legal institutions and the gradual assumption of a new content by those that are already in existence. No legal historian will admit that the basic legal relations in Germany, let us say, of the sixteenth century, coincide with those of the fifteenth, or that the changes, some of which were very sweeping ones, took place solely as a result of legislation, which was enacted very rarely and was not very sweeping. Does this not hold true for the nineteenth century as well, a period which was so highly agitated socially, economically, and politically that one may say that until that time mankind had never experienced its like? It is a question of what one means by development. The family law has undergone development. This means exactly what it meant in the Middle Ages, i.e. that the relations of husband and wife, of parents and children, now bear a different stamp. Ownership of land has undergone development even apart from the fact that the soil was freed by statute and by administrative action from the burdens and charges resting upon it; this means that there is a different system of landholding in vogue because different kinds of real and obligatory rights have been established with reference to the soil, and also because the economy of the peasant and of the great landowner has undergone a change. The law of contract has undergone development; this development is based on the fact that new kinds of contracts have come into use and that the contracts of the traditional kind now have a different content. The law of inheritance has undergone development; this means, chiefly, that division of inheritance, testaments, and other dispositions *mortis causa* now have a content quite different from that which they had a century ago. Compared with these revolutionary changes, the changes brought about by legislation are negligible.

The sociology of law then must begin with the ascertainment of the living law. Its attention will be directed primarily to the concrete, not the abstract. It is only the concrete that can be observed. What the anatomist places under the microscope is not human tissue in the abstract but a specific tissue of a specific human being; the physiologist likewise does not study the functions of the liver of mammals in the abstract, but those of a specific liver of a specific mammal. Only when he has completed the observation of the concrete does he ask whether it is universally valid, and this fact, too, he endeavors to establish by means of a series of concrete observations, for which he has to find specific methods. The same may be said of the investigator of law. He must first concern himself with concrete usages, relations of domination, legal relations, contracts, articles of association, dispositions by last will and testament. It is not true, therefore, that the investigation of the living law is concerned only with "customary law" or with "business usage." If one does any thinking at all when one uses these words — which is not always the case — one will realize that they do not refer to the concrete, but to that which has been universalized. But only the concrete usages, the relations of domination, the legal relations, the contracts, the articles of association, the dispositions by last will and testament, yield the rules according to which men regulate their conduct. And it is only on the basis of these rules that the norms for decision that the courts apply and the statutory provisions that alone have hitherto occupied the attention of jurists arise. The great majority of judicial decisions are based on the concrete usages, relations of possession, contracts, Articles of association, and dispositions by last will and testament, that the courts have found to exist. If we would comprehend the universalizations, the reductions to unity, and the other methods of finding norms that the judge and the lawgiver employ, we must first of all know the basis upon which they were carried out. The more we know of the Roman banking system, the better shall we understand *receptum* and *litteris contrahere*[1]. Does this not hold true for the law of our day? To this ext ent Savigny was right when he said that the law — and by law he means above all the legal proposition — can be understood only from its historical connection; but the historical connection does not lie in the hoary past, but in the present, out of which the legal proposition grows.

But the scientific significance of the living law is not confined to its influence upon the norms for decision which the courts apply or upon the content of statutes. The knowledge of the living law has an independent value, and this consists in the fact that it constitutes the foundation of the legal order of human society. In order to acquire a knowledge of this order we must know the usages, relations of domination, legal relations, contracts, articles of association, declarations by last will and testament, quite independently of the question whether they have already found expression in a judicial decision or in a statute or whether they will ever find it. The provisions contained in the new German Commercial Code regulating stock exchanges, banks, publishing houses, and other supplementary provisions were full of gaps when they were enacted and, for the most part, have become antiquated today. Modern commerce, especially the export trade, has meanwhile created an enormous number of new forms, which ought to be the subject matter of scientific study as well as those that have been enumerated in the statute. Very much that is of genuine value can be found on this point in the literature on the science of commerce that is blossoming forth so abundantly. A part of the order in the sphere of mining and navigation has been made accessible to legal science through mining law, maritime law, and the law of inland navigation, but for the most part this has long since become antiquated. The factory, the bank, the railroad, the

1. *receptum* and *litteris contrahere*：承保与通过文书订立契约（斜体为拉丁文）

great landed estate, the labor union, the association of employers, and a thousand other forms of life — each of these likewise has an order, and this order has a legal side as well as that of the mercantile establishment, which is being regulated in detail only by the Commercial Code. In addition there are countless forms in which the activity of these associations manifests itself outwardly, above all the contracts. In studying the manufacturing establishment, the legal investigator must pursue the countless, highly intricate paths that lead from the acceptance of the order to the delivery of the finished products to the customer, to wit the position of the representative and of the commercial traveler, the three departments that are to be found in every manufacturing establishment (the sales department, the technical department, and the manufacturing department), the arrival of the orders, the preparation and the preservation of drawings, the computation of the cost of the undertaking, the sale price, the calculation for the purpose of checking up, the execution of the order on the basis of the drawings, the functions of the manufacturing department, of the mas ter workman the management of the warehouse, the computation of wages by the piece and by time, the distribution of wages among the individual workmen, the importance of the certificate showing that material has been handed over, the price list, the supervision at the gates by porters. Of equal importance for the legal side of the order of the undertaking is the keeping of books, the taking of inventories, the supervision over the warehouse, the preservation of drawings and models, the employment of workmen and of apprentices, the working regulations, and the committees of the workmen.

Economists, it is true, have often been engaged in investigations of the kind demanded here. But this has by no means rendered the work of the jurist superfluous. The jurist and the economist are dealing everywhere with the same social phenomena. Property, money, bills of exchange, share companies, credit, law and right of inheritance — it would be difficult to find a single object that the science of law is not concerned with as much as economics. But the jurist and the economist are dealing with different aspects of the same social phenomena. One concerns himself with their economic significance and scope; the other, with their legal regulation and their legal consequences. Though the jurist can be taught much by the economist, and the economist by the jurist, the questions which the identical objects of investigation pose to their respective sciences are absolutely distinct; and for this very reason no part of the labor which is necessary for both may be thrust upon one of them alone.

The investigation of the living law will of course render neither the historical nor the ethnological method superfluous; for we can learn the laws governing the development of society only by studying the historic and the prehistoric (ethnological) facts. But the historical and ethnological methods are indispensable, too, for the understanding of the state of the law of the present time. It is true we shall never understand the past but through the present; but the path to the understanding of the innermost nature of the present lies through the understanding of the past. Within every part of the present lies its entire past, which can be clearly discerned by the eye that is able to look into these depths. This truth was not hidden from the eyes of the great founders of the Historical School, and for this reason their object was by no means, as is generally believed today, to create a legal science which in its essence is a history of law, but a historical science of law. It is true, in the main they were occupied not even with legal history but with legal antiquities, and substituted dialectic speculations for historical legal science or — and this is not much bet ter — Schelling's philosophy. They, too, were children of their time. But they wrote a legend in large letters above the gate of entrance to their school which stated what their goal was. No one however was able to read and interpret the inscription. And this fact is just as characteristic as is the other fact that at a later time the *Zeitschrift für geschichtliche*

Rechtswissenschaft[1] became a *Zeitschrift für Rechtsgeschichte*[2].

In order to understand the actual state of the law we must institute an investigation as to the contribution that is being made by society itself as well as by state law, and also as to the actual influence of the state upon social law. We must know what kinds of marriages and families exist in a country, what kinds of contracts are being entered into, what their content is as a general rule, what kinds of declarations by last will and testament are being drawn up, how all of these things ought to be adjudged according to the law that is in force in the courts and other tribunals, how they are actually being adjudged, and to what extent these judgments and other decisions are actually effective. An investigation of this sort will reveal that although the legislation of two different countries may be identical, eg of France and Roumania, the law of one country may differ from that of the other; that in spite of the fact that the courts and other tribunals of Bohemia, Dalmatia, and Galicia apply the same code, the law of these countries is by no means the same; and that because of the differences in the actual state of the law, there is no uniform law even in the various parts of Germany in spite of the Civil Code, quite apart from the particular divergencies of legislation.

Of course our knowledge in this sphere will always remain full of gaps, and unsatisfactory, and doubtless it is much easier and much more pleasant to study a few codes together with illustrative material and explanatory notes than to ascertain the actual state of the law. But it certainly is not the function of science to seek easy and pleasant tasks but great and productive ones. We know in part, and the science of law is no exception to this; the more truly scientific it will become, the more perfect it will be.

This exposition would altogether fail of its purpose if it were

---

1. *Zeitschrift für geschichtliche Rechtswissenschaft*：〈德〉历史法学杂志
2. *Zeitschrift für Rechtsgeschichte*：〈德〉法学历史杂志

understood to convey the idea that I mean to say that the methods which I have indicated in any way exhaust the methodology of the sociology of law. New scientific aims will always make new scientific methods necessary. For this reason, in order to prove that the possibilities are unlimited, I wish to point out a few things. Political geography as created by Ratzel and as it is understood today by Brunhes in France is in fact sociology with a geographic method. As early as the fifties of the last century Le Play, a Frenchman, in his *science social* based his investigations at all points on the local conditions of social life, and the school which he founded is zealously continuing the work he began. In his book on irrigation in Spain, Egypt, and Algiers, which is at least as interesting, even to the jurist, as any work on the history of law or on ethnology, Brunhes points out that there is a great number of legal formations which are associated everywhere with the kind and nature of the irrigation plants and the amount of their output. The reason why the Arabs of the desert do not recognize property rights in the sandy plain of the desert but only in the ttees of the oases cannot be given by ethnology and legal history but only by the peculiar economic institutions of the desert.

Many decades ago Ofner of Vienna pointed out the possibility of instituting a direct investigation of the sense of law and right (*Rechtsgefühl*) by means of juristic experiment. A year ago Kobler discussed the idea in detail in the Vienna *Juristische Blätter*[1], and actually instituted experiments in the *Freie juristische Vereinigung*[2], which he himself had founded. Actual or fictitious law cases, even entire court proceedings, are being submitted to the persons who are being used for the experiment, who must not be jurists, and who are requested to express an opinion on them. They can do this only by relying on their sense of law and right. Is not everyone reminded of

1. *Juristische Blätter*：〈德〉《法学通报》
2. *Freie juristische Vereinigung*：〈德〉自由法律协会

the psychometry of the school of Fechner and Wundt? These tests are open to the same objections that have been urged against psychometry. The person who permits himself to be used for the experiment is not in his usual frame of mind, and he knows, too, that his judgment does not decide the case; the fictitious case arouses no passions, does not agitate the emotions, but addresses itself to the intellect alone. These are sources of error which a correct method must compute and take into account. In spite of this however the attempt will produce valuable results, provided one does not forget about the sources of error.

Method is as infinite as science itself.

术语汇编与简释

accessories (Zubehör)：从物

从物是指在两个独立物结合使用中处于附属地位，起辅助和配合作用的物。从物并非主物的构成部分但从属于主物，从物依照交易习惯或当事人约定通常配合主物发挥效用，例如遥控器通常是电视机的从物。对于主物的处分一般情况下及于从物，从物上的权利随主物权利的转移而转移。

actio：诉讼；诉权

诉讼是指纠纷当事人通过将争议提交给法院裁判的方式来解决纠纷。诉权是指当事人提起诉讼的权利，即当事人请求法院解决纠纷的权利。

allgemeines Staatsrecht：〈德〉狭义公法

狭义公法是法律科学的第一个分支，其漠视研究成果的实践应用，追求的是纯科学的目标。

assignment of an obligatory right：债权让与

债权让与是指在不改变债的内容的前提下，债关系中权利主体发生变更，原债权人（让与人）以合同将债权移转于新债权人(受让人)。

Collcctivism：集体主义

集体主义表达的是个人主义所倡导的个体思维的对立面，不同于社会主义与共产主义。集体主义尝试向社会引入一些在现存社区中可以完全实现的原则。尽管集体主义与个人主义存在明显冲突，但是他们都不过是一种与基于财产所有权的法律秩序相反倾向的表达。

common law (getneines Recht)：普通法

普通法赖以存在的基础是判例法。英国普通法不但是英格兰、爱尔兰、威尔士的法律，而且在苏格兰法律中也占有极大的比重。此外，其还是美国法以及几乎所有英属殖民地法律的重要组成部分。普通法是远比罗马法发展程度更高、更理性与更强大的法律体。

counter performance：对待给付

对待给付是指债权债务关系中，为了获得他人对自己的给付，自己对对方所为的给付。给付是指债务人实现债的内容的行为或不行为。

culpa in contrahendo：〈拉〉缔约过失

缔约过失是指缔约当事人违反依诚实信用原则所应承担的先合同义务，造成对方信赖利益损失的行为。

customary law：习惯法

习惯法是独立于国家制定法之外与民族的法律意识相符的规范。这些规范不仅具有法律价值，同时也被用于指导人们的行事与生活方式。习惯法既是行为规则，也是裁判规则。习惯法既非纯粹的道德规范，也不是完全的法律规范，而是介于道德与法律之间的准法规范。

doctrine of correality and solidarity：连带责任

连带责任亦称“连带债务”。“民事责任”的一种。指数个债务人就同一债务各负全部给付的一种责任形式。即债权人可对债务人中的一人，数人或全体，同时或先后请求全部或部分给付的一种债务形式。如合伙债务的债权人，对于合伙成员的一人、数人或全体，均可请求其同时或先后，部分或全部地清偿合伙债务。

ecclesiastical law：教会法

教会法泛指罗马天主教、东正教以及基督教的其他一些教派（如新教的圣公会和加尔文教等）的各种法规。

equity law：衡平法

衡平法并不是独立的法律体系，其可以理解为普通法的补充。如果没有衡平法，普通法将是僵化的法律体系，无法适应现实生活的要求。衡平法的一原则是法律第一，公平第二。衡平法大体包括信托法、担保法、特定履行等，因而衡平法也包括少量的法律规范和救济。

German popular law：德国民间法

德国民间法起源于曾属于罗马且法律发展高度发达的区域。德国民间法受到罗马法与教会法的影响，包含大量非本土的东西，特别是许多国家法、先前非法律的东西以及后来从未变成法律的东西。

glossators：注释法学派

注释法学派是指 11 世纪兴起于欧洲的，用注释或文字解释研究罗马法、特别是《查士丁尼法典》的一个法学家派别。

Haftung：〈德〉责任

责任存在于债权人获取清偿前其占有的物与债务人。责任的范围、内容和持续期间由债务的范围、内容和持续时间决定。

Hand muss Hand wahren：〈德〉"以手护手"原则

"以手护手"法律命题是间接事实信赖的一种应用。如果该所有人将物委托于占有人保管，第三人与善意地占有人缔结的契约对于所有人是有效的。其理由是善意购买者基于信赖占有人保管的所建立的一种间接事实状态而作出的算计。

human Associations：人类联合体

人类社会是彼此具有相互关系的人类联合体的集合。构成人类社会的人类联合体性质迥异。国家、民族、国家联合体、宗教团体、教会、教派、公司、社会阶层、职业团体、政党等构成了一个社会。这些联合体彼此之间的作用与反作用清晰可见。人类联合体包括原生性联合体与非原生性联合体。

in iure：**〈拉〉法律审**

法律审与事实审相对，法律审主要指审判时处理案件法律适用问题，事实审指审判时处理案件事实认定问题。

Individualism：**个人主义**

个人主义的顶点是如下的原则：每一个体都是其自身的目的，其不屈服于任何力量而为他所有。也就是说，其不受使自己受控于他人意志的支配，也不受使自己受控于联合体意志的支配。个人主义瓦解了习惯建立的依附关系。

ius civile：**〈拉〉市民法**

市民法是古老的罗马法制，与城邦相联系，主要来源于一种家庭法律制度，是在氏族群体生活和交往中形成的一系列关系的总和，也是一种跨家际社会秩序的习俗规范。

juristic Law：**法学家法**

法学家法由法学家通过普遍化创造的裁判规范构成。法学家不能发布命令，其只能发现法律，从社会关系中提炼出法律。法学家法不能超越其来源的社会关系。

Kauf brichtnicht Miete：**〈德〉买卖不破租赁**

买卖不破租赁是指租赁物在租赁期间发生所有权变动的，不影响租赁合同的效力，此条规则主要适用于不动产，尤其是房屋租赁。

legal norms：**法律规范**

法律规范是一种运用到实践中的法律命令，即使没有明确的成文规定，其也在确定的（也许规模较小）联合体获得普遍遵从。法律规范构成社会内部秩序的基础，制裁并非法律规范的特性。

legal propositions：**法律命题**

法律命题是制定法卷册或法律书籍中精确、具有普遍约束的法律规则的表达。联合体中一旦存在生效的法律命题，则这些法律命题就可以产生出法律规范。但法律规范的数量都大大多于法律命题。

living law：**活法**

活法的科学意义并不限于对法院所适用的裁判规范或对制定法内容的影响。活法的知识具有独立的价值，其构成了人类社会法律秩序的基础。

mancipatio：**〈拉〉要式买卖**

要式买卖是指以一定形式为成立要件的买卖，比如必须采取书面形式，属于要式法律行为的一种。

possession：**占有**

占有在某种意义上是占有者根据物的经济目的使用与利用占有物的法律事实。每一法律体系都保护占有者对物的经济利用。占有是对物的纯粹经济关系的描述，与所有权与其他物权存在着区分。

practical juristic science：**实用法学**

实用法学不同于法律科学，是使法律推动日常生活法律所需的技艺。实用法学源自塑造法律体系从而使其实际可行的需要。实用法学技术的两个分支日趋重要，一是源自于裁判法律争议需要的司法技术；二是草拟法律文件的技术。

private law：私法

私法具有组织内容，其总是关注人类联合体，决定着个人在人类工作群体中的位置以及人类群体和其利用的工具间的关系。私法主要是创立联合体而不是个人的权利与义务。

projection：法律投射

法律投射位于法律适用与法律发现之间。其有时更多具有法律适用的特性，有时更具有法律发现的特性。除了那些审判活动不同于法律适用的场合外，法律投射是法官的创造性活动。

real rights of usufruct：不动产用益权

不动产用益权是指对自己或他人所有的不动产，在一定范围内进行使用、收益的权利。

force of law：既判力

既判力是指生效判决对双方当事人和法院所具有的强制拘束力。法院作出的终局判决一旦生效，当事人和法院都应受该判决内容的拘束，当事人不得在以后的诉讼中主张与该判决相反的内容，法院也不得在以后的诉讼中作出与该判决冲突的判断。

reliance on collateral facts：外部事实信赖

外部事实信赖是指行为人对于成文法规或交易观念上的一定权利、法律关系，其他法律上视为重要要素之外部要件事实为信赖。

res mancipi：要式物

要式物是指需通过要式买卖等特定方式转让的物。

Roman juristic science：罗马法学

罗马法学独立于其他任何法源创造了自己的法律素材。罗马法主要根源于自有的法学家法，亦即法学家自己创设的法学家法。罗马法并未书写成文，而是通过法学家的解释构建的法。

Sociological Science of Law：法律社会学

法律社会学是理论性法律科学，其最主要功能就是将规制、命令与决定社会的那部分法律从纯粹的裁判规范中区分出来，并进而彰显其组织力。

State Law：国家法

国家法是由国家创制之法，其并非指形式上而是指内容上由国家创制之法。国家法的形成不仅可以采取制定法的形式，也可采取行政法规、治安条例、地方执法官法和法官法的形式。

stipulatio：要式口约

要式口约是指双方当事人用特定的语言，经问答相符而订立的单务严法契约，是罗马法上口头契约中最重要、使用最广泛的一种类型。要约者是债权人（*stipulator*），承诺者（*sponsor, promittor*）是债务人。要式口约源于《十二铜表法》以前的神前宣誓，但神前宣誓并不具有法律效力，仅靠道德宗教进行约束，后来宣誓的方式为问答所取代，法律也认可了其效力，即形成了要式口约。

Tatbe stand (constitutive facts)：构成要件事实

构成要件事实是指行为人的行为满足了法律规定的某种行为特定构成要件，具备了构成法律规定的某种行为的基本事实特征。

The Corpus iuriscivilis：《民法大全》

《民法大全》包含一本名为《法学阶梯》的教科书，源自法学著作《学说汇编》的摘录以及名为《法典》的法规。《民法大全》的内容是法学家法，他们一部分是以文学形式呈现，一部分是以答复与裁决形式予以阐明。

the jurata：合意咨审制（英格兰古法）

由12人宣誓组成，不同于依据亨利二世的法令建立的咨审团(assiza)。是在亨利二世法令规定不由咨审团审理的诉讼形式中，由当事人请求组成的陪审团，但为了免于重召一个新的陪审团的不便，当事人一般请求由咨审团作为普通法陪审团(jurata)参审。

the jurisprudence of conceptions：概念法学

概念法学于19世纪中叶以后由历史法学演变而来的“潘德克顿法学”，它以罗马《学说汇纂》为其理论体系和概念术语的历史基础，强调对法律概念的分析和构造法律的结构体系。

the theory of the sources of the law：法源理论

法源，基本含义是法的来源或法的栖身之所。法的渊源一词法源于欧洲大陆古罗马的Fontes iuris，普遍使用法的渊源一词的是英美法系的学者。法的渊源是法理学中的重要概念。

Trust Transactio：信托交易

信托交易是一种契约，这种交易中的正义要素与契约中的正义要素完全相同：所有者对自己财产的处分权。

Usage：习惯

习惯非指法律命题的习惯性应用，其意旨过去的惯例可以成为未来的规范。习惯决定了联合体头领与成员间的地位、地位优越者与低微者的关系以及联合体每一成员的角色。习惯创造了每一个原生性联合体的秩序，是联合体生活不可或缺的根基。

writ：令状

在英国，法庭的运作取决于原告为其诉因获取恰当的令状。

也就是说，不能获取恰当的令状将导致原告败诉。在中世纪早期，令状可因任何看似正当的诉求而被签发。但随着时间推移，获取令状变得越来越困难，只有常规的令状才较容易获取，而获得一个新型令状变得日益困难。

Eugen Ehrlich
Fundamental Principles of the Sociology of Law

图书在版编目（CIP）数据

法律社会学基本原理 = Fundamental Principles of the Sociology of Law：导读注释版：英文 /（奥）尤根·埃利希著；曹阳注释．—上海：上海译文出版社，2022.10

（世界学术经典系列）

ISBN 978-7-5327-9120-0

Ⅰ.①法… Ⅱ.①尤… ②曹… Ⅲ.①法律社会学—英文 Ⅳ.①D90-052

中国版本图书馆CIP数据核字（2022）第143005号

法律社会学基本原理
［奥］尤根·埃利希　著　曹　阳　导读　注释
责任编辑 / 谭春惠　装帧设计 / 张志全工作室

上海译文出版社有限公司出版、发行
网址：www.yiwen.com.cn
201101 上海市闵行区号景路159弄B座
江阴市机关印刷服务有限公司印刷

开本 890×1240　1/32　印张 19.5　插页 6　字数 556,000
2022年10月第1版　2022年10月第1次印刷
印数：0,001 — 1,500 册

ISBN 978-7-5327-9120-0/D·146
定价：158.00元

Fundamental Principles of the Sociology of Law

图书在版编目(CIP)数据

World Academic Classics
世界学术经典·英文版

Marxism
马克思主义

The Communist Manifesto (Marx & Engels)
共产党宣言（马克思、恩格斯）

Chinese Classics
中国经典

论语（汉英对照）
The Analects of Confucius

道德经（汉英对照）
Dao De Jing

孟子（汉英对照）
Mencius

庄子（汉英对照）
Zhuangzi

孙子兵法（汉英对照）
Sun Tzu on the Art of War

大学·中庸（汉英对照）
The Great Learning & The Doctrine of the Mean

Philosophy
哲　学

Republic (Plato)
理想国（柏拉图）

Metaphysics (Aristotle)
形而上学（亚里士多德）

Meditations on First Philosophy (René Descartes)
第一哲学沉思录（笛卡尔）

A Discourse on Method (René Descartes)
方法论（笛卡尔）

Pascal's Pensées (Blaise Pascal)
思想录（帕斯卡尔）

A Treatise of Human Nature (David Hume)
人性论（休谟）

Critique of Pure Reason (Kant)
纯粹理性批判（康德）

Critique of Judgment (Kant)
判断力批判（康德）

The Phenomenology of Mind (Hegel)
精神现象学（黑格尔）

The Logic of Hegel (Hegel)
小逻辑（黑格尔）

The World as Will and Representation (Schopenhauer)
作为意志与表象的世界（叔本华）

Thus Spake Zarathustra (Nietzsche)
查拉图斯特拉如是说（尼采）

Either / Or (Kierkegaard)
非此即彼（克尔凯郭尔）

Ideas: General Introduction to Pure Phenomenology (Husserl)
纯粹现象学导论（胡塞尔）

On First Philosophy (Husserl)
论第一哲学（胡塞尔）

Tractatus Logico Philosophicus (Wittgenstein)
逻辑哲学论（维特根斯坦）

Philosophical Investigations (Wittgenstein)
哲学研究（维特根斯坦）

Pragmatism (William James)
实用主义（威廉·詹姆斯）

Reconstruction in Philosophy (John Dewey)
哲学的改造（杜威）

Time and Free Will (Henri Bergson)
时间与自由意志（柏格森）

A Discourse on the Positive Spirit (Auguste Comte)
论实证精神（孔德）

Novum Organum (Francis Bacon)
新工具（培根）

Ethics
伦理学

The Nicomachean Ethics of Aristotle (Aristotle)
尼各马可伦理学（亚里士多德）

The Theory of Moral Sentiments (Adam Smith)
道德情操论（亚当·斯密）

A Discourse on Inequality (Rousseau)
论人类不平等的起源与基础（卢梭）

Critique of Practical Reason (Kant)
实践理性批判（康德）

Utilitarianism (Mill)
功利主义（密尔）

Principia Ethica (Moore)
伦理学原理（摩尔）

Religion
宗教学

Confessions (St. Augustine)
忏悔录（圣·奥古斯丁）

Basic Writings of Saint Thomas Aquinas (Thomas Aquinas)
圣托马斯基本著作（阿奎那）

Basic Theological Writings (Martin Luther)
路德基本著作选（马丁·路德）

The Courage to Be (Paul Tillich)
存在的勇气（蒂利希）

The Essence of Christianity (Ludwig Feuerbach)
基督教的本质（费尔巴哈）

Politics
政治学

The Politics of Aristotle (Aristotle)
政治学（亚里士多德）

The Prince (Machiavelli)
君主论（马基雅维利）

The Social Contract (Rousseau)
社会契约论（卢梭）

Leviathan (Thomas Hobbes)
利维坦（霍布斯）

Two Treatises of Government (John Locke)
政府论（洛克）

The Spirit of the Laws (Montesquieu)
论法的精神（孟德斯鸠）

Democracy in America (Tocqueville)
论美国民主（托克维尔）

Considerations on Representative Government (Mill)
代议制政府（密尔）

The Federalist Papers (Hamilton)
联邦党人文集（汉密尔顿）

The Ancien Régime and the Revolution (Tocqueville)
旧制度与大革命（托克维尔）

Utopia (Thomas More)
乌托邦（莫尔）

On Liberty (Mill)
论自由（密尔）

Reflections on the Revolution in France (Edmund Burke)
评法国革命（伯克）

The Will to Power (Nietzsche)
权力意志（尼采）

On War (Carl von Clausewitz)
战争论（克劳塞维茨）

Mutual Aid: A Factor of Evolution (Kropotkin)
互助论（克鲁泡特金）

Economics
经济学

The Economics of Welfare (Pigou)
福利经济学（庇古）

Principles of Economics (Alfred Marshall)
经济学原理（马歇尔）

The General Theory of Employment, Interest and Money (Keynes)
就业、利息与货币通论（凯恩斯）

The Theory of Economic Development (Schumpeter)
经济发展理论（熊彼特）

An Inquiry into the Nature and Causes of the Wealth of Nations (Adam Smith)
国民财富的性质和原因的研究（亚当·斯密）

Capitalism, Socialism and Democracy (Schumpeter)
资本主义、社会主义与民主（熊彼特）

An Essay on Population (Thomas Robert Malthus)
人口原理（马尔萨斯）

The Principles of Scientific Management (Frederick Winslow Taylor)
科学管理原理（泰勒）

Sociology
社会学

Suicide: A Study in Sociology (Durkheim)
自杀：社会学研究（迪尔凯姆）

The Protestant Ethic and the Spirit of Capitalism (Max Weber)
新教伦理与资本主义精神（韦伯）

The Philosophy of Money (Georg Simmel)
货币哲学（西美尔）

The Mind and Society: A Treatise on General Sociology (Vilfredo Pareto)
思想与社会：社会学总论（帕累托）

Ideology and Utopia (Mannheim)
意识形态与乌托邦（曼海姆）

First Principles (Herbert Spencer)
基本原理（斯宾塞）

The Theory of the Leisure Class (Thorstein B. Veblen)
论闲逸阶级（凡勃伦）

Anthropology
人类学

The Golden Bough (James George Frazer)
金枝（詹姆斯·乔治·弗雷泽）

Argonauts of the Western Pacific (Malinowski)
西太平洋的航海者（马林诺夫斯基）

Structure and Function in Primitive Society (Radcliffe-Brown)
原始社会的结构和功能（拉德克利夫–布朗）

Race, Language and Culture (Franz Boas)
种族、语言与文化（弗朗茨·博厄斯）

The Savage Mind (Claude Lévi-Strauss)
野性思维（克劳德·列维–斯特劳斯）

Psychology
心理学

The Principles of Psychology (William James)
心理学原理（威廉·詹姆斯）

Principles of Physiological Psychology (Wundt)
生理心理学原理（冯特）

The Interpretation of Dreams (Sigmund Freud)
释梦（弗洛伊德）

The Archetypes and the Collective Unconscious (Jung)
原型与集体无意识（荣格）

Law
法　学

Ancient Law (Maine)
古代法（梅因）

English Law and Political Philosophy (Maitland)
英国法律与政治哲学（梅特兰）

Lectures on Jurisprudence (Austin)
法理学演讲录（奥斯丁）

Fundamental Principles of the Sociology of Law (Ehrlich)
法律社会学基本原理（埃利希）

History
历史学

The Histories (Herodotus)
历史（希罗多德）

The Peloponnesian War (Thucydides)
伯罗奔尼撒战争史（修昔底德）

The Annals of Imperial Rome (Tacitus)
编年史（塔西佗）

The City of God (St. Augustine)
上帝之城（圣·奥古斯丁）

On Heroes, Hero Worship, and the Heroic in History (Thomas Carlyle)
论历史上的英雄、英雄崇拜和英雄业绩（卡莱尔）

The Idea of History (Collingwood)
历史的观念（科林伍德）

History of Civilization in Europe (Francois Guizot)
欧洲文明史（基佐）

The Influence of Sea Power (Alfred T. Mahan)
海权对历史的影响（马汉）

Theory & History of Historiography (Benedetto Croce)
史学理论与史学史（克罗齐）

A Short Account of the Destruction of the Indies (Bartolomé de Las Cases)
西印度毁灭述略（卡萨斯）

Literary Theory and Aesthetics
文学理论与美学

On the Art of Poetry (Aristotle)
诗学（亚里士多德）

On the Art of Poetry (Horace)
诗艺（贺拉斯）

On the Sublime (Longinus)
论崇高（朗吉努斯）

Theory of Aesthetic / History of Aesthetic (Benedetto Croce)
美学理论 / 美学史（克罗齐）

Hegel's Aesthetics Lectures on Fine Art (Hegel)
黑格尔美学讲演录（黑格尔）

The Birth of Tragedy (Friedrich Nietzsche)
悲剧的诞生（尼采）

Linguistics
语言学

Course in General Linguistics (Saussure)
普通语言学教程（索绪尔）

On Language (Wilhelm von Humboldt)
论语言（威廉·冯·洪堡特）

Scientific Philosophy
自然科学哲学

On the Origin of Species (Charles Darwin)
物种起源（查尔斯·达尔文）

Mathematical Principles of Natural Philosophy and Its System of the World (Issac Newton)
自然哲学的数学原理（牛顿）

Natural History (Pliny the Elder)
自然史（老普林尼）